The Oxford Companion to the Economics of China

Shenggen Fan is Director General of the International Food Policy Research Institute.

Ravi Kanbur is T.H. Lee Professor of World Affairs, International Professor of Applied Economics and Management, and Professor of Economics at Cornell University.

Shang-Jin Wei is N. T. Wang Professor of Chinese Business and Economy at Columbia University's Graduate School of Business and School of International and Public Affairs, and a former Chief Economist of Asian Development Bank.

Xiaobo Zhang is National one thousand-talent program Chair and Professor of Economics at the School of Development, Peking University and senior research fellow at the International Food Policy Research Institute (IFPRI).

The Oxford Companion to the Economics of China

Edited by
Shenggen Fan
Ravi Kanbur
Shang-Jin Wei
Xiaobo Zhang

OXFORD
UNIVERSITY PRESS

Great Clarendon Street, Oxford, OX2 6DP,
United Kingdom

Oxford University Press is a department of the University of Oxford.
It furthers the University's objective of excellence in research, scholarship,
and education by publishing worldwide. Oxford is a registered trade mark of
Oxford University Press in the UK and in certain other countries

Published in the United States of America by Oxford University Press
198 Madison Avenue, New York, NY 10016, United States of America

British Library Cataloguing in Publication Data

Data available

Library of Congress Cataloging in Publication Data

Data available

ISBN 978–0–19–967820–4 (Hbk.)
ISBN 978–0–19–882553–1 (Pbk.)

PREFACE

This compendium of entries, together with an overview, provides a new collection of perspectives on the Chinese economy's past, present, and future. The entries are brief but wide ranging, covering China's aggregate performance, the main sectoral trends, issues of inequality and environment in its many dimensions, and China's role in the world economy. The contributors of these entries include: the best of young Chinese researchers based in China and outside; renowned academics from the top universities in China, Europe, and North America; present and past senior officials of international agencies like the World Bank and the International Monetary Fund; senior Chinese government officials from the Centre and the Provinces; and four recipients of the Nobel Prize in Economics. Other than the requirement that the entry be analytical and not polemical, the contributors were given freedom to put forward their particular perspective on a topic. The entries are not therefore surveys of the literature. Rather, they constitute a picture of the concerns of modern economics as it is applied to China, as seen by the leading economists working on China. We hope that this *Companion* will contribute to analysis and to the policy discourse as China looks ahead to the next thirty-five years, approaching the 100th anniversary of the People's Republic in 2049.

Shenggen Fan
Ravi Kanbur
Shang-Jin Wei
Xiaobo Zhang

■ ACKNOWLEDGEMENTS

The Editors would like to thank Sue Snyder of Cornell University for being the administrative anchor of the China Companion project, and for managing the correspondence with over 100 authors. The Companion could not have been produced without her help. Translation support from Sam Zhang is gratefully acknowledged. Shenggen Fan would also like to acknowledge the assistance provided by Joanna Brzeska to him in reviewing and editing part of the volume.

■ CONTENTS

■ LIST OF FIGURES

■ LIST OF TABLES

LIST OF CONTRIBUTORS

Franklin Allen, Imperial College London

Douglas Almond, Columbia University

Kym Anderson, University of Adelaide

Pranab Bardhan, University of California, Berkeley

Chad P. Bown, The World Bank

Loren Brandt, University of Toronto

Deborah Bräutigam, Johns Hopkins University/SAIS

Fang Cai, Chinese Academy of Social Science

Hongbin Cai, Peking University

Ximing Cai, University of Illinois

Xi Chen, Yale University

Menzie D. Chinn, University of Wisconsin

Simon Cox, Former Asia Economics Editor, *The Economist*

Zhongren Cui, Guangxi Development Research Center

Alan de Brauw, International Food Policy Research Institute (IFPRI)

Peikun Dai, Anhui Development Research Center

Sylvie Démurger, Centre National de la Recherche Scientifique (CNRS)

Yongheng Deng, National University of Singapore

Chengri Ding, University of Maryland

David Dollar, Brookings Institution

Xiao-yuan Dong, University of Winnipeg

Julan Du, Chinese University of Hong Kong

Ying Du, National Development and Reform Commission

Richard A. Easterlin, University of Southern California

Shenggen Fan, International Food Policy Research Institute

Hanming Fang, University of Pennsylvania

Robert W. Fogel (Deceased)

Ross Garnaut, University of Melbourne

Roger Gordon, University of California, San Diego

Nathaniel Grotte, University of Chicago

Wanda Guo, China Development Institute (CDI)

Gordon H. Hanson, University of California, San Diego

Ann Harrison, University of Pennsylvania, The Wharton School

Dong He, Hong Kong Monetary Authority

James J. Heckman, University of Chicago

J. Vernon Henderson, London School of Economics

Trevor Houser, Peter G. Peterson Institute for International Economics

Jikan Huang, Chinese Academy of Sciences

Yasheng Huang, MIT Sloan School of Management

Yiping Huang, Peking University

Ravi Kanbur, Cornell University

John Knight, University of Oxford

Samuel Krumholz, UCLA Luskin School of Public Affairs

Haizheng Li, Georgia Institute of Technology

Hongbin Li, Tsinghua University

Wei Li, Cheung Kong GSB

Edwin Lim, CERAP

Justin Yifu Lin, Peking University

Shuanglin Lin, Peking University and University of Nebraska Omaha

Gordon G. Liu, Peking University

Qinyi Liu, Hunan University, China

Feng Lu, Peking University

Yi Lu, National University of Singapore

Xiaopeng Luo, Zhejiang University

Guonan Ma, Bruegel

Aaditya Mattoo, The World Bank

Lingsheng Meng, Tsinghua University

Xin Meng, Australian National University

Michelle Miro, University of Illinois

Victor Nee, Cornell University

Sonja Opper, Lund University

Keijiro Otsuka, National Graduate Institute for Policy Studies (GRIPS)

Yao Pan, Aalto University

Albert Park, Hong Kong University of Science and Technology

Dwight Perkins, Harvard University

Eswar Prasad, Cornell University

Ye Qi, Tsinghua University

Jun 'QJ' Qian, Shanghai Advanced Institute of Finance, Shanghai Jiaotong University

Nancy Qian, Yale University

Yingyi Qian, Tsinghua University

Dongyu Qu, Chinese Academy of Agricultural Sciences (CAAS)

Futian Qu, Nanjing Agricultural University

Martin Ravallion, Georgetown University

Carl Riskin, Queens College and Columbia University

Peter E. Robertson, University of Western Australia

Nouriel Roubini, New York University

Scott Rozelle, Stanford University

Jinchuan Shi, Zhejiang University

Stephen C. Smith, George Washington University

Ligang Song, The Australian National University

Lina Song, University of Nottingham

Zheng Song, Chicago Booth

Michael Spence, New York University

Joseph E. Stiglitz, Columbia University

Kjetil Storesletten, University of Oslo

Arvind Subramanian, Peterson Institute of International Economics

Laixiang Sun, SOAS and University of London

Jie Tang, Shenzhen Government

Zhigang Tao, University of Hong Kong

Guoqiang Tian, Texas A&M University

Kai-yuen Tsui, Chinese University of Hong Kong

Calum G. Turvey, Cornell University

Baorui Wan, Ministry of Agriculture

Hua Wang, The World Bank

Jici Wang, Peking University

Jing Wang, University of Western Ontario

Rong Wang, Peking University

Yikai Wang, University of Zurich

Sangui Wang, Renmin University of China

Shang-Jin Wei, Asian Development Bank

John Whalley, University of Western Ontario

Adam Wolfe, New York University

Yanrui Wu, University of Western Australia

Qingsheng Xie, Guizhou University of China

Yu Xie, University of Michigan

Bin Xu, China Europe International Business School

Chenggang Xu, University of Hong Kong

Chenhua Yang, Development Research Centre

Dennis Tao Yang, University of Virginia

Yang Yao, CCER, Peking University

Junjian Yi, University of Chicago

Boyang Zhang, Cornell University

Chuanting Zhang, Policy Research Centre of Shandong Province

Weiying Zhang, Peking University

Xiaobo Zhang, Peking University and International Food Policy Research Institute

Changwen Zhao, China State Development Research Center

Yaohui Zhao, Peking University

Funing Zhong, Nanjing Agricultural University

Ling Zhu, Chinese Academy of Social Sciences (CESS)

Fabrizio Zilibotti, University of Zurich

Chen Zongsheng Nankai University

Huang Zuhui, Zhejiang University

The economics of China
Successes and challenges

Shenggen Fan, Ravi Kanbur, Shang-Jin Wei, and Xiaobo Zhang

0.1 Introduction

It is now the fourth decade since the start of China's economic reforms launched the country on perhaps the most spectacular growth and poverty reduction performance in the history of the world. This achievement has been accompanied by equally dramatic outcomes in other economic spheres. There has been growth in exports, infrastructure, reserves, foreign direct investment, and development assistance. But, at the same time, there has been growth in inequality, spatial divergence, corruption, an underclass of migrant workers, environmental pollution, and carbon emissions. These twin dimensions frame the economics of China as it looks ahead to the next four decades, approaching the 100th anniversary of the People's Republic in 2049.

This chapter introduces the *Oxford Companion to the Economics of China*; a new collection of perspectives on the Chinese economy's past, present, and future. The entries are brief but wide ranging, covering China's aggregate performance, the main sectoral trends, issues of inequality in its many dimensions, and China's role in the world economy. The contributors of these entries include: the best of young Chinese researchers based in China and outside; renowned academics from the top universities in China, Europe, and North America; present and past senior officials of international agencies like the World Bank and the International Monetary Fund; senior Chinese government officials from the Centre and the Provinces; and four recipients of the Nobel Prize in Economics. Other than the requirement that the entry be analytical and not polemical, the contributors were given freedom to put forwards their particular perspective on a topic. The entries are not therefore surveys of the literature. Rather, they constitute a picture of the concerns of modern economics as it is applied to China's problems, as seen by the leading economists working on China.

This introduction cannot, should not, and does not summarize or synthesize the entries in the *Companion*. Rather, in what follows we provide our own perspectives on the economics of China—the past experience and the future prospects. While the entries in the *Companion* provide some of the input to our discussion, we rely also on the broader literature on Chinese economic development. Section 1.2 begins the exercise (1.2.1) with an account of how the broad aggregates of the Chinese economy have moved in the last thirty-five years, setting out the remarkable acceleration in growth and trade that the reform process unleashed. The section then moves on to take a more sectoral perspective (1.2.2) on these developments, looking at movements in agriculture and industry in particular. Finally, based on this aggregate picture, Section 1.2.3 highlights emerging issues for the future.

Our reading of China's economic development raises two major sets of issues, one of which is inward looking, and the other of which is outward looking. While Chinese aggregate development is impressive, and has led to dramatic poverty reduction, it has also led to a set of issues which Section 1.3 discusses under the heading of 'Domestic Challenges'. Section 1.3.1 takes up the sharp rise in interpersonal inequality in China, and its many dimensions, such as the growing underclass in urban areas. Section 1.3.2 takes a different cut at the inequality question by considering some non-income dimensions of well-being. Section 1.3.3 specifically addresses an important aspect of non-income well-being, environmental sustainability. Section 1.3.4 focuses on the spatial dimension of inequality, which has been an important one in China historically.

The outward oriented set of issues are considered in Section 1.4, under the heading 'China and the World'. Section 1.4.1 addresses the past, present, and future of China's integration into the global economy, looking at trade, investment, and financial flows. Section 1.4.2 assesses specifically China's engagement with the developing world through aid, investment, and trade. Section 1.4.3 turns its attention to China's role in global agencies such as the World Bank and the International Monetary Fund, and more generally in creating global public goods and addressing global externalities such as carbon emissions and financial contagion.

Section 1.5 pulls together the threads by providing a perspective on how the experiences and lessons of the past thirty-five years frame the challenges faced by China in the coming thirty-five years to 2049.

0.2 Chinese performance and the China model

0.2.1 GROWTH AND POVERTY REDUCTION

Since the late 1970s, China has grown at an average annual rate of around 10 per cent for more than three decades. Starting from being a poor and insular nation, it has become the second largest economy, the largest trading nation, and the most popular destination of foreign direct investment in the world. Many economists are optimistic about China's growth potential (Lin; Fogel and Grotte, *this volume*). China is set to surpass the USA as the leading economy in a decade.

The Chinese growth miracle started with agriculture in the late 1970s. The essence of the reform was decollectivization of agricultural production and land user rights. The most important part of the reform was officially called the household responsibility system (HRS). HRS granted farmers land cultivation rights and empowered them to make their own production decisions. With better aligned incentives, agricultural production and rural incomes witnessed a dramatic increase in the ensuing years. During the first period of HRS implementation between 1978 and 1984, output in the Chinese agricultural sector increased by more than 61 per cent and HRS accounted for 49 per cent of the output growth (Lin, 1992). Within a few years, hundreds of millions of farmers were released from their land, providing the non-farm sector with a seemingly unlimited labour supply.

In the mid-1980s, township and village-owned enterprises (TVEs) took off under the dual-track reform. Concerned about the potentially catastrophic consequence of fully liberalizing prices and privatizing the state-owned enterprises (SOEs) en masse, China adopted a gradual and pragmatic approach by allowing the TVEs to operate at the margin. Because TVEs were largely labour intensive in line with China's comparative advantage at the time, they immediately blossomed once they were allowed to access quotas of raw materials unused by SOEs. The TVE sector outpaced the state sector in both growth rate and productivity. As a result of the TVE sector's fast growth, the non-state sector's share of industrial output increased from 22 per cent in 1978 to 47 per cent in 1991, while the state sector's share declined from 78 per cent to 53 per cent in the same period (Xu and Qian, 1993). TVE development peaked in the mid-1990s. Employment in the TVE sector increased from 30 million in 1980 to 129 million in 1995. TVEs' share of gross domestic product (GDP) rose from 14.3 per cent in 1980 to 37.5 per cent in 1995.

The reform of industrial sectors in urban areas started in earnest only in the late 1980s, and was pursued along two dimensions. On the one hand, entry barriers in most sectors were reduced substantially so that many de novo private firms were born, although many were often nominally associated with local government ownership. On the other hand, the reform of existing state-owned enterprises (SOEs) was executed by following a strategy of 'grasping the big, and letting go of the small'. That is, while a small number of very large firms in what the government considered 'strategic sectors' were kept in majority state ownership, a large number of small and medium-sized enterprises were privatized or at least their ownership was transferred from the central government to local governments.

By the mid-1990s, the private sector also witnessed dramatic growth. Seeing the dynamics of the private sector, the government started to reform TVEs and SOEs. By the late 1990s and early 2000s, most TVEs and SOEs had been privatized. Accordingly, TVE employment plummeted from 129 million in 1995 to merely 6 million in 2011, while SOE employment shrank from 113 million in 1995 to 67 million in 2011. In the short term, the reform was a painful process; millions of urban workers were retrenched. Eventually, most of the lost jobs in TVEs and SOEs were picked up by the dynamic private sector. By 2011, 193 million people worked in private enterprises or were self-employed, about three times the workforce of SOEs (CNBS, 2012).

China's economic growth was not geographically even. In order to better utilize China's comparative advantage of cheap labour in the international market, China adopted an export-oriented development strategy. It set up numerous special zones in the coastal provinces to attract foreign direct investment (FDI). From 1978 to the mid-2000s, the coastal areas attracted the majority of FDI and created millions of jobs. China's entry to the World Trade Organization (WTO) further increased the trend to global integration. As the coastal provinces became a focus of growth, workers from interior regions migrated there to seek better-paid jobs. The total number of migrants increased by nearly fivefold from merely 25 million in 1990 to 145 million in 2009 (CNBS, 2010; Meng, *this volume*).

For nearly two decades, it seemed that China had inexhaustible surplus labour. But signs of labour shortages started to emerge in the mid-2000s. Since 2004, wages for unskilled workers have had double digit growth rates, indicating that China perhaps has passed the Lewis turning point, and that the era of surplus labour is over (Zhang et al., 2011). Because remittances from migrant workers accounted for a large share of rural income, rising wages for unskilled labour boosted rural income. In the past several years, rural income growth overtook its urban counterpart after lagging behind for two decades.

The trends of poverty reduction mirrored China's growth patterns. Rapid economic growth contributed to massive poverty reduction. Since the late 1970s, more than 600 million Chinese have escaped from poverty (Ravallion and Chen, 2007; Park and Wang, *this volume*). At the onset of economic reform in the late 1970s, more than half of the population lived under the international '$1 per day' poverty line. By 2010, the incidence of poverty had dropped to about 10 per cent. There is no doubt that both the scale and speed of poverty reduction in China are unparalleled in human history.

However, the progress against poverty has been uneven over time and across the country. Most of the drop in poverty happened in the early 1980s when the HRS reform took place. Consequently, the rural poverty rate dropped sharply from 76 per cent in 1980 to 24 per cent in 1986 based on the international poverty line of $1 per day (Ravallion and Chen, 2007). In other words, more than 400 million people moved out of poverty in a short, six-year spell. Agricultural growth played a key role in China's massive poverty reduction. Afterwards, however, the pace of poverty reduction stalled in the 1990s and early 2000s during the period of SOE reform. Urban poverty emerged as a problem (Fang et al., 2002; Appleton et al., 2010). In the past decade, thanks to rising wages and the introduction of social safety net programmes, the poverty rate has shown a steady decline (Park and Wang *this volume*). Yet, there are still pockets of poverty, mainly concentrated in the western region.

Accompanied by economic growth, many social indicators have also improved. According to the China Population Census in 1981 and 2010, the infant mortality rate dropped from 39.1 per thousand to 13.1 per thousand from 1981 to 2010, while the illiteracy rate declined from 34.8 per cent to 4.9 per cent. Life expectancy in China witnessed a remarkable improvement from as low as 35 years in 1949, to 68 years in 1981 and 75 years in 2010. Chinese life expectancy was more than eight years longer than Russia's and only four years below the USA's. Given that China's per capita GDP is only one-fifth of that in the USA, China's record in improving life expectancy is truly remarkable.

0.2.2 STRUCTURAL TRANSFORMATION

China's remarkable development path since the late 1970s is marked by a significant transformation of its economic and demographic structure. This process involves a shift from a predominantly agricultural and rural economy to an urban-based, industrialized one. A corresponding change in the demographic structure has also taken place as a more urban population is increasingly employed in services and industry.

During the last thirty-five years, growth in China's agricultural sector has hovered around 4 per cent per year, whereas the services and industrial sectors in China grew much faster (two to five times) than agriculture. An extensive body of literature has attributed this rapid growth to a combination of factors, including improved sectoral productivity and increased input use. Increased productivity growth in both agriculture and non-agriculture has been associated with a decline in agriculture's share of economic activity as resources, such as labour and capital, are reallocated to higher-productivity sectors (Dekle and Vandenbroucke, 2012).

The central focus of the Chinese economy has rapidly shifted away from agriculture towards industry and services. In the 1960s, agriculture contributed approximately 40 per cent of GDP, but by 2011 agriculture's share of GDP had fallen to 10 per cent. Over the last three decades, industry has steadily continued to contribute 40–50 per cent of GDP, and the services sector has nearly doubled its share of GDP from 24 per cent in 1970 to 43 per cent in 2011. However, in terms of share of GDP, the services sector in China remains far smaller than in other emerging economies such as Brazil, India, and South Africa, where services contribute 67, 55, and 67 per cent of GDP, respectively. In fact, the size of China's services sector in relation to other sectors is on par with poorer economies such as Cambodia, Vietnam, and Ethiopia although China's rather low share may reflect a strong performance in the industrial sector.

Structural changes across sectors have been accompanied by significant restructuring within China's agricultural sector. What was once an overwhelmingly grain-focused sector has steadily been moving towards one that increasingly includes higher-valued cash crops (such as oil seeds, fruits, and vegetables), livestock, and aquaculture products. During the last several decades, the production of these high-value agricultural products recorded growth rates that often exceeded those of staple crops such as rice and wheat (Huang et al., 2012). In fact, the share of agricultural output value coming from crops decreased from 82 per cent in 1970 to 55 per cent in 2010, compared to an increase from 2 per cent to 10 per cent by fisheries and 14 to 31 per cent by livestock. This structural transformation can also be seen within crop farming as the share of land allocated to staple crops such as rice and wheat has decreased while it has increased for cash crops such as vegetables.

Similar structural changes occurred in manufacturing and service sectors. As described by Yu (2012), China's manufacturing sector experienced rapid structural shifts in four phases. From 1978 to 1985, China was still a resource-based economy, producing and exporting resource-based goods, such as coal, oil, and gasoline. During 1986–95, China witnessed rapid growth in labour-intensive exports. From 1996 to 2000, the main export from China was electrical machinery and transport equipment. During the last decade, China has recorded rapid export growth in high-technology products, such as life-science equipment, electronics, and IT products. The service sector has also been transformed from small informal service activities and state-owned trading, marketing, and education/health services to a dynamic, more informal, and private owned sector (Zhang and Evenett, 2010).

Structural changes can also be observed in employment patterns. In 1980, agriculture was a major employer, with 70 per cent of the country's workforce engaged in agricultural activities. A much smaller percentage of the workforce was employed in the industry and service sectors, 18 per cent and 13 per cent, respectively. By 2010, the industrial landscape had also experienced a large-scale movement from agriculture to industry and services. Agriculture still employs the largest share of the workforce but the percentage has declined to 38 per cent. In contrast, employment in industry and services has been on the rise, increasing to 29 per cent and 35 per cent of the workforce. As workers exit agriculture and migrate to urban centres for employment in industry and services, China's population is becoming more urban. The share of the population living in urban areas rose from 19 per cent to 50 per cent between 1980 and 2011, and forecasts indicate that approximately 77 per cent of the population will live in urban areas by 2050 (United Nations Population Division, 2012). Indeed, the number of people living in rural areas has fallen since the early 1990s at an increasingly higher rate and this trend is projected to continue in the future.

As labour becomes more expensive and moves out of agriculture in China, a mechanization revolution is taking place within the agricultural sector in the form of the emergence of private mechanized service providers. Numbering in the tens of thousands, these farmer companies are fulfilling the country's need to replace increasingly expensive labour with machinery by travelling year-round, across provinces, to provide farmers with land preparation and harvesting services at a competitive price (Yang et al., 2013). Rice production in China, for example, is modernizing across the entire value chain. In addition to the doubling of farm equipment holdings in China between 2004 and 2009, rice mills are consolidating and modernizing technologically and the rice value chain is becoming geographically longer but shorter in terms of participants (Reardon et al., 2012).

0.2.3 THE CHINESE ECONOMIC MODEL

The successful expansion and development of the Chinese economy during the past several decades is undeniable. China's development trajectory has been guided by a series of gradual reforms that focused on transforming from central planning to a more market-based and equitable economy. This raises the question as to what extent China's experience can serve as a model that other developing countries can follow.

0.3 Model of economic development

Over the last three decades, the Chinese government has implemented a broad spectrum of economic reforms that were situated in a framework of transforming the economy from central planning to a more efficient, market-driven, and (more recently) equitable system. A significant common denominator across these reforms was the adoption of a gradual and progressive approach that was based on evidence from local experiments, often dubbed 'crossing the river by touching the stones', in key areas, such as trade, governance, and ownership structures.

Consider the example of rural reform. Initially, the decentralization of agricultural production and management systems happened in Xiaogang Village of Anhui Province. Later, the government ran some pilots of the same kind of reform in remote areas (Du, 2010). Once evidence from these pilots showed that decollectivization successfully stimulated production incentives and encouraged more efficient resource allocation; the reforms were sanctioned by the central government and then scaled-up nationally. As a complement to the change in the ownership structure, the central government also promoted village self-governance on an experimental basis, which allowed for the testing of procedures and logistics. What started as makeshift, locally driven organizations in a few villages became a ten-year pilot scheme under the Draft Organic Law of Village Committees, followed by a nationwide roll-out of village elections (O'Brian and Li, 2000; Qian, *this volume*).

The opening of China's economy to foreign trade was also implemented through a gradual, experimental approach that saw the establishment of Special Economic Zones

(SEZs) in a handful of provinces. Characterized by preferential policies (such as lower tax rates) and institutional autonomy, the SEZs were established to stimulate joint ventures and foreign direct investment, serving as a springboard to increase China's exports and technology development (Lin and Wang, 2009; Zeng, 2010). The SEZs successfully tested a more liberalized economy in a few places before expanding the reforms to other areas in various forms, including high-tech and free trade zones.

These various pilots and experiments allowed the government to test heterogeneous structures that best suited China's unique economic and political characteristics. Such careful experimentation at the local level was essential for the successful design, sequencing, and implementation of reforms. It allowed for mid-course corrections and provided the time to build the necessary institutions, help stakeholders adjust to the new system, and secure political support (Bruce and Li, 2009; Zhang et al., 2010; Xing and Zhang, 2013).

Although the size and structure of China's economy and population differ in many respects from other developing countries, its pragmatic and gradual approach to economic reforms offers useful lessons. Rather than immediately implementing all reforms or unwaveringly following universal prescriptions under one 'ideological' path, China's central government progressively introduced policies, building on previous reforms and continually capitalizing on China's changing comparative advantage. This approach allowed the Chinese central authorities to develop rather unorthodox policy measures that differed from those that would have been prescribed by outsiders (Rodrik, 2005). A dual-track approach to many reforms enabled the government to integrate and smoothly transition between new and old policy initiatives—for example, providing the necessary protection to nonviable firms in priority sectors and, simultaneously, liberalizing labour-intensive sectors in which China had a comparative advantage. Good initial conditions in rural infrastructure, agricultural research, and extension services, and the capacity of institutions also played a key role. In addition, adjustments were made along the way to account for unanticipated developments, including the recent introduction of policies that focus on eliminating disparities between regions and population groups (Li et al., 2013).

Looking ahead, the question for analysts and policy makers is how the China model will address a range of challenges that have emerged alongside the undoubted successes of the past thirty-five years. We turn now to these domestic and international challenges.

0.4 Domestic challenges

0.4.1 INCOME INEQUALITY

During the planned economic era, China was one of the world's most egalitarian societies. In 1981, the Gini coefficient in rural and urban areas was low at 0.25 and 0.18, respectively (Ravallion and Chen, 2007). However, there was a large rural–urban gap because of the *Hukou* system put place in the late 1950s. Under the *Hukou* system, urban residents enjoyed the privilege of guaranteed jobs and a cradle-to-grave social welfare system, but rural residents were confined to their birth places. In 1981, per capita urban income was about three times rural income. As a result, the overall Gini coefficient (0.28) exceeded that of either urban or rural China, taken separately (Riskin, *this volume*). Of course, national income inequality, even at 0.28, was low when compared to China's subsequent changes or to most other countries.

During the HRS reform period, rural incomes rose twice as fast as their urban counterparts. Consequently, the rural–urban gap narrowed, lowering overall inequality. In 1988, the Gini coefficient fell to 0.21 (Knight, *this volume*). However, since that time unfavourable farm prices and the coastal development strategies have once again widened the rural–urban gap. The national Gini rose to 0.45 in 2001 (Ravallion and Chen, 2007). Based on survey data for 2007 from the Chinese Household Income Project (CHIP), Li et al. (2013) estimated a national Gini of 0.47.

Estimates based on a few recent nationally representative surveys independently undertaken by Chinese universities suggest the income distribution problem is even more serious (Xie et al., 2013). Three surveys, the China Family Panel Studies (CFPS by Peking University, 2010 and 2012), the Chinese General Social Survey (CGSS, 2010) by Renmin University, and the Chinese Household Finance Survey (CHFS, 2011) by Southwestern University of Finance and Economics, all report China's national Gini coefficient over 0.5 in 2010. In particular, the estimate based on CHFS reached 0.6, making China one of the most unequal societies in the world. It is widely speculated that the national surveys have seriously undercounted the high-income groups. A recent study (Zhang et al., 2014) demonstrates that the official surveys may underestimate the number of poor as well—poverty prevalence at the national, rural, and urban levels based on the CFPS, CGSS, and CHFS were much higher than official estimates and those based on the CHIP, a subsample of national surveys.

Not only has overall income inequality worsened, so has inequality within urban and rural areas. According to an estimate based on the CFPS, the rural and urban Gini coefficients were as high as 0.50 and 0.48 in 2010, reflecting a rapid escalation from low levels of within-group inequality in the 1980s (Xie et al., 2013). The rapid increase in urban inequality was closely associated with the massive retrenchment of SOE workers in the 1990s. As most of the laid-off SOE workers were in their 40s or 50s, it was difficult for them to find jobs that were better paid than their previous ones. Meanwhile, the remaining urban workers could command higher wages because skill premiums had increased since China's opening up, in particular its accession to the WTO in 2002 (Song, *this volume*). In addition, there was a shift in government policy in favour of the state sector. In the past decades, workers in SOEs enjoyed more lucrative pay than their counterparts in private enterprises owing to the increasing monopoly power of SOEs. All these factors contributed to the escalation of urban inequality.

Regarding rural inequality, non-farm employment is a major contributing factor. The share of wage income inequality in overall rural income inequality rose from 21 per cent in 1988 to 41 per cent in 2007 (Knight, *this volume*). Since wage income mainly came from local non-farm jobs and remittance, the uneven distribution of non-farm job opportunities across regions plays a significant part in explaining rising rural inequality. The contribution of between-province inequality to total rural inequality increased from 22 per cent in 1988 to 39 per cent in 2007 (Sicular et al., 2007).

As China enters the stage of development beyond the Lewis turning point where surplus labour is exhausted, in principle the market force of rising wages should place a downward pressure on national income inequality. Because of the large share of wage income in total rural income, rising real wages could play an important role in narrowing the rural–urban gap and overall income inequality. Indeed, in the past several years, rural income grew faster than urban income. An estimate based on the second wave of CFPS reports that the national Gini dropped slightly from 0.51 in 2010 to 0.49 in 2012 (Xie et al., 2013). Although China's income inequality remains at a globally high level, at least the worsening trend seems to have been subdued, if not reversed.

However, market forces alone may not be strong enough to reduce the high income inequality before government transfers. Various government policies can help speed up the process (Riskin, *this volume*). For example, introducing more competition to the SOE sector could help dissipate their monopoly rents and cut their wage advantages relative to private firms, and the elimination of the *Hukou* system will promote permanent migration and narrow the rural–urban income gap.

0.4.2 NON-INCOME DIMENSIONS

China's growth model is not an entirely happy story. Despite the multiplication of real incomes in the past three decades, China's life satisfaction did not improve (Easterlin, *this volume*). A large annual survey conducted by China's Central TV (Wei and Zhang, 2013) disclosed that the average happiness score has steadily declined from 2005 to 2011. How is it possible for Chinese people to feel more miserable amid the marked improvement in material living conditions? There are many potential explanations. Here we list a few.

First, happiness draws from relative comparisons. As income increases, people's aspirations aim for a new target. 'Relative deprivation' is a widespread phenomenon (Chen, *this volume*). For example, when someone sees his neighbours suddenly getting rich, he may feel relatively deprived and less happy even though his own income has not changed at all. This example highlights that both relative income and chosen reference groups shape happiness. As a matter of fact, it is local income inequality that matters more to happiness than national inequality (Knight, *this volume*). Xing et al. (2009) found that within-village inequality increased from 0.44 in 2004 to 0.49 in 2006 in Guizhou. The rising inequality within a community negates the positive force of income growth on happiness.

Second, the underlying reasons for inequality also matter to happiness. The large rural–urban gap in income and access to public service have been a defining feature of the contemporary Chinese economy, generating a major source of resentment for rural residents. Although during the reform period health indicators have improved, their rural–urban gap has also widened. For example, the ratio of infant mortality in rural areas relative to urban areas increased from 1.7 in 1981 to 2.8 in 2000 (Kanbur and Zhang, 2005). Uneven access to healthcare was the major cause. For instance, in cities, the out-of-pocket expense in total healthcare expense was 44 per cent in cities and 87 per cent in the countryside. The rural–urban gap in the number of hospital beds and healthcare professionals per 1,000 people grew in the reform period. By 1998, the gap had increased by more than fivefold. During the past decade, China has introduced a new rural cooperative medical system intended to make healthcare more affordable for the rural poor. However, the findings on the impact of this programme are mixed (Lei and Lin, 2009; Babiarz et al., 2010).

Thanks to the nine-year mandatory education law introduced in 1986, illiteracy has largely been eliminated in both rural and urban areas (Li, *this volume*). However, the disparity in access to higher education has widened. In the late 1970s, most of the college students came from rural areas. However, the proportion of rural students dropped to only 10 per cent in the elite universities in recent years (Cai, *this volume*). There is an emerging trend that many rich families send their children abroad for college, even high school education. The number studying abroad has increased at an annual rate of 25 per cent in the past decade (Li, *this volume*). Of course, the proportion of students studying abroad among rural families is much lower than their urban counterparts. The recent rise in real wages for unskilled labour in combination with high college tuition fees induce many rural youngsters to drop out of school at an early age and migrate to the cities for work (Rozelle et al., 2013). In the short run, such a decision may seem to be sensible. But in the long run, as China develops, the demand for skilled employees will eventually exceed that for unskilled labour. Many unskilled jobs will disappear, making many of the currently unskilled workers unemployable and trapping them in poverty. The widening gap in education between rural and urban areas will impede social mobility and enlarge income inequality, greatly increasing China's chances of falling into a middle-income trap.

0.4.3 ENVIRONMENTAL SUSTAINABILITY

Some undesirable outcomes of growth negatively affect people's life satisfaction. Environmental problems and food safety are now among the top concerns of urban residents. The heavy smog in Beijing highlights the seriousness of the problem. Two Chinese cities command the top places in lists of the world's ten most polluted places.[1] Air pollution has

---

[1] <http://www.time.com/time/specials/2007/completelist/0,29569,1661031,00.html>.

become a national problem. A recent report released by China's Ministry of Environmental Protection (MEP) found that only 17 out of 113 major cities in China met air quality standards in 2012.[2] It has been widely documented in the public health literature that air pollution significantly increases the risks of respiratory diseases (Almond, *this volume*). When people are confined to their apartments due to fears of polluted air, they are more likely to voice their complaints.

Water pollution is also a serious problem. The MEP report revealed that 57.3 per cent of ground water in 198 cities was 'bad' or 'seriously bad' and about one-third of national major rivers were deemed 'polluted' or 'seriously polluted'. Of 4,000 water treatment plans, 1,000 did not meet the national standards.[3] Not surprisingly, pollution has replaced land disputes as the leading cause of social unrest in China.

As China became the 'world's factory', it also earned the title of the largest carbon dioxide emitter in the world, accounting for 29 per cent of world emissions in 2011. China contributed to a large share of the incremental increase in CO_2 emissions. Given China's reliance on an export-oriented development strategy, it would be a great challenge for China to reduce CO_2 emissions without compromising its growth.

Contaminated water and soil due to industrial pollution and overuse of fertilizers and pesticides have also led to a food safety problem. According to a recent report, more than 44 per cent of the rice in Guizhou Province contained cadmium levels exceeding the national standards.[4] In addition, as the food supply chain extends, the chance of fraud and deception in food processing increases. There have been numerous media reports on food safety problems, such as the deadly baby formula scandal and thousands of sick babies.[5] The concerns for food safety would of course comprise part of general concerns about quality of life.

0.4.4 REGIONAL DIVERGENCE AND THE PROVINCIAL PERSPECTIVE

Regional balance and regional divergence is a major policy issue in China. The roots of this concern go back many hundreds, if not thousands, of years. For example, the Berkeley historian Roy Bin Wong (2011) has highlighted spatial dimensions and concerns in the economic policies of the eighteenth-century Qing empire in the context of the broad sweep of Chinese history:

---

[2] <http://www.guardian.co.uk/environment/chinas-choice/2013/jun/07/chinas-environmental-problems-grim-ministry-report>.

[3] 'Water pollution: A Bay of Pigs moment', <http://www.economist.com/blogs/analects/2013/03/water-pollution>, 12 March 2013.

[4] <http://www.foodsafetynews.com/2013/06/director-general-of-fao-expresses-worry-about-food-safety-and-pollution-in-china/#.UbhwfflQGB8>.

[5] <http://blogs.wsj.com/chinarealtime/2013/05/21/why-americans-should-worry-about-chinas-food-safety-problems/>.

Chinese officials understood that the maritime regions of the empire posed different opportunities and challenges than the landlocked interior. . . . The state moreover showed special awareness of the needs of more peripheral and poorer regions to which it sent resources in efforts to make the agrarian economy more viable for populations that were in some places growing quickly because of migration. . . . Ideas about promoting food supply security and the importance of a materially secure population to the political fortunes of rulers go back to pre-imperial Chinese political thought and took various institutional forms over the two thousand years in which imperial rule was the norm more often than not. (Wong, 2011: 105–6)

The needs of a fissiparous empire facing continuous challenges from the outside, with some of the dynasties themselves being from 'beyond the Great Wall' (e.g. Mongols and their descendents in the north), meant that the state of well-being in all parts of China has been a deep rooted concern in policy making.

It is this historical context that has framed the story of regional divergence in China since the revolution. Kanbur and Zhang (2005) and Fan et al. (2011) have documented the evolution of spatial inequality in China during this period using inequality decomposition methods, focusing on population weighted mean consumption across provinces, and across rural and urban areas within provinces. Kanbur and Zhang (2005) identify three phases of regional inequality trends from 1952 to 2000, and Fan et al. (2011) suggest a possible new trend in the latest data. As measured in these studies, regional inequality rose precipitously during the Great Leap Forward and the Great Famine, peaking in 1960. As the economy and society recovered from the Great Famine inequality fell, but began rising sharply again at the start of the Cultural Revolution in 1967. After the reforms began in 1978, with their initial focus on agricultural production, regional inequality fell until the mid-1980s.

However, after the mid-1980s China decentralized and opened up, and inequality, especially inter-provincial inequality, rose sharply. The coastal provinces pulled ahead while the inland provinces lagged behind. The econometric analysis in Kanbur and Zhang (2005) identifies measures of decentralization and measures of openness as the key correlates of rising spatial inequality. In the dynamics of the process, it can be seen how decentralization and openness interacted. Opening up provided the initial boost to coastal provinces. More of their rising revenues were left with them under the new dispensation of decentralization. This allowed them to invest further in infrastructure and to attract industry to build on their natural comparative advantage of location, and the spiral was set in motion.

In the face of this rising inequality, it is perhaps not surprising given the historical context elucidated by Wong (2011) that the government began an active programme of investment in the lagging regions in the form of a 'western development strategy' (also known as 'Go West'). As summarized by Fan et al. (2011: 52) based on the work of Yao (2009):

Between 2000 and 2005, the central government started 70 main construction projects and the total amount of investment in western regions reached one trillion Yuan (Yao, 2009). More than one third of funds raised by long term government bonds for construction were directed to the western regions at this time, and from 2002 to 2005 the percent of funds from these bonds directed to the region reached 40% (Yao, 2009).

These investments and other major trends such as the tightening of labour markets in rural areas are having their effect. Fan et al. (2011) identify a possible fourth phase of regional inequality: 'overall, regional inequality has leveled off and even slightly declined since the mid-2000s'.

A particular feature of this *Companion* is the perspective it provides from across a range of provinces. The twelve entries in Part XV range from coastal provinces such as Guangdong and Jiangsu to inland provinces such as Sichuan and Guizhou. Many of these entries are written by local policy makers and analysts, providing a window into local concerns and aspirations. In the fast growing regions like Guangdong, a new generation of policy problem issues has been identified:

As the origin of China's market economic reform, Guangdong has encountered almost all of the conflicts, problems, and challenges that have occurred during the socioeconomic development of the nation. . . . how should the next round of reforms be initiated to mitigate conflicts and improve the economic competitiveness of the province? . . . Guangdong is currently at a critical juncture for the transformation of its economic structure and growth model, and acceleration of its social reform. Therefore, the next round of reforms should be staged not only in the economic domain, but also within the government system. (Guo Wanda, *this volume, entry on Guangdong*)

For Sichuan province, on the other hand, much of the policy making is now seen through the prism of the consequences of and responses to the massive earthquake of 2008:

On Monday, May 12, 2008, an earthquake that registered 8.0 on the Richter scale struck Sichuan, with its epicenter in Wenchuan County. This earthquake, the most devastating natural disaster in the area since 1949, resulted in 69,227 casualties with 374,643 people injured and 17,923 missing. Residential, transportation, and industrial infrastructure was thoroughly damaged. The direct loss was reported to have exceeded RMB 1 trillion. . . . After the event, the Sichuan government adopted the following guiding principles towards reconstruction: develop industry, support job creation, assist the poor, protect the environment, and facilitate social development. (Changwen Zhao, *this volume, entry on Sichuan*)

Perhaps the most consistent theme in the provincial entries in Part XV is the combination of good governance to address development and distributional issues. In this they are consistent with the more macro perspective provided in Fan et al. (2011), where it is argued that apart from market reform to aid the equalization of wages across the country, infrastructure investment, social protection, and governance reform will be the key components of managing regional divergence in China. And it does appear that, after a period of increasing geographical inequality, government policy has now returned to the historical norm of concerns about disparities in well-being across the vastness of China.

China is vast internally, but it is also a growing force in global markets and global institutions. Its actions now affect global trends as much as global trends affect its own economic performance. The next section therefore turns to China's international challenges.

0.5 **China and the world**

0.5.1 INTERNATIONAL TRADE AND CAPITAL FLOWS

If one thinks Chinese GDP growth is impressive, the growth of its international trade (exports and imports) is even more astonishing. Since 1980, its trade volume has roughly doubled once every four years. In 1990, Chinese exports ranked 14th in the world and its imports ranked 17th, smaller than Belgium. In 2012, China was the world's largest exporter and the second largest importer. If one were to follow a conventional measure of openness by looking at the ratio of total trade to GDP, China (at close to 70 per cent) is substantially more open than the USA (at about 20 per cent) or Japan (at about 30 per cent). How has China achieved such a rapid rise in trade openness? What does the conventional measure of trade openness fail to capture in the Chinese case?

To understand China's growth in trade openness, beyond looking at the falling tariffs and non-tariff barriers, four factors are especially important: de-monopolization, foreign direct investment, the WTO accession, and global value chains.

Before 1980, China was economically closed. Besides traditional trade barriers, state monopoly in trading rights was a key barrier to trade. As a rule, a majority of Chinese firms could not directly engage in exports and imports. If they traded at all, they did so indirectly by going through a state-owned trading company. This raised the cost of participating in international trade, leading to a smaller volume of trade. This also reduced the learning Chinese firms could have obtained from dealing with international clients or global suppliers directly. The country undertook several stages to de-monopolize the state trading rights by progressively granting more firms the right to trade directly. This contributed greatly to expanding trade volume.

Foreign firms, either wholly owned or joint ventures with Chinese firms, are another major contributor to Chinese export expansion. In the early days of the reform, most Chinese firms lacked the technical, marketing, or managerial know-how to export successfully to the world market. Foreign firms bridge that gap by taking designs, machines, market orders, and sometimes even foreign-made intermediate goods to China, as well as organizing production in China. In much of the 1990s and 2000s, exports by foreign invested firms accounted for over 50 per cent of China's overall exports. At the same time, imports by foreign invested firms also accounted for a big (50 per cent) share of the country's overall import shares.

The accession to the World Trade Organization (WTO) in 2001 was another watershed event on China's road to becoming a great trading nation. Even in the years leading up to the WTO accession, it had engaged in a large number of trade and industrial reforms, inspired by market access and other demands from trading partner countries. This included massive reductions in tariff levels, eliminating or reducing non-tariff barriers, and importantly making the regulatory regimes of firms more transparent. Many of the reforms were in fact demanded by domestic firms, including and maybe especially by private sector firms; the negotiations for WTO membership became an opportunity or a commitment device to undertake these reforms. The end results benefitted not just firms in trading partners or multinational firms in China, but also Chinese firms in general. Interestingly, even though China's WTO accession required one-sided reforms—China needed to undertake reforms to satisfy the demands of existing members of the WTO while trading partners did not need to do anything—the trade reforms provided a substantial boost to both exports and imports. When import competing sectors shrink, domestic resources (including labour, raw materials, and capital) have to be redeployed to other sectors, including sectors that produce for the world market. Calibrations by Ju et al. (2012) suggest that the WTO accession may account for one-third or one-half of the observed growth in China's trade expansion (in both exports and imports).

To understand China's trade expansion, one cannot ignore the country's active participation in global value chains (GVCs). With the reductions in policy-induced trade barriers, improvement in shipping and other transportation technologies, and reductions in communication costs, production in most sectors has become increasingly segmented across national borders. Over the last two decades, China has become one of the most notable participants in GVCs. For example, most iPhones and iPads sold in the world are technically produced in and exported by China. But of course, the actual production utilizes designs from the USA and key components from Japan, Korea, Taiwan, and several other economies. Participation in GVCs allows China to be a major producer and exporter of products that would normally be considered sophisticated or advanced such as telecommunication equipment, computers, and chemical products (see Koopman et al., 2012).

These four factors—'democratization' of trading rights, inward foreign direct investment, WTO accession, and participation in GVCs—have, at different stages, contributed to the astonishing growth in the country's overall trade volumes.

0.6 International capital flows

China's composition of capital inflows is quite distinct: it is overwhelmingly dominated by inward FDI, with comparatively little foreign portfolio inflows or borrowing from foreign banks. The volume of FDI is an outcome of the country's deliberate policy to attract foreign firms to come to China for their technology and for their managerial and marketing know-how. At the time of writing, China is the largest developing country recipient of FDI. Even as a share of GDP, China attracts more FDI than India, Brazil, or Russia. China's relatively small volumes of foreign bank borrowing and foreign portfolio inflows are the outcomes of its capital control policies, which have been liberalized at a deliberately slow pace.

While the capital control regimes carry some efficiency costs, they also bring benefits in terms of financial stability. China managed to escape from the worst of the Asian financial crisis of 1997–99 and the global financial crisis of 2007–09 in large part thanks to its capital control regimes. In planning for its financial liberalization programmes in the years ahead, this tradeoff between financial stability and economic efficiency needs to be borne in mind. In particular, liberalization of capital controls needs to be commensurate with the country's financial supervisory and regulatory capacity and the private sector's risk management capacity.

China's participation in GVCs implies that the share of China's domestic value in its exports is low. Koopman et al. (2012) estimated that on average, the domestic value share of exports is about 50 per cent. The share is much lower in sectors that are conventionally thought to be sophisticated because they are more likely to use a high share of imported components and machineries. Understanding GVCs could correct misperceptions about bilateral trade imbalances. For example, much of China's exports to the USA reflects indirect exports of value added to the USA by Japan, Korea, Taiwan, and other economies. In comparison, most of the Chinese imports from the USA actually reflect the US domestic value added. According to Koopman et al. (2012), the China–US bilateral surplus in value added terms is about 25 per cent less than the bilateral surplus in gross trade.

The Chinese current account surplus is not a mystery. Two factors are especially noteworthy. The first is China's accession to the WTO in late 2001, which, by itself, tends to reduce the domestic return to capital, generating incentives for the country to hold a greater portion of its wealth in foreign assets during a transitional period of about six to seven years. Research by Ju et al. (2012) suggests that this has contributed one-third of the surplus we observe.

The second factor is a rising ratio of marrying-age young men to young women since 2002. This imbalance has caused young men, and especially their parents, to raise their savings rate in order to compete better in the marriage market. The same force has also contributed to a rise in corporate savings because more parents with an unmarried son and more young men themselves have chosen to be entrepreneurs. Given the difficulty in getting a bank loan, new entrepreneurs and small firms must rely on their own savings to finance their operation and expansion. Wei and Zhang (2011) and Du and Wei (2013) estimate that this force has accounted for another one-third of the current account surplus.

To be sure, other factors also matter. Collectively, they account for the remaining one-third of the surplus. Because the gradual reforms associated with the WTO accession have been completed, the part of the surplus due to this factor is naturally winding down. In contrast, because the sex ratio imbalance will rise over the next decade, the part of the surplus due to this factor is not going away any time soon.

0.6.1 CHINA AND THE DEVELOPING WORLD

With a per capita income of just over $6,000 at official exchange rates, China is classified as an Upper Middle Income Country. Its per capita income is four times that of India, eight times that of Bangladesh, and twelve times that of Ethiopia. Chinese officials sometimes refer to China as the 'world's largest developing country' (Mitchell, 2006). If so, it is clearly *primus inter pares* in its relations with many if not most other developing countries, be they political or economic relations. Our focus here is primarily on economic relations between China and other low income countries. We will highlight two aspects of the relationships—first, China as a comparator and guide for other developing countries and, second, Chinese trade, investment, and aid, particularly in relation to Africa.

It is interesting to begin by noting the tradition of comparison between the two giants of the developing world, India and China, as reflected in the entry in this volume by Pranab Bardhan. India entered its economic reform phase a decade after China, and has had historically high growth rates, especially in the 2000s before the global financial crisis, but these growth rates have been significantly below those of China, and the gap in per capita income has widened over the years. At the same time, social indicators in China have by and large been at higher levels, and have improved faster, than those in India.

Amartya Sen (2011), in particular, has highlighted a range of differences in achievement between the two countries. Life expectancy is 73.5 years in China and 64.4 years in India; adult literacy rates are 94 per cent and 74 per cent, respectively; triple vaccination immunization rates for children are 97 per cent and 66 per cent. Of course some of this is explained simply by the fact that China has a much higher income level than India. But the burden of Sen's argument is that income alone cannot explain variations in social indicators—how that income is used matters as well. He points out that public expenditure on social sectors in India lags behind that in China. However, as Sen has also pointed out in his writings, the Great Famine of 1959–62 killed more than 30 million people in China, whereas the Indian political system, backed by a free press, has ensured that such a massive catastrophe has not happened in India since independence. Sen has helped to crystallize a debate on the advantages of the Indian system in preventing famines while at the same time allowing widespread 'silent hunger' in the form of malnutrition. For India as for other developing countries, comparisons with China are very much part of the policy debate.

More generally in the realm of economic policy, Chinese success has acted as a role model for other developing countries, and has also entered the debate on the relevance of the 'Washington Consensus' for development strategy. As developed by Justin Lin, in his entry in this volume and in Lin (2012), the Chinese experience leads to a significant modification of the tenets of the Washington Consensus. While market discipline and market mechanisms are not jettisoned by any means, purposive involvement of the state in helping structural transformation, including through industrial policy, is the lesson that is being drawn across the developing world from the Chinese experience.

But it is not only the impact of China's experience on development thinking that has been important. The direct effect of China on trade, investment, and aid has also been significant. As Mitchell (2006) notes, among the top ten sources of China's oil imports are Angola, Sudan, Equatorial Guinea, and Indonesia. China has equity oil stakes in many Latin American countries, including Venezuela. It is a major purchaser of a range of minerals from Brazil. It accounts for 40 per cent of Chile's copper exports. The net result of these relationships is that growth in many developing countries is directly linked to healthy growth in China, and the pattern of that growth matters too. If China switches its pattern of demand from industrial to a more consumer-oriented structure, then this could have repercussions, including perhaps opening up export opportunities for some countries. This effect could be further strengthened by rising wages in China allowing some countries to occupy export niches previously taken up by Chinese light manufacturing.

China itself has also begun to invest in developing countries, and this investment goes beyond that associated with oil and natural resources. In particular, China's economic relations with Africa have garnered a lot of interest in the analytical and in the popular discourse. Deborah Brautigam, a contributor to this Companion, quotes Chinese figures that show that:

as of end 2011, 15.6% of their Africa investment is in manufacturing and 30.6% in mining, with finance at 19.5% and construction at 16.4%. From what I can see, there is far more manufacturing investment from China than from the United States. (Brautigam, 2013: np)

Brautigam's work details the relationship at the country-specific level as well, including in Ethiopia:

when Ethiopia's economy began to grow at Asian rates, the Chinese saw increased opportunities. Not all were in the direction stereotypes would have predicted. For example, while Chinese petroleum companies have done work in Ethiopia, this has been largely under contract for others. Rather, the Chinese unleashed a variety of state-sponsored tools for building economic ties. (Brautigam, 2012: np).

Not all Chinese investment in Africa has come without adverse comment or reaction. Although there is little in the way of systematic evidence, journalistic reporting is pointing to growing tensions. In its survey of China in Africa, the *Economist* magazine paints a cautionary picture: 'Once feted as saviours in Africa, Chinese have come to be viewed with mixed feelings—especially in smaller countries where China's weight is felt all the more. . . . Chinese expatriates in Africa come from a rough-and-tumble, anything-goes business culture that cares little about rules and regulations. Local sensitivities are routinely ignored at home, and so abroad' (*Economist*, 2011).

Thus an interesting connection is made between the improvement of governance within China and improved practices in Chinese investment abroad.

Finally, Chinese aid to Africa (and elsewhere) is increasingly coming under scrutiny, and is discussed in Deborah Brautigam's entry in the *Companion*. Chinese official aid expenditures on grants and interest free loans were estimated to be $2.7 billion in 2011. Adding in concessional loans would increase this to $6 billion. There is considerable discussion among the 'traditional' OECD donors on Chinese aid practices. For example, China typically does not put economic and especially political conditions on aid, a stance which is greatly welcomed by aid recipients, and it emphasizes economic infrastructure as opposed to broader issues of governance. Thus in the aid arena, as in the arena of economic policies, Chinese practice differs from the norm and is leading to a healthy debate on the best methods of delivering development assistance.

China's growing importance in development assistance is one aspect of a more extensive, and intensive, engagement with institutions of global governance, and we turn now to an exploration of these challenges.

0.6.2 INTERNATIONAL INSTITUTIONS AND GLOBAL GOVERNANCE

China's participation in the international economic governance system has evolved in three stages. Before the 1980s, as a first stage, the country chose to stay out of the international system, as reflected in its low trading volume, minimum cross-border capital flows, and economic mismanagement at home. In the second stage, from 1980 to sometime close to 2010, China has been a follower of international rules set largely by the USA and other systemically important economies. This was not done with resentment. In fact, both the government and the private sector often invoke a need to 'follow the common international norms and practices' as a roadmap for economic reforms at home, which has greatly benefited the Chinese economy. In more recent years, China may be entering a third stage, actively seeking to be one of the rule makers. An example is China's suggestion that the dominant position of the US dollar in international trade settlement and as a reserve currency can be revised and re-visited in ways that might be beneficial to developing countries in general. China has also started to promote the internationalization of its currency, apparently ahead of other countries at a similar or even somewhat higher stage of economic development.

To understand the Chinese approach to economic reforms, it is important to appreciate the role of digesting and following international norms and rules. Of course, China does not blindly follow foreign advice or foreign models. Its reform programmes have many distinct features such as the dual-track reforms, special economic zones, and super-national treatment of foreign firms operating in China. Nonetheless, examples of international practices and norms often shorten the country's learning curve significantly.

The WTO accession is a good example of reformers in the government using the pressure of international rules and that of trading partners to further the goals of domestic reforms. China used to have a very complex and non-transparent web of government regulations, many of which were either not published or contradictory to each other. The main beneficiaries of the opacity were a small number of politically connected firms and bureaucrats who yielded enormous discretionary power. The main victims were domestic private firms, and many unborn and still-born entrepreneurs, in addition to multinational firms operating in China or wanting to do business with Chinese firms. As part of the WTO accession negotiation, China had to make the regulatory regime much more transparent. While foreign firms were the principle vocal proponents of the reform, the largest beneficiaries were in fact domestic Chinese firms. In that sense, the WTO accession is a significant event for China in ways beyond lower import trade barriers.

In the years leading up to China's membership in the WTO, there were concerns (mostly outside China) that China will be involved in so many trade disputes that it will overwhelm the WTO's young dispute settlement mechanism (DSM). The fear is that not only will many countries bring cases against China to the DSM but China will also bring an equal number of cases against other member countries. In the six years after China's membership, it was surprising to find that at least half of this fear had not been realized. China chose not to bring any cases against other countries in spite of it being subjected to many cases brought by the USA, the European Union, and some other economies. Because the system is new and novel to China, it apparently decided to observe and learn. However, in 2007, China brought its first case (against the USA). It has apparently now decided to be as active in initiating complaints as it is in receiving them.

Since the onset of the North Atlantic financial crisis, because China has emerged relatively stronger than most high-income countries, the global crisis has led to some re-thinking in China about its relationship with the international economic system. In particular, it is more willing to question whether the rules that have been governing the international economy as conceived and championed by the USA and other leading industrial economies are optimal for the world economy. China's surpassing of Japan as the world's second largest economy since 2011 has added to its confidence. As a result, China has started to demand a more significant role in the rule-making process. A visible but perhaps less significant part of the process is in the personnel areas of international organizations. Chinese nationals became deputy secretary general of the United Nations in charge of economic affairs, deputy managing director of the International Monetary Fund, senior vice president and the chief economist of the World Bank, vice president of the Asian Development Bank, and so on. This is not as significant as it may have appeared in part because nationals of India, an economy half the size of China, held similar positions long before Chinese nationals did.

A more important part of the process is the generation of ideas on the agenda of major international fora. In March 2009, the governor of China's central bank opined that an international monetary system that depends so heavily on a single reserve currency, the US dollar, is inherently risky and could make the consequence of a financial crisis worse than it otherwise would be, and advocated a move to a greater use of the IMF's special drawing rights (SDRs) as a reserve currency. When the call for greater SDR use did not receive the necessary political support from the USA (unsurprisingly), the Chinese central bank and the Chinese government started to do something that is at least partly within their power—to promote greater international use of the renminbi (RMB) as a currency for trade settlement, for denominating financial swap lines among central banks, and for limited use as a reserve currency by other central banks.

The promotion of the internationalization of the RMB is unusual in several ways. First, almost all other countries at China's stage of economic development are resigned to using other countries' currencies, typically those of a few high-income countries with a deep and liquid capital market, for all international transactions in both goods and services trade and financial trade. In fact, the US dollar alone takes up about 70 per cent of global non-gold foreign exchange reserves. A small number of other currencies, the euro, the Japanese yen, Swiss franc, and pound sterling, in particular, take up the majority of the remaining 30 per cent. Due to concerns about potential complications for domestic monetary policy operations, Japan actively discouraged any international use of its currency during its peak economic miracle years. (When it changed its mind and started to promote internationalization of the yen in the 1990s, it made little progress.) The world market for international currencies appeared to be settled in its equilibrium without much appetite for a new currency. So China's move is unusual and unprecedented when benchmarked to other countries' experiences.

Second, China's promotion of RMB internationalization is not without risk. From the perspective of safeguarding financial stability, the optimal sequence of reforms dictates that China needs to address the governance problems within its banking sector as each of its large majority state-owned banks represents a potential systemic risk, to have market determined interest rates and exchange rates, and to strengthen its domestic financial supervisory capacity before it can safely lift capital controls which would be a prerequisite for any true internationalization of the RMB (Wei, 2013). Instead, in an eagerness to promote the global use of the RMB, China has selectively and creatively opened its capital controls through the use of a qualified foreign institutional investors (QFII) scheme and qualified domestic institutional investors (QDII) scheme, and the use of Hong Kong based financial institutions to undertake RMB-related financial transactions otherwise not allowed by the capital controls regimes. These experiments have gone reasonably smoothly and are in accordance with China's well-practised gradualist style of reforms. China is now contemplating a bolder move to lift most of the remaining measures of capital controls in the next few years. If that policy change proves to be premature, China might risk a financial crisis of the kind that Thailand or Korea experienced during 1997–99. On the other hand, if that policy change succeeds, the Chinese currency could become a serious rival to the US dollar, or at least displace the euro and the yen over time as a major alternative to the US dollar. Perhaps more significantly, ideas coming out of Beijing on reforming the international economic system may attract a more attentive audience.

0.7 Conclusion: emerging issues and future challenges

China is now at a crossroads. After more than three decades of growth based on removing policy distortions to realize its comparative advantage, government investment in infrastructure to boost aggregate demand and productivity, and promotion of exports and foreign investment, this growth model has shown signs of diminishing returns. There are two paths ahead. China can be another South Korea, which is embarking on a transition to a more innovation-based growth model, or it can become Argentina, which used to have a more promising and favourable future than most other developing countries, but managed to squander the opportunity and has been stuck in a middle-income trap. Of course, China wishes to take the first path. It could adjust its growth model, developing more domestic demand and cultivating legal and education systems that are compatible with an innovation-based growth model.

To stay on an upward trajectory of economic growth, the Chinese economy has to face a host of emerging challenges. First, the growing demands of an increasingly affluent and urban population threaten to undermine an already stressed natural resource base. Especially pressing environmental issues include climate change, air pollution, water scarcity and pollution, and land degradation. These environmental challenges are exacerbated by government policies that distort prices for energy, water, and land.

Second, inequalities across and within regions have been on the rise, raising concerns over the potential impact that such disparities could have on future economic growth, social equity, and political stability (OECD, 2012; Fan et al., 2011). Although less prosperous regions have experienced increased economic growth during the last decade as a result of preferential policies and investments under the 'Western development strategy', regional disparities continue to be on the rise (Golley, 2007). The government's recent Income Redistribution Plan—which calls for state-owned companies to pay higher taxes and dividends, increase minimum wage, and improve access to the healthcare and pension system (especially for migrants)—is a significant step by the government to rebalance China's growth and spread wealth more evenly. However, the plan's vague wording and lack of specific directives could act as a potential impediment to its implementation.

Third, China's large network of state-owned enterprises—which hold monopolies in 'strategic sectors' such as banking, telecommunications, energy, and utilities—distort the balanced development of China's economy due to weak corporate governance structures and subsidized inputs. For example, state-owned enterprises have access to low interest loans from the state-dominated banking sector, while (often more efficient) private small and medium-sized enterprises are turned away. Such preferential access to cheap credit for state-owned enterprises stifles competition and innovation from the private sector (both domestic and foreign) and encourages the inefficient allocation of resources, over-investment, and overcapacity in industrial production (World Bank, 2013a; Chen et al., 2011). At the same time, the monopolistic and weak corporate governance structures of SOEs have bred special interest groups of political and economic elites who have profited from preferential treatment.

While the enormity of the challenges China faces cannot be overstated, no one should underestimate China's ability to rise to the challenges either. After all, the reforms and transitions of the last three decades and half were no easy feat. What are the things China can do that could enhance the chance of success in its quest to become the next Korea? The reform process can continue to put greater focus on supporting the equitable and sustainable growth of China's economy. The increasingly scarce and degraded state of natural resources demands policies that strengthen environmental regulations and their supervision. More efficient and sustainable management of natural resources can also be supported through reforms to resource pricing systems so that consumers receive the proper signals about the true cost of resource use. In terms of inequality, policies are needed to equalize opportunities for income generation, including greater access to education—especially among the rural poor—and the elimination of restrictions on rural–urban migration. By spreading wealth more evenly, the government hopes to rebalance China's economy so that economic growth originates more from domestic consumption and demand. The gradual removal of institutional barriers—including the liberalization of interest rates and reduction of input subsidies—alongside the privatization and restructuring of SOEs will help to create a vibrant and innovative private sector that can compete on an equal footing with state-owned enterprises. These latter reforms will inevitably face opposition from the politically and economically influential individuals who stand to lose their privileged (and profitable) position within the SOE apparatus.

The Chinese model of development is not a silver bullet of development policies that can be easily replicated in other developing countries. Rather, China's development experience should be seen as a process towards a more efficient, market-driven, and lately equitable final goal through gradual reforms, experimentation, and learning-by-doing.

Going forwards, whether China can succeed in its transition to a new growth model, and how it decides to meet countless challenges that will undoubtedly emerge, will have socioeconomic consequences not only for the Chinese but also for the rest of the world.

■ REFERENCES

Almond, Douglas. This volume, pp. 436–440.

Appleton, Simon, Lina Song, and Qingjie Xia. 2010. Growing out of poverty: trends and patterns of urban poverty in China 1988–2002. *World Development* 38(5), 665–78.

Babiarz, Kimberly Singer, Grant Miller, Hongmei Yi, Linxiu Zhang, and Scott Rozelle. 2010. New evidence on the impact of China's New Rural Cooperative Medical Scheme and its implications for rural primary healthcare: multivariate difference-in-difference analysis. *BMJ* 341: c5617.

Brautigam, Deborah. 2012. Ethiopia's Partnership with China. <http://www.guardian.co.uk/global-development/poverty-matters/2011/dec/30/china-ethiopia-business-opportunities> 24 January.

Brautigam, Deborah. 2013. Obama, China and Africa: Manufacturing. <http://www.chinaafricarealstory.com/> July1.

Bruce, J. and Z. Li. 2009. 'Crossing the River While Feeling the Rocks' Incremental Land Reform and its Impact on Rural Welfare in China. IFPRI Discussion Paper 926. Washington, DC: International Food Policy Research Institute.

Cai, Hongbin. This volume, pp. 428–432.

Chen, Xi. This volume, pp. 406–410.

Chen, S., G. Jefferson, and J. Zhang. 2011. Structural change, productivity growth and industrial transformation in China. *China Economic Review* 22(1), 133–50.

China National Bureau of Statistics (CNBS). Various years. *China Statistical Yearbook*. Beijing: China Statistical Press.

Dekle, R. and G. Vandenbroucke. 2012. A quantitative analysis of China's structural transformation. *Journal of Economic Dynamics and Control* 36, 119–35.

Du, R. 2010. The course of China's rural reform. In *Narratives of Chinese Economic Reforms: How Does China Cross the River?* edited by X. Zhang, S. Fan, and A. De Haan, 15–29. Singapore: World Scientific Publishing.

Du, Qingyuan and Shang-Jin Wei. 2013. A Theory of the Competitive Saving Motive. NBER Working Paper # 18911.

Easterlin. This volume, pp. 401–405.

The Economist. 2011. 'The Chinese in Africa.' April 20, <http://www.economist.com/node/18586448?story_id=18586448>.

Fan, Shenggen, Ravi Kanbur, and Xiaobo Zhang. 2011. China's regional disparities: experience and policy. *Review of Development Finance* 1(1), 47–56.

Fang, Cheng, Xiaobo Zhang, and Shenggen Fan. 2002. The emerging urban poverty and inequality in China: evidence from Household Survey. *China Economic Review* 13(4), 430–43.

Fogel, Robert and Nathaniel Grotte. This volume, pp. 66–69.

Golley, J. 2007. China's Western Development Strategy and nature versus nurture. *Journal of Chinese Economic and Business Studies* 5(2), 115–29.

Huang, Jikun, Xiaobing Wang, and Huanguang Qiu. 2012. *Small-Scale Farmers in China in the Face of Modernisation and Globalization*. London/The Hague: International Institute for Environment and Development/HIVOS Citation (IIED)/HIVOS.

Jiandong Ju, Kang Shi, and Shang-Jin Wei. 2012. Trade Reforms and Current Account Imbalances: When Does the General Equilibrium Effect Overturn a Partial Equilibrium Intuition? NBER Working Paper # 18653.

Kanbur, Ravi and Xiaobo Zhang. 2005. Fifty years of regional inequality in China: a journey through revolution, reform and openness. *Review of Development Economics* 9(1), 87–106.

Knight, John. This volume, pp. 422–427.

Koopman, Robert, Zhi Wang, and Shang-Jin Wei. 2012. Estimating domestic content in exports when processing trade is pervasive. *Journal of Development Economics* 99(1): 178–89.

Lei, Xiaoyan and Wanchun Lin. 2009. The New Cooperative Medical Scheme in rural China: does more coverage mean more service and better health? *Health Economics* Supplement 2, S25–46.

Li, Haizheng. This volume, pp. 465–471.

Li, S., L. Chuliang, and T. Sicular. 2013. 'Overview: income inequality and poverty in China, 2002–2007.' In *Rising Inequality in China: Challenge to the Harmonious Society*, edited by Li Shi, Hiroshi Sato, and Terry Sicular, 24–59. Cambridge and New York: Cambridge University Press.

Lin, Justin Yifu. This volume, pp. 251–255.

Lin, Justin Yifu. 1992. Rural reforms and agricultural growth in China. *American Economic Review*. 82(1), 34–51.

Lin, Justin Yifu. 2012. *New Structural Economics: A Framework for Rethinking Development and Policy*. Washington, DC: The World Bank.

Lin, Justin Yifu and Y. Wang. 2009. China's Integration with the World: Development as a Process of Learning and Industrial Upgrading. Policy Research Working Paper Series 4799. Washington, DC: World Bank.

Meng, Xin. This volume, pp. 382–387.

Mitchell, Derek J. 2006. China and the Developing World. <http://csis.org/files/media/csis/pubs/090212_06china_developing.pdf>.

OECD. 2012. *China in Focus: Lessons and Challenges*. Paris: OECD.

O'Brien, Kevin J. and Lianjiang Li. 2000. Accommodating 'democracy' in a one-party state: introducing village elections in China. *The China Quarterly* 162, 465–89.

Qian, N. This volume, pp. 330–333.

Ravallion, Martin and Shaohua Chen. 2007. China's (uneven) progress against poverty. *Journal of Development Economics* 82(1), 1–42.

Reardon, T., K. Chen, B. Minten, and L. Adriano. 2012. *The Quiet Revolution in Staple Food Value Chains Enter the Dragon, the Elephant, and the Tiger*. Mandaluyong City, Philippines: Asian Development Bank.

Riskin, Carl. This volume, pp. 417–421.

Rodrik, D. 2005. Growth strategies. In *Handbook of Economic Growth*, edited by P. Aghion and S. Durlauf. Edition 1, Volume 1. Amsterdam: North Holland.

Rozelle, Scott, Linxiu Zhang, Hongmei Yi, Renfu Luo, and Changfang Liu. 2013. The Human Capital Roots of the Middle Income Trap: Education, Nutrition and Health Inequality in China, paper presented at Conference on the Study of Inequality in China, 17 June, Beijing.

Sen, Amartya. 2011. Quality of life: India vs. China. *New York Review of Books*, May 12.

Sicular, Terry, Ximing Yue, Björn Gustafsson, and Shi Li. 2007. The urban–rural income gap and inequality in China. *Review of Income and Wealth* 53(1), 93–126.

Shang-Jin Wei. 2013. Chinese financial sector reforms: Five tasks and the optimal sequence. Mimeograph. Columbia University.

Shang-Jin Wei. and Xiaobo Zhang. 2011. Sex Ratios, Entrepreneurship, and Economic Growth in the People's Republic of China. NBER Working Paper # 16800.

Song, Lina. This volume, pp. 230–234.

United Nations Population Division. 2012. World urbanization prospects: the 2011 revision. New York: United Nations Population Division. <http://esa.un.org/unpd/wup/unup/index_panel1.html> accessed 12 June 2013.

Wei, Shang-Jin and Xiaobo Zhang. 2011. 'The competitive saving motive: evidence from rising sex ratios and savings rates in China. *Journal of Political Economy* 119(3), 511–64.

Wei, Shang-Jin and Xiaobo Zhang. 2013. Immiserizing Growth: Some Evidence (from China with Hope for Love). Memo.

Wong, R. Bin. 2011. Social spending in contemporary China: historical priorities and contemporary possibilities. In *History, Historians, and Development Policy*, edited by C. A. Bayly et al., 117–21. Manchester: Manchester University Press.

World Bank. 2013. *World Bank Development Indicators*. Washington, DC: World Bank. <http://data.world-bank.org/data-catalog/world-development-indicators> accessed 10 June 2013.

World Bank. 2013a. *China 2030 Building a Modern, Harmonious, and Creative Society*. Washington, DC: World Bank.

Xie, Yu, Xiaobo Zhang, Qi Xu, and Chunni Zhang. 2013. Income distribution. In: Yu Xie, Xiaobo Zhang, Qiang Ren. and Jianxin Li. *China Livelihood Report 2012*, 27–50. Beijing: Peking University Press. [In Chinese.]

Xing, L., S. Fan, X. Luo, and X. Zhang. 2009. Community poverty and inequality in Western China: A tale of three villages in Guizhou Province. *China Economic Review* 20(2), 338–49.

Xing, Haipeng and Xiaobo Zhang. 2013. The Logic of Adaptive Sequential Experimentation in Policy Design. International Food Policy Research Institute Discussion Paper No. 01273.

Xu, Cheng-Gang and Qian, Yingyi. 1993. Why China's economic reforms differ: The M-form hierarchy and entry/expansion of the non-state sector. *The Economics of Transition* 1(2), 135–70.

Yang, J., Z. Huang, X. Zhang, and T. Reardon. 2013. The rapid rise of cross-regional agricultural mechanization services in China. *American Journal of Agricultural Economics* (Papers and Proceedings), 1–7. October 2013.

Yao, Y. 2009. The political economy of government policies toward regional inequality in China. In *Reshaping Economic Geography in East Asia*, edited by Yukon Huang and Alessandro M. Bocchi, 218–40. Washington, DC: World Bank.Yu, Miaojie. 2012. Industrial Structural Upgrading and Poverty Reduction in China. China Center for Economic Research, <http://mjyu.ccer.edu.cn/Yu_UNIDO.pdf>, accessed 10 May 2014.

Zeng, D. 2010. How do special economic zones and industrial clusters drive China's rapid development? In *Building Engines for Growth and Competitiveness in China* edited by D. Zheng (ed.), ch. 1. Washington, DC: World Bank.

Zhang, Chunni, Qi Xu, Xiang Zhou, Xiaobo Zhang, and Yu Xie. 2014. An Evaluation of Poverty Prevalence in China: New Evidence from Four Recent Surveys. *China Economic Review*, forthcoming.

Zhang, Liping and Simon J. Evenett. 2010. The Growth of China's Services Sector and Associated Trade: Complementarities between Structural Change and Sustainability. International Institute for Sustainable Development. <http://www.iisd.org/pdf/2010/sts_4_growth_china_services_sector.pdf> accessed 10 May 2014.

Zhang, X. B., A. de Haan, and S. Fan. 2010. *Narratives of Chinese Economic Reforms: How Does China Cross the River?* Singapore: World Scientific Publishing.

Zhang, X., J. Yang, and S. Wang. 2011. China has reached the Lewis turning point. *China Economic Review* 22(4), 542–54.

Part I
The China Model

1 From a manipulated revolution to manipulated marketization

A logic of the Chinese model

Xiaopeng Luo

Historically, the central authority of the Chinese Empire was empowered by its capacity to manipulate family competition through the Imperial Examination System. While this group selection mechanism (Wilson, 2012) effectively supported political centralization, it stifled regional competition, a critical group selection mechanism for political development. The collective identity system in contemporary China that was established after the Great Famine of 1959–60 has empowered the Chinese state to undertake large-scale social experiments through collectivity, including regional competition. Both Mao's Cultural Revolution and Deng Xiaoping's marketization were based on this so-called Danwei Society (a unit which works). As China has shown to the world in the last five decades, its collective identity system has legitimized and empowered the central authority to manipulate group selections for radical social changes in very different directions.

The collective identity system embodies two historical commitments made by the communist revolution: to build a strong modern state, and to build an equal society. While Mao's manipulated revolution failed to deliver an equal society, the legitimacy and the capacity of the party state remained strong, partly because the first promise was not totally broken, and partly because the sunk cost of the socialist experiment was too high for a complete reverse.

The political continuity of China's radical social changes from state socialism to state capitalism that has taken place in the last three decades has been remarkable. This continuity comes from the fact that both the political leadership and the state capacity were quite ready to adopt the global trends. Culturally, the state authority was not only rooted in a particular ideology, but also rooted in the traditional belief system that 'idealizes benevolent paternalistic leadership and the dependency between leaders and followers' (Pye, 1986). Institutionally, the state is capable of manipulating social change in opposite directions because the collective identity system in the Danwei Society has a built-in mechanism that substitutes social privilege with economic discretion (Luo, 1994, 2004). The tradability between social entitlements and economic freedom created great flexibility within the system.

The collective identity system of the Danwei Society was not designed by the top elites; it evolved because China could not afford an equal socialist entitlement system for its huge population. Consequently, social and economic entitlements were structured in a form very different from that of the Soviet Union and other East European countries. A unified social and economic hierarchy was formed, and rules and principles were set for how resources were to be allocated among the collective units with no exit freedom for individuals after the Great Famine of 1959–60. Therefore all collective entitlements were strictly attached to the ranked work units and localities. Birth rights play a critical role in defining social entitlements. A child whose mother is a peasant must inherit her rural status, which was at the bottom in the Danwei Society.

However, there were rules of social mobility in the Mao era set up for both individuals and collectives. These rules legitimized and institutionalized the state power to manipulate collectivity for both political and economic purposes. Individuals could move up the social hierarchy through education and political promotion. Rural collectives could move up to urban collectives through economic opportunities, such as state acquisition of land for industrial or urban developments. For urban industrial units, mobility was set for both moving up and down. For those units positioned at lower ranks, fewer resources were allocated by the state, but more economic discretion was permitted. So if greater economic freedom led to high profitability, these units had to be moved up to the next higher rank so that the state could take a higher rent while the members were allowed to enjoy higher social entitlements, but less economic discretion. Likewise, if profitability declined significantly, the collective could be demoted, which meant greater economic discretion but fewer social entitlements.

This trading of collective economic discretion with social entitlement was rooted in China's long tradition of trading wealth with social status by families, and in the Danwei Society of modern China this became a key mechanism in manipulating collectivity by the state.

The fatal weakness of sharing rents through hierarchy in the Danwei Society lay in the counterproductive incentive of collective farming. Because, for those failed rural collectives, the state was obliged to provide a minimal food supply to keep people alive. As the radicalism caused more rural collectives to fail, the state's obligation led to a heavy financial burden, and it gave peasants a painful but powerful lever to resist the collective farming system. After years of unremitting resistance, the collective farming system was dismantled.

The agricultural de-collectivization through the so called Household Responsibility System (HRS) in the early 1980s marks the beginning of the transition from a manipulated revolution to manipulated marketization. The principle of allocating most economic residuals to the state in the Danwei Society was reversed by the early years of the reforms. In order to increase productivity, the state had to allow most agricultural residuals to be retained by rural households and invested the rents to expand freedom. The fiscal decentralization which paralleled the HRS also followed the same principle: local governments were given more control over marginal revenues, which encouraged them to compete in improving their protection of property rights (Luo, 1986).

Encouraging rural collectives and local governments to buy economic freedom from the state was a successful strategy in the early years of the reforms because it was a process of Pareto improvement (everyone gains but not at the expense of others). This characteristic was clearly demonstrated by the process of agricultural de-collectivization. The HRS was first initiated in poor areas but initially strongly resisted by relatively rich provinces where the rural collectives were enjoying higher incomes through industrial activities. A significant part of the industrial revenue was used to subsidize their grain production, which was heavily taxed by the state through low procurement prices. The success of the HRS in poorer areas dramatically increased grain supply, therefore greatly reducing the state procurement from the rich collectives, so they were able to free up more labour and financial resources to expand industrial activities. As a result, the freedom bought by the peasants from the state in the poor areas actually enhanced the freedom of the peasants in the rich areas.

The rural de-collectivization combined with fiscal decentralization had led to a boom in rural industrialization, driven by the explosive growth of non-state enterprises and the rapid increase of rural savings. However, the bottleneck preventing peasants from further expanding their economic opportunity was the privilege of the urban sectors to access state rationed capital goods—which were underpriced. The dual-track price reform, initiated in the mid-1980s, released this bottleneck by allowing state enterprises to sell their products to peasants at market value after fulfilling output quotas. This reform established a new rule for the Danwei Society to expand economic freedom because it essentially allowed the rural sector and the private sector to buy more market power not only from the state, but also from the privileged urban sectors.

This strategy of marketization was very controversial because the distribution of rents from this transaction between the state sector and non-state sectors was neither well regulated nor transparent. While such transactions increased the economic freedom of the non-state sectors, it also created opportunities for rent seeking and corruption, thereby creating opportunities to enlarge social inequality. However, this principle was extensively applied by the state to manipulate all factor markets to the benefit of the state and the urban sectors from 1993 onwards, further empowering the state to systematically manipulate the process of marketization. As this preference dominated domestic investment, most of the rents generated from the marketization tended not to create more jobs for the huge rural labour force freed by the de-collectivization. Rural underemployment remained the largest challenge for the policy makers.

Zhao Ziyang's strategy of opening up whole coastal areas for FDI in export manufactures had created an opportunity for the state to shy away from the severe urban bias. Taking advantage of the rapid increase in export demand and FDI, the state was able to further increase its share of rent in the economy through manipulating regional completion. In the tax reform of 1994, the rules of fiscal decentralization were changed to the benefit of the central power. A remarkably high growth rate of 18 per cent was imposed on the provinces for submitting revenue to the central government, setting out a regressive taxation across China (Zhang, 2006). This is because the local governments had no authority to cut urban entitlements, so those counties that were able to attract more private investment could afford to lower the local tax rate. The advantage of rich areas' lower effective tax rates was reinforced by the manipulated liberalization of the labour market across regions, because peasant workers coming to the coastal provinces and large cities from the inner provinces were forced to take unfair wages far below their urban counterparts. The implicit per capita labour tax rate on a migrant worker was estimated to be more than 100 per cent.

Despite its unfairness, the so-called 'peasant worker' system implied a new rule of manipulated marketization. By paying substantial labour taxes to the local governments where migrant workers found jobs, the peasants actually extended their economic freedom in the Danwei Society, which previously gave no jobs to outsiders. However, employment was not to be translated into local citizenship. This interregional trade in labour was not totally based on reciprocity, because the central and the local governments were the main beneficiaries. In many areas, local citizens became victims of excessive industrial development as the quality of local life and the environment were ruined.

Because the state could benefit so much from export-driven growth, there was no incentive for both the central and local governments to enhance labour rights, set fair rules for emigration, and implement more balanced exchange rates and trade policies. The rapid increase of China's trade surplus was translated into a huge domestic money supply to fuel government investment. Internationally, the surplus was translated into China's huge foreign currency reserve, primarily in the form of the US treasury bonds, which severely distorted the global capital cost and asset markets (Ferguson and Schularick, 2007).

The great power of the Chinese state to manipulate collective identities was demonstrated by the fact that, on an annual basis, more than 150 million rural labourers had to leave their native villages to find a job with no hope of achieving citizenship where they worked. The 'peasant worker' system essentially became a state slavery system. The participation in the global economy of this giant, cheap labour force has not only changed the landscape of the global economy, but also caused a huge economic imbalance both for the Chinese economy and for the world economy. The tension that resulted from this imbalance was the main source of the liquidity flood and debt tsunami that brought down the global finance system in 2008.

The transit from a manipulated revolution to a manipulated marketization is a big jump towards freedom for China. However, the current social and political crises have shown that without building up capacity for self-governance within both society and localities, manipulated social changes, even in the right direction, can be very costly, and potentially self-destructive, as was shown by the Cultural Revolution (1966–76). How to transform the manipulated Chinese society into an autonomous society remains a great challenge for the Chinese elites.

■ **REFERENCES**

Ferguson, Niall and Moritz Schularick. 2007. 'Chimerica' and the global asset market boom. *International Finance* 10(3): 215–39.

Luo, Xiaopeng. 1986, Ownership and status stratification. In *China's Rural Industry—Structure, Development, and Reform*, edited by Byrd and Lin, ch. 7. Oxford: Oxford University Press.

Luo, Xiaopeng. 1994. China's Reforms and the Hierarchical Property Rights. Modern China Research 41.

Luo, Xiaopeng. 2004. Economic growth under unlimited supply of cheap 'migrant labour': origins, characteristics and prospects of China's economic growth model in the last decade. Paper presented in the international conference 'Globalization, Smallholder Farmers, and Market Integration', Nanjing, China, 8–9 November.

Pye, Lucian. 1965. *Political Culture and Political Development*. Princeton, NJ: Princeton University Press.

Wilson, Edward O. 2012. *The Social Conquest of Earth*. New York and London: W.W. Norton & Company.

Zhang, Xiaobo. 2006. Fiscal decentralization and political centralization in China: Implications for growth and inequality. *Journal of Comparative Economics* 34(4): 713–26.

2 Transition to a market economy
Explaining the successes and failures

Joseph E. Stiglitz

China has grown remarkably since it began its transition to a market economy more than three decades ago—far better than Russia.[1] The reasons for this hold important lessons for economics.

There are two categories of explanations for the differences in performance: (a) the two countries faced different circumstances; (b) they undertook different policies. It is impossible to fully untangle the explanations: differences in circumstances would naturally lead to differences in policies. Independent of circumstance, however, various economists did support highly different policies—in pacing, sequencing, and priorities. Some called for shock therapy, focusing on macroeconomic adjustments; others for gradualism, focusing more on microeconomic issues. Different economists held contradicting opinions on privatization—a high priority for Washington Consensus supporters—and on institutions, competition, the role of government, and the pace of liberalization for capital and financial markets and trade.

At least through the first decades of transition, the contrast in the policy bundles pursued by the two countries could not have been greater. Russia followed, though imperfectly, the Washington Consensus shock therapy policies; China followed an alternative course. Inevitably then, the advocates of Washington Consensus[2] policies attribute Russia's (comparative and absolute) failures either to deficiencies in following the prescriptions, or to its different circumstances.

The real flaw, I argue, is with the Washington Consensus and the policies based on it. If anything, the circumstances favoured Russia. Further, even if Russia imperfectly

---

[1] This chapter is based on previous work (listed in the references) by the author and several co-authors (Karla Hoff, Yingyi Qian, David Ellerman, Athar Hussain, Sergio Godoy, and Nicholas Stern) to whom he is greatly indebted.

[2] There is no way of simply and accurately summarizing the policies advocated by the 'shock therapists' and the international financial institutions. Still, it is useful to group the two strategies according to some basic themes. See Stiglitz (2008).

followed the Washington Consensus policies, China's successful policies deviated from them even more. In fact, there is a causal link between Russia's policies and its poor performance, an interpretation consistent with cross-country and time-series empirical work.

A purported defence of the *economic* failure is that there was a political transformation going on as well, which the economic transformation was responsible for 'locking in'. But the strategy failed to create a vibrant democratic Russia, and the economic strategy may in fact have contributed to this political failure.

2.1 **The contrasting performance**

Russia's performance in the initial years of transition was particularly disappointing: between 1990 and 1999, real GDP per capita fell by 38 per cent. There were concomitant indicators of failure, such as a decline of three years in life expectancy and large outmigration of some of the country's most talented individuals. The country deindustrialized, becoming increasingly simply an exporter of raw materials (especially oil and gas).

Of course, Russia had inherited a distorted economic system. Capital and labour had been misallocated; innovation had been suppressed. But in a sense, that only meant it had more room for improvement. Replacing an inefficient economic system (central planning with decentralization; quotas with market-based incentives) *should* have ensured that the country's resources were better used. Output should have gone up.

By contrast, in the same period, China's per capita income more than doubled, and life expectancy increased by two years. Technical capacities grew. By 2010, it was becoming a technological leader in some fields. As it restructured its economy away from primary production, China became the largest producer of industrial goods.

2.2 **The flawed economic model**

Russia's failed policies were overly influenced by the neoclassical model, which ignored market frictions (imperfect information, imperfect competition, imperfect markets). In reality, social and private returns were often not aligned. While the advocates of rapid transition prided themselves in at last providing incentives to market participants, what they did not realize was that those incentives were, in many cases, perverse; they were directed more at asset-stripping than at wealth creation.

The irony was that while these policies' proponents often talked about the importance of 'governance', they failed to note pervasive problems of *corporate governance* that can arise when there are inadequate corporate governance statutes.[3] By contrast, the critics of shock therapy stressed the importance of the 'institutional infrastructure', including corporate governance.

Still another flaw in the Washington Consensus was the belief that as government activities (such as providing credit, inputs, etc.) were stripped away, *competitive and efficient* markets would spontaneously arise to fill the gap. Typically they did not. The absence of capital markets (banks) that were experienced in project selection and monitoring and contract enforcement, combined with weak entrepreneurship, meant that when jobs and enterprises were destroyed, new ones were not created.[4]

The advocates of shock therapy also underestimated the importance of social capital in making economies (and societies more generally) function. The Soviet Union had done much to destroy civil society and civic engagement. Even if appropriate legal structures had been put into place, they would have been an imperfect substitute. But transition under shock therapy eviscerated social capital even more and did not create the 'institutional infrastructure' necessary for an effectively functioning market economy—or for democracy.

So too, overly simplistic macro-models that paid insufficient attention to credit and credit institutions led to monetary policies that for a time moved much of Russia back to an inefficient barter system (all in the name of taming inflation).

As a result, Washington Consensus policies (including privatization and liberalization) did not bring the promised benefits. This should not have been a surprise, considering there was little theory and no historical basis for shock therapists' faith in rapid privatization. By contrast, there was ample historical evidence of the problems facing societies in the absence of good legal and financial institutions.

Just as the advocates of the shock therapy model were excessively optimistic about the results they expected, they were excessively pessimistic about the ad hoc nature of the Chinese reforms. But the 'partial' reforms were effective. (a) China's move to the individual responsibility system provided effective incentives in the agriculture sector, even though it did not entail *full* privatization. It provided most of the benefits that would have been achieved with full privatization, without the adverse political and social consequences. (b) China put more emphasis on competition than privatization, especially in the early stages.[5] Both were necessary to achieve the full benefits of a market, and priorities had to be contingent on local circumstances. Township and village enterprises involved continued public ownership (though at the local level),

---

[3] Berle and Means (1932) stressed the importance of the separation of ownership and control; the economics of information put the theory of corporate governance on rigorous theoretical foundations, see for example Stiglitz (1985).

[4] Ellerman and I (2000) also emphasized the consequences of the absence of small enterprises in the Soviet regime.

[5] Something Arrow and I had suggested in a 1980 conference with Chinese officials. See my 1980 paper.

but provided the basis for vigorous competition. (c) One of the original challenges was how to move from the distorted price system under the old regime to a more market-based price system. The Chinese cleverly used a two-part price system—though conventional wisdom at the time argued against these kinds of pricing mechanisms. (d) China was slow to move to trade liberalization—and even now has not fully liberalized its capital account. Strong government intervention enabled the country to avoid the instability (and often high unemployment) that marked those who liberalized too rapidly. It provided time for development of a domestic entrepreneurial class. (e) Industrialization was also aided by strong industrial policies, including the management of the exchange rate (to keep it competitive)—policies that were eschewed by the Washington Consensus.

2.3 **The flawed political model**

There was a naïve belief that a newly established class of wealthy individuals would have incentives to create the legal and institutional infrastructure that would enable a market economy to function well. There were at least four key flaws. (a) Those with economic power wish to perpetuate it, devising rules that benefit themselves, but would not necessarily make the economic system work better. Wealthy individuals use their wealth, including through political influence, to enhance their rents: monopolists oppose strong competition laws; financiers, laws that circumscribe their abuses of information asymmetries and market power. (b) With capital market liberalization, the rich in Russia could take their money out of the country and invest it in a place where there were good protections, meanwhile taking advantage of their superior ability at asset stripping. (c) As a result, there was an economic and political equilibrium in which Russia remained 'lawless' (Hoff and Stiglitz 2004a, 2004b). (d) There are further difficulties in leaving a 'lawless' state: those that follow may try to recapture proceeds that are viewed as not gainfully gotten. Illegitimate privatization thus made the process of transition to a rule of law more difficult (Hoff and Stiglitz, 2007).

2.4 **Alternative explanations**

Supporters of Washington Consensus policies suggest that China's task in transition was easier: it was a less developed, more agrarian economy. But on average, less developed countries (with the exception of the East Asian countries that did not follow the Washington Consensus prescriptions) have not done well. Development is difficult. Transition is difficult. It is illogical to suggest that combining the two would make both tasks easier. And there is little evidence that the ease of transition is related to the size of an economy's agrarian sector.

Many of the studies of transition occurred in the early years. It was not clear then whether the tortoise or the hare would win: even if fast reformers among the FSU and Eastern Europe appeared to be doing well early on, would they be able to sustain their advantage? One of the few studies to be done later on was that of Godoy and Stiglitz (2007), which concludes that the tortoises did win—speed of privatization was negatively correlated with longer-run performance—and that institutions mattered. As time went on, the significance of initial conditions (emphasized in the earlier literature) disappeared.[6]

2.5 **Concluding remarks**

The end of Communism and the transition from Communism to the market economy was one of history's most important economic episodes. Standard theory had little to say about how to manage that transition, but that did not stop many economists from providing advice. Much of that was wrong; in some cases, it was counterproductive. The contrast between Russia and China is testimony to the benefits of pragmatism and against the reliance on simplistic neoclassical models. The limitations of those models were well known before the transition: if those models had been right, market socialism would have been far more successful (Stiglitz, 1994). Chinese leaders understood that transition required institutional innovations and, untethered by the dictates of neoclassical economics, were able to devise pragmatic solutions that provided the basis of that country's three decades of unprecedented growth.

■ REFERENCES

Berle, Adolf A. and Gardner C. Means. 1932. *The Modern Corporation and Private Property*. New York: Macmillan.

Ellerman, David and J. E. Stiglitz. 2000. New bridges across the chasm: macro- and micro-strategies for Russia and other transitional economies. *Zagreb International Review of Economics and Business* 3(1), 41–72.

Godoy, S. and J. E. Stiglitz. 2007. Growth, initial conditions, law and speed of privatization in transition countries: 11 years later. *Transition and Beyond*, edited by S. Estrin et al., 89–117. Hampshire, England: Palgrave Macmillan.

Hoff, K. and J. E. Stiglitz. 2004a. The transition process in post-communist societies: towards a political economy of property rights. In *Toward Pro-Poor Policies: Aid, Institutions and Globalization*, edited by B. Tungodden, N. Stern, and I. Kolstad, 231–45. Oxford University Press: World Bank.

---

[6] As they note, empirical work in this area is plagued by a host of econometric problems. See for example the discussion in Hoff and Stiglitz (2004a, 2004b, 2007).

Hoff, K. and J. E. Stiglitz. 2004b. After the Big Bang? Obstacles to the emergence of the rule of law in post-communist societies. *American Economic Review* 94(3), 753–63.

Hoff, K. and J. E. Stiglitz. 2007. Exiting a lawless state. *Economic Journal* 118(531), 1474–97.

Stiglitz, J. E. 1980. Information, Planning and Incentives, presented at the CSCCRP Sino-American Conference on Alternative Development Strategies in Wingspread, Racine, WI, November 1980. (Reprinted in *Selected Works on Economics of Joseph E. Stiglitz* (Chinese), Beijing: China Financial Publishing House, 2006.)

Stiglitz, J. E. 1985. Credit markets and the control of capital. *Journal of Money, Banking, and Credit* 17(2), 133–52.

Stiglitz, J. E. 1994. *Wither Socialism*. Cambridge, MA: MIT Press.

Stiglitz, J. E. 2008. Is there a post-Washington Consensus consensus? In *The Washington Consensus Reconsidered: Towards a New Global Governance*, edited by Narcis Serra and Joseph E. Stiglitz, 41–56. New York: Oxford University Press.

3 Chinese residents' rising income growth and distribution inequality

Chen Zongsheng

China has achieved significant economic and social development since its reform and opening up, changing from a less-developed country with relatively low income into the world's second largest economic entity.[1] In 1978, China had a GDP of just $147.3 billion, occupying 1.75 per cent of the world's total GDP. By 2010, China's GDP reached $5.47 trillion and, by 2011, it reached $5.88 trillion, surpassing Japan and becoming the second highest in the world. With GDP per capita rising from $300 to more than $5,000 in 2011, China became a fledgling middle-income economy, and correspondingly, the living standards of Chinese people have risen dramatically. At the same time, however, these have been accompanied by a worsening income distribution.

In the past three decades, China has experienced a three-stage transition of their guiding principles and institutional frameworks of income distribution reform. The main trend began with the abolition of egalitarianism to a focus on economic efficiency instead, and then a gradual move towards a particular emphasis on equality. During the first stage, 1978–92, the distribution of income was primarily measured by labour, along with several complementary forms of distribution. This was designed to maintain the balance between equality and efficiency. The 13th National Congress of the Chinese Communist Party (CCP) acknowledged the rationality and legitimacy of non-labour factors to participate in income distribution. The Congress claimed to 'reflect social justice under the prerequisite of facilitating efficiency', abolished egalitarianism, and established the principle of 'more pay for more work', so as to encourage economic efficiency and develop productive forces. While incomes increased at different rates for different groups of people, the expansion of income discrepancies attracted widespread concern. As a result, during the late period of the first stage, the 14th National Congress came up with the principle of 'balanced efficiency and fairness'.

---

[1] Thanks are due to Dr Qingbin Li for his dedication in preparing related materials for this chapter.

The second transition stage covers the period from the 3rd Plenary Session of the 14th Central Committee in 1992 to the 3rd Plenary Session of the 16th Central Committee in 2003. Within the framework of a market economy, the government announced its intention to 'to combine the principles of distributing by labor and distributing by factors', as well as the principle of distributing income according to the contribution made to production. The government stressed the idea that the initial distribution should focus on efficiency with an application of market power, while redistribution should centre on equality, so as to enhance the government's regulatory power in income distribution.

The period from the 4th Plenary Session of the 16th Central Committee in 2004 onward has seen the third stage. Based on general distribution principles, the government changed the mantra of 'distribute according to [the contribution to] production' from a principle into a system. Moreover, the government stressed that the income distribution system should focus more on social equality. They proposed that 'both initial distribution and redistribution should reach a balance between efficiency and equality, and redistribution should pay more attention to equality', instead of the old saying of 'prioritize efficiency with due consideration to fairness'.

The reform and adjustment of the income distribution system greatly excited the people, and improved their standards of living to a large extent. Generally speaking, the income standards of citizens moved from a position of adequate standards of food and clothing to the early stages of prosperity, marching towards the goal of an overall well-off society, even starting to evolve towards a model of diversification. A widely used method is to measure the income standard of urban citizens in terms of urban disposable income per capita, while the income situation of rural citizens is measured by net income per capita. As shown by the data in Figures 3.1, 3.2, and 3.3, the incomes of both urban and rural areas have experienced rapid growth, regardless of whether they are measured by nominal value or by a standard value based on a benchmark year. Specifically, urban disposable income per capita reached 20,000 yuan (19,109.4 yuan) in 2010, which was 55.6 times that of 1978 levels when measured by nominal value, and still 7.65 times more when measured by standard value—less volatility, but a higher stable growth rate. Meanwhile, the rural net income per capita increased by 42.3 times from 1979 to 2010 in nominal value terms, and 7.5 times in standard value terms. Even though the development of rural areas fell a little behind that of urban areas, both without doubt experienced significant growth. Such results are among the most important achievements of China's economic reform and opening up during the thirty years since they first began.

During this time, which has seen economic and social development, fast reform and economic development, and the breaking away from egalitarianism, it is natural that income distribution exhibits a degree of volatility. In most years, the income gap has been correlated with the degree of economic development. But some important phenomena have appeared recently that threaten to impede economic development as well as the harmony of society and thus deserves serious attention.

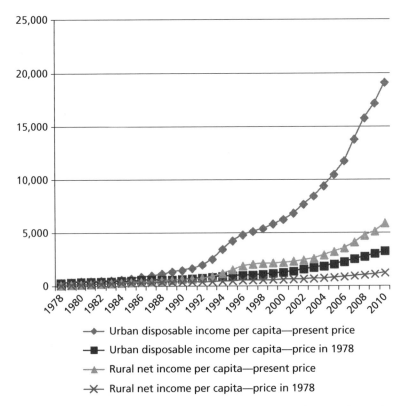

Figure 3.1. Income growth of China's urban and rural areas after reform and opening up (1978–2010) (measured in both standard and present prices)

Source: China Statistic Yearbook 2011.

First, the income gap between citizens is experiencing an increasing trend, with the Gini index increasing from an egalitarian standard of 0.2 to a recent result of 0.45. Second, both urban and rural areas are experiencing a trend of growing internal income gaps, with the Gini index rising from 0.2 to 0.39 (2005) in urban areas, and from 0.3 to 0.4 in rural areas. Moreover, the income gap within rural areas has been greater than the urban gap in the years 1978–2013. The good news is that the trend in the income gap has been alleviating in recent years, but this requires further verification. Third, a significant income gap formed between rural and urban areas after China's reform and opening up. Using the income ratios of the two areas as a somewhat imprecise measurement, urban disposable income per capita reached over three times the amount of rural net income per capita in 2002, and this ratio remained around 3.2 in subsequent years. Although the disparities between the two areas seem to be a bit lower than the measurement of the Gini index, the general trend remains the same. An important point is that the income gap between rural and urban areas contributes to more than half of the whole income

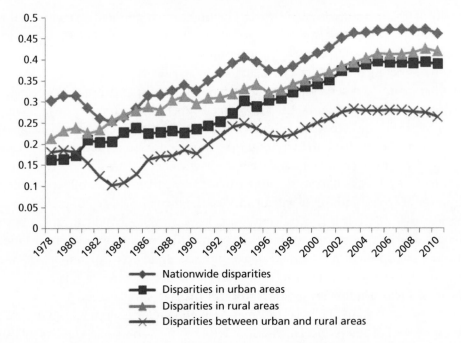

Figure 3.2. China's income gap after reform and opening up (1978–2010) (measured according to the Gini index)

Note: Income standards are measured by disposable income in urban areas and net income in rural areas.

Source: Chen and Gao (2012).

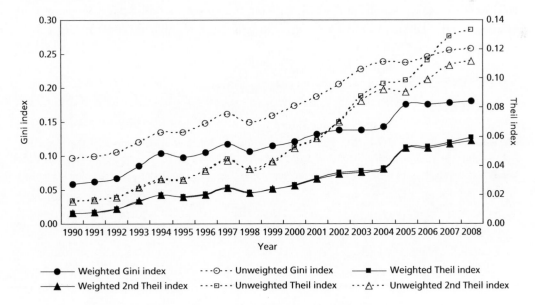

Figure 3.3. China's income gap at the level of industries (1990–2008)

Source: Wu (2011).

disparity of China. The household (*Hukou*) registration systems and several related wel-fare systems are primarily responsible for the formation of China's dual structure. These institutional factors are mainly restricting the movement of rural surplus labour, and sub-stantially restricting income improvement for rural residents.

Another topic that deserves our special attention is the disparity between wages across industries. As shown in Figures 3.1–3.3, China is experiencing a rapid rise in industrial income disparities, by both weighted and unweighted calculations. Industrial income dis-parities should be divided into two categories: the reasonable ones and the unreasonable ones. The disparity in technological development and creative standards between indus-tries will cause a reasonable income disparity with a positive effect; while the monopol-istic power of typical industries will also widen the income gap, creating unreasonable disparities that may result in a collective loss of social welfare. Actually, the industrial income and profit disparities of China at the current time mainly originate from monop-olistic power. Therefore an important step in suppressing an ever-expanding income gap in industry is to deepen the reform of the market economy system, particularly by regu-lating monopolistic industries and their workers, managers, and executives.

Thus the crucial point of China's income distribution reform has not been to enhance the income level of any particular class, but rather to focus on regulating and adjusting the order and relationships of income distributions, in order to eliminate the income gap caused by a dual economic structure, abnormally high incomes, and especially monop-olies and corruption. Generally speaking, equality should be achieved systematically in the initial distribution of wealth, with effective redistribution only acting as a safeguard role. Ideally, wealth would be distributed along a bell curve, with fewer people at the extremes and a larger middle class. Surely, this is not a feasible short-term target, but rather a good long-term goal.

■ **REFERENCES**

Chen, Zongsheng and Yuwei Gao. 2012. Public ownership income distribution inverted-u hypothesis: discus-sions and tests. *Comparative Economics & Social Systems* 2012(2), 18–28.

Wu, Peng. 2011. A Research on the Industrial Income Differences of China. Doctoral Dissertation of Nankai University.

4 The influence of foreign economists in the early stages of China's reforms

Edwin Lim

Despite widespread admiration of their success, the process by which Chinese economic reforms evolved is not well documented or understood. One common misconception outside China is that the reforms were entirely home-grown and evolved without the benefit of modern mainstream economics.[1] In fact, China's leaders actively sought and used the expertise of foreign economists during the early stages of the reforms.

Deng Xiaoping's enthusiasm for reform was motivated in no small part by his discovery on visits abroad of how far China had fallen behind the rest of the world. Learning and using the experience of foreign countries was a key element of his vision for China.[2] While Chinese reform is often rightly characterized as a series of experiments, including the household responsibility system, the dual-track approach, and the Special Economic Zones, the framework for these experiments was the senior leadership's evolving strategy of moving from central planning to a market economy.

In this chapter I will describe some of the ways in which foreign economists contributed to the reform process, drawing mainly on my experience in the World Bank during the 1980's.[3]

---

[1] For example: 'There has not been a greater instance of poverty reduction in history than that of China in the quarter century since the late 1970s. Yet can anyone name the (Western) economists or the piece of research that played an instrumental role in China's reforms?' (Rodrik, 2010: 33).

[2] 'Recently our comrades had a look abroad. The more we see the more we realize how backward we are ... We must be self-reliant, struggle to build our own country; at the same time, we need to sincerely learn all the advanced things of foreign countries. The world is changing every day, new things are continuously emerging. We cannot close the door. Unless we exercise our brains we will be doomed to backwardness forever.' Deng Xiaoping in 1978, *South China Elites Weekly*, 17 August 2004.

[3] I was responsible for the World Bank's economic work on China between 1980 and 1990. Lead author of the 1981 and 1985 studies and involved in most of the other World Bank activities discussed in this chapter was Adrian Wood, who left after the second study to resume his academic career in the UK. A fuller account is available, in Chinese, in the preface I was asked to write for a book to mark the 30th anniversary of China's reforms and openness: *Fifty Economists Looking at the Thirty Years: Recollection and Analysis* (2008) China Economic Publishing. I am grateful for Professors Wu Jinglian and Zhao Renwei for explaining the Chinese perspective on many of the events described in it and in the present chapter.

As I shall show, the Bank played an important role, both as a direct provider of economic advice and as a facilitator of advice from economists outside the Bank. Its influence owed much not only to the ability of the many excellent economists on its staff, but also to the wisdom and open-mindedness of the Chinese officials and economists involved in the reform process. A particularly vital role was played by Zhao Ziyang, Premier from 1980 to 1987 and head of the System Reform Commission, who personally led the assimilation of foreign economic ideas and experience, and whose remarkable understanding of economic principles was noted by many of the foreign economists who met him.[4]

4.1 Soviet and East European economists

The initial opening to foreign economic ideas was to other socialist countries. Between 1979 and the early 1980s, there were several exchanges between China and the Soviet Union and Eastern Europe. Of particular importance were the visits of the Polish economist Wlodek Brus in December 1979 and the Czech economist Ota Sik in June 1981.

Their lectures led to the invitation of a team of East European economists and practitioners in July 1982 to discuss reform ideas and experiences with Chinese economists. A small conference was held at the mountain resort of Moganshan. The foreign team, organized by the World Bank, was led by Brus and included another Pole, a Czech, and a Hungarian (most of them by that time emigrés), as well as an American (David Granick) specializing in socialist economic reforms.

The outcome of these exchanges was the rejection of the Soviet and East European approach to reform. In these countries, all reform attempts had failed. What was there for China to learn from this, except to seek another way? One issue of debate was the speed of reform. Based on the many failures of partial reforms in the 1970s, the consensus of the European economists, even in 1982, was for a 'comprehensive, once and for all' reform. After touring China, however, the European economists changed their minds. They saw that the success of the rural reforms provided impetus for further reform which did not exist in Europe, and they recognized that it would be less risky for China as a low-income developing country to continue its step-by-step approach.[5]

More positively, the East European economists brought to China a new level of understanding of the problems of a planned economy. The dissection of the socialist planned economic system using modern analytical techniques reached new heights in the work of Janos Kornai, who visited China in 1985 for the Bashan Lun conference (see the next but

---

[4] For example, Milton Friedman, who met privately for two hours with Zhao, reported that 'he displayed a sophisticated understanding of the economic situation and how the market operated'. See Friedman and Friedman (1999: 543).

[5] As reported by Xue Muqiao, Liao Jili, and Liu Zhoufu, the three senior Chinese participants in the conference, to Chinese leaders in August 1982.

one section). Concepts such as investment hunger, a shortage economy, and soft budget constraints illuminated and deepened understanding of familiar problems.

These insights of East European economists demonstrated to their Chinese counterparts that the dysfunctionality of a planned economy was systemic. The many economic problems which they had attributed to policy mistakes were actually inherent defects of the planned economic system and could be overcome only through fundamental reform. Thus, by the mid-1980s, having abandoned the idea of further tinkering with the central planning system, the thinking of Chinese reformers had moved decisively towards a market economy and reliance on the tools of mainstream economics.

4.2 The economic work of the World Bank[6]

Two major studies that brought mainstream economics into the reform policy debate in China were prepared by the World Bank.[7] The first, in 1981, was a requirement for access to Bank loans. Its analysis of China's development trajectory caught the attention of Chinese leaders. In May 1983, Deng Xiaoping and Zhao Ziyang met with a Bank delegation led by President Clausen. Deng explained that China had decided to launch a development programme aimed at quadrupling the gross value of industrial and agricultural output between 1980 and 2000. He had found the first report of the World Bank interesting and useful, and proposed that the Bank should undertake another study to address key development issues China might face in the next twenty years, to suggest alternative ways based on international experience for China to achieve its development goal, and to analyse the feasibility of achieving that goal.

Both the first World Bank study, and the second, published in 1985, involved teams of about thirty people—not only general and sector economists but also specialists in a wide range of areas, from education, health, and population to railways, ports, and petroleum. The teams visited Gansu, Hubei, Jiangsu, Beijing, and Shanghai for extensive field research. To learn about economic investigations by foreign economists, Chinese counterpart teams attended every meeting, received all the data provided and saw every draft. A Chinese industrial economist who worked closely with the first World Bank economic team was Zhu Rongji, China's Premier from 1998 to 2003.

These two reports brought the concepts and methods of economics to a wider audience in China, and enabled Chinese leaders and decision makers to learn about their

[6] Accounts of the influence of the World Bank's economic work in China can be found in Jacobsonand Oksenberg (1990); Stern and Ferreira (1997); and Vogel (2011: ch. 16, 'Accelerating Economic Growth and Opening, 1982–1989').

[7] *China: Socialist Economic Development*, World Bank, issued in 1981 but available publicly only in 1983; and *China: Long Term Development Issues and Options*, 1985, Johns Hopkins University Press.

application to a case study they knew well—the Chinese economy. That they found the conclusions and recommendations of the Bank reports generally persuasive and useful reassured them about the relevance of modern mainstream economics to China. The 1985 report was particularly influential.[8] It endorsed the possibility of rapid future growth and the feasibility of quadrupling production over twenty years. However, it also identified an alternative development path, involving a greater emphasis on services and more efficient resource use. The report was sent by Premier Zhao to all economic ministries and was an input into China's 7th Five Year Plan (1986–90).

4.3 Learning through international conferences

Chinese leaders wanted not only to get ideas from prominent foreign academics and practitioners but also to give young Chinese economists the opportunity to learn through discussions and debate. The latter half of the 1980s thus saw the start of a series of international conferences on specific topics of concern to Chinese policy makers. One of the first and most important of them is now widely known in China as the 'Bashan Lun (Boat) Conference'.

The initiative came from Premier Zhao in his capacity as head of the System Reform Commission. His request was for the World Bank to organize an international conference to discuss the following topics: how to manage a market economy; issues related to the transition from a centrally planned economy to a market economy; and international experiences in integrating plan and market.

The purpose was not only to invite foreign experts to lecture, but also to provide an opportunity for in-depth exchanges between the Chinese and foreign participants. The conference took place in September 1985. The foreign participants first met Premier Zhao in Beijing, when he explained what he was seeking from the conference. They then flew to Chongqing and boarded a Yangtze River tourist boat called the Bashan for a seven day trip to Wuhan. The unusual venue allowed the Chinese participants, including many senior officials, to be fully available for a week, uninterrupted by their normal responsibilities, and thus for continuous exchange between Chinese and foreign participants. It was an intensive week, with plenary sessions, small-group discussions, and private conversations which lasted into the night.

On the boat were virtually all the top Chinese economists of the time, including An Zhiwen, Xue Muqiao, Ma Hong, Liu Guoguang, and Tong Dalin. Mid-level participants included Gao Shangquan, Wu Jinglian, Xiang Huaicheng, and Zhao Renwei, while younger participants included Guo Shuqing and Lou Jiwei. The foreign participants included

---

[8] Wu Jinglian reports that Ma Hong, who was then Minister in charge of DRC, highlighted sections of the report for reading by Premier Zhao.

three eminent macro-economists: Nobel laureate James Tobin, Sir Alec Cairncross, and Otmar Emminger (a former head of Germany's central bank). Cairncross and Emminger both had experience of managing the de-control of prices and freeing up of markets after the Second World War in the UK and Germany. Other foreign participants were Brus and Kornai, who talked mainly about the micro-economic requirements for transition from a centrally planned economy to a market economy.

The most important contribution of the Bashan Lun conference was a better understanding of the functioning of a market economy. Although the Chinese leaders had already decided in 1984 to break through the limitation of a centrally planned system, there was relatively little understanding of how a market economy works. It was therefore very useful for the foreign participants to explain how the theory and practice of macro-management had moved from the laissez-faire approach of the 1920s and 1930s to the aggregate demand management and activist macro-economic policies of the 1980s. Most of the discussions were on indirect control of the market economy through the combined use of fiscal, monetary, and income policies.

Chinese leaders also asked successful practitioners of development in other countries to serve as advisers. One was Goh Keng Swee, the architect of Singapore's rapid growth, who was invited by Deng in 1984 to advise on the Special Economic Zones (SEZs). In the late 1980s and early 1990s, international conferences continued to be a channel for Chinese officials and economists to learn about international reforms and development experiences. But the subjects of these conferences moved from broad strategic reform policy to more specific issues. For instance, participants at a conference on enterprise governance and management in 1986 included Herbert Simon, Peter Drucker, and heads of SOEs from Germany, Brazil, Bulgaria, and Yugoslavia. In 1993, when overheating and inflation were again emerging as a problem in macro-management, a workshop was organized in Cambridge, MA, by Harvard's HIID, China's DRC, and the World Bank, followed later that year by a conference in Dalian on macro-management and stabilization.

Exchanges and dialogue with foreign economists and economic practitioners have continued since then, but mainly organized by Chinese economists themselves, with different foreign institutions, at various levels, and for different purposes. Indeed, the growing number of Chinese economists trained in the best universities in the world since the 1990s helps to explain, and their dominant influence on policy today reflects, the currently high status of mainstream economics in China.[9]

---

[9] Sending students to study abroad was an important element of learning foreign ideas and experiences orchestrated by Deng Xiaoping, as reflected in his directive of 1979 to the Ministry of Education (regarding the work of Tsinghua University) to significantly expand the number of students to be sent abroad. According to Chinese statistics, a total of more than one million Chinese students studied abroad during 1979–2007, a quarter of whom had returned to China.

4.4 **Concluding remarks**

China's economic reforms, like all successful such reforms, were initiated, owned and managed by the country's own leaders and economists. However, in a break from its rejection over the previous five centuries of foreign ideas and institutions, China's reforms started with an intellectual opening. The process of assimilating foreign ideas and experience was orchestrated by Deng Xiaoping, and in economics was led by Zhao Ziyang. They and other Chinese leaders took every opportunity to get the input of foreign economists, though they were also discriminating in what parts of it they accepted. The World Bank contributed substantially to this process, largely because of the way in which it was used by China, whose leaders came to see the Bank as more valuable to them as a channel for economic ideas than as a source of cheap capital.

■ **REFERENCES**

Friedman, Milton and Rose Friedman. 1999. *Two Lucky People: Memoirs*. Chicago: University of Chicago Press.

Jacobson, Harold K. and Michel Oksenberg. 1990. *China's Participation in the IMF, the World Bank and GATT: Toward a Global Economic Order*. Ann Arbor: University of Michigan Press.

Rodrik, Dani. 2010. Diagnostics before Prescription. *Journal of Economic Perspectives*, 24(3), 33–44.

Stern, Nicholas and Francisco Ferreira. 1997. The World Bank as 'intellectual actor'. In *The World Bank: Its First Half Century. Volume 2*, edited by Devesh Kapur, J. P. Lewis, and Richard Webb. Washington, DC: Brookings Institution.

Vogel, Ezra. 2011. *Deng Xiaoping and the Transformation of China*. Cambridge, MA: Belknap Harvard.

5 China and India
The pattern of recent growth and governance in a comparative political economy perspective

Pranab Bardhan

The two largest countries of the world with ancient agrarian civilizations, with many centuries of dominance in the world economy in the past and recently with impressive economic growth performance, draw obvious comparison. Over the last more than sixty years these two neighbouring countries having adopted sharply divergent political and economic systems also provides a point of reference in any study of comparative systems. This short chapter will first briefly describe their patterns of economic growth primarily in the last three decades and the implications of these patterns for the massive poverty and inequality existing the two countries, and then move on to discuss the nature of governance in both public and private spheres which shape those patterns.

In 1820 China and India contributed about half of world income (measured in 1990 prices), in 1950 they contributed less than 10 per cent (the preceding century in the case of China and nearly two centuries in the case of India included rather unpleasant encounters with international powers), and a very rough projection is that in 2025 the two countries will contribute about one-third of world income (China much more than India). In the 1870s as well as the 1970s per capita income in comparable prices was somewhat higher in India, but since then China has shot ahead. Even accounting for some possible overstatement in the Chinese official rates of growth, per capita income has grown at least twice as fast in China than in India over the last three decades.

In the sectoral pattern of growth China has excelled particularly in manufacture, India more in services. China is widely regarded as the manufacturing centre of the world (although this is not yet quite true in manufacturing value added, the share of US or EU in world manufacturing value added is still much higher than that of China). In India there has been dramatic growth in the modern service sub-sectors such as software, communications, and finance, but nearly 60 per cent of service sector income is still generated in the informal sector (only a small part of which is linked with the formal sector). In terms of sub-sectors, Chinese expansion, at least in the initial years, has been more in labour-intensive activities (the production of clothing, shoes, toys, furniture, etc.) which employed large numbers of the unskilled poor; in India expansion has been more in skill-intensive and capital-intensive activities (such as software, pharmaceuticals, or cars and car parts). All the service sector activities enabled by information technology employ only about half of 1 per cent of the total labour force in India.

Contrary to popular impressions, in both countries the growth has not been mainly externally driven. The mainspring of growth in China has been domestic investment, and in India domestic investment and consumption. Even though foreign trade and investment have led to significant technological and managerial upgrading in China, their growth has contributed only modestly to aggregate economic growth. Even during the high global expansion of trade in the period 2002–07, the increase in exports (in domestic value added terms) contributed only a little above a quarter of total real GDP growth in China in the period, substantially less than the contribution of domestic investment. Chinese domestic saving and investment rates are significantly higher than in India. Household saving rates may be slightly higher in India, but enterprise and public saving rates are much higher in China. The consequent lower cost of capital (along with more decentralized financing and management, better cost recovery from user fees, and more peremptory land acquisition) have enabled China to build growth-enhancing infrastructure (highways, railways, ports, power plants, etc.) at a much faster pace than India.

According to World Bank estimates, taking a crude but common poverty line (like, say, $1 a day per capita at 2005 prices), the percentage of people below that line was about 73 per cent (probably an overestimate) in 1981 in China (42 per cent in India); it went down to 7 per cent in 2008 in China (21 per cent in India)—a dramatic decline in China, a significant one in India. There is statistical evidence to suggest that most of the dramatic poverty reduction in China has been due to agricultural growth and public investment in rural infrastructure, not globalization (as is commonly believed). The non-income indicators of poverty (in terms of basic health, nutrition, and education) continue to be dismal in India. On some of these indicators India today is where China was at the beginning of 1970s (a beneficial part of the socialist legacy in China). The environmental consequences of growth (such as air and water pollution), which the poor bear the brunt of, may be larger in absolute terms in China, simply because of the more rapid industrialization and urbanization there, but broad estimates of proportional damage and depletion (in terms of annual percentage of national income) seem to be similar in the two countries. Whether the Chinese central government's energetic countermeasures in limiting environmental degradation launched in recent years will succeed in making a big dent on the problem remains to be seen. Indian countermeasures have yet not reached the Chinese scale, but the environmental movement is more active as a watchdog in India.

Inequality has gone up in both countries, partly as a result of sectoral transformation (as the less unequal agricultural sector declines in importance in terms of income but not commensurately in terms of the people whose livelihoods still depend on it), and partly due to a rise in the skill premium in wages and rental incomes from land and other appreciating assets. Contrary to popular opinion, globalization may not be the most important factor in raising inequality. For example, inequality within China is less in the more globally exposed coastal areas than in the interior areas. Urban–rural disparity is higher in China than in India (within China it is wider in the interior areas than in the coastal areas).

More than income inequality, of greater interest ethically and politically is inequality of opportunity. There are no direct measures of this inequality, but in these two countries it is likely to depend on inequality in the distribution of land, education, and social status. Most estimates suggest that inequality in land and education is much worse in India than in China (largely because of the much larger population of landless and illiterate or semi-literate in India). The level of inequality in social status is also likely to be worse in India, partly on account of the legacy of the caste system in India (but the trend over time is in a positive direction with movements towards political equality brought about by democracy leading to changes in social status and occupational distribution). The picture of gender inequality is mixed: in terms of a gender imbalance in the survival of children, it is worse in China (in the 0–5 age group, for 100 girls there are now 122 boys in China, 109 boys in India), but in terms of female literacy, maternal mortality, or female participation in the labour force, China is far ahead.

In matters of governance the dominant issue in public discussion in both countries is the rampant corruption of public officials and politicians. It is, of course, difficult to get reliable estimates of comparative corruption. There are some reasons why incentives for corruption may be somewhat less in China: the punishment is severe (in many cases, execution); Chinese politicians, unlike their Indian counterparts, do not have to procure funds for the increasingly expensive general elections; since career advancement of local officials depends on local area economic performance (unlike in India where promotion is mostly seniority-based and, with frequent transfers, there is no incentive to develop a stake in the local economy), so the Chinese local official, even while stealing, may take care not to steal too much. On the other hand, democratic India has more institutionalized mechanisms for checking corruption (the Right to Information Act, a free media, and a more vigorous tradition of investigative journalism, an active NGO movement as watchdog, etc.). In fact the connection between business and politics being tighter and less subject to public scrutiny in China, 'crony capitalism' is much more evident there. In India in the allocation of scarce public resources (land, mining rights, telecommunication spectrums, etc.) there have been many accusations of official corruption. But with powerful political families controlling some of the monopoly state-owned enterprises in China and 'princelings' running private enterprises and real estate companies, Chinese politicians have got away with more opportunities for converting their political oligarchic power into massive wealth. The Sanghai-based Hurun Report suggests that in 2011 the seventy richest delegates to the National People's Congress (China's equivalent of Parliament) had a net worth of about $90 billion. Just to get an idea of comparative scale, if you look at the accounts of (declared) assets of the members of the Indian Parliament, the corresponding total wealth of the seventy richest Indian delegates will be much less than half a billion dollars. While crony capitalism is not absent in India, the Indian private corporate sector has a longer tradition of vigorous autonomous development and is comparatively less dependent on political rent-seeking. As the state-owned and politically connected private firms in China become 'too big to fail', it may hurt productivity by blocking entry and exit of firms.

At the local level of governance, decentralization has been more effective in China in both social service delivery and local business development. The incentives and resources for sub-national governments to pursue local development projects are much stronger in China than in India. Of total government expenditure, more than 50 per cent is spent at the sub-provincial level in China, the corresponding percentage in India is nearer 5 per cent. Inter-area competition and market integration through the development of infrastructure and trade are much stronger in China. But the capture of local governments by a locally powerful elite is pervasive in both countries. Except in a small number of states in India, the local landed interests and local middlemen and contractors often divert much of the money coming from above away from the intended beneficiaries of development projects. In China, local officials in collusion with local business often hurt the poor through arbitrary land acquisition, toxic pollution, and violations of safety regulations in factories and mines. In both countries this is possible because of accountability failures (largely due to a lack of democratic processes in China and weak sub-provincial democracy in most regions in India).

The issue of accountability brings us directly to the question of the relation between democracy (or lack of it) and development. For some years now it has been the conviction of the Chinese elite (often termed 'the Beijing Consensus') that authoritarianism is good for development. This is a false and pernicious idea. Examples are easy to find that authoritarianism is neither necessary nor sufficient for development. The relationship between democracy and development is more complex than is portrayed in much of the simplistic discussion both in China and the West. Democracies make fewer catastrophic mistakes (of the kind China has made far too often in the last fifty years), they manage social conflicts (of which India with a more heterogeneous population has more) better, and with popular social movements they keep capitalist excesses somewhat in check. But the Indian experience suggests that democracies easily lend themselves to a form of competitive populism where many of the scarce resources are frittered away in short-run subsidies and handouts (the promise of free water and electricity is a frequent electoral gesture in many Indian state elections), which hurt the cause of long-run pro-poor investments (for example in roads, irrigation, water, and electricity). The pragmatic and professional Chinese leadership often shows an ability to take quick and decisive actions more readily than Indian leaders, but faced with a crisis or political shock, they often over-react, suppress information, and act heavy-handedly, which raises the danger of instability. For all its apparent 'messiness' the Indian democratic governments are in a deeper sense less fragile, as they draw their strength from a legitimacy derived through democratic pluralism. In the long run, democracies may also foster more innovativeness by inducing more free flow of information and creativity.

Both China and India have had an impressive economic performance in recent decades, but they are both hobbled by their different types of structural weaknesses and accountability failures.

Part II
Future Prospects for China

6 Will China continue to prosper?

Simon Cox

Economic forecasts are both unreliable and indispensable. Policy makers cannot trust them. But they cannot live without them either. Certainly in China's case, economic soothsaying has proved influential even when it was entirely spurious. In 1957, Chairman Mao Zedong projected that China could increase its steel output by over 700 per cent in 15 years, overtaking Britain. His boast set the stage for the disastrous Great Leap Forward. Even now, appeals to the distant future remain an important part of China's policy making rituals. In his final speech as general secretary of China's Communist Party, Hu Jintao said that China should aim to double its per capita income from 2010 to 2020.

Will China fulfil that aim? Or will Hu's target prove as elusive as Mao's industrial dreams? In answering this question, academic economists provide surprisingly little guidance. Despite a voluminous literature on the empirical correlates of growth and the necessary conditions for economic catch-up, academics have largely fought shy of making long-term growth projections.

One exception is Robert Lucas, who published an informal, turn-of-the-millennium piece, sketching out one vision of development in the twenty-first century (Lucas, 2000). His sketch was based on the simplest possible model of economic 'convergence', the idea that latecomers to industrialization grow faster than the countries that preceded them. In this model, a catch-up economy's growth is a simple function of its distance from the leading economy.

China has successfully narrowed that gap in recent decades. In 2000 its per capita income was only 8 per cent of America's.[1] By 2010, it was almost 19 per cent. Lucas's simple model can be calibrated to fit this period of convergence.[2] Thus calibrated, it can then provide a simple benchmark for China's growth prospects from 2010 to 2020.

According to this benchmark, China's per capita growth can be expected to slow steadily as it narrows the gap with the USA. From an average of 9.3 per cent over the years 2001

---

[1] In this chapter, per capita income is always calculated in 2005 PPP dollars, based on the Penn World Tables (PWT), Version 7.1, unless otherwise noted.

[2] The projection assumes that US per capita income grows by 2 per cent a year. The growth equation takes the form: China's per capita income growth = $2 - 3.45*\ln$(China's per capita income/US per capita income).

to 2010 growth will slow to about 7.3 per cent on average from 2011 to 2020. But that would still be just fast enough to double China's per capita income, in keeping with Hu's target.

This optimistic projection reflects one stark fact and one strong assumption. The stark fact is that China still has plenty of room to grow: the gap between its income and the USA's remains wide. The strong assumption is that China's growth will remain a constant proportion of this diminishing gap—that China's convergence in this decade will be as successful as its convergence last decade.

Sceptics cite a variety of reasons to doubt this assumption. In the past decade, they point out, China's growth has been flattered by excessive rates of investment. In the decade ahead, they add, China's demographics will prove less favourable. Finally, as China advances, it will fall foul of the so-called 'middle-income trap' that has interrupted the progress of other once-promising countries. This chapter will examine each danger in turn.

6.1 **Excessive investment**

The backyard furnaces promoted by Mao during the Great Leap Forward failed miserably to fulfil his wish of surpassing Britain's steel output. But today China is by far the biggest steelmaker in the world, producing 65 times as much as the UK in 2010. This enormous expansion in industrial capacity reflects one of the most striking features of China's economy: its extraordinary rates of investment. In 2011 it invested almost half of its GDP, a higher share than either Japan or South Korea during their eras of rapid growth.

Many economists argue that such a high rate of capital spending poses a threat to China's future growth. They fear it will result in widespread overcapacity, a wave of bad loans, and an investment bust, from which China's growth will struggle to recover.

The problem can be divided into two separable issues. First, is China's heavy investment wasteful and inefficient? Second, must it result in a 'bust'? Those who answer yes to the first question typically also answer yes to the second. But Chinese investment can be wasteful without being unsustainable.

China's investment does appear to be inefficient. More precisely, it suffers from what economists call 'dynamic inefficiency'. China's level of capital spending consistently exceeds its capital income; it invests more in its capital stock year-by-year than it earns from it (He et al., 2007). By investing less, China could increase consumption in the present without reducing it in the future.

But although China's investment rate is inefficiently high, its saving rate is even higher. Indeed, China has exported over $2 trillion of excess saving to the rest of the world since 1994 through its persistent current account surpluses. China's investment splurge is thus different from the spending booms, fed by foreign capital inflows, that preceded Asia's financial crises in 1997–98. China's capital spending may be squandering resources. But they are resources that China has already set aside.

China's dynamic inefficiency may help to explain why it seems so prone to bubbles in everything from property to caterpillar fungus. Such economies are, in effect, trying excessively hard to transfer resources from the present to the future. Productive investment is the best vehicle for this transfer. But if such investments are either unavailable or inaccessible, savers will seek alternative stores of value.

Some of China's apparently worthless assets—such as Ordos, a notorious 'ghost' city in Inner Mongolia—function as vehicles for its prodigious saving. Lavishly built, but lightly inhabited, Ordos was intended to soak up windfall earnings from Mongolia's mining boom that would otherwise leave the province. Viewed from this perspective, China's extravagant but vacant properties are like the family jewellery that lies unworn and unseen in the safe.

6.2 Ageing

By investing in infrastructure, property, and factories, China is using today's resources to make provision for the future. This provision may be excessive, as critics allege. But China, it should be noted, will also face unaccustomed burdens in the future, thanks to a second worrying trend: the ageing of its population. The percentage of working-age Chinese began to fall in 2011 and the absolute number (aged 15–59) began to shrink the following year.

This ageing will depress two important ratios: the ratio of workers to dependants and the ratio of labour to capital. As China's dependency ratio rises, the household saving rate may fall, because families will have fewer breadwinners for every mouth to feed. That will limit the amount of resources available for investment.

In addition, as labour becomes more scarce, wages will rise. If they rise fast enough, they will claim a bigger share of China's national income, at the expense of profits.[3] That should reduce China's high rate of investment, because much of the country's capital spending is financed out of corporate saving.

To some extent, then, the first two worries about China's prospects offset each other. China's investment (where it is not entirely unproductive) should help it meet its demographic burdens. Conversely, those demographic burdens will steadily erode China's willingness and ability to persist with such high rates of investment.

---

[3] This requires a low elasticity of substitution between capital and labour, contrary to the assumptions of the conventional Cobb–Douglas production function, but in keeping with the decline in China's wage share in recent years.

6.3 **The middle-income trap**

When a migrant worker leaves China's farms to find work in industry or services, China's productivity jumps. But China will eventually exhaust this straightforward source of productivity improvement. To sustain its progress, it will need to find another engine of development. The shift from one development phase to another is not always easy. It constitutes a 'thrilling jump', according to Cai (2012), that not every economy succeeds in making. Some fall instead into a 'middle-income trap'.

The spectre of a middle-income trap haunts many discussions of China's future. The trap helped motivate the 'China 2030' report, produced jointly by the World Bank and the Development Research Centre, a government think-tank. The report pointed out that 101 economies qualified as middle-income in 1960. But only thirteen of them blossomed into high-income economies by 2008. 'Growing up is hard to do,' it concluded.

But the evidence for a middle-income trap is not as strong as the report implies. Its definition of middle-income covered a vast range of income levels, from as little as $600 per capita in 1960 to as much as $13,300 per capita in 2008. (Both amounts are expressed in 1990 Geary–Khamis dollars.) In principle, therefore, an economy at the low end of middle-income status in 1960 could grow by over 6 per cent for forty-eight years and still fail to graduate into the charmed circle of high-income countries by 2008.

To gauge China's prospects more precisely, it is useful to see how other countries have fared after reaching China's stage of development. For this purpose, China's 'stage of development' is defined as a per capita income between 18.9 per cent and 25 per cent of the US level. This definition is in keeping with Lucas's model (and others), which assume that a country's room for growth is governed not by its absolute level of income, but by its distance from the leading economies.

Figure 6.1 shows how the average economy has fared after reaching China's stage of development. The average is based on forty-two economies in the Penn World Tables that reached this threshold at some point. (It excludes countries with populations smaller than Singapore's. Because many of the forty-two economies reached China's stage of development quite recently, they do not all have many years of subsequent progress to track.)

Nonetheless the figure paints a happier picture than one might expect, given all the talk of a middle-income trap. It shows that the average country continues to catch up with America, even forty years after reaching China's current stage of development. Averaging across the enormous variety of cases, there is no obvious point at which convergence tends to slow or stop—no identifiable 'jump' from one development phase to the next.

It seems that the phases of development do not proceed in a polite and orderly sequence, one after the other. They intermingle and overlap. At any point in time, some parts of a national economy will be leading, others lagging.

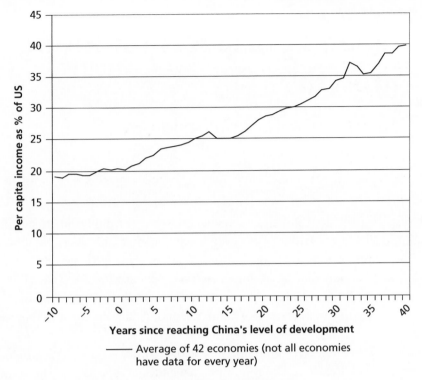

Figure 6.1. Years since reaching China's level of development

This seems true, at least, of China. Some parts of its economy are still reaping the 'easy' productivity gains that result from moving labour between agriculture, industry, and services. But this kind of development contributed only 1.4 percentage points of China's growth from 1995 to 2012 (Kuijs, 2013). The bulk of China's growth is already coming from elsewhere, principally productivity improvements within industry. In that sense, most of China's economy has already made the thrilling jump from one development phase to the next.

■ REFERENCES

Cai, F. 2012. Is there a 'middle-income trap'? Theories, experiences and relevance to China. *China & World Economy* 20(1); 49–61.

He, D., W. Zhang, and J. Shek. 2007. How efficient has been China's investment?' *Pacific Economic Review* 12(5); 597–617.

Kuijs, L. 2013. Personal communication with author

Lucas Jr, R. E. 2000. Some macroeconomics for the 21st century. *Journal of Economic Perspectives* 14(1); 159–68.

7 China's prospects for future growth

Robert W. Fogel and Nathaniel Grotte

In the 1950s, the early days of the phenomenal growth that would come to be known as the 'Asian Miracle', few would have believed it possible that China's economy would be predicted to represent 40 per cent of global GDP a century later (Fogel, 2007). This prediction is based not only on China's anticipated rise, but also the relative decline of current economic powerhouses such as the eurozone countries. To contextualize this shift, it is worth considering a few aspects of China's economic development in the twentieth century.

The mid-1960s marked the beginning a period of vigorous economic growth for many Asian nations, including Hong Kong, Taiwan, Thailand, and especially Japan, which went from a war-ravaged country to the second largest economy in the world in the span of four decades, increasing per capita income tenfold. Many economists were sceptical that this level of growth could be sustained for a variety of reasons, including the supposition that the growth depended mainly on investment in capital rather than improvements in efficiency.

In fact, these investments resulted in efficiency improvements, and Chinese economic growth did not slow down. In addition, China invested heavily in promoting education in the 1970s and 1980s, raising the ratios of school-age students enrolled in schools dramatically. This increase in educational levels was promoted by both business and political leaders who recognized not only that they had to expand the supply of highly trained technicians, but that the demand for high-tech consumer products required well-educated consumers. The quality of labour has risen not only because of education, but also because of on-the-job training, increased experience, improved health, and increased longevity.

Even though the extent of China's economic growth was slow to be understood, it nevertheless influenced economic thought. A new wave of papers from growth theorists appeared in the mid-1980s responding to new patterns of growth in the economies of the USA and Europe. This attention, in part, turned to Indonesia, Malaysia, and Thailand. China began to attract attention in the 1980s.

Table 7.1 The global distribution of gross domestic product (GDP) in 2040, by grouping of nations

Grouping	Population (in millions)	Percent of total	GDP (in billions of $)	Percent of total
United States	392	5	41,944	14
European Union	376	4	15,040	5
India	1,522	17	36,528	12
China	1,455	17	123,675	40
Japan	108	1	5,292	2
6 South East Asian Countries	516	6	35,604	12
Subtotals	4,369	50	258,083	85
Rest of the world	4,332	50	49,774	16
World	8,701	100	307,857	101

Source: Fogel (2007).

Table 7.1 presents our predictions for the global economy of 2040. As important as China's actions will be to their future economic growth, what the rest of the word does, or fails to do, will also be important. In 2000, the EU population exceeded that of the USA by about a third. By 2040, the EU's population is predicted to be somewhat smaller than that of the USA, a result primarily of stagnating fertility rates. In recent decades, these rates have fallen below the level necessary to maintain population levels. A corresponding implication of this is the rapid ageing of the European population. Italy and Germany will see median ages around 50 years by 2040. As a result, the ratio of citizens working to those not in the labour force will dip dramatically, which will slow opportunities for economic expansion.

Recent World Bank data put China's fertility rate at a low 1.61 births per woman (and falling), which is well below the level of 2.1 needed to maintain population size.[1]

China has made, and should continue to make, great investments in the human capital of its citizens, greatly enhancing the quality of labour through education. In 1998, President Jiang Zemin called for massive increases in higher-education enrollments. The response was swift: over the next four years, enrollment in higher education increased by 165 per cent, from 3.4 million to 9.0 million.[2] Data from the USA indicate that college-educated workers are three times as productive, and a high school graduate is 1.8 times as productive, as a worker with less than a ninth grade education. These investments are a substantial part of what makes our estimates for China's future possible.

[1] <http://data.worldbank.org/indicator/SP.DYN.TFRT.IN>.
[2] *China Statistical Yearbook 2003*. Beijing: China Statistics Press.

In 2011, China's urban population surpassed its rural population for the first time in history, reflecting a shift of labour from agriculture to industrial work.[3] This sort of internal migration has been well understood by scholars of modern economic growth, who have identified that the agricultural share of the labour force declined but labour productivity in agriculture rose. In the quarter century between 1978 and 2003, growth in Chinese labour productivity has been high not only in agriculture, but in services and industry as well, averaging about 6 per cent per annum. At the national level, output per worker grew by 9 per cent, because the level of output per worker was much higher in industry and services than in agriculture. Hence, by shifting workers from agriculture, which contained the majority of workers, the economy gained an additional boost in the annual national growth rate (Fogel, 2007). That being said, productivity in rural areas continues to grow, and that sector is responsible for about a third of Chinese economic growth.

Also important for the future of China's growth is what Nobel laureate Simon Kuznets characterized as 'substantial changes in the organization of society—an emergence of new institutions and a diminished importance of the old'. It may be a surprise to some outsiders, but China's present-day political system is not the monolith it is often believed to be. Often it is local governments, rather than Beijing, that are behind the most successful initiatives. China is certainly not an open democracy, but there is more criticism and debate than some realize. Today, one sees open discussion at high levels. One example is the annual meeting of the Chinese Economists Society, where there are always individuals who are very critical of the Chinese government. For example, they will point out that recent decisions by the finance ministers are flawed, or call attention to issues of equity. They might even publish a critical letter in a Beijing newspaper. Instead of cracking down on this sort of speech, the finance minister is more likely to call them up and ask to set up a meeting. It may not be well known, but this sort of back-and-forth is happening more and more often, and Chinese economic planning has become much more responsive and open to new ideas than in the past.

An explosion of academic interest in China's economy (including the present volume) speaks to global interest in the development of its economy. It may seem a small point, but this interest is possible largely because of the availability of quality economic data—something that could not be taken for granted thirty years ago when Simon Kuznets, in his Nobel speech, bemoaned the lack of such data for developing countries, which tended to have a much poorer supply than developed countries—'a parallel,' he observed, 'to the smaller relative supply of material capital'. Some improvement in this area had been observed, but not for China, which, in Kuznets' opinion, 'view data as useful to their enemies (internal or external) and are therefore either not revealed by government or possibly not even collected'.[4]

---

[3] <http://www.forbes.com/sites/afontevecchia/2012/01/17/china-the-bullish-case-for-a-soft-landing/>.
[4] <http://www.nobelprize.org/nobel_prizes/economics/laureates/1971/kuznets-lecture.html>.

Chinese officials have taken Kuznets' concerns to heart. There is good evidence to believe that the statistics coming out of China are reliable, and Chinese officials have every reason to want them to be. If anything, it is likely that Chinese statisticians are underestimating economic progress—especially in the service sector, where small firms often fail to report numbers to the government. This sort of underestimation happens in the USA as well, where improvements in services such as education and healthcare are not adequately accounted for.

And for the rest of the world? China's current growth rates and expected future growth does not, of course, preclude labour productivity and per capita income from growing elsewhere. We predict that Europe, for example, will likely grow at rates that are, by past standards, not bad—on the order of 1.8 per cent per annum. The European market will be about 60 per cent larger in 2040 than it was in 2000. America's market will be over 300 per cent larger; India's will be over 1,400 per cent larger—and China's will be 2,400 per cent larger. Indeed, the Chinese market in 2040 by itself will probably be larger than the combined markets of the USA, the European Union, India, and Japan. Even if English continues to be the principal commercial language in the coming decades, it would nevertheless behoove MBA students to learn a little Mandarin.

■ **REFERENCE**

Fogel, R. W. 2007. Capitalism and democracy in 2040. *Daedalus* 136(3), 87–95.

8 China's future performance and development challenges

Dwight Perkins

China's high gross domestic product (GDP) growth experience has lasted longer (over three decades) and has involved faster average growth in income per capita than in any other country in world history. In thinking about China over the coming one to two decades, many analysts simply project forwards China's growth during the recent past with results that are dramatic. In 2011 China's GDP converted to US dollars at the official exchange rate of $7.5 trillion (RMB47.156 trillion), or roughly half that of the USA, and at purchasing power parity prices it was a significantly higher share of the US level. Over the thirty-three years of reform beginning in 1978, the annual average growth rate according to official statistics was 9.6 per cent. If one projects this growth rate forwards one or two decades one gets a GDP figure for 2021 of US$19 trillion and for 2031 of US$47 trillion (at 2011 prices) or more than three times the current GDP of the USA.

China may well someday reach GDP levels of this magnitude but there are ample reasons for believing that it will take much longer than one or two decades to do so. Countries on the economic frontier, such as the USA, may grow at a steady rate for a century or more, but that has not been the experience of countries attempting to catch up with those on the frontier. For those attempting to catch up in the latter half of the twentieth century, if they had the right foundations and the right policies they grew very rapidly for two or three decades but then slowed down. Among China's East Asian neighbours this slowdown occurred at around US$13,000 per capita in year 2000 purchasing power parity terms. In countries around the world which managed to reach a per capita income of $20,000 or more, almost all experienced a reduction in their GDP growth rate when they reached between $10,000 and $16,000 per capita. Slowing down did not mean that they faced major crises such as prolonged recessions, the GDP growth rates in East Asia were still relatively high by international standards at 4–5 per cent a year for a time, but they were no longer at near double digit rates and they never returned to such rates on a sustained basis.

GDP growth in China is likely to decelerate markedly within the next decade and possibly within the next few years and that will have profound implications for China's

influence on the world economy as well as for the standard of living and economic structure of China's own economy. The reasons for this deceleration can best be understood by
looking first at supply side issues and then turning to the demand side where China's gross
domestic expenditure structure is unique.[1]

8.1 **Supply side sources of growth deceleration**

On the supply side, the starting point for an analysis of the future is the growth accounting equation that relates the growth rate of GDP to the growth rate of the labour force, the
growth rate of capital (including human capital), and the productivity growth of those
inputs (called total factor productivity or TFP). At this general level, we already know
what is likely to happen to the growth rate of the labour force because most of those who
will enter the labour force over the coming two decades have already been born. The one
child family policy ensures that China's labour force will stop growing within the coming
decade. The rate of increase in the education of that labour force will also slow because
China has already approached universal education through nine grades and is not far from
achieving the same through secondary school. The share of the relevant age cohorts in universities will continue to rise but not at the rapid rates of the past three decades. The growth
rate of the capital stock in recent years has been faster than the growth rate of GDP but this
too will come to an end because the rate of gross capital formation is already at an unusual
and probably unsustainable 50 per cent of GDP. We shall return to why the investment in
capital at this level is not likely to be sustainable when we look at demand side issues.

  With the growth rate of capital and labour inputs slowing down, sustaining the near
two-digit GDP growth rates of the past implies that total factor productivity growth will
have to accelerate to levels higher than anything achieved to date. But one source of TFP
growth is almost certain to slow—the productivity that comes from shifting large numbers of labourers out of low productivity occupations (mainly agriculture where much
labour is under-employed) into higher productivity tasks, mostly in the urban areas.
There are still far more people in the rural areas than are needed in agriculture but most
of those who are farming are ageing and are not likely to migrate out. In contrast, virtually
all of those between the ages 18 and 40 have already left the countryside for jobs in the
cities. Many have left their children back in the village and that means migration will continue as these children reach working age. The number of migrants, however, is likely to

---

[1] For those interested in pursuing the issues discussed in this short chapter in greater depth, they are
referred to longer works of the author including Dwight H. Perkins, China's investment and GDP growth
boom: when and how will it end? In *China's Economic Development: Past, Present, and Future*, edited by Masahiko Aoki, Chong-en Bai, Fang Cai, and Yingyi Qian, Palgrave: International Economic Association, 2012;
and Barry Eichengreen, Dwight H. Perkins, and Kwanho Shin, *From Miracle to Maturity: The Growth of the
Korean Economy*. Cambridge, MA: Distributed by Harvard University Press, 2012.

be smaller than in the past decades that saw nearly 300 million workers and their families leave agriculture and related rural occupations.

At a level that is difficult to quantify, much of the rise in productivity in China over the past three decades has come about because of reforms that involved the dismantling of the inefficient Soviet style economic system in favour of a reliance on market forces and competition. The dismantling of the rural communes in favour of household-based agriculture, the abandonment of the centrally directed administrative allocation of industrial inputs and output in favour of market allocation, the encouragement of foreign direct investment, and other similar reforms had a profound impact on productivity. Going forwards, however, the reforms required involve refining the market system to make it more efficient and that is likely to be a slower process. China, like all economies that approach high income status, will also have to rely more on its own research and development efforts rather than on making modest adjustments to imported technologies. China, with the rapid expansion and rising quality of its education and research institutions, is well placed to do this, but developing new technologies on one's own involves making mistakes and is inevitably slower than adapting someone else's technologies.

There is another structural change on the supply side that is likely to reduce the GDP growth rate. In the early stages of catch up growth, the share of manufacturing in GDP and manufacturing employment in total employment rises rapidly, but both of these shares reach a peak when per capita income reaches a certain level (less than $14,000 per capita in most countries in year 2000 PPP prices). The actual number of people in the labour force in manufacturing then begins to decline while the output value of manufacturing continues to rise but at a slower rate. The service sectors then experience a rise in their share in GDP and an even larger rise in their share of the labour force. Since the service sectors tend to grow more slowly than manufacturing grew in its early stages (in part because TFP in services tends to be lower than in manufacturing), the shift towards services also slows the GDP growth rate.

8.2 Demand side sources of growth deceleration

The supply side explanations for GDP growth deceleration are common to most countries. On the demand side China is facing a problem that is unprecedented in the experience of other economies. China's share of household consumption in GDP started the reform period in 1978 at a fairly low level when compared with other nations and that share has fallen steadily ever since. By 2010 the share had reached 33.8 per cent of GDP, down from a reform period peak of 52.5 per cent in 1981. This share in most countries is around 60 per cent and in the USA it is around 70 per cent. A full explanation of the reasons for this low and declining level are beyond the scope of this short chapter but the combination of low income growth (relative to the GDP growth rate) due to the large overhang of surplus labour in the countryside plus a high savings rate due to a weak social safety net are the main causes.

The gap in China between consumption and the level of total aggregate demand required to sustain the full employment of resources (other than structural unemployment) was filled by a steadily rising level of investment. Gross capital formation as a share of GDP rose from a low of 31.9 per cent of GDP in 1982 to 48.6 per cent of GDP in 2010. Much of this rise occurred after the year 2000. An investment share of this magnitude could not be sustained by the increase in Chinese consumer demand or government consumption with the exception of consumer demand in one area. There was a huge pent up demand for housing in urban China. Urban housing investment had been virtually absent during the two decades prior to the reform period and urban housing space per capita had fallen to 3.6 square metres. There was also a huge pent up demand for infrastructure because China prior to 1978, following the Soviet approach to infrastructure, avoided investing in the sector until transport bottlenecks and the like became so severe that they had no choice.

Beginning in the reform period but particularly during the period from 1998 to 2011, China invested heavily in both housing and infrastructure. Much of the housing investment was private and some of it was speculative investment to take advantage of rising real estate prices while infrastructure investment was mostly public. Both were massive in scale. The total available urban housing per capita rose to 31.6 square metres or nearly 100 square metres for a family of three in 2010. China's road system was converted from a limited number of two lane paved and overcrowded highways to a multi-lane modern limited access highway system longer than the interstate system of the USA. Feeder roads were expanded and paved. New modern airport terminals were built in all provincial capitals, a high speed passenger rail system covering the whole country was begun along with a large scale water system designed to move the surplus water of the Yangtze River to the parched cities and farms of north China, and much more. This massive investment in housing and infrastructure, however, is reaching saturation levels in many areas and it is unlikely that investment levels of this magnitude can be justified by high investment returns going forwards. Real estate prices are already beginning to decline among other reasons. Thus on the demand side as well as the supply side, the GDP growth rate is likely to slow.

8.3 The implications of decelerating growth

The Chinese government and the Chinese Communist Party for the past three decades have justified their rule in large part because their ability to produce a high growth rate has led to rapidly rising incomes and has each year absorbed ten million or more migrants from the countryside into higher paying urban employment. Slower GDP growth, however, is not likely to threaten this justification for their rule if growth continues at a respectable rate of say 5 per cent a year for another two decades. The surplus of labour in the countryside has fallen and there are now labour shortages that are leading to accelerated wages and hence incomes and that will continue even at a slower GDP growth rate. There is a clear need to provide housing and other services for the migrants that until now have been largely neglected and that will justify continued large government investments in housing, healthcare, and education, although not as much housing investment as in the recent past. A major problem roughly two decades from now will be that the one child family policies that contributed to the large demographic dividend of the past two decades will give way to a major problem of a large ageing population and a shrinking labour force to support those elderly. Even with continued fairly rapid growth, meeting the future needs of both the working and elderly households will become a major challenge. If growth were to slow markedly below 5 per cent or 6 per cent a year, however, the working population in less than two decades would be pitted against the ageing population in a struggle for a share of a pie that was no longer growing and a challenge would become a crisis.

9 Rebalancing China's growth

Ligang Song

The call to rebalance economic growth in China is primarily motivated by the structural problems within China as well as in its economic relations with the rest of the world. China's international payments surpluses during the first decade of the twenty-first century have corresponded with deepening domestic structural risks to China's economic growth and development. These structural challenges include the composition of growth resulting from China's dynamic internal transformation, China's trade orientation, the trajectory and intensity of resource use and CO_2 emissions, welfare problems of distribution, and international market constraints. It is thought to be necessary for China to confront these challenges now in order to put the growth path on a more sustainable trajectory for the future. However, China faces huge challenges in addressing its economic imbalances and sustaining growth against a backdrop of heightened domestic and international uncertainty (Deer and Song, 2012).

The role of policy should be to design and implement a framework that reduces distortions, encourages and rewards innovation, equalizes access to education, employment, a social safety net, and capital for investment, while minimizing rent seeking opportunities. The desire to achieve such an environment will create a demand for institutional reforms that can facilitate these processes of structural change in the least disruptive fashion (McKay and Song, 2012).

Unbalanced domestic expenditure refers to China's high, and growing, share of investment relative to consumption in the expenditure measure of GDP. The external payment imbalance refers to China's current account, trade account, and private financial account surpluses. While the list of Chinese economic characteristics that deserve the label 'unbalanced' are legion—including the level of the exchange rate, the urban–rural income divide, the coast–hinterland divide, and asymmetries in the degree of access to credit, education, social security and housing—at some level they all relate to and inform the basic macro-economic structure and the external payments position.

Catch-up growth driven by rapid capital accumulation can be sustained for decades in capital-poor transitional economies with an abundant supply of labour. China's still relatively low level of income per capita and capital stock per worker, in addition to its relatively low (policy suppressed) urbanization rate and the relative backwardness of its central and interior provinces, argue that concentrated growth on the Chinese mainland could potentially continue for longer than it did for its neighbours, including Chinese Taiwan and South Korea.

China's investment-led growth model is coming under increasing scrutiny due to the increasingly unhelpful international environment in which it finds itself now, in addition to the sheer heft that China exercises as the world's largest manufacturing exporter, pollution emitter, and commodity consumer. Furthermore, the costs of resource intensive growth—via high pollution and energy intensity—are becoming increasingly apparent. The low share of household consumption in total expenditure is a result of both a high marginal propensity to save and the low wage share of income at the national level, and until recently declining real rural incomes.

China's total manufacturing trade balance was in net surplus from as early as 1994, but this was concentrated in lower value added manufactures and was initially offset by a net deficit in heavier machinery and transport sectors. However, the machinery and transport equipment balance turned to surplus and rose sharply from 2004 to 2008. This turnaround in the machinery and transport equipment balance was the result of rising investment in heavy industry in the early 2000s (Anderson, 2008), which led to a sharp rise in heavy manufactured goods output and an expanding market share abroad and import substitution at home when capacity came on stream from 2004. Yet this sharp rise in output was not matched by an equivalent rise in domestic or foreign demand and, thus, the rise in market share led to falling prices, a lower rate of profit, and continual deterioration of China's terms of trade (McKay and Song, 2010).

The legacy of China's pre-reform heavy industrial structure and its institutional and policy architecture have led to a pattern of growth marked by widening imbalances that are more pronounced than those seen in other industrialization drives, and which were not present in the initial stages of China's reform. China's domestic expenditure and external imbalances widened in the 2000s as a result of China's stalled institutional reforms in the 1990s, and this has reinforced an investment-led industrial structure, especially in heavy industrial production and real estate development. The current growth pattern highlights the opportunity costs of stalled structural reform areas, such as the migration and labour market systems, vertical fiscal relations, state-enterprises, and the financial system.

Three sets of market-enhancing institutional reforms are therefore necessary: reform of the labour system, reform of the financial system, and reform of the government system, particularly in regards to the local government and state enterprise sectors. The interdependence of the Chinese economy with the world economy also suggests the significance of these channels for international rebalancing (Deer and Song, 2012).

The key is shifting the economic environment and incentive structure within which China's economic entities operate. The rebalancing policy objectives are to raise the domestic absorptive capacity of China's economy, through raising the relative share of consumption in final expenditure, rather than by seeking to reduce the net role of exports; and to direct resources further away from the relatively inefficient into the more product-ive sectors of the economy through an improved market mechanism.

The effective (as opposed to spatial) urbanization of China's migrant workers is the most effective and realistic mid-term policy strategy for rebalancing China's macro-economy. Institutional reform can accelerate the long-run processes of migration and urbanization in China, which would raise domestic demand and, thus, reduce both the internal and the external imbalances in China's macro-economy and shift the current unbalanced industrial structure. A policy of urbanizing rural migrant workers by remov-ing threshold barriers to urban residency and ensuring equal access to social housing, education, healthcare, and social protection are likely to raise consumption by migrant workers (Song et al., 2010).

The process of urbanization requires investment in urban infrastructure (such as mass transit and utility provision) and in service industries. The effect, combined with higher domestic consumption by migrant workers, would be to raise growth and enhance struc-tural change. Urbanizing China's rural migrant workers would also help to integrate Chi-na's still segmented labour markets and provide a basis for long-term real wages to rise. Real wage gains can accelerate structural change by raising household consumption in domestic demand and by providing a basis for real currency appreciation. That can help shift China's industrial structure towards the tertiary sectors, which would benefit from the broader and deeper consumption basket of the better remunerated household sector.

Capital market reforms are necessary for China to rebalance in three related areas: the allocation of capital, the cost of capital, and the link between domestic financial reform and exchange arrangements. Although China's bank-dominated financial system deep-ened its asset base considerably over the reform period, China's system of formal credit allocation has remained narrow, and is mainly directed to the state-sector as state owned banks (SOBs) continue to dominate the sector. China's state-owned commercial banking sector allocates capital at rates which are low relative to those prevailing in private mar-kets or a broad indicator such as the growth rate of nominal GDP, which reinforces the wider structure of investment and expenditure imbalances.

It will be difficult to develop domestic financial markets without further liberalization of the foreign exchange system or of financial (capital) account controls. The two spheres are mutually reinforcing, even circular. The exchange rate remains the anchor for China's monetary policy and any move towards a flexible currency needs to be accompanied by a shift to a different anchor. Current efforts to build up the interbank lending market and thereby establish a benchmark short-term interest rate to serve as this anchor shows some promise. A feasible reform would be to seek to incorporate China's large informal finan-cial sector into the official financial system, in tandem with a removal of administrative ceilings on bank deposit rates and floor lending rates. The objective would be to cre-ate a legal sector of smaller non-bank financial lending and deposit institutions. These firms would compete with the banking system to provide market-based contract terms for households and small and medium-sized enterprises (SMEs).

Following fiscal reforms in 1994, the majority of government revenues have been collected by the central government, while local governments have remained responsible for the majority of public and social expenditure, especially on healthcare and education. As a consequence of this fiscal and governmental system, not only do local governments have a powerful incentive to maximize growth, but they have an overriding fiscal incentive to do so through driving new investments, such as in real estate, in which they have direct or indirect claims to income, rather than through raising consumption.

The current pattern of local government investment—and outlays, more broadly—could be better directed to meeting the needs of China's current urban and migrant populations by directing more expenditure to social housing, and educational and social services (such as healthcare, retirement income, transportation, unemployment insurance, public space, and environmental amenity). There is much more to be done to reform the fiscal system at central and local government levels, including shifting the current land-transaction tax system to a property valuation and rates system.

SOEs have accounted for much of the sharp rise in heavy industrial profits and enterprise savings in the period since 2000. The monopoly position of China's SOEs also poses a longer-term challenge to the reform of China's industrial structure towards a more balanced trajectory. However, they also suggest an inefficient allocation of capital across sectors, which also reflect the still large distortions in China's factor markets, which cumulatively benefit the SOE sector disproportionately (Huang and Wang, 2010).

The pressures that are currently building will ultimately convince China to accelerate the pace of structural adjustment including the pace of liberalizing its capital account with the full convertibility and 'internationalization' of the RMB. China's eventual success in achieving the objective of rebalancing will also depend on how China's major trading partners seek to overcome their own structural problems. The global economy will be challenged to maintain the rate of expansion required to return balance sheets to health while demand centres and relative prices continue to shift.

Tackling China's economic imbalances necessitates economic policy reform to facilitate a more sustainable pattern of growth that will fundamentally alter China's industrial structure and its trade orientation. Rebalancing will direct a new pattern of growth, which requires a major alteration of the current industrial structure and the institutional arrangements associated with it, thereby leading to slower but higher quality growth consistent with the ultimate objective of China's economic transformation: to achieve an improved standard of living for the Chinese people in the most efficient and equitable way.

▪ REFERENCES

Anderson, Jonathan. 2008. China's industrial investment boom and the Renminbi. In *Debating China's Exchange Rate Policy*, edited by Morris Goldstein and Nicholas Lardy, 61–69. Washington, DC: Peterson Institute for International Economics.

Deer, Luke and Ligang Song. 2012. China's approach to rebalancing: a conceptual and policy framework. *China & World Economy* 20(1), 1–26.

Huang, Yiping and Bijun Wang. 2010. Cost distortions and structural imbalances in China. *China & World Economy* 18(4), 1–17.

McKay, Huw and Ligang Song. 2010. China as a global manufacturing powerhouse: strategic considerations and structural adjustment. *China & World Economy* 18(1), 1–32.

McKay, Huw and Ligang Song. 2012. Rebalancing the Chinese economy to sustain long-term growth. In *Rebalancing and Sustaining Growth in China*, edited by Huw McKay and Ligang Song, 1–18. Canberra: Australian National University Press.

Song, Ligang, Jiang Wu, and Yongsheng Zhang. 2010. Urbanisation of migrant workers and expansion of domestic demand. *Social Sciences in China* 31(3), 194–216.

10 China's middle-income transition and evolving inclusive growth strategy

Michael Spence

China is entering a middle-income transition, defined as the phase of growth that takes the per capita income from 4000 dollars to about 10,000 dollars. Most countries that enter this phase slow down. At least statistically, it is fraught with difficulty. The exceptions, the predecessors that sustained high growth in the middle-income transition, are Japan, Korea, the Taiwanese economy, Singapore, and Hong Kong. None was at the scale or complexity of the Chinese case.

In this transition in China, there are several parallel structural changes supported by public investment and policy initiatives that need to happen. Very labour intensive process manufacturing and assembly will move inland and eventually to countries at earlier stages of development, and lower per capita incomes. Urbanization will continue and accelerate, with massive required investments in urban infrastructure. Sustainably financing models of urban development will have to be created. Probably the municipal bond markets will be created with appropriate legal and regulatory underpinnings. Land sales have been an important source of revenue for urban infrastructure, but that is not a sustainable financing mechanism.

Tens of millions of lower skilled jobs will move to earlier-stage developing countries and that represents a huge opportunity for them. Justin Lin, the chief economist at the World Bank, estimates that 85 million jobs in this category will migrate away from China in the next few years. With per capita incomes of 5,000 dollars and rising, China will lose its comparative advantage in this type of economic activity.

The employment engine for people moving from rural to urban areas has been a concern, because it used to be the labour intensive export sector. In fact, employment for the less skilled new arrivals will shift away from the labour intensive component of the export sector, towards the lower skilled end of the urban service sectors, which will expand rapidly. It is important that this works. Without it, the remaining rural population could be stranded away from the modern urban economy. The alternative would be to subsidize the labour intensive tradable sector until urbanization has progressed further, either directly or through control of the exchange rate. This is a bad idea as it will cause a slowing down of the structural shifts to higher value added activity which in turn is required to support the rising incomes.

A key feature of the transition in China, as it was in previous cases, is an expansion of the market side of the economy relative to the state directed part. Essentially, the economy needs to change its mode of value creation towards capital, human capital, and knowledge intensive activity. As part of that process, services will expand in general and even within the manufacturing supply chains. The policies required to support this element of transformation are heavy investment in human capital, expansion of basic and applied research, and legal institutions and regulatory structures that support entry and exit, innovation, patents and intellectual property, and more generally the dynamic aspects of competition. Financial sector development is also a prerequisite at this stage, and I will return to that a little later.

The Chinese economy is large, though not yet rich. In fact it is the second or third largest economy in the world after the USA and Europe, if you count the latter as a single economy. It is not too much less than half the size of the two advanced economy giants. If growth is maintained in the range above 7 per cent, that difference can be expected to shrink and disappear over a decade or a little more, roughly the same time period as a relatively high speed middle-income transition would entail. With growing size and wealth, the growth drivers also change. The expansion of the domestic economy and domestic demand will be an increasingly important driver of growth, in China and broadly in the global economy. China is now the leading export destination for India, Brazil, Argentina, Australia, Japan in the near future, and a host of other countries in Asia.

There is a challenge in this area. The large supply of labour in the rural areas has held down wage growth following the pattern described by W. Arthur Lewis. This has caused labour income and household disposable income to decline as a fraction of national income. In addition, the household savings rate is very high, of the order of 30 per cent of disposable income. This puts consumption at around 40 per cent of GDP. In fact, to allow the domestic economy to deliver an appropriate share of aggregate demand and growth, consumption has to rise, and that means that disposable income as a fraction of national income has to rise and the savings rate probably should fall.

Building up the social security and insurance systems without taking on the style of an advanced country, unfunded liabilities will be part of the programme and may reduce the precautionary self-insurance component of savings. On the income side, the Lewis pattern seems to have broken within the last year and a half. Wages are rising very quickly in the coastal areas (20–30 per cent a year in the Pearl River Delta). While that presents transitional difficulties for businesses, it actually helps with the structural transformation and the expansion of the right kind of domestic demand.

China has been an economy with export diversification and very high levels of public and private investment as the growth drivers. The shift towards consumption is crucial, in part because there is a dangerous expansion of low return investments (on auto-pilot) in the state-owned and public sectors, exacerbated by the investment-oriented fiscal stimulus that was part of the response to the crisis of 2008–09. An investment-led growth model is fine if the private and social returns are high, but becomes an unsustainable growth pattern if the system allows the returns to fall. Household demand is important not just for its aggregate size, but because that demand will guide the structural evolution of the composition of the supply side of the economy.

The investment decisions in the public sector need to be subject to a rigorous process to ensure that low return investments are screened out.

The state-owned enterprise sector since the 1990s has shed its social insurance functions and has become more efficient. But it is still large, accounting for more than half the net fixed assets in the economy. For a variety of reasons, it is unlikely to be privatized. But it needs to be exposed to competition within the SOE group and more importantly from the private sector. Further, the dividends from the state-owned enterprises should be made larger (that is retained earnings should be less—currently dividends are probably less than 15 per cent of earnings) and flow to the government budget. That would put the SOEs on an equal footing with the private sector in terms of raising capital where risk adjusted rates of return are the key determinants of capital allocation. To accomplish these coordinated changes, financial sector development and shifts in corporate governance are important ingredients in the structural change in the 12th Five Year Plan and the middle-income transition.

In addition, the social insurance functions that used to be lodged in enterprises (almost all the large ones were state-owned) prior to the reforms of the 1990s, have not been completely rebuilt, although there has been progress. Incomplete access and coverage in areas such as pensions, healthcare, education, and unemployment in part explains the rising inequality and related social tensions. These are, of course, exacerbated by corruption among local officials that has not been adequately reigned in.

To summarize, the key elements in the coming transition are:

1. deepening of the capital, human capital, and technology base of the economy to support higher value added activities and higher incomes;

2. a rise in the portion of income going to households and a likely increase in consumption (the alternative being high return investment);

3. an economy that is driven less by investment and external demand and more by domestic demand;

4. the movement offshore of lower value added labour intensive parts of the tradeable side of the economy;

5. expansion of the service side of the economy in both the tradeable and non-tradeable sectors;

6. rapid urbanization, labour mobility, and the elimination of the system of household registration or *Hukou* that affects mobility and access to key services such as education;

7. a system change with respect to the allocation of capital to ensure a high return on investment;

8. the expansion of the market side of the economy, competition, entry and exit and innovation; state directed activity should decline in relative importance;

9. appreciation of the currency at a pace that maintains the pressure for structural change and movement into high value added sectors, without going so quickly as to outrun the capacity of the economy to generate new or replacement employment;

10. resist the tendency to promote domestic innovation by restricting market access of foreign firms—because such a policy will ultimately slow innovation by reducing competition and lowering the rate of inbound knowledge and technology transfer;

11. social policies designed to deal with security and equality or distributional issues;

12. an aggressive move to increase environmental protection;

13. increased energy efficiency going beyond the natural tendency of energy intensity to decline with rising incomes.

All of this is captured in the 12th Five Year Plan. But it is complex. There are elements of potential resistance. Thus the risks are largely in the area of implementation.

In assessing these risks, it is useful to employ a simple three-part framework: resources, competence, and political will. China has a huge state balance sheet relative to the size of the economy. It is also healthy, featuring low levels of debt and other liabilities. It also has a wide range of choice with respect to policy instruments and investments. I would say that resources are not the central issue.

The policy reforms are led by an elite meritocracy. This group has demonstrated great skill in the past, navigating the country through complex structural change. There is no particular reason to think that there is a lack of understanding of the key requirements in this transition.

Political will is a more complex issue with several parts.

The labour intensive export sector will resist structural change and the appreciation of the currency. The state-owned enterprises are powerful and will want to maintain their privileged position and their control over resources and retained earnings. Both these elements are unlikely to be strong enough to reduce reform momentum.

There is a part of the political spectrum that does not want the marketization and reform process to go forwards, and would prefer a more enduring dominant role of the state in the economy. The rising inequality and social tensions are used to buttress this case. The progressive reform movement correctly views a move back in that direction as deleterious to the prospects for growth and development.

In China, these issues are sorted out within the Communist Party. The Party remains the driving force for economic, system, and political reform. It has the key role of constraining corruption and adapting the political structures to accommodate a growing range of voices. With still relatively weak institutional safeguards, the Party is the principal constraining factor with respect to market and governmental misbehaviour and excesses. Notwithstanding internal tensions within the Party, some of them ideological in nature, it has proved quite flexible and adaptable on these dimensions, and the reform momentum has been maintained. Its continued ability to do that is a critical element of the implementation of the plan and the transition to a middle-income.

Many knowledgeable analysts believe that at this stage, economic and political change will have to go hand in hand. The old mantra was economic development first and political change later. That of course has not been the reality, with consultative political mechanisms being instituted in parallel with economic development and reform. But the belief is that the pace of political change in the direction of a more decentralized system of social choice (one might call this democracy) will (and needs to) accelerate, to accompany expanding individual and economic freedom of choice and action.

■ REFERENCE

Lewis, W. Arthur. 1954. Economic development with unlimited supplies of labor. *Manchester School of Economic and Social Studies* 22, 139–91.

11 China's consumer revolution

Yanrui Wu

With the largest single consumer group on earth, the Chinese market has for a long time attracted the attention of researchers as well as business analysts worldwide. In 2012 China's GDP per capita reached US$6,000 and hence the country joined the group of the so-called 'upper middle income' economies according to the World Bank (2010). In the same year, China overtook the United States to become the world's largest commodity trader. Businessmen and policy makers are all excited about the potential purchasing power and the resultant opportunities in the world's second largest economy. This short chapter aims to present a review of the main works addressing China's consumer revolution. The rest of the text begins with a survey of the literature addressing the general consumption issues. Then it discusses more specific topics including consumer behaviour, the new rich, e-consumers, gender and consumer cohorts, and advertising and marketing. Finally it ends with a description of some emerging issues in China's consumer market.

11.1 General studies

Over the years several authors have published works titled 'China's consumer revolution' which have broader coverage of the topics in this field. Cao and Myers (1998) examined urban consumption patterns in the 1990s, and particularly observed the revival of the traditional gift-giving culture in coastal China. They argued that gift-giving between the Chinese people can strengthen their social, economic, and political ties. Li (1998) focused on Chinese consumers and consumer behaviour, and targeted at a marketing audience in the business world. Wu (1999) presented a comprehensive analysis of household survey data. He covered both urban and rural families and the emerging new riches in China in the 1990s. In a volume edited by Davis (2000), fourteen scholars dealt with various issues associated with urban consumers in China, such as luxury housing, white wedding gowns, McDonald's, premium cigarettes, and bowling. More recent studies include Tang (2009), Tian and Dong (2010), and Wu (2013). Tang edited a book exploring China's changing business environment and the evolution of the Chinese consumer market in different sectors. Implications for global suppliers are also discussed in the book. Tian and Dong focused on consumers' attitudes towards foreign brands. Their analysis is based on survey responses from and interviews with Chinese consumers in both rural and urban areas. Wu presented a comprehensive list of references with short descriptions which is a good reading guide for students and newcomers in this field.

11.2 **Consumer behaviour**

There is a large pool of literature on consumer behaviour in China. It involves the application of modern econometric methods and survey data of consumers and households. The analytical issues cover consumer decision-making styles, food safety, consumer–brand relationship, rural and urban consumers, away-from-home-consumption, and so on. It is found that consumer behaviour is affected by the differences in consumer purchasing power as well as the maturity of the market. In China the traditional Chinese culture and values continue to influence consumer decision-making styles. Chinese consumers' behaviour is also affected by safety concerns, choice of lifestyles, and access to information. For example, Zhang (2010) found that social norms and other people's opinions are the primary determinants that influence the Chinese consumers' decision to purchase. Zhang considered case studies of mobile phone users. Due to the problem of power imbalance and asymmetric information in the Chinese consumer market, team purchasing has emerged. It acts as a form of consumer empowerment through team buyers' collective actions such as information collection, product evaluation, and fraud detection. The increasing power of consumers in the Chinese marketplace also appears in the form of consumers' rising awareness of their rights and growing readiness to take court action against suppliers. Researchers have also endeavoured to compare Chinese consumers with their peers in other countries, particularly consumers in the developed world. Bian and Veloutsou (2007) attempted to identify the demographic characteristics of the consumers who purchase counterfeit brands in the UK and China. They also examined consumers' views on counterfeit brands, genuine brands, and non-logo products.

11.3 **The new rich**

China's new middle class, or the new rich, are the trend setters in the country's current consumer revolution. Middle class consumers are often associated with demand for luxury goods and conspicuous consumption. Many of them belong to the one-child generation in China due to the implementation of the one-child family policy thirty years ago. Zhan and He (2012) showed that luxury goods are not necessarily extravagant purchases in China. They argue that social influence is an important factor affecting luxury consumption. They also found that uniqueness is more important and, hence, as knowledge about different luxury brands accumulates, consumers tend to view the best-known brands more negatively. Degen (2009) argued that Chinese consumers' motivation to buy luxury brands has its roots in Confucian values and individual desire for social recognition. Thus studying the changes in culture and values and their roots is vital for an understanding of the behaviour of China's new rich.

11.4 **E-consumers**

At the end of 2012, China's Internet users (or netizens) numbered more than half a billion. E-commerce and associated consumption activities have expanded rapidly in the country. A new strand of the literature has also emerged. It deals with various issues such as e-consumers' behaviour, credit card users, and mobile banking. While growing rapidly, e-commerce in China is still influenced by consumer trust, the price of goods, and knowledge about computers and online currency clearance. The growth of e-commerce has also brought new challenges within the economy. One of those is the management of consumer credit risks. China is yet to establish a comprehensive national consumer credit database. Wang et al. (2011) examined consumer credit card debt behaviour and its correlation with demographics, credit card features, attitude, and personality factors. They found that the latter two factors are the key factors affecting credit card debt in China. They also showed that some credit card features give consumers an illusion of income and hence effectively help to facilitate consumer credit card debt problems.

11.5 **Gender and consumer cohorts**

Consumption can be gender-related or cohort-specific. For this reason, men's lifestyle magazines have in recent years become increasingly popular in China while similar products for women have a long history in the country. Another phenomenal development is the full bloom of beauty pageants. Some authors call this 'meinu jingji' (or the beauty economy) (Xu and Feiner, 2007). They believe that the beauty pageants are symbolic of China's neoliberal policies. As for online and mobile banking, Chinese users are predominantly male, not necessarily young nor highly educated as perceived in Western societies. Differences in generational cohorts could also lead to variations in consumer values and behaviour. For example, older consumers could feel younger than their actual life age. Thus their consumption pattern may be affected by their self-perceived age (Ying and Yao, 2010). Due to rapid ageing of the population, older consumers will be a significant force for consumption in the Chinese market and hence further research into their behaviour is important for marketing and the delivery of consumer services. Furthermore, due to the one-child family policy, children are treated as 'little emperors' in their families and hence may have a significant influence on the families' budget and spending. Thus young consumers or children also play an important and unique role in China's consumer market.

11.6 Advertising and marketing

Associated with the consumer revolution is the boom in product advertising and marketing in China. Therefore the literature in this field has expanded too. Researchers have so far focused on various channels of advertising such as magazines, newspapers, TVs, and the Internet. For example, Ying and Sun (2010) analysed consumers' beliefs and attitudes towards online advertising across different cultures. They found that Romanians tended to view online advertising more positively and were more likely to read online advertisements than Chinese, whereas Chinese were more likely to buy online than Romanians. Marketing and culture are intrinsically linked. Hopkins (2007) observed that, when consumption is used to display personal or gender identity, marketing tactics affecting the associations of goods and identity can influence consumption. Geng et al. (2008) showed that Chinese consumers are more positive about marketing but less positive about consumerism than their Canadian counterparts. They also found that Chinese consumers are less likely to complain and are more supportive of government actions and public resolution than Canadian consumers. These differences may be due to different cultural values (e.g. individualism) and the role of government institutions according to Geng et al. In addition, China is vast and diverse. Thus advertising and marketing strategies should reflect differences based on geographic locations and ethnic backgrounds. Finally, in the Chinese context, Guanxi and hence its investment strategy may also have significant effects on customer loyalty.

11.7 Emerging issues

After three decades of high growth, the Chinese economy is now in the process of transition from the 'world's factory' to the 'world's market'. It can be anticipated that China's growth will be more demand-driven in the coming decades and thus consumption in the country is to expand substantially. With the growth of domestic consumption, new consumer-related issues are emerging in China and becoming topics for future research. Those topics include green consumption, eco-tourism, credit card risk, and consumer privacy protection, to cite a few. Several pioneering studies have already explored sustainable consumption (Liu et al., 2012), compared Chinese consumers with others in terms of 'socially responsible' consumption (Jun and She, 2011) and examined consumer credit card debt behaviour (Wang et al., 2011). It can be anticipated that this type of study will be expanded in the future.

■ REFERENCES

Bian, Xuemei and Cleopatra Veloutsou. 2007. Consumers' attitudes regarding non-deceptive counterfeit brands in the UK and China. *Journal of Brand Management* 14(3), 211–22.

Cao, Linda and R. H. Myers. 1998. China's consumer revolution: The 1990s and beyond. *Journal of Contemporary China* 7(18), 351–68.

Davis, Deborah S. (ed.) 2000. *The Consumer Revolution in Urban China*. Stanford, CA: University of California Press.

Degen, Ronald Jean. 2009. Opportunity for luxury brands in China. *IUP Journal of Brand Management* 6(3/4), 75–85.

Geng, Cui, Tsang-sing Chan, and Annamma Joy. 2008. Consumers' attitudes toward marketing: A cross-cultural study of China and Canada. *Journal of International Consumer Marketing* 20(3/4), 81–93.

Hopkins, Barbara E. 2007. Western cosmetics in the gendered development of consumer culture in China. *Feminist Economics* 13(3/4), 287–306.

Jun, Yan and Qiuling She. 2011. Developing a trichotomy model to measure socially responsible behavior in China. *International Journal of Market Research* 53(2), 253–74.

Li, Conghua. 1998. *China: The consumer revolution*. Singapore: John Wiley & Sons.

Liu, Xianbing, Can Wang, Tomohiro Shishime, and Tetsuro Fujitsuka. 2012. Sustainable consumption: Green purchasing behaviors of urban residents in China. *Sustainable Development* 20(4), 293–308.

Tang, Lei. (ed.) 2009. *The Chinese Consumer Market: Opportunities and risks*. Cambridge, UK: Chandos.

Tian, Kelly and Lily Dong. 2010. *Consumer-Citizens of China: The Role of Foreign Brands in the Imagined Future China*. London and New York: Routledge.

Wang, Lili, Wei Lu, and Naresh K. Malhotra. 2011. Demographics, attitude, personality and credit card features correlate with credit card debt: A view from China. *Journal of Economic Psychology* 32(1), 179–93.

World Bank. 2010. *Gross national income per capita 2010, Atlas method and PPP*, online resources (<www.worldbank.org>).

Wu, Yanrui. 1999. *China's Consumer Revolution: The Emerging Patterns of Wealth and Expenditure*. London and New York: Edward Elgar.

Wu, Yanrui. 2013. Consumer society. In *Oxford Bibliographies in Chinese Studies* edited by Tim Wright. Oxford: Oxford University Press.

Xu, Gary and Susan Feiner. 2007. Meinu Jingji / China's beauty economy: Buying looks, shifting value, and changing place. *Feminist Economics* 13(3/4), 307–23.

Ying, Wang and Sun Shaojing. 2010. Modeling online advertising: A cross-cultural comparison between China and Romania, *Journal of Marketing Communications* 16(5), 271–85.

Ying, Bin and Rui Yao. 2010. Self-perceived age and attitudes toward marketing of older consumers in China. *Journal of Family and Economic Issues* 31(3), 318–27.

Zhan, Lingjing and Yanqun He. 2012. Understanding luxury consumption in China: Consumer perceptions of best-known brands. *Journal of Business Research* 65(10), 1452–60.

Zhang, Xin An. 2010. Zhongguo Xiaofeizhe de Guke Jiazhi Xingcheng Jizhi: Yi Shouji Wei Duixiang de Shizheng Yanjiu (Customer value formation mechanism in China: An empirical study of mobile phone users). *Guan Li Shi Jie* (Management World) 25(1), 107–21.

12 Future strategy for growth and inclusion

Guoqiang Tian

When it comes to the future development strategy, it is necessary to first evaluate the effects of China's reform over the past thirty years. The achievements are without doubt remarkable and unquestionable. According to the studies by Maddison (2003: 30) and other economic historians, for the past 1,000 years, China's per capita GDP was in a state of almost horizontal development in terms of real purchasing power. The year of 1978 was a turning point, since that time the per capita GDP has practically entered a vertical rising phase and China began to maintain an average annual economic growth rate of nearly 10 per cent, which promoted China to being the world's second largest economy and will possibly see China being the world's largest economy in the next ten to twenty years. On the other hand, in accordance with the purchasing power parity, China was the world's largest economy once before in 1820, at which time its GDP accounted for about one-third of the world's GDP. Therefore in a sense, the enormous growth of China's economy over the past thirty years can be defined as a return to its being the world's largest economy.

However, the development model that has been sustaining the economic growth and tremendous achievements of China over the past thirty years is now confronted with a series of uncertainties and major challenges. First, the world is undergoing a period of tremendous change and adjustment following the global financial crisis and the European sovereign debt crisis; the competition and reshuffling of power among emerging economies is still unfolding; the open external environment enjoyed by China for a long time is starting to become rigid; and it is increasingly difficult to maintain the export-oriented development mode. Second, China itself is also faced with deep-seated problems which can be described as an over-emphasis on the government versus an under-emphasis on the market; an over-emphasis on development versus an under-emphasis on public service; and an over-emphasis on enriching the state versus an under-emphasis on enriching the people, which introduce many obstacles to the transformation to a domestic demand-led development mode. It is therefore necessary to carry out deep socio-economic transition and development. Third, due to the law of diminishing marginal returns, China is facing the practical problems of a recession in demographic, resources, energy, and environmental returns and China's extensive economic growth mode and development pattern driven by low cost factors is undergoing a severe test. As such, and with its entry into the group of middle-income countries, China is now facing the enormous pressure of economic slowdown and surging social problems in the context of constantly decreasing demographic, resources, and environmental returns. In 2012, China's economic growth rate declined to around 8 per cent. If the traditional model of imbalanced, uncoordinated, and unsustainable economic development cannot be fundamentally reformed, China will face a higher risk of economic downturn in the future.

How to effectively cope with this unfavourable situation? The solution lies in vigorously promoting the transformation of China's economic reform from the liberalization phase to the marketization and privatization phases in order to achieve the transition from the model of factor-driven economic development to the models of efficiency-driven and innovation-driven economic development in China. Meanwhile, it is necessary to clarify the governance boundary among government, market, and society in order to achieve the comprehensive governance and coordinated development of economy, politics, society, and culture as well as to promote the inclusion of economic and social development. This is the road China must follow in order to grow from a middle-income country to a high-income country.

In this early stage, China's economic reform emphasizes economic liberalization that features recognizing individual interests, implementing decentralized decision making and introducing various incentive mechanisms, so that the country's comparative advantages can be freed from the restrictions of a rigid system. At the same time, the co-existence of and competition among different forms of ownerships lead to the flourishing of the non-state-owned economy, including collective economy, private economy, township enterprises, foreign-funded enterprises, and joint ventures. This has brought great changes to the economic system, thus laying a foundation and accumulating experience for accelerating the transition towards a market mechanism.

The second phase of China's economic reform focuses on market-oriented economic reform. It began with the government's declaration that the goal of China's economic system reform is to establish a socialist market economy system, as put forward at the 14th National Congress of the Communist Party of China in 1992. The primary task in this phase is to establish the basic framework of a market economy in order to facilitate the emergence of a competitive market price system through price system reform, thus achieving efficiency. So far, China's market economy is still not fully developed and the efficiency-driven development model has not yet been well established, let alone the innovation-driven development model.

Looking into the future, China must achieve three major tasks in economy.

First, in the context of a gradual loss of low-cost advantage, China should establish new efficiency-driven advantages based on an effective market mechanism to achieve intensive development. This requires further deepening market-oriented reform, defining a reasonable and clear boundary between government and the market, and shifting away from the pattern of a strong government and a weak market, so as to let the market play a greater fundamental role in resource allocation, especially in those markets which currently have a monopoly and those where there is excessive administrative intervention, such as the land, labour, and financial markets.

The reason for this is that factor price distortion is highly contagious and spreading, and a series of micro behaviour distortions underlie the macro-economic imbalances. Currently, many factor markets in China are distorted by the government, thus leading to a distortion of the three basic roles of market price in conveying information, providing incentives, and determining income distribution. The transformation of the economic development pattern should actually be the outcome of the play of the market and the free choice of market entities under the constraint of factor scarcity.

From the perspective of government functions, due to the historical existence of a planned economy, the Chinese government retains its strong role as an omnipotent and development-oriented government, which has resulted in the current extensive development model of high rent-seeking and low efficiency under excessive government intervention in the economy, as well as the three sets of 'over-emphasis' versus 'under-emphasis', namely, an over-emphasis on the government versus an under-emphasis on the market; an over-emphasis on enriching the state versus an under-emphasis on enriching the people; and an over-emphasis on development versus an under-emphasis on public service. There is thus an urgent need to change the current over-playing, under-playing, and mis-playing of the government role in the transformation from an omnipotent government to a limited government and from a development-oriented government to a public service-oriented government. That is to say, the primary role of government is to formulate basic rules, guarantee social order and stability, as well as supply public goods and services, which can be summarized with two words: 'maintenance' and 'service'. Only in this way can the government and the market be respectively placed in their proper positions to ensure a truly effective market.

Second, in the context of draining existing growth momentum, China should search for stronger private sector-based and innovation-driven growth engines to achieve sustainable development. This requires eliminating the excessive dependence of economic development on traditional factors such as population, resources, and capital, while turning to innovation factors such as high-tech, high-quality human capital and intellectual property, as well as the more important entrepreneurship for economic growth. Just as Schumpeter (2007: 113) pointed out, innovation occurs in its real sense only when scientific knowledge and technological inventions are converted into business activities by entrepreneurs. This also needs to allow full play to the role of market, enterprises, and entrepreneurs, and to further expand and develop the private sector.

A review of economic development practice all over the world shows that due to incentives and information, the private economy tends to be more efficient and innovative than the state-owned economy. This is also the reason why the private economy is the main force for national innovation in developed countries. The primary role of government is to provide an institutional environment conducive to innovation and entrepreneurship, rather than to lead the innovation and to specify technical routes and product line through administrative orders or subsidies. A competitive modern market economy system is the basic condition for innovation, while innovation led by enterprises is the key to achieving 'independent innovation' and constructing 'an innovative country'.

Moreover, as the private-owned, private-operated, and private-profiting economic entity, the private economy is more in line with the theme of the times—inclusive growth. It also helps to return wealth to the people, share wealth among the people, and promotes the implementation of the development strategy by raising the prosperity of the nation by enriching its people. This goes back to the logical proposition that 'to enrich the people, private rights need to be assigned'. Broadly speaking, so-called private rights are mainly reflected in the following three aspects: ensuring free economic choice, giving and protecting the private property, and guaranteeing the basic survival rights of individuals. In China, there is still much room for improvement in these aspects.

It is beyond doubt that transformations to efficiency-driven and innovation-driven economic development both require the full play of the market. However, some scholars advocating the 'China model' do not agree with or even oppose such a viewpoint, but believe that a powerful government has been the most critical force for the achievements of China's reform and opening up over the past thirty years. There is no denying the fact that government plays an interim and special role in the process of institutional transition, but government intervention as a transitional institutional arrangement should be gradually relaxed and removed, otherwise it may slip into the path of national crony capitalism. This is not only the experience of the modern market economy, but also the wisdom of ancient Chinese philosophy. As Sima Qian, a great Chinese historian in the Han Dynasty, pointed out in his work *Biography of Merchants* in *Records of the Grand Historian* 2000 years ago, 'The master way of management is to follow the natural law and not to intervene, to lead with interests comes second, to teach with morals comes third, to rule by regulations comes next and to compete for profits comes last.' The great Chinese philosopher Lao Tzu in the Spring and Autumn and Warring States Periods also proposed that a government should 'Reign the state with fairness, use martial forces with tactics of surprise, and govern the people with non-intervention' in his work *Tao Te Ching* (ch. 57). In common parlance, that means to be righteous in deed, flexible in practice, and minimal in intervention. Of course, non-intervention governance does not imply absolute inaction in governance. It requires the construction of an administration team and the administrative efficacy of government, as well as the establishment of rules, that is, the basic legal institutional arrangements.

Third, China's transition and development is a systematic issue that calls for promoting the comprehensive governance and coordinated development of the economy, politics, society, and culture, and defining a reasonable and clear governance boundary between the government, market, and society. It is also necessary to establish an effective market, a limited government and a harmonious society, increase people's sense of happiness and realize scientific development, thus achieving the sustainable development of China's economy and long-term social stability. This is because, as mentioned earlier in this chapter, China's socioeconomic transition and development have reached a crucial point and entered a critical stage after more than thirty years of reform and opening up, where socioeconomic problems are interwoven with deep-seated political and cultural problems that can no longer be solved by reform of the economic system alone. Moreover, neither the total GDP nor the ranking or share of GDP in the world can fully and accurately reflect the level of socioeconomic development and national happiness.

In the medium and long term, it is not a question of 'if' but 'how' China will become the world's largest economy. It is thus necessary for China to truly realize the vision and goal of building a harmonious society, instead of letting it stay as slogans and words. The priority of China's reform for the next step is to further deepen and intensify market-oriented reform in order to achieve the transition from factor-driven to efficiency-driven and innovation-driven economic development, and at the same time define a reasonable boundary between government, society, and market, and unswervingly follow the path of economic marketization, social rule of law, and political democracy. Otherwise, China is likely to fall into the 'middle-income trap' or 'transition trap'. To the world, China's successful transition is an opportunity rather than a threat. On the other hand, should China fail in its transition, that would truly be a disaster for the whole world.

■ **REFERENCES**

Lao Tzu, *Tao Te Ching*, Chapter 57.

Maddison, A. 2003. *The World Economy: A Millennial Perspective*, Chinese version translated by X. Wu, X. Xu, Y. Ye, and F. Shi, Peking University Press.

Schumpeter, J. A. 2007. *The Theory of Economic Development: An Inquiry Into Profits, Capital, Credit, Interest, and the Business Cycle*, Chinese version translated by H. Ye, China Social Sciences Press.

Sima Qian, *Records of the Grand Historian, Biographies of Merchants*.

G. Tian, J. Xia and X. Chen, On economic inherent logic of prospering the nation through enriching its people, *Academic Monthly* 45(11), 66.

Part III
China and the Global Economy

13 The global impact of China's growth

Peter E. Robertson

13.1 Introduction

Over the last two decades China's growth rate has matched, if not exceeded, the peak growth rates of the Asian miracle economies. The result has been the largest fall in absolute poverty in human history, and the emergence of a new 'economic superpower'. Because of its size, China is the subject of extensive introspection over world issues such as: manufacturing jobs; wages; investment and savings imbalances; exchange rates; environmental issues; as well as the balance of defence capabilities.[1] Nevertheless, despite the popularity of 'China Bashing' in the media, relatively little analytical work exists on the overall economic impact of China's growth on the rest of the world—at least relative to its importance.

The two quintessential issues in the existing literature are: (i) concern from other manufacturing exporting economies that their export prices are eroded by Chinese competition, and; (ii) fear that Chinese exports have hurt domestic imports competing with manufacturing in developed countries. Both concerns stem from the massive export-based growth in China. Perhaps ironically, economic theory tells us that this export-biased growth has eroded China's terms-of-trade and generated welfare gains for its trade partners. In what follows I consider how these differing views stand up against the evidence.

13.2 How big is China?

Since China's size is the key issue it is useful to note that 'economic size' is a surprisingly difficult thing to quantify. First, in order to compare economies we must convert their

---

[1] Some of these aspects of China's international impact are discussed elsewhere in this volume. For additional discussions, see for example Tyers and Zhang (2011) for a survey of exchange rate management issues, Yang (2012) on global imbalances, Li et al. (2011) on global research and education, McKibbin et al. (2008) and Weber et al. (2008) on global environmental issues, and Friedberg (2011) for a highly readable discussion of international security issues.

GDP from domestic currency units into a common currency. It is well known that market exchange rates do not properly weight differences in living costs, may fluctuate by large amounts, and may be subject to manipulation by governments.

Thus, when comparing real incomes across countries, analysts often use Purchasing Power Parity (PPP) exchange rates. The World Bank's estimate of China's GDP in $PPP places China's GDP at approximately 75 per cent of the USA's GDP in 2011. Other studies, however, argue that this estimate understates China's size by 50 per cent (Feenstra et al., 2012). Hence there is an important measurement issue.

Second it is not obvious that these PPP exchange rates are the best ones to use to measure the size of China's economic impact on the world economy. Their principle purpose is to measure the costs of living for the purpose of welfare comparisons. If, however, we wish only to know China's ability to affect world prices through its potential to supply or demand goods and services on world markets, then standard exchange rate measures are, arguably, the more appropriate measure.

China's GDP at current market exchange rates, however, is only half the size of the USA's.[2] Thus taking into account both of these conceptual and methodological issues, we are left with estimates of China's relative size that have a disturbingly large range of 50–125 per cent of the USA's GDP.

An alternative indicator of China's size relative to the world economy is the relative size of its trade flows. According to the World Bank, China's merchandise exports represent 9 per cent of the world total, the same as the USA, despite being half its size.

Trade flows, however, are recorded as gross values whereas the actual contribution of a country to world supply is represented by the value added content of its exports. This distinction is important for China, since much of China's exports represent assembly and packaging of imported components—the last stage of the 'Asian value chain'. Koopman et al. (2012) estimate that the value added share of China's exports for 2004 was 62.8 per cent which is somewhat smaller than those of the USA (74.6 per cent) and Japan (84.9 per cent).[3] The classic example is the iPad, where Chinese value added is estimated at just 2 per cent of the total price (Kraemer et al., 2011).

The cautionary tale from this discussion is that it is quite difficult to quantify China's size. Nevertheless it is clear that there has been rapid increase in the size of China's economy over the last two decades, moving from a negligible fraction of world trade and output to its current level. Using market exchange rates China is still the second largest country in the world, passing Germany in 2007 and Japan in 2010, and accounts for 10 per cent of world output and 9 per cent of world trade.

---

[2] It would be even smaller if we used an average exchange rate over say 5 or 10 years, since the renminbi has appreciated sharply against the US dollar since 2005.

[3] This points to an interesting question of China's importance in facilitating the fragmentation of production globally and in particular the Asian production hub. Haddad (2007) and Hanson (2012) offer some useful discussions of these trends. Also see Schott (2006).

13.3 **Quantifying the impact on world trade flows**

Being large is a necessary condition for a country to have a non-negligible impact on the world prices, but it is not sufficient. The impact of one economy's growth on the world economy is transmitted through its impact on the terms of trade—which depends on the bias of its growth. (Hicks, 1953; Corden, 1956; Bhagwati, 1958). In China's case there appears to have been a strong export bias, so that China's growth has most likely caused an improvement in the terms of trade for its trade partners (Amiti and Freund, 2010; Harris et al., 2011).

For manufactured importing countries, such as the USA, this may cause structural adjustment, but also improve welfare. But for other manufacturing exporters, that is, those competing with China in export markets, the terms-of-trade decline is causing welfare losses.[4]

An extensive literature exists trying to assess the quantitative implications of these two effects on trade flows, (Ahearne et al., 2003; Lall and Albaladejo, 2004; Roland-Holst and Weiss, 2005; Coxhead, 2007; Eichengreen et al., 2007; Athukorala, 2010; Hanson and Robertson, 2010). Overall the evidence is mixed. For example Lall and Albaladejo (2004) find evidence of strong competitive effects but Hanson and Robertson (2010) find that, for the countries with the most similar trade patterns to China, its growth represents only a small negative shock in export demand. Eichengreen et al. (2007) find a positive effect on the exports of high income Asian economies that are significant exporters of capital goods, and a strong negative effect on low income Asian countries that are dependent on the production and exports of consumer goods.

Athukorala (2010), however, argues that these studies fail to take into account the complex Asian production networks. He finds that China's exports to third country markets have had complementary effects on Asian exports due to the effect of components trade, and that the impact of China's growth on Asia is overwhelmingly positive.

Another limitation of this gravity literature is that it is focused on trade flows only. To that end Wood and Mayer (2011) use a factor content approach, familiar from the 'trade–wage' literature, to examine the impact of China's emergence on the industry composition in other countries.

Wood and Mayer argue that an upper estimate of the effect of a world with China, relative to one without out it, would be to increase the world share of basic skilled workers by approximately 10 per cent. They find that this would reduce the output shares of other countries' primary and manufacturing sectors by up to only 1–3.5 per cent, with the Asian economies being the most severely affected.

---

[4] An alternative mechanism emphasized in new trade theory is that restructuring of industries may cause changes in average productivity at the industry level as marginal firms enter or exit. Hiseh and Ossa (2011) attempt to quantify these effects but find that they are very small.

In contrast Autor et al. (2012) assess the impact of China's import penetration on USA manufacturing, focusing not just on wage effects but also on regional employment effects. They find that the rising exposure to Chinese import competition explains between 33–55 per cent of the US manufacturing employment decline between 1990 and 2000. This is a dramatic contrast with much of the earlier trade–wage literature that found minimal effects on wages from trade in the USA, though this can be accounted for by the fact that China is now much larger than it was when most of trade–wage studies were undertaken.

13.4 **General equilibrium, trade, and world growth**

A limitation of the literature discussed above is that it is does not inform us about global growth or the welfare effects of China's growth. To complete the picture, a greater theoretical structure is required that allows us to map changes in the terms-of-trade onto economy-wide adjustments and factor returns. This is where computable general equilibrium (CGE) models are particularly useful, allowing us to quantify the theory that is at the core of our understanding about how growth in one country can affect another.

Dimaranan et al. (2007) consider Chinese productivity increases that amount to a 40 per cent increase in income for China. They find relatively large income gains for some neighbouring Asian economies, particularly Malaysia, Taiwan, and Hong Kong, and resource exporters such as Australia and Canada.[5] These gains are in the order of a 0.4-0.8 per cent increase in the countries' incomes, which represents 1–2 per cent of China's growth. Conversely they find modest losses for other neighbouring countries such as Singapore, Thailand, and the Philippines. The average gain is 0.5 per cent of GDP for lower income countries and 0.6 per cent for middle income countries, and approximately no change for the more developed countries as a whole, including the USA.

Harris et al. (2010), however, find much larger impacts on the USA. They consider the impact of a decade of China's growth, 1996–2005 which amounts to an 80 per cent increase in China's GDP above the world growth trend. They find that this increases the USA's GDP by 3.2 percentage points. This represents an annualized additional growth benefit to the USA of 0.32 percentage points per year. This is a significant boost for an economy with a long run growth rate of just under 2 per cent per year.[6] They also find that the bias of China's growth is crucial for generating these terms-of-trade effects—a result that is emphasized by di Giovanni et al. (2012).

---

[5] For our purposes, however, this study muddies the water a little since its results are for China and India together.

[6] A feature of their model is that allows import prices to affect investment costs, and hence equilibrium capital–labour ratios. Thus the model relates terms-of-trade effects induced by China's growth into long-run growth in the USA.

Robertson and Xu (2010) employ a similar model to assess the impact of China's growth on other Asian economies. They find a 12 per cent increase in per capita incomes for the more developed Asian economies, or approximately 1.2 percentage points of growth per year. They also find more modest but still positive gains for the ASEAN group, which contrasts with some of the previous studies that showed terms-of-trade declines.

Some of these differences in the impacts on GDP may be accounted for by the difference between short-run and long-run analyses in these studies. Moreover, all these CGE studies find that China's growth results in significant reductions in the output of manufacturing in other countries—whether the gains are positive or negative. This reiterates the point that, while terms-of-trade improvements may hurt import competing sectors through Rybczynski effects, this is also part of the process whereby terms-of-trade gains are realized.[7]

13.5 Conclusion

The closest precedent for China's rise and integration into the world economy is the USA, which emerged at the start of the twentieth century as the world's largest industrial nation. The USA's growth also created significant adjustments to the world economy, but a century ago it would have been hard to imagine the dominance that the USA would exert over the next 100 years.

China's continued rise may pose just as many economic challenges and create as many or more benefits. Currently, however, China's size on the world market is still only half the size of the USA. A robust theme in the literature discussed in this chapter is that the countries most affected by China so far are its neighbouring Asian economies and the resource exporting countries. This confirms that China's main influence, so far, has been as a regional force rather than global one. Nevertheless at least some studies suggest that the terms-of-trade impacts have been quite large and that China's growth has been an important source of growth for Asia economies and other economies, including the USA.

■ REFERENCES

Ahearne, A. G., J. G. Fernald, P. Loungani, and J. W. Schindler. 2003. China and Emerging Asia: Comrades or Competitiors? Federal Reserve Bank of Chicago, Working Paper 03-27.

Amiti, Mary and Caroline Freund. 2010. The Anatomy of China's Export Growth. In *China's Growing Role in World Trade*, edited by Robert C. Feenstra and Shang-Jin Wei, (eds), 35-56. National Bureau of Economic Research.

[7] For example Harris et al. (2011) find a large contraction in manufactured durables output in the USA—similar to that reported by Autor et al. (2012)—but this was associated with significant income gains.

Athukorala, Prema-chandra. 2010. The rise of China and East Asian export performance: is the crowding-out fear warranted? *The World Economy* 32(2), 234–66.

Autor, David H., David Dorn, and Gordon H. Hanson. 2012. The China Syndrome: Local Labor Market Effects of Import Competition in the United States. NBER Working Paper 18054.

Bhagwati, J. 1958. Immiserizing growth: a geometrical note. *The Review of Economic Studies* 25(3), 201–5.

Coxhead, I. 2007. A new resource curse? Impacts of China's boom on comparative advantage and resource dependence in Southeast Asia. *World Development* 35(7), 1099–119.

Corden, W. M. 1956. Economic expansion and international trade: a geometric approach. *Oxford Economic Papers* 8(2), 223–8.

di Giovanni, J., A. A. Levchenko, and J. Zhang. 2012. The Global Welfare Impact of China: Trade Integration and Technological Change. CEPR Discussion Paper No. DP9683.

Dimaranan, Betina, Elena Ianchovichina, and Will Martin. 2007. China, India, and the Future of the World Economy: Fierce Competition or Shared Growth? Policy Research Working Paper 4304.

Eichengreen, Barry, Rhee, Yeongseop, and Tong, Hui. 2007. China and the exports of other Asian countries. *Review of World Economics* 143(2), 201–26.

Feenstra, Robert C., Hong Ma, J. Peter Neary, and D.S. Prasada Rao. 2012. Who Shrunk China? Puzzles in the Measurement of Real GDP. NBER Working Paper No. 17729.

Friedberg, Aaron L. 2011. *A Contest for Supremacy: China, America, and the Struggle for Mastery in Asia.* New York: W.W. Norton.

Haddad, M. 2007. Trade Integration in East Asia: The Role of China and Production Networks. World Bank Policy Research Working Papers No. 4160 Washington, DC: The World Bank.

Hanson, Gordon H. 2012. The Rise of Middle Kingdoms: Emerging Economies in Global Trade, NBER Working Paper 17961.

Hanson, Gordon H. and Raymond Robertson. 2010. China and the manufacturing exports of other developing countries. In *China's Growing Role in World Trade*, edited by Robert C. Feenstra and Shang-Jin Wei (eds), 137-59. University of Chicago Press.

Harris, Richard G., Peter E. Robertson, and Jessica Xu. 2011. The international effects of China's growth, trade and education booms. *The World Economy* 34(10), 1703–25.

Hicks, John 1953. An Inaugural Lecture. *Oxford Economic Papers* 5 (2), 117–35.

Hsieh, Chang-Tai and Ralph Ossa. 2011. A Global View of Productivity Growth in China. NBER Working Paper No. 16778.

Koopman, Robert, Zhi Wang, and Shang-Jin Wei. 2012. How Much of Chinese Exports is Really Made in China? Assessing Domestic Value-Added When Processing Trade is Pervasive. NBER Working Paper 14109.

Kraemer, K., G. Linden, and J. Dedrick 2011. Capturing Value in Global Networks: Apple's iPad and iPhone. Mimeo, University of California, Irvine.

Lall, Sanjaya and Albaladejo, Manuel. 2004. China's competitive performance: a threat to East Asian manufactured exports. *World Development* 32(9), 1441–66.

Li, Yao Amber, John Whalley, Shunming Zhang, and Xiliang Zhao. 2011. The higher educational transformation of China and its global implications. *The World Economy* 34(4), 516–45.

McKibbin, Warwick, Peter Wilcoxen, and Wing Thye Woo. 2008. China Can Grow and Still Help Prevent the Tragedy of the CO_2 Commons. CAMA Working Papers 2008–2014, Australian National University, Centre for Applied Macroeconomic Analysis.

Robertson, Peter E. and Jessica Xu. 2010. In China's Wake: Has Asia Gained from China's Growth. Economics, University of Western Australia Business School Discussion Papers, 10.15.

Roland-Holst, D. and J. Weiss. 2005. People's Republic of China and its neighbours: evidence on regional trade and investment effects. *Asian-Pacific Economic Literature* 19(2), 18–35.

Schott, Peter K. 2006. The Relative Sophistication of Chinese Exports. NBER Working Papers 12173, National Bureau of Economic Research.

Tyers, Rod and Ying Zhang. 2011. Appreciating the Renminbi. *The World Economy*. 34(2), 265–97.

Tyers, R., Y. Zhang, and T. S. Cheong. 2013. China's Saving and Global Economic Performance. University of Western Australia, Economics Discussion paper 13.20.

Weber, C. L., G. P. Peters, D. Guan, and K. Hubacek. 2008. The contribution of Chinese exports to climate change. *Energy Policy*, 36(9), 3572–7.

Wood, Adrian and Jörg Mayer. 2011. Has China de-industrialised other developing countries? *Review of World Economics* 147(2), 325–50.

Yang, Dennis Tao. 2012. Aggregate savings and external imbalances in China. *Journal of Economic Perspectives* 26(4), 125–46.

14 Effects of China's trade on other countries

Gordon H. Hanson

Over a breathtakingly short period of time, China has become a global manufacturing powerhouse. In 1980, shortly after the end of the Mao Zedong era, China accounted for 11 per cent of valued added in manufacturing by low- and middle-income countries. By 1990, after ten years of reform and opening, China's share had reached 17 per cent; by 2000, eight years after Deng Xiaoping's famous 'southern tour' accelerated China's liberalization of foreign trade and investment (Naughton, 2007), China's share had surged to 32 per cent; and by 2011, a decade following China's accession to the World Trade Organisation (WTO), it had reach 48 per cent. Today, China accounts for 14 per cent of global manufacturing exports, up from 2 per cent in 1990.

The image of China as a low-end producer doing little more than assembling parts and components imported from advanced economies is now antiquated. China is rapidly moving up the value chain within industries, and expanding into more sophisticated goods across industries (Amiti and Freund, 2010; Hanson, 2012). The share of domestic value added in China's exports rose from 50 per cent in 1997 to over 60 per cent in 2007 (Koopmans et al., 2012) and has even increased by larger amounts (32 per cent in 2000 to 46 per cent in 2006) in China's export processing sector (Kee and Tang, 2012), which does specialize in assembly. As testimony to its industrial prowess, China is home to the world's largest telecommunications manufacturer (Huawei) and its second largest producer of personal computers and related equipment (Lenovo).

The unleashing of China's productive potential represents a major shock to the global economy. The origins of this shock lie in the manner in which Mao kept China far inside the global technology frontier and the speed with which Deng's reforms initiated a process of technological convergence. Between 1992 and 2007, the median Chinese manufacturing plant had average annual growth in total factor productivity (TFP) of 15 per cent (Hseih and Klenow, 2009). Given that productivity levels in China remain far behind the United States, the catch-up phase of the country's economic growth may be far from over (Song et al., 2011).

The academic literature is just beginning to assess what China's emergence means for the global economy. With China's strong specialization in manufacturing—which during the 2000s accounted for an average of 83 per cent of its exports, placing it among the world's most manufacturing oriented countries—its growth would appear to be a negative terms-of-trade shock for other export manufacturers and a positive terms-of-trade shock for countries that produce the raw materials and commodities used in manufacturing (Devlin et al., 2005). When apparel and textile quotas under the Multi-Fiber Arrangement were lifted, China's exports in these sectors expanded at the expense of other developing countries (Brambilla et al., 2010), an outcome possibly intensified by the entry of new, more productive firms (Khandelwal et al., 2011).

More generally, manufacturing oriented emerging economies appear to have had slower export growth as a result of China's surge (Hanson and Robertson, 2010). These affects appear to be larger for countries whose manufacturing sectors compete directly with China's export processing plants, such as Mexico's maquiladoras (Utar and Torres Ruiz, 2012). Other work suggests that China's impact on its competitors is more complex, helping attract foreign direct investment (FDI) to countries in Asia that are part of the same global supply chains, while diverting FDI away from countries outside the region (Eichengreen and Tong, 2007). Which countries gain and which lose from China's growth may therefore be a function not just of whether a country has a comparative advantage in manufacturing or in raw materials but of the specific production networks in which a country's industries participate.

What is perhaps most surprising about recent research is how small the estimated global welfare impacts of China's rise appear to be. Hsieh and Ossa (2012) and di Giovanni et al. (2011) calibrate global general equilibrium models of trade and find that welfare changes caused by China's recent productivity growth are modest everywhere except in China. These findings are consistent with analysis of a wide class of trade models that show the static gains from trade to be small (Arkolakis et al., 2012). It is worth noting that these models ignore any impact of China on the pace of global innovation, which could generate dynamic gains from trade. They also fail to account for impacts of trading with China on the distribution of income within countries, an issue at the centre of public discussions about globalization. Empirical work has focused much more on the impacts of trade on innovation and distribution.

Departing from structural models, a new strand of research looks for evidence of China's economic impact in how firms, industries, or regions adjust to trade shocks. Bernard et al. (2006) show that during the 1990s US manufacturing plants in sectors exposed to larger increases in imports from low-wage countries, including China, were more likely to exit and, among those not exiting, more likely to cut employment or switch industries. In Europe, exposure to trade with China has encouraged surviving firms to increase the production of patents and raise their TFP, using innovation as a strategy to escape low-wage-country import competition (Bloom et al., 2011).

Shocks to firms and industries are transmitted to labour markets thereby affecting wages and employment. In the United States, Ebenstein et al. (2010) suggest that trade with low-wage countries affects wages at the occupation rather than industry level, owing to the mobility of workers across industries.[1] Autor et al. (2013a) find that within industries there is considerable hetereogeneity in how workers are affected by import competition. Workers who in 1991 were employed in industries that saw larger increases in imports from China over the ensuing two decades were more likely to leave their initial employers, exit their initial industries, or depart manufacturing altogether. For low-wage workers and workers with weak attachment to the labour force, greater exposure to trade with China means significant decreases in their long-run earnings and greater reliance on government-provided disability insurance as their primary source of income.

Because industries tend to be geographically concentrated, regions differ in their exposure to trade, creating a spatial dimension in adjustment to trade shocks. Exploiting regional variation in US manufacturing specialization, Autor et al. (2013b) estimate that increased import competition from China can account for about one-fifth of the decline in US manufacturing employment over the period 1992–2007. Regions more exposed to trade with China also saw significant increases in government transfers per capita, suggesting that import competition has consequences for fiscal balances, as well. For policy makers contemplating trade actions against China, these distributional effects of trade may be what is foremost in their minds, rather than the apparently modest, positive net changes in welfare.

Important for understanding China's medium-run impact on the United States are the large imbalances between aggregate exports and aggregate imports in the two countries. During the 2000s, China's average current account surplus was 5 per cent of its GDP, a figure equal to the US current account deficit over the same period. Currently, for the United States, China's growth means a major shift in global supply, without an offsetting shift in global demand: US manufacturing imports from China are five times US manufacturing exports to China. For countries running trade surpluses, the situation is completely different. In Germany, for instance, regions specialized in producing the machine tools and other capital goods that China imports have seen significant increases in manufacturing employment associated with trade with China (Dauth et al., 2012). Over time, of course, global imbalances will ease, and indeed may already have begun to do so. However, the magnitude of the recent imbalances suggests that some countries, such as the United States, may have front-loaded the consumption gains from trade with China, whereas other countries, such as Germany, may have front-loaded the innovation gains from China trade. These differences in adjustment could have long-run consequences for the impact of trade on these economies.

---

[1] Not surprisingly, Liu and Trefler (2008) find little impact of service outsourcing to China on US labour markets, as these services' trade flows remain quite small.

■ REFERENCES

Amiti, Mary, and Caroline Freund. 2010. An anatomy of China's export growth. In *China's Growing Role in World Trade*, edited by Robert Feenstra and Shang-Jin Wei (eds), 35-62. Chicago: NBER and University of Chicago Press.

Arkolakis, Costas, Arnaud Costinot, and Andres Rodriguez-Clare. 2012. New trade models, same old gains? *American Economic Review* 102(1), 94–130.

Autor, David H., David Dorn, and Gordon H. Hanson. 2013a. Adjustment to Trade: Worker Level Evidence. Mimeo, MIT and UC San Diego.

Autor, David H., David Dorn, and Gordon H. Hanson. 2013b. The China Syndrome: local labor market effects of import competition in the United States. *American Economic Review*, 103(6), 2121–68.

Bernard, Andrew B., J. Bradford Jensen, and Peter K. Schott. 2006. Survival of the best fit: exposure to low-wage countries and the (uneven) growth of U.S. manufacturing plants. *Journal of International Economics* 68(1), 219–37.

Bloom, Nicholas, Mirko Draca, and John Van Reenen. 2011. Trade Induced Technical Change? The Impact of Chinese Imports on Diffusion, Innovation, and Productivity. Mimeo, Stanford University.

Brambilla, Irene, Amit Khandelwal, and Peter Schott. 2010. China's experience under the multi-fiber arrangement (MFA) and the agreement on textiles and clothing (ATC). In *China's Growing Role in World Trade*, edited by Robert Feenstra and Shang Jin Wei (eds), 345–87. Chicago: University of Chicago Press and the NBER.

Dauth, Wolfgang, Sebastian Findeisen, and Jens Suedekum. 2012. The Rise of the East and the Far East: German Labor Markets and Trade Integration. Mimeo, IAB.

Devlin, Robert, Antoni Estevadeordal, and Andrés Rodriguez-Clare. 2005. *The Emergence of China: Opportunities and Challenges for Latin America and the Caribbean*. Washington, DC: Inter-American Development Bank.

di Giovanni, Julian, Andrei Levchenko, and Jing Zhang. 2011. The Global Welfare Impact of China: Trade Integration and Technological Change. Mimeo, University of Michigan.

Ebenstein, Avraham, Ann Harrison, Margaret McMillan, and Shannon Phillips. 2010. Estimating the Impact of Trade and Offshoring on American Workers Using the Current Population Surveys. Mimeo, UC Berkeley.

Eichengreen, Barry, and Hui Tong. 2007. Is China's FDI coming at the expense of other countries? *Journal of the Japanese and International Economies* 21(2), 153–72.

Hanson, Gordon. 2012. The rise of middle kingdoms: emerging economies in global trade. *Journal of Economic Perspectives* 26(2), 41–64.

Hanson, Gordon H. and Raymond Robertson. 2010. China and the manufacturing exports of other developing countries. In *China's Growing Role in World Trade*, Robert Feenstra and Shang Jin Wei (eds), 137–59. Chicago: University of Chicago Press and the NBER.

Hsieh, Chang-Tai, and Peter J. Klenow. 2009. Misallocation and manufacturing TFP in China and India. *Quarterly Journal of Economics* 124(4), 1403–48.

Hsieh, Chang-Tai, and Ralph Ossa. 2012. A Global View of Productivity Growth in China. NBER Working Paper No. 16778.

Kee, Hiau Looi and Heiwai Tang. 2012. Domestic Value Added in Chinese Exports. Mimeo, the World Bank.

Khandelwal, Amit, Peter Schott, and Shang Jin Wei. 2011. Trade Liberalization and Embedded Institutional Reform: Evidence from Chinese Exporters. NBER Working Paper No. 17524.

Koopmans, Robert, Zhi Wang, and Shang-Jin Wei. 2012. Estimating domestic content in trade when processing trade is pervasive. *Journal of Development Economics*, forthcoming.

Liu, Runjuan and Daniel Trefler. 2008. Mucho Ado about Nothing: American Jobs and the Rise of Service Outsourcing to China and India. NBER Working Paper No. 14061.

Naughton, Barry. 2007. *The Chinese Economy: Transitions and Growth*. Cambridge, MA: MIT Press.

Song, Zheng, Kjetil Storesletten, and Fabrizio Zilibotti. 2011. Growing Like China. *American Economic Review* 101(1), 196–233.

Utar, Hale and Luis B. Torres Ruiz. 2012. International Competition and Industrial Evolution: Evidence from the Impact of Chinese Competition on Mexican Maquiladoras. Mimeo, University of Colorado.

15 The internationalization of the renminbi

Dong He

15.1 Introduction

Since 2009, the internationalization of the Chinese yuan, or the renminbi, has become an increasingly important subject in the economics of China. On the surface, internationalization of the renminbi means the currency is used as a unit of account, medium of exchange, and store of value in international trade and financial transactions. Beneath the surface, it means that non-Chinese residents hold renminbi-denominated assets and liabilities, both on-balance sheet and off-balance sheet. Seen from this perspective, the analytical questions in understanding the process of renminbi internationalization include at least the following: Why do non-Chinese residents have incentives to hold renminbi-denominated assets and liabilities? How do non-Chinese residents acquire renminbi-denominated assets and liabilities? Does this not require convertibility of the renminbi under the capital account of the balance of payments? What are the roles of official policies and market forces in driving the process of renminbi internationalization?

At the outset, it is useful to dispel the popular notion that China cannot possibly internationalize its currency or become a reserve currency issuing country because it runs current account surpluses. This argument is predicated on the assumption that a country can only supply its currency for international use by running current account deficits. However, a country can also supply its currency for international use through the capital account. In effect, a reserve currency country plays the role of a bank to the rest of the world: it issues short-term liabilities that non-residents would use for international trade and investment, and it also invests in other countries, perhaps in less liquid forms, such as foreign direct investments. In other words, issuing reserve currency is a process of financial intermediation through the international balance sheet of the reserve currency country. Historically, Great Britain and the United States gained reserve currency status while running current account surpluses.

15.2 **The context**

Renminbi internationalization was put on the policy agenda by the Chinese authorities in the aftermath of the global financial crisis of 2007–09. As banks scrambled for liquidity, US dollar funding markets and foreign exchange swap markets seized up in late 2008. The resulting 'dollar shortage' threatened to stifle international trade. This experience has highlighted the danger of relying excessively on one reserve currency in international trade and payments, and the possible benefits of using a wider array of currencies, including emerging market currencies, especially in transactions between emerging markets (Zhou, 2012).

More broadly, the spread of the trans-Atlantic financial crisis globally was seen as an intrinsic defect of the international monetary system, where domestic policy objectives of the major reserve currency country override its obligations to maintain global monetary and financial stability. A more diversified system to supply global liquidity can be seen as an interim solution before the arrival of a truly super-national reserve currency (Zhou, 2009).

15.3 **The role of official policies**

Whether or not a currency is used extensively for international transactions is primarily determined by market forces. Seen in this light, renminbi internationalization is more a process of dismantling extant restrictions against its international use. Since mid-2009, the Chinese authorities have acted quickly to remove restrictions against the use of renminbi in current account transactions, and have gradually expanded the scope for the use of renminbi in capital account transactions.

The major challenge in managing the process is to delineate the relationship between currency internationalization and capital account liberalization. While it is commonly taken for granted that capital account convertibility is a pre-requisite for currency internationalization, the Chinese authorities have argued that currency internationalization and capital account liberalization should be mutually reinforcing processes (Zhou 2012). Currency internationalization is seen as an integral component of the broad financial sector reform and development agenda, and can be made consistent with the 'proactive, gradualist, and controllable' approach to capital account liberalization.

As a bare minimum, international use of the domestic currency requires that offshore banks need to be able to keep and have access to clearing balances with onshore banks. In other words, some degree of non-resident convertibility of the renminbi has to be granted to offshore banks. Before July 2009, offshore banks generally could not maintain and have access to renminbi balances kept with onshore banks. With the launch of a pilot scheme of renminbi trade settlement in July 2009, overseas banks could open correspondent accounts with banks inside China. From August 2010 onwards overseas nonbank institutions accepting payments for exports to China in renminbi can deposit the proceeds from such transactions on accounts with banks inside China.

Once cross-border payment flows in renminbi are made possible, non-residents would need the means to acquire renminbi assets and liabilities. The Chinese authorities allowed the settlement of current account balances as the first major source and use of renminbi funds: payment by onshore firms for imports from overseas would be sources of renminbi funds for non-residents, and payment by offshore firms for imports from China would be uses of renminbi funds by non-residents. Before the launch of the pilot scheme of renminbi trade settlement in July 2009, no firm in China could use the renminbi to settle payments with overseas counterparties. Under the pilot scheme, 365 firms were included in the list of firms eligible to choose to the renminbi for trade settlement. A year later, in June 2010, coverage of the pilot scheme was expanded to twenty provinces, allowing all firms in those provinces to settle imports and services trade in renminbi, and more than 60,000 firms to settle exports of goods in renminbi. In August 2011, coverage of the scheme expanded further to all provinces; and finally in February 2012, all current account transactions by all mainland firms could now be invoiced and settled in renminbi.

The Chinese authorities also gradually expanded the scope of using renminbi to acquire assets and liabilities by non-residents through direct and portfolio investments. In August 2010, the People's Bank of China (PBoC) announced a pilot scheme for eligible offshore financial institutions involved in renminbi trade settlement to make use of their renminbi funds to invest in the onshore interbank bond market. In January 2011 and October 2011, administrative rules for the use of renminbi by Chinese enterprises to conduct overseas direct investments, and administrative rules for conducting foreign direct investments in China by foreign firms in renminbi, respectively, were promulgated. A further channel of portfolio flows in renminbi was opened up when the so-called renminbi Qualified Foreign Institutional Investor (R-QFII) scheme was announced in December 2011, under which Hong Kong-based brokerage firms could offer to non-Chinese residents renminbi investment products, subject to an aggregate quota, that are invested in onshore bond and stock markets.

To support the international use of the renminbi and to provide a contingent source of liquidity, the PBoC has also set up bilateral local currency swap facilities with overseas central banks and monetary authorities. By June 2012, eighteen agreements for such facilities have been assigned, with the total amount reaching RMB1.6 trillion.

15.4 **Incentives**

Market forces have responded quickly to official policies. According to the PBoC statistics, 8 per cent of China's merchandise and service trade in 2011 was settled in renminbi, a sharp rise from 2 per cent in 2010. In 2011, foreign investors settled 12 per cent of their direct investments in China in renminbi, and Chinese investors settled 5 per cent of their direct investments overseas in renminbi. At the same time, non-Chinese residents' holdings of renminbi deposits and bonds also grew rapidly. Renminbi customer deposits of Hong Kong banks increased from RMB315 billion yuan at the end of 2010 to RMB588 billion yuan at the end of 2011. According to Bank of International Settlements (BIS) international securities data, renminbi offshore bonds outstanding at the end of 2011 amounted to some RMB320 billion yuan.

Non-Chinese residents have strong incentives to increase their exposure to renminbi assets and liabilities because the starting positions are in all likelihood significantly below their desired or optimal portfolio allocations into the renminbi. And such optimal allocations are likely to grow with the increasing weight of the Chinese economy in global production and trade. Some critics, such as Garber (2011), have taken one-way speculative positioning due to strong renminbi appreciation expectations as the main impetus for international use of the renminbi. However, the underlying incentive to increase exposure to renminbi assets and liabilities by non-Chinese residents is likely to remain strong, not easily reversed by cyclical fluctuations in exchange rate expectations.

From the point of view of Chinese residents, internationalizing the renminbi can be expected to help to reduce the currency mismatch of China's international balance sheet. Because of both current account surpluses and capital inflows, on the one hand, and the controls and the consequent lack of internationalization of the renminbi, on the other, Chinese residents bear all the risk of an appreciation. Denominating China's claims on the rest of the world, or allowing non-residents to borrow, in renminbi would reduce this currency exposure (Cheung et al., 2011). Offshore renminbi bond markets would allow governments and firms outside of China to borrow in renminbi and thereby allow Chinese life insurers and pension funds to diversify credit while matching renminbi liabilities.

15.5 The role of offshore markets

Judging from the experience of the US dollar and other major reserve currencies, currency internationalization is accompanied by the development of offshore markets of that currency. As He and McCauley (2010) have argued, offshore markets perform essential economic functions, including separation of currency and country risks and the diversification of operational risks.

Hong Kong was the first place outside Mainland China to have renminbi banking, supported by a clearing arrangement provided by the PBoC. Since 2004, Hong Kong has progressively developed into a renminbi offshore centre, with the scope of its renminbi banking business expanding from personal deposits, to bonds, to trade credit and project financing, and to interbank trading. Since July 2010, Hong Kong has produced a second set of spot and forward exchange rates for the renminbi, dubbed the CNH, for delivery of renminbi against dollars outside Mainland China. A second set of renminbi yield curves has also been formed in Hong Kong with the active issuance of bonds by the Chinese Ministry of Finance and firms from both inside and outside China. These offshore renminbi exchange and interest rates have retained a spread over, but have tended to move in tandem with, onshore rates.

At present, the renminbi balance sheet of banks in Hong Kong serves as a conduit for net renminbi lending from the rest of the world to the mainland. Renminbi bonds issued by non-banks and held outside the banking system tend also to result in a net renminbi claim of the rest of the world on China. However, as the expected path of the renminbi exchange rate shows much less consistent appreciation, non-resident borrowing in renminbi looks to be less discouraged by one-way expectations on the exchange rate. Indeed, loans and advances in renminbi booked by Hong Kong banks grew rapidly in the first half of 2012. In this case, the renminbi offshore market in Hong Kong (and in other financial centres) can be expected to evolve along the paths of the other types of offshore markets (He and McCauley 2012). Over time, the renminbi offshore market is likely to predominantly play the role of intermediary between non-mainland Chinese borrowers and lenders.

15.6 **Prospects**

The experience since 2009 shows that facilitating the internationalization of the renminbi requires a deliberate pace of institutional reforms and policy liberalization, which in turn would be conducive to a more open and market-based financial system in China. In the long run, the status of the renminbi as an international currency will depend on the size of the Chinese economy and the sophistication of renminbi financial markets. As long as the Chinese economy continues a fast pace of growth and further integrates with the global community, the prospect for the renminbi is bright.

■ **REFERENCES**

Cheung, Yin-Wong, Guonan Ma, and Robert McCauley. 2011. Renminbising China's foreign assets. *Pacific Economic Review* 16(1), 1–17.

Garber, Peter. 2011. What Currently Drives CNH Market Equilibrium? A CGS/IIGG Working Paper, Council on Foreign Relations, November.

He, Dong and Robert McCauley. 2010. Offshore Markets for the Domestic Currency: Monetary and Financial Stability Issues. BIS Working Papers, no 320, September.

He, Dong and Robert McCauley. 2012. Eurodollar Banking and Currency Internationalisation. *BIS Quarterly Review,* Bank for International Settlements, June.

Zhou, Xiaochuan. 2009. Thoughts on reforming the international monetary system. 23 March, the People's Bank of China (in Chinese).

Zhou, Xiaochuan. 2012. Special Interview—everything about the renminbi. *Century Weekly,* 2 January, published by Caixin Media (in Chinese).

16 Antidumping and other trade disputes

Chad P. Bown

16.1 Introduction: what is antidumping and why is it used?

Antidumping is an import-restricting policy. National governments ultimately administer and apply antidumping subject to the guidance of international rules. Antidumping use has been permitted under both the 1947 General Agreement on Tariffs and Trade (GATT) Article VI and since 1995 under the World Trade Organization (WTO) Agreement on Antidumping. 'Appropriate' use of antidumping can ultimately be enforceable under the WTO's Dispute Settlement Understanding.

The three primary legal elements that governments must satisfy in order to justify imposition of new antidumping trade barriers are that (1) there are 'dumped' imports, (2) there is 'injury' to a domestic industry that produces a competing product, and (3) the dumped imports are a significant cause of that injury. Evidence of dumping requires one of three forms—an exporting firm charging a price in a foreign market that is (i) lower than a constructed measure of its costs, (ii) lower than the selling price of the same good in its home market, or (iii) lower than the selling price of the same good in a third market. Evidence of injury to the domestic industry can be justified through any number of traditional economic indicators, such as a reduction in domestic industry profits, sales, employment, capacity utilization, etc.

Despite antidumping laws being around for more than a century and their legal appearance as a well-articulated policy instrument, economists have difficulty positing a rationale for their existence. First, the legal criterion for 'dumping' penalizes the kind of profit-maximizing behaviour (e.g. price discrimination, short-run pricing below average cost) that many legal systems in market economies find perfectly permissible if the competition is between purely domestic firms. Second, the legal criterion for 'injury' penalizes an outcome predicted by virtually all basic models of international trade. When an economy voluntarily liberalizes, imports increase and industries that face new competition shrink and their resources are reallocated.

As such, many economists interpret antidumping as simply an extraordinarily flexible tool by which governments can be legally permitted to impose new import protection. Nowhere is this flexibility more evident than with respect to China's experience. Sometimes antidumping is imposed against a single export source; at other times it is imposed against multiple trading partners. Sometimes it is imposed narrowly on one product; at other times it is imposed more broadly on a larger industry. Sometimes it is imposed as an import tariff in which the domestic government accrues the rents; at other times it is imposed as a 'price undertaking' in which the foreign firms are allocated the rents. Sometimes it is imposed in response to macro-economic shocks; at other times it is imposed to respond to narrow political interests. Sometimes it is imposed only for a few months; at other times it can last for decades.

16.2 China as a target of trading partner's antidumping import restrictions

China has been the most frequent target for applied new import restrictions for virtually every major user of antidumping over the period 1995–2011 (Bown, 2010, 2011a, 2011b, 2013). This is the case for high-income, historical users of antidumping with already low most-favoured nation (MFN) tariffs—for example the USA, the European Union, Canada, Australia—whose overall application has been in recent decline. It is also true for the major emerging market 'new users'—for example Argentina, Brazil, India, Indonesia, South Africa, and Turkey—a number of which have seen their application of antidumping steadily increase during this same period when they have undergone a broader process of trade liberalization.

The black lines in Figure 16.1 illustrate that a much larger (and growing) share of China's exports to major *emerging* markets are becoming subject to antidumping than its share of exports to high-income markets. This phenomenon gained prominence around the time of China's WTO accession in 2001, and it re-occurred during the Great Recession. By the end of 2011, over 10 per cent of China's exports to major emerging markets were subject to antidumping and related temporary trade barriers (TTBs), compared to less than 5 per cent of its exports to high-income markets.

China's export experience with foreign antidumping has historical parallels with Japan, South Korea, and Taiwan, China. These three economies had similar export-led growth strategies and also became substantial targets of antidumping in the 1980s and 1990s as their trading partners sought to slow down the domestic (and incumbent foreign) suppliers' adjustment to new sources of competition.

Nevertheless, Figure 16.1 reveals one unique aspect of China's experience through the sharp increase in emerging markets' antidumping against China's exports beginning

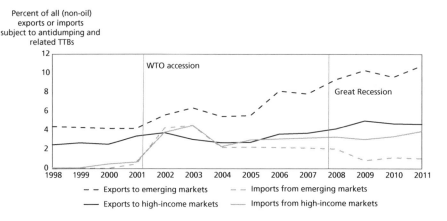

Figure 16.1. China's exports and imports subject to antidumping and related TTBs, 1998–2011

Source: Bown (2013: figs 1 and 2), trade-weighted estimates calculated from data at the 6-digit HS level compiled by the author from Bown (2012).

TTBs = temporary trade barriers and include antidumping, safeguards, and countervailing duties. Exports shares calculated from the import data and TTB policy use of six emerging markets (Argentina, Brazil, India, Indonesia, South Africa, Turkey) and six high-income markets (Australia, Canada, European Union, Japan, South Korea, United States).

after 2000. Only after China's 2001 WTO accession were trading partners required to offer China's exporters the same MFN import tariff treatment that they grant other WTO members. A partial explanation for the sharp increase in foreign antidumping against China's exports around the time of China's accession is due to trading partners 'converting' other pre-2001 discriminatory trade barriers into potentially WTO-consistent antidumping.

16.3 **China as a user of antidumping import restrictions**

As China substantially liberalized its import tariffs during the 1990s in the run-up to its WTO accession, it also established an antidumping policy regime and subsequently applied its first antidumping tariff on imports in 1998. As the grey lines in Figure 16.1 illustrate, by the end of 2011, almost 4 per cent of China's imports from high-income trading partners were subject to antidumping or a related temporary trade barrier, much less than China applied to imports from other emerging markets (1.1 per cent).

The first decade of China's antidumping use was overwhelmingly dominated by its domestic chemicals industry (Bown, 2010) and trade barriers applied against multiple sources. Beginning in the financial crisis of 2008–09, new Chinese industries—ranging from agriculture ('chicken feet') to automobiles—began to use antidumping, more frequently targeting singular sources. Some have argued that the recent shift in use is motivated by retaliation (Chandra, 2011).[1]

16.4 **Key policy issues**

While being a substantial target of foreign antidumping is but a small price that China may have willingly paid for its integration into global markets over the previous twenty years, there are a number of looming policy issues likely to impact how China's exports are affected by antidumping over the next twenty years.

First, the rapid increase in antidumping has led to a large 'stock' of China's exports becoming subject to such barriers (see again Figure 16.1). Such barriers could end after five years under the 'Sunset Review' provisions that the WTO put into effect in 1995. Nevertheless, such provisions appear to be less and less binding for all countries over time. The policy implication is that temporary trade barriers such as antidumping are becoming more and more permanent.

Second, in terms of new barriers, many existing WTO members were granted the ability to treat China as a non-market economy (NME) during antidumping investigations under the terms of its accession. NME status has contributed to the high incidence of antidumping confronting China's exports. An open question is whether China's NME status will expire quietly or whether trading partners replace it with something else. Many of China's trading partners remain deeply concerned with perceived unfair 'subsidies'; whether such subsidies are due to the role of China's state-owned enterprises (SOEs), intervention in foreign exchange markets, and alleged currency undervaluation that implicitly subsidizes exports, or something else. The subsidies issue may impact future antidumping use directly or indirectly by pushing governments towards substitutable policies such as countervailing duties.

The key policy question for China is how to address these issues. One choice for China is to ignore them altogether and to simply accept these particular trade barriers as the cost of a relatively liberal multilateral trading system that has otherwise largely accommodated China's export-led growth. A second choice is to take matters into one's 'own hands' and use antidumping retaliation to discipline antidumping use abroad (Blonigen and Bown, 2003). A third option for China is to continue its increasing use of WTO dispute settlement to press for legal decisions that might remove existing barriers and jurisprudence that might reshape how future policies

---

[1] Interestingly, however, these claims of retaliation were not motivated by the USA's use of antidumping policy but instead the USA's use of an alternative temporary trade barrier policy; that is, the China-specific safeguard that was applied to imports of tyres in 2009. For a discussion of the policy, see Bown (2010) and Bown and Crowley (2010).

are implemented. A final alternative is negotiation. While antidumping reform has not been a major part of the Doha Round, the number of issues involved and the possibility of reciprocal tradeoffs could require that antidumping be best handled through placement on a multilateral agenda.

■ REFERENCES

Blonigen, Bruce A. and Chad P. Bown. 2003. Antidumping and retaliation threats. *Journal of International Economics* 60(2), 249–73.

Bown, Chad P. 2010. China's WTO entry: antidumping, safeguards, and dispute settlement. In *China's Growing Role in World Trade*, edited by Robert C. Feenstra and Shang-Jin Wei (eds), 281–337. University of Chicago Press.

Bown, Chad P. 2011a. Taking stock of antidumping, safeguards and countervailing duties, 1990-2009. *The World Economy* 34(12), 1955–98.

Bown, Chad P. (ed.). 2011b. *The Great Recession and Import Protection: The Role of Temporary Trade Barriers*. London, UK: CEPR and the World Bank.

Bown, Chad P. 2012. *Temporary Trade Barriers Database*, The World Bank, May. Available at <http://econ.worldbank.org/ttbd/>.

Bown, Chad P. 2013. Emerging economies and the emergence of south-south protectionism. *Journal of World Trade* 47(1), 1–44.

Bown, Chad P. and Meredith A. Crowley. 2010. China's export growth and the China safeguard: threats to the world trading system? *Canadian Journal of Economics* 43(4), 1353–88.

Chandra, Piyush. 2011. China: A sleeping giant of temporary trade barriers? In *The Great Recession and Import Protection: The Role of Temporary Trade Barriers*, edited by Chad P. Bown. London, UK: CEPR and the World Bank.

17 US–China economic relations

Stephen C. Smith and Yao Pan

US–China economic relations encompass three primary areas: international trade in goods and services, foreign direct investment (FDI), and portfolio investment.[1] These three relationships are understood in their institutional and regulatory environments. These three spheres also interact with one another: in some cases providing substitute means to achieve objectives; in other cases, one relationship works much better if features of another relationship are also working well, in which case they are complements. They are also affected by non-economic relations. Throughout this entry, we attempt to present views from China and the USA in a balanced way.[2]

Differences between the countries' economic and political systems are a significant feature of the bilateral economic relationships, which are sometimes contentious.[3] At the same time, the impacts of these differences are easily overstated; contention has emerged in a similar way between the USA and other fast-growing economies with state-led development strategies, such as Japan and South Korea in the 1980s.

17.1 International trade in goods and services

In 1980, shortly after the beginning of reforms,[4] China's exports to the USA stood at $2.43 billion, or 0.61 per cent of GDP in 2005 dollars. For the USA, exports to China were $7.86 billion, or a paltry 0.14 per cent of GDP in comparable 2005 dollars. Over the next three decades, the levels of exports and corresponding imports changed dramatically, with a chronic trade deficit, as seen in Figure 17.1. This observation led to many calls in the USA

[1] We have benefited from perspectives gained from the annual 'Conference on China's Development and US-China Economic Relations' (2008–2011) at GWU's Institute for International Economic Policy (IIEP); see <http://www.gwu.edu/~iiep/G2_at_GW/G2_at_GW_2011.cfm>. Research support from IIEP is gratefully acknowledged.

[2] This has required some translations from original Chinese media sources, as noted.

[3] Yasheng Huang, book and talk at 2010 Conference on China's Development and US–China Economic Relations at GWU, 'Capitalism with Chinese Characteristics'.

[4] The history of China's market reforms—and reasons for their emergence and path taken—are examined in Chapters 2, 4, 23, 68, and 88, this volume.

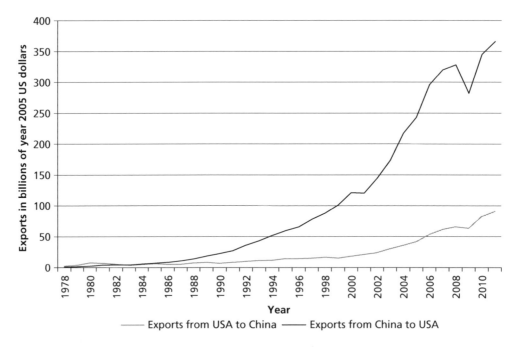

Figure 17.1. Annual exports from China to the USA, and from the USA to China, 1978–2011

Source: UN COMTRADE database via World Integrated Trade Solution (WITS).

for measures in response to (if not to retaliate for) perceived unfair trade policies and practices on the part of China.

Over time, the composition of exports also changed significantly. Manufactured exports from China to the USA became increasingly sophisticated as measured by technology content and value added. While predominantly attention has been paid to trends in merchandise exports, trends in the services sector are also informative. The USA maintains an increasing trade surplus in the service sector.[5]

By design, the WTO is the main regulatory mechanism of China–US trade.[6] Indeed, as trade relations have been fraught with disagreements, both sides have appealed to the WTO. China brought ten complaints to the WTO in the decade since its accession in 2001 with eight of them being lodged against the USA, while the United States brought thirty-four complaints, of which fifteen were against China.[7]

Bilateral China–US talks are arguably more important than WTO action. This view grew as it became increasingly clear that the WTO Doha Round of negotiations—initiated just

---

[5] Data source: United Nations Service Trade Statistics Database.
[6] See Chapter 18, this volume.
[7] Data source: WTO website <http://www.wto.org/>.

after China's accession—were likely to end in failure. Indeed, this failure to make further progress put the WTO role in question. Government positions revealed sharp differences but also a mutual goal of smooth trading relationships, from which both sides could gain.

The US perspective has focused on the criticism that China effectively subsidizes its exports and maintains an artificially undervalued currency, flouting WTO treaty agreements and unfairly harming US producers.[8]

A widely accepted argument is that if China's artificial import barriers are reduced, net imports must increase.[9] As noted by Fred Bergsten,[10] 'Surplus China and deficit America . . . appear to recognize that it would be a huge mistake, and indeed again unsustainable, for China to resume its reliance on export-led growth and ever-rising trade surpluses or for the United States to become once again the "global consumer of last resort" and run huge current account deficits. Instead, China must expand domestic (especially consumer) demand and the United States must re-orient toward exports and productive investment.'

In contrast, as argued by Shang-Jin Wei, 'If import barriers are reduced . . . an export expansion triggered by trade liberalization could more than offset the increase in imports. . . . Because the expanding export sector (e.g. garments) is less capital intensive than the contracting import-competing sector (e.g. semi-conductor products), in order to fully absorb all the capital [savings], the export sector has to expand by an extent greater than the increase in the imports of the capital intensive goods.'[11]

Further, as noted by the *China Daily*, 'Traditional measures in international trade assume the value of exports comes solely from the exporting countries. These measures cannot fully reflect China's position in its trade with other countries. Better measures should be based on value-added, as proposed by [the] WTO and OECD. . . . Under these new measures, the trade [im]balance between [the] US and China will be significantly downsized.'[12] As noted by Deming Chen, 'The trade [im]balance between [the] US and China mainly comes from processing trade and is due to different positions in the industry value chain. . . . The trade between [the] US and State Owned Enterprise in China is balanced in general. 75 per cent of trade imbalance comes from the processing trade in

---

[8] Details of exchange rate management—and the active debate on whether the renminbi is overvalued and if so by how much—are outside the scope of this review. See Chapter 15, this volume.

[9] For a forceful example see the presentation of Tim Punke, 'The US–China Relationship—Redefining the Terms', at the September 2011 Conference on China's Development and US–China Economic Relations, at GWU.

[10] Fred Bergsten, 'The United States–China Economic Relationship and the Strategic and Economic Dialogue', presentation at November 2009 Conference on China's Development and US–China Economic Relations, at GWU.

[11] Shang-Jin Wei, 'Trade Reforms and Current Account Imbalances: When Can the Common Sense Be Wrong?' a paper presented at the September 2011 Conference on China's Development and US–China Economic Relations, at GWU.

[12] *China Daily*, 1 June 2012; translation by Yao Pan.

Foreign Owned Enterprises and 60 per cent of these FOEs are from [the] US. Moreover, China also wants to import from [the] US, but [the] US imposed export restrictions [on] China for high-tech products.'[13]

In summarizing the exchange rate and trade balance debate, Premier Jiabao Wen 'pointed out that China's international balance of payments, particularly in trade and goods, is "approaching basic equilibrium", citing figures to say that the current account surplus of China in 2011 only accounted for 2.8 per cent of its GDP, below the 3 per cent level that is internationally recognized as appropriate.'[14]

Overall, statements from China emphasize mutual rebalancing. As stated by Xiaochuan Zhou,[15] 'China has proposed a policy bundle that . . . includes increasing domestic demand, boosting rural consumption, promoting growth of the service industry, correcting "encourage export and limit import" policies, and adjusting exchange rate[s].'

These disagreements show that, while Figure 17.1 appears to tell a straightforward story, interpretation of the figures is fraught with complexity. For example, a significant portion of China's recorded exports may represent intra-corporate transfers from subsidiaries in China to US parent companies.[16]

17.2 **Foreign direct investment (FDI)**

FDI from US multinational corporation parent companies in their subsidiaries in China has also grown dramatically since 1985, as seen in Figure 17.2.

The US FDI stock in China represented 1.27 per cent of total US FDI in 2010; and FDI from China to the US economy represented 1.06 per cent of its total FDI.[17] The difference in FDI stocks and flows across the countries is very large. Some reflect the different stages of development. Approximately 10 per cent of the FDI stock in China originates from the USA. Bijian Zheng, an advisor to China's leadership, argued in 2012 that, 'Mutual FDI between China and [the] US will be the focus of the cooperation in the future.'[18]

It appears likely that investment from China to the USA will rise in the coming decade. As noted by Yukon Huang, 'Rising labor costs in China combined with the benefits of

---

[13] Deming Chen (Minister of the Chinese Ministry of Commerce) quoted in the *Shanghai Financial News*, 20 March 2012; translation by Yao Pan.

[14] 'Wen urges co-operation to address Sino-US trade imbalance', *Xinhua News Agency*, 14 March 2012, Translation by Yao Pan.

[15] *Chinanews.com*, December 12, 2007, Translation by Yao Pan.

[16] According to US Census Bureau, Related Party Database, 28 per cent of US goods imported from China were intra-firm in 2011.

[17] Source for total inward/outward FDI stock China or US: UNCTADstat.

[18] Bijian Zheng, quoted from *China Chinanews.com*; translation by Yao Pan. See:'中美专家"居安思危"望创造新利益汇合'.

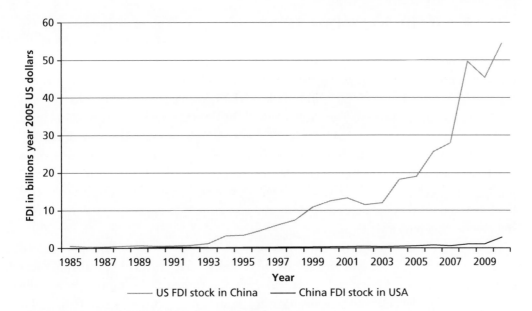

Figure 17.2. FDI stocks between the USA and China

Source: International Direct Investments Statistics database, OECD Statistics; data do not include Hong Kong.

proximity to technology centers and more sophisticated markets are starting to generate proposals to produce more in the US. This provides an option similar to the relocation of Japanese auto plants to the USA which helped to ameliorate tensions.'[19]

Trade, investment, and financial relations are interconnected; as Caihua Zhu argued, 'FDI is a very important tool in mediating the imbalance of International Payment between the two nations . . . [the] trade surplus with the U.S. will not decrease suddenly because it takes time for China to consume more and the U.S. to save more . . . China's fast economic growth ensures sustainable FDI inflows (including from the U.S.) into China. Thus, learning from the experience of Japan in the middle of [the] 1980s, China needs to expand its overseas investment, especially investment in the U.S. to alleviate great pressures on its domestic monetary policy and exchange rate resulting from the tremendous holding of foreign reserves...'[20]

Premier Jiabao Wen also represented China's official view in a 2012 interview: 'Cooperation is the way to address trade imbalance between China and the United States as well as the difficulties and frictions arising from it . . . The United States should open its exports to China and ease related restrictions while promoting two-way investment.'[21]

---

[19] Yukon Huang, 'Will the US and China Ever Invest in Each Other?' *Financial Times*, 25 July 2012.

[20] Caihua Zhu: 'Constraints by US against China investment in the US', presentation at the October 2010 Conference on China's Development and US–China Economic Relations, at GWU.

[21] 'Wen urges co-operation to address Sino-US trade imbalance', Xinhua news agency, 14 March 2012, Translation by Yao Pan.

17.3 **Portfolio investment**

Purchases from China of US government securities comprise a major part of the bilateral portfolio flow. This has brought benefits and costs to both parties.[22] The practice has probably served to keep the renminbi low. The USA has benefited because China's purchases have helped keep US interest rates low. But according to a widespread interpretation, China's export growth has been higher because the flow raises the price of US dollars relative to the renminbi, and the result has been harm to American producers. Such purchases have similarly helped to sterilize net export inflows to China, helping to keep inflation in check. It is a classic development strategy to keep export surpluses abroad until such time as they are needed for domestic investments (including human capital) of sufficiently high return.

Fred Bergsten has argued, 'The two governments will need to take further policy steps to sustain and build on this progress. . . . China has blocked further appreciation of its exchange rate against the dollar. . . . For its part, the United States must substantially reduce its budget deficits as soon as the recovery permits if it is to avoid a renewed escalation of its external imbalances.'

As a final note, other aspects of US–China relations also play important roles. In particular, disagreements concerning protection of intellectual property rights (IPRs) in China have become increasingly sharp. Interactions between the countries' individual responses to the global financial crisis appear to have been more cooperative. At the same time, China's growing role in global (economic) governance, and the diplomatic objectives to project influence, also influence the shape of negotiations over economic relations. If a US–China 'G2' is ever to rival the role of the G8 or G20, a great deal of economic and diplomatic progress must be made.

---

[22] Yongtu Long (Secretary-General, Boao Forum For Asia), *Sohu Finance*, 12 December 2008.

18 China and the WTO

Aaditya Mattoo and Arvind Subramanian

Beginning in the 1990s, when it was becoming clear that China represented a huge market access opportunity, the USA and the EU launched efforts to reduce China's trade barriers.[1] This initiative was aided by the fact that the Chinese leadership, or at least some parts of it under Zhu Rongji, wanted to use the World Trade Organization (WTO) as a means for furthering domestic reform and anchoring it in the WTO. A broader strategic goal was 'to facilitate the peaceful emergence of China as a great trading nation—and to avoid the trade tensions associated with the emergence of major new traders in the past' (Bhattasali et al., 2004).

World Trade Organization accession was the watershed in emerging China's international economic integration. Accommodating a dominant China may well turn out to be a watershed for the multilateral trading system.

18.1 The accession: how the WTO changed China

The accession deal gave China reasonably assured access to foreign markets in return for significant but not complete liberalization of its own market. Thus, China received most-favoured-nation (MFN) treatment in foreign markets, and was freed from onerous, one-sided review procedures, such as the former annual review of MFN in the United States. WTO members agreed to refrain from invoking non-application provisions of the type widely invoked against Japan when it joined the GATT. Significantly, quotas on textiles and clothing originally imposed under the Multi-Fiber Arrangement were abolished.

World Trade Organization members did retain the right to revert to temporary protection. Until 2013, product-specific transitional safeguard provisions could be applied by any WTO Member, and then even trigger actions against the diversion of Chinese exports to other markets. China also remains vulnerable until 2016 to antidumping action because its non-market economy status increases the likelihood and magnitude of antidumping duties. Finally, members initially retained the right to impose special safeguards on textiles and clothing.

---

[1] This article draws upon Bhattasali et al. (2004) and Mattoo and Subramanian (2012).

As far as China's own trade reform is concerned, accession was a process rather than an event. In the period leading up to its accession, China had already significantly reduced barriers to trade. In its accessions agreement, China committed to gradually liberalizing further in industry, agriculture, and services. In manufacturing, average tariffs had fallen from 46.5 per cent in 1992 to around 13 per cent in 2001; with the full implementation of China's accession commitments, they fell further to 6.9 per cent. The effective degree of liberalization was even greater because of the abolition of non-tariff barriers such as designated trading, quotas, and licences. The transparency and predictability of China's trade policy were greatly enhanced through both the general WTO policy rules, such as the need to publish trade rules and regulations, and some of the specific commitments made by China, such as the binding of its entire tariff schedule for goods.

The average rate of protection in rice, wheat, and maize did not have to be significantly reduced because either the system of state trading operated to tax exports (in the case of rice) or because imports (of wheat and maize) were expected to exceed the agreed tariff-rate quota reasonably frequently, allowing for the imposition of higher tariffs. China promised to refrain from using export subsidies on agricultural goods and it has accepted a limit of 8.5 per cent on de minimis domestic support (compared to the usual 10 per cent limit for developing countries).

China's commitments on services represent the most radical services reform programme negotiated in the WTO. These commitments encompassed whole swathes of the economy which had previously been closed to foreign participation, ranging from transport and telecommunications to finance and retail. In banking, for example, foreign banks had been virtually shut out at the time of accession, but China committed to eliminate all restrictions over the next seven years. In more sensitive areas, such as basic telecommunications and life insurance too, entry was liberalized even though China continued to prohibit majority foreign ownership.

18.2 Transitional stalemate: the elephant in the green room

Within a decade of its accession, China's dramatic growth has transformed the negotiating dynamic in the WTO. A significant but publicly unacknowledged impediment to concluding the Doha negotiations is the WTO members' difficulty in coming to terms with China's trade juggernaut and the policies, such as the managed exchange rate, that are perceived to fuel it but are not part of the Doha agenda. In manufacturing trade, China's share in the major import markets has doubled between 2001 and 2009, and in some of the most important world markets, China now accounts for more than a fifth of total manufacturing imports. Furthermore, China looms especially large in the markets of major trading partners in sectors where protection is greatest, and its share has increased dramatically over the course of the Doha Round.

The fear persists that China will gain even greater market share as a result of any trade liberalization in the Doha Round. One sign of this fear is that industrial and especially developing countries are increasingly resorting to contingent protection against imports from China (Bown, 2010). But recourse to this instrument will become more difficult when China attains market economy status in 2016. Moreover, the product-specific transitional safeguards that were negotiated at the time of China's WTO accession expired in 2013. This leaves countries even more anxious about competition from China.

18.3 Looking ahead: how China will change the WTO

The challenge of accommodating China will be greater in the future. As discussed in Subramanian (2011), within the next twenty years China is likely to be even more economically dominant: by 2030, its market-based GDP is projected to equal that of the USA, its purchasing power parity-based GDP to be twice that of the USA, China's trade in goods to be nearly twice that of the USA and Europe.

The trading system has accommodated an emerging China. How will it adapt to and be shaped by a dominant China? China's trade-dependence will tend to create a strong stake for China in maintaining an open trading and financial system. Post-World War II, the USA fashioned such a system out of enlightened self-interest. China's interest in this system might be much more existential and strong because of its low level of income.

But that cannot be taken for granted. The temptation to exercise power need not stem from some sinister motive on the part of China but simply from the fact that increased size confers greater market power. Economic self-interest then dictates that a country exploit this power to improve its welfare by influencing its terms-of-trade, by increasing the price of its exports and/or reducing the price of its imports (including raw materials) (Bagwell and Staiger, 1999). If the previous bargain struck at the time of China's WTO accession is no longer an equilibrium, then a new bargain may need to be struck, which would reflect China's increased size.

18.3.1 WILL CHINA ADHERE TO ITS EXISTING OBLIGATIONS?

From the Chinese perspective, there will inevitably be a weighing of the benefits of adhering to multilateral principles and processes—in terms of economic efficiency, low transactions costs, and minimal political frictions—and of seeking more advantageous bilateral or plurilateral deals by exploiting its growing economic heft.

In this context, it is encouraging that China is becoming more of a routine participant in WTO dispute settlement proceedings both as an initiator of disputes and as a respondent. It is also encouraging that, so far, China has largely agreed to comply with the terms of WTO dispute settlement proceedings. For example, of the eight cases brought by the United States, three have been resolved by a memorandum of understanding, two are pending decision, and in three China has alleged compliance with the decision of the Dispute Settlement Body.

There are, however, still concerns. On intellectual property rights (IPRs), China faces a particular challenge in reconciling the WTO obligations on the protection of with its goal of improving access to cutting-edge technologies for its national firms. Here it is relevant that China's dominance will be associated at least initially not with technological leadership—as in the case of its predecessors Britain and the USA—but with technological catch-up. The use of exchange rates to tax imports and subsidize exports reflects a continued desire to pursue proactive trade and industrial policy while WTO rules constrain the use of more explicit policy instruments (Rodrik, 2009). In services, China's far-reaching promises to rapidly liberalize conflict with both protectionist and prudential goals. Measures affecting trading rights and distribution services for certain publications and audiovisual entertainment were clearly protectionist, as a WTO panel ruled, but it is harder to determine whether China's decision to impose minimum working capital requirements for each direct branch of a foreign bank located in China is to ensure financial stability or to inhibit foreign competition. Finally, export restrictions China has maintained on a number of raw materials which are used to produce everyday items as well as technology products were also found by a WTO panel to be inconsistent with its obligations.

18.3.2 A NEW CHINA ROUND OF NEGOTIATIONS?

The time may have come for an initiative on multilateral trade negotiations that builds on but redefines the Doha Agenda and that would anchor China more fully in the multilateral trading system. Such an initiative would have two pillars.

Large parts of the current Doha Agenda, such as the market access negotiations in manufacturing, agriculture, and services, as well as the domestic support issues in agriculture, remain relevant, perhaps even more so in the context of a rising China. For example, exporters of services from other countries have a strong interest in further liberalization of the huge and growing but still protected Chinese market. Moreover, China itself is developing an interest in exporting services—its exports of services have grown at over 18 per cent per annum over the last decade. There may be a basis for a bargain, especially if industrial countries and larger emerging market countries are willing to lock-in openness to cross-border trade in business services and allow Chinese FDI without creating implicit barriers. In agriculture, China's subsidies to farmers increased six-fold between 2008 and 2010 and were higher than those of the USA (OECD, 2011). In this respect, China seems to be conforming to a broader trend whereby countries, as they become richer, switch from taxing to subsidizing agriculture. These developments make the domestic support elements of the agricultural negotiations even more relevant.

But any meaningful deal needs to cover at least some of the elements outlined in the following paragraphs.

18.3.2.1 Security of access to food, energy, and other resources

China will be a large importer of energy and foodstuffs in the medium term. It has a big incentive to ensure that partner countries do not restrict their exports of these commodities. At the same time, China's restrictions on exports of rare earths have created anxiety in the rest of the world because it is the almost exclusive supplier of these minerals which are crucial to the global electronics, defence, and renewable energy industries. The Doha round has been devoted to traditional forms of protection. It would be in China's interest to enlarge the trade agenda so that trade barriers, both on imports and exports, are put on the trade agenda.

18.3.2.2 Security of access for foreign investments

In some cases, Chinese foreign investment has provoked anxiety and protectionist sentiment. Mutually beneficial bargains are there for the making. The WTO is an appropriate forum for such deals because it already regulates private and government investments in key service sectors, such as telecommunications, transport, and finance. One way to manage such investments would be to require countries importing capital, such as the USA and EU members, not to impose undue restrictions on investments. In return, China and other investing countries would commit to following certain criteria—transparency, an arms-length relationship with governments, and the pursuit of purely commercial objectives.

18.3.2.3 Limits to climate change-motivated trade action

Even though the climate change talks have lost momentum, policy action to address climate change is likely in the future. Under the range of likely emissions reductions being envisaged by the major industrial countries, there will be calls to offset the competitiveness pressure of imports from countries which make less ambitious reductions. As part of any international agreement on climate change, China could seek to negotiate rules in the WTO that would either prohibit all forms of carbon-based border tax adjustment, or at most only allow the least damaging options under the strictest conditions.

18.3.2.4 **Government procurement**

Government procurement, estimated to be 15–20 per cent of GDP in the OECD economies and an even larger share of GDP in the emerging markets, has largely escaped WTO rules. Given the evidence of opacity, lack of accountability, and discrimination in national procurement regimes, there are bound to be huge mutual benefits from liberalization. A subset of, mostly industrial, countries are parties to the Agreement on Government Procurement and have promised not to discriminate against each other. But non-members like China are not assured of fair treatment in other countries. China has an obvious incentive to gain assured access to the procurement markets of industrial and larger developing countries and this is consistent with China being a competitive supplier across the board. At the same time, trading partners have a big stake in liberalizing China's large and highly protected government procurement.

18.3.2.5 **Exchange rates**

As noted above, the perceived undervaluation of major currencies, especially the Chinese renminbi, is a central concern not just for industrial countries, but also for developing countries (see Mattoo, Mishra, and Subramanian, 2012). For a number of domestic reasons, China will want to change its exchange rate policies. But these changes might not happen quickly enough and a multilateral effort by trading partners to secure new rules against undervaluation might be a useful complement to the domestic imperatives faced by China to appreciate its currency. A multilateral approach is also needed to preempt the type of unilateral action of the kind that is being contemplated by Brazil and the USA, and hence to avoid the dangers of retaliation and escalation. One possibility going forwards would be for the IMF and the WTO to cooperate on exchange-rate issues.

18.4 **Conclusion**

The idea is now gaining ground that the Trans-Pacific Partnership (TPP) with the USA in the lead and based on the idea of open regionalism could be an alternative to the multilateralism of the WTO and also as the best way of engaging China on trade issues. The problem with this approach is that China would never agree to just fall in line with rules developed during a negotiation in which it has not participated. Worse, TPP could also provoke China into playing the regionalism game in a way that could fundamentally fragment the trading system.

A better way of keeping China anchored in the multilateral system would be for China's trading partners to say that 'not only in our dealings with you but also amongst ourselves, we will embrace multilateralism'. This would signal a belief in the intrinsic worth of multilateralism rather than just as an instrument to contain China. One goal of such restraint today would be to prevent a dominant China tomorrow from pursuing preferential arrangements in the future that disadvantage excluded countries.

A modicum of trust between trading partners based on broadly similar domestic institutional frameworks is necessary for international cooperation. In the case of China, the pervasive and often non-transparent role for the state in economic activity is sometimes seen as inconsistent with justiciable international rules and commitments. The approach suggested here is to decompose state involvement into its constituent elements—state purchases in the form of government procurement, state investments through sovereign wealth funds—and to suggest how these elements might be the focus of international rules. Our approach does not offer a perfect solution, but a combination of such an approach combined with progressive change in the basis of the Chinese economy seems the best way forward.

■ REFERENCES

Bagwell, Kyle and Robert W. Staiger. 1999. An economic theory of GATT. *American Economic Review* 89(1), 215–48.

Bhattasali, Deepak, Shantong Li, and Will Martin. 2004. *China and the WTO: Accession, Policy Reform and Poverty Reduction Strategies*. Washington, DC: World Bank and Oxford University Press.

Bown, Chad. 2010. Taking Stock of Antidumping, Safeguards, and Countervailing Duties, 1990–2009. World Bank Policy Research Working Paper 5436. Washington: World Bank.

Mattoo, Aaditya and Arvind Subramanian. 2012. China and the World Trading System, forthcoming in *World Economy*.

Mattoo, Aaditya, Prachi Mishra, and Arvind Subramanian. 2012. Spillover Effects of Exchange Rates: A Study of the Renminbi. Peterson Institute for International Economics Working Paper 12–14, and World Bank Policy Research Working Paper 5989, Washington, DC.

OECD. 2011. *Agricultural Policy Monitoring and Evaluation 2011: OECD Countries and Emerging Economies*. Paris: OECD, available at <http://www.oecd.org/document/32/0,3746,en_2649_37401_48625184_1_1_1_37401,00.html#country>.

Rodrik, Dani. 2009. Making Room for China in the World Economy. Paper prepared for the AEA session on 'Growth in a Partially De-Globalized World.'

Subramanian, Arvind. 2011. *Eclipse: Living in the Shadow of China's Economic Dominance*. Washington, DC: Peterson Institute of International Economics.

19 China's aid policy

Deborah Bräutigam

19.1 A brief history of Chinese aid

China's aid programme began in 1950, with transfers to North Korea. During that decade, aid was focused on China's Asian neighbours: Burma, Cambodia, North Vietnam, Nepal, and Sri Lanka (Bartke, 1989). China also began providing aid to 'friendly' countries in North Africa: Egypt (1956), and Algeria (1958). During the 1960s, China's aid programme targeted African countries with socialist governments: Guinea, Ghana, Mali, Tanzania, and Zambia. As more countries emerged from colonialism, however, aid evolved to become an active component of Beijing's diplomacy. Aid diplomacy was instrumental in the 1971 United Nations vote that removed Taiwan from membership, and admitted China.

By 1975, China had aid programmes in more African countries than did the USA (Bräutigam, 1998). Between 1970 and 1975, China funded and built the 1860 km Tanzania–Zambia railway line, with 10 kilometres of tunnels and 300 bridges. The railway enabled landlocked Zambia to export its copper without going through Rhodesia (later, Zimbabwe) and South Africa, both controlled at the time by hostile regimes. In 1978, China was giving aid to sixty-six countries. Chinese teams completed 470 projects between 1971 and 1978. Between 1967 and 1976, aid averaged around 5 per cent of government expenditure (Bräutigam, 2011: 41). When China began to focus on its own modernization under Deng Xiaoping, this level was judged to be unsustainable.

Chinese premier Zhao Ziyang announced a major reform in 1982, during a historic trip to eleven African countries. China's aid would become part of a larger system of 'cooperation' that would be 'practical . . . take a variety of forms' and be based on 'mutual benefit' (Bräutigam, 2011: 53). Much as experimentation characterized China's own development, Chinese officials launched different experiments in aid: debt–equity swaps, funds for joint ventures, trilateral cooperation with the United Nations Development Program, and the Food and Agriculture Organization, and so on. Chinese companies also began offering management and technical assistance for completed aid projects: stadiums, sugar factories, conference centres.

19.2 **Organization of aid**

China's broad aid policy is set by the State Council, while details have been handled by a series of changing institutions. China's first dedicated office for aid, the State Administration (later, Commission) of Foreign Economic Relations, was set up in 1960 directly under the State Council. Decisions on new aid agreements were made jointly by the Ministry of Foreign Affairs and the Commission. To manage the large increase in foreign aid projects, in 1970 the Commission was upgraded to become the Ministry of Foreign Economic Relations, and all provinces and many large state-owned companies were also tasked with setting up provincial offices for foreign economic and technical cooperation. During China's post-Mao reforms, the Ministry of Foreign Economic Relations was merged with the Ministry of Trade in 1982 to become the Ministry of Foreign Economic Relations and Trade (MOFERT). The foreign economic and technical cooperation offices were transformed into companies. For example, China Civil Engineering Construction Corporation was formerly the cooperation office of the Ministry of Railways, and China Road and Bridge Corporation was the cooperation office of the Ministry of Communications. In 1993, MOFERT became the Ministry of Foreign Trade and Economic Cooperation (MOFTEC), and in 2003, it became simply the Ministry of Commerce, with foreign aid handled by a vice-minister who oversees the Department of Aid to Foreign Countries (Bräutigam, 2011).

In 2012, the Department described its tasks as follows: 'To formulate and implement plans and policies of foreign aid, to boost the reform on China's foreign aid methods, to organize negotiations on foreign aid and sign related agreements, to tackle inter-governmental aid affairs; to formulate and implement foreign aid plans; to supervise and inspect the implementation of foreign aid projects' (MOFCOM, 2012). The Department has fifteen divisions, and a staff of about seventy professionals. Another dozen or so researchers work on foreign aid issues in MOFCOM's 'think-tank', the Chinese Academy of International Trade and Economic Cooperation (CAITEC). MOFCOM also has three semi-autonomous entities that manage some aspects of the aid programme. The Executive Bureau of International Economic Cooperation handles tenders for 'complete plant' aid projects, procurement, and quality control. China International Center for Economic and Technical Exchanges manages aid-in-kind (such as a shipment of fertilizer), and the Academy of International Business Officials is responsible for coordinating short-term training courses.

Other parts of the Chinese government are also involved in some aspects of foreign aid implementation. China's Export-Import Bank has a small window for interest-subsidized, concessional foreign aid loans, which complement its main export credit function. The aid loans are specifically made for the purpose of promoting economic development and improved living standards in the recipient country, whereas export credits are simply to promote exports and do not need to have a developmental purpose. China's Ministry of Health is in charge of overseas medical teams, which are organized and funded by its provincial-level branches, in long-term 'twinning' arrangements with particular countries. Host countries house the doctors (who serve for two years), and usually pay their airfares and a stipend. The Ministry of Education manages the scholarship programme for students from developing countries doing degree programmes in China. Beijing usually pays the tuition, airfares, and housing, and gives students a small stipend (Brautigam, 2011). In 2008, MOFCOM, the Ministry of Foreign Affairs, and the Ministry of Finance established an official inter-agency taskforce to help coordinate the expanded aid activities (State Council, 2011).

19.3 **Instruments**

China's aid is provided through grants, zero-interest loans, and interest-subsidized concessional loans (*youhui daikuan*). Grants finance small and medium-sized social development projects, humanitarian assistance, training and technical cooperation, and in-kind assistance. Zero-interest loans pay for public works (including stadiums and conference centres) and light industry, while concessional loans offer finance for productive projects that can earn an income and therefore make repayments (joint ventures, shrimp farming, cotton mills, etc.), larger economic infrastructure (toll roads, power plants), or the import of Chinese equipment or technical services, such as telecommunications or green energy systems. Interest-subsidized concessional loans have fixed interest rates, generally 2–3 per cent, and are usually repayable over 15–20 years, which includes a grace period of 5–7 years (State Council, 2011: 5). China also provides assistance through funding university scholarships, overseas medical teams, and debt relief. A youth volunteer programme was launched in 2002.

In addition, China has a number of instruments for supporting its firms' business overseas that are sometimes confused with its official aid programme. For example, one department in China's Eximbank manages projects financed by concessional aid and preferential export credits, but the vast majority of loans and guarantees issued by China Eximbank are at non-concessional market rates, generally the London Interbank Offered Rate (LIBOR) plus a margin. China Eximbank also offers preferential export buyer's credits (*youhui maifan xindai*) which are similar to the concessional loans in structure, but are subsidized through a different budget line, and offered solely to promote exports. China Development Bank (CDB) lends to foreign governments, but at commercial rates. CDB manages the China Africa Development Fund, which provides equity for investment. Both China Eximbank and CDB have offered large lines of credit, at commercial rates, secured by exports, and usually used to finance imports from China or work by Chinese contractors. These are called resources-for-infrastructure loans, or 'mutual benefit loans' (*huhui daikuan*). While potentially developmental, none of these qualify as official aid.

19.4 **Scope and volume**

China's *Statistical Yearbook* publishes annual figures for government expenditures on external assistance. Instructions issued by the Ministry of Finance in 1998 state that these figures include complete plant (turn-key) projects financed with grants and zero-interest loans, in-kind aid, military assistance, and cash aid, as well as training programmes inside China and the costs of Chinese technical assistance overseas, plus the interest rate subsidy for concessional loans, some costs of Chinese firms in foreign-aid funded joint ventures, and overheads for companies carrying out aid projects (Kobayashi, 2008: 2–3). These figures do not include the costs of health teams sent by the provinces, China's scholarship programmes, or refugee expenses inside China.

In 2011, for the first time, the Chinese government published official figures on the accumulated amount of aid commitments between the 1950s and the end of 2009 (State Council, 2011).[1] Chinese total aid commitments were 256.29 billion yuan, including 106.2 billion yuan in grants, 76.54 billion yuan in interest-free loans, and 73.55 billion yuan in concessional loans. A debt relief programme led to the cancellation of 25.58 billion yuan of overdue interest-free loans in 50 countries (2000–09), the majority (35) in Africa. In 2009, Africa received nearly half (45.7%) of China's official total aid (including concessional loans).

Chinese aid has been on an upward trajectory for several decades. Between 2004 and 2009, China's overall aid commitments grew at an average rate of 29.4 per cent (State Council, 2011: 3). Published figures for the Ministry of Finance's budgeted aid expenditures show that disbursements grew at an average annual rate of 17.3 per cent during that period. The foreign aid role of China Eximbank has expanded considerably. For example, by March 2000, China Eximbank had financed 60 projects in 31 countries, with total concessional loan commitments of only $US470, or 3.9 billion yuan (Zhang, 2000). By the end of 2009, China Eximbank had committed concessional loan financing to 325 projects, worth 73.55 billion yuan, in 76 countries (State Council, 2011: 5).

In 2012 China's annual official aid expenditure was 16.7 billion yuan, or US$2.7. However, this figure includes only the grants, interest-free loans, and the interest subsidy for concessional loans. Including the value of China's concessional loans would make China's annual aid disbursement (gross) in 2012 around $6.3 billion.[2]

---

[1] These figures were not adjusted for inflation. They refer to commitments rather than disbursements (personal email communication, MOFCOM official, 2 May 2011).

[2] Unless otherwise stated, figures in this paragraph are the author's calculations based on Bräutigam (2011: 317).

19.5 **Differences from OECD-DAC**

The eight broad principles that have governed Chinese aid since 1964 emphasize equality, mutual benefit, local ownership, and respect for the sovereignty of the host government, with no political conditionality. Loans are to be non-conditional, interest-free, or low-interest, and easily rescheduled. Projects will use high-quality materials from China, have quick results, and boost self-reliance. Chinese experts will transfer their expertise 'fully' and live at the same standard as their local counterparts.

For donors from wealthy countries, the Organization of Economic Cooperation and Development (OECD) Development Assistance Committee (DAC) sets rules and norms for foreign aid. China's aid differs from these norms in four main respects. First, all OECD-DAC members are transparent about reporting aid figures, while China is far less so. Second, most OECD-DAC members impose economic and political conditions on at least some of their aid, to some countries; China famously does not. Third, while many OECD-DAC members still tie their food aid, technical assistance, and some procurement to their own firms and citizens, they are working to reduce tying levels; China is not. Finally, the content of aid differs, with China consistently emphasizing economic infra-structure and productive projects (agriculture, manufacturing) while the OECD-DAC members have regularly changed their emphasis from infrastructure, to basic needs, to policy reform, and governance.

■ **REFERENCES**

Bartke, Wolfgang. 1989. *The Economic Aid of the PR China to Developing and Socialist Countries* revised edn. Munich: K G Saur Verlag Gmbh & Co.

Bräutigam, Deborah. 1998. *Chinese Aid and African Development: Exporting Green Revolution.* New York: St. Martin's Press.

Bräutigam, Deborah. 2011. *The Dragon's Gift: The Real Story of China in Africa.* Oxford: Oxford University Press.

Kobayashi, Takaaki. 2008. Evolution of China's Aid Policy. Japan Bank for International Cooperation Working Paper No. 27, Tokyo, April.

MOFCOM. 2012. Department of Aid to Foreign Countries: Functions. <http://yws2.mofcom.gov.cn/> accessed 8 February 2012.

State Council. 2011. China's Foreign Aid. Information Office of the State Council, the People's Republic of China, Beijing, April 2011.

Zhang, Dingmin. 2000. Bank Finances Plant in Mali. *China Daily*, 22 March, 5.

Part IV
Trade and the Chinese Economy

20 The Chinese exchange rate and global imbalances

Menzie D. Chinn

20.1 Introduction

China's current account and exchange rate have loomed large in debates surrounding the development and impact of global imbalances. In Section 20.2, I examine the determinants of the Chinese current account and exchange rates, treating them as endogenous variables. In Section 20.3, I consider the exchange rate as at least partly exogenous, subject to the control of the policy authorities. Section 20.4 concludes.[1]

20.2 The current account and exchange rate as equilibrium outcomes

20.2.1 INTERPRETATIONS OF THE IMBALANCES

Global imbalances typically pertained to the development of large current account surpluses and deficits during the first decade of the 2000s. Although there are many conventional models of the current account, there is no single standard theory or hypothesis that convincingly explains the unprecedented scale and persistence of the imbalances observed over the past decade.

Prominent explanations include (1) trends in national saving and investment rates, (2) the global saving glut, and (3) distortions in financial markets. These explanations are not mutually exclusive. However, what is true is that China does figure in most of these explanations.

The saving–investment approach takes a perspective from the national saving identity which states that the current account is equal to the budget balance and the private

[1] Extremely helpful comments were received from Luis Catao, Steve Phillips, Eswar Prasad, and Shang-Jin Wei. Chinn acknowledges the financial support of the faculty research funds of the University of Wisconsin.

saving–investment gap. This is a tautology, unless one imposes some structure and causality. A systematic approach involves modelling the current account by explicitly focusing on the determinants of private investment and saving, and adding those variables to the budget balance. The 'global saving glut' explanation was first expounded by Bernanke (2005). This argument views excess saving from Asian emerging market countries, driven by rising savings and collapsing investment in the aftermath of the financial crisis, as the cause of the US current account deficit. The burgeoning surpluses of the oil exporters, ranging from the Persian Gulf countries to Russia, also play a role. From this perspective, the US external imbalance is a problem made abroad; the lack of well-developed and open financial markets encourages countries with excess savings to seek financial intermediation in well-developed financial systems such as the USA. This view implies that a solution may only arise in the longer term, as better developed financial systems mitigate this excess savings problem.

The Caballero–Farhi–Gourinchas (2008) hypothesis recasts the saving glut problem as one that asserts that countries with more developed financial markets should have weaker current accounts. As the authors state, 'capital flows from China, with its underdeveloped capital markets, to the United States, which has a comparative advantage in producing safe financial assets'.[2] Obstfeld and Rogoff (2010) are sceptical that such factors are important.

20.2.2 EMPIRICAL ASSESSMENTS

Chinn et al. (2014) examine a sample of twenty-three industrial and eighty-six developing countries over the four decades 1970–2008, with the aim of explaining current account balances. They find the effect of financial development, its interactions with legal development and capital account openness, are supportive of the Caballero et al. interpretation of global imbalances with statistically significant coefficients for the sub-sample of emerging markets; those with better developed financial markets and legal institutions or open capital accounts tend to have weaker current account balances, or experience the least tendency for capital to flow out.

Nonetheless, emerging market economies appear to have run unusually large surpluses in the 2001–05 period, consistent with the idea that they were fixated on minimizing financing vulnerabilities and accumulating reserves following the Asian crisis. Such behaviour is not evident for emerging markets as a group in 2006–08, with the exception of China, which does seem to run significantly larger surpluses than is explainable using observed variables.

---

[2] Caballero et al. (2008) model the saving glut explanation as a shortage of assets in the developing world. Mendoza et al. (2009) model financial development as the increase in the degree of enforcement of financial contracts.

The cross-country perspective highlights the fact that China's recent behaviour is anomalous. The unique aspect of Chinese behaviour extends to both saving and investment. While the level of China's national investment has been fairly high in recent years, that of national saving has been even higher. Hence, understanding the impact of financial globalization on China requires an examination of the growth imbalances that have contributed to China's unique saving behaviour. While household saving was the main contributor to the aggregate saving before 2000 (see Chamon and Prasad, 2010), both household and corporate saving have been major contributors since then (Ma and Yi, 2010; Prasad, 2011), although household behaviour remains more anomalous (Bayoumi et al., 2011). Over the last few years, household saving has again become the largest contributor. However, it is also noteworthy that during the same period, government saving has been rising rapidly after having played a minor role.[3]

More recent assessments have sought to augment these current account regressions with new variables, such as proxy measures for social protection—which has been viewed as particularly important in the Chinese context—as well as foreign exchange intervention (see IMF, 2012, Gagnon, 2012). These variables explain an increased proportion of the surge in the Chinese current account during the 2000s.

20.2.3 THE EXCHANGE RATE

The determinants of the current account and the real exchange rate should in principle be the same. Indeed, as noted in Cheung et al. (2010), budget balances or government spending, net foreign assets, and measures of income per capita often make it into empirical models of the RMB.

The most prominent assessments of the Chinese real exchange rate have focused on the price approach, linking in particular the real exchange rate to per capita income. This relationship—the Penn effect—is the robust empirical positive association between national price levels and real per capita incomes across countries documented by a series of studies.[4] Typically, this relationship has been rationalized by the Balassa (1964) and Samuelson (1964) models, which incorporate internal and external balance. In the short- to medium-term, however, these conditions are not guaranteed. Thus, this estimated exchange rate measure is properly interpreted as a long-run measure and is ill-suited (on its own) to analysing short-run phenomena.

---

[3] See Ma and Yi (2010). Du and Wei (2010) and Wei and Zhang (2011) identify the sex ratio as a specific demographic factor that drives Chinese saving behaviour.

[4] Kravis et al. (1978); Summers and Heston (1991).

Cheung et al. (2010) find the estimated degree of RMB undervaluation in 2006 is quantitatively large at the 50 per cent plus level.[5] Nonetheless, there is a high level of (sampling) uncertainty surrounding the point estimate, and the estimated misalignment is not statistically significant at conventional levels. Moreover, using the post-2005 International Comparison Program benchmark data, they find a much smaller degree of misalignment, down in single digits.

20.3 The exchange rate as a policy instrument

A common interpretation holds that the exchange rate is managed by the Chinese authorities in a manner that affects the trade balance, either for mercantilist reasons, or as a means of self-insurance. In the former perspective, the developing countries of East Asia have followed an export-led development strategy based upon currency undervaluation. The second interpretation attributes the motivation for large-scale reserve accumulation to the desire for self-insurance. Foreign exchange reserves can reduce the probability of an output drop induced by capital flight or sudden stop. This self-insurance motivation rose substantially in the wake of the East Asian crises (Aizenman and Marion 2003; Aizenman and Lee, 2007).

Once one takes the exchange rate as a quasi-exogenous variable, then one can ask how the trade balance, roughly equal to the current account, behaves in response to exchange rate changes in a partial equilibrium context. Several studies have examined Chinese trade flows over the period ranging from the mid-1990s to the mid-2000s (Garcia-Herrero and Koivu, 2007; Marquez and Schindler, 2007; Aziz and Li, 2008). Generally, some amount of disaggregation is necessary to obtain sensible results (for instance, into ordinary and processing trade flows). While it is possible to explain exports, imports often exhibit unexpected signs with respect to price or income.

The difficulty in interpreting the results regarding price elasticity arises partly because of the role of China in the integrated production chain. Only a portion of the total value of exports constitutes Chinese value added; the rest is accounted for by imported components. One can account for the impact of vertical specialization directly by creating value-added trade-weighted real exchange rates (Bems and Johnson, 2012).

Using conventional price measures, Cheung et al. (2012) find that for exports, while there is some diversity of responses to income and exchange rate variables, Chinese trade flow behaviour largely accords with conventional wisdom: higher rest of world income results in higher Chinese exports, while a stronger RMB results in lower exports. However, the income elasticity is imprecisely estimated, varying widely depending upon the

---

[5] These results are robust to the inclusion of additional regressors (capital controls, institutional development).

inclusion or exclusion of a linear time trend. In addition, the price elasticity varies widely between goods exported from SOEs, foreign invested firms, and private firms. The latter appear to behave in a more price-sensitive fashion than the other firm types. As their share of exports continues to rise, one should expect the overall price elasticity to increase, holding all else constant. For Chinese real exports, they find that the income elasticity is approximately six, while the exchange rate elasticity is near unity—after accounting for entry into the WTO.

In line with previous studies, Cheung et al. (2012) do not always obtain sensible import estimates; manufactured imports, which constitute about 70 per cent of Chinese imports, exhibit a positive (rather than negative) price elasticity, except when relative productivity is included. Productivity enters either because it proxies for supply, or because the CPI-deflated real exchange rate variable is a poor proxy for the relevant real exchange rate (either the producer price index (PPI) deflated or unit labour cost deflated).

20.4 **Concluding thoughts**

The global imbalances of the 2000s have been associated with oil exporting nations and China. Two, not necessarily exclusive, ways of looking at the role of China is to focus on saving and investment behaviour, or on the exchange rate. The substantial reduction of the Chinese current account surplus in 2011–12 in the absence of substantially faster currency appreciation suggests that exchange rates are in and of themselves only one important factor. However, that observation does not imply that the exchange rate is unimportant as a determinant of the current account.

■ REFERENCES

Aizenman, Joshua and Jaewoo Lee. 2007. International reserves: precautionary versus mercantilist views, theory and evidence. *Open Economies Review* 18(2), 191–214.

Aizenman, Joseph and Nancy P. Marion. 2003.'The high demand for international reserves in the Far East: What's going on? *Journal of the Japanese and International Economies* 17(3), 370–400.

Aziz, Jahangir and Xiangming Li. 2008. China's changing trade elasticities. *China and the World Economy* 16(3), 1–21.

Balassa, Bela. 1964. The purchasing power parity doctrine: a reappraisal. *JPE* 72(6), 584–96.

Bayoumi, Tamim, Hui Tong, and Shang-Jin Wei. 2011. The Chinese corporate savings puzzle: a firm-level cross-country perspective. In *Capitalizing China*, edited by Joseph P. H. Fan and Randall Morck. University of Chicago Press.

Bems, Rudolfs, and Robert C. Johnson. 2012. Value-Added Exchange Rates. *NBER Working Paper* No.18498.

Bernanke, Benjamin. 2005. The Global Saving Glut and the U.S. Current Account. Remarks at the Sandridge Lecture, Richmond, VA, 10 March.

Caballero, Ricardo, Emmanuel Farhi, and Pierre-Olivier Gourinchas. 2008. An equilibrium model of 'global imbalances' and low interest rates. *American Economic Review* 98(1), 358–93.

Chamon, Marcos and Eswar Prasad. 2010. Why are saving rates of urban households in China rising. *American Economic Journal: Macroeconomics* 2(1), 93–130.

Cheung, Yin-Wong, Menzie Chinn, and Eiji Fujii. 2010. China's current account and exchange rate. *China's Growing Role in World Trade*, edited by Rob Feenstra and Shang-Jin Wei, 231–71. University of Chicago Press for NBER.

Cheung, Yin-Wong, Menzie Chinn, and XingWang Qian. 2012. Are Chinese trade flows different? *Journal of International Money and Finance* 31(8), 2127–46.

Chinn, Menzie D., Barry Eichengreen, and Hiro Ito. 2014. A forensic analysis of global imbalances. *Oxford Economic Papers* 66(2), 465–90.

Du, Qingyuan and Shang-jin Wei. 2010. A Sexually Unbalanced Model of Current Account Imbalances. NBER Working Paper No. 16000.

Gagnon, Joseph. 2012,'Global Imbalances and Foreign Asset Expansion by Developing Economy Central Banks. Working Paper No. 12–15. Washington, DC: Peterson Institute for International Economics, March.

Garcia-Herrero, Alicia and Tuuli Koivu., 2007. Can the Chinese Trade Surplus Be Reduced through Exchange Rate Policy? BOFIT Discussion Papers No. 2007–2006. Helsinki: Bank of Finland, March.

IMF. 2012. External Balance Assessment (EBA): Technical Background of the Pilot Methodology. Mimeo. Washington, DC: IMF, August.

Kravis, Irving B., Alan Heston, and Robert Summers. 1978. *International Comparisons of Real Product and Purchasing Power*. Baltimore MD: The Johns Hopkins University Press.

Ma, Guonan and Wang Yi. 2010. China's High Saving Rate: Myth and Reality. BIS Working Paper No. 312, June.

Marquez, Jaime and John W. Schindler. 2007. Exchange-rate effects on China's trade. *Research in Economics* 15(5), 837–53.

Mendoza, Enrique G., Vincenzo Quadrini, and Jose-Victor Ríos-Rull. 2009. Financial integration, financial deepness and global imbalances. *Journal of Political Economics* 117(3), 317–416.

Obstfeld, Maurice and Kenneth Rogoff. 2010. Global imbalances and the financial crisis: products of common causes. In *Asia and the Global Financial Crisis*, edied by Reuven Glick and Mark M. Spiegel. SF: Federal Reserve Bank of San Francisco.

Prasad, Eswar. 2011. Rebalancing growth in Asia. *International Finance* 14(1), 27–66.

Samuelson, Paul. 1964. Theoretical notes on trade problems. *Review of Economics and Statistics* 46, 145–154.

Summers, Robert and Alan Heston. 1991. The Penn World Table (Mark5): an expanded set of international comparisons. *Quarterly Journal of Economics* 106(2), 327–68.

Wei, Shang-jin and Xiaobo Zhang. 2011. The competitive saving motive: evidence from rising sex ratios and savings rates in China. *Journal of Political Economics* 119(3), 511–64.

21 Using tax-based instruments for innovative China's trade rebalancing

John Whalley and Jing Wang

The large Chinese trade imbalance has been discussed extensively in recent years, as has rebalancing in general at G20 summits and specifically at the G20 meeting in Pittsburgh in September 2009 as part of the Framework for Strong, Sustainable, and Balanced Growth (FSSBG).[1] Rebalancing refers to the reduction of large aggregate imbalances, covering trade (and current account) imbalances, public sector deficits, and high savings rates in some countries and low savings rates in others.

Whalley and Wang (2011) have evaluated the joint impacts of exchange rate appreciation on trade flows and country surpluses using a general equilibrium model with both trade structure and monetary structure. Their simulation results suggested that the impacts of RMB appreciation on the surplus are proportionally larger than on imports or exports, and China's trade surplus would fall by 12.7 per cent, 25.8 per cent, and 53.7 per cent with appreciations of RMB of 5 per cent, 10 per cent, and 20 per cent respectively. Increasing China's money stock has similar effects on trade surplus and trade flows as RMB appreciation. But as far as external sector imbalances are concerned, concrete proposals for policy changes outside of exchange rate adjustments to address rebalancing are few.

The literature has thus centred in the main on exchange rate adjustment which has generated pressure on China for exchange rate appreciation. China has therefore been on the defence on these issues. There is little chance that the Chinese government will accept a large currency appreciation at the present time, given that the RMB had appreciated cumulatively by 31.5 per cent against the US dollar between July 2005 and February 2012. During this process of RMB appreciation, China's trade surplus has expanded even more quickly from US$102 billion in 2005 to US$298 billion in 2008, and shrank to US$155 billion in 2011.[2] Another concern of the government is the shock to the domestic economy

[1] We are grateful to the Ontario Research Fund for financial support.

[2] Source: 2009–2011 National Economic and Social Development Statistical Communique of PRC, National Bureau of Statistics of China.

from exchange rate fluctuations. Mao and Whalley (2011) argue that a 10 per cent appreciation in the real RMB exchange rate would cause a net employment decline in Chinese manufacturing industries of between 4.1 per cent and 5.3 per cent.

Here we suggest that innovative tax-based initiatives could be pursued by China which might aid rebalancing and also have the effect of alleviating exchange rate pressures. Since China introduced its value added tax in 1994, like most countries around the world, it has operated as a tax on imports with exports remaining tax free. This implies a destination basis for the tax, as opposed to an origin basis, a system which has imports tax free but exports taxed. The proposal made here is that if China were to switch its value added tax (VAT) regime from the current destination basis (DB) to an origin basis (OB), the effect would be both to significantly reduce China's trade imbalance and also increase China's and world welfare.

This effect reflects the feature that, under a VAT destination basis, imports are taxed while input taxes are rebated (as currently), while under an origin basis, imports enter tax free but exports receive no tax rebate. Previous academic research on VAT has stressed the neutrality of impacts on trade for movements between these two bases, but for this to occur trade must be balanced.[3] In the presence of a significant Chinese trade surplus, using an equal yield origin basis expands the tax base, allows tax rates to be lowered, generates efficiency gains, and can also reduce the trade surplus and achieve some degree of rebalancing.

China is unique in having two separate components of their VAT; one applying to domestic transactions (or domestic VAT) and one applying to international trade transactions (import VAT and export refunds). VAT, introduced in 1994, is one of the most important Chinese taxes in revenue terms. VAT revenues increased quickly after its 1994 introduction, and VAT has been the largest tax revenue source in China in recent years.

Chinese domestic VAT revenues increased from 233.9 billion RMB in 1994 to 24,266.6 billion RMB in 2011, and import VAT revenues increased from 32.3 billion RMB in 1994 to 1,356.0 billion RMB in 2011, or 42-fold.[4] In 2011, Chinese domestic VAT and import VAT contributed 27 per cent and 15 per cent to national tax revenues respectively. These two parts of the VAT thus provided nearly 42 per cent of national government revenues.

China's VAT is administered by the State Administration of Taxation (the import VAT is collected by customs on its behalf), and revenues are shared between the central government (75 per cent) and local governments (25 per cent). According to the Provisional Regulation of the People's Republic of China (PRC) on VAT, value added tax, as in other

---

[3] See Krauss and Johnson (1974), Whalley (1979), Grossman (1980), Lockwood et al. (1994), and Genser (1998).

[4] Data Source: 1994–1998 Tax Revenue Statistics, State Administration of Taxation, China. <http://www.chinatax.gov.cn/n8136506/n8136593/n8137633/n8138817/8224324.html>. 'Structural Analysis on 2011 Tax Revenue Growth'. Ministry of Finance, People's Republic of China, <http://szs.mof.gov.cn/zhengwuxinxi/gongzuodongtai/201202/t20120214_628,012.html>.

countries, is to be paid by enterprises or individuals who sell merchandise, provide processing, repair, or assembling services, or import goods into the PRC. The tax is thus based on the added value derived from production, the selling of merchandise, and providing industrial repair or assembly services. For different taxable goods and services, different tax rates (including zero rates) apply. VAT is the major source of revenue for all government levels in China, and particularly the central government.

China's VAT began on an experimental basis in the 1980s in selected provinces, when China began to implement VAT on twenty-four specified taxable items. In 1994, with the goal of building up the socialist market economy, the wider tax system was changed, and a State Council decree enacting a broader VAT on 'The Provisional Regulation of the People's Republic of China on Value Added Tax' came into effect. In 2004, China made further changes to the VAT system. A scheme of 'increment deduction', which shifts the previous production-based VAT regime to a consumption-based VAT, allowing enterprises to deduct the full amount of the input tax, was introduced for eight industries. It was then extended to twenty-six industrial cities in the Central Chinese provinces in 2007. China implemented further VAT changes nationwide in 2009, as part of a national move from a production-based VAT to one which is consumption-based. With the exception of a few industries, all industries in China are now able to offset the full amount of input VAT paid on newly purchased machinery and equipment against VAT collected when they sell their products.

But returning to rebalancing and the external sector, China's VAT effectively operates on a destination basis, so China imposes not only tariffs but also import-related VAT on imported goods as part of its general trade regime. An import-related consumption tax is also levied on certain goods. For exports, China applies a zero-rated VAT with the exception of certain restricted or prohibited goods and technologies. Effectively, there is no VAT on exports, and VAT already paid is refunded as an export tax rebate.

The Chinese government began to implement export tax rebates in April 1985, using a 'full refund' principle established in 1988. After further tax reform in 1994, the new VAT was introduced and export goods were to receive a full export rebate reflecting the tax paid on inputs. To implement the initial export tax rebates, the central government earmarked funds for the purpose, but the obligation turned out to be too great to fulfil. Consequently, in 1995 and 1996 the government twice reduced the export tax rebate rate. Since then, China has operated a separate partial export rebate system, disconnected from domestic VAT, which uses separate export rebate rates which change often (and by product) according to the economic situation. But even though VAT in China is administered as two separate elements, the net joint effect is to operate a destination-based tax as discussed above, creating the opportunity to move to an effective origin-based tax by eliminating the export rebate component of the tax and removing taxes on imports.

Li and Whalley (2012a) analyse the potential impacts of the Chinese VAT regime changing from a destination basis to an origin basis on China's trade surplus using a standard general equilibrium model. With the trade surplus being endogenously determined in their model, they conduct a simulation of a Chinese VAT basis switch under two scenarios: an equal yield format with endogenous tax rates for the new regime, and a fixed tax rate format. Their results suggest that the effect of China's VAT regime switching would be both to significantly reduce China's trade imbalance by over 40 per cent and also increase China's and the world's welfare.

Wider significance of this kind of analysis may lead to joint global tax-based approaches to rebalancing. China and Germany (and the EU more broadly) have already instituted destination-based VAT, while the USA has no federal broadly based indirect tax. If Germany, with a large trade surplus like China, switched to an origin-based VAT, similar effects of reducing the global trade imbalance and increasing its own and the world's welfare would follow. Were the USA to adopt a destination-based VAT, given their trade deficit, then again a similar accumulation of effects could follow. Li and Whalley (2012b) analyse the impact on imbalances of joint VAT regime changes by involving the USA adopting destination-based VAT while China and Germany adopt origin-based VAT. Their simulation results show that the net effect of the three largest trading partners jointly using tax-based rebalancing could be substantial with imbalances falling by between 7.3 per cent and 15.9 per cent depending on different US VAT rates.

Trade rebalancing has become a major focus of discussion in the G20, and is now taken as a global objective after the 2008 financial crisis. Here we suggest that the G20 summit discussions may consider alternative instruments, especially indirect tax instruments such as VAT, instead of focusing on members adjusting exchange rates. International policy cooperation on tax basis arrangements may be more politically feasible than exchange rate adjustments.

Further, China would possibly be more willing to adopt tax based initiatives than currency revaluation. As the advantages of VAT are widely acknowledged in both developed and developing countries (Kononova and Whalley, 2009), the Chinese government laid an emphasis on using VAT to reform its tax system and tax policies have been actively carried out to improve China's economic restructuring. After implementing many significant measures in the manufacturing sector, China extended VAT to the service sector by issuing Pilot Proposals for the Change from Business Tax to Value-Added Tax in November 2011. Its pilot project launched in Shanghai in 2012, used VAT instead of business tax levied on transportation, R&D, cultural and creative industries, logistics, assurance service, and consulting.

Thus, we suggest that for China, with a large trade surplus, switching their VAT basis from a destination to an origin base may be a significant accompanying measure yielding substantial reductions in China's trade imbalance of over 40 per cent and also welfare gains both for China and the world. It might be a positive move for China to consider, and it may also weaken international pressure on the RMB.

■ REFERENCES

Genser B. 1998. A generalized equivalence property of mixed international VAT regimes. *Journal of Economics* 98(2), 253–62.

Grossman G. M. 1980. Border tax adjustments: do they distort trade? *Journal of International Economics* 10(1), 117–28.

Kononova V. and J. Whalley. 2009. Recent Russian Debate on Moving from VAT to Sales Taxes and Its Global Implications. NBER Working Paper No. 15615.

Krauss, M. B. and H. G. Johnson. 1974. *General Equilibrium Analysis*. Sydney: Allen & Unwin.

Li, C. and J. Whalley. 2012a. Rebalancing and the Chinese VAT: Some Numerical Simulation Results. *China Economic Review* 23(2), 316–24.

Li, C. and J. Whalley. 2012b. Indirect Tax Initiatives and Global Rebalancing. NBER Working Paper No.17919.

Lockwood B., D. Meza, and G. D. Myles. 1994. When Are origin and destination regimes equivalent? *International Tax and Public Finance* 2(1), 5–24.

Mao R. and J. Whalley. 2011. Ownership Characteristics, Real Exchange Rate Movements and Labor Market Adjustment in China. NBER Working Paper No. 17565.

Whalley J. 1979. Uniform domestic tax rates, trade distortions and economic integration. *Journal of Public Economics* 11(2), 213–21.

Whalley, J. and L. Wang. 2011. The impact of renminbi appreciation on trade flows and reserve accumulation in a monetary trade model. *Economic Modelling* 28(1–2), 614–21.

22 China's evolving trade composition

Kym Anderson

China is a densely populated country, with more than three times the people per square mile than the rest of the world.[1] For that reason standard trade theory suggests China would begin to industrialize, and to become a net importer of primary products and a net exporter of unskilled labour-intensive manufactures, at an early stage of economic development when wages are still low (Krueger, 1977; Leamer, 1987). Then over time, as industrial and human capital per worker grew more rapidly there than in the rest of the world, China's exports would be expected to move towards more capital-intensive manufactured parts, finished goods, and perhaps services. Unless productivity in primary sectors grew much faster in China than elsewhere, the country would lose competitiveness in agricultural and mineral products.

Those expectations are largely supported by China's trade data, with one important exception. Table 22.1(a) reveals that, even before the economy gradually opened up to trade, the share of manufactures in China's merchandise exports grew from 15 per cent in the first third of the twentieth century to 30 per cent by the mid-1950s and nearly 50 per cent by the late 1970s. But by 1987 that share was two-thirds, and it reached 93 per cent by 2011. Hence the share of primary products in China's exports has fallen over that period from 85 per cent to just 7 per cent.

The share contributed by the labour-intensive textiles and clothing sub-sector over the past 100 years has traced an inverted-U shape, beginning at 6 per cent, gradually rising to 36 per cent in 1987, but then falling rapidly since then to 6 per cent again by 2011. That peak is very similar to the 35 per cent experienced by Korea in the 1970s and by Japan in the 1920s to 1950s (Anderson and Park, 1989). However, the peak was maintained for a much shorter time in China than in those earlier industrializing countries, thanks to the fragmentation of industrial production processes in recent years that has led to very rapid growth in other intra-industry trade.

Within the primary goods sector, the share of fuel and minerals in China's total exports has fallen from one-third to one-twenty-fifth over the past century, and that of farm

[1] The author is grateful for funding from the Australian Research Council.

Table 22.1 Sectoral shares of merchandise exports and 'revealed' comparative advantage indexes,[a] China, 1910–2011

(a) Sectoral shares of merchandise exports (per cent)

	Exports as % of GDP	Primary products				Manufactured products	
		Agriculture and food[b]		Fuels and minerals[b]		Textiles and clothing	Other manufactures
1910–29	na	51		34		6	9
1955–57	6	55		15		14	16
1965–69	4	51	(21)	5		20	24
1975–77	5	38	(13)	16		21	25
1984–86	12	22	(6)	24		29	25
1987	16	20	(6)	14		36	30
1990	17	16	(1)	13	(7)	27	44
2000	23	7	(–2)	5	(–10)	21	67
2005	37	4	(–3)	4	(–15)	7	85
2011	30	3	(–5)	4	(–20)	6	87

(b) 'Revealed' comparative advantage indexes[a]

	Agriculture and food	Fuels and minerals	Textiles and clothing	Other manufactures
1965–69	2.1	0.3	3.3	0.4
1975–77	2.2	0.7	3.9	0.5
1984–86	1.4	1.1	5.1	0.5
1987	1.3	0.7	6.5	0.5
1990	1.3	0.7	3.2	0.7
2000	0.7	0.3	2.8	1.0
2005	0.5	0.2	3.2	1.3
2011	0.4	0.1	3.3	1.4

[a] Sectoral share of total merchandise exports in China relative to that sector's share for the world.
[b] Sectoral exports net of imports, as a share of total merchandise exports are given in parentheses.
Source: Updated from Anderson (1990: table 3.7) using the World Bank's *World Development Indicators* and the World Trade Organization's *International Trade Statistics*.

products has fallen from a little over one-half to one-thirtieth (Table 22.1(a)). Those shares have tended to decline in the rest of the world too, but not as much as in China. As a consequence, China's 'revealed' comparative advantage indexes for both farming and mining products have declined from above to far below one (Table 22.1(b)). Notice also from the second part of Table 22.1 that China's index of 'revealed' comparative advantage in textiles and clothing has halved since 1987 while that for other manufactures has almost trebled.

The important exceptional feature of China's commodity trade is exposed by data on imports of primary goods. While the share of fuel and minerals in China's total merchandise imports has grown from 6 per cent to 24 per cent over the two decades to 2011, the share of farm products in total imports has *declined* rather than grown. If one looks at exports net of imports as a share of total exports, as shown in parentheses in Table 22.1(a), the two sub-sectors both trend downwards and switch from positive to negative numbers at the turn of the century. However, the extent of that trend is very modest in the case of farm products. This is also revealed in China's trade specialization index, defined as net exports as a ratio of exports plus imports for each sub-sector (and hence begin confined between +1 and –1): for mining products that fell from +0.6 in 1980–84 to –0.5 by 2000–04, while for farm products the fall over that period was only from +0.09 to –0.16 (Sandri et al., 2006). Indeed China's overall agricultural self-sufficiency was never more than 1 point away from 100 per cent in each of the decades of the 1960s, 1970s, 1980s, and 1990s, and was still 98 per cent in 2000–04 (Anderson, 2009: table 4).

Why has China's trade in farm products undergone so little transformation? There are two major explanations. One is that China has made very substantial investments in agricultural research. New data compiled by Pardey et al. (2012) show China's share of global public agricultural R&D investment rising from 5 per cent in the 1960s and 1970s to almost 10 per cent in the 1990s and to 19 per cent by 2008. As a consequence, China's cereal yields per hectare have grown at 2.9 per cent per annum during 1961–2010, compared with 1.6 per cent for the rest of the world. Productivity growth has been particularly rapid in the two decades since 1990: farm land productivity grew at 4.0 per cent per annum in China but at an average of only 1.6 per cent elsewhere, and the farm labour productivity growth difference has been even more startling: 3.9 per cent in China and just 0.8 per cent in the rest of the world.

The other key contributor to China's capacity to maintain agricultural self-sufficiency for so long despite rapid industrialization has to do with changes in governmental distortions to incentives since the country's reforms began at the end of the 1970s. Agricultural production and exports were in effect taxed very heavily prior to the 1980s while domestic consumers of farm products were subsidized, but during the 1980s and early 1990s those distortions were gradually phased out. The farm policies took numerous forms but included export restrictions and requirements to deliver part of the crop to the government at below-market prices. Agriculture was also discouraged indirectly by manufacturing protection policies and an overvalued exchange rate. When taken together, it meant the price of farm relative to non-farm tradeable products within China was only half what it was at the country's border in the 1980s, that is, the relative rate of assistance to agriculture was around –0.5. Indeed it had been as low as –0.6 in the early 1980s, but it gradually approached zero between the late 1980s to the late 1990s (Figure 22.1). The consumer subsidy equivalent on farm products also gradually diminished over that period (the negative of the consumer tax equivalent shown in Figure 22.1). Those changes in incentives

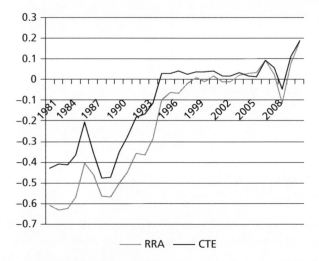

Figure 22.1. Relative Rate of Assistance (RRA) to agriculture and consumer tax equivalent on farm products, China, 1981–2010

[a] The RRA is defined as $[(100 + NRAag^t)/(100 + NRAnonag^t)-1]$, where $NRAag^t$ and $NRAnonag^t$, respectively, are the NRAs for the tradeable segments of the agricultural and non-agricultural sectors.

Source: Anderson and Nelgen (2013).

would have had a major impact in terms of encouraging production and discouraging domestic consumption of farm products during the 1980s and 1990s, thus contributing to the country's agricultural self-sufficiency.

The tendency for a country to gradually change from effectively taxing to subsidizing farmers relative to manufacturers in the course of its economic development has been observed in numerous relatively densely populated countries as they industrialize, including in Northeast Asia (Anderson et al., 1986)—and for reasons that can be explained using modern political economy theory (Anderson et al., 2013). A critical question is: will China also succumb to that political pressure? The answer matters not only for China but also for the rest of the world, given that China accounts for about one-fifth of global food production and consumption.

The Relative Rate of Assistance (RRA) evidence presented in Figure 22.2 suggests China is indeed on such a trajectory. The numerator of the RRA, the agricultural nominal rate of assistance, has risen for China from –3 to 21 per cent between 1999 and 2010 (Anderson and Nelgen, 2013, based on PSE estimates by OECD 2012). This has been sufficient for China to maintain self-sufficiency over the past decade in all key food products except soybean (whose tariff is bound in the WTO at 3 per cent and which mostly goes into livestock feed and so helps maintain apparent self-sufficiency in meat and milk). Some of this support has come in the form of domestic farm subsidies, the rest in import restrictions. Ample scope for raising such support remains within China's

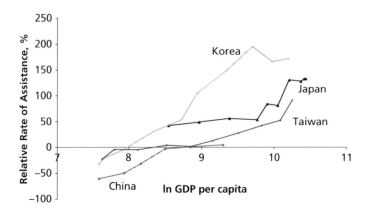

Figure 22.2. Relative Rate of Assistance to agriculture (per cent) and log of real GDP per capita, China (1981–2010) and Northeast Asian economies (1955–2004)

Source: Updated from Anderson (2009), using new estimates from Anderson and Nelgen (2013).

WTO commitments, so if there is to be any restraint to continuing on this economically wasteful path, it will have to come from domestic leadership. Thankfully the emergence of new, lower-cost social protection mechanisms involving conditional cash e-transfers are becoming available, but it remains to be seen whether China's leaders make use of them to re-instrument their support for rural communities away from traditional market-distorting measures.

■ REFERENCES

Anderson, K. 1990. *Changing Comparative Advantages in China: Effects on Food, Feed and Fibre Markets*, Paris: OECD (in English and French; published also in Chinese by Economic Science Press for China's State Planning Commission, 1992).

Anderson, K. 2009. Distorted agricultural incentives and economic development: Asia's experience. *The World Economy* 32(3), 351–84.

Anderson, K. and S. Nelgen. 2013. *Updated National and Global Estimates of Distortions to Agricultural Incentives, 1955 to 2011*, World Bank, Washington DC, updated in June at <http://www.worldbank.org/agdistortions>.

Anderson, K. and Y. I. Park. 1989. China and the international relocation of world textile and clothing activity. *Weltwirtschaftliches Archiv* 125(1), 129–48.

Anderson, K., Y. Hayami and others. 1986. *The Political Economy of Agricultural Protection: East Asia in International Perspective*. Boston, London and Sydney: Allen and Unwin (and Tianjin: People's Publishing House, expanded Chinese edition translated by F. Cai, 1996).

Anderson, K., G. Rausser, and J. Swinnen. 2013. Political economy of public policies: insights from distortions to agricultural and food markets. *Journal of Economic Literature* 51(2), 423–77.

Krueger, A. O. 1977. *Growth, Distortions and Patterns of Trade Among Many Countries*. Princeton, NJ: International Finance Section.

Leamer, E. E. 1987. Paths of development in the three-factor, n-good general equilibrium model. *Journal of Political Economy* 95(5), 961–99.

Pardey, P. G., J. M. Alston, and C. Chan-Kang. 2012. Agricultural Production, Productivity and R&D over the Past Half Century: An Emerging New World Order. Staff Paper P12–17, Department of Applied Economics, University of Minnesota, St. Paul MN, September.

Sandri, D., E. Valenzuela, and K. Anderson. 2006. Compendium of National Economic and Trade Indicators by Region, 1960 to 2004. Agricultural Distortions Working Paper 01, World Bank, Washington DC, October. <http://www.worldbank.org/agdistortions>.

23 Trade policy reform and trade volume

Bin Xu

China started reforming its foreign trade system in 1978. Before 1978, China had a foreign trade regime modelled after the Soviet Union in the 1950s, which was an extreme form of import substitution. In that regime, the central government, through the Ministry of Foreign Trade (later changed to the Ministry of Foreign Economic Relations and Trade, or MOFERT), monopolized China's foreign trade. The Ministry exercised control of foreign trade through a handful of foreign trade corporations that specialized in trade in defined product categories. The foreign trade corporations imported and exported according to the national economic plan. The purpose of imports was primarily to overcome bottlenecks due to limited domestic production capability. Exports were perceived mainly, if not exclusively, as a means of financing imports (Lardy, 1992).

In 1978, Deng Xiaoping launched China's economic reform and opening-up. Reform of the foreign trade system became one of the priorities. To achieve the goal of 'four modernizations', China needed foreign exchange for the importation of machinery and technology, which required exports to grow more rapidly. In 1978, China only exported US$9.8 billion, ranked as the world's thirty-second exporting country.

The first step in the reform was to decentralize foreign trading authority. In 1979 a dozen national foreign trade corporations handled all foreign trade transactions in China. By the mid-1980s the MOFERT had approved the creation of 800 separate import and export corporations, each authorized to engage in international trade transactions within specified product ranges. Towards the end of the 1980s, the number of trading companies had increased to more than 5,000 (Lardy, 1992).

One important feature of China's trade reform in the 1980s was the phasing out of direct quantitative decisions and the increasing use of conventional trade policies such as tariffs and non-tariff barriers. In the pre-reform era, tariffs served mainly as a source of government revenue. Beginning in 1980, changes in tariff rates became more frequent and of greater importance in influencing the volume and commodity composition of both exports and imports (Lardy, 1992). The government also instituted a system of import and export licences to control the volume and commodity composition of trade. In 1985, China established a system of indirect tax rebates for exports.

Another important dimension of China's trade reform in the 1980s was the relaxation of exchange control. Before reform, all foreign exchange from exporting had to be turned over to the state through the Bank of China, and all imports were fulfilled according to the import plan with the foreign exchange allocated to it by the Bank of China. Starting from the early 1980s, exporters were allowed to retain a share of their foreign exchange earnings (Shan, 1989).

In the 1980s, China established economic zones that were largely free from import and export restrictions, which include the four special economic zones on the southeast coast and the fourteen coastal cities designated as open cities. In 1984, the state approved two schemes designed to facilitate exports based on processing or assembly activity, which were known as 'processing with supplied materials' and 'processing with imported materials' (World Bank, 1994). Processing exports grew rapidly, accounting for 40.9 per cent of China's total exports in 1990 (Table 23.1).

China continued its trade reform in the 1990s. During this period, China made great progress in reducing the coverage of non-tariff barriers and lowering tariffs. The number of products subject to import quotas and licences fell from 1,247 in 1992 to 261 in 1999. The import coverage of all non-tariff barriers fell from 32.5 per cent in 1996 to 21.6 per cent in 2001. China's average applied most-favoured-nation (MFN) tariff rate was cut from around 50 per cent in the early 1980s to 15.6 per cent in 2001. Another important feature was the substantial reduction in the dispersion of tariff rates, with the standard deviation falling from 32.1 per cent in 1992 to 10 per cent in 2001 (Ianchovichina and Martin, 2004).

In the 1990s, China greatly increased its openness to foreign direct investment (FDI). FDI was attracted by economic zones established in high technology, free-trade zones, and bonded areas. These zones particularly attracted FDI engaged in processing trade. As Table 23.1 shows, the share of exports by foreign invested enterprises (FIEs) in total

Table 23.1 China's trade volume

	Exports (billion $)	Imports (billion $)	Share of processing exports (%)	Share of exports by FIEs (%)	Exports-GDP ratio (%)	Share in world exports (%)	Rank in world exports
1980	18.1	20.0	5.1	0.0	6.0	0.9	26
1985	27.4	42.3	12.1	1.1	9.0	1.4	17
1990	62.1	53.3	40.9	12.6	16.0	1.8	15
1995	148.8	132.1	49.5	31.5	20.5	2.9	11
2000	249.2	225.1	55.2	47.9	20.8	3.9	7
2005	762.0	660.0	54.7	58.3	33.9	7.3	3
2010	1577.9	1394.8	46.9	54.6	26.7	10.4	1

Source: China Trade and External Economic Statistical Yearbook 2011.

exports increased from 12.6 per cent in 1990 to 47.9 per cent in 2000, and the share of processing exports in total exports increased from 40.9 per cent in 1990 to 55.2 per cent in 2000.

China reformed its foreign exchange rate to promote exports. In the pre-reform era China had fixed the exchange rate at an overvalued level which subsidized imports and hurt exports. In 1981, the government instituted a dual exchange rate system in which an internal settlement rate was set at RMB 2.8 to US$1 as compared to the official exchange rate of RMB 1.5. Since then, the official exchange rate had devalued towards the internal settlement rate, and the dual-rate system was abandoned in 1985 as the two rates merged (Shan, 1989). In 1986, China introduced a formal secondary market for foreign exchange known as the swap market where the swap rate was much higher than the official exchange rate. In 1994 the government unified the two rates at the secondary market exchange rate of RMB8.7. It was estimated that, in real terms, China's currency devalued by more than 70 per cent between 1980 and 1995 (Lardy, 2002).

Another policy that promoted exports was an export tax rebate. An export tax rebate is the money the tax authority returns to exporting enterprises for the indirect tax they pay in the production and distribution process. In 1994, China implemented a major tax system reform by introducing a new value added tax (VAT). The basic VAT rate was 17 per cent, and a lower VAT rate of 13 per cent was set for foodstuffs, utilities, newspapers, and agricultural production inputs. For export products, the VAT rate was zero and hence they would get a 17 per cent or 13 per cent VAT rebate in accordance with the tax rate paid. Because the amount of tax rebate was too much of a burden for the central government, the rebate rates were decreased from 17 per cent (13 per cent) to 10 per cent (6 per cent) in 1995 and 1996. From 1998 to 1999, however, the government increased the export rebate rates nine times to counter the negative impact of the Asian financial crisis on exports (Cui, 2003).

In December 2001, China became a member of the World Trade Organization (WTO). Membership of the WTO has acted as a catalyst for trade policy reform in China. China's average applied MFN tariff rate was cut from 15.6 per cent in 2001 to 9.5 per cent in 2009. The average applied MFN tariff rate for agricultural products was cut from 23.1 per cent in 2001 to 15.2 per cent in 2009. The average applied MFN tariff rate for non-agricultural products was cut from 14.4 per cent in 2001 to 8.6 per cent in 2009. Up to 1 January 2005, China had, in accordance with the Informational Technology Agreement (ITA), eliminated tariffs for all ITA products (WTO, 2006, 2008, 2010).

At the time of China's accession to the WTO, import quotas were applied to a number of products, including motor vehicles, petroleum products, natural rubber products, cameras, and wrist watches. As a commitment to the WTO, China had eliminated all the import quotas by 1 January 2005. Moreover, the number of products partially and fully covered by import licensing was reduced from 214 in 2002 to 82 in 2005; the remaining products covered by import licensing were mainly chemicals and chemical products.

Since 2005, import prohibitions and licensing have been reduced progressively, and the administration of the import licensing regime has also been simplified. China still maintains import prohibitions on some products on grounds of public interest, environmental protection, or in accordance with international commitments. Tariff rate quotas still exist for some agricultural products and chemical fertilizers. China has improved the administration of the tariff rate quota system and has increased quota levels gradually (WTO, 2006, 2008, 2010).

Before 2008, China provided tax concessions to foreign-invested enterprises (FIEs) based on their export performance. A reduction of 50 per cent of the normal income tax rate of 33 per cent can be obtained by FIEs that export over 70 per cent of their production volume for the year; the reduction applies after the income tax holiday period expires. In addition, FIEs established in the special economic zones or economic and technology development zones, or any other FIEs otherwise enjoying an income tax rate of 15 per cent, pay income tax at 10 per cent if the same export requirement is met (WTO, 2006). With the entry into force of the Enterprises Income Tax Law in 2008, tax incentives given to FIEs based on export performance were removed (WTO, 2008).

China officially abolished subsidies for exports of industrial goods in 1991. China states that it has followed a commitment made upon joining the WTO that it does not maintain or introduce any export subsidies to its agricultural products (WTO, 2010). However, China promotes exports through measures such as: export credits, and export credit insurance; public information services; assistance for exporters to explore international markets; setting up institutions to promote trade by developing foreign trade relations, sponsoring exhibitions, providing information and advisory services; and facilitating exports by small and medium-sized enterprises (WTO, 2006). The Export-Import Bank of China was established in 1994 to provide export credit. The China Export & Credit Insurance Corporation was established in 2001 to promote exports, in particular high value added and high-tech capital goods. The twenty-first century witnessed China's becoming a global platform for exports of manufactured products. With multinational enterprises moving their factories to China, China saw a further increase in processing trade activity (Table 23.1). In 2009, foreign invested enterprises conducted over 50 per cent of China's foreign trade and around 84 per cent of its processing trade (WTO, 2010).

China still uses various export restrictions, including prohibitions, licensing, quotas, taxes, and less-than-full VAT rebates, to manage certain exports on the grounds of natural resource and energy conservation. China's export taxes, in the form of statutory rates and interim rates, are levied on an MFN basis. Most export taxes involve ad valorem rates ranging from 0 to 40 per cent; the simple average was around 13.5 per cent in 2009. China also levies special export taxes with a view to curtailing exports of certain products. In 2009, thirty-five products, mainly fertilizers, were subject to special export taxes. Including special export taxes, the simple average export tax rate was around 20 per cent in 2009 (WTO, 2010). China has two export licensing regimes: export quotas and export licences.

Export quotas apply to exports under quantitative restrictions, which are either allocated by the government or through a bidding process. In both cases, after the exporter obtains a quota, a licence is issued. The value of exports subject to licensing accounted for 4.1 per cent of total exports in 2004, down from 9.5 per cent in 1999 and 48.3 per cent in 1992 (WTO, 2006). The number of products subject to export quotas and licensing increased, however, from 332 in 2002 to 447 in 2007 (WTO, 2008).

In sum, China's trade reform since 1978 has transformed its trading system from a central planning system to a market-oriented system and has significantly reduced trade barriers, making China one of the more open large economies in the world. China's trade volume increased from $38.1 billion in 1980 to $2972.7 billion in 2010 (Table 23.1). In 2010, China overtook Germany to become the world's largest exporter. China remains the world's second largest importer, behind the USA.

■ REFERENCES

Cui, Zhiyuan. 2003. China's export tax rebate policy. *China: An International Journal* 1(2): 339–49.
Ianchovichina, Elena and Will Marin. 2004. Impacts of China's accession to the World Trade Organization. *The World Bank Economic Review* 18(1): 3–27.
Lardy, Nicholas R. 1992. *Foreign Trade and Economic Reform in 1978–1990*. New York: Cambridge University Press.
Lardy, Nicholas R. 2002. *Integrating China into the Global Economy*. Washington, DC: Brookings Institution Press.
Shan, Weijian. 1989. Reforms of China's Foreign trade system: experiences and prospects. *China Economic Review* 1(1): 33–55.
World Bank. 1994. *China: Foreign Trade Reform*. Washington, DC: The World Bank.
WTO. 2006. *Trade Policy Review—China*. Washington, DC: World Trade Organization.
WTO. 2008. *Trade Policy Review—China*. Washington, DC: World Trade Organization.
WTO. 2010. *Trade Policy Review—China*. Washington, DC: World Trade Organization.

24 Trade and industrial policy
China in the 1990s to today

Ann Harrison

The Chinese government has intervened extensively to promote industrialization in China, relying on a range of policy instruments. These instruments include a general welcoming of foreign direct investment (FDI) across China, both tariff protection and liberalization, and tax subsidies to promote both foreign and domestic investment. Industrial policies have also included a range of non-price measures, such as low-cost or even free infrastructure for new investors, directed credit for favoured sectors, favourable procurement policies, subsidized energy provision, inexpensive real-estate, and tax rebates to exporters. In this entry, we first document the tax and tariff incentives offered to manufacturing firms in China during the last two decades. We then review the emerging evidence for the impact of tax incentives and tariff protection on firm performance. We restrict our discussion to tariffs and taxes because our information on these is the most reliable, significant in scope, and quantifiable.

24.1 Trade and industrial policies: the early reform years

While this survey is primarily focused on the last fifteen years, it is instructive to quickly review China's integration into the world economy over the last several decades. China's transition from a highly centralized, monopolistic trade regime with extensive import and export controls began at the end of 1978. Figure 24.1 shows that the share of trade (exports plus imports) in GDP terms for China was less than 10 per cent in the 1970s, but increased rapidly as the regime liberalized. By the mid-1990s, the share of trade in terms of GDP had reached over forty percentage points.

Naughton (1996) documents the transition to a more open trade and foreign investment regime from 1978 onwards. The government began to dismantle the foreign trade monopolies, and opened up trade and foreign investment. Elements of the trade and

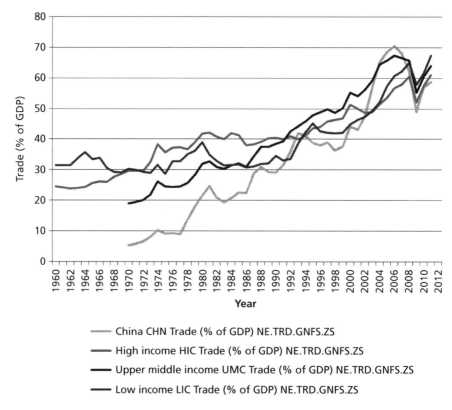

Figure 24.1. Trade (Exports + Imports) as a percentage of GDP: China versus the world

investment reforms included exchange rate devaluation, relaxing the rules on currency convertibility, increasing the number of foreign trade corporations from twelve national monopolies to many thousands, reducing non-tariff barriers, and gradually reducing tariffs and freeing up import prices. One important feature of the reforms was its dualistic nature, similar to other types of dual-track reforms introduced in China during the last several decades. A separate, export-promoting regime was created alongside the existing import-substituting regime. The export-promoting regime eased both the statutory and administrative costs of exporting and importing for foreign invested enterprises (FIEs) and domestic exporting firms.

In 1980 the government established the first four Special Economic Zones and extended these to fourteen coastal cities in 1984 (Brandt et al., 2012). Foreign investment inflows were encouraged to bring in capital, and the government began a policy of sometimes explicit and at other times implicit bargaining to grant domestic market access to foreign companies in exchange for technological know-how. Duty free importation was also allowed outside special zones, particularly for targeted foreign firms.

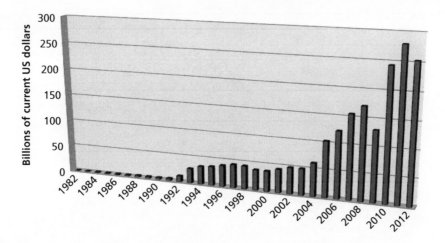

Figure 24.2. Net FDI inflows to China, 1982–2012

Naughton (1996) observes that the dualistic trading regimes allowed China to create a virtual giant export processing zone which operated alongside a fairly protected domestic economy. The firms in this giant zone were frequently but not always located along the southern coasts, since admission to the zone was determined by firm status rather than strictly by location. Writing in the mid-1990s, Naughton expected that China's spectacular double digit export growth would slow down, noting that 'it is likely to decelerate over the medium term, since the pace of structural change will slow down and China's size will tend to make the country proportionately less deeply involved in the world economy'. Yet as Figure 24.1 shows, after the mid-1990s China's integration into the global economy resumed at an accelerated pace, with trade growing to 70 per cent of GDP immediately before the financial crisis in 2007. One factor that has facilitated the continued growth in trade is the spectacular rise in inward foreign investment, which is documented in Figure 24.2. Major reforms to encourage incoming foreign investment were introduced in 1986 and 1991. Inducements to foreign investors included duty drawbacks, tariff exemptions, subsidies, infrastructure provisions, and tax holidays.

24.2 **Trade and industrial policies: 1998–2007**

Chinese manufacturing firms generally benefited from high tariffs, particularly prior to WTO entry. Until 1990, average tariffs on manufacturing in China were as high as 50 per cent. The summary statistics for tariff levels from 1998 and 2007 appear in Table 24.1. The highest tariffs in 1998 were on food processing (32.8 per cent), food (30.1 per cent), beverages (45.3 per cent), tobacco (65 per cent), and textiles and apparel (25.4 to 32.6 per

Table 24.1 Average final goods tariffs by industry

Industry	1998 tariff	2003 tariff	2007 tariff
Processing food from agricultural products	32.83	21.48	19.46
Foodstuff	30.06	19.67	16.82
Beverages	45.33	23.21	16.69
Manufacture of tobacco products	65	43.67	41
Manufacture of textiles	25.43	14.45	10.75
Manufacture of textile wearing apparel, footwear	32.58	19.73	16.37
Manufacture of leather, fur, feather	24.41	17.75	16.14
Processing of timber, manufacture of wood, bamboo	13.8	7.31	5.46
Manufacture of furniture	22	9.41	3.49
Manufacture of paper and paper products	18.89	9.74	6.15
Printing, reproduction of recording media	21.91	11.55	6.96
Manufacture of articles for culture, education, and sporting activity	20.78	12.25	8.7
Processing of petroleum, coking, processing of nuclear fuel	6.54	5.9	5.91
Manufacture of raw chemical materials and chemical products	12.22	9.65	8.27
Manufacture of medicines	9.69	5.1	5.09
Manufacture of chemical fibres	17.56	7.64	5.13
Manufacture of rubber	18.68	15.67	14.93
Manufacture of plastics	17.67	10.82	9.37
Manufacture of non-metallic mineral products	15.34	11.72	11.22
Smelting and pressing of non-ferrous metals	9.13	5.53	5.37
Smelting and pressing of metals	7.54	5.25	5.14
Manufacture of metal products	15.74	11.68	10.93
Manufacture of general purpose machinery	14.63	9.31	8.73
Manufacture of special purpose machinery	12.91	8.23	7.77
Manufacture of transport equipment	27.87	16.96	12.32
Manufacture of electrical machinery and equipment	17.02	10.71	10.5
Manufacture of electronic equipment	14.62	6.13	4.36
Measuring, cultural and office equipment	14	8.58	8.2
Manufacture of artwork and other manufacturing	21.83	16.22	15.11

Source: Cai et al. (2012)

cent). Table also indicates significant heterogeneity in protection across sectors, with the highest tariffs in food and beverages and single digit tariffs in other sectors such as electronic equipment.

The period between 1998 and 2007 witnessed many policy shifts as China experimented with different industrial policies. China's accession to the WTO in December 2001 led to significant reductions in tariffs during the sample period, with the greatest declines in tariffs occurring in those sectors with the highest initial levels of protection. From 1998 to 2007, the overall average of final goods tariffs decreased by almost 50 per cent, which is a significant change over a short time period. While the level of tariffs fell significantly during the next nine years, the pattern of protection remained similar. In 2007, the highest tariffs remained in food processing, beverages, tobacco, and apparel.

China has implemented a range of different instruments to attract foreign investors, and these incentives could be considered a major pillar of China's industrial policy. Many foreign investors in China over the last two decades faced much lower corporate tax rates than domestic enterprises. While the standard tax rate across all firms during the sample period was 33 per cent, many foreign-owned firms were granted tax subsidies in the form of tax holidays.[1] The trends show a steady increase in subsidized foreign investment between 1998 and 2007. While in the 1990s the majority of foreign firms paid the statutory tax rate, by the end of the sample period, the majority of foreign investors received some form of a tax subsidy.

The policy environment was reversed beginning in 2008, with a gradual phase-out of these tax advantages for multinational firms. Before 2008, foreign investors received a 15 per cent corporate tax rate while domestic enterprises faced a regular 33 per cent corporate tax rate. Starting in January 2008, the new corporate tax policy aims to achieve gradual tax harmonization. Foreign-invested firms that previously received preferential corporate tax rates are expected to return to the regular tax rate within 5 years. In 2008, the tax rate increased from 15 per cent to 18 per cent; in 2009, the rate increased to 20 per cent; in 2010, the corporate tax rate reached 22 per cent and finally reached 25 per cent in 2012.

Many domestic and foreign firms also benefited from reductions in value added taxes, rather than through reductions on corporate income taxes. However, fewer foreign firms receive subsidies in the form of exemptions on value added taxes than via tax holidays. These exemptions increased until 2003, then declined. Income tax holidays were a more pervasive form of incentives until the 2008 tax reform aimed at normalizing corporate tax rates across foreign and domestic enterprises.

---

[1] While it is difficult to exactly estimate the extent of tax holidays, Du et al. (2012) report trends in both subsidized and non-subsidized foreign investment.

Cai et al. (2012) report the pattern of tariff and tax incentives during this period. In particular, they explore whether tax and tariff incentives were biased in favour of exports, skill-intensity, R&D intensity, or labour intensity. They find that tariffs were higher on less skill-intensive, and less R&D intensive goods. Tariffs were also higher in sectors with a higher export share. Nevertheless, the correlation coefficients are generally low, in most cases significantly below 10 per cent. Such low correlation coefficients suggest that apart from exporting sectors, which were targeted for special treatment, other targeting was not systematic.

The pattern for income tax holidays is consistent with the pattern of tariff protection. Just like tariffs, taxes were lowest (and consequently tax holidays were highest) on export-intensive goods. Taxes were higher on skill-intensive and R&D intensive goods, consistent with lower protection for those types of goods.

To summarize across both tariffs and taxes, tariff and tax policies have been biased towards export-oriented sectors. To a lesser extent, the government also supported unskilled-intensive sectors, and sectors with low R&D intensity, which are sectors where China was most likely to have an actual or a latent comparative advantage. One puzzle is why tax and tariff support has been highest in sectors where the country is likely to already possess comparative advantage. The data are consistent with other evidence showing greater protection where countries have a comparative advantage (for example, garments and textiles in Mexico and Morocco; see Hanson and Harrison (1999a, 1999b)). One possibility is that current comparative advantage is a good proxy for latent comparative advantage, particularly when sectors are broadly defined. Another possibility is that tariffs are initially imposed in areas of latent comparative advantage but protection becomes entrenched as comparative advantage shifts into different types of goods.

24.3 **Impact of trade and industrial policies on performance**

An extensive literature explores the role of trade liberalization and its impact on productivity for both developed and developing countries. This literature is reviewed in detail in Harrison and Rodriguez Clare (2010). However, there are very few studies that estimate the impact of tariff reductions on firm-level productivity in China. This is surprising, given China's highly visible entry into the WTO, the subsequent declines in tariffs (Table 24.1), and the extensive evidence on the linkages between tariff changes and firm performance in other parts of the world.

One exception is the forthcoming study on the linkages between output tariffs, input tariffs, and processing trade in China by Miaojie Yu (forthcoming). Yu merges Chinese census data with firm-specific measures of final goods and imported intermediate input trade to calculate firm-specific final goods and input tariffs. Yu finds that contrary to the results for Indonesia in Amiti and Konings (2007) and Topalova and Khandwal (2011) for India, reductions in final goods tariffs in China increased productivity more for processing firms than did reductions in intermediate input tariffs. Yu attributes this result in large part to the fact that firms under the processing trade regime were exempted from tariffs on intermediate inputs.

Du, Harrison, and Jefferson (forthcoming) also test for the effects of input tariffs on productivity, and find negative but less significant effects of input tariffs on productivity—possibly because systems to reimburse firms for input taxes were in place and many exporters were granted exemptions on input tariffs. Exploiting the exogenous change in trade policies with China's entry into the WTO at the end of 2001, they find that the magnitude of backward linkages—indicating spillovers from foreign firms to their domestic suppliers—increased with trade liberalization.

There is now a significant body of research exploring, in both China and elsewhere, whether there are technology spillovers from incoming foreign investment. Researchers distinguish between horizontal linkages, which indicate benefits from firms located in the same sector, and vertical linkages. Vertical linkages indicate benefits from either foreign investors who purchase inputs from domestic suppliers (backward linkages) or from foreign firms supplying inputs to domestic enterprises (forward linkages). There is now a substantial literature for China which suggests that horizontal linkages were less important but vertical linkages are quite important.

For backward linkages, Du et al. (2012) find that a one percentage point increase in backward FDI is associated with a 0.8–0.9 percentage point increase in output. These magnitudes are twice as large as those found by Blalock and Gertler (2008) for Indonesia but smaller than Javorcik's (2004) findings for Lithuania. Du et al. also find that the most significant beneficiaries from foreign investors in China have been the state owned enterprises (SOEs). While SOEs in China generally exhibit worse performance than private enterprises, they benefit greatly from forming joint ventures with foreign firms. Du et al. find that foreign equity participation is associated with an improvement in productivity which is twenty times greater for SOEs. The much larger and statistically significant coefficient associated with foreign equity participation in SOEs is consistent with the hypothesis that firms with foreign equity have played an important role in improving the performance of some SOEs.

As in many other policy arenas, the Chinese government has actively developed its trade and industrial policies in conjunction with policy experiments. For example, the government typically introduces a new policy such as a value added tax incentive in some regions or provinces, and then extends that policy to the rest of the country if it proves to be successful. As an illustration, in 2004, the Chinese government implemented a value added tax reform in three northeast provinces which removes fixed asset investment from the value added tax base. The objective of the 2004 reform was to encourage firms to raise investment on fixed assets for production (excluding structures) and to upgrade their machinery and equipment.

Cai and Harrison (2011) evaluate the impact of this policy, whose goal was to encourage technology upgrading, particularly in the backward northeast provinces. Cai and Harrison find employment fell significantly in the treated provinces and sectors. The reform reduced the total number of employees for all types of firms. This experiment has since been extended to the rest of China.

The evidence suggests varied success with industrial promotion policies in China. The use of tax holidays for exporters and FDI promotion led to significantly better outcomes than higher tariffs or VAT rebates in backward provinces. The results consistently show that tax concessions to exporters and FDI promotion, rather than tariff protection, were associated with improved productivity performance in China. One interpretation (see Aghion et al., 2012) is that industrial policies which promote competition are more likely to successfully improve performance. China's most successful industrial promotion policies have been those which target foreign investment and exporters, consistent with the importance of combining competition with industrial policy.

■ REFERENCES

Aghion, Philippe, Mathias Dewatripont, Luosha Du, Ann Harrison, and Patrick Legros. 2012. Industrial Policy and Competition. NBER Working Paper.

Amiti, M., and J. Konings. 2007. Trade liberalization, intermediate inputs and productivity. *American Economic Review* 97(5), 1611–38.

Blalock, Garrick, and Paul J. Gertler. 2008. Welfare gains from foreign direct investment through technology transfer to local suppliers. *Journal of International Economics* 74(2), 402–21.

Brandt, Loren, Johannes Van Biesebroeck, Luhang Wang, and Yifan Zhang. 2012. WTO Accession and Performance of Chinese Manufacturing Firms. CEPR Discussion Paper 9166.

Cai, Jing and Ann Harrison. 2011. The Value-Added Tax Reform Puzzle. NBER Working Paper 17532.

Cai, Jing, Ann Harrison, and Justin Yifu Lin. 2012. Patterns of Trade and Tax Interventions and Firm Performance in China, Working Paper.

Du, Luosha, Ann Harrison, and Gary Jefferson. 2012. Testing for horizontal and vertical foreign investment spillovers in China, 1998–2007. *Journal of Asian Economics*, Volume 23(3), 234–243.

Du, Luosha, Ann Harrison, and Gary Jefferson. Forthcoming. FDI spillovers and industrial policy: The role of tariffs and tax holidays. *World Development*.

Hanson, Gordon, and Ann Harrison. 1999a. Trade liberalization and wage inequality in Mexico. *Industrial and Labor Relations Review* 52(2), 271–88.

Hanson, Gordon, and Ann Harrison. 1999b. Who gains from trade reform? some remaining puzzles. *Journal of Development Economics* 59, 125–54.

Harrison, A. E. and A. Rodriguez-Clare. 2010, Trade, foreign investment, and industrial policy for developing countries. In *Handbook of Development Economics, 5*, edited by Dani Rodrik and Mark Rosenzweig, 4039–214. Amsterdam: North Holland.

Javorcik, Beata Smarzynska. 2004. Does foreign direct investment increase the productivity of domestic firms? In search of spillovers through backward linkages. *The American Economic Review* 94(3), 605–27.

Naughton, Barry. 1996. China's Emergence and Prospects as a Trading Nation. Brookings Papers on Economic Activity.

Topalova, P. and A. Khandelwal. 2011. Trade liberalization and firm productivity: the case of India. *The Review of Economics and Statistics*, 93(3), 995–1009.

Yu, M. L. forthcoming. Processing trade, tariff reductions, and firm productivity: evidence from Chinese products. *Economic Journal*.

Part V
Macro-economics and Finance

25 China

International macro-economic impact of domestic change

Ross Garnaut

China's size and deepening integration into the international economy have made changes in its domestic macro-economic development and performance a major influence on global economic developments. This became apparent during the Asian Financial Crisis of the late 1990s, became part of attempts to explain the Great Crash of 2008, and will be felt more powerfully as China's new model of economic growth after 2011 changes the structure of Chinese expenditure and incomes.

This chapter focuses mainly on how China's macro-economic development is affecting savings, investment, and capital flows into the international economy. China now has by far the largest absolute savings of any country, nearly two and a half times the United States in 2012. Chinese savings represented about 7.6 per cent of global GDP, compared with 3.1 per cent for the United States. (Here I use standard national accounts data in US dollars from IMF sources. All data are from the Fund's October 2013 World Economic Outlook database.) Chinese savings are mostly invested at home, with the current account surplus (the excess of savings over investment) representing about 2.3 per cent of Chinese and 0.33 per cent of global GDP. This outcome in 2012 was down from a Chinese surplus of 10.1 per cent of GDP in 2007, but still made China the second largest source of surplus savings for international investment after Germany (Ma and McCawley, 2013).

Let us look at what has driven the changes in Chinese savings, investment, and current account surpluses through the late twentieth and early twenty-first centuries, examine recent developments in Chinese economic policy and structure, and seek insights for future developments from this analysis.

For nearly two decades of Chinese reform from its beginning in 1978, the Chinese fiscal and monetary authorities found it difficult to keep demand growth on a steady path as market exchange became increasingly important. Chinese investment and savings shares of GDP fluctuated around one-third rising slowly to about two-fifths in the early 1990s. Periods of current account surplus were interrupted by deficits in times of exceptionally strong growth in domestic demand, peaking at 3.7 per cent of GDP in 1985. The episodes of strong demand and current payments deficits were often accompanied by inflation at rates well into double digits. Payments deficits and high inflation led to the application of controls on expenditure which cut across the market-oriented reforms and brought excessive growth to a bumpy end. The tendency to periodic inflation was associated with subsequent currency depreciation.

Increasing use of variations in interest rates and other macro-economic instruments was effective in establishing greater stability in the second half of the 1990s. Greater macro-economic stability encouraged and was for a while supported in 1995 by the replacement of a dual exchange rate comprising an overvalued fixed exchange rate and low 'grey market' rate, by an integrated system with a de facto peg to the US dollar near the low 'grey market' rate. Market-oriented macro-economic intervention and the pegged exchange rate seemed to establish a new era of more stable economic growth. The last annual current account deficit was in 1993 (1.3 per cent of GDP) and the last year of double digit inflation was 1995 (17.1 per cent increase in the CPI).

Stability was challenged by the Asian Financial Crisis that emerged in Thailand in mid-1997 and spread quickly through the rest of Southeast Asia and Korea, reaching its greatest depths in mid-1998. In China, as in all Western Pacific economies, exports fell sharply and currencies came under speculative attack (McLeod and Garnaut 1998; Arndt and Hill, 1999). Huge depreciations of all other currencies in the region, including those of the Western Pacific's developed economies, Japan, Australia, and New Zealand, reduced the competitiveness of trade-exposed industry in China. Slowing of export growth and pessimism about East Asian prospects led to contractive tendencies in China as well as speculative capital outflow. The Chinese authorities responded to the crisis by maintaining the fixed exchange rate against the strong US dollar. This implied large currency appreciation on a trade-weighted basis. Growth in economic activity and employment was supported by massive fiscal and monetary expansion that temporarily reduced the trade and current account surpluses. China entered a period of deflation on the broadly based price indicators, extending from 1998 to 2002. The long deflation combined with an acceleration of productivity growth after China's entry into the World Trade Organization (WTO) in 2001 to restore China's international competitiveness.

The massive Keynesian expansion with a high fixed exchange rate was risky, because of the additional stress that it placed on the financing of external payments when China's initial external reserves were of modest dimension. It was successful in maintaining Chinese economic growth at a high level. China's holding of the US dollar peg and its maintenance of growth in domestic demand helped to put a floor under levels of economic activity, exchange rates against external currencies, and volumes of foreign trade through the Western Pacific and was important in truncating the East Asian crisis. Other Western Pacific economies returned to strong economic growth from 2000, just in time to support the renewal of strong export growth in China and to take pressure off the fixed exchange rate before doubts about the durability of the strategy became overwhelming.

The massive expansion changed the structure of Chinese growth. It mainly took the form of increased expenditure through state-related activities and enterprises. This broke what had been considerable momentum in the expansion of the private economy. It ushered in a period of higher investment emphasizing heavy industry and infrastructure. Strong growth of capital-intensive state-related economic activity and reforms to improve their commercial performance increased profits as a share of national income, with a high proportion of savings being retained within enterprises. The savings share of GDP rose prodigiously, to half in 2006 and a peak of 53.4 per cent in 2008. Investment also increased as a share of GDP, but more moderately, to 43 per cent in 2006 and a peak of 48.9 per cent in 2011.

Rapid Chinese economic growth from the mid-1980s has been described as following a 'Lewisian' model (Lewis, 1954; Ranis and Fei, 1961). A rapidly expanding, highly productive modern non-farm economy drew large amounts of labour from the countryside where its marginal productivity was low. For a considerable period, this occurred without large increases in rural or urban wages for low-skilled labour. Productivity growth in the modern sector exceeded the rate of increase in wages, leading to an increasing profit share of GDP. A high proportion of incremental profits was saved and reinvested in the enterprise within which it was generated, so that the savings and investment shares of GDP increased. Higher investment, in turn, supported high rates of growth in economic activity. The consumption share of GDP fell with the wages share to levels that were unknown in the history of modern economic development in a substantial economy.

China's labour force growth slowed from the early twenty-first century as the low fertility of the early reform period reduced the number of new entrants. By 2013, the absolute size of the labour force was shrinking (Cai, 2010; Cai and Lu, 2013). Increasing investment in education was focused on a declining number of young people, causing the supply of low-skilled workers to decline more rapidly.

The combination of slow growth in the low-skilled labour force and sustained strong growth in modern sector economic activity eventually removed the abundance of labour supply from the countryside. Shortages of low-skilled labour and rising wages appeared in coastal industrial cities in 2004 and spread until wages were rising more rapidly than productivity through almost all of the national economy. China had entered a 'Lewisian turning period' of economic development (Garnaut and Huang, 2006; Cai, 2010; Garnaut, 2010). It was a turning period and not a turning point because the growing scarcity of labour and rising wages arose at different times and in different degrees across an immense and weakly integrated labour market.

Chinese structural adjustment was accelerated in a non-inflationary way by the commencement of renminbi appreciation against the US dollar from 2005. The appreciation had accumulated to a little over 7 per cent by the time that it was suspended for two years due to the global financial crisis in 2008.

Rising real wages stopped the increases in the profit, savings, and investment shares of GDP but did not immediately reverse them. By the time of its peak in 2007 China had by far the world's largest current account surplus as a share of GDP by a considerable margin. The availability of surplus capital from China with a high proportion being invested in US government securities assisted the expansion of expenditure on housing, consumption, and military and other government activities and allowed US taxes to fall without upward pressure on long-term interest rates in the developed world. This contributed to the Great Crash of 2008 and the subsequent long recession (Garnaut with Llewellyn Smith, 2009).

The Great Crash brought rapid, internationally oriented growth to a sudden stop. Exports stopped growing. Thirty million of the several hundred million rural residents working in the industrial cities went home and stayed there for a considerable time. Growth in wages went into reverse. The Chinese authorities responded with an enlarged version of the Keynesian expansion of the late twentieth century. Again it was successful in quickly restoring growth and contributed to the stabilization of Western Pacific and this time also to global economic activity. The pre-Crash pattern of growth was re-established from late 2009.

Rapid investment-led growth was criticized with increasing intensity from the early twenty-first century for its effects in increasing inequality in the distribution of income and wealth, for its neglect of growth of services, and for its damage to the domestic and global natural environment. Prior to the Great Crash, the government had articulated new policies that elevated the priority of improving public services in rural areas, reducing inequality in the distribution of income and wealth and easing pressure on the environment. The new priorities were reflected to some extent in the allocation of resources before 2008, but responses to the crisis delayed their main impact.

The new priorities were prominent in the 12th Five-year Plan for 2011–15 and by 2012 were being reflected in the national economic data. Policy now generally reinforced changes occurring as a result of the turning period in the labour market. The wages and consumption shares of GDP began to rise. The savings share stabilized at a high level and fell moderately from 2009. The investment share rose with the policy response to the Great Crash and then stabilized at a high level. The current account surplus fell sharply to 4.9 per cent in 2009, 4.0 per cent in 2010, and around 2 per cent since then. The energy and metals intensity of economic activity and the coal share of energy use (crucial to domestic and international environmental effects) all fell sharply after 2011.

These changes in China's macro-economic development are so large that they amount to a new model of economic growth (Garnaut et al., 2013). If sustained under the influence of growing labour scarcity and government policy it would see the moderation of aggregate growth of output from an average of nearly 10 per cent in the 33 years to 2011 to around 7–8 per cent. It would see the investment and savings shares of GDP fall steadily to perhaps three-quarters of their peak levels. The current account surplus would depend on the relative size of the cutbacks in savings and investment shares of GDP but would tend to stabilize near the low levels of 2011–13. China would become a proportionately smaller contributor of surplus savings to world capital markets at a time when the normalization of monetary policies in developed countries is placing upward pressure on global interest rates on long-term debt. China would be delivering the international macro-economic change that the USA and some other developed countries had been seeking, but perhaps at the cost of the developed countries' own economic growth.

■ REFERENCES

Arndt, H. W. and H. Hill (eds). 1999. *Southeast Asia's Economic Crisis: Origins, Lessons and the Way Forward*, Singapore: Institute of Southeast Asian Studies.

Cai, F. 2010. Demographic transition, demographic dividend and Lewis turning point in China. *China Economic Journal* 3(2), 107–119.

Cai, F. and L. Yang. 2013, The end of China's demographic dividend: the perspective of potential economic growth. In *China: A New Model for Growth and Development*, edited by Ligang Song, Ross Garnaut, and Fang Cai, ch. 4. Canberra and Beijing: ANU E-Press and China Social Science Academic Press.

Garnaut, R. 2010. Macro-economic implications of the turning point. *China Economic Journal*. 3(2), 181–190.

Garnaut, R. Cai, and L. Song. 2006. China's new strategy for long-term growth and development. In *China: A New Model for Growth and Development*, edited by Ligang Song, Ross Garnaut, and Fang Cai, ch. 1. Canberra and Beijing: ANU E-Press and China Social Sciences Academic Press.

Garnaut, R. and Y. Huang. 2013. In *The Turning Point in China's Economic Development*, edited by Ross Garnaut and Ligang Song. Canberra and Beijing: ANU E-Press and China Social Sciences Academic Press.

Garnaut, R. and D. Llewellyn Smith. 2009. *The Great Crash of 2008*. Melbourne: Melbourne University Publishing.

Lewis, W. A. 1954. Economic development with unlimited supplies of labour. Manchester School of Economics and Social Sciences, Vol. XXII (May).

Ma, G. and R. N. McCawley. 2013. Global and Euro Imbalances, BIS Working Paper No. 424, Bank of International Settlements, September.

McLeod, R. and R. Garnaut. (eds). 1998. *East Asia in Crisis: From Being a Miracle to Needing One*. London and New York: Routledge.

Ranis, G. and J. C. H. Fei. 1961. A theory of economic development. *The American Economic Review* 51(4), 333–565.

26 Chinese tax structure

Roger Gordon and Wei Li

The Chinese tax structure has changed dramatically since the introduction of economic reforms in the early 1980s.[1] Initially, the tax structure was typical of those seen in the poorest countries. Excise taxes were a primary source of revenue, with tax rates varying dramatically by type of good, with most revenue coming from the manufacturing sector and more specifically from state-owned firms. Corporate income taxes were an additional important source of revenue. The corporate tax rate of 55 per cent was among the highest in the world. Tariffs (and implicit tariffs through monopoly control over international trade) were also important. Financial repression was an implicit source of revenue, with interest rates on bank deposits at times far below those available abroad.

At this point, the Chinese tax structure roughly corresponds to that seen in the most developed countries. As of 1994, excise taxes were replaced by a value added tax (VAT): the VAT rate of 17 per cent is typical among richer countries. Also in 1994, the corporate tax rate fell to 33 per cent, a rate which again is typical. A personal income tax has been introduced and gradually expanded. It still is a secondary source of tax revenue, but its role is growing quickly. China has also introduced a Social Security programme for urban residents, financed by a payroll tax. China has joined the WTO, and as a result tariff rates have fallen dramatically.

Tax revenue has grown during the reform period from a low of 10 per cent of GDP, a figure typical among the poorest countries, to the present figure of 19 per cent of GDP, a figure more typical of middle-income countries.

This growth in revenue inspite of stable tax rates since 1994 implies a steady fall in tax evasion. With similar tax rates but still roughly half the tax revenue seen among the richest countries, however, evasion rates still remain high relative to those in these richest countries.

Increasing overall revenue, though, does not necessarily signal a closer link between a firm's tax payments and its statutory tax base. If a firm's reported sales or profits are hard to verify, for example, tax authorities could be assessing tax based on other more easily observed attributes of firms, for example their physical capital stock and/or

[1] The first author would like to thank CKGSB for its hospitality and financial support during the period this paper was written. The views are those of the authors, and not necessarily those of CKGSB.

their labour force. In ongoing work, we have attempted to infer the information used by the tax authorities when collecting taxes from individual firms by regressing each firm's tax payments against its reported sales and profits, along with their capital stock and labour force. We find in the late 1990s and early 2000s that factor inputs are a more useful tool to explain actual tax payments than are reported sales and profits (the reputed tax bases). In more recent years, though, sales and profits have played an increasingly important role in explaining tax payments, suggesting that tax payments are increasingly being based on the statutes rather than on the discretion of tax officials.

The rise in tax revenue with stable tax rates suggests a steady fall in the efficiency costs of the tax system. Firms have fewer opportunities to avoid tax, for example by shifting income across subsidiaries facing different tax provisions, or from the corporate to the personal tax base.

One unusual aspect of the Chinese tax structure to date is the division of revenue between the national and local governments. This division may initially have been a source of strength, but it increasingly presents fiscal challenges for the Chinese government.

At the beginning of the reforms, the national government received all the tax revenue from state-owned firms. Lower levels of government received corporate tax revenue and much of the excise tax revenue from firms they were responsible for establishing, and later from privately owned firms once their entry was permitted. Business taxes on non-industrial (largely services) firms and agricultural taxes all went to local governments. A personal income tax was later introduced, with the revenue split 60/40 between central and local governments.

There were several key advantages of this allocation of tax revenue. First, poorer countries typically face great difficulty collecting taxes from small firms, given the ease with which these firms can either hide their existence from the tax authorities, or hide their taxable income, perhaps through the use of cash sales. Local governments, being 'closer to the ground', should find it easier to monitor local activity than would the national government. As the nominal owner of many of these firms (or the one whose regulations can block entry), local governments have additional access to information about the taxable activity of these firms. When they are the owner, they can provide incentives to the managers of these firms to comply with the tax law.[2]

An additional advantage of allocating revenue from new firms to local governments is that these governments, as a result, have a strong incentive to encourage the entry and growth of new firms. The data show that township and village enterprises (TVEs) entered rapidly and grew quickly, in spite of the then punitive tax rates that, in theory, should have discouraged entry. Local governments seem to have been successful in designing the

---

[2] In all firms, information flow is facilitated by the appointment of a party representative within each firm, who has nominal oversight over the firm's manager.

incentives on TVE managers to act in the interest of the local government as owner and recipient of the firms' tax revenue.

One problem that was quickly recognized, though, is that local governments were hiding the economic activity of locally owned firms from the national government, in order to retain more of the tax revenue at the local level. In response to this conflict of interest between national and local governments, the national government in 1994 took over responsibility for tax assessments on these non-state firms, returning to local governments their share of this tax revenue. In addition, existing excise taxes were largely replaced by a VAT, with only a quarter of the resulting revenue going to local governments. The result was a dramatic jump in national tax revenue, and a dramatic loss in local tax revenue.

This loss in local governments' tax revenue only worsened over time due to a series of subsequent tax reforms. One such reform around 2005 eliminated the remaining taxes on agriculture. At roughly the same time, corporate tax revenue from all new firms started to go to the national government rather than to local governments. Recently, firms subject to the business tax (where revenue went entirely to local governments) instead became subject to value added tax (where local governments receive only a quarter of the resulting revenue).

One response by local governments to this loss in tax revenue was to impose user fees on those receiving local public services. Students in local schools have at times been subject to tuition and/or fees for supplies. Those receiving medical care largely pay the cost for this service. Tolls on the main local roads can be very high.

In addition, local governments have developed a new source of revenue: land sales. Under the initial economic reforms, farmland was leased to farmers for an extended time period. However, officially the local government retained ownership of land. Local governments could seize agricultural land through the equivalent of eminent domain, compensating farmers based on the estimated value of this land in terms of its agricultural use.

Local governments could then lease or sell the acquired land to non-agricultural users, potentially at a price far above that paid to the farmers. If the land were rented, local governments would have a continuing source of revenue. Local officials, though, have a short time horizon, since they typically hold their positions in a specific jurisdiction for only three to five years. As a result, officials have largely auctioned (long-term leases to) the land they seize rather than rented it, thereby obtaining control of the full value of the land while they hold their position in that jurisdiction. In the first half of 2013, revenue from land auctions accounted for more than 46 per cent of the total revenue of local governments in China.[3]

Hong Kong has used a similar source of government revenue through its monopoly control over the land market. In Hong Kong, the government has maintained strict limits on urban development, keeping land prices high.

---

[3] Source: <http://news.xinhuanet.com/house/bj/2013-08-13/c_125,157,780.htm>, accessed on 19 August 2013.

Local officials in China, though, have an incentive to sell as much land as they can while they remain in office. Presumably as a result, the national government has limited the level of land sales that can take place each year in any given jurisdiction.

Chinese local officials have an additional reason to shift land from agricultural to non-agricultural uses. Agricultural production is no longer taxed in China, while the income generated through other uses of land does generate local tax revenue. Land sales have, as a result, been continuing at a rapid rate. This source of local revenue will quickly be depleted, as the amount of land remaining in agriculture continues to shrink.

Another problem with the existing sources of local tax revenue is that effective local tax rates vary dramatically by industry. Agriculture is untaxed; the business tax (largely on the service sector) was retained in full by local governments; VAT is only partially retained by local governments and is collected from only a subset of industries and only from the headquarters of a firm rather than from each plant; while the allocation of the corporate tax from a firm depends on the origins of that firm. Local governments therefore have strong financial incentives to favour those firms paying higher tax rates, particularly firms in the service sector who are subject to the business tax. The service sector includes firms involved with real estate development, reinforcing the incentive to take land out of agriculture (where the returns are untaxed), and sell it to developers.

The sources of local government revenue not only induce local governments to favour some industries over others but also affect their incentives to provide local public services. There are clear incentives to provide services to firms facing high local tax rates, since the resulting improvement in firm performance increases the local tax base. Since agriculture is now untaxed, though, there are no such incentives to provide services to farmers.

In other countries, the incentive to provide services to households in part comes from the incentive to attract more residents to the jurisdiction, thereby increasing the local tax base.[4] The *Hukou* household registration system in China, however, heavily restricts migration across jurisdictions, leaving the local population largely unresponsive to the quality of local public services.[5] As a result, providing local public services to households generates little or no compensating increase in local tax revenue, which discourages the provision of such services, and weakens any incentive to oversee the quality of those services that are provided.

---

[4] Formally, the forecast is that new residents in equilibrium will face taxes equal to the marginal cost of providing them with local public services. If revenue were higher than the cost of services, then other communities have an incentive to compete by offering a better deal. In contrast, when revenue is less than the cost of local public services, the jurisdiction has an incentive to cut back on services (or discourage such individuals from residing in the jurisdiction).

[5] Those with higher education, however, can move much more easily, discouraging jurisdictions who might lose educated individuals from providing them the needed education, while encouraging the receiving jurisdictions to provide high quality services to this mobile sub-population.

There is now serious discussion about introducing a property tax in China. With a property tax, revenue is the same regardless of where the property is used, as long as property is allocated to the highest bidder. Local governments would then have an incentive to make the jurisdiction a more attractive place to locate, in order to drive up property values. Such a change in the Chinese tax structure would bring this structure yet closer to that seen in other richer countries.

27 Government expenditure

Shuanglin Lin

Through allocating resources, providing public goods and services, and affecting aggregate demand, government expenditure plays an important role in promoting economic development and social justice. Official government expenditure in China includes budgetary and extra-budgetary expenditure. There is also off-budget expenditure, which is outside of the government monitoring system. Based on international standards, China's government expenditure should also include subsidies to state-owned enterprises and social security expenditure. This chapter will discuss budgetary and extra-budgetary expenditure, the composition of government budgetary expenditure, and the challenges to China's government spending.

27.1 Government budgetary expenditure

Budgetary expenditure is proposed by the administrative branch of the government and approved the National People's Congress. China's fiscal year starts on 1 January each year, but the budget is approved in March at the annual meeting of the National People's Congress. China's provincial governments have no authority to establish tax laws or to issue debt, and their budgets are balanced through central government subsidies. Provincial government budgets must be approved by the central government.

Since the establishment of the People's Republic of China in 1949, China's economic system has changed from being market-oriented to being centrally planned, and then back to being market-oriented. Government expenditures have fluctuated along with the changes in the economic system. In the early 1950s, the government faced economic reconstruction, and government expenditures increased rapidly. The government expenditure share of GDP was 25.3 per cent in 1952 and reached 29 per cent in 1956. In 1957, China completed socialist reform, eliminating all private enterprises and establishing state-owned and collectively owned enterprises in urban areas. In 1958, China established collective farms in rural areas, called the people's communes. A centrally planned economic system was established. Soon afterwards, the Chinese leader Mao Zedong launched the Great Leap Forward movement (1958–60) in an effort to catch up, in a short period of time, with industrialized countries. Government expenditure increased dramatically. The share of GDP was 30.6 per cent in 1958, 37.7 per cent in 1959, and 44.2 per cent in 1960, the highest ever. The Great Leap Forward movement failed.

Starting from 1961, the Chinese economy entered a five-year period of adjustment and reform by providing factory workers with material incentives to work and allocating a small piece of land to farmers to grow what they wanted. Government expenditure as a share of GDP decreased to 29.2 per cent in 1961 and to 26.8 per cent in 1965. With these reforms, the economy soon recovered. However, Mao viewed the reforms as a departure from the socialist system. In 1966, Mao launched the Great Proletariat Cultural Revolution to prevent China from heading towards capitalism. As a result of this move, the economy was paralysed. Government expenditure as a share of GDP remained at 20–30 per cent in the 1960s and the 1970s.

In 1978, China started market-oriented economic reforms. Government expenditure as a share of GDP declined steadily for many years, from 31 per cent in 1978 to 22.4 per cent in 1985, 16.6 per cent in 1990, and 14 per cent in 1992. However, these reforms resulted in a large decline in government revenue and expenditure. In 1994, the government launched tax reforms to strengthen the government's tax collection and central government's fiscal power. Government expenditure as a share of GDP increased from 11.7 per cent in 1995 to 17.8 per cent in 2000, and to 22.4 per cent in 2010. Figure 27.1 shows the ratio of government budgetary expenditures to GDP from 1950 to 2010.

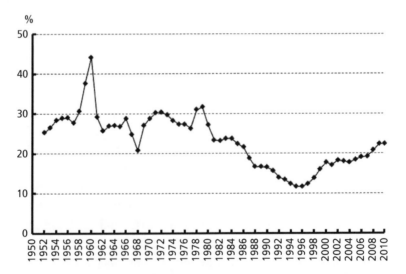

Figure 27.1. Ratio of government budgetary expenditure to GDP, 1950–2010

Source: China National Bureau of Statistics, *Statistical Yearbook of China*, 2000–2011.

27.2 **Government extra-budgetary expenditure**

Extra-budgetary expenditure is directly controlled by local governments, government agencies, and government institutions, and it does not need to be approved by the higher level of government. Extra-budgetary expenditure is financed by extra-budgetary revenue, which is non-tax revenue collected by local governments, central government agencies, and government institutions.

Extra-budgetary expenditure by local governments (particularly county-level and township-level) mainly includes subsidies for agricultural production services to set up small businesses, irrigation and water conservancy construction, public welfare undertakings in rural areas, urban utilities, construction, maintenance, and technology improvement of local state-owned enterprises. Extra-budgetary expenditure by state-owned enterprises includes the renovation of capital equipment, employee benefits, and staff bonuses. Extra-budgetary expenditure of administrative and operative units includes employee benefits and construction.

Extra-budgetary expenditure has existed since the establishment of the PRC. It was small in the beginning, experienced dramatic increases in the early 1990s, and has since declined in recent years. The ratio of extra-budgetary expenditure to GDP was 13.9 per cent in 1982, 15.3 per cent in 1985, and 13.7 per cent in 1992, compared to the ratio of budgetary expenditure to GDP of 14 per cent!

The coverage of extra-budgetary expenditure was significantly adjusted in 1993. For example, the innovation fund and the major repair fund for the state-owned enterprises were no longer listed as extra-budgetary funds. Beginning in 1997, government managed funds (e.g. the highway construction fund, railway construction fund, and electricity power construction fund) were excluded from extra-budgetary revenue and expenditure and included in extra-budgetary revenue and expenditure. Thus, the data later than 1993 are not comparable to earlier years. The ratio of extra-budgetary expenditure to GDP has declined. It was 3.8 per cent in 1993, 5.7 per cent in 1996, and 4.0 per cent in 2000, and declined to 1.83 per cent in 2009.[1] The data for 2010 were not available at the time of writing.

Extra-budgetary expenditure is classified into the following categories: investment in fixed assets, expenditure for city maintenance, administrative and operative expenditure, expenditure by township governments, and other expenditure.

27.3 **Other government expenditure**

The measurement of China's government expenditure is slightly different from many other countries. For example, in many countries, such as the USA, the UK, and Russia, social

---

[1] See China National Statistical Bureau, *Statistical Yearbook of China*, Beijing: Statistical Publishing House, 2011.

security expenditure is included in total government expenditure. However, in China social security expenditure for enterprise workers is not included in the total of government expenditure. Also, in China government subsidies to loss-making enterprises have been treated as negative revenue (deducted from total government revenue), instead of expenditure. For a more accurate comparison of the size of China's government expenditure with the rest of the world, it is necessary to include social security expenditure and subsidies to loss-making enterprises in China's total government expenditure.

Social security expenditure includes basic pension insurance, unemployment insurance, medical insurance, work injury insurance, and maternity insurance. Social security account revenue has grown rapidly, from 18.7 billion yuan in 1990 (accounting for 1 per cent of GDP) to 1369.6 billion yuan in 2008 (accounting for 4.4 per cent of GDP), and to 1882.3 billion yuan in 2010 (accounting for 4.7 per cent of GDP).

The subsidies to loss-making state-owned enterprises were large in the 1980s and the early 1990s, but have declined substantially in recent years, along with the privatization of unprofitable SOEs and the reduction of the social security burdens of the existing SOEs. For example, the subsidies to loss-making SOEs accounted for 25 per cent of total expenditure in 1985, 20.5 per cent in 1990, and 0.5 per cent in 2007. The data for 2010 were not available at the time of writing.

The ratio of total government expenditure (budgetary expenditure, extra-budgetary expenditure, social security expenditure, subsidies to SOEs) to GDP was 37.1 per cent in 1982, 43.4 per cent in 1985, 34 per cent in 1990, and 30.6 per cent in 1992. After adjustment for the coverage of extra-budgetary expenditure, the extra-budgetary share of GDP, as well as the total government expenditure share of GDP declined sharply. The ratio of total government expenditures to GDP was 19.7 per cent in 1993, 24.4 per cent in 2000, and 24.1 per cent in 2007. It is estimated to be about 30 per cent in 2010.

In addition to budgetary and extra-budgetary expenditure, there is also off-budgetary expenditure in China's local government and government agencies and institutions. Off-budgetary expenditure consists of expenditure not included in either budgetary expenditure or extra-budgetary expenditure, and most of it is illegal and financed by unreported revenue (e.g. fees and revenue from land sales). No one knows exactly how large off-budgetary government expenditure has been; it is estimated at around 5 per cent of GDP.

Adding off-budgetary expenditure, the total government share in GDP should be around 35 per cent. In 2007, the total government share in GDP was 43.81 per cent in Germany, 37.15 per cent in the USA, 20.89 per cent in Thailand, 15.18 per cent in Singapore.[2] Thus, China's government expenditure is not low for this stage of development.

---

[2] See International Monetary Fund (2008), *Government Finance Yearbook 2008.*

27.4 **Composition of government budgetary expenditure**

In 2007, the government reclassified its expenditure. The most noticeable change is the replacement of government administrative expenditure by expenditure for general public services, and many areas of government expenditure, such as education, healthcare, and environmental protection are now shown separately. According to the 2008 *Statistical Yearbook of China*, government expenditure is classified into the following fourteen main categories: (1) general public services; (2) foreign affairs; (3) national defence; (4) public security; (5) education; (6) science and technology; (7) culture, sport, and media; (8) social safety net and employment effort; (9) medical and healthcare; (10) environment protection; (11) urban and rural community affairs; (12) agriculture, forestry, and water conservancy; (13) transportation; and (14) industry, commerce, and banking.

In 2010, the shares of major items in total government expenditure are illustrated in Figure 27.2. The share of education in total government expenditure was 14 per cent, general public services 10.4 per cent, social safety net and employment effort 10.2 per cent, agriculture, forestry, and water conservancy 9 per cent, urban and rural community affairs 6.7 per cent, public security 6.1 per cent, transportation 6.1 per cent, national defence 5.9 per cent, medical and healthcare 5.3 per cent, and environmental protection 2.7 per cent.

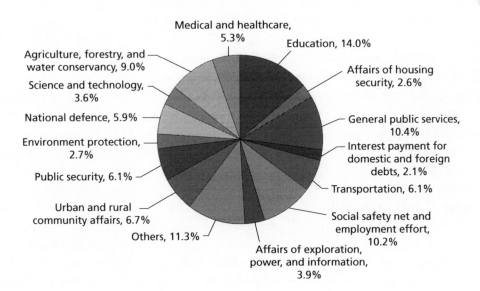

Figure 27.2. Composition of total government expenditure in 2010

Source: China National Statistical Bureau, *Statistical Yearbook of China*, Beijing: Statistical Publishing House, 2011.

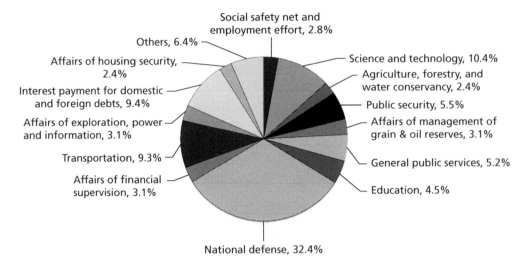

Figure 27.3. Composition of central government expenditure

Source: China National Statistical Bureau, *Statistical Yearbook of China*, Beijing: Statistical Publishing House, 2011.

Figure 27.3 shows the shares of major central government expenditures in total central government expenditures in 2010. Defence expenditures accounted for 32.4 per cent of total central government expenditures, science and technology 10.49 per cent, interest payments on domestic and foreign debt were 9.4 per cent, transportation stood at 9.3 per cent, public security 5.5 per cent, general public services 5.2 per cent, education 4.5 per cent, and social safety net and employment effort 2.8 per cent.

Local government expenditures mainly include sixteen items: (1) capital construction; (2) enterprise innovation funds; (3) science and technology funds; (4) additional appropriation for enterprises' short-term funds; (5) geological prospecting expenses; (6) operating expenses of the department of industry; (7) transportation and commerce; (8) agricultural production support and agriculture operating expenses; (9) operating expenses for culture education, science, and healthcare; (10) pensions and relief funds for social welfare; (11) government administration; (12) price subsidies; (13) urban maintain and construction expenditure; (14) supporting underdeveloped areas; (15) simple construction in commerce department; and (16) other miscellaneous expenditures.

Figure 27.4 shows the major items of local government expenditure as a share of total local government expenditure. The proportion of total local government expenditure spent on education was 16 per cent, general public services 11.5 per cent, social safety net and employment effort 11.7 per cent, agriculture, forestry, and water conservancy 10.5 per cent, urban and rural community affairs 8.1 per cent, medical and healthcare 6.4 per cent, public security 6.3 per cent, transportation 5.4 per cent, and environmental protection 3.2 per cent.

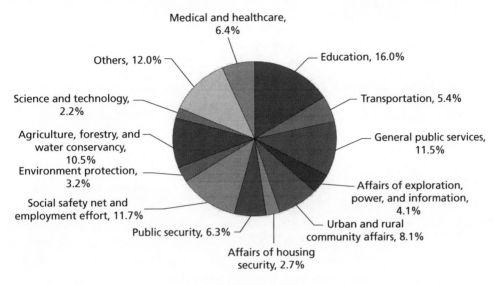

Figure 27.4. Share of major items in total local government expenditure

Source: China National Statistical Bureau, *Statistical Yearbook of China*, Beijing: Statistical Publishing House, 2011.

27.5 **Challenges to China's government expenditure**

China faces problems in the allocation of government expenditure. First, the government spends too little on education, healthcare, and scientific development. For example, in 2010 China's education expenditure accounted for 3.13 per cent of GDP, lower than the world average. To achieve sustainable development, China must spend more in key areas, such as education, health, and sciences.

Second, central government does not take enough expenditure responsibility. China's public expenditure system has been distorted by the unbalanced fiscal responsibilities of different government levels. In 2010, local governments directly received 48.9 per cent of total tax revenue, but undertook 82.2 per cent of total expenditure. They rely heavily on central government for transfers.

Third, government expenditure lacks transparency, something which is undermined by the antiquated system of classifying expenditure. In particular, the existence of off-budgetary government expenditure makes it difficult to determine the allocation of government expenditure.

28 China's high saving puzzle

Guonan Ma and Dennis Tao Yang

Over the past two decades, one defining feature of the Chinese economy has been its extraordinarily high and rising saving rate (Ma and Wang, 2010; Yang et al., 2012; Yang, 2012).[1] China saves more than half of its GDP, exceeding all OECD economies, overtaking Singapore as the top Asian saver, and ranking the highest among all global economies of meaningful size. China is an outlier in the prediction of aggregate saving from a wide range of empirical models. Moreover, China's saving rate has been exceptionally high relative to its own history. Its gross national saving rate fluctuated at around 35–40 per cent per cent of GDP in 1980–99, followed by a persistent upsurge reaching 53 per cent of GDP in 2010.

Framing the Chinese economy in the context of its saving–investment balance is useful. By definition, aggregate saving plus consumption is equal to GDP; thus, a high and rising saving rate implies a low and falling consumption rate. China's aggregate consumption to GDP ratio declined from 62 per cent in 1992 to 47 per cent in 2010. However, China's private consumption has been anything but weak. Consumption expenditure grew at some 8 per cent annually in real terms during the same period, as testified by the tripling or quadrupling in the penetration of consumer durables, such as colour TVs, refrigerators, washing machines, air conditioning, and cars.

The declining consumption share is attributable to the fact that the Chinese economy grew even faster than consumption. During the same period, China's annual GDP growth hovered at around 10 per cent per annum, mainly powered by still stronger investment spending. Gross capital formation increased at a breakneck speed of over 12 per cent per annum over these two decades, as its share in terms of GDP rose from 38 per cent to a staggering 48 per cent by 2010. Remarkably, China's high and rising saving rate—from 36 per cent of GDP in 1992 to 53 per cent in 2010—exceeded the country's high level of investment, causing a saving–investment gap. Accordingly, China's current account surplus surged from around 1 per cent of GDP to a peak of 10 per cent in 2007, before settling back towards 5 per cent in 2010. In consequence, within a decade, China swung from a net debtor nation of 10 per cent of GDP to a net creditor of 30 per cent.

---

[1] The views expressed here are those of the authors and do not necessarily reflect those of the BIS.

Therefore, such high and rising saving holds the key to understanding China's economic performance and imbalances. These savings levels helped to finance strong growth, while keeping average inflation at 2 per cent over the past decade. China's internal imbalances, a profile of domestic demand driven by 'over-investment', have more to do with high saving and little to do with 'anaemic' consumer spending. The country's external imbalances, large current account surpluses underpinned by an export-led growth model, relate more to high savings rather than under-investment. Thus, any meaningful rebalancing of the Chinese economy begs the puzzling question of why China incurs great savings.

Solving this puzzle has proven difficult. The composition of China's rising gross national savings level defies any simplistic interpretations. All three sectors in the Chinese economy—household, corporate, and government—are high savers (see Figure 28.1). Individually, these sectors may not be exceptional: as a share of GDP, China's corporate saving at best rivals that of Japan, household saving is below that of India, and government saving is less than that of Korea. However, these combined and simultaneous high savings levels distinguish China from its international peers.

The evolving contributions of these three sectors of Chinese savers to aggregate saving also challenge conventional wisdom. During much of the 1990s, China's aggregate saving changed little in relation to output, with modest falling household and government saving, but with this offset by noticeably advancing corporate saving. However, from 2000 to 2008, gross national saving rose from 37 per cent to 53 per cent of GDP. The change in the aggregate saving rate over time can be decomposed into the changes in individual average saving rates and income shares of the three sectors. A decomposition analysis for this period reveals three major sources of increased saving: (a) a sharp rise in the share of disposable income of the enterprise in GDP; (b) an increase in the household saving rate; and (c) an increase in the government saving rate. All three sectors help drive up aggregate saving in China.

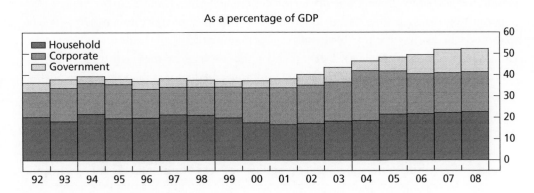

Figure 28.1. Gross national savings by sector, as a percentage of GDP

Sources: ADB; OECD; national data; authors' own estimates.

At least three sets of related questions are important for understanding the high and rising Chinese saving puzzle. First, what are the key driving forces behind the individual saving components and their interactions? Second, what are the prospects for China's gross national saving rate? Third, what government policies are useful for rebalancing the Chinese economy?

A growing body of literature aims to solve this puzzle. Although intense efforts have been allocated to the study of Chinese household saving behaviour during the 2000s, it is noteworthy that household saving is only one component of aggregate saving. Chinese urban household surveys suggest a U-shaped age-saving profile in recent years, which sharply contrasts the hump-shaped saving patterns implied by the life-cycle hypothesis. A flattened age–earning profile associated with structural changes in the Chinese labour market, serious gender imbalances leading to greater competition in the marriage market, and reduced pension benefits during economic transition are some of the recent advances towards understanding China's rising household propensity to save. Controversy remains over whether the improving but still limited access to consumer credit and low interest rates help drive personal savings upwards. Finally, China's worsening income inequality can lift the household propensity for saving.

Corporate saving is the sum of depreciation and retained earnings. Rising corporate earnings were mainly facilitated by enhanced corporate efficiency owing to massive enterprise restructuring in the late 1990s, slow wage growth capped by a large labour pool, and export expansion associated with China's 2001 World Trade Organization (WTO) accession. Controversy remains over the roles of monopoly, subsidies, difficult external financing, and low dividends in boosting retained corporate earnings. However, the central question is not whether these distortions exist, but whether they worsened to become a principal driver behind the increase in corporate profits. With regard to the government, the rise in taxes on production, income taxes, social insurance contributions, and revenues from land sales far exceeded the moderate growth in its consumption. As a result, the government savings rate increased from 3.3 per cent of GDP in 2000 to 8.4 per cent in 2008.

Some progress has been made in understanding corporate and government saving behaviour. Nevertheless, few attempts have explored the potential economy-wide forces influencing Chinese aggregate saving in a consistent manner. For instance, rapid growth and industrialization, a sizeable pool of surplus labour, and a compressed demographic transition, together with developments in education and housing ownership reforms, may have combined to accentuate a complex transition process that features a falling labour share, boosts corporate profits, and weakens the state company-based social safety net. All of these jointly increase the aggregate savings rate. China's WTO entry might accommodate this transition through increased foreign direct investment and expanding overseas export markets, thereby helping to explain the concurrent rising savings rate and strong consumer spending.

Much remains unexplored and to be learned, but the cumulative research efforts thus far should allow a glimpse at the medium-term prospects for the Chinese savings rate.

We judge that this savings rate is probably approaching a plateau and will likely trend lower in the coming decade. If China's pool of surplus labour substantially diminishes in future years, one would expect an increased wage share in the Chinese economy, boosting consumption and dampening corporate profits. Should the anticipated acceleration of China's population ageing set in later in this decade, output growth may slow and public social spending may rise. Large corporate efficiency gains from painful restructuring may be a one-off, and so may be the positive income shock emanating from the WTO accession, especially following the global financial crisis.

In general, a gradual easing of China's savings rate from its current high level should eventually imply both a more balanced domestic demand and current account, given its already very high investment rate. However, in reality, rebalancing China's growth model is easier said than done, given the inherent tensions among internal and external rebalancing and growth. History shows that an increase in consumption with a decline in saving relative to GDP often relates to a measurable growth slowdown. In addition, domestic rebalancing does not necessarily bring about external rebalancing. Indeed, the Japanese experiences in the 1980s show that, during its transition from a mainly investment-driven model towards a more consumption-oriented economy (domestic rebalancing), its current account surplus widened considerably and persistently as the economy slowed.

Three sets of government policies can facilitate the anticipated transition to a lower savings rate. First, a wide range of deregulations could be the most useful measure to manage tensions between growth and rebalancing. These deregulations may include cutting entry barriers to the labour-intensive services sector, improving access to external financing for small firms, and reducing frictions in rural–urban labour migration. These pro-growth measures support jobs and wages, promoting consumption and easing corporate saving. Second, policies may aim to strengthen the social safety net covering healthcare, pensions, and low-income support. An expanded poverty reduction programme is also helpful. However, care must be taken to focus on a broader and more efficient coverage of basic social services, and avoid unsustainable generous welfare schemes. Third, checks should be put in place to restrain the government tendency to keep to itself a large portion of the growth dividend, without providing sufficient social services accordingly. Tax cuts and administrative fee reductions would be a good start in this regard.

■ REFERENCES

Ma, Guonan and Yi Wang. 2010. China's high saving rate: myth and reality. *International Economics* 122, 5–40.

Yang, Dennis T. 2012. Aggregate savings and external imbalances in China. *Journal of Economic Perspectives* 26, 125–46.

Yang, Dennis T., Junsen Zhang, and Shaojie Zhou. 2012, Why are saving rates so high in China? In *Capitalizing China*, edited by Joseph Fan and Randall Morck. University of Chicago Press.

29 Monetary policy in China

Eswar Prasad and Boyang Zhang

China's increasing openness to trade and financial flows and the economy's gradual transition to a market-oriented one has increased the importance of developing an effective monetary policy framework. Monetary policy plays a crucial role in macro-economic and financial stability, helps to promote the efficient allocation of resources, and serves as a buffer against internal and external shocks. China's monetary policy framework has evolved over time but remains constrained by a managed exchange rate regime, institutional weaknesses, and an underdeveloped financial system that reduces the potency of the monetary transmission mechanism.

29.1 Current state of monetary and exchange rate policies

The main nominal anchor for China's monetary policy has been the nominal exchange rate, which was pegged to the dollar from the mid-1990s until July 2005 (Naughton, 2007). In that month, the renminbi was revalued against the US dollar by about 2 per cent and, according to the People's Bank of China (PBC), the currency was thereafter managed against an undisclosed basket of currencies. In practice, the renminbi has remained tightly managed against the dollar, with the PBC subsequently indicating that on any given trading day the bilateral exchange rate would be allowed to float within a band of 0.3 per cent relative to the closing price of the previous day. The renminbi was re-pegged to the dollar during the global financial crisis and then once again allowed to appreciate against the dollar starting in June 2010. In April 2012, the floating band was widened to 1.0 per cent per day (People's Bank of China, 2012).

The exchange rate regime has restricted the PBC's ability to use the conventional monetary policy instrument of the policy interest rate. Until the end of 2011, there were strong pressures on the renminbi to appreciate. The PBC had to intervene heavily in the foreign exchange markets to prevent further nominal appreciation of the renminbi. This has led to a dramatic accumulation of foreign exchange reserves, from a level of $156 billion in 2000 to $3.2 trillion as of the second quarter of 2012 (Prasad, 2011; Prasad and

Ye, 2012). While China does have capital controls in place, these controls have become increasingly porous over time, compromising the independence of monetary policy (Prasad and Wei, 2007).

A further constraint is that, until recently, banks' deposit and lending rates were directly controlled by the government. Since 2003, interest rates have been progressively liberalized and the situation now is that the baseline deposit rate constitutes a ceiling for deposit rates and the lending rate is in principle fully determined by the market. Thus, in principle, banks can set interest rates more freely than in the past although the baseline deposit rate is still set by the government and cannot be increased by competition for deposits among banks. In practice, actual lending and deposit rates do still cluster around the baseline rates, suggesting that distorted incentives and noncompetitive behaviour have dampened the effects of interest rate liberalization. For instance, as noted by Prasad (2009), state-owned banks (which still dominate the banking system) have a strong incentive to lend to state-owned enterprises, as such loans are effectively backed by the government.

Figure 29.1 shows that the baseline deposit and lending rates have moved in lockstep, and with limited variation, over the last decade. Real interest rates, shown in Figure 29.2, are of course more volatile. It is interesting to note that the real deposit rate has been low or negative for much of the last decade, with the rate being especially low (largely negative) in 2004 and 2007. In those years, the real lending rate was also quite low. Many authors have argued that the low deposit rates, which cannot be increased when banks compete for deposits due to the deposit rate ceiling, effectively impose a tax on households and is

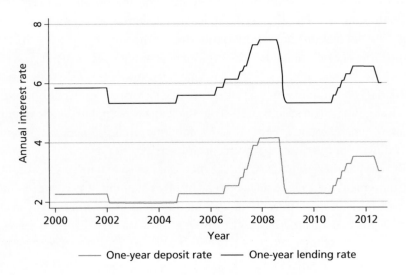

Figure 29.1. Benchmark nominal deposit and lending rates (in percent)

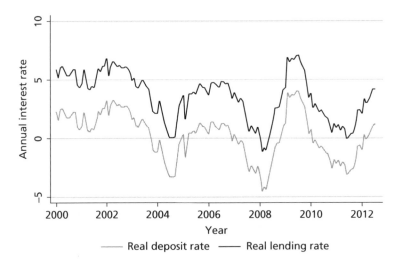

Figure 29.2. Real deposit and lending rates (in percent)

a sign of financial repression (see, e.g., Prasad, 2009; Lardy, 2008, 2012). The absence of other avenues, such as corporate bond markets, for less-risky saving opportunities has kept Chinese households in the thrall of banks despite low returns on savings.

In market economies, policy interest rates typically affect the interbank lending market and, through that channel, eventually affect real economic activity. In China, the large banks have a broad base of retail deposits that tend to be weakly interest-elastic, making these banks less sensitive to changes in baseline rates. By contrast, the smaller banks, such as joint stock commercial banks, tend to rely more on the interbank markets for their short-term funding and liquidity needs. These smaller banks are therefore more sensitive to interest rate fluctuations but the five large state-owned banks, which still account for about two-thirds of assets and liabilities in China's banking system, are far less sensitive.

Given the weaknesses in the interest rate channel of monetary transmission, the PBC has tended to rely on quantity measures. These take the form of guidance on credit expansion as well as guidance on specific industries that banks are encouraged to offer more (or less) credit to, depending on broader macro-economic circumstances as well as concerns about slowdowns (or overheating) in specific industries.

The PBC has another policy instrument that it has used extensively in recent years—reserve requirements as a percentage of deposits. By changing reserve requirements, the PBC can effectively drain or inject liquidity into the banking system. Banks can also place additional deposits with the PBC, constituting excess reserves. Excess reserves may be considered a liquidity buffer and may also reflect weak credit demand conditions.

During the last decade, reserve requirements were used as a monetary management tool and to sterilize the effects of foreign exchange market intervention. Consequently,

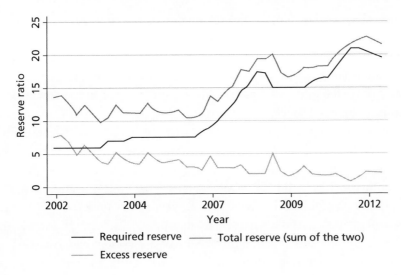

Figure 29.3. Reserve ratios (in percent)

the required reserve ratio rose sharply over the last decade (Figure 29.3). The cuts in this ratio during the worst of the global financial crisis and more recently in response to the economic slowdown of 2012 indicate that this ratio is used as a policy tool to both tighten and ease monetary policy. The excess reserves ratio has gently trended downward over time but is somewhat volatile, indicating that banks use this as a liquidity management tool. The rates of remuneration on required and excess reserves were 1.62 per cent and 0.72 per cent, respectively, as of September 2012. The PBC has also used changes in these rates to signal its monetary policy intentions.

During the previous decade, the PBC reached a limit in terms of sterilized intervention through the purchase of government bonds as the supply of those bonds was rather limited given the low level of explicit central government debt (less than 20 per cent of GDP). This led the PBC to issue its own short-maturity bills and to use those as a sterilization tool, by varying both the quantity and rate of remuneration on those bills. The total amount of outstanding PBC bills peaked in 2008 at around $700 billion (the yield on those bonds at the time was about 4 per cent). More recently, the outstanding stock of PBC bills has diminished substantially. In January 2013, the PBC announced the adoption of two new quantitative policy tools—Short-term Liquidity Operations (SLO) and Standing Lending Facility (SLF).

The picture that emerges from this discussion is of a heavily constrained monetary policy framework where the nominal exchange rate remains the key nominal anchor and a variety of mostly quantitative tools are used to implement monetary policy.

This combination of policies has delivered relatively moderate inflation over the last decade. But it does have a price in terms of economic welfare and efficiency. An independent interest rate policy is a key tool for improving domestic macro-economic management and promoting stable growth and low inflation. As the Chinese economy becomes more complex and market-oriented, it will become harder to manage through command and control methods than it was in the past. And, as it becomes more exposed to global influences through its rising trade and financial links to the world economy, it will also become more exposed to external shocks.

Monetary policy is typically the first line of defence against macro-economic shocks, both internal and external. Hence, having an independent monetary policy is important for overall macro-economic stability. Monetary policy independence is, however, a mirage if the central bank is mandated to attain an exchange rate objective. A more flexible exchange rate is a prerequisite for an independent monetary policy.

Independent interest rate policy, in turn, is a key input to financial sector reforms. Chinese banks have still not developed appreciable risk-assessment expertise or been given the right incentives to lend on commercial principles. Using interest rate policy, rather than government directives, to guide credit expansion is essential to encourage banks to become more robust financial institutions. Trying to foster the commercial orientation of the banking sector in the absence of monetary policy tools to guide credit and money growth is one of the factors holding back banking reforms.

Goodfriend and Prasad (2007) argue that China should eventually adopt an explicit inflation objective—a long-run range for the inflation rate and an explicit acknowledgement that low inflation is the priority of monetary policy—as a new anchor for monetary policy. An inflation objective, coupled with exchange rate flexibility, would work best to stabilize domestic demand in response to internal and external macro-economic shocks. Indeed, focusing on inflation stability is the best way for monetary policy to achieve broader objectives such as financial stability and high employment growth. Over time, the inflation objective would provide a basis for currency flexibility. Thus, exchange rate reform will be seen as a key component of an overall reform strategy that is in China's short- and long-term interests.

■ REFERENCES

Goodfriend, Marvin and Eswar Prasad. 2007. A framework for independent monetary policy in China. *CESifo Economic Studies* 53(1), 2–41.

Lardy, Nicholas. 2008. Financial Repression in China. *Policy Brief 08–8I*, Washington DC: Peterson Institute for International Economics.

Lardy, Nicholas. 2012. Sustaining China's Economic Growth After the Global Financial Crisis. Washington DC: Peterson Institute for International Economics.

Naughton, Barry. 2007. *The Chinese Economy: Transitions and Growth*. Cambridge, MA: MIT Press.

People's Bank of China. 2012. *Highlights of China's Monetary Policy in the Second Quarter of 2012*, Beijing: PBC.

Prasad, Eswar. 2009. Is the Chinese growth miracle built to last. *China Economic Review* 20, 103–23.

Prasad, Eswar. 2011. Role Reversal in Global Finance. NBER Working Paper No. 17497.

Prasad, Eswar and Shang-Jin Wei. 2007. China's approach to capital inflows: patterns and possible explanations. In *Capital Controls and Capital Flows in Emerging Economies: Policies, Practices, and Consequences*, edited by Sebastian Edwards. Chicago: University of Chicago Press.

Prasad, Eswar and Lei Ye. 2012. *The Renminbi's Role in the Global Monetary System*. Washington DC: Brookings Institution.

30 China's inflation in the post-reform period

Feng Lu

30.1 Overview

In a similar way to other economies adopting a paper money system, the contemporary Chinese economy faces the troubles of inflation. The causes and expressions of inflation, however, differ between the different institutional settings. As China is transforming from a planned economy to an open market economy, inflation that was previously hidden has gradually been transformed into ordinary inflation, reflected by the growth of various general price indexes. For the past decade or so, inflation in China was also manifested in the raising of various asset prices, making the issue of inflation more complicated. There are debates among the opinions of monetarists and structuralists with regard to the underlying causes of inflation. The policy measures adopted by the government to combat inflation in China are much diversified and go beyond the scope of most conventional textbooks on macro-economics.

During the planning period of the 1950s to the 1970s, the prices for most goods and services were determined by the administration in China. As a result, there were limited observed price changes, but widespread shortages and disequilibrium in supply and demand, as demonstrated through 'hidden and repressed inflation' (Kornai, 1980; Nuti, 1986: 37–82). Only one price hike occurred in the aftermath of the Great Leap Forward in the late 1950s, which led to unprecedented expansion in industrial investment, especially in steel related sectors, severe crop failures, and famines in the early 1960s. The annual growth rate of total credit was 76 per cent, 63 per cent, and 21 per cent in 1958, 1959, and 1960 respectively, while the credit growth rate for industrial sectors was 194 per cent, 186 per cent, and 43 per cent, respectively (Ming Su, 2007: 1060). The growth rate of the consumer price index (CPI) was 16 per cent in 1961 but fell quickly to 3.8 per cent in 1962 and –3.9 per cent in 1963.

In the post-reform period, the institutional setting in China changed from a planned system to a market regime and the prices of most goods and services were gradually liberalized by the early 1990s. China established its stock market in the early 1990s and also implemented housing reforms in the 1990s. Along with this process, inflation was

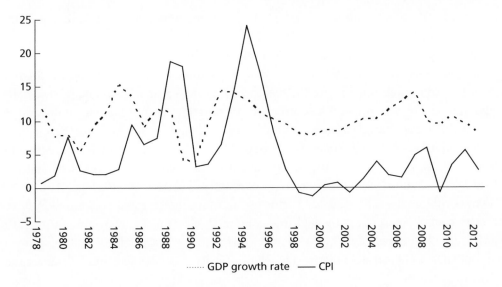

Figure 30.1. Annual change of GDP growth rate and consumer price index in China, 1978–2012 (%)

Source: Various volumes of *China Statistical Yearbook*, China Statistical Bureau.

increasingly reflected in the surges of various general price measurements. As shown by the CPI and GDP growth rates in Figure 30.1, the Chinese economy experienced four rounds of inflation in the post-reform period.

30.2 The first inflation in the early 1980s

The first wave of inflation in China's post-reform period occurred in the early 1980s when CPI grew at 7.5 per cent in 1980. In view of the fact that most goods and services were still administratively controlled at that time, the real inflation pressure was higher than the growth rate of CPI in 1980 alone indicates. The major driving force for the first round of inflation was the so-called 'New Great Leap forward', which was formulated in 1977–78. The plan dictated that China would build 120 large-scale projects. To implement the plan, China's government commissioned 22 large imported projects totalling $7.8 billion in 1978 (Xin Su, 2007: 480–1), that was equal to almost 80 per cent of China's total export revenue that year. It was this plan that provided the main impetus for the aggregate demand shock that resulted in the inflation.

The surge in investment put pressure on the fiscal balance and the money supply. The growth rate of money in circulation increased by 27 per cent and 29 per cent in 1979 and 1980, respectively, which were the highest since the Great Leap Forward campaign in the late 1950s and early 1960s (Ming Su, 2007: 1059–63). Although China registered a fiscal surplus of 1.01 billion yuan in 1978, the balance turned into deficit of 20.6 billion yuan, equivalent of 5.2 per cent of GDP in 1979.

The policy makers decided to deal with excessive expansion and inflation by establishing the powerful Financial and Economic Committee of the State Council in March 1979. The Committee put forward the 'eight words principle', of 'adjustment, reform, consolidation and enhancement'. The entrenchment programme continued until the end of 1980 at which the Central Committee of the Chinese Communist Party (CCP) decided to 'further adjust the national economy'. The major measures adopted include: (1) reduction of the scale of fixed asset investment and infrastructure investment projects; (2) cutting defence and administrative expenditure; (3) strengthening the credit management, freezing of corporate deposits, and hard selling of treasury bonds totalling 4.8 billion yuan to state owned enterprises. Through the combined effects of the above measures, CPI declined to 2.5 per cent and 2.0 per cent in 1982 and 1983, respectively, and the growth rates of GDP and fixed asset investment fell drastically to 5.2 per cent and 5.5 per cent in 1981, respectively.

30.3 The second wave of inflation in the mid and late 1980s

The Chinese macro-economy entered a new phase of tremendous expansion in the mid and late 1980s. During the period of 1983–88, the growth rate averaged 11.44 per cent. In particular, the economy grew by15.2 per cent in 1984, a record high, and 13.5 per cent in 1985. CPI increased by 9.3 per cent in 1985 from 2.7 per cent in 1984, and then slowed to 6.5 per cent and 7.3 per cent in 1986 and 1987, before surging to around 18.8 per cent in 1988. Although the expansion of economic activity slowed down drastically in 1989, CPI grew by 18 per cent due to the lagged effects of inflation.

This episode of inflation was caused by various factors. CCP announced an ambitious plan in 1982 to quadruple the total economic scale by the end of the twentieth century. It decided to speed up reform in urban areas in 1984. The pro-reform and development environment encouraged local governments and enterprises to quickly expand investment. Inflation was also fuelled by excessive growth in the number of loans. In 1984 and 1985, total credit increased by 35 per cent and 30 per cent, respectively (Ming Su, 2007: 53–4). Differing opinions in academic and policy making circles, regarding how to assess the risk of inflation in an environment of rapid growth, probably delayed the necessary policy measures to control inflation (Hong Liu, 2002: 247–70). The announcement in August 1988 of a decision to push forwards the reform of price liberalization in a loose monetary environment was interpreted by the general public as a signal of another round of inflation, triggering panic buying and even a bank run that immediately resulted in the most dangerous period of inflation in China's post-reform era.

Anti-inflation policy underwent a tortuous process in this period. In late 1984 and 1985, the State Council held three meetings of provincial governors, requiring local governments to take measures to control the excessive expansion of investment and consumption. The People' Bank of China (PBC), the central bank in China, strengthened controls on credit quotas and twice increased the interest rates for both deposit and loans. As a result the inflation and GDP growth rate declined to 6.5 per cent and 8.8 per cent in 1986.

Facing a rapid decline in money aggregates and a drastic slowing-down of real economic activity in the first quarter of 1986, the policy makers were worried about an overshooting of the entrenchment policy and started to relax the supply of credit and money in the second quarter of 1986. As a result, M0 and M1 growth rates bounced back to around 30 per cent in early 1987, CPI and RPI also reversed their early declining trend and picked up to around 6–7 per cent in early 1987 and close to 10 per cent at the beginning of 1988, from 2–3 per cent in the summer 1986. GDP growth rate rose to 11.6 per cent in 1987.

At the beginning of 1988, the mainstream opinion viewed inflation as a structural price escalation resulting from a poor harvest in the agricultural sector. The policy makers decided to implement a dual breakthrough of reform on prices and wages. Because the macro-economic environment was under pressure due to the excessive money supply and widespread inflationary expectation, the price reform measures served to signal to the general public another round of inflation and triggered panic buying in the market and even a bank run. The monthly CPI rose from 10 per cent in early 1988 to nearly 28 per cent in early 1989. This serious level of inflation, coupled with the corruption related to the dual-track price system, caused widespread social discontent and instability.

Endorsed by the 3rd Session of the 13th CCP Conference, the government's policy priority shifted to rectifying the problem of inflation in September 1988. The austerity programme of so-called 'forced landing' included various measures aiming at fighting inflation and controlling excessive aggregate demand. First, the programme drastically reduced the fixed asset investment scale and stopped the examination and approval of investment projects outside the plan. Second, the 'forced landing' programme controlled institutional procurement, and strengthened price regulation, including placing a temporary price ceiling on vital production materials. Third, the programme introduced strict control on the expansion of credit and temporarily blocked credit to township and village enterprises. Fourth, it raised the required reserve ratio of commercial banks and twice raised interest rates. The banks provided inflation-proof interest rates for three-year saving deposits.

Inflation was quickly brought under control but economic growth was severely interrupted. Nominal fixed asset investment declined from 25.4 in 1988 to –7.4 per cent in

1989 and 2.4 per cent in 1990. The GDP growth rate fell from 11.3 per cent in 1988 to 4.1 per cent in 1989 and 3.8 per cent in 1990. The CPI growth rate fell from 18.8 per cent in 1988 to 18 per cent in 1989 and 3.1 per cent in 1990.

30.4 The third wave of inflation in the first half of the 1990s

In 1990, the government started to exit from the extremely tight macro-economic policy introduced at the end of 1988 which produced only modest effects. The macro-economy began to recover in 1991, mainly driven by the brisk pace of the non-state-owned firms. After the famous southern tour by Deng Xiaoping in the early 1992, economic reform was revitalized.

Driven by the reform breakthrough and the impetus of economic recovery, the Chinese economy quickly entered a new phase of rapid growth and inflation. In 1992 and 1993, M1 increased by 35.9 per cent and 38.8 per cent respectively and M2 grew by 31.3 per cent and 37.3 per cent respectively. The growth rates of nominal fixed asset investment surged to 44.4 per cent and 61.8 per cent in 1992 and 1993. During a four-year period from 1992 to1995, China's GDP growth rates were 14.2 per cent, 14.0 per cent, 13.1 per cent, and 10.9 per cent respectively, while CPI grew by 6.4 per cent, 14.7 per cent, 24.1 per cent, and 17.1 per cent, respectively. In 1994 inflation reached a record high for the entire post-reform period.

The policy makers decided to implement sixteen points of tightening policy by announcing 'the opinion regarding the current economic situation and strengthening the macro-economic adjustment and control by Central Committee of CCP' in June 1993. The measures included raising interest rates, issuing treasury bonds to finance fiscal deficits, requiring local authorities to sell a quota of treasury bonds, reducing bank loans and interbank lending, requiring that a firm's initial public offering on the stock market was first approved by government agencies, reducing fixed asset investments and administrative expenditure by 20 per cent, and temporarily suspending new price reform measures, and so forth.

The novelty with this new round of tightening policies was that it was coupled with a new wave of bold economic reform measures. The 3rd Session of the 14th CCP Conference in November 1993 launched comprehensive reforms in the areas of public finance and taxation, finance, and the exchange rate regime, SOE reforms and social securities, and so on. Implementation of the reform measures laid the foundation for the so-called socialist market economic system.

The comprehensive tightening policies gradually took effect in the next two to three years. The growth rates of M1 and M2 declined to 18.9 per cent and 25.3 per cent in 1996. The growth rates of GDP and nominal fixed asset investment fell to 10 per cent and

14.8 per cent in 1996. The growth rate of CPI also decreased to 8.3 per cent in 1996. Due to changes in the internal and external environment, Chinese macro-economic growth slowed further and eventually entered mild deflation in 1998–99.

30.5 The new inflation in the recent decade

China's economy witnessed an unprecedented boom in the early years of the twenty-first century. The average real GDP growth rate in 2000–10 was 10.4 per cent, and for the period 2003–07 was 11.6 per cent. In addition, due to the real appreciation of the Chinese currency, RMB, the average growth rate of GDP measured in US dollars was 17.2 per cent during 2000–10. Per capita GDP in US dollars increased from about $1,000 in 2000 to more than $4,000 in 2010 (Feng Lu, 2012: 40–51). China has become the most important contributing country to global economic growth in terms of the incremental growth of various bulk commodities, capital formation, aggregate demand, and international trade.

China's inflation in the recent decade has presented a new pattern with various characteristics. First, inflation has manifested not only in periodic rises in the conventional goods and services price indices, but is also reflected in a distinct surge in asset prices. Monthly CPI increased by more than 5 per cent in the third quarter of 2004 and at the end of 2010, and exceeded 8 per cent in the first quarter of 2008. There were five years in the recent decade (2004, 2007–08, 2010–11) in which the GDP deflator ranged between 6.7 per cent and 7.8 per cent. The rise in asset prices is also indicative of the inflationary pressure during the period. The Shanghai Stock Exchange Composite Index surged from 1,300 at the beginning of 2006 to 6,250 in October 2007. Commodity housing prices increased several-fold in the decade 2000–10.

Second, the source of monetary expansion underpinning inflation has been largely transformed. In the 1980s and 1990s, there were two main channels through which excessive expansion of PBC's balance sheet was transmitted into inflationary pressure. The first is monetization of fiscal deficits. When excessive fiscal deficits occurred and the capability of the government to issue treasury bonds was restricted in the 1980s, the deficits had to be financed through a withdrawal from the central bank which caused inflationary pressure. The second channel related to a situation in which the central bank was under pressure to provide excessive loans to the state-owned commercial banks to present them from becoming insolvent. The root cause for this situation was that numerous state-owned enterprises (SOEs) were unable to compete in the new market environment, and banks were obliged to provide loans for SOEs to allow them to survive as the large-scale exit of SOEs was politically unacceptable before the major SOE reform in the late 1990s. The third channel relevant in the recent period is relatively new. The massive accumulation of a foreign exchange reserve replaced the excessive liquidity provision to the treasury and commercial banks as the most important single source for the excessive balance sheet expansion of the PBC. During 2003–12, broad money (M2) increased by 2.3 times and the total assets of the PBC increased by 2.75 times while the proportion of foreign exchange reserve in the total PBC asset increased from 54.3 per cent to 71.7 per cent. The external imbalance has become a major driving force behind internal imbalance and domestic inflation.

Third, the policy instruments adopted in China's macro-economic management, called 'macro-adjustment and control (MAC)', were much more diversified. Apart from the conventional monetary and fiscal measures, the sectoral and quantitative policy tools were also frequently adopted as MAC policy instruments. The sectoral and quantitative policy tools range from restrictions or even a temporary prohibition on investing in specific sectors, raising the required capital ratio for investment in specific sectors, to a tightening of the regulations on environment protection or the provision of urgent subsidies for the production of certain agricultural products and so on. In dealing with inflationary problems, the Chinese government occasionally used administrative policy tools of such as a temporary suspension of land supply for urban investment, temporary price freezes, and the like, especially if the situation of inflation were viewed as particularly serious or urgent (Feng Lu, 2013).

Although the diversified policy instruments made positive contributions to maintaining macro-economic stability, they produced various side-effects on the normal functioning of the market. They were also detrimental to fully utilizing the adjustment functions of the price mechanism by interest rates and exchange rates, in coordinating the Chinese open macro-economy. Excessive dependency on diversified MAC tools has not been helpful for improving the market mechanism. The new Chinese government formed in early 2013 placed a high priority on the reform agenda in the areas of fiscal, financial, and macro-economic policies. Should these reforms be appropriately designed and implemented, the Chinese economy will be in a better position to prevent and combat inflation in future.

■ **REFERENCES**

Kornai, J. 1980. *Economics of Shortage.* Amsterdam: North Holland.
Hong Liu. 2002. *The Academic and Critical Biography in the Contemporary China: Jinglian Wu.* The Shaan Xi Normal University Press.
Feng Lu. 2012. China's contribution to the world: Economic growth, resource consumption and global imbalance. *China Economist* 7(4), 40–51.
Feng Lu. 2013. Macro Adjustment & Control (MAC)—Aggregate Demand Management with China's Style (2000–2010). CCER Discussion Paper Series (In English), No.E2013004.
Nuti, D. M. 1986. Hidden and repressed inflation in Soviet-type economies: Definitions, measurements and stabilization. *Contributions to Political Economy* 5(1), 37–82.
Ming, Su. (ed.) 2007. *China Financial Statistics (1949–2005), Vol. II.* Beijing: China Finance Press.
Xin, Su. 2007. *Economic History of New China.* Beijing: Press of Party School of Central Committee of CCP.

31 Local government debts

Yiping Huang

China's public debt stood at 15.5 per cent of GDP at the end of 2012, which contrasts sharply with both the USA, which has been under the pressure of high debt burdens, and the eurozone, which has been suffering from debt crises. However, pubic debt does not fully capture the potential liabilities of the Chinese government. Important components of contingent liabilities include non-performing loans of financial institutions, funding gaps of the pension system, losses of the state-owned enterprises (SOEs), and local government liabilities. If all explicit and implicit debts are taken into account, total government liabilities could amount to above 100 per cent of GDP at the end of 2012, according to some economic analyses (see, for instance, Chang et al., 2013).

In recent years, local government debt has become a key source of concern in terms of the fiscal sustainability in China. This is primarily because local government liabilities grew exponentially after the global financial crisis. According to an official audit in early 2011 by the National Audit Office (NAO), total borrowing by the Local Government Investment Vehicles (LGIVs) totalled ¥10.7 trillion, equivalent to 27 per cent of GDP in that year. Different from traditional local SOEs, LGIVs are the entities set up by local governments for infrastructure development. Their liabilities accumulated rapidly after 2008 as part of the government's broad stimulus package to boost economic growth. LGIV borrowing increased by about ¥6 trillion during the 2009–10 period. In 2011, new bank lending to LGIVs rose only by ¥300 million. However, LGIVs' borrowing did not stop. Instead, they tapped into the newly developed shadow banking businesses, such as by issuing those high-return wealth management products (WMPs). Bond issuance also rose significantly in recent years, to ¥1.25 trillion in 2012, doubling the level of the previous year. This was in addition to ¥250 billion issued by the Ministry of Finance (MOF) on behalf of various local governments.

There was wide suspicion that the 2011 audit result significantly underestimated the actual liabilities of local government. This doubt was later reinforced when it became clear that there were no systemic data on shadow banking transactions. In mid-2013, soon after taking office, the Li Keqiang government ordered a thorough survey of the situation. Some economists estimated that total LGIV borrowing rose to ¥19 trillion at the end of 2012, equivalent to 37 per cent of GDP (Zhang et al., 2013).

According to the Budget Law, local governments are not allowed to run a budget deficit. Many local governments, however, routinely overspend for several reasons. One import-ant reason is that, since the 1994 tax reform, there is a serious mismatch between revenue and responsibility at the local level. The reform divided tax revenue into three groups: the first group, including revenue from consumption taxes, vehicle purchase taxes, and tariffs, goes to central government; the second group, including revenues from business, resources, land use and property taxes, goes to local government; and the third group, including revenue from value added and income taxes, is shared by both the central and local government. In 2011, for instance, central government received 54.2 per cent of total fiscal revenue. In contrast, local governments are responsible for more than 70 per cent of spending, resulting in a figure which is often greater than the amount of fiscal revenue available to them, including the 47.8 per cent of total fiscal revenue they receive in the first round of distribution plus the transfer payment from central government in the second round.

The transfer system was set up to address local fiscal inadequacy, ensure sufficient pub-lic services, and reduce regional disparities. However, it suffers from a number of defi-ciencies, preventing it from being a predictable and reliable source of finance (Shah and Shen, 2006). These include: (1) a complex and opaque system with few individuals know-ing about all the programmes and their underlying allocation basis; (2) a lack of central coordination and transparency (only 22.5 per cent of total intergovernmental subsidies from central government were audited in 2003); and (3) a lack of a regulatory framework to ensure accountability and results.

Local governments have to find their own ways to fill this funding gap. In addition to their regular fiscal responsibilities, local government has another driver which encour-ages them to overspend—to boost economic growth. Economic studies reveal that GDP growth was often seen as one of the most important determinants of career advancement for senior local officials (see, for instance, Li and Zhou, 2005). Therefore, senior local gov-ernment officials often act more like corporate executives than public servants, trying to attract more investment projects to their own regions and, at times, making local govern-ment investments themselves.

A thirst for revenue sometimes led to peculiar government behaviour. In some places, local governments have assigned explicit quotas for traffic fines and fines for violating the One-child Policy. Another common practice is to sell land (strictly speaking, selling the leasing rights of land). According to the Chinese Constitution, rural land is owned by a collective and urban land is owned by the state. However, a change of land uses, from arable to construction for example, requires approval by local government. In recent years in some municipalities, land sales revenue has often accounted for one-third or even one-half of a local government's total revenue. Taking 2012 as an example, local governments' direct fiscal revenue was ¥6.1 trillion, the transfer payment from central government was ¥4.5 trillion, and revenue from land sales was ¥2.7 trillion. Land sales revenue accounted for about 20 per cent of total local government revenue in that year, and had been slightly below 25 per cent in 2011.

The so-called soft budget constraint enables the LGIVs and other local government entities to borrow extremely large amounts from banks, other financial institutions, and capital markets. Although local governments are not officially permitted to incur budget deficits, they can borrow without constraint because there are no separate balance sheets for individual local governments. A widely accepted assumption is that if a local government fails to repay a debt, the central government has to step in and pick up the bill. The soft budget constraint for local government borrowing led to a serious moral hazard problem and caused significant consequences—both borrowers and lenders tend to relax their risk controls due to available 'third-party insurance' (central government's implicit guarantee). Governor Zhou Xiaochuan of the People's Bank of China (PBC) once blamed the local government's soft budget constraint for the loss of controls over bank credit and other monetary variables (Zhou Xiaochuan 2012). A more direct consequence of the soft budget constraint for the local government is the rapid accumulation of local government liabilities.

The 2011 government audit revealed some detailed information about local government borrowing. Of the total borrowing, which was likely under-reported, bank loans, bond issuance, and borrowing from higher levels of the government contributed 79 per cent, 7 per cent, and 4 per cent, respectively. In terms of borrowers, LGIVs, local government agencies and departments, and subsidized government organizations and entities accounted for 47 per cent, 23.3 per cent, and 16 per cent, respectively. Again, municipal-level governments incurred the largest amount of borrowing, accounting for 43 per cent of the total debt outstanding, followed by provincial governments (30 per cent) and county governments (27 per cent). And, finally, roughly half of the debt (49 per cent) was incurred during the 2009–10 investment boom, and more than half was used for local infrastructure development—urban infrastructure and transportation together accounted for 55 per cent of total debt, while 9 per cent was social spending.

At the time of 2011 audit, NAO discovered that nearly half of local government borrowing would mature during 2011 and 2012. It was impossible for those debts to be to repaid as most of the infrastructure projects were on-going. For instance, total local government debt issued to fund the construction of expressways was ¥1.1 trillion. Most of this debt relies on rollovers (issuing new debt to repay old debt) for repayment. In 2010, the rollover rate of expressway debt was as high as 55 per cent. This practice is likely to continue in the coming years as most of the original borrowing will mature before 2016.

A study of data on 869 LGIVs, which accounted for 72 per cent of total LGIV debt in 2012, reveals that the total debt rose by 39 per cent during 2011–12, despite a sudden halt placed on new bank lending (Zhang et al., 2013). The same study also found that over half of LGIV debt would have been at risk of default in 2012 and that 70 per cent would have defaulted without government support in the case of a liquidity crisis. In the earlier audit, the NAO also identified several major risks associated with local government debt. The first was a lack of transparency and the non-compliance of local government financing. The second was exclusion of debt issuance and repayment plans from the budgets of most local governments. And, finally, the third was a lack of proper corporate governance at most LGIVs.

Clearly, local government debts are a major threat to the sustainability of China's fiscal system. But it is likely that this is a flow problem, not a stock problem. At this stage, the Chinese government still has enough room and means to contain the risks of local government debt. To start with, China still has large state-owned assets totalling ¥53.4 trillion in 2009, of which ¥27.9 trillion belonged to central government while ¥25.5 trillion belonged to local governments (Chang et al., 2013). The central government also maintains a generally healthy fiscal position in most years. Meanwhile, a large proportion of the local government debts is backed by some sort of asset and, therefore, is not a net liability. In addition, an study based on China's national balance sheet estimated China's total national assets at ¥294 trillion in 2008 (Cao et al., 2012). Of this, corporates held the largest share, at 42 per cent, followed by households (21 per cent), commercial banks (25 per cent), government (8.3 per cent), and overseas holdings (4 per cent). It also put total national liabilities at ¥153 trillion that year. Thus, the country had net assets of ¥141 trillion.

However, if the central government fails to curb the rapid expansion of irresponsible borrowing by local governments, then liabilities could quickly outgrow the government's assets and China could suffer a debt crisis, with serious and widespread implications for economic activities, financial institutions, social welfare systems, and political stability.

The Li Keqiang government has started to take action to pull together effective fiscal reform programmes to reduce fiscal risk. One likely step to be undertaken in the coming years to reduce the mismatch of revenue and responsibility at the local level is to shift some spending responsibilities, such as those on legal, education, healthcare, and social welfare systems, back to the central government. In order to effectively contain the risks of local government debts, however, important policy changes will be needed in at least three areas. First, the promotion schemes for government officials should be amended to deemphasize the importance of GDP growth. This would mean that local officials would not be so enthusiastic about expanding investment projects in order to boost GDP growth. Second, the central government needs to create reliable and sustainable revenue sources for the local governments which are compatible with their responsibilities. This could involve some kind of further decentralization of fiscal revenue. In particular, the local governments should not be left to find additional resources themselves to fulfil policy responsibilities introduced by the central government. And, third, local governments should have their own independent balance sheets and become accountable for all their fiscal liabilities. Their borrowing behaviour would then be properly disciplined by the financial markets, both in terms of how much they can raise and at what cost.

■ REFERENCES

Cao, Y. et al. 2012. *Restoring the National Fiscal Health*, Beijing: Bank of China.

Chang, J., L. Yang, and Y. Huang. 2013. How big is the Chinese government debt? *China Economic Journal*, 6(2-3),152–171.

Li, H and L. Zhou. 2005. Political turnover and economic performance: The incentive role of personnel control in China. *Journal of Public Economics* 89(9–10), 1734–62.

Shah, A. and C. Shen. 2006. Reform of the intergovernmental transfer system in China. Policy Research Working Paper Series 4100. Washington DC: The World Bank.

Zhang, Z., C. Hua, and W. Chen. 2013. China's heavy LGFV debt burden, *Asia Special Report*. Hong Kong: Nomura Global Markets Research.

Zhou, X. 2012. Characteristics of China's monetary policy in the new century, Speech at the Caixin Annual Conference China and the World. 17 November 2012, Beijing.

32 China is headed for a financial crisis and a sharp slowdown

Nouriel Roubini and Adam Wolfe

32.1 China's solution to the global financial crisis—overinvestment

When the global recession caused China's net exports to plummet from 7.7 per cent of GDP in 2008 to 4.3 per cent in 2009, China reacted not by raising the consumption share of GDP—which has remained at 35 per cent since 2008—but instead by further increasing the gross capital formation share of GDP from 43.8 per cent to 47.2 per cent in 2009 alone. Thus, the collapse of net exports did not lead to a severe recession—as occurred in Japan, Germany, emerging Asia, and other export-led economies. However, the shift towards investment has continued well beyond the rebound in Chinese growth that began in Q2 2009. Fixed investment increased further to 49.2 per cent of GDP in 2011, a record high for any major economy, largely due to state intervention to ensure that cheap capital was available for infrastructure spending, commercial and residential real estate investment, and capacity expansions for state-owned enterprises.

No country in the world can be productive enough to take almost 50 per cent of GDP and reinvest it into new capital stock without eventually facing massive overcapacity, a non-performing loan problem for the banking system and a surge in public debt through contingent liabilities. In the last fifty years, all historical episodes of excessive investment have ended with a hard landing, a financial crisis and/or a long period of low growth. And these hard landings have occurred not only in cases of housing booms, which always end with a crash, but even in episodes of overinvestment in manufacturing and industrial capacity: from the Soviet Union in the 1960s–80s, to Latin America in the 1970s–early 1980s, to Japan in the 1980s, to the USA in the 1990s, to East Asia in the 1990s. Chinese rebalancing away from investment is inevitable, and so are the consequences for growth. Rebalancing away from investment-led growth, whether by policy design or policy mistake, invariably results in slower GDP growth. In a sample of twenty-four countries that have seen a structural peak in their investment share of GDP since 1980, growth slowed from an average 5.5 per cent in the three years preceding the peak to 0.9 per cent in the three years afterwards.[1]

China's post-2007 investment boom is showing similar signs of instability, as the productivity of those investments continues to decline. The efficiency of capital accumulation can be estimated by the incremental capital–output ratio (ICOR), or how many marginal units of investment are required to produce one additional unit of GDP. From 2000 through 2007, China achieved an average 10.5 per cent GDP growth rate with an average 39.8 per cent investment rate and had an ICOR of 3.9. Most emerging markets have ICORs in the 3.7 to 5.8 range, meaning that China was one of the most productive investors in the emerging markets space before the global financial crisis. However, from 2008 through to 2011, China invested an average 47.5 per cent of its GDP each year, but only managed to generate 9.6 per cent growth and an ICOR of 5.0. In other words, whereas it used to take 3.8 units of investment to produce one unit of GDP, after the global financial crisis it took 5.0 units for China to produce the same output. In 2012, an investment rate of 48 per cent of GDP produced only 7.7 per cent GDP growth, meaning China's ICOR rose to about 6.2. In terms of investment productivity, China's response to the global financial crisis pushed it from top of the class to failing in four years.

Looking at an example at the micro level can provide a better sense of why the productivity of Chinese investment is falling. Poor investment does not appear to be a problem with China's massive airport construction binge so far. On the demand side, passenger traffic at China's airports increased by 230 per cent between 2003 and 2011, reaching 280 million, and the existing supply seems fairly well matched to demand. In 2010, China's sixteen busiest airports (9 per cent of the total) handled 67.7 per cent of total air traffic in the country, and the top fifty-one airports (29 per cent of the total) handled 95.2 per cent of total passenger traffic. This is similar to the USA, where the busiest 9 per cent of airports accounted for 76 per cent of the passenger traffic and the top 29 per cent of airports accounted for 89 per cent of the total. Since the value of a network tends to increase along with its density, although with decreasing returns to scale, and Chinese demand for air transport is growing, further expansion of the airport network makes sense. However, the current rate of expansion looks unsustainable. First of all, the growth rate in passenger traffic is levelling off as the base becomes bigger. From 2003 through 2007, passenger traffic increased at a compound annual rate of 21.3 per cent; from 2007 to 2011, this slipped to 11.1 per cent. As the flow of new demand slows, the rate of the growth of new supply should as well. It is already difficult to imagine that the forty-five airports scheduled to come on line before 2015, most of which are in areas

---

[1] The countries in which investment as a share of GDP reached a structural, though not necessarily permanent, peak are Argentina, Australia, Austria, Bolivia, Chile, Denmark, Finland, Hong Kong, Iceland, Indonesia, Ireland, Israel, Japan, South Korea, Malaysia, Mexico, Norway, the Philippines, Portugal, Singapore, Spain, Sweden, Thailand, and Vietnam, according to IMF data in the World Economic Outlook database.

of low-population density, will generate sufficient productivity gains to justify their expense when 71 per cent of the existing network is barely being used at all. It is even more difficult to believe that China can increase this figure to forty-six airports next year, which is what would be necessary for the flow of investment to increase (assuming all airports are of equal value and they are constructed at a linear rate). Furthermore, the value of a dense airport network will be undermined to some extent by China's simultaneous drive to build the world's largest high-speed train network, which will also compete with China's new highways.

32.2 Chinese overinvestment is not due to measurement error

We do not believe that China is a special case, and its period of overinvestment will end just like every other in the history of the world. However, some argue that China *is* different because either its capital stock is low, suggesting plenty of room for further investment, or its investment level is being significantly overstated because consumption is systematically undercounted by the National Bureau of Statistics.

A low capital stock has not prevented similar investment busts in emerging markets in the past. Capital investments are undertaken to increase the productivity of labour, as new transport networks allow labour to move to areas where production is located, new electricity capacity allows those production clusters to increase output, and so on. Investment helps to narrow the gap in labour productivity with the lead country, but as this process plays out the incremental gains from new investment become smaller and more difficult to achieve. This does not mean that China should stop adding to its capital stock at a rapid rate any time soon, but the annual increase in those additions should become smaller as the potential returns take longer to materialize. Instead the flow of Chinese investment continues to grow.

The various arguments that Chinese consumption is significantly understated tend to hinge on the differential between the growth rates of retail sales and private consumption, the vast amount of undercounted wealth in China, and/or rapidly rising wages. First, retail sales are not equivalent to consumption, as the data are captured at the point of sale, not final use, which means that government and wholesale purchases are included in the series. Likewise, while the incomes of China's elite are clearly understated, the sampling method of Wang and Woo (2010), on which the estimates that consumption is understated by up to 20 per cent are based, is problematic. Data based on non-random sampling and self-reporting to an acquaintance should be subject to an even larger margin of error than the household survey data collected by the National Bureau of Statistics. Finally, while wages have been rising rapidly, especially for migrant workers in the coastal provinces, none of the available data suggest that total wage growth outstripped GDP until at least 2012. We agree that consumption is slightly undercounted, mostly due to household services going under reported, but this is likely only a percentage point or two of GDP.

32.3 Still, China faces a different kind of crisis

In 2013–16, after years of falling returns on its capital investments and rising capital structure and maturity mismatches, China appears poised for a financial crisis and/or a sustained period of below-potential growth. However, China's financial crisis is unlikely to be like those we have seen in other emerging markets because of its persistent current account surplus, closed capital account, state-ownership of the banking sector, and a near limitless ability of the People's Bank of China (PBC) to create liquidity.

Alongside lower returns on its capital investments, China has also seen a sharp rise in its gross total debt stock, which we estimate increased from 168 per cent of GDP at the end of 2007 to 223 per cent of GDP in 2012. Most of the increase in debt stock occurred from Q4 2008 through the end of 2009; however, since 2010 China has seen a large increase in the complexity of debt instruments in the shadow banking system. This financial innovation has done nothing to allocate capital more efficiently in China, but rather was a response aimed to circumvent the state intervention intended to control credit growth. Domestic savings trapped in the country by the closed capital account have always sought higher real returns than the negative rates available on bank deposits. Thus property became a major savings vehicle, especially after the domestic equity market collapsed in late 2007. Government restrictions that made it more difficult to invest in property after 2009 encouraged the creation of new financial products to tap this pool of savings, much of which was directed to property developers, heavy industrial producers, and other sectors that faced similar regulatory constraints on their borrowing. Banks and trust companies thus matched return-starved savers with capital-starved borrowers through wealth management products and other fixed-income products that are not recorded on bank balance sheets. These products are extremely risky—most offer extremely short maturities even though they are backing long-term products—and they are unlikely to remain off-balance sheet in a crisis. Worryingly, the issuing of wealth management products and non-bank lending jumped sharply in 2012.

The bust is more likely to look like Japan's post-bubble collapse, although lost decades due to deflation exacerbating a 'balance sheet recession' are unlikely. By definition, a current account surplus means that China continues to have excess savings even as its investment rate has increased beyond the point of sustainability, and the surplus is likely to widen as investment falls more sharply than savings in an economic downturn. Alongside a closed capital account, this should ensure that there is a pool of savings available to refinance China's debt stock without a sudden stop. State-ownership of the banking sector, while a contributing factor in creating the problem, will also help to ensure that those rollovers go smoothly. Meanwhile, even in a situation in which China's overall balance of payments falls into deficit, as it did briefly in Q2 2012, the PBC can lower banks' required reserve ratios and sell its foreign assets to create RMB and ensure sufficient liquidity in the system.

While the endgame may not be as severe as in other emerging markets, China is well on its way towards an investment bust from which its financial system is unlikely to escape unscathed. We expect consumption to hold up rather well through this process, growing around its trend rate of 7–9 per cent annually in real terms, but we do not think it is possible for consumption to accelerate by the 1.5 percentage points required to maintain steady headline GDP growth for every percentage point that investment is expected to slow. The labour market will be hit by a slowdown in construction activity, and high-net worth households are likely to face negative wealth effects from falling property values. Government policies and increased subsidies may be able to offset some of these effects, but we expect Chinese GDP growth to slip to 4–6 per cent sometime not too long after 2013.

■ **REFERENCE**

Wang, Xiaolu and Wing Thye Woo. 2010. The Size and Distribution of Hidden Household Income in China. Working Paper.

33 How can China's financial system help to transform its economy?

Franklin Allen and Jun 'QJ' Qian

33.1 Funding the hybrid sector

Our definition of the hybrid sector includes all non-state, non-listed firms, including privately or individually owned firms, and firms that are partially owned by local governments (e.g. Township Village Enterprises or TVEs).[1] In earlier work (Allen et al., 2005, 2008) we show that the growth of this sector has been much higher than that of the state sector and the listed sector, and it has contributed most of China's economic growth. Over the period 1990–2010, the hybrid sector has employed an average of over 77 per cent of all non-agricultural workers, while TVEs have been the most important employers providing (non-agricultural) jobs for residents in the rural areas.

Firms from the hybrid sector do not raise external funds from markets; we also find that most of the bank credit goes to the state and listed sectors. Beyond internal funds, these firms rely on 'alternative financing channels' that include all the non-bank, non-market sources. The most successful part of the financial system, in terms of supporting the growth of the overall economy, is this alternative financial sector, including many types (including informal) of private credit agencies and related financial intermediaries, and coalitions of various forms among firms, investors, and local governments. Many of these financing mechanisms rely on governance mechanisms *outside* the formal legal system, such as competition in product and input markets as well as among different coalitions and informal institutions, and trust, reputation, and relationships. The alternative financial sector, along with the non-legal governance mechanisms, is the main force behind the phenomenal growth of the hybrid sector. In fact, Allen and Qian (2010) argue that conducting business outside

[1] We wish to thank Ravi Kanbar for helpful comments, and Boston College and the Wharton Financial Institutions Center for financial support. The authors are responsible for all remaining errors.

the legal system in fast-growing economies such as China can actually be superior to using the law as the basis for finance and commerce. Going forwards, the co-existence of the alternative financial sector with banks and markets can continue to fuel the growth of the hybrid sector.

33.2 **More financial products and further development of financial markets**

The Shanghai and Shenzhen Stock Exchanges were established in 1990. The real estate market also went from nonexistent in the early 1990s to one that is currently comparable in size with the stock market. Both the stock and real estate markets have experienced major corrections during the past decade, and are characterized by high volatilities and speculative short-term behaviour. An important lesson from the evolution of financial markets around the globe is that these markets do not provide sufficient diversification of risks for investors and firms. Other types of markets and more financial products including derivatives need to be developed. Doing this can enhance the risk management capabilities of China's financial institutions. Deep and efficient markets can provide an alternative to banks for raising large amounts of capital.

The government bond market is the largest fixed income securities market; the second largest component is called 'policy financial bonds', with proceeds invested in government-run projects and industries such as infrastructure construction. In terms of the amount of outstanding bonds at the end of 2008, the corporate bond market is less than one-quarter of the size of the government bond market; the growth of the corporate bond market, however, has picked up pace in the past few years.

We attribute the (relatively) poor performance of the stock market in recent years to a number of factors. A significant problem for corporate governance is the large overhang of nontradeable shares owned by government entities. The good news is that many of these shares have been floated on the market through the share reform carried out during recent years. Other ways to reform the stock market include the listing of more firms from the hybrid sector. The establishment of the 'Growth Enterprises Market' provides an example in this regard. More legal and business (accounting and finance) professionals should be trained. In most developed countries institutional investors, such as mutual funds and hedge funds, play an important role. This leads markets to have a higher degree of efficiency than if they are dominated by individual investors. There are also advantages in terms of corporate governance if institutional investors actively monitor firms' managers as blockholders. Currently institutional investors are relatively small in terms of assets held given their early stage of development in China. However, they are expanding dramatically and this trend should continue.

33.3 **Private equity/venture capital and the funding of new industries**

Dubbed as the 'world's manufacturer', China has been successful in expanding low cost, labour-intensive industries over the past three decades. However, as income level rises so do labour costs, and China cannot rely on these industries to sustain growth and provide the bulk of employment opportunities in the long run. Hence, it is crucial for China to develop new industries and become a world leader in these sectors. Allen and Gale (1999, 2000a) argue that markets are better than banks for funding new industries, because evaluation of these industries based on experience is difficult, and there is a wide diversity of opinion. Investors can gather information at a low cost and those that anticipate high profits can provide finance through the markets to the firms operating in the new industries. A key part of this process is the PE/VC sectors: venture capitalists are able to raise high levels of funds in the USA because of the prospect that successful firms will be able to undertake an IPO and the existence of an active IPO market.

These facts imply that the development of active PE and VC markets can increase the financing for China's new industries. What is unusual about China is that it currently has the ability to develop both traditional industries, such as manufacturing, and new, high-tech industries, such as aerospace, bio-genetics, and green energy products. This is different from the experience of South Korea and Taiwan in the 1970s, as they focused on developing manufacturing industries first. Allen and Gale also argue that banks are better than financial markets for funding mature industries because there is wide agreement on how they are best managed, so the delegation of the investment decision to a bank works well. This delegation process, and the economies of scale in information acquisition through delegation, makes bank-based systems more efficient in terms of financing growth in these industries.

33.4 **Funding social safety networks and local governments**

As compared to many developed economies, households in China have much higher savings rates, and much of the savings are for precautionary reasons such as medical expenses. Thus, to encourage domestic consumption social safety net programmes should be further developed. Financial institutions such as insurance companies and asset management industries including pension funds can play a major role. With a rapidly ageing population and the growth of household disposable income, further development of a multi-pillar pension system, including individual accounts with employees' self-contributed (tax exempt) funds that can be directly invested in the financial markets, can lead to the development of both the financial and fiscal systems.

Other non-bank financial institutions such as insurance companies also play an important role in the development of social safety networks. In terms of the ratio of total assets managed by insurance companies over GDP, China's insurance industry (about 10 per cent of GDP) is significantly smaller than that of other Asian economies (South Korea, Taiwan, and Singapore, all over 30 per cent). The insurance industry is also significantly smaller compared to China's banking industry, and property insurance is particularly underdeveloped due to the fact that the private real estate market was only recently established. Only 4 per cent of the total population was covered by life insurance, and insurance premiums were only 3.2 per cent of GDP in 2008, standing far behind the global average figure of over 7 per cent; coverage ratios for property insurance are even lower.

Finally, local governments are important providers of social welfare services and programmes, and it is important that they should be able to raise revenues independently. According to the model in developed countries such as the USA, their revenue sources include taxes on consumption and property taxes. In addition, local governments should be allowed to raise funds through financial markets, such as by issuing municipal bonds while pursuing a balanced budget fiscal approach.

33.5 **Preventing financial vrises**

In recent years, banking crises have often been preceded by abnormal price rises ('bubbles') in the real estate and/or stock markets. Allen and Gale (2000b) provide a theory of bubbles and crises based on the existence of an agency problem. Many investors in real estate and stock markets obtain their investment funds from external sources. If the providers of the funds are unable to observe the characteristics of the investment, there is a classic risk-shifting problem due to limited liabilities. Risk shifting increases the return to risky assets and causes investors to bid up asset prices above their fundamental values. A crucial determinant for asset prices is the amount of credit that is provided for speculative investment.

If the non-performing loans in the banking sector of China spike up and/or if economic growth slows significantly then there may be a banking crisis. However, given its strong financial position, the government can prevent this situation from getting out of control. Bubbles and crashes in real estate markets could cause a banking crisis that will be more damaging to the real economy. Booming real estate markets attract speculative money into properties with a large amount coming from banks. The agency problem in real estate lending and investment mentioned above worsens this problem. If the real estate market falls significantly within a short period of time, defaults on bank loans could be large enough to trigger a banking crisis. Given the fact investors may borrow (from banks) to finance their investment, a future stock market crash could also have serious consequences. Therefore, a banking crisis triggered by crashes in the real estate and/or stock markets represents the most serious risk of a financial crisis in China.

A new breed of financial crises emerged starting in the 1980s. A common precursor was financial liberalization and significant credit expansion and subsequent stock market crashes and banking crises. In emerging markets this is often accompanied by an exchange rate crisis ('twin crises') as governments choose between lowering interest rates to ease the banking crisis or raising them to defend the home currency. Finally, a significant fall in output occurs and the economies enter a recession. China has experienced a large increase in its foreign exchange reserves since 2001. This experience is not unique for China. Many East Asian countries have experienced similar problems induced by large (private) capital inflows starting in the late 1980s.

To offset the inflationary effect of the increasing foreign reserves, the central bank can sterilize the foreign assets by taking opposite actions with domestic assets, or implement other contractionary monetary policies. In China's case, the major sterilization tools are open market operations and raising required reserve ratios. To make sterilization effective, China also has to impose tight capital controls, though such controls are somewhat porous. A better solution for China and for a more balanced world of capital flows, would be to develop RMB as one of the world's major reserve currencies and hence reduce the incentives of all surplus countries to hoard US dollars and invest in safe dollar-denominated assets.

The rapid increase in foreign exchange reserves in recent years suggests there is a lot of speculative money in China in anticipation of an RMB revaluation. If there is a significant future revaluation or if after some time it becomes clear that there will not be one, then much of this money may be withdrawn. If the central bank and government allow the currency to float so that they do not use up the exchange reserves, then any falls in the value of the RMB may occur quickly and this may limit further outflows. If they try to limit the exchange rate movement, there may be a classic currency crisis. This in turn may trigger a banking crisis if there are large withdrawals from banks. Quickly adopting a full float can help to avoid a twin crisis, and thus reduce the overall economic costs of the currency crisis.

■ REFERENCES

Allen, Franklin and Douglas Gale. 1999. Diversity of opinion and financing of new technologies. *Journal of Financial Intermediation* 8, 68–89.

Allen, Franklin and Douglas Gale. 2000a. *Comparing Financial Systems*, Cambridge, MA: MIT Press.

Allen, Franklin and Douglas Gale. 2000b. Bubbles and crises. *Economic Journal* 110, 236–55.

Allen, Franklin and Jun Qian. 2010. Comparing legal and alternative institutions in commerce. In *Global Perspectives on the Rule of Law*, edited by Heckman et al. Routledge-Cavendish.

Allen, Franklin, Jun Qian, and Meijun Qian. 2005. Law, finance, and economic growth in China. *Journal of Financial Economics* 77, 57–116.

Allen, Franklin, Jun Qian, and Meijun Qian. 2008. China's financial system: past, present, and future. In *China's Great Economic Transformation*, edited by L. Brandt and T. Rawski. Cambridge: Cambridge University Press.

Part VI
Urbanization

34 Urbanization in China

J. Vernon Henderson

China's economic achievements since 1978 have been remarkable: the transformation to an export, consumer-good-oriented economy with an emerging service sector and 8.5 per cent annual growth rates in per capita income. Key to this transformation has been urbanization. The rapid growth of the service and export sector and the move from capital-intensive heavy industry to lighter, more labour-intensive manufacturing are sustained by a movement of labour out of rural activities into cities. Cities with their agglomeration economies and knowledge spillovers are viewed as the engines of growth in developing countries. In China, in 1978 17 per cent of the population was urbanized. By 2010 the rate was over 45 per cent with a corresponding rise in the share of migrant workers in the urban labour force from under 0.5 per cent in 1978 to about 46 per cent in 2010.

China's urbanization process has distinct features and challenges. Foremost are the restraints imposed on migration out of the rural and into the urban sector in China, compared to other countries. Despite the changes, these restraints delayed and distorted the urbanization process. Perhaps more critically, the nature of the restraints may be largely responsible for China's extraordinary degree of income and social inequality. In addition there are concerns about the development of an economically healthy urban economic hierarchy, emerging out of the Maoist era.

34.1 Urbanization policy and the *Hukou* system

In 1978 China had nearly 300 million workers in agriculture and a rural sector that was almost entirely agriculture based, in contrast to the rest of the world. While the surplus of labour in agriculture and the lack of rural sector industry and services were well recognized, the prescription was not to encourage widespread urbanization. Rather it was to move, in relative terms, the workforce out of farming, but to limit population movements. As formulated in the early 1980s (and reflected in the 1982 national plan), there was development of town and village enterprises (TVEs) whereby workers 'leave the land but not the village' with a policy that any population moves should be short distance into smaller cities. Moves into bigger cities were to be strictly limited and any longer distance migration should be temporary.

The mechanism of control was the household registration system, or the *Hukou* system. Under the *Hukou* system a person is a citizen of the village or urban district where their parent (until recently mother) is a citizen. Until the early 2000s, changes in citizenship were very limited. The most fundamental division remains between those with urban and rural *Hukou*. Traditionally urban *Hukou* holders were entitled to a job, housing, a set of food rations (until 1992), and public services in their locality. Rural *Hukou* holders had land allocations, food allocations, and services. Legal migration required a set of permissions from the place a person left, the place they went to, and fees. Most critically, a migrant moving to a city was entitled to nothing in the city—no jobs, job training and placement services, formal sector housing, or, in particular, urban services such as access to schooling and healthcare. Today permission to move and the payment of fees are no longer required but access to urban goods and services remains restricted. Rural migrants live in dorms and in 'urban villages' on land still under rural control, which in many cases are essentially urban slums. Lack of local *Hukou* means migrants may still be denied basic public services including schooling for their children. In smaller and medium-size cities there has been greater integration, especially among rural versus urban *Hukou* holders from the local area. There are more opportunities to convert *Hukou* status and many cities have partially followed State Council directives to open urban services to migrants, although this is less true in the biggest cities.

In 1978, the beginning of the reform era, the urban–rural consumption ratio was roughly 2.1:1. That gap in real income is an inducement to migrate, where migration acts as the arbitrage mechanism in national labour markets. However, weighing against that were quotas that limited arbitrage. More recently the limiting factor has been the cost of migration, relative to costs in other countries. What sets China aside are two things. First is the limit on access to public services, such as schooling for children. Second are the rural sector anchors: there is little ability to sell rights to rural land leaseholds or implicit shares in TVEs, and in some cases even housing. So the move to the city has to be achieved without resources and involves abandoning effective claims in rural areas.

34.2 Outcomes of restrained migration

These limits on migration have a number of potential outcomes. First is under-urbanization. Arguably, China remains under-urbanized at 45 per cent versus, for its income level, an expected rate of 55 per cent or more. There are still over 300 million workers in agriculture, an absolute size which is bigger than it was in 1978. However this surplus is a stock problem that is likely to be solved by ageing. Even in middle-income rural areas, most young people leave the village after middle or high school, at age 16–18.

And they leave with little or no knowledge of farming. Sometimes only the tails of the distribution are left—the very poor or untalented and children of rich rural families who manage their family's holdings. As the stock of rural workers ages and retires, time may solve the surplus labour problem.

A second outcome is related to the initial policy of keeping movements off the farm localized. The TVE movement was very successful until the late 1990s. Townships grew into county cities and county cities into prefectures with localized agglomerations of TVEs. This became on-the-spot urbanization: urbanization without long distance migration. However, the result was that by 1990 China's urban population was, on a world scale, disproportionately housed in smaller cities. Econometric evidence suggests there were significant productivity losses in exploiting urban scale economies, from cities being undersized at almost all points of the urban hierarchy. Again, time seems to be solving the problem; today's migrants are focused on moving to bigger cities.

What seems to be ongoing and is yet to diminish is the urban–rural consumption gap. From a level of 2.1 in 1978, this gap has climbed to well over 3, at a level of development where this gap would be expected to be sharply declining and converging to 1. In places such as South Korea or Taiwan, let alone developed countries such as the USA and Japan, the ratio is at or close to 1. This is not just a problem of excessively costly migration. It is a problem of under-development of capital in the rural sector—inferior schools and schooling opportunities and strong biases in the capital market towards the urban sector.

34.3 **The urban hierarchy**

In contrast to 1990, the size distribution of China's cities today is similar to the rest of the world, with perhaps a modest lack of big cities, although not necessarily mega-cities. There may still be non-competitive smaller cities in parts of the country whose economic fortunes may continue to decline, but perhaps no more than in other countries— competition produces losers as well as winners. China initially inherited unusual production patterns in its cities. Medium and larger cities under Maoist decentralized planning tended to produce almost the entire range of manufactured products. In contrast is the pattern in market economies where smaller and medium-size cities specialized in a narrow set of interrelated products, so that countries have cities that are highly specialize in textile, apparel, steel, wood producing, automobile, insurance, healthcare, entertainment, and so on. Even in 2000 in China, many cities continued to support non-competitive industries in their cities, sometimes financed by non-performing loans issued by state banks. Newer cities in China seem to be more specialized, some narrowly so; and older cities are shedding un-profitable industries. Increased degrees of urban specialization have been well documented.

Within the urban hierarchy, development changes the role of the largest cities. In China in 1978 the central cities of the largest urban areas were manufacturing zones, much like cities in the West in 1900. The centres of large urban areas are high-cost locations for standardized manufacturing, relative to any scale benefits they experience. With development and the building of transport infrastructure, manufacturing typically decentralizes in two stages, as well documented in the USA, South Korea, Indonesia, and India. First, there is the decentralization to the suburban or peri-urban areas of large cities followed by decentralization away from the largest metropolitan areas into smaller cities and the rural sector. The largest urban areas become centres of financial and business services, as well as housing the arts and cultural centres and in some cases high-tech activity.

China's largest cities centres have de-industrialized over the last twenty years, with the construction of ring roads and highways and better use of the railway network. In 1990 in provincial level cities and provincial capitals, the city centre (urban districts) contained about 85 per cent of all manufacturing GDP in their prefectures, while today those same areas have at most 50 per cent. However, the second stage of deindustrialization out of the largest cities has been slow to develop. These cities are now relatively less manufacturing intensive than other urban areas, but they still have huge manufacturing bases. The slower development of a large service sector in the largest cities may be due to the slow development of financial and legal institutions, as discussed in the next section.

34.4 **Two policy dilemmas**

One aspect of urbanization in China that is similar to the rest of the world, especially in countries that are yet to democratize, is favouring of the largest cities: biases in fiscal allocations and biases in capital markets controlled by the state. Analysis of this and reasons for it can be found in the literature.[1] Bias is difficult to prove, since it requires an evaluation of whether allocations are optimal or not. Evidence would be a difference in the rates of return to capital or the extent of non-performing loans in bigger versus smaller cities and rural areas. Such evidence exists for China but the data are from the late 1990s. Certainly FDI and fixed capital allocations are heavily weighted towards the largest cities, despite the relative deindustrialization of these cities. The showcase infrastructure investments in Shanghai and Beijing are well known examples of this phenomenon.

---

[1] A full set of references and data sources for this essay can be found in two papers by J. Vernon Henderson, 'Evaluating China's urbanization experience and prospects. In *Globalization and the Rural-Urban Divide*, edited by M. Gopinath and H. Kim. Seoul National University Press, 2009 and Urban and regional development. In *Medium and Long Term Development and Transformation of the Chinese Economy*, edited by E. Lim and M. Spence. China CITIC Press, 2011.

The dilemma that favouritism imposes is that it creates jobs and draws in migrants. However, favoured cities wish to resist in-migration and so make living conditions for migrants difficult. In China, for the largest cities, this is called a policy of 'raising the door sills' to restrain in-migration. The dilemma then is one of favouritism versus inequality and 'social harmony'. To reduce inequality is to reduce the double divide: the divide between conditions in the urban and rural sectors and the divide within cities between local *Hukou* holders and migrants. Migration into favoured cities is restrained by the second divisive factor. Eliminating that divide without eliminating favouritism would lead to even more migration into the biggest cities, and a pathway to over-populated mega-cities, such as Greater Jakarta or Mexico City. For example in China, the annual increase of migrants from outside the province into Beijing and Shanghai from 2000 to 2005 averaged 6.6 per cent and 8.1 per cent a year respectively in a context where at least 25 per cent of the population has non-local *Hukou*. The danger is that these cities will grow to become over-populated mega-cities with the attendant problems of congestion, pollution, poor health conditions, and high costs of living.

A related dilemma concerns state control of the financial sector and legal system. Global cities offer legally enforceable contracts and competitive financial markets. For Shanghai and Beijing to compete with such cities, including Hong Kong, for international financial and business services would require reforms in China that are slow to emerge. For the moment that limits the economic development of the biggest cities in China and may explain their on-going reliance on manufacturing.[2]

---

[2] Additional references of interest include: N. Baum-Snow, L. Brandt, J. V. Henderson, M. Turner, and Q. Zhang, Roads, Railways and Decentralization of Chinese Cities. mimeo, 2012; F. Cai, *Floating Population: Urbanization with Chinese Characteristics.* CASS, 2006; K. W. Chan, The Chinese Hukou System at 50. *Eurasian Geography and Economics* (2009) 50: 197–221; Fujita, M. and D. Hu, Regional disparities in China: the effects of globalization and economic liberalization. *Annals of Regional Science* (2001) 35: 3–37; J. R. Logan (ed.), *Urban China in Transition.* Wiley-Blackwell, 2008—see especially the chapters by M. Zhou and C. Cai, W. Wu and E. Rosenbaum, and Y. Zhou and J.R. Logan.

35 Urban wages in China

Lina Song

Urban wages in China reflect both a dualistic model of development and a transition from institutionally determined wages to market determined wages. There was no labour market in Communist China. A system of standardized wage scales was established in 1956 and applied to the country's state sector, largely equivalent to the urban sector. This system was much influenced by the Soviet model, and remained in place throughout the pre-reform period.

Urban labour was classified into two categories, staff (干部) and workers (工人). Wages were structured accordingly. Administrative personnel ('staff') were sub-divided into twenty salary grades, technicians (also 'staff') into seventeen grades, and manual employees ('workers') into eight grades. Wage tables laid down the wage payments for each grade. There were only slight regional (cost of living) and industrial variations. Workers were divided into broad occupations, and each occupation spanned a number of grades (Appleton et al., 2010). During the Cultural Revolution (1966–76) wage policy was strongly egalitarian. The need for material incentives was denied; and bonuses based on work performance were abolished.

In the same period, especially after 1958 when a residential status (*Hukou*) system was enforced, rural–urban migration was curbed. The *Hukou* system functioned as a de facto internal passport system. It provided the state with the means of preventing a permanent change of residence, and in particular of curbing permanent rural–urban migration. Even temporary migration was made extremely difficult by the urban rationing of grain and basic foods, housing, and other necessities. Consequently, the wage sector during the period was only open to those who dwelled in, and were registered in, urban areas.

In the 1980s, under the reform programme, firms were granted some autonomy to remunerate workers according to their productivity through bonuses. Bonuses were initially limited to no more than 5 per cent of a state-owned enterprise's total wage expenditure, but the limit was gradually abolished (Meng, 2000: 83). The most important feature of 1980s reform was to allow a non-state-owned sector to develop. At the same time rural to urban labour migration started due to a loosening of strict control. By the early 1990s, a large-scale wave of migration had begun. The urban wage structure became complex, with urban residents working in state-owned enterprises co-existing with other residents in non-state enterprises and with rural–urban migrants.

Around 1997, a phase of radical urban reform started; with the retrenchment of almost half of all workers in state-owned enterprises. As a result of these major policy changes, a 'labour market' outside state control seemed to be emerging from the 1990s.

There are two entirely different perspectives on the consequences of the labour policy developments. On the first view, the availability of migrants prepared to work for low wages provides potential competition for urban residents. Urban retrenchment creates an opportunity for firms to renegotiate old contracts, both formal and implicit, and may force urban residents to compete with migrants for work. On the alternative view, these developments simply create a labour market with tiers distinguished by the degree of state protection (Appleton et al., 2002, 2004; Meng and Zhang, 2001). Urban residents who kept their jobs were able to continue to be employed on preferential terms while retrenched urban workers might have suffered prolonged unemployment or entered a secondary (not state-owned) labour market. The retrenchment policy and the consequent rise in urban unemployment lead to tighter controls on migrants, aimed at restricting their numbers and in this way assisting those who were laid-off.

Earlier studies of the labour market in the mid-1990s, just prior to the introduction of the redundancy policy, found clear evidence of segmented wages between urban workers and migrants (Knight and Song, 1999a, 1999b). This arose from the political and institutional arrangements which gave urban residents privileged access to secure employment at above market-clearing wages and which controlled the flow of peasants to the cities, allowing rural migrants to fill only the jobs that urban dwellers did not want.[1]

With the mass retrenchment of the second half of the 1990s, a further distinction between workers became potentially important—that between urban residents who had suffered retrenchment and those who had never lost their job. Consequently, three tiers could be identified in the urban labour market: non-retrenched urban workers, retrenched and re-employed urban workers, and rural–urban migrants.

The highest-paid tier consists of those urban workers who were not made redundant during the 1990s. Even after standardizing for their personal characteristics (and occupations), this group were paid more than either migrants or urban workers who were re-employed after being made redundant (Appleton et al., 2002).[2] The wage structure for the 'highest tier' in a labour market was conventional. Human capital— proxied by education, good health, and experience—was rewarded and there were

---

[1] However, Dong and Bowles (2002) found no evidence of labour market segmentation between firms of different ownership categories.

[2] The latter wage differential does not appear to reflect selectivity, as it might if the 'less able' workers were more likely to be sacked. It is less clear where the two lower tiers of the labour market—migrants and re-employed urban workers—stand in relation to each other. Their average wage rates are quite similar. However, they appear to be paid according to rather different wage structures, making it unlikely that they can be regarded as jointly forming a single 'secondary' labour market.

predictable occupational differentials. Some other wage differentials—such as differences in underlying productivity—may be less justified but are nonetheless unsurprising. Men, Communist Party members, and workers in centrally owned SOEs all appear to earn wage premiums. By contrast, the cross-sectional wage structures for migrants and re-employed workers were significantly different. Within both these tiers, there were no premiums for Communist Party membership or for employment in central SOEs. One might ascribe this to the effect of greater competition eroding wage differentials not related to productivity. Where the migrants and re-employed workers do differ, however, is in terms of wage differentials by education and occupation. For migrants, these differentials resemble those estimated for non-retrenched urban workers. For the re-employed, there appear to be no returns to education and few significant occupational differentials. The results for these re-employed workers suggest that the labour market they face is a fierce one that is not working well for them. The lack of rewards for productivity may imply that their employers still lack information on this, or that the workers are forced by limited opportunities to accept low-grade jobs in which their productive characteristics have little value.

The three tiers identified may prove to be a transitional phenomenon. Using a national representative household survey, Appleton et al. (2005) found that China's urban labour market appears to be evolving towards a structure similar to that found in OECD countries. It is experiencing the emergence of a mixed economy and growing dominance of services. The rising share of workers employed in the private sector will increase the extent to which pay is determined by productivity. There has been an erosion of the premium paid to state-sector employees. Changes in ownership between 1998 and 2002 due to restructuring allowed the effects of ownership on wages to be estimated, controlling for any selectivity effects. These estimates imply that some of the apparent wage differentials by ownership may reflect selectivity effects, with more-productive workers gravitating to enterprises with foreign involvement and less-productive workers being found in urban collectives.

The shift in employment from primary and secondary to tertiary (service) sectors has also been mirrored in the urban wage structure. Manufacturing workers appeared to be favoured over those in many service sectors in 1988, but this ceased to be true during the 1990s. In addition, the gap between blue-collar and white-collar workers has widened. Some of China's recent industrial transformation has occurred through the painful progress of retrenchment in the state-owned sector, particularly in unprofitable heavy industry. While rising unemployment in the late 1990s was accompanied by real wage increases, there is evidence from the 1998–2002 panel that higher provincial unemployment has exerted a moderating effect on wages. The resulting 'wage curve' is somewhat flatter than commonly found in other countries, but is nonetheless clearly discernible (Appleton et al., 2005).

The transition to market-determined wages has seen a widening in urban wage gaps, including some defined by worker characteristics such as sex and party membership that, prima facie, are not related to productivity. Dong and Zhang (2009) used firm-level data to analyse male–female wage differences in Chinese industry in the late 1990s. Their estimates suggested that employers' discrimination against women was not a significant source of the gender wage gap in Chinese state-owned enterprises. Instead, they found that the gender gap in wages for unskilled workers was less than the gender gap in productivity. This implies that women in the state-owned sector benefited from its egalitarian wage structure, receiving wage premiums and accounting for a disproportionate share of the sector's labour surplus.

The wage premium for Communist Party membership rose in urban China during the period of pro-market reform, paradoxically given the lessening of direct Communist Party influence on promotion. However, there are some signs that the rise may be ending. When using party membership as a time-varying determinant of wages, entrance to the Party in the period 1998–2002 was associated with only a moderate rise in wages. These lower estimates compared to the cross-sectional results may reflect Party membership being a signal of pre-existing higher productivity. Alternatively, it may be that the next generation of Party members is less able to secure the privileges enjoyed by those who entered at a time when the Party and the state had a greater role in the allocation of labour. Moreover, membership of the smaller 'democratic' parties appears to bring similar benefits to membership of the Communist Party, perhaps indicating that the benefits are in terms of access to networks rather than political power relations per se (Appleton et al., 2009).

The widening inequality in urban wages during reform has attracted considerable attention and concern. Some insight into this is provided by analysis of the Chinese Household Income Project Surveys for 1988, 1995, 1999, 2002, and 2008 (Appleton et al., 2014). Breakdowns based on quantile regressions using data from the wage surveys suggest that initially, from 1988 to 1995, the rise was entirely due to changes in the wage structure rather than changes in the characteristics of workers. Most notably among the changes in the wage structure were increased returns to factors bearing on productivity, such as education and experience, but also widening occupational and industrial pay gaps. In the second half of the 1990s, these trends continued and explained two-thirds of the widening of urban wage gaps. But changes in worker characteristics—due to educational expansion and industrial restructuring—also played a role, accounting for the residual third. The rise in wage inequality seems to have paused from 1999 to 2002, but then resumed, once again largely driven by changes in the wage structure. This time, however, changes in the returns to education were seen to equalize but were outweighed by rising wage differentials due to occupation, industry, and provincial location.

■ REFERENCES

Appleton, Simon, John Knight, Lina Song, and Qingjie Xia. 2002. Labour retrenchment in China: determinants and consequences. *China Economic Review* 13(2–3): 252–76.

Appleton, S., J. Knight, L. Song, and Q. Xia. 2004. Contrasting paradigms: segmentation and competitiveness in the formation of the Chinese labour market. *Journal of Chinese Economic and Business Studies* 2(3), 185–206.

Appleton, S., L. Song, and Q. Xia. 2005. Has China crossed the river? the evolution of wage structure in China. *Journal of Comparative Economics* 33(4), 644–63.

Appleton, S., J. Knight, L. Song, and Q. Xia. 2009. The economics of Communist Party Membership: the curious case of rising numbers and wage premium during China's transition. *Journal of Development Studies* 45(2), 256–75.

Appleton, S., J. Knight, and L. Song. 2010. China's labour market: evolution and impediments. In *China and the World Economy*, edited by David Greenaway, Chris Milner, and Shujie Yao. Palgrave Macmillan.

Appleton, S., L. Song, and Q. Xia. 2014. Understanding urban wage inequality in China 1988–2008: Evidence from quantile analysis. *World Development 62,1–14.*

Dong, Xiao-yuan and Liqin Zhang. 2009. Economic transition and gender differentials in wages and productivity: evidence from Chinese manufacturing enterprises. *Journal of Development Economics* 88(1), 144–56.

Harris, John and Michael Todaro. 1970. Migration, unemployment and development: a two-sector analysis. *The American Economic Review* 60(1),126–42.

Knight, John and Lina Song. 1999a. Employment constraints and sub-optimality in Chinese enterprises. *Oxford Economic Papers* 51(2), 284–99.

Knight John and Lina Song. 1999b. *The Rural–Urban Divide, Economic Disparities and Interactions in China.* New York and Oxford: Oxford University Press.

Meng, X. 2000. *Labour Market Reform in China.* London: Cambridge University Press.

Knight, John, Lina Song, and Huaibin Jia. 1999. Chinese rural migrants in urban enterprises: three perspectives. In *The Workers' State Meets the Market: Labour in China's Transition* edited by Cook and Maurer-Fazio. London: Frank Cass.

Meng, Xin and Junsen Zhang. 2001. The two-tier labour market in urban China: occupational segregation and wage differentials between urban residents and rural migrants. *Journal of Comparative Economics* 29, 485–504.

36 Local investment climates and competition among cities

David Dollar

China started its period of reform and opening up with a number of distinctive characteristics. With about a fifth of the world's population, China has only 7 per cent of the arable land; its per capita resource endowment in oil, iron, copper, and other minerals is low. Hence the country's comparative advantage does not lie in agriculture and other primary products. Nevertheless, China began its reform with 80 per cent of the population in rural areas because the pre-reform system had maintained a rigorous household registration (*Hukou*) system that prevented rural–urban migration. Under the planned economy, the government had invested significantly in state-owned industrial enterprises. Because of concerns about security, this investment was concentrated in inland cities. So, China began its economic reform with very little industry in the coastal provinces that would be its best location economically in an era of globalization. Guangdong and Fujian provinces, close to the dynamic economies of Hong Kong and Taiwan, had virtually no industry at all.

Under the planned economy China was largely cut off from global trade and investment. In the 1950s it imported machinery and technology from the Soviet Union, but after the break between the two Communist giants around 1960, China entered a two-decade period of almost complete isolation. The legacy of isolation and Cultural Revolution was that China at the end of the 1970s was poorer than sub-Saharan Africa, backwards technologically, and in poor fiscal and financial condition.

After the death of Mao Zedong a wide range of Communist Party officials, led by Deng Xiaoping, wanted to take the economy in a different direction. Deng believed that it was particularly important to open up the country to foreign ideas and technology. This notion was still controversial, however, given the legacy of Western intervention in China. Controversial new directions in Communist Party policy were often first tried out on an experimental basis in a few locations, with good results then being scaled up to a larger level. In the case of opening up to foreign investment and trade, the party decided in 1979 to open four special economic zones that would be able to attract foreign investment and would have streamlined procedures for importing machinery and materials to be used in processing trade for export. Three of these cities were in Guangdong, one in Fujian. Other cities quickly wanted to be involved in the experiment. In 1984 fourteen more cities were given the same opportunities as the special zones. In 1993 this was expanded to the more than thirty provincial capitals plus five inland cities along the Yangzi River and nine border cities (Eckaus 1997). Thus, within a relatively short period of time dozens of Chinese cities had opened up to foreign trade and investment.

The implicit contract between the central leaders and these local governments was clear. The government 'has no money. So we will give you a policy that allows you to charge ahead and cut through your own difficult road,' was what Deng told Party leaders at a policy meeting on the special zones in 1979 (Vogel, 2011: 398). The central government did not have the resources to finance capital and technology imports. But local governments were encouraged to attract foreign investment. This policy set off intense competition among local governments to attract investment. Foreign investors were interested in entering the China market, and they had a large number of cities to choose from. Investors were naturally attracted to cities that could streamline their local bureaucracy and centralize decision-making in a small number of government offices—the proverbial one-stop shop.

Deng's governing style encouraged this competition. According to Vogel (2011: 699–700), 'Deng pulled back on the governing structure that tried to penetrate everywhere. Instead of setting tight rules that local areas had to follow, he established a system in which governing teams, selected by the next higher level, were given considerable independence as long as they managed to bring rapid growth. . . . In Deng's era and in the decades after Deng, those judgments [on local government performance] were based overwhelmingly on how much the team contributed to China's overall economic growth.'

Cities such as Shenzhen, Dongguan, Foshan, and Xiamen developed reputations for being hospitable to foreign investors and for having local officials who could help investors cut through bureaucratic problems. These successes naturally spread to other cities since local officials everywhere knew that much of the prospect for career advancement would depend on investment and growth. In the early 2000s the World Bank surveyed more than 10,000 firms in 120 Chinese cities and found considerable variation in local investment climates, with the better ones comparing very favourably with countries at a higher level of development (World Bank, 2004).

Another key aspect of local investment climates in China was economic infrastructure. China began its reform with very poor infrastructure and fiscal constraints that limited the state's ability to finance improvements. A number of early policy decisions were key to resolving these bottlenecks. In the mid-1980s the State Council allowed investment in the power sector to proceed on a cost-recovery basis. This resulted for a time in a dual-pricing system in which 'old power' was relatively cheap for the state enterprises, while 'new power' was priced to provide an adequate return to investors. Naturally new power spread very quickly. The price of power has often been high in China by international standards, but it is available and reliable. Similarly with roads: China has developed the most extensive system of toll roads in the world, with tolls that are high relative to per capita GDP. This practical approach to infrastructure pricing enabled the key economic infrastructure (power, roads, ports) to expand quickly (Dollar, 2008). Much of the financial responsibility for this development rests at the local level. Cities that could attract some initial foreign investment through better administration then had the capacity to finance investments in power and transport, and the revenue from those investments spurred further infrastructure investment.

A final key ingredient for China's industrial development was labour. Some of the locations that have risen to industrial prominence were little villages or towns, with small populations, at the beginning of reform. The *Hukou* system has continued to prevent permanent rural–urban migration, but local authorities were able to get around this constraint through the use of migrant workers. Employers could recruit rural workers to come and work in factories, hotels/restaurants, and construction activities. These migrants were typically young workers. They were not allowed to bring families with them and they were not registered urban residents, so they were not entitled to a full range of urban services. This system was very favourable for the rapid expansion of industrial activity. Cities could attract workers who would live in dormitories or on construction sites. There was no need to provide permanent housing; nor did they make claims on the social services of the city government.

The number of migrant workers has risen from basically zero at the beginning of the reform to 253 million in 2011, according to official statistics. The latter number is more than 40 per cent of today's urban workforce. Most of the increase in the urban workforce since the beginning of the reform period has come from migrant workers. The migrant worker phenomenon is likely a key reason why labour's share of GDP has fallen during China's reform and is now below 50 per cent, low by international standards.

One of the key reasons for China's overall growth has been this system in which local governments are given considerable autonomy, localities then compete intensely for investment and growth, and local officials are evaluated and promoted primarily on the basis of these economic results. While the system has been very effective at generating investment and growth, it does present some challenges for the future.

First, this model tends to undervalue factors other than growth. China's development has taken a heavy toll on the environment. It has many of the most air-polluted cities in the world and serious problems with polluted rivers and lakes. If local officials are rewarded for investment and growth during their typical five-year tenure in a position, they are not going to put much weight on environmental considerations, especially ones whose main impact is long term. There has been much discussion within the party about broadening the criteria for evaluating local officials, but in fact growth has remained the key evaluation criterion, along with political stability.

Second, the *Hukou* system is a key factor behind the large rise in inequality that has occurred during China's reform. The average urban–rural income gap has risen above 3:1, one of the largest in the world. The *Hukou* system puts labour at a disadvantage and locks the rural population out of better education and health services that are a foundation of human capital. There is continual discussion of reform of the *Hukou* system but local governments generally oppose reform. Treating the vast migrant population as citizens would mean putting more local fiscal resources into education, health, social security, and housing.

A third issue is that the current system skews incentives towards investment. China's overall investment rate has risen throughout the reform period and reached nearly 50 per cent of GDP in recent years. This raises questions about whether all this investment will in fact bear fruit in the future. For long-term growth, innovation and human capital accumulation are key. But a local official trying to increase growth over a five-year period is not going to put much weight on those factors: they both take too long to pay off. The surest way to increase growth quickly would be new investment projects: constructing infrastructure and attracting factories to use it. Thus the growth model does not put sufficient weight on human capital development and foundations of innovation such as intellectual property rights and a deep financial system.

A final point is that the decentralized governance model in China favours results over rules. This approach creates a good environment for corruption. Cities have to be careful not to have too much corruption as that can be a factor which deters investment. But certain types of corruption have flourished. All land in China is owned by the state. Farmers have use rights over agricultural land. But the government can take this land away with arbitrarily determined compensation. Many of the social and political disputes in China involve dispossessed farmers disgruntled at losing their land with poor compensation. Once local government has taken this land, it can auction it to developers and industrialists who pay the market price. If local officials pocket some or all of the difference between the compensation and the market price, this is a form of corruption that interferes little with the efficiency of investment, but rather is in the nature of a pure transfer from poor peasants to relatively well-off local officials.

In summary, local autonomy and the incentives to create good local investment climates have been an important feature of China's reform and its resulting success in achieving investment and growth. At the same time this system contributes to some of the key challenges that China now faces, including environmental degradation, rising inequality, lack of innovation, and government corruption.

■ REFERENCES

Dollar, David. 2008. Lessons from China for Africa. Policy Research Working Paper 4531, World Bank.

Eckaus, Richard S. 1997. China. In *Going Global: Transition from Plan to Market in the World Economy*, edited by Padma Desai. Cambridge, MA: MIT Press.

Vogel, Ezra F. 2011. *Deng Xiaoping and the Transformation of China*. Cambridge, MA: Harvard University Press.

World Bank. 2004. *World Development Report: A Better Investment Climate for Everyone*. Washington, DC: World Bank.

37 The value of land and housing in China's residential market

Yongheng Deng

China's nascent residential housing market has experienced a slow start since the Central Government introduced a series of residential housing and housing finance reform measures back in the 1980s. Although China's first residential mortgage loan was issued in 1986 by the China Construction Bank, the residential housing finance market did not play a visible role in the Chinese housing sector for another decade (Deng et al., 2005; Deng and Liu, 2009). In 1998, the State Council issued the 23rd Decree, which is regarded as a milestone of Chinese housing reform. Work units were no longer allowed to develop new residential housing units for their employees in any form. Starting from that point, China's residential housing market took off with unparalleled speed with respect to both price level and market scale. House prices across thirty-five major markets in China have risen by almost 200 per cent since the first quarter of 2004, with about 60 per cent of that increase occurring since the first quarter of 2007 (see Wu et al., 2012). There were two sharp periods of land price escalation in early 2007 and during 2009–10. Real constant quality prices fell after both surges. The most recent data for 2013 show a resurgence in price growth in 2013. The dramatic rise and fall of prices in China's housing and land markets have attracted global attention.

What can we learn from observing such an extraordinary shift in the housing and land markets in China? There is a large and impressive literature on measuring real estate (housing) prices in developed markets (Case and Shiller, 1989; Englund et al., 1998; Deng and Quigley, 2008). Some recent studies apply these pricing frameworks to value the prices in China's nascent housing market (see, for example, Wu et al., 2014). Based on a new and unique dataset on residential land markets across thirty-five major Chinese cities, Deng et al. (2012) reported that even with the recent pullback in land prices in 2011 observed in many markets, the average annual compound rate of real constant quality land price growth still is above 10 per cent in the typical market and exceeds 20 per cent per annum in eleven cities over the sample period from 2003 to 2011. Extremely high rates of price appreciation are not restricted to the big coastal region markets such as Beijing and Shanghai, which experienced real annual growth rates of 20.2 per cent and 23.7

per cent, respectively. In fact, the city of Hefei, the capital of Anhui province in central China, has the highest real annual average growth rate of 30.1 per cent over the sample period from 2004 to 2011. In addition, the markets of Changsha, Chongqing, Lanzhou, Nanjing, and Tianjin are almost indistinguishable from Beijing and Shanghai in the magnitudes of their land price growth. A natural question to ask is what has driven such a phenomenal boom in China's land and housing markets in recent years.

In one of the recent studies on China's residential real estate market, Deng et al. (2014) showed that large state-owned enterprises (SOEs) that are directly controlled by the central government play a major role in fuelling the surge in land prices in major Chinese cities. During the period when the central government implemented its macro-economic stimulus policies towards the end of 2008, the central government ordered its SOE banks to lend, and they lent; but primarily to the central government's non-financial SOEs. The central government ordered its non-financial SOEs to invest, and they invested; but investments were heavily concentrated in real estate and land markets. This led a substantial and rapid GDP growth in 2009, effectively countering the effects of the global financial crisis that affected many other countries that year. However, the study pointed out that the success of the Chinese stimulus through its SOE channel may well disguise a curse, as it may strengthen the flow of credit into already cash-flush central government directly controlled large SOEs, which were almost certainly not credit constrained at the time.

Local political economy factors also contribute to recent surges in land prices. For example, local government's heavy dependency on land sales revenue as an important off-budget funding source is one of them. The growth in real estate land prices would directly lead to more funds for local governments. Higher investment by the local government in infrastructure and real estate will raise local land prices and thus local governments' revenues from land sales, which subsequently allow them to spend more to promote growth. As a result, Deng et al. (2014) found that from 2000 to 2009, prefectural officers' spending on urban infrastructure tilts towards transportation and is biased against other long-term intangible development such as environmental amenities.

Deng et al. (2012) also find that while there are strong common year effects in land price appreciation, city-specific effects cannot explain any of the variation. Thus, prices tend to move in the same way across most markets in a given year, possibly due to shifts in the Chinese macro environment, government policy measures, or national market sentiment. There also is large mean reversion in annual price growth, of the order of 35 per cent. This is quite different from the US housing markets. Mean reversion in Chinese land price growth is larger if land prices were increasing in the previous year, suggesting that the Chinese government intervenes regularly to tame the property market.

Urban economics theory has long suggested that the price of land is a basic indicator of the attractiveness and the economic value of a specific location and the improvement (the building) on that site. However, real estate is a bundle of land and improvements, the value of land and land leverage ratio (i.e. the ratio of the land transaction price to the weighted average price of matched housing projects) will also affect the cost and affordability of housing in the urban cities. Wu et al. (2012) reported that the land leverage ratio in China's major housing markets has risen sharply in recent years. In early 2010, it constituted over 60 per cent on average of house value in Beijing, for example. Land prices are also quite volatile—three to five times more so than house prices according to the data. The data suggest that the volatility in house prices appears to be driven by the land market, not by other factors of production.

One of the traditional metrics to examine housing market sustainability and housing affordability is the measure of price-to-rent ratio. The price-to-rent ratios in Beijing and Shanghai climbed to 45.9 and 45.5, respectively, in the first quarter of 2010. The largest increase is in Hangzhou, where the price-to-rent ratio doubled to 65.5 in the first quarter of 2010 (from 31.8 in the first quarter of 2007). Using an asset market approach to compute the value of housing services (Poterba, 1984), Wu et al. (2012) concluded that the high expectation about strong appreciation in land and housing markets appears to drive the unprecedented high price-to-rent ratios in major Chinese housing markets. Their calculation suggested that even a modest decline in expected appreciation would lead to large house price declines of over 40 per cent in markets such as Beijing.

Economic theory predicts a strong link between housing wealth, financial wealth, and consumer spending (Case et al., 2005). Although an abrupt collapse in house price is unlikely to irreparably damage China's financing and banking industry, a fall in property prices will mean a significant loss of wealth for many Chinese. The typical Chinese household has access to only a very limited means to store wealth. In recent years, many Chinese households have become house price dependent by storing most of their wealth in real estate. A collapse in house prices will erode wealth and aggregate demand, possibly worse than has been witnessed in the Western world during the recent subprime crisis.

How can China's housing market risk under uncertainty be better managed? Can land market prices serve as a leading indicator to predict the future course of the housing market? Based on a preliminary analysis using a unique and rich dataset on local residential land and housing markets across thirty-five major Chinese cities, we found that a positive signal of a land price surge may push up the neighbourhood housing prices when the transmission peaks nine months later, that is, a 1 per cent positive signal of a land price hike leads to an average 3 per cent increase in house prices within the neighbourhood over a 2–3 kilometres radius nine months later. There is much more to be done to gain a better understanding of the economic value of land and housing in China, which can help the government to formulate a more sensible macro prudential policy regarding the land and housing market development and regulation in China.

■ **REFERENCES**

Case, Karl E. and Robert J. Shiller. 1989. The efficiency of the market for single-family homes. *American Economic Review* 79(1), 125–37.

Case, Karl E., John M. Quigley, and Robert J. Shiller. 2005. Comparing wealth effects: the stock market versus the housing market. *Advances in Macroeconomics* 5(1), 1–32.

Deng, Yongheng and John M. Quigley. 2008. Index revision, house price risk,and the market for house price derivatives. *Journal of Real Estate Finance and Economics* 37(3), 191–209.

Deng, Yongheng and Peng Liu. 2009. Mortgage prepayment and default behavior with embedded forward contract risks in China's housing market. *Journal of Real Estate Finance and Economics* 38(3), 214–40.

Deng, Yongheng, Della Zheng, and Changfeng Ling. 2005. An early assessment of residential mortgage performance in China. *Journal of Real Estate Finance and Economics* 31(2), 117–36.

Deng, Yongheng, Joseph Gyourko, and Jing Wu. 2012. Land and House Price Measurement in China. In *Property Markets and Financial Stability* edited by A. Heath, F. Packer, and C. Windsor. Canberra: The Reserve Bank of Australia.

Deng, Yongheng, Randall Morck, Jing Wu, and Bernard Yeung. 2014. China's pseudo-monetary policy. Forthcoming in *Review of Finance*.

Englund, Peter, John M. Quigley, and Christian L. Redfearn. 1998. Improved price indexes for real estate: measuring the course of Swedish housing prices. *Journal of Urban Economics* 44(2), 171–96.

Poterba, James. 1984. Tax subsidies to owner-occupied housing: an asset market approach. *Quarterly Journal of Economics* 94(4), 729–52.

Wu, Jing, Yongheng Deng, and Hongyu Liu. 2014. House price index construction in the nascent housing market: the case of China. *Journal of Real Estate Finance and Economics* 48(3), 522–45.

Wu, Jing, Joseph Gyourko, and Yongheng Deng. 2012. Evaluating conditions in major Chinese housing markets. *Regional Science and Urban Economics* 42(3), 531–43.

38 The urban pension system

Zheng Song, Kjetil Storesletten, Yikai Wang,
and Fabrizio Zilibotti

The pre-1997 urban pension system was primarily based on state and urban collective enterprises in a centrally planned economy. Retirees received pensions from their employers, with replacement rates that could be as high as 80 per cent (see, e.g., Sin, 2005; Salditt et al., 2007). The coverage was low in the work-unit-based system, though. Many non-state-owned enterprises had no pension scheme for their employees. The coverage rate, measured by the ratio of the number of workers covered by the system to urban employment, was merely 44 per cent in 1992 according to the *China Statistical Yearbook 2009*. The rapid expansion of the private sector caused a growing disproportion between the numbers of contributors and beneficiaries and, therefore, severe financial distress for the old system (Zhao and Xu 2002). To deal with the issue, the government initiated a transition from the traditional system to a public pension system in the early 1990s. The new system was implemented nationwide after the State Council issued 'A Decision on Establishing a Unified Basic Pension System for Enterprise Workers (Document 26)' in 1997.

The reformed system mainly consists of two pillars. The first pillar, funded by 17 per cent wage taxes paid by enterprises, guarantees a replacement rate of 20 per cent of local average wage for retirees with a minimum of fifteen years' worth of contributions. It is worth emphasizing that the pension funds are managed by local governments (previously at the city level and now at the provincial level). The second pillar provides pensions from individual accounts financed by a contribution of 3 per cent and 8 per cent wage taxes paid by enterprises and workers, respectively. There is a third pillar adding to individual accounts through voluntary contributions. The return of individual accounts is adjusted according to bank deposit rates. The system also defines monthly pension benefits from individual accounts equalling the account balance at retirement divided by 120. The targeted replacement rate of the system is 58.5 per cent.[1]

More recently, a new reform was implemented after the State Council issued 'A Decision on Improving the Basic Pension System for Enterprise Workers (Document 38)' in

---

[1] Suppose that the wage growth rate is equal to the interest rate. For a worker who contributes to the system for thirty-five years (from age 25 to 60), her pension benefits should be equal to 20 per cent of the local average wages (the first pillar) plus 38.5 per cent of her wage before retirement.

2005. The reform adjusted the proportion of taxes paid by enterprises and individuals and the proportion of the contribution for individual accounts. Individual accounts are now funded by a wage tax of 8 per cent paid by workers only.[2]

Two features of the current urban pension system are particularly important. First, the pension reform was cohort-specific. There were three types of cohorts when the pension reform took place: cohorts entering the labour market after 1997 (*Xinren*), cohorts retiring before 1997 (*Laoren*), and cohorts in between (*Zhongren*). Pension contributions and benefits of *Xinren* are entirely determined by the new rule. According to Item 5 in Document 26, the government commits to pay *Laoren* the same pension benefits as those in the old system subject to an annual adjustment for wage growth and inflation. For *Zhongren*, their contributions follow the new rule, while their benefits consist of two components: (1) pensions from the new system identical to those for *Xinren*, and (2) a transitional pension that smooths the pension gap between *Laoren* and *Xinren*.

Second, like private savings, pension funds are allowed to invest in domestic stock markets. The baseline model assumes the annual rate of returns to pension funds to be 2.5 per cent, which is identical to the rate of return to private savings. According to the latest information released by the National Council for Social Security Fund, the average share of pension funds invested in stock markets was 19.22 per cent in 2003–11. If 20 per cent of pension funds have access to the market with an annual return of 6 per cent and the rest of the funds gain an annual return of 1.75 per cent as one-year bank deposits, the average annual rate of return would be equal to 2.6 per cent (Song et al., 2012).

It is also worth emphasizing that the actual urban pension system deviates from statutory regulations in a number of ways and Song et al. (2012) have developed a model to capture some major discrepancies. First, the individual accounts are basically empty (Song et al., 2012). Despite the recent efforts made by the central government to fund these empty individual accounts, there are only 270 billion RMB in all the individual accounts of around 200 million workers participating in the urban pension system.[3]

Second, the statutory contribution rate including both basic pensions and individual accounts is 28 per cent, of which 20 per cent should be paid by firms and 8 per cent should be paid by workers (see the discussion on Documents 26 and 38 earlier in this chapter). However, there is evidence that a significant share of the contributions is evaded.

---

[2] The reform also adjusted the pension benefits. The replacement rate of an individual is now determined by years of contribution: a one year contribution increases the replacement rate of a wage index averaged from local and individual wages by one percentage point. However, the article did not state explicitly how to compute the wage index. In practice, the index appears to differ across provinces. For instance, the increase in the average pension benefits per retiree in 2011 was almost the same across Beijing and GanSu (the monthly increase was RMB210 in Beijing and RMB196 in GanSu), though the average wage in Beijing is more than twice as high as that in GanSu and the gap has been rather stable over time.

[3] The figure of 270 billion RMB comes from the information released by the Ministry of Human Resources and Social Security in the 2012 National People's Congress. Source: <http://lianghui.people.com.cn/2012npc/GB/239293/17320248.html.>

For instance, in the annual National Industrial Survey—which includes all state-owned manufacturing enterprises and all private manufacturing enterprises with revenue above 5 million RMB—the average pension contributions paid by firms in 2004–07 amounts to 11 per cent of average wages, 9 percentage points below the statutory rate.[4] Most evasion is by privately owned firms, whose contribution rate is a merely 7 per cent. Therefore, the actual contribution rate is substantially lower than the statutory rate even for workers participating in the system.[5]

Finally, although the coverage rate of the urban pension system is still relatively low, it has grown from about 40 per cent in 1998 to 57 per cent in 2009, where we measure the coverage rate by the number of employees participating in the pension system as a share of the number of urban employees.[6]

38.1 **The rural pension system**

The pre-2009 rural pension programme had two features. First, it was 'fully funded' in the sense that pension benefits were essentially determined by contributions to individual accounts. Second, the coverage rate was low since farmers had no incentive to participate. A pilot pension programme was launched for rural residents in 2009. Like those in the urban pension system, the new rural programme has two benefit components. The first is referred to as basic pension, mainly financed by the Ministry of Finance, and the second is a pension from an individual account. If a migrant worker who joined the urban pension system returns to her home town, the money accumulated in her account will be transferred to her new account in the rural pension programme. The programme was first implemented in 10 per cent of cities and counties on a trial basis. The government set a target of extending the programme to 60 per cent of cities and counties in 2011. Many of the cities and counties report high participation rates (above 80 per cent). This is not surprising since the programme is heavily subsidized (more details are given in the following paragraphs).

We will now lay out some basic features of the new programme upon which our model is based. According to 'Instructions on New Rural Pension Experiments' issued by the State Council in 2009, the new programme pays a basic pension of RMB55 ($8.7) per month. Suppose that the rural wage equals the rural per capita annual net income, which was RMB5,153 in 2009 (*China Statistical Yearbook 2010*). Then, the basic pension would correspond to a replacement rate of 12.8 per cent. Notice that provinces are allowed to choose more generous rural pensions. So, the replacement rate of 9 per cent should be

[4] In addition, with a labour income share less of than 20 per cent, wages appear to be severely underreported.
[5] Song et al. (2012) find an actual contribution rate of 19.4 per cent.
[6] Both numbers are obtained from the *China Statistical Yearbook 2010*.

viewed as a lower boundary.[7] In practice, some places set a much higher basic pension standard. Beijing, for instance, increased the level to RMB280. The monthly basic pension in Shanghai has a range from RMB150 to RMB300, depending on age, years of contribution, and status in the old pension programme.[8] Since the rural per capita net income in Beijing and Shanghai is about 1.4 times higher than the average level in China, a monthly pension of RMB280 would imply a replacement rate of 27.2 per cent. In the quantitative exercise, we then set the replacement rate to 20 per cent to match the average of the basic level of 12.8 per cent and the high level of 27.2 per cent.[9] According to our model simulations, on the contribution side, rural residents in principle should contribute 4 per cent to 8 per cent of the local average income per capita in the previous year.[10]

The current pension programme heavily relies on government subsidy. *China Statistical Yearbook 2010* reports a rural population of 712.88 million. According to the 2005 one-percent population survey, 13.7 per cent of the rural population is above age 60. These two numbers give a rural population of 97.66 million who are entitled to a basic pension. This, in turn, implies an annual government subsidy of 64.46 billion RMB, if the monthly basic pension is set to RMB55. The central government revenue was 3,592 billion RMB in 2009. So, a full-coverage rural pension programme in 2009 would require a subsidy which can be mneasured as a 1.8 per cent share of central government revenue and a 0.19 per cent share of GDP.

■ **REFERENCES**

Salditt, Felix, Peter Whiteford, and Willem Adema. 2007. Pension Reform in China: Progress and Prospects. OECD Social, Employment and Migration Working Paper 53.

[7] The Ministry of Human Resources and Social Security has made it clear that there is no upper boundary for the basic pension and local governments may increase the basic pension according to their public financing capacity.

[8] See 'Detailed Rules for the Implementation of Beijing Urban–Rural Household Pension Plans', Beijing Municipal Labor and Social Security Bureau, 2009 and 'Implementation Guidelines of State Council's Instructions on New Rural Pension Experiments', Shanghai Municipal Government, 2010.

[9] All rural residents above age sixty are entitled to the basic pension. The only condition is that children of a basic pension recipient, if any, should participate in the programme. In practice, the basic pension might be contingent on years of contribution and status in the old pension programme (see the given example from Shanghai). In addition, a recent official policy report from the Ministry of Human Resources and Social Security (<http://news.qq.com/a/20090806/000974.htm>) states that under the new system, a rural worker paying an annual contribution rate of 4 per cent for fifteen years should be entitled to pension benefits with a replacement rate of 25 per cent.

[10] Rural residents are allowed to contribute more. But the contribution rate cannot exceed 15 per cent for each person. Moreover, to be eligible for a pension from individual account, a rural resident must contribute to the programme for at least fifteen years. The monthly pension benefit is set equal to the accumulated money in an individual account divided by 139 (the same rule as applied to the urban pension programme).

Sin, Yvonne. 2005. China: Pension Liabilities and Reform Options for Old Age Insurance. World Bank Working Paper No. 2005–2001.

Song, Zheng, Kjetil Storesletten, Yikai Wang, and Fabrizio Zilibotti. 2012. Sharing high growth across generations: pensions and demographic transition in China. Forthcoming *American Economic Journal: Macroeconomics*.

Zhao, Yaohui and Jianguo Xu. 2002. China's urban pension system: reforms and problems. *The Cato Journal* 21(3), 395–414.

Part VII
Industry and Markets

39 Development strategy and industrialization

Justin Yifu Lin

In this chapter, I will first discuss economic development and industrialization in the context of the New Structural Economics (Lin 2012a) and then use this framework to explain China's extraordinary rise from being a poor and insular nation thirty years ago to being the second largest and one of the most dynamic economies in the world today. I will also point out the remaining challenges for China's industrialization and lessons for other developing countries.

Economic development is a process of continuous technological innovation, industrial upgrading, and structural transformation. For the New Structural Economics, the starting point in analysing a country's economic development is its factor endowments (such as land, labour, and other resources). A country's factor endowments are fixed in a specific time, but can evolve over time, and determine a country's total budget, relative factor prices, and comparative advantage at that specific time. Countries at different stages of development have different economic structures due to distinct factor endowments. For countries at early stages of development, factor endowments typically reflect a scarcity of capital and an abundance of labour or natural resources. Only labour- and resource-intensive industries will have comparative advantage in open, competitive markets (Heckscher and Ohlin, 1991; Ju et al., 2009).

At the other extreme, in high-income countries, capital—not labour or resources—is typically the most abundant factor endowment. These countries tend to have comparative advantage in capital-intensive industries. Situated on the global technological and industrial frontier, they rely on creative destruction or the invention of new technology and products to achieve technological innovation and industrial upgrading (Schumpeter, 1942). Firms engaged in upgrading must undertake risky research and development activities that generate non-rival, public knowledge that benefits other firms in the economy (Aghion and Howitt, 1992).

For a developing country to reach the income levels of advanced countries, it must upgrade its industrial structure to the same relative capital intensity of advanced countries. But to do so, it must first close its endowment gap with advanced countries. The fastest way for a country to accumulate capital and upgrade the endowment structure is to follow its comparative advantage and to rely on a competitive market as the mechanism for allocating resources at each stage of its development. In this way, the economy will be most competitive, create most economic surplus, and save and invest the most. Upgrading the industrial structure can be accelerated by the advantage of backwardness, that is, when developing countries can take advantage of the availability of technologies and industries already developed by more advanced countries (Gerschenkron, 1962; Krugman, 1979). Using available technologies and entering existing industries in line with their comparative advantage, while relying on market forces to foster competition, is what has allowed Japan and other East Asian economies to sustain dynamic growth and converge to high-income countries within one or two generations (Lin, 2009).

After recovering from the Civil War, China started its modernization drive in 1953 with an inaugural five-year plan. A desire to catch up with the industrialized advanced countries quickly led the political elites in China to prioritize the development of large, heavy, advanced industries, which were the basis of military strength and economic power. But China was a lower-income, agrarian economy at that time, and, given China's employment structure and income level, such an industrialization strategy defied the country's comparative advantage. Firms in the government's priority industries were not viable on the open, competitive market. To implement this comparative-advantage defying (CAD) strategy, the Chinese government needed to protect the priority industries by giving non-viable firms in those industries a monopoly and by subsidizing them through various price distortions, including suppressed interest rates, an overvalued exchange rate, and lower prices for inputs. The price distortions created shortages, and the government was obliged to use administrative measures to mobilize and allocate resources directly to non-viable firms (Lin and Li, 2009).

Labour-intensive sectors in which China had a comparative advantage were repressed. Despite a very respectable average annual GDP growth rate of 6.1 per cent from 1952 to 1978 and the establishment of large modern industries, the Chinese economy did not take off and China remained essentially a closed economy, with 71.3 per cent of its labour force still in traditional agriculture.

In 1978, Deng Xiaoping initiated a pragmatic, gradual, dual-track approach to transition from a planned economy to a market economy. The government continued to provide the necessary protection to non-viable firms in the priority sectors and, simultaneously, liberalized the entry of private enterprises, joint ventures, and foreign direct investment (FDI) in labour-intensive sectors in which China had a comparative advantage, but that were repressed before the transition. This transition strategy allowed China both to maintain stability by avoiding the collapse of old priority industries and to achieve dynamic growth by simultaneously pursuing a comparative advantage following (CAF) strategy and tapping the advantage of backwardness in the industrial upgrading process. This strategy also allowed China to use the gains it realized from dynamic growth to compensate those that were negatively affected by the transition, reducing their resistance to reform (Lau et al., 2000).

Since the implementation of these reforms China has moved gradually but steadily towards being a well-functioning market economy. This transition facilitated the rapid growth of its international trade, the dramatic increase in its trade dependence ratio, and the large inflows of FDI. Moreover, China's manufactured exports were upgraded from simple toys, textiles, and other cheap products in the 1980s and 1990s, to high-value and technologically sophisticated machinery and information and communication technology products in the 2000s. As a result, annual GDP growth averaged 9.9 per cent over the 32-year period, an estimated 627 million people were lifted from poverty, and China surpassed Japan to become the second largest economy in the world (World Bank, 2011).

Looking forwards, China still has the potential to rely on the advantage of backwardness to accelerate growth. The income gap between China and the USA is a proxy for the large technological gap that still exists between China and the advanced industrialized countries more broadly. In 2008, China's per capita income was 21 per cent of that of the USA, measured in purchasing power parity, similar to Japan in 1951, Korea in 1977, and Taiwan, China, in 1975 (Maddison, 2011). The average growth rate of Japan from 1951 to 1971 was 9.2 per cent, the average growth rate of Taiwan, China, 1975–95 was 8.3 per cent, and the average growth rate of Korea 1977–97 was 7.6 per cent. After 20 years of rapid growth, the per capita income in Japan, Taiwan, and Korea increased from 21 per cent of that of the USA to 65.6 per cent, 54.2 per cent, and 50.2 per cent, respectively. Given its growth experience, China has the potential to achieve another 20 years of 8 per cent growth if it continues to follow the CAF strategy, upgrade its industries, and tap into the advantage of backwardness. By 2030 China's per capita income measured in purchasing power parity may reach about 50 per cent of the per capita income of the USA (Lin 2012b).

To achieve this goal, China needs to overcome a number of structural problems, particularly the disparity in income distribution, the imbalance between consumption and savings, and the external trade surplus. When the transition started in 1979, China was a relatively egalitarian society. With rapid growth, income distribution has become increasingly unequal. The Gini coefficient, a measurement of income inequality, increased from 0.31 in 1981 to 0.47 in 2008 (Chen and Ravallion, 2010). Meanwhile, household consumption as a percentage of GDP dropped from about 50 per cent to roughly 35 per cent, whereas the fixed asset investment increased from around 30 per cent to more than 45 per cent of GDP. The Chinese trade balance as a percentage of GDP has grown from almost nothing in 1982 to 9 per cent in 2007.

These structural problems are the result of policy distortions intended to maintain stability during China's dual-track transition process. Although most distortions have been removed, the major distortions remaining include the concentration of financial services in the four large state-owned banks, the almost zero royalty on natural resources, and the monopoly of the major service industries, including telecommunication, power, and banking. These distortions contribute to stability during China's transition process. They also contribute to rising income disparity and other imbalances in the economy. Therefore, it is imperative for China to address the structural imbalances, by removing the remaining distortions in the finance, natural resources, and service sectors so as to complete the transition to a well-functioning market economy (Lin, 2012b).

Along with its increasing its income and shrinking its technological gap with advanced countries, China also needs to become more of an innovator in its own right so as to gradually shift from absorbing existing technologies to being an indigenous innovator of new technology if it is to drive its growth.

There are many useful lessons that can be drawn from China's experiences over the past half century. Every developing country has the opportunity to accelerate its growth if it follows a CAF strategy at each stage of development and if it can tap into the advantage of backwardness. Avoiding CAD strategies and the distortions they entail will ensure a well-functioning market, which in turn will compel firms to enter industries consistent with the country's comparative advantages. If a developing country follows its comparative advantage in technological and industrial development, it will be competitive in domestic and international markets. It will grow, accumulate capital, and upgrade its endowment structure. Once upgraded, the economy's comparative advantage will change and its infrastructure will need to be modified accordingly. In the process it is desirable for the state to play a proactive, facilitating role, such as by compensating for externalities created by pioneer firms in the process of industrial upgrading, or by coordinating investments in soft and hard infrastructure. Through the appropriate functions of competitive markets and a proactive, facilitating state, a developing country can tap the potential of the advantage of backwardness and achieve dynamic growth (Lin, 2012a).

Many developing countries, as a result of their governments' previous CAD strategies, suffer from distortions and have firms that are non-viable in competitive markets. These developing countries can learn from China's reform experience by adopting a dual-track approach—providing some transitory protections to non-viable firms to maintain stability, but liberalizing entry into sectors in which the country has comparative advantages. Such an approach can improve the resource allocation and tap the advantage of backwardness. For developing countries now fighting to eradicate poverty and close the income gap with high-income countries, the lessons from China's transition and development will help them realize their potential.

■ REFERENCES

Aghion, P. and P. Howitt. 1992. A model of growth through creative destruction. *Econometrica* 60(2), 323–51.

Chen, S. and M. Ravallion. 2010. The developing world is poorer than we thought, but no less successful in the fight against poverty. *The Quarterly Journal of Economics* 125(4), 1577–625.

Gerschenkron, A. 1962. *Economic Backwardness in Historical Perspective: A Book of Essays*. Cambridge, MA: Belknap Press of Harvard University Press.

Heckscher, E. F. and B. Ohlin. 1991. *Heckscher–Ohlin Trade Theory*. Cambridge, MA: MIT Press.

Ju, J., J. Y. Lin, and Y. Wang. 2009. Endowment Structures, Industrial Dynamics, and Economic Growth. Policy Research Working Papers 5055, Washington, DC: World Bank.

Krugman, P. 1979. A model of innovation, technology transfer, and the world distribution of income. *Journal of Political Economy* 87(2), 253–66.

Lau, L. J., Y. Qian, and G. Roland. 2000. Reform without losers: an interpretation of China's dual-track approach to transition. *Journal of Political Economy* 108(1), 120–43.

Lin, J. Y. 1992. Rural reforms and agricultural growth in China. *American Economic Review* 82(1), 34–51.

Lin, J. Y. 2003. Development strategy, viability and economic convergence. *Economic Development and Cultural Change* 53(2), 277–308.

Lin, J. Y. 2009. *Economic Development and Transition: Thought, Strategy, and Viability*. Cambridge: Cambridge University Press.

Lin, J. Y. 2012a. *New Structural Economics: A Framework for Rethinking Development and Policy*. Washington, DC: World Bank.

Lin, J. Y. 2012b. *Demystifying the Chinese Economy*. Cambridge: Cambridge University Press.

Lin, J. Y. and F. Li. 2009. Development Strategy, Viability, and Economic Distortions in Developing Countries. *Policy Research Working Paper* 4906, Washington, DC: World Bank.

Maddison, A. 2011. *Historical Statistics of the World Economy: 1–2008 AD*. Available at <http://www.ggdc.net/maddison/Historical_Statistics/horizontal-file_02-2010.xls>, accessed 22 February 2012.

Schumpeter, J. A. 1942. *Capitalism, Socialism and Democracy*. New York: Harper and Brothers.

World Bank. 2011. *World Development Indicators*. Washington, DC: World Bank.

40 Industrial upgrading and productivity growth in China

Loren Brandt

China's manufacturing sector has played an important role in the economy's growth for the last three decades, expanding at a rate nearly at par with the rest of the economy. Currently, manufacturing contributes in upwards of 35 per cent of GDP, and is the source of nearly 90 per cent of its exports. Despite massive layoffs from the state manufacturing sector beginning in the mid-1990s, manufacturing has continued to absorb new workers, and in 2010 total employment was over110–120 million.[1]

Concerned about manufacturing's future prospects, recent policy initiatives of the central government, including the 12th Five-Year Plan for Science and Industry, and the Five-Year Plan for National Strategic Emerging Industries, call for new national efforts to upgrade China's industries. These efforts are based on a view of limited upgrading and development of innovative capacity, especially in 'Chinese' firms, and increases in labour and capital—not productivity growth—as the key source of growth in the Chinese economy.[2] These views, as well as nationalist and strategic concerns, are playing into China's current big push for 'indigenous' innovation and the development of ambitious plans in priority areas extending from energy resources to biotechnology to IT—initiatives that often envisage restricted roles for multinationals. As part of these efforts, the Chinese government is also promoting a big outward push by domestic firms.

The perception of limited upgrading in China's manufacturing may be off the mark however (Breznitz and Murphree, 2012). So may be the government's assessment of the critical constraints on upgrading and innovation by Chinese firms, and the kinds of policies and investments it is promoting to foster new innovation. Both have potentially important implications for China's future ability to sustain current growth rates. Recent

---

[1] These estimates are based on the sum of urban manufacturing employment, manufacturing employment in the TVE (township and village enterprise) sector, and individuals self-employed in manufacturing. On manufacturing employment in China, see Bannister and Cook (2011).

[2] Frequently cited in support of such a perspective are the country's deficit in international technology transfer payments, the 'limited' transfer by foreign firms of cutting edge technology to the local economy, the small number of national champions with international brand-name recognition, and a low (albeit rising) share of GDP directed towards R&D.

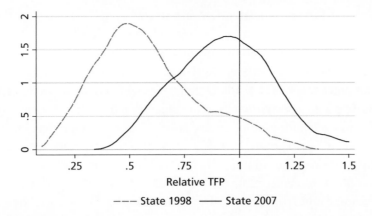

Figure 40.1. Distribution of relative productivity of state-owned enterprises (foreign-invested firms normalized to 1)

research (Brandt et al., 2012a) points to impressive growth in productivity in Chinese manufacturing in the previous decade and a half that is comparable or higher than rates observed in Japan, Taiwan, or Korea over similar extended periods in their development.[3] This growth is relatively broad based, and cuts across sectors, regions, and ownership groups. Figure 40.1, for example, clearly illustrates the narrowing of the productivity gap between state-owned enterprises (SOEs) and foreign-invested firms at the four-digit industry level between 1998 and 2007. In 1998, productivity of an SOE was only half or so of that of a foreign firm within the same sector, but by 2007, this gap had reduced to less than 10 per cent. Product upgrading in the form of cost *and* quality innovation that is allowing firms to capture a rising market share in demanding international markets is also clearly evident in China's export behaviour (Schott, 2008; Mandel, 2013). Exports, however, only make up a sixth of China's manufacturing output, which points to the importance of upgrading in the context of China's rapidly growing domestic market.

Equally telling, productivity growth is occurring less through the upgrading efforts and improvements in 'continuing' or 'surviving' firms, and much more because of 'creative destruction' and the dynamic process of entry and exit. Between 1995 and 2010, for example, more than a million new manufacturing firms have been established, the majority of which are private. Exits have also been common. When new (old) firms enter (exit) the productivity distribution at levels higher (lower) than incumbent firms, total productivity rises; new firms also contribute positively to productivity growth. Recent estimates (Brandt et al., 2012a) suggest that this margin may be the source of as much as 60 per cent of productivity growth in manufacturing since the mid-1990s.

[3] On the much larger role of productivity growth in aggregate economic growth than is typically offered, see Zhu (2012).

This perspective focuses our attention on the role of market liberalization and the dynamics of competition in China as key drivers.[4] This process began in the early 1980s with the rise of the TVE sector and the introduction of the dual-track system (Naughton, 1995), and accelerated in the 1990s as a host of internal and external barriers came down. China did not enter the World Trade Organization (WTO) until 2001, but tariffs and non-tariff barriers actually experienced a much larger reduction before entry than after. Between 1992 and 2000, for example, average tariffs fell from 43 per cent to 18 per cent, and then further to 7 per cent by 2010.[5] With tariff reductions passed on almost in full to lower domestic prices, the 'productivity threshold' that entering firms must achieve in order to be profitable has been rising (Brandt et al., 2012b).

Due to its size and rapid per capita GDP growth, China has become the largest market in the world for a growing list of various products. Demand for mobile handsets, for example, grew from 35 million in 2000 to 225 million in 2010, or 20 per cent of global demand; in automobiles, more than 11 million passenger cars were sold in 2010 compared to slightly more than a million in 2000; and in the case of excavators, domestic sales increased from 9,000 to 215,000 over the same period. Twenty years ago, these markets were often highly segmented between the products of domestic firms and multinationals—domestic firms serving the low end and multinationals serving the higher end through either imports or production in China—but increasingly, intense competition can be observed emerging between these two (Brandt and Thun, 2010).

To be successful, investments to upgrade the local capabilities of both types firms are required. For domestic firms, upgrading to improve product quality and variety, and thereby avoid the intense competition at the lower end of the market, has become essential. For foreign firms, investment is needed in local sourcing, as well as developing local R&D capabilities to modify products in ways that make them more appealing to local customers. One major foreign auto original equipment manufacturer (OEM), for example, developed a five-year plan in the mid-2000s to lower their production costs in China by 45 per cent through exactly such measures (Interview, July 2006).

In the Chinese context, the interactions and spillovers between these two types of firms are especially important. This expands the pool of upgrading opportunities for OEMs and suppliers.[6] Increasingly, Chinese firms are able to leverage the benefits from participating in multiple value chains, for example, supplying local Chinese firms, more demanding local foreign firms producing in China, and also for the export market. Each of these channels requires different kinds of know-how and capabilities. Moreover, through mobility

---

[4] See Sutton (1998) and Brandt et al. (2008) for a more general discussion on the links.

[5] As Branstetter and Lardy (2008) argue, accession to the WTO represents 'a watershed, not a sea change'.

[6] Also important are extra-firm ties with universities, research institutions, and consulting companies, which help to define a network of institutions that interact as a collective system to generate and use knowledge (Freeman, 1991).

in the labour market, knowledge and experience acquired in foreign firms is being more broadly disseminated through the economy. This kind of behaviour is pervasive.

Despite its depth, this process is highly uneven across sectors, with a host of restrictions and constraints continuing to impede the upgrading process and the reallocation of resources (skilled labour, capital, energy, and raw materials) to the most productive of firms. Note, for example, the wide dispersion across sectors in the productivity gap between state and foreign firms in 2007 in Figure 40.1. Hsieh and Klenow (2009) estimate that total factor productivity (TFP) in industry could be raised by as much as 25 per cent if misallocation *within* sectors could be lowered to the levels within sectors observed in the USA. There may be even larger gains for *inter-sector* reallocation, which are excluded from these calculations.

These distortions are most likely due to continued imperfections in capital markets, regulatory restrictions on entry that preserve existing market power, difficulty of firm exit, policy preferences in key sectors for state-owned or state-linked firms, as well as continued subsidies to exporters. The state has retreated from many sectors, but in those where it has remained, it often dominates. At the two-digit level, in 2010 for example, the five sectors (out of a total of thirty-six) in which state firms have the highest revenue from output represent nearly two-thirds of total state output in industry. Moreover, the average state share in these sectors is 60.1 per cent, compared to an average of 24.4 per cent over all thirty-six sectors. These sectors include power generation, transportation equipment, iron and steel, petroleum, and coal mining. State entry in newly emerging sectors is also prominent.

Much more work needs to be done to identify these factors, but a number of things point to the likelihood that such impediments are largely policy related and tied up in China's political economy, especially the government's non-economic objectives, at both the local and central level. In some circles in China, there are growing concerns of a return to highly *dirigisme* economic policies (World Bank, 2012). In all likelihood, the costs for the economy are very high. There are also dynamic implications, as perceived constraints on future firm growth may be impeding the investment incentives of the most dynamic firms in R&D, worker training, capital equipment, and so on because of lower expected returns.

The automobile industry, the heavy construction equipment sector, and telecoms provide a revealing contrast in the ability of domestic (Chinese-owned) firms to emerge in the context of highly competitive domestic markets (Brandt and Thun, 2014). In heavy construction, a mix of private and state-linked firms such as Sany, Zoomlion, Longgong, Liugong, and Xiagong have emerged since the late 1990s and are successfully competing with multinationals such as Volvo, Caterpillar, and Komatsu in a growing array of products and product-market segments in both China and now in other emerging markets.[7] Amongst Chinese firms, there is also growing market consolidation that is bottom-up as

---

[7] Major products of the heavy construction equipment sector include wheel-loaders, excavators, and motor-graders.

opposed to top-down and government-directed. Telecoms equipment, on the other hand, has parallels with heavy construction equipment, with local equipment manufacturers such as Huawei and ZTE successfully leveraging early market opportunities in lower-tier cities in their upgrading efforts.[8]

Contrast this experience with the auto sector, where Chinese firms continue to experience difficulties in competing domestically, let alone globally. Once again high on the agenda of policy makers in Beijing is a top-down, administrative-led consolidation of market players that is simultaneously encouraging overseas acquisitions. Two leading Chinese OEMs, BYD and Chery, are also facing serious financial difficulties, and have been increasingly dependent on subsidies. In handsets, government policy through the early 2000s restricted the development of local firms through restrictions on licensing, and only innovations of MTK (Taiwan)—in the baseband chipset—and Google—through Android—lowered barriers to entry, and significantly opened the door for new Chinese firms to emerge. Underlying these differences between sectors are several decades of state policies relating to freedom of entry, foreign direct investment (FDI), forms of technology transfer, tariffs, bankruptcy, and mergers and acquisitions that are influencing the incentives and channels of upgrading, and the ability of highly competitive indigenous firms to emerge.

Some of the same factors at work in industry help to explain even weaker performance in services, which now constitute upwards of 45 per cent of GDP. Earlier estimates by Holz (2006) and Bosworth and Collins (2008) suggest that productivity growth in services may be only 15–20 per cent of that in manufacturing. Services contribute directly to GDP, but are also an important input into manufacturing. The most recent national input–output table for China shows that the contribution of services (direct and indirect through their contribution to other intermediate goods) to manufacturing is 40 per cent. In general, the reform and restructuring of services, for example transportation, telecom, retail and wholesale trade, and financial services, lags behind reforms in manufacturing by a wide margin. Largely non-tradeable, high prices in these sectors can be linked directly to low productivity. Industry and manufacturing are important, but China's ability to remain competitive and sustain robust growth will depend as much, if not more, on productivity performance in services, and here the record has not been promising.

■ **REFERENCES**

Bannister, Judith and George Cook. 2011. China's employment and compensation costs in manufacturing through 2008. *Monthly Labor Review* 3, 39–52.

Bosworth, Barry, and Susan M. Collins. 2008. Accounting for growth: comparing China and India. *Journal of Economic Perspectives* 22(1), 45–66.

---

[8] In this context, it is interesting to note that Huawei, prevented by government procurement policy from entering the domestic 2G equipment market, turned to countries in Africa and Latin America to find opportunities to expand.

Brandt, Loren, Thomas Rawski, and John Sutton. 2008. Industrial development in China. In *China's Great Economic Transformation*, edited by Loren Brandt and Thomas G. Rawski, 569–632. Cambridge and New York: Cambridge University Press.

Brandt, Loren and Eric Thun. 2010. The fight for the middle: upgrading, competition, and industrial development in China. *World Development* 38(11), 1555–74.

Brandt, Loren and Eric Thun. 2014. Constructing a Ladder for Growth: Policy, Markets and Industrial Upgrading in China.

Brandt, Loren, Johannes Van Biesebroeck, and Yifan Zhang. 2012a. Creative accounting or creative destruction? firm-level productivity growth in Chinese manufacturing. *Journal of Development Economics* 97(2), 339–51.

Brandt, Loren, Johannes Van Biesebroeck, Yifan Zhang, and Luhang Wang. 2012b. WTO Accession and Firm-level Productivity in Chinese Manufacturing. CEPR Discussion Paper Series, No. 9166.

Branstetter, Lee and Nicholas R. Lardy. 2008. China's embrace of globalization. In *China's Great Economic Transformation*, edited by Loren Brandt and Thomas G. Rawski, 633–82. Cambridge and New York: Cambridge University Press.

Breznitz, Dan and Michael Murphree. 2012. *Run of the Red Queen: Government, Innovation, Globalization, and Economic Growth in China*. New Haven, CT: Yale University Press.

Freeman, C. 1991. Networks of innovators: a synthesis of research issues. *Research Policy* 20, 499–51.

Holz, Carsten A. 2006. Measuring Chinese Productivity Growth, 1952–2005 (22 July). Available at SSRN: <http://ssrn.com/abstract=928568 or http://dx.doi.org/10.2139/ssrn.928568>.

Hsieh, Chang-tai and Peter Klenow. 2009. Misallocation and manufacturing TFP in China and India. *Quarterly Journal of Economics* 74(4), 1403–48.

Mandel, Benjamin R. 2013. Chinese Exports and U.S. Import Prices. Staff Report No. 591. Federal Reserve Bank of New York.

Naughton, Barry. 1995. *Growing Out of the Plan: Chinese Economic Reform, 1978–1993*. Cambridge, UK and New York: Cambridge University Press.

Schott, Peter. 2008. The relative sophistication of Chinese exports. *Economic Policy* 23(53), 5–49.

Sutton, John. 1998. *Technology and Market Structure: Theory and History*. Cambridge and London: MIT Press.

World Bank. 2012. The World Bank and Development Research Center of the State Council, the People's Republic of China. *China 2030: Building a Modern, Harmonious, and Creative High-Income Society*. <http://www.worldbank.org/content/dam/Worldbank/document/China-2030-complete.pdf> accessed 18 December 2012.

Zhu, Xiaodong. 2012. Understanding China's growth: past, present, and future.' *Journal of Economic Perspectives* 26(4), 103–24.

41 Making clusters innovative?

A Chinese observation

Jici Wang

41.1 The puzzles in Chinese industrial agglomeration

This chapter provides an insight into the chaotic cluster concept, the mixed cluster phenomenon, and popular cluster policy in China.

A voluminous literature addresses the importance of industrial agglomeration. A cluster is a 'visual thing' yet the benefits realized from geographical clustering only arise within certain industries at certain stages of development in certain places and under the right conditions. In order to establish a clearer point of departure, this chapter defines an ideal industrial cluster as a group of proximate and inter-related firms and associated institutions that generates external economies, possibly creates opportunities for mutual learning, and enhances cooperation and innovation (Wang, 2007).

Industrial agglomeration is a ubiquitous phenomenon in China. On the one hand, a large number of industrial parks and zones have been created by central and local governments. Enterprises have gathered in these parks and zones, which include eighty-eight national high-tech development zones and 128 national economic and technology development zones in cities. Some industrial clusters have formed within the zones. A fine geographical division of labour within and between industrial clusters has occurred in various sectors, segregating enterprises by technological level and creativity. On the other hand, a number of local labour-intensive industrial districts engage in the manufacture of apparel, footwear, furniture, TV sets, home appliances, toys, motorcycles, musical instruments, and other common goods. Most of the country's exported goods have been produced in coastal clusters, but have been gradually drifting inland. As a kind of industrial cluster in China, the notion of industrial districts can be traced back to Marshallian and Italian discourses (Marshall, 1890; Becattini, 1990; Wang et al, 2001).

The importance of local synergy and rivalry has been stressed in Porter's (1990) work on industrial clusters and restated in his 'Regions and the New Economics of Competition' (Porter, 2001). The literature on industrial districts has hailed the importance of local relationships for competing in the global economy (Becattini, 1990). However, the theoretical underpinning of these studies may not exist in China. Industrial clusters do not automatically lead to innovation; rather, they become supply-chain cities for multinational corporations, where knowledge is hidden in the final products. Central and local governments often intervene by constructing various industrial parks and collecting an ideal assortment of local firms there, which creates geographical proximity without any incentive to collaborate or innovate together.

In China, local entrepreneurs and officials have backed policies that promote the notion of clustering. This has stirred interest in a high number of relevant ministries as well. Guangdong was the first province to formulate policies and measures to create local specialized industrial districts. In 1999, the Office of Science and Technology of Guangdong province pointed out the importance of clustering in a technology-oriented economy in its 10th Five-Year Plan. Guangdong's local governments have constructed efficient innovation centres—specialized towns—since 2000. Many other provinces, such as Zhejiang, and the Industrial Associations of many sectors at the state level, such as for textiles, footwear, jewellery, musical instruments, and so on, also pay close attention to upgrading industrial districts.

China's cluster-related development is complex. To explain it, one must analyse the following contrasting pairs of ideas: industrial parks versus industrial clusters, state-intervention versus market-mechanisms, and multinational corporation (MNC)-led versus home-grown technology strategies. A defining feature of clusters is willingness among entrepreneurs to coordinate diverse production activities in order to reduce transaction costs, create local capabilities, and spawn a shared vision of business growth and potential among various technological trajectories.

The eventual competitiveness of the cluster is strengthened by appropriate public intervention. What is the main task—to make new low-road-clusters continually, or to breed new innovative clusters and to innovate within existing clusters? This is the key question to be answered by China.

41.2 The trajectories and prospects of Chinese industrial clusters

Have the Chinese industrial clusters formed due to internal forces, external forces, or interaction between the two? The effect of rapid cross-border dispersion from international outsourcing by MNCs co-exists with local effects of external economies. In a context of increasing integration with global networks, the origins of China's clusters differ case by case, reflecting complex transitional institutions. These clusters serve both domestic and foreign markets (Wang et al., 2001).

The emergence of these clusters is related to global outsourcing, China's opening up and economic reforms, local entrepreneurship rooted within each particular area, and the transformation of state-owned firms (Figure 41.1). The concentrated dispersion caused by offshore outsourcing deserves further research (Giuliani et al., 2005).

The key issue of China's cluster development is the impact that MNCs have on the competitiveness of Chinese clusters. In a developmental scenario, MNCs become deeply embedded in the local economy through the creation of a network of sophisticated, interdependent linkages that support the expansion of local firms and generate self-sustaining growth of the local cluster as a whole. In a dependent scenario on the other hand, flexibility has negative connotations. A local cluster is a set of weak nodes within a wide network of powerful multinationals (Wang and Wang, 1998). For China, there is a long way to go until market mechanisms can independently facilitate competitive clusters with a high exchange of social capital in the firms' interactions.

MNCs may help the emergence of new clusters and the development of those already in existence. Beijing's 125-acre (50-hectare) Xingwang Park, sponsored by Nokia, was developed as the 'Nokia Centre for Logistics Excellence' and there are over thirty suppliers based at the Park. Clearly there are many benefits of 'non-cluster economies of traded interdependencies among firms in clusters' (Yeung et al., 2005). In Tianjin and Guangzhou, the success of the automobile industry clusters demonstrate that scale economies are a sufficient condition for related firms to join the anchor firm's cluster (Kuchiki and Tsuji, 2008). In Hangji of Yangzhou city, Colgate acquired Sanxiao Group in 2003 and gained access to the low-cost toothbrush suppliers in a cluster known as 'Toothbrush City' (Wang, 2009). Impressed by how production sub-contractors in the cluster could

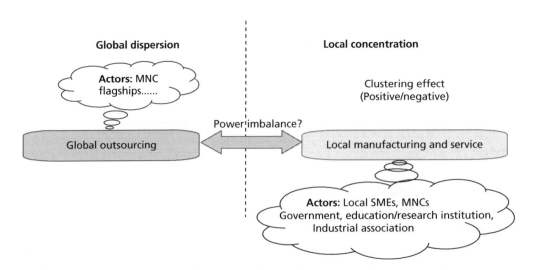

Figure 41.1. Background of cluster formation in China

take orders of any size and accept quick changes of product models or designs, investors related to Taiwanese PC (personal computers) chose to invest in a cluster in Dongguan city in Southern China in the late 1980s, moving to Suzhou in the mid-1990s and Chongqing more recently.

There are many effects of MNCs on local clusters. As a study of the Zhongguancun high-tech cluster shows, the relationship between MNCs and local firms in Chinese clusters is usually hierarchical, but can also be interdependent and evolutionary. MNCs provide local firms with vital technological and organizational training, which the local firms use strategically to develop their market networks and innovative capacity in their home market. The learning capacity of local firms is vastly improved by the presence of similar enterprises, research and development facilities, and an enabling environment created by local governments (Zhou and Tong, 2003).

Export-oriented industrial districts (a type of cluster) tend to be priority outsourcing partners for multinationals. Local producers do not simply export into an anonymous global market; often they feed into chains that are governed by powerful global players (Schmitz, 2006). Agencies playing the role of purchase and production organizers maintain close contact with multinational flagships. They keep one foot in their local community and the other in a broader network of international traders and customers. They collect information from the market so that local producers can better adapt to it. However, the intermediary may also be opportunistic, driving down the purchase price and reducing market efficiency; this has been the case with the Dongguan footwear cluster.

Dongguan in Guangdong Province has become the world's largest hub of commodity shoes. With more than one million employees, Dongguan's annual output of shoes exceeds one billion pairs. It currently houses five shoe material markets, 650 shoe trading and pattern design centres, 1,800 factories, about 2,000 firms supplying leather, shoe machines, and so on, and 3,000 ancillary shops dealing in leather, shoes, and hardware. However, most of the shoe factories are just assembly plants. Mass production is determined by large orders from big traders. Such made-to-order production requires raw materials from outside, and in most cases depends on outside technical support provided by R&D institutions of the parent company. In 2000, Dongguan's footwear production began a downward turn. According to a report in 2009, about 25 per cent of Dongguan's shoe manufacturers have relocated to Vietnam, India, Myanmar, and other countries, and another 50 per cent moved to Hunan, Jiangxi, Guangxi, Henan, and other provinces. Facing the outflow of manufacturers, Dongguan's footwear-related businesses are seeking to upgrade their industry. As some big footwear events in Dongguan show, the city will become a global headquarters for R&D centres and footwear enterprises.

In sum, insertion into global value chains will bring opportunities for small local firms in Chinese clusters for learning and upgrading, but multinational power may dilute local ambition to creatively upgrade the production system by any means possible. Therefore, a persistent problem for China's industrial clusters will be the transition from production capacity to capacity for innovation. Some clusters in China are beginning to accumulate significant innovative capabilities. This is an urgent task.

■ REFERENCES

Becattini, G. 1990. The Marshallian industrial district as a socio-economic notion. In *Industrial Districts and Inter-Firm Co-operation in Italy*, edited by F. Pyke, G. Becattini, and W. Sengenberger. Geneva: IILS.

Giuliani, E., C. Pietrobelli, R. Rabellotti. 2005. Upgrading in global value chains: Lessons from Latin American clusters. *World Development* 33(4), 549–73.

He, C, Y. Wei, F. Pan. 2007. Geographical concentration of industries in China: the importance of spatial and industrial scale. *Eurasian Geography and Economics* 48(5), 603–25.

Kuchiki, A. and M. Tsuji. (eds) 2008. *The Flowchart Approach to Industrial Cluster Policy*, IDE-JETRO Series, Palgrave Macmillan.

Marshall, A. 1890. *The Principle of Economics*, London: Macmillan,.

Porter, M. 1990 *The Competitive Advantage of Nations*, London: Macmillan.

Porter, M. 2001. Regions and the new economics of competition. In *Global City-Regions*,edited by A. J. Scott. Oxford: Oxford University Press.

Schmitz, A. 2006. Regional systems and global chains. In *Keynote Papers and Section Papers' Abstracts*. Beijing: The fifth international conference on industrial clustering and regional development, pp. 1–18.

Wang J. et al. 2001. *Innovative Space: Industry Cluster and Regional Development*, Beijing University Press. [In Chinese.]

Wang, J. 2007. Industrial clusters in China: the low road vs. the high road in cluster development. In *Development on the Ground: Clusters, Networks and Regions in Emerging Economies*, edited by Allen Scott and G. Garofoli, 145–64. London: Routeledge.

Wang, J. 2009. New phenomena and challenges of clusters in China in the new era of globalization. In *Asian Industrial Clusters, Global Competitiveness and New Policy Initiatives* edited by B. Ganne and Y. Lecler, 195–212. Singapore: World Scientific Publishing.

Wang, J., et al. 2010. *Beyond Clusters: The Theory and Practice of China's Industry Cluster Development*, Science Press. [In Chinese.]

Wang, J. C. and J. X. Wang. 1998. An analysis of new-tech agglomeration in Beijing: a new industrial district in the making?'*Environment and Planning A* 30(4), 681–701.

Yeung, H., W. Liu, and P. Dicken. 2005. Transnational corporations and network effects of a local manufacturing cluster in mobile telecommunication equipment in China. *World Development* 34(3), 520–40.

Zhou, Y. and X. Tong. 2003. An Innovation region in China: interaction between multinational corporations and local firms in a high-tech cluster in Beijing. *Economic Geography* 79(2), 129–52.

42 Markets and institutional change in China

Victor Nee and Sonja Opper

The state's involvement in launching and guiding economic reform when departing from centrally planned economies is undeniably essential, but the degree of state guidance has differed markedly between the top-down big-bang approach in Eastern and Central European economies and China's more evolutionary approach. The leaders of China's reform relied on gradual market liberalization while postponing large-scale privatization of the state-owned sector until the mid-1990s, two decades after the start of the reform. An unintended consequence of the reformers' decision to institute market liberalization was the new structural autonomy that decentralized product markets provided to economic actors outside of the state-controlled economy. The expansion of decentralized markets empowered entrepreneurs to pursue opportunities for profits independently of the state's allocation system for production factors. In their search for pathways to grow a private manufacturing economy, swarms of entrepreneurs experimented with institutional innovations that enabled them to bypass the state's allocation system and secure control of upstream factor resources and downstream distribution. Neither difficulties in accessing scarce government-controlled resources, nor the absence of a legal and regulatory framework supportive of private enterprise, posed an effective constraint on the rise of private manufacturing. By the time private enterprise finally received constitutional protection guaranteeing equal status with government-owned firms (in 2004), and the implementation of China's first Property Rights Law (in 2007), a substantial private sector of 5.5 million private companies with more than $1.3 trillion of registered capital already employed close to 75 million workers (*Annual Report of Non-State-Owned Economy in China*, 2008: 76).

42.1 Rise of private manufacturing firms

The rise of a dynamic private manufacturing economy in China as the main driver of capitalist economic development provides a good example of how the emergence of markets provided the necessary incentives and opportunities for economic actors to decouple from the main pillars of China's economic system: household farming in the countryside, and state-owned and collective firm manufacturing in the urban sector. First, the gradual replacement of central planning by market mechanisms *shifted power* from bureaucrats and central planners to producers. This implies that producers were facing a greater set of choices, which allowed them to develop new forms of production. Through market exchange, economic actors were able to informally work out new institutional arrangements for cooperation outside the boundaries of the established system of state production and allocation. Second, the rise of free markets provided *incentives* for institutional innovation as rewards were increasingly based on performance rather than the strength of political connections. Finally, markets endogenously expand the *opportunities* for entrepreneurs and firms to identify new markets and prospects for profit making.

Clearly, with factor and product markets evolving outside of the state's allocation system, strategic interests not aligned with the structure of opportunity legitimized by the state became decoupled from formal rules mandated by the state-owned economy. This decoupling process typically followed four stages: First, shifts in *market competition* provided incentives for economic actors to develop bottom-up institutional arrangements to secure gains from emergent opportunity structures. Second, *entrepreneurial action* generated institutional innovations and, through a process of trial and error, successful solutions diffused through the regional economy. Third, *mutual monitoring and enforcement* in crosscutting networks of like-minded actors reinforced novel behavioural strategies and norms. Fourth, through *mimicking*, swarms of followers piled in and, following tipping points, a self-reinforcing social movement dynamic evolved, which in turn facilitated local collective action to lobby for changes in the formal rules consonant with informal norms. Industry-based associations and lobbyists acted as agents representing social interests. Politicians eventually responded to bottom-up innovations by changing the formal rules to accommodate and regulate emerging economic realities.

In an established economic order dominated by state-owned enterprises and banks, entrepreneurs endogenously developed economic institutions that enabled them to compete and cooperate in spite of discriminatory rules that privileged the state-owned firms. These endogenous institutions—that is, private capital market, labour markets, industrial clusters, distribution networks, markets for innovation—enabled private enterprises to surmount barriers to market entry in China's transition economy. In this way, despite discriminatory treatment by the state, weak property rights, and stigmatized status on the periphery of the favoured state-owned firms, it was the private enterprise economy that emerged as the fastest-growing sector. By 2010, through bottom-up endogenous processes, private industrial firms and family-run businesses had developed into a key economic sector employing more than 160 million people (*China Statistical Yearbook 2011*).

42.2 **Informal norms, business networks, and economic institutions**

Avinash Dixit (2004: 3) makes plain that 'economic activity does not grind to a halt because government cannot or does not provide an adequate underpinning of law. Too much potential value would go unrealized; therefore groups and societies have much to gain if they create alternative institutions to provide the necessary economic governance.' Just as informal norms enable, motivate, and guide economic transactions in societies with well-established legal systems, such socially sanctioned expectations arise to facilitate economic activity when economic actors cannot rely on the legal system to litigate the resolution of disputes over property rights and contracts. The informal norms that play such a pervasive and important role in enabling and guiding private economic growth in transition economies seem to operate effectively beyond the shadow of the law. Not surprisingly, this includes both the illegitimate shadow economy controlled by criminal elements and legitimate private firms that develop into leading manufacturing and technology firms such as Alibaba.com and Geely Automobiles. As the general manager of a chemical company in Zhejiang Province noted, 'There are so many problems with legal implementation. It is easier to get together a circle of friends who inform each other.'

A broad consensus across the social sciences agrees that social norms and networks are mainly effective in the governance of exchange in close-knit communities of like-minded economic actors. If the total gains from cooperation exceed the costs, private orders relying on norms and networks can provide stable institutional arrangements for economic actors to sustain repeat transactions (Bernstein, 1992; Nee, 1998; Nee and Ingram, 1998). Entrepreneurs in China's transition economy rely on informal norms to secure trust, acquire information, and make cooperation possible in a competitive economy. Without contract law, missing property rights protection and, in spite of discriminatory government policies, entrepreneurs founded firms and built businesses on the basis of social norms enforced through sanctions embedded in multiplex business networks. Only after the private enterprise economy was already well established as an irrepressible and powerful engine of economic growth did the state begin to enact, ex post, the formal rules and policies that cumulatively conferred legitimacy, formal legal rights, and equality to private firms.

This is consistent with the causal sequence in the rise of political and economic institutions in the West. Norms often precede laws, and only become formalized once a 'norm becomes firmer' and once 'there is growing support to formalize it through the promulgation of laws' (Axelrod, 1986: 1106). It is well known that commercial law often builds on established and widely accepted business law. Worldwide, the inception of securities markets was not usually preceded or even accompanied by formal state-mandated rules protecting shareholder rights (Nee and Opper, 2009). Good formal institutions have typically followed, rather than preceded, economic development (Glaeser et al., 2004).

The behaviour of economic actors frequently bears little resemblance to the formal rules mandated by the state. Instead, the actual conduct of business and organizational practices conform to informal norms reflecting the private expectations and interests of economic actors. In departures from central planning, the actual business practices of economic actors are often at odds with the goals formulated by politicians and the existing rules of the game.

Informal norms operating in the shadows of the state can both limit and sustain economic development. On the one hand, decoupling entrepreneurial action from formal rules can give rise to an inefficient allocation of resources when economic actors collude to secure resources from government for their group, resulting in structural rigidities and economic stagnation (Olson, 1982). Mafia-like business networks in Russia's transition economy operated to obstruct reformers' 'big-bang' strategy to quickly institute a market economy. The rise of dense industrial clusters of private manufacturers in China contributed to three decades of economic growth through rapid accumulation of wealth and provision of non-farm employment.

Given the enormous variability of possible outcomes from the interaction between informal business norms and formal rules, a central problem for a theory of institutional change is to better specify the nature of the relationship. Most importantly, it is crucial to understand under which conditions a change of informal institutions, as observed for China's private firm economy, is likely to precede formal adjustments to state laws and regulations. In *Capitalism from Below*, Nee and Opper (2012) employ a Schelling-type frequency dependent utility model to detail the scope conditions under which informal norms successfully decouple from formal rules. Whether opposition norms reach tipping points, where a de-coupling from existing laws becomes individually rational, rests on a set of three distinct factors: first, a decoupling becomes more likely the smaller the expected sanctions from government and local enforcement agencies in case of defection. Second, the expected utility of defection (assuming others defect as well) needs to be larger than in a case of norm compliance. Lastly, local network externalities in close-knit, geographically confined areas can speed up the diffusion of new local behavioural patterns.

Building on these factors, Della Posta et al. (2014) develop an agent-based model showing that the diffusion of opposition norms can accelerate rapidly if expected utilities, sanctions, and network externalities are conducive. In fact, their model confirms that cases of endogenous institutional change, initiated by the spread of informal opposition norms, are far more widespread than state-centred theories of institutional change would predict. It fits their model that Wenzhou municipality, a place historically neglected by state investment, was among the first to experience the rise of a private sector economy. While there was virtually no employment outside of the farming sector (making a decoupling from existing institutions very desirable), the local government had little incentive to sanction entrepreneurial activity due to tight fiscal constraints. Here and elsewhere, it was through the innovative activities of marginalized social actors, operating within close-knit networks, that private firm development has spread and gradually diffused in the Yangzi Delta region.

42.3 **Endogenous institutional change and capitalist economic development**

What lessons do we draw from the emergence and development of capitalism in China? The theory of endogenous institutional change very briefly outlined here turns on mechanisms that are general. Nee and Opper (2012) show that entrepreneurs are the key agents driving institutional innovations that enable capitalist economic development; once established, these emergent economic institutions facilitate additional bursts of entrepreneurial action that lead to a series of tipping points in the growth of a market capitalist economy. Within business communities, multiplex networks provide the sinews of enforceable trust and the conduits of information flow that allow for cooperation in competitive markets. Emergent social norms are effectively enforced through mechanisms as common and universal as social approval (reputation, status) and punishment (bilateral sanctions, accurate negative gossip, and community sanctions). Thus, a dynamic process, starting with small numbers of marginal economic actors in peripheral locations, gave rise to a social movement-like growth and diffusion of entrepreneurship across the regional economy.

In the private enterprise manufacturing economy all of the key factors required for successful entrepreneurship could be found and secured through network ties and bottom-up institutional arrangements. Producers in industrial clusters benefited from a stable chain of suppliers that offered the mix of technical support and the material inputs needed for flexible and adaptive production. With networks connecting producers with upstream and downstream markets, the advantages of industrial clusters go well beyond the specialization effects of the work process and knowledge spillovers. Equally importantly, the spatial proximity in cluster locations provides fertile ground for the face-to-face interactions required to develop generally accepted business norms. Mechanisms such as personalized exchange, mutual dependence in multiplex business relations, and community sanctions provide the social glue that binds principals and agents to contracts—implicit and formal—and foster cooperative forms of conflict resolution. Without close-knit and highly specialized business communities, it is doubtful whether entrepreneurs could have so effectively developed the norms required to survive and thrive outside the state's production system.

Nee and Opper (2012) detail how, once the private enterprise economy was an emergent social and economic force in China, political elites in central and local government then put in place the legal and regulatory structures to legitimize private enterprise as an organizational form and model of economic development. In other words, in the years after the state-initiated economic reforms, bottom-up institutional innovations in the private sector initially enabled the development of a dynamic capitalist economy, and then the political elite followed up with accommodative change of formal rules legitimizing what had already taken place on the ground in order to enable the gains in productivity to be channelled into taxable revenue.

■ REFERENCES

Annual Report of Non-State-Owned Economy in China. 2008. No. 5 (2007–2008). Beijing: Social Sciences Academic Press. [In Chinese.]

Axelrod, Robert. 1986. An evolutionary approach to norms. *The American Political Science Review* 80, 1095–111.

Bernstein, Lisa. 1992. Opting out of the legal system: extralegal contractual relations in the diamond industry. *Journal of Legal Studies* 21, 115–57.

China Statistical Yearbook 2011. Beijing: China Statistics Press.

Della Posta, Daniel J., Victor Nee, and Sonja Opper. 2014. Endogenous Institutional Change. Cornell University, Center for the Study of Economy and Society, Working Paper No 69.

Dixit, Avinash K. 2004. *Lawlessness and Economics: Alternative Modes of Governance.* Princeton, NJ: Princeton University Press.

Glaeser, Edward L., Rafael La Porta, Florencio Lopez-de-Silanes, and Andrei Shleifer. 2004. Do institutions cause growth? *Journal of Economic Growth* 9: 271–303.

Nee, Victor. 1998. Norms and networks in economic and organizational performance. *American Economic Review: Papers and Proceedings* 88, 85–9.

Nee, Victor, and Paul Ingram. 1998. Embeddedness and beyond: institutions, exchange and social structure. In *The New Institutionalism in Sociology*, edited by Mary Brinton and Victor Nee, 19–45. New York: Russell Sage Foundation.

Nee, Victor and Sonja Opper. 2009. Bureaucracy and financial markets. *Kyklos*, 62(2), 293–315.

Nee, Victor and Sonja Opper. 2012. *Capitalism from Below: Markets and Institutional Change in China.* Cambridge, MA: Harvard University Press.

Olson, Mancur. 1982. *The Rise and Decline of Nations: Economic Growth, Stagflation, and Social Rigidities.* New Haven, CT: Yale University Press.

43 Economic institutions and their impacts on firm strategies and performance

Julan Du, Yi Lu, and Zhigang Tao

43.1 Introduction

Being the world's second-largest country by land area, it is quite natural for China to exhibit significant variations in economic development across regions just because of its sheer geographic size. Differences in natural endowments such as arable land, natural resources, and transport facilities to other parts of the country certainly explain some of these variations in regional economic development. In a series of works, mostly among the three authors of this chapter, but also with various other co-authors (mainly, Yi Che of Shanghai Jiaotong University and Ivan Png of the National University of Singapore; see the references for the complete list), it can be shown, however, that the regional variations in the quality of economic institutions, including primarily property rights protection and contract enforcement, play an equally important, if not greater, role in accounting for the regional variations in economic development.

43.2 Why economic institutions matter

For quite some time, the proposition that economic institutions matter for China's economic growth seemed to be a rather unlikely one judging by the record of the Chinese economy over the last thirty years. This is because, until recently, China provided little formal protection of private property. Private enterprises were not even formally permitted to exist until 1988 with the enactment of the Private Enterprise Administration Act, which was ten years after the start of China's economic reform. Only in 2004 did China make landmark amendments to its constitution to recognize and protect private property rights. Meanwhile, there have been persistent concerns about the quality of China's contracting institutions in resolving business disputes. China's formal legal institutions (i.e. courts) are far from being independent and impartial because the judicial system is under the direct control of the ruling Communist Party and governments. Yet, on aggregate, China's economic performance has been nothing less than spectacular. Combined, the Chinese experience seems to suggest the unimportance of economic institutions for economic growth, what is also known as the China puzzle.

It is our conjecture, however, that China's economic development could be concentrated in those regions where institutions are reasonably good, or concentrated among industries for which institutions are less important. In other words, the so-called China puzzle may not hold, once we look beyond the macro-level stylized facts and start uncovering micro-level evidence of the impact of economic institutions on firm strategies and performance.

Fortunately, the quality of economic institutions has been the focus of several surveys, for example, the investment climate surveys by the World Bank and the surveys of China's private enterprises. Quite a number of survey questions have been used to measure the quality of economic institutions as a reflection of the complexity of the subjects being measured. According to North (1991), property rights protection concerns the economic institutions constraining government expropriation. So the following measures for the quality of property rights protection are used, based on replies to the relevant survey questions: (1) the severity of extra-legal payments (*Tan Pai*) and informal levies (*Za Fei*) in the regions where private enterprises operate as a measure of the severity of government expropriation; (2) the proportion of entrepreneurs requesting government help in cases of business disputes in each region as a measure of the government's helping hand in upholding property rights; (3) the proportion of private entrepreneurs answering affirmatively to the question of whether it is necessary to have stricter policies against government corruption in the region as an indicator of the degree of government corruption. Contract enforcement concerns the economic institutions facilitating effective resolution of business disputes (see North, 1991). Hence the following measures of the quality of contracting institutions are used, based on replies to the relevant survey questions: (1) the proportion of private entrepreneurs answering affirmatively to the question of whether they use the courts to resolve business disputes; (2) the likelihood that the legal system will uphold their contracts and property rights in business disputes; and (3) the percentage of business disputes encountered by a firm that are settled by the courts as opposed to government arbitration and private resolution. Indeed, the above measures of de facto property rights protection and contract enforcement exhibit wide variations across the regions despite the fact that China is a unitary state with uniform laws across the country. Compared with cross-country studies that suffer from the difficulties of controlling for political, cultural, and religious differences between countries, examining the cross-region variations in economic institutions in China allows a natural experiment to be conducted, focusing on de facto law enforcement after holding constant de jure legal codes.

As much of China's economic growth over the last thirty years has been driven by the emergence and development of foreign multinationals operating in China and China's indigenous private enterprises, which are most sensitive to the quality of economic institutions, this study focuses on the impacts of economic institutions on firm strategies and performance for these two types of firms, and in particular, China's indigenous private enterprises.

43.3 The impact of economic institutions on firm strategies

Attracting foreign direct investment (FDI) is a top priority for many developing countries that are lacking the capital required for development. Understanding why capital does not flow from rich countries to poor ones where the return on capital is expected to be higher is also a top research topic (the well known Lucas paradox). We conjecture, however, that while developing countries enjoy great market potential, cost advantages, and possibly agglomeration economies, they suffer from having poor economic institutions, which explains the limited flow of capital from rich countries to poorer ones. As the largest FDI recipient among developing countries, China—characterized by large cross-region variations in economic institutions and FDI inflow—offers an ideal setting for testing this conjecture.

Specifically, using a dataset of 6,288 US multinationals investing in various regions in China for the period of 1993–2001, Du et al. (2008) investigate the impacts of economic institutions on the choice of location for FDI. While controlling for the traditional factors determining this choice (such as market potential, costs of production, and agglomeration economies), they find that US multinationals prefer to invest in those regions that have better protection for property rights, a lower degree of government intervention in business operations, a lower level of government corruption, and better contract enforcement. Their results offer a possible partial solution to the Lucas paradox and provide useful policy suggestions for developing countries.

In three separate studies, we find that, for China's indigenous private enterprises, the quality of regional economic institutions has a significant impact on their business organization and level of family control.

One puzzling feature of firms in developing economies is that they are much more diversified than their counterparts in developed economies. One obvious and important difference between these two types of economies is the quality of institutions constraining government expropriation of private property. Indeed it has been argued that diversified firms may thrive in situations of severe government expropriation, as they could leverage their expertise in dealing with corrupt government officials across multiple lines of business. Albeit a reasonable conjecture, there is little rigorous empirical work on the relationship between government expropriation and firm diversification. Du et al. (2012a) fill in the void in the literature by utilizing the cross-region variations in China on the one hand and addressing the empirical estimation issues on the other. Specifically, using a dataset of China's private enterprises, they find that firms reporting more severe government expropriation are more diversified in terms of business scope. In order to conclude that the protection of property rights shapes firm diversification, they carry out a series of analyses to address the issues of omitted variables bias and reverse causality, and their results remain robust.

Aside from the horizontal scope of firm, Du et al. (2012b) also examine the impact of contracting institutions on the vertical boundary of firms. This is a significant departure from existing studies that are primarily focused on factors at the level of the transaction parties, such as asset specificity and contractual incompleteness, in explaining the choice between make and buy. Du et al. (2012b) argue that if contracts cannot be reliably supported by contracting institutions, a situation which is typical in developing economies, the transacting parties can engage in ex post opportunistic behaviour no matter how excellent the factors are at the transaction parties' level. Vertical integration serves as an organizational solution to weak contracting institutions. In other words, poor contracting institutions add to market transaction costs, and give rise to the prevalence of vertical integration. Using a World Bank survey dataset of Chinese firms, Du et al. (2012b) indeed find that firms located in regions with poorer contracting institutions are more vertically integrated. Their results are robust to various checks, including those for dealing with omitted variable bias and reverse causality.

Family control of business is prevalent in developing economies. One of the leading theories suggests that it is a response to weak contract enforcement in such economies, under which it is difficult to rely on professional managers or attract investment from external investors. Lu and Tao (2009) provide the first test of this theory using a dataset of China's private enterprises. They find that firms located in regions with weaker contract enforcement indeed have greater family control in various business decision making, including those in operations, wages, and benefits; human resource management; and long-term development planning.

43.4 The impact of economic institutions on firm performance

Firm survival is obviously an important indicator of firm performance. It impacts not only on current competition but also on future entrepreneurial activities. The existing literature consists mainly of studies using data from developed countries which focus on industry-level and firm-level determinants for firm survival. However, we believe that for newly established firms in developing countries, the quality of economic institutions is definitely an important determinant of firm survival. Using data from manufacturing firms in China for the 1998–2005 period, Che et al. (2011) find that institutional quality does have a significant and positive impact on the survival of private enterprises. Their results, which are robust to the inclusion of both firm- and industry-level determinants, uncover a much-neglected factor for firm survival and hold policy implications for the developing economies.

Another important measure of firm performance is firm productivity, which is often used to measure economic growth at the micro-level. Using a World Bank dataset of Chinese firms, Lu et al. (2013) find that firms located in regions with better property rights protection enjoy faster growth in firm productivity. Their results, which are robust to various controls including especially different methods for dealing with the endogeneity problems, lend strong support to the proposition that the quality of economic institutions still matters in China (or there is no such China puzzle of unimportance of institutions for economic performance).

43.5 Conclusion

To summarize, the authors' research has shown that, in addition to factors such as internal and external market integration and incentive motivation, economic institutions are important for economic growth in China by casting significant impacts on firm strategies and performance, thereby negating the so-called China puzzle. Our research implies that China would have grown even more rapidly and healthily if it had better economic institutions. Future research will be directed at understanding the process of institutional changes in China.

■ **REFERENCES**

Che, Yi, Yi Lu, and Zhigang Tao. 2011. Institutions and Frm Survival: Evidence from China's Industries, Working Paper.

Du, Julan, Yi Lu, and Zhigang Tao. 2008. Economic institutions and FDI location choice: evidence from U.S. multinationals in China, *Journal of Comparative Economics* 36(3), 412–29.

Du, Julan, Yi Lu, and Zhigang Tao. 2012a. Property Rights Protection and Diversification: Evidence from China's Private Firms, Working Paper.

Du, Julan, Yi Lu, and Zhigang Tao. 2012b. Contracting institutions and vertical integration: evidence from China's manufacturing firms. *Journal of Comparative Economics* 40(1), 89–107.

Lu, Yi and Zhigang Tao. 2009. Contract enforcement and family control of business, *Journal of Comparative Economics* 37(4), 597–609.

Lu, Yi, Ivan Png, and Zhigang Tao. 2013. Do institutions not matter in China? Evidence from manufacturing enterprises. *Journal of Comparative Economics* 41(1), 74–90.

North, Douglass C. 1991. Institutions. *Journal of Economic Perspectives* 5, 97–112.

44 Insurance markets in China

Hanming Fang

Even though Chinese merchants practised risk transfer and distribution as early as 3000 BC,[1] modern insurance markets in China are still in their infancy relative to advanced market economies. In this chapter, I provide a brief description of a variety of insurance markets in China and discuss the issues of future development.[2]

44.1 Health insurance market

China's current health insurance system consists of three layers: basic health insurance; employer-supplemented health insurance; and individual-supplemented health insurance.

44.1.1 BASIC HEALTH INSURANCE

The basic health insurance in China is implemented under a prefecture- or county-level planning framework, where the planning units have discretion over policy details and are responsible for balancing their own budget. It consists of three parts: the urban employee basic health insurance (UEBHI), the urban resident basic health insurance (URBHI), and the new cooperative medical scheme (NCMS) for rural populations.

The UEBHI is compulsory for all urban firms and non-profit organizations, and optional for township and individually owned businesses. Usually the employee and the employer respectively contribute 2 per cent and 6 per cent of the employee's wage towards the premium. Benefits are subject to a cap, varying from 30 to 300 thousand yuan per year depending on the local policy. At the end of 2011, 252 million urban employees participated in UEBHI.

---

[1] See, for example, Vaughan, E. J., 1997, *Risk Management*, New York: Wiley.
[2] I am grateful to Qing Gong for excellent research assistance in the preparation of this article.

Urban residents not covered by the UEBHI can participate in URBHI by paying the premium themselves, which is smaller than that for the UEBHI but the benefits are also significantly lower. At the end of 2010, 221 million urban residents participated in URBHI.

The NCMS was initiated by the State Council in 2002 to reduce illness-induced poverty in rural areas. Rural households voluntarily participate by paying an annual premium, usually less than 300 yuan, more than half of which is subsidized by the central and local governments. At the end of 2011, 832 million individuals, or 97.5 per cent of China's rural population, participated in NCMS.

44.1.2 EMPLOYER-SUPPLEMENTED HEALTH INSURANCE

To provide additional benefits for employees, employers can provide a supplemented health insurance by purchasing a scheme from a commercial insurance company, establishing an account itself, or, if the employer is already in the basic health insurance programme, paying additional premiums to the local health insurance administrative agency. To encourage provision, funds used for supplemented health insurance are tax deductible up to a limit.

44.1.3 INDIVIDUAL-SUPPLEMENTED HEALTH INSURANCE

Individuals can also purchase insurance directly from insurance companies. Commercial health insurance is a relatively small component of China's personal insurance market, comprising only 6.37 per cent of total personal insurance revenues in 2010.[3]

One important issue is that China's basic health insurance system is financed at the prefecture or county level, where the local planning units balance their own budgets with very limited transfer from the central government. Consequently, excess demand for reimbursements relative to collected premiums often result in insufficient funds being available to reimburse all covered expenses. Low planning levels also render significant regional variations in policy details; for example, the caps on annual reimbursements in more developed counties can be ten times as high as those in less developed counties. Moreover, the basic health insurance in one region often cannot be used for medical expenses incurred outside region, which creates barriers to labour mobility.

---

[3] See *China Insurance Yearbook 2011*.

44.2 **Life insurance market**

As of the end of 2011, there are sixty-one commercial life insurance companies in China, of which twenty-five are foreign firms. The total life insurance revenue from premium payments reached about 640 billion yuan in 2011, with the Chinese companies accounting for close to 95 per cent of the market share.[4] The Chinese life insurance market is highly concentrated. The largest three insurers, China Life, China Pacific Insurance (Life), and Ping An Insurance, make up more than half of total revenues, although their market share decreased in recent years.[5]

Despite steady growth during the past decade, the Chinese life insurance market still lags behind the global average in insurance penetration (the ratio of total premium revenue over GDP) and density (the ratio of total premium revenue over total population). In 2010, insurance penetration in China was 2.62 per cent and the insurance density was 783 yuan, both well below the global average of 4.0 per cent and US $364.3.[6]

High concentration in China's life insurance market leads to limited innovation in life insurance products, and low service quality. Misleading sales tactics, frequent charges of extra fees, and complicated claim procedures are common complaints.

44.3 **Property insurance market**

As of 2011, China has fifty-nine property insurance companies, including twenty-one foreign insurers. Property insurance currently accounts for about one-third of total insurance revenues. The number of property insurance companies has been steadily increasing, yet the property insurance market is even more concentrated than the life insurance market. The top three companies have always been People's Insurance, China Pacific Insurance (Property), and Ping An Property Insurance, taking two-thirds of total property insurance revenues. Foreign property insurers, despite their numbers, generate far smaller revenues. The payment rate for property insurance in China is fairly stable at around 50 per cent.

The penetration and density of property insurance in China are low, both absolutely and relatively. The 2011 property insurance revenue is only 1 per cent of GDP, while the

---

[4] See *China Insurance Yearbook 2011* and China Insurance Regulatory Commission at <http://www.circ.gov.cn/web/site0/tab61/i191553.htm>.

[5] Author's calculation using China Insurance Regulatory Commission statistics.

[6] World Insurance in 2010: Premium Back to Growth—Capital Increases. Swiss Re Sigma Report, No.2/2011, pp. 20.

average is 2.9 per cent globally and 3 per cent for emerging markets.[7] Insurance density was US$ 56.5 in 2011, much lower than the US$ 263 world average but slightly higher than the US$ 49 emerging market average.[8]

Automobile insurance is the dominant type of property insurance sold in China, largely due to the dramatic growth in the number of vehicles and increasing participation rates in recent years. Demand was boosted further when auto liability insurance became compulsory in 2006,[9] which generates over 77 per cent of property insurance revenues (Wang, 2011: 34). Even though the China Insurance Regulatory Commission (CIRC) regulation requires that the insurance companies set the premium to just break even, it does not stop the companies from making huge profits from auto insurance.[10]

High concentration in the Chinese property insurance market significantly hinders the competition, resulting in poor service quality and delay in reimbursement.

44.4 **Agricultural insurance**

There are twenty-one companies in China offering various agricultural insurances, the largest being PICC-Property and Casualty Company, China United Property Insurance, An-Hua Agricultural Insurance, and Sunshine Agricultural Insurance. The top three companies account for close to 80 per cent of the market. Premium revenue of agricultural insurances amounted to 13.59 billion yuan in 2010; and total claims reached 9.60 billion, covering 129 million rural households and 680 million acres of crop, oil, or cotton.

The fact that agricultural insurance in China is a policy-driven public service requires complicated coordination among several government departments including those in the CIRC, the Ministry of Agriculture, the Ministry of Finance, and the National Development and Reform Commission; and also among different levels of governments—the state, the province, and the prefecture or county—because all three levels of the government contribute to some of the premium subsidies to the farmers. Since local governments are required to match central government subsidies for some insurance, they are sometimes unwilling to promote agricultural insurances. Even with considerable government subsidies, some farmers do not trust the insurance companies and are therefore reluctant

---

[7] Source: Author's calculation using figures in table 4 and GDP and population data from *China Statistical Yearbook 2011*. Figures for 2011 are from The People's Republic of China Economic and Social Development Statistics Report for 2011 (February 2012), at <http://www.stats.gov.cn/tjgb/ndtjgb/qgndtjgb/t20120222_402786440.htm>

[8] World Insurance in 2010: Premium Back to Growth—Capital Increases. Swiss Re Sigma Report, No.2/2011, pp. 37.

[9] Auto liability insurance is the first compulsory insurance in China as required by the Road Traffic Safety Law enacted in 2006.

[10] The Provision on Mandatory Motor Vehicle Traffic Accident Liability Insurance, Chapter 2, Section 6, at <http://www.gov.cn/zwgk/2012-04/30/content_2125893.htm>.

to purchase insurance (Cai et al., 2014). Due to its voluntary participation nature, there are also widespread adverse selection and moral hazard problems, and sometimes even fraud, in agricultural insurance.

44.5 **Social insurance programmes**

The Chinese social insurance system consists of five basic insurances: pension, unemployment insurance, health insurance, work injury insurance, and maternity insurance. The first two and the other three are usually combined as two bundles. The pension system and health insurance are the two pillars of China's social insurance programme. The basic health insurance programme was discussed in detail in the first section of this chapter. In this section we will focus on China's pension system.

China's current pension system is planned at the province level and administered at the prefecture level. Policies are kept uniform within each province, but the detailed figures may vary across prefectures. All firms are compulsory participants. The firm pays 20 per cent of an employee's wage income as the monthly premium that goes into the social pension fund, which is run as a pay-as-you-go system. The employee pays another 8 per cent that goes into his/her personal account (at least in principle).[11] The expected national average replacement rate is 70 per cent. By the end of 2011, 216 million urban employees participated in the pension programme.[12] Similar to the basic health insurance system, there are also employer-supplemented and individual-supplemented pension programmes. These are provided by commercial insurance companies or industrial associations and are not part of China's social insurance system.

Many of the designed features of the pension system were not implemented in practice. For example, funds in the personal accounts (8 per cent paid by the employee) of working participants were often used to pay for the pensions of retirees. The system also faces significant financial stress as the Chinese population is expected to decline and enter an ageing period in 2030. The social pension fund in China is sponsored by central government budgets. A recent study projects that with low mortality and low fertility, China's pension deficit rate will amount to 59.9 per cent if the retirement age remains constant (Yi Zheng, 2011). Several measures have been taken to prevent huge deficits in future: in 2001, the central government used the sale of state shares to supplement social pension funds.

Another problem with China's current pension system is inequality among participants because benefits and costs for participants differ greatly across types of employers and

---

[11] Monthly contributions into pension funds are subject to a ceiling: individuals and firms shall, respectively, pay no more than 8 per cent and 20 per cent of *three* times the local average wage for each participant.

[12] Employees working for non-profit organizations and some government agencies (*Shi Ye Dan Wei*) have their own more generous pension system.

regions. Government employees enjoy more generous pension plans supported by local fiscal budgets. Because the system is planned at the province level and managed locally, policies and rules may vary even within the same province. The regional variations in the pension system add to China's already severe regional inequalities.

44.6 **Conclusion**

Despite the rapid growth in recent years, there are still many areas where Chinese insurance markets need to further develop. The existing markets are dominated by few large majority state-owned insurance companies, leading to limited product innovation and poor customer services. While CIRC has attempted to reduce many forms of malpractices committed by the insurance companies, more competition from the entry of financially strong private companies is needed to drive down the abnormally high profit margin in Chinese insurance markets. There are also several important insurance markets that are non-existent or tiny in China. For example, the private annuity insurance market in China is very small. Homeowners' insurance, which is huge in other countries, is also small. Commercial insurance, used frequently in other market economies to hedge against price risks, is also only at the early stages of development in China.

▓ REFERENCES

Cai, Hongbin, Yuyu Chen, Hanming Fang, and Li-An Zhou. 2014. The effect of microinsurance on economic activities: evidence from a randomized natural field experiment. Forthcoming, *Review of Economics and Statistics.*

Wang, Xujin. 2011. *Property Insurance*, Beijing: Peking University Press.

Yi, Zheng. 2011. Effects of demographic and retirement-age policies on future pension deficits, with an application to China. *Population and Development Review* 37(3), 553–69.

45 The future of private and state-owned enterprises in China

Weiying Zhang

45.1 The reform of SOEs

To understand the future of private and state-owned enterprises (SOEs) in China, we need to understand how the reform of SOEs has proceeded and the private sector has emerged.

Before Deng Xiaoping's reform, the Chinese economy, like all other socialist countries, was monopolized by the state sector. There were no private enterprises at all. Naturally, the reform of SOEs and the development of private businesses have been the major components of transition from the planned economy to a market-based economy.

The reform of SOEs of the past three decades has seen three phases: 1978–92, 1992–2003, and 2003–12. The underlying doctrines and policy instruments of reform differ across the three phases.

In the first phase, from the beginning to 1992, both the reform leaders and most economists believed that SOEs could be made efficient through improving management and introducing competition, and there was no need to change state ownership. With this doctrine, the official reform policies were *zhengqi fengkai* (separating firms from the government) and *fangquan rangli*, that is, through various measures, granting the necessary autonomies to enterprises so that managers could make business decisions according to supply and demand, and to allow enterprises to keep part of their profits so that both management and workers could be motivated to work hard.

It should be said that this kind of reform policy achieved some positive results (Groves et al., 1994; Zhang,1997). However, the overall performance of SOE reform was not satisfactory. By the late 1980s, facing strong competition from non-state firms (mainly township and village-owned enterprises, TVEs) and foreign-invested joint-ventures, SOEs were not just less efficient and less competitive, but most of them could not survive without government subsidies and bank loan support. By the early 1990s, many SOEs were heavily over-indebted and technically bankrupt. This directly threatened the stability of the banking system. For local governments, the role of SOEs changed from revenue contributors to financial burden. In 1992, the total loss of all loss-making SOEs exceeded the total profits of all profit-making SOEs.

The unsatisfactory result of SOE reform in the 1980s offered a valuable lesson. By the early 1990s, many government officials and economists had realized that SOE reform could go no further without fundamental changes in ownership structure. After Deng Xiaoping's southern visit in Spring 1992, calling for a return to the reform road, 'Socialist Market Economy' was adopted as the reform goal by the Central Committee of CCP at its 14th National Conference. The reform doctrine changed and ownership reform of SOEs began. Although 'maintaining the dominant position of state ownership' was still the official principle, various measures of privatization and partial privatization of SOEs were encouraged, or at least tolerated, under the umbrella of 'building-up of modern corporate system with well-defined property rights, clear responsibility, separation of firms from government and scientific management'. Many local governments initiated privatization campaigns. By 1997, most county-level government-controlled SOEs and TVEs were fully or partially privatized. In 1998, partially triggered by the Asian Financial Crisis, the central government launched a pilot project of corporatization of 1,000 large SOEs. By 2003, most large SOEs controlled by municipal, provincial, and even the central government had been corporatized through ownership diversification and stock-listing. SOEs gradually retreated from competitive sectors.

The change of SOE reform policies with 1992 as a turning point means that in the first phase the state sector continued to expand, while in the second phase the state sector shrank. For example, employees of the state economic sector increased year by year to 80 million in 1992 from 60 million in 1978. However, after 1992, the number went down year by year to only 30 million in 2004, just half of that in 1978 (*China Statistical Year Book* 2005).

The SOE reform began its third phase in 2003 when Hu Jingtao's regime took office. In that year, SASAC (the State Assets Supervision and Administration Committee) was established and the State Reform Commission was merged into the State Development Commission (thereafter renamed as SDRC). Since then, apart from state-owned banks and financial institutions being listed in stock exchanges after introducing international strategic investors, the reform lost momentum. This will be discussed further later in this chapter.

45.2 Development of private enterprises

The development of private enterprises in China has run in parallel with SOE reform. Consistent with the official doctrine of the early stage that only publicly owned firms were compatible with socialism, private enterprises were legally prohibited until 1988.

Although in practice the spontaneous emergence of private enterprises was tolerated by some local governments due to employment pressure, the central government tried to crack down on them from time to time. The legalization of private enterprises was a long process involving several administrative and legislative steps. Self-employed businesses were legalized in 1982. Privately owned enterprises obtained legal status only in 1988 after a long debate. Even after that, they were still discriminated against politically and administratively. Following the event on 4 June 1989, the government launched another crack-down on the private sector. Naturally, almost all non-state enterprises established in 1980s were registered as 'collective firms' (TVEs in rural area), although many of them were in fact privately owned and controlled.

The year of 1992 was also a turning point for the development of private enterprises. With Deng Xiaoping's new reform push, the government reversed its anti-private policy. Private enterprises were less discriminated against and even encouraged. More and more new private enterprises were established. A greater number of existing collective enterprises and TVEs took off their 'red-cap' to become legally private. Many small and some middle-sized SOEs were transferred into private hands through various privatization programmes.

By the turn of century, private enterprises had emerged as the dominant ownership form of newly established firms in China. For example, from 2000 to 2001, the number of private firms increased by 15.1 per cent. However, during the same period, the total number of firms of all ownership forms was reduced by 4.1 per cent. The development of private enterprises was further promoted by a boom in hi-tech industries and by the internet, particularly after China entered the World Trade Organization (WTO) in 2001. The share of private enterprises in total industrial output rose to 30.5 per cent by 2010 from 6.1 per cent in 2001 (*China Statistical Yearbook 2011*).

With the development of the private sector, three dominant groups of entrepreneurs have emerged, roughly in this order: (1) peasants-turned entrepreneurs; (2) officials-turned entrepreneurs; and (3) overseas-returnees and engineers-turned entrepreneurs (Zhang et al., 2010). These three generations of entrepreneurs differ in their educational backgrounds, initial businesses, firms' ownership and governance style, financing, and in particular their connections to government. However, they are now merging into a joint force for growth.

45.3 SOEs: from retreat to expansion

When Hu Jingtao's regime took power in 2003, it was expected that the economic reform would be continued and deepened. What has happened is that the reform has become stagnant and has seen setbacks in some respects since 2005. While the private sector has still been organically growing, SOEs have become more aggressive and more dominant in a number of key sectors. SASAC's goal has been to make SOEs bigger and stronger. It has made SOEs more dominant in key industries by administratively reorganizing 196 of its central government-controlled SOEs into 120 between 2003 and 2010. SOEs in state-monopolized industries, such as petroleum and gas, and electricity, have expanded their monopoly into both downstream and upstream sectors, which crowded out private enterprises or made it more difficult for them to survive. In Shanxi Province, a major area of coal production, SOEs compulsorily took over almost all private mines in 2009/2010. Such compulsory mergers and acquisitions (M&As) have also taken place in other sectors (such as steel and civil aviation) and in other regions (Unirule Institite, 2011).

This has been called 'the phenomenon of *guojin mintui*', meaning the state expands and the private sector retreats. It has occurred for several reasons. First, the leading politicians, on the whole, are no longer market-oriented reformers but more orthodox socialists. Second, SOEs have become the powerful vested interest groups in both political and economical life. Third, public opinion has switched to favouring SOEs since 2005. And finally, the recent global financial crisis has made the so-called 'Chinese Model'—characterized by a big state sector and strong government intervention—more attractive and legitimate. This partially explains why SOEs have become more aggressive and tyrannical since 2008.

45.4 The possible future scenario

The economic reform of more than thirty years has dramatically changed the ownership structure of enterprises in China. Although private enterprises have been discriminated against compared to SOEs, and *guojin mintui* appeared in the past few years, the general trend has been for the state domain to shrink while the private domain has expanded. The share of SOEs in industrial output had declined to 26.6 per cent in 2010 from 80.7 per cent in 1978, while the share of private enterprises had climbed to 30.5 per cent from nothing in the same period. Among thirty-nine two-digit industries, SOEs had left twenty industries by 2010 (output share is less than 20 per cent) (Li Zhaoxi, 2012). In terms of GDP, today, roughly speaking, SOEs contribute less than 40 per cent and non-state enterprises contribute more than 60 per cent.

Nevertheless, SOEs still play a crucial role in key industries such as energy, raw materials, and equipment manufacturing. SOEs even hold monopoly positions in financial systems, telecommunications, oil and gas, and major public utilities. In other words, SOEs still control the lifeblood of the Chinese economy even after more than thirty years.

Furthermore, there is no level playing field between SOEs and private enterprises. SOEs are still privileged and private enterprises are heavily discriminated against in terms of financing, market entry, taxation, and many other respects, both legally and administratively. The key industries are still not open to private enterprises.

More importantly, private property rights in China remain unsecured, although the protection of private property rights was explicitly written into the 2004 Constitution. Government policies towards private enterprises have been constantly changing and unpredictable. Confiscations of private property through various means have been observed from time to time. The mass emigration of business people in the past few years shows that entrepreneurs are not very confident about the future.

The stagnation of reform over the recent few years has worried many people. Even Prime Minister Wen Jiabo has repeatedly called for deepening reform. However, his arguments remain on paper and have not yet been seen in practice. This shows that the current Chinese leadership is fragmented and there is no united reform-oriented leadership.

The future of private and state-owned enterprises depends on what the next generation of leaders will do: will they restart the economic reform and initiate political reform or will they continue to run the country in the style of the current leaders according to the so-called Chinese model? While it is risky to make a prediction, I have some confidence that changes will come.

First, and most importantly, the current slowdown in economic growth shows that China cannot sustain its high growth without fundamental change in its growth model. The high growth of the past three decades has been based on low labour costs and was export-driven. As labour costs increase (the annual increase was around 15 per cent in the past decade) and exporting becomes more difficult, Chinese enterprises must be more innovative. The success of this transformation depends on the activation of private entrepreneurship, not the expansion of SOEs, as SOEs cannot be innovative.

Second, SOEs's monopoly in key industries has caused wide resentment. Consumers complain about the higher cost and lower quality of services; entrepreneurs criticize monopolies for unfair competition; and the public accuse them of cronyism. Chinese people now even ask for SOEs' monopoly profits to be shared as they are unhappy that the profits are all returned to the SOE. All these show that SOEs are becoming less popular.

Recently the State Council announced a new thirty-six-item policy for the development of private enterprises, which allows private enterprises to enter all industries. While the policy is not easy to implement given that many administrative barriers exist, it signals that the above two considerations have drawn the attention of the top leaders.

Third, various studies show that SOEs are less efficient than private enterprises. Some of them are profitable on paper only because (1) of their monopoly position; (2) of higher commodity prices in recent years; and (3) they use many free or quasi-free inputs (Unirule Institite, 2011). SOEs are also highly indebted for excessive expansion and cheap loans. As the economy slows down, their profits will go down and even turn into a loss, and non-performance loans will re-appear. If that happens, the government will be forced to privatize these SOEs, as in the 1990s.

Fourth, China is building a nationwide social security net. However, the social security fund is already in deficit. Surely, as the population is ageing, the deficit will be huge. The only solution is to transform the state shares in SOEs into a social security fund or raise funds through the privatization of SOEs. In fact, the transformation of shares has already begun.

The above four reasons will drive the government back to the interrupted privatization process sooner or later, and allow more room for the development of private enterprises. The government will have to do this to maintain political stability.

The privatization of current SOEs is simply a political decision and technically it is not difficult. Given that most operating SOEs are already listed on stock exchanges, what the government needs to do is just to release its shares to the markets or distribute its shares to households.

It is possible that within ten to twenty years, the share of SOEs in GDP will decline to 10 per cent or less. China will become a market economy based private ownership.

Of course, given the uncertainty of Chinese politics, other scenarios are also possible. However, if private enterprises cannot become a dominant player, I believe, the Chinese economy will face major problems in the future.

■ REFERENCES

Groves, T., Yongmiao Hong, John McMillan, and Barry Naughton. 1994. Autonomy and incentives in Chinese state enterprises. *Quarterly Journal of Economics* 109, 183–209.

Unirule Institute of Economics. 2011. The nature, perfomance and reform of the state-owned enterprises. *The Review of New Political Economy* 19, 6–133.

Zhang, Weiying. 1997. Decision rights, residual claim and performance: a theory of how China's state enterprise reform works. *China Economic Review* 8(1), 67–82.

Zhang, Weiying, W. W. Cooper, Honghui Deng, Barnett R. Parker, and T. Ruefli. 2010. Entrepreneurial talents and economic development in China. *Socio-Economic Planning Sciences* 44(4), 178–92.

Zhaoxi, Li. 2012. State Ownership Policy and State-Owned Enterprise Reform: Development, Problems, and Policy Proposals. Working Paper, Cairncross Foundation, Beijing.

46 Political economy of privatization in China

Yasheng Huang

An observer of the Chinese economy in 2012 confronts a profound puzzle. On the one hand, the analyst knows that China has privatized on a massive scale. In the late 1990s between 30 to 40 million workers were laid off due to the restructuring and privatization of state-owned enterprises (SOEs). Even the most radical shock therapies in other transition economies pale in comparison.

But the same analyst also sees that SOEs have never been as powerful as they are today. The entire banking sector is controlled by the state and they are among the largest banks in the world. This is also true of the telecommunications sector. Every year the top Chinese firms that make it into the *Fortune* magazine lists of the globally most competitive companies are almost exclusively SOEs. One of these two contradictory facts has to give way and it is one that says that China has implemented transformative privatization.

China did privatize. This is not in dispute. What is in dispute is how transformative Chinese privatization has been. Many believe that Chinese reforms have been transformative. One leading China economist proclaimed that the process of transition was already complete. The remaining challenge was one of economic development (Naughton, 2007). The argument in this chapter is that this judgement is premature.

Chinese privatization is best described as being stealthy in nature and tactical in objective. It can be described as stealthy because Chinese privatization has largely been an implicitly permissive policy rather than an explicitly supportive policy. Privatization was permitted ex post even though the privatization practices occurred on an enormous scale. This is in contrast with India. India did not privatize aggressively. Between 1991 and 2000, only forty-eight companies were privatized. But India established a government agency with the dedicated task of privatizing the Indian economy—known as the Ministry of Disinvestment. One implication of stealth privatization is that private property rights cannot be fully secure. Stealth privatization has left a lot of discretion in the hands of the state. What the state has—tacitly—conceded can also be regained.

Tactical privatization refers to the idea that the state never fully embraced privatization as a policy goal in and of itself. Privatization was intended as an instrument in the service of a larger goal. The goal of the Chinese state is to maintain political control. Maintaining political control in turn requires maintaining economic control of vital sectors of the economy. Viewed this way, the privatization programme of the late 1990s was really a means to fund those SOEs the state intended to control and to reduce operational and managerial complexities so that the state could focus on operating and managing fewer and larger firms. Tactical privatization did not reduce the power of the state; it funded and made smarter the power of the Chinese state.

The first section of this chapter provides more details on stealth privatization. The second section discusses tactical privatization and the third section concludes by drawing some broad implications of this way of viewing Chinese privatization experience.

46.1 **Stealth privatization**

Stealth privatization has two effects. One is that China's privatization is hard to observe, which has led several economists to conclude that China has transitioned without privatization (Stiglitz, 2006). Qian (1999) observed that China did not privatize a single SOE before 1992. The other effect is that private property rights are not secure. This is probably one situation where practice does not make perfect: a lot of privatization practices do not translate into secure private property rights.

China did not privatize through conventional methods. One privatization instrument was through foreign direct investment (FDI). Many foreign firms entered China through joint ventures (JVs). A conventional JV involves an agreement between independent firms to jointly fund and operate a new project and a new line of business. But many JV deals involving SOEs are really acquisition deals. In this type of acquisition, the Chinese firm capitalizes its main operating assets, product lines, and distribution networks as equity stakes in a joint venture. Often the original firm is left with the non-operating assets, such as employee housing, cafeterias, medical facilities, and debt.

In transactions involving JV acquisitions, the shareholders of the investing SOEs make the same calculation as they would under conventional acquisitions. They believe that the future operating income from Chinese management will be less than the dividend income from their shares of the future income generated by foreign management. The reason for the preponderance of a JV format rather than straightforward acquisitions is because of legal and regulatory requirements imposed by the Chinese government. The underlying economics is similar in both types of acquisition (Huang, 2003).

The Chinese have coined a specific term to refer to JV acquisition—grafted JVs. The word, graft, as Gallagher (2001) explains, comes from horticulture—'the grafting of a new branch to the trunk of a sickly tree in order to revive it'. This is a vivid and apt description of the insolvency-induced FDI inflows of the 1990s. The insolvency-induced FDI also gave rise to a phenomenon widely reported in the Chinese press at the time—the operating assets were often capitalized at a fraction of their book value. In Russia, foreigners paid only a fraction of presumptive book value (Boycko et al., 1995), but foreigners bought Russian assets at the time of a catastrophic economic decline, episodic macro-economic and financial instability, and the paralysis and even collapse of the state in some regions of the country. The JV acquisitions described here have occurred in China at a time of surging economic growth and a generally stable political environment. The first documented instances of such FDI acquisitions of SOEs took place as early as 1984. Privatization of this sort long predates what many economists view as the turning point in Chinese privatization experience—the 1997 15th Party Congress (Huang, 2003).

The second method of privatization is through corruption—stealth privatization by definition. Because privatization policy is not an explicitly stated goal of the Chinese government, the pricing and the valuation of the assets held by the SOEs are often undertaken 'under the table'. Although there are state-sponsored asset exchanges in Chinese cities, they are mostly illiquid and very few genuine sales go through them. Few are scalable. Both the supply and the demand sides of the asset sales on these exchanges are highly fragmented, private, personal, and network-driven, unlike a true exchange which is characterized by transparency, disclosure, and impersonal transactions.

Corruption is an inevitable result of informal privatization practices. Raymond Fisman and Yongxiang Wang (2011) provide statistical evidence that under-pricing occurred in more than 70 per cent of the deals. In the absence of a political mandate supporting privatization, corruption acts as an incentive for privatization. Because privatization is not an explicitly stated goal of the government, there are substantial political risks for bureaucrats who permit or promote privatization. Then the rational behaviour is to demand a large financial payoff to offset the political risks inherent in the stealth privatization. Stealth privatization begets corruption.

And corruption makes privatization even more 'stealthy'. There is a feedback loop mechanism here. Because privatization is not fully accepted as a legitimate policy, it tends to be informal, personal, and negotiated—and therefore corrupt. The corruption of the process then further undermines the legitimacy of the entire programme. In the past decade, the Chinese government has arrested, prosecuted, and sentenced to long jail terms many entrepreneurs and government officials on corruption charges.

This political economy feedback loop leads to private property rights—never fully secure in the current political system—being perceived as even more insecure. Recent press reports reveal that 60–70% of China's richest entrepreneurs are now contemplating an exit option of leaving China altogether. There are incipient signs of some capital flight in the country's balance of payment statistics. Net errors and omissions—in the negative direction—have increased, despite the fact that the policy discussions are dominated by whether or not the the Chinese currency should appreciate further and the fact that the currency has appreciated substantially since 2005.

46.2 **Tactical privatization**

While stealth privatization occurred throughout the reform era, the scale of privatization has increased substantially since 1997. In 1997, the Communist Party formally adopted what was known as 'Grasping the big and letting go of the small', a more explicit and a more explicitly stated privatization programme. The Chinese state no longer just permitted privatization ex post; it began to do so ex ante. Qian (1999) proclaimed, 'It is quite remarkable for China to have overcome ideological and political opposition to embrace the market system and private ownership without a political revolution.'

Had Qian been right in 1999, one would not have seen a stronger, better-financed and expanding state sector in 2014. In important ways, the Chinese state is far more consistent both in its pronouncements and in its policy practices than outside economists often credit. Many economists assumed that the Communist Party in 1997 endorsed a full privatization programme, when in fact the Chinese state has done exactly what it said it would do in 1997. 'Letting go of the small' meant that the government supported privatization of individually small but numerically numerous SOEs. These are labour-intensive firms and singling them out for privatization, with no established social protection in place, led to massive unemployment, social instability, and wrenching human costs. (Coincidentally and concurrently, the Chinese state tightened its political and security controls in order to suppress dissent.)

'Letting go of the small' directly contradicts a popular hypothesis as to why China had resisted explicit privatization before 1997—maintaining employment. That hypothesis would predict that the Chinese state would privatize capital-intensive firms first, not labour-intensive firms. The Chinese state did exactly the opposite. According to a government estimate, small SOEs only accounted for some 18 per cent of the assets in the state sector as of 1997 (State Development and Planning Commission, 1998).

A superior hypothesis is illustrated by the first part of the Chinese privatization formula—'Grasping the big'. 'Grasping the big' meant restructuring, consolidating, and strengthening China's largest SOEs. 'Letting go of the small' is the tactic employed to 'grasp the big'. It reduced and ended government subsidies and social liabilities. It also reduced operating and managerial complexities. Instead of managing tens of thousands of small firms scattered around the country, the Chinese state could now focus on only a few thousand firms. Taken together 'Grasping the big and letting go of the small' really means a massive reallocation of financial, human, and managerial resources away from the small SOEs to a handful of the largest SOEs.

46.3 **Implications**

There has not been a Thatcherian revolution in China. The goal of the Chinese state is not to 'starve the beast'. 'Stuff the beast' is a more accurate description of the goal of Chinese policy. The Chinese state sector is more streamlined and on a far stronger financial footing than ever. The asset base of the firms directly managed by the State Asset Supervision and Administration Commission (SASAC) more than tripled from 7.1 trillion yuan in 2003 to 21 trillion yuan in 2009.[1]

The best description of the Chinese economy today is that it is a commanding-heights state-capitalist economy. While GDP growth has been extremely fast during this commanding-heights phase of Chinese reforms, other indicators bode less well. The labour share of GDP dropped sharply during this period. So did the consumption share of GDP. Now with anaemic growth in the USA and Europe on the edge of a deepening crisis, the fragility of the commanding-heights approach is again exposed. It is not a question of *if* but of *when* China will have to undertake a genuine privatization programme that has as its core the goal of creating a vibrant private sector rather than strengthening political control. There is no third way.

■ REFERENCES

Boycko, Maxim, Andrei Shleifer, and Robert W. Vishny. 1995. *Privatizing Russia*. Cambridge, MA: MIT Press.

Fisman, Raymond and Yongxiang Wang. 2011. Evidence on the existence and the impact of corruption in state asset sales in China. Working Paper, Columbia Business School.

Gallagher, Mary. 2001. Grafted Capitalism: Ownership Change and Labor Relations in the PRC. Paper prepared for the conference 'Uneven Transition in China: Reform and Inequality', Ann Arbor, 7 April.

Huang, Yasheng. 2003. *Selling China*. New York: Cambridge University Press.

Naughton, Barry. 2007. *The Chinese Economy: Transitions and Growth*. Cambridge, MA: MIT Press.

Qian, Yingyi. 1999. The Institutional Foundations of China's Market Transition. Paper read at The World Bank Annual Conference on Development Economics, 28–30 April, Washington, DC.

State Development and Planning Commission. 1998. *Report on Chinese Industrial Development*. Beijing: Zhongguo jingji chubanshe.

Stiglitz, Joseph E. 2006. The Transition from communism to market: A reappraisal after 15 Years. In *European Bank for Reconstruction and Development Annual Meeting*. London.

[1] His comment was widely reported in the Chinese media. See for example <http://finance.qq.com/a/20100915/001683.htm>.

Part VIII

Agriculture and Rural Development

47 Food security and agriculture in China

Laixiang Sun

47.1 Introduction

For thousands of years, grain and vegetables have dominated food calorie supply in China. According to the Chinese farm survey of John Buck (1937) in the 1930s, grain and vegetables accounted for 97 per cent of food calorie supply. FAO's Food Balance Sheets showed that up to 1985, grain and vegetables still accounted for more than 90 per cent of food calorie supply and after 20 year of impressive income growth, this figure was still at the level of 78 per cent in 2005, far higher than the level of rich developed countries. This gap is expected to significantly narrow in the coming decades owing to the surge in meat consumption of the poor segments of the population (Fischer et al., 2007; Keyzer et al., 2005). According to our estimation, meat consumption per capita in China will increase from 46 kg in 2005 to 75 kg in 2030. If fishery products are included, the figure will rise from 60 kg in 2005 to 100 kg in 2030. This means that by 2030 China will need to produce 265 million more pigs a year, 7–8 billion more poultry, and 8–10 billion more fish. Drawing on the headline concern over 'who will feed China' in the mid-1990s, a major challenge for Chinese agriculture in the coming decades is: who will feed China's livestock? In other words, can China's farmers feed the animals required to meet the accelerating demand for meat and dairy products and to what extent will China depend on international feed and meat markets to fill the supply–demand gaps?

This and other new challenges for the coming decades are shaped by the following forces: a growing population that is expected to exceed 1,435 million by 2030, increasing urbanization of more than 60 per cent by 2030, and rising incomes as the country's economic growth benefits more and more people. At the same time, industrialization and climate change are expected to lead to a loss of fertile cropland in the traditional suburb areas and trade liberalization and technological progress will continue to shape further change. Understanding the interactions among these driving forces and their impacts on farmers and consumers across the diverse 2,885 counties that make up the countryside of China is not easy. Setting the right agricultural policies is even harder.

47.2 **Modelling future scenarios of Chinese agriculture**

To help identify the most effective policies and analyse their potential impacts on different parts of China, researchers from the International Institute for Applied Systems Analysis (IIASA), the Centre for World Food Studies of the Free University Amsterdam (SOW-VU), the Centre for Chinese Agricultural Policy of the Chinese Academy of Sciences (CCAP-CAS), and an other five research partner institutions developed the most detailed model of Chinese agriculture yet available in a series of projects starting in 2001.[1] Known first as Chinagro-I and then Chinagro-II, the model provides informative analysis down to county level and helps researchers analyse consumer and producer behaviour, government policies, and markets.

In more detail, Chinagro-II is a 17-commodity, 8-region general equilibrium welfare model. Farm supply is represented at county level (2,885, virtually all), and accommodates for every county outputs of 28 activities and 9 land use types and livestock systems. Consumption is depicted at regional level, separately for the urban and the rural population, each divided into three income groups, and domestic trade is interregional. The model describes the price-based interaction between the supply behaviour of farmers, the demand behaviour of consumers, and the trade flows connecting them. Farmers maximize their revenue by optimally allocating labour and equipment to cropping and livestock systems, at exogenously specified land resources, stable capacities, and levels of technology, while taking the buying and selling prices in the county as given. In addition to purchased inputs, local inputs such as crop residuals, grass, organic manure, and household waste contribute to the production process. Consumers maximize their utility, at given prices, by optimally allocating their expenditures according to a utility function that is quasi-linear, that is, linear with a unit coefficient in part of non-food consumption and obeying a linear expenditure system in food commodities and the remainder of non-food consumption. Trade between regions in China and with the rest of the world is cost minimizing at given world prices and import and export tariff rates. The impact of China's imports and exports on the world market is assessed by coupling Chinagro-II and the GTAP-model of world trade.[2] Through its significant geographic detail, the model can incorporate location-specific information on climate, resources, and technology while its equilibrium structure enables it to represent coordination flows among the various agents and describe market clearing at different levels (Fischer et al., 2007; Keyzer and van Veen, 2005).

---

[1] This series of projects has been sponsored by the European Commission (ICA4-CT-2001–10085, the CHINAGRO project; 044255, the CATSEI project), the Natural Science Foundation of China (#70024001, 40921140410), the Netherlands Ministry of Agriculture, Nature Management and Food Quality, and Chinese Academy of Sciences (CXTD-Z2005–1).

[2] Global Trade Analysis Project, see Hertel (1997).

The baseline scenario of Chinagro-II is defined by a coherent set of assumptions about the central (most plausible) tendencies of exogenous driving forces, which include non-agricultural output growth, population growth, urbanization and interregional migration, international prices, changes in land and water resources and stable capacities, adjustment of food preferences, technical progress, and trade liberalization. The base year for the model simulation is 2005. The model is partially verified based on available data for 2010. Scenario analysis is conducted for 2010, 2020, and 2030.

The simulation of the baseline scenario shows that, on one hand, self-sufficiency in rice, wheat, vegetables, and fruits will be maintained and China will also be able to export significant amount of vegetables and fruits in 2020 and 2030. On the other hand, for animal feed China will further increase its reliance on the world market, especially owing to the fact that the availability of traditional feed (such as crop residuals, grass, household waste) cannot expand at the same rates as the livestock sector. We classify the tradeable feed into three commodities: maize, carbohydrate feed, and protein feed, in which carbohydrate feed covers feed types other than maize that are relatively rich in carbohydrates, such as those based on tubers and minor grains, while protein feed covers feed types that are relatively rich in proteins such as soybean, oilseed cakes, and wheat and rice bran. Although maize was actually exported in 2005 and 2010, for 2030 the baseline simulation indicates a substantial import volume at about 15.8 million tons, presuming that government tariff policies will indeed allow large volumes of imports at relatively low tariff rates. Imports of carbohydrate feed, expressed in grain equivalent, are projected to go up to 14 million tons from the 2005 level of 1 million tons; and imports of protein feed, expressed in cake equivalent, increase from 24 to 58 million tons. The latter flow looks huge but please note that world trade in soybean cake is already quite large, with about 125 million tons in 2008 (Keyzer and van Veen, 2010).[3] In addition, it is worth noting the growing importance of world trade in dried distillers grain with solubles (DDGs), the major by-product from maize-based bioethanol production which is rich in proteins.

Considered as a share of domestic demand in China, these import volumes are not excessive. The largest shares are found for edible oils and protein feeds, at 52 per cent and 42 per cent, respectively. All other shares are below 20 per cent. Owing to China's large non-agricultural trade surplus, there will be no problem for China to finance such imports. However, these amounts are substantial for the world market. China's imports of carbohydrate and protein feed may imply a claim to 30–40 per cent of total world trade and the share of maize and edible oil imports could amount to 15–20 per cent of the global market. China's efforts to secure part of its agricultural imports via leasing or obtaining land in other continents should be viewed in this context. Based on coupled

---

[3] We apply a cake content of 0.82 to the 65 million tons of soybeans in the trade.

simulations with the worldwide GTAP model, the effect of China's import increases on world feed prices is estimated at about 5 per cent. This is a significant effect and will definitely lead to more pressure on world agricultural markets. On the other hand, it will encourage feed production in major exporting countries and stimulate the emergence of new feed markets such as DDGs and other by-products of bio-fuel production. In this sense it will not necessarily lead to turmoil.

Alongside the economic and trade impacts on and from the development of China's agriculture sector, we also explored its social and environmental implications. For example, the research team looks into the fertilizer issues in a spatially explicit way, both via model simulations and via specific studies. Simulations show steady and significant surpluses for nitrogen and phosphates on the vast majority of grid-cells of cropland, and deficits for potassium. The simulations pinpoint the areas that suffer from excessive fertilizer application and the resulting environmental damage and waste of the precious resources of nitrogen and phosphorous. Policy actions should combine the improvement of practices in fertilizer application, technical measures to reduce losses, and spatial reallocation of the production of livestock (Fischer et al., 2009, 2010).

47.3 **Conclusion**

China's agriculture has been growing in a healthy manner for the last three and a half decades. Food production is rising and the food chain is becoming more efficient. Trade patterns have been changing accordingly and in line with the comparative advantage of the country. China is exporting more labour-intensive fruits and vegetables as well as high value added commodities while it is importing more land-intensive agricultural products such as soybeans, cotton, sugar, and dairy. In terms of a trade regime, China moved from one under bureaucratic control to one in which the private sector takes a major responsibility for imports and exports.

The chief challenge for Chinese agriculture in the future is that China will have to meet the rising demand for meat with less land, less water, and less labour while trying to address the environmental problems caused by the intensive application of chemical fertilizers and by rapid industrialization. As a consequence, trade with world food and feed markets will have to expand. The simulation of our integrated modelling shows that China is likely to become an even greater importer of edible oil, carbohydrates, and protein feeds than it is today, and will probably expand its imports of maize for livestock feeds. Although these imports remain moderate relative to China's size, they are large as a fraction of world trade. This will increase pressure on the world markets of these commodities; nevertheless the net effects will remain limited because agriculture in both China and the rest of world will respond and adjust.

■ REFERENCES

Buck, J. L. 1937. *Land Utilization in China.* Chicago: University of Chicago Press.

Fischer, G., J. Huang, M. A. Keyzer, H. Qiu, L. Sun, and W. C. M. van Veen. 2007. China's Agricultural Prospects and Challenges: Report on scenario simulations until 2030 with the Chinagro welfare model covering national, regional and county level. Research Report, SOW-VU, Free University, Amsterdam, The Netherlands.

Fischer, G., T. Ermolieva, Y. Ermoliv, and L. Sun. 2009. Risk-adjusted approaches for planning sustainable agriculture. *Stochastic Environmental Research and Risk Assessment* 23(4), 441–50.

Fischer, G., W. Winiwarter, T. Ermolieva, G.-Y. Cao, H. Qiu, Z. Klimont, D. Wiberg, and F. Wagner. 2010. Integrated modeling framework for assessment and mitigation of nitrogen pollution from agriculture: Concept and case study for China. *Agriculture, Ecosystems and Environment* 136(1–2), 116–24.

Hertel, T. W. (ed.) 1997. *Global Trade Analysis: Modeling and Applications.* Cambridge: Cambridge University Press.

Keyzer, M. A. and W. van Veen. 2005. Towards a spatially and socially explicit agricultural policy analysis for China: specification of the Chinagro models. Working Paper 05–02, SOW-VU, Free University, Amsterdam, The Netherlands.

Keyzer, M. A. and W. van Veen. 2010. China's food demand, supply and trade in 2030: simulations with Chinagro II model. Presentation at CATSEI Final Policy Forum, Beijing, 19 November 2010.

Keyzer, M. A., M. D. Merbis, I. F. P. W. Pavel, and C. F. A. van Wesenbeeck. 2005. Diet shifts towards meat and the effects on cereal use: can we feed the animals in 2030? *Ecological Economics* 55(2), 187–202.

48 Food security in China

Funing Zhong

The FAO definition reads: 'Food security exists when all people, at all times, have physical, social and economic access to sufficient, safe and nutritious food that meets their dietary needs and food preferences for an active and healthy life' (FAO, 2011). There is no doubt that food security has always been one of the top policy issues in China where 22 per cent of the world's population depends on about 10 per cent of the world's total arable land, and per capita fresh water availability is only about a quarter of the world's average.

However, it should be noted that food security is expressed as 'grain security' in Chinese terms,[1] suggesting some differences in policy implications. In addition to the coverage of crops, there are significant differences in policy objectives and tools. The formal policy is best documented in 'Grain Law (draft for public opinions)' released by the State Council (Legislative Affairs Office of the State Council, 2012). In the draft document grain is re-iterated and re-emphasized as a 'specific commodity crucial to the national economy and people's lives', and the state would adhere to the 'principle of basic self-reliance'. The draft document further stipulates that the state would 'coordinate the market mechanisms linking grain production, marketing and consumption, in order to ensure basic balance in total demand and supply, as well as basically ensuring stabilized prices'. It has been confirmed that: (1) grain security relies on domestic production; and (2) government interventions in marketing and trade are among the chosen policy tools.

The inclusion of market intervention in the toolbox to achieve grain security has been deeply rooted ever since the founding of the People's Republic. During World War II and the subsequent civil war, China suffered severely from hyper-inflation (Xu, 1983), which largely contributed to the overthrow of the Guomindang government. Having learned the importance of ensuring food security, one of the top tasks facing the new government in the early 1950s was to stabilize food prices in the newly controlled cities. The new

---

[1] In official Chinese statistics, grain includes cereals (such as rice, wheat, corn, and coarse grains), beans, and tubers. Soybeans are counted as beans and hence grain crops, not oil-bearing crops that consist mainly of peanuts and rapeseeds. Food is a more general term, including grains, edible oil, vegetables, and fruits, as well as animal products. The emphasis on grain security reflects the fact that staple food has long been considered a basic necessity in human consumption and hence a policy focal point regarding national security.

government responded with interventions in grain marketing and quickly succeeded with a large quantity of grain being procured from farmers at a low price. Thanks to the re-distribution of farmland through the land reform programme, agricultural production recovered very quickly, and farmers were willing to deliver the requested grain to the government at prices below market levels, at least for a short time (Zhong, 2004).

The state control on grain marketing soon became an even more important policy tool as China adopted the Russian-style 'heavy industry first' development strategy. With support from the population, the government determined to mobilize all available resources to build up the heavy industrial sectors as a way to achieve modernization. In a poor peasant economy, one necessity to mobilize all available resources at that time required restricting consumption in general, and extracting agricultural surplus in particular. It seemed that the state monopoly in grain marketing was the most convenient tool to serve both these ends. While the compulsory marketing system enabled the government to procure grain from farmers and ration it to urban residents at low prices, the resulting surplus in the form of industrial profits was retained by the government for investment.

Of course, low procurement prices might depress farmers' incentives for grain production and meet with resistance. To ensure that production and procurement fell in line with state plans, farmers were organized into cooperatives and then communes which it was relatively easy to put under administrative control and political pressure. A rationing system was strictly implemented in the urban/industrial sectors, in order to ensure relatively fair and equal access for all consumers given the limited total supply and low incomes. However, even with considerable pressure, the procurement scheme was unable to ensure a minimum and adequate supply for the growing population. In practice, the administered quota price had to be raised periodically, and a premium had to be added to encourage above-quota delivery.

The ongoing reform began with an increase of 20 per cent in procurement prices in 1979 alone, and the above-quota premium was raised from 30 per cent to 50 per cent at the same time. While the quota price was increased periodically afterwards, the volumes of the quota were gradually reduced, permitting farmers to sell their surplus on the free market at higher prices. The procurement system was replaced with 'contracted purchases' in 1986, but the nature of compulsory delivery at a price below market level remained the same. When food prices surged at the end of 1993, the government blamed a shortage in domestic production instead of double-digit inflation, and responded by introducing the 'provincial governors' responsibility' system, holding all provincial governments responsible for balancing grain demand with the local supply.

The situation in the grain market changed dramatically in December 1996 as prices for major grain crops declined by 40 per cent in a month, and stayed at the same low level for several years. The seemingly long-term surplus led to the abolition of the 'contracted purchasing' system in the mid-1990s. At the same time, a special grain inventory system, which had been introduced in 1990 to smooth fluctuations in production, was enhanced with 'grain risk funds' to purchase excess supply in the market.

As a result of low prices over a number of years, grain production continuously declined from the 1998 peak level by 16 per cent in five years. Alarmed by the risk of serious shortages in domestic production, the government initiated a new package of policies, which have been in place since the end of 2002, with the goal of securing domestic food supply. The new package was started in a few provinces as a subsidy programme for grain producers, and was extended to cover the whole country within a few years. Minimum price schemes were introduced in 2004 for selected grain crops in selected areas, such as corn in northeast China and rice in several northeast, central, and southern provinces, while 'temporary stock', another price support measure, was periodically carried out for corn produced in northeast China. In addition, the agricultural tax was phased out in 2004–06 to provide better incentives for agricultural production in general, and grain producers benefited more than other farmers since the agricultural tax had been levied on arable land, more than 60 per cent of which was devoted to grain crops.

The policy focusing on domestic production was accompanied by public investment in agricultural R&D, infrastructure, and the development of modern input sectors. China was the first country to develop and widely adopt dwarf and semi-dwarf varieties of rice and wheat in the 1960s, and hybrid rice in the 1970s. Irrigated area tripled in the latter half of the twentieth century, covering more than 40 per cent of arable land and 73 per cent of cereals production in China by 1998 (Cai and Rosegrant, 2004). By 2009, the irrigated area was further increased by 10 per cent, despite a 5–6 per cent decline in total arable land in the previous ten years. There were also a substantial increase in the use of modern inputs. The total use of chemical fertilizers increased from 8.8 million metric tons (mmt) in 1978 to 54 mmt in 2009, expanding by more than 5 times in 31 years, and the total power of agricultural machinery increased from 117 million kilowatts (kw) to 875 million kw, representing a 6.5 fold increase in 31 years.

Given the policy of priority and fuelled by public investment, grain production has shown remarkable growth in China, both before and during the reform. Total output has increased from 163.92 mmt in 1952, the year marking the beginning of recovery from war, to 304.77 mmt in 1978, the year marking the start of the ongoing reform, to 571.21 mmt in 2011. Such impressive success in grain production is solely attributable to yield growth, as arable land has continuously shifted to more profitable cash crops, as well as being lost to industrialization and urbanization (Carter et al., 2012).

However, despite the remarkable increase in domestic grain production, food imports have significantly increased in the last few years. Imports of soybeans and edible oils rose quickly from 1.1 mmt and 2.6 mmt in 1996 to 54.8 mmt and 6.87 mmt in 2010, respectively. As soybean is considered a grain crop, the grain self-sufficiency rate has already been well below the target of 95 per cent set by the government in its 1996 White Paper (State

Council Information Office, 1996). Moreover, China has turned into a net importer of two major cereal crops—rice and corn—since the 2009/10 marketing year. This increasing reliance on the world food market is viewed by the government as alarming, and the issue of grain security has re-emerged as a hot topic.

The challenges are apparent. On the supply side, farmland will continue to disappear due to rapid urbanization and shifts to non-grain crops; water shortages are likely to become more and more severe; pollution and deterioration will further reduce arable land and worsen the quality of remaining land, and improving yields will become increasingly difficult at the current high levels of inputs and yields. On the demand side, the population is likely to continue to increase in the near future; along with rapid income growth, leading to higher demand for food and changing diets towards more animal products. As a result, the imbalance between domestic supply and demand is likely to widen due to basic market forces.

There are two other challenges as well. First, production costs increase so quickly that domestic market prices are going to exceed those in the world market, resulting in growing pressures from imports. Second, as price support is not permitted, the traditional target of keeping prices affordable for the poor becomes less and less compatible with providing adequate incentives to producers. Therefore, restricted by WTO commitments, China is no longer able to pursue its dual objectives of self-reliance and low prices at the same time, even if it is willing to accept efficiency losses.

What alternatives are left for China? China may have to re-define its policy objectives regarding grain security, reducing the target set for self-sufficiency or excluding soybeans from the coverage. More importantly, China should formally, though gradually, accept the position of a net food importer and change its policy objective and tools accordingly. Consumers' access to food supply should not be restricted to domestic production, as increasing grain production in other parts of the world is equally important. The increases in total world supply may improve food security for all countries participating in the trading system, and China is capable of playing an important role in helping many countries increase their grain production through technology transfer and investment.

Increasing domestic grain production is still a desired policy objective, and public investments in R&D and infrastructure are better tools.[2] The development of high and super-high yield varieties through biotechnology, and the improvement of low-yield farmland through infrastructural investments, are the two approaches that should be put at the top of the public investment agenda. These measures are much better than market interventions that may compromise the long-term objective of food security. To help the poor, targeted income support is also to be preferred over price control.

---

[2] For example, see the CPC Central Committee (2012).

■ REFERENCES

Cai, X. and M. Rosegrant. 2004. China's water and food: an outlook to the future. In *Dare to Dream: Vision of 2050 Agriculture in China*, edited by T. C. Tso and He Kang. Beijing: China Agricultural University Press

Carter, C. A., F. Zhong, and J. Zhu. 2012. Advances in China's agriculture and global implications. *Applied Economic Perspectives and Policy* 34(1), 1–36.

CPC Central Committee. 2012. Some points in speeding agricultural R&D innovation and continuously enhancing capacity in supply of agricultural products. CPC Document, 2 February 2012. <http://www.china.com.cn/policy/txt/2012-02/02/content_24528271.htm>.

FAO. 2011. FAO Practical Guide: Basic Concepts of Food Security. (PDF). <http://www.fao.org/docrep/013/al936e/al936e00.pdf>. Retrieved 13 November 2011.

Legislative Affairs Office of the State Council. 2012. Grain Law (draft for public opinions), <http://www.chinalaw.gov.cn/article/cazjgg/201202/20120200360700.shtml>. 21 February.

State Council Information Office. 1996. The Grain Issue in China (White Paper). <http://www.chinagate.com.cn>.

Xu, D. 1983. *Zhongguo Jindai Nongye Shengchan He Maoyi Tongji Ziliao (Statistical Data of Agricultural Production and Trade in Modern China)*. Shanghai: Shanghai People's Press

Zhong, F. 2004. The political economy of China's grain marketing system. In *China's Domestic Grain Marketing Reform and Integration*, edited by Chen Chunlai and Christopher Findlay. Canberra: Asia Pacific Press.

49 Farm size and long-term prospects for Chinese agriculture

Keijiro Otsuka

49.1 Introduction

In the process of the economic development in Asia which accompanied continuous increases in the real wage rate, the comparative advantage of the economy in most Asian countries has been shifting from agriculture to non-agricultural sectors. A part of the reason is the small farm size in Asia, which requires labour-intensive cultivation (Otsuka, 2013). In order to reduce labour costs, farm size expansion and large mechanization must take place, as land and machinery are complementary (Otsuka et al., 2013). Any expansion of farm size, however, is difficult to realize due to imperfections in the land market (Otsuka, 2007). Moreover, as Johnson (1991) forcefully argues, agricultural support policies to reduce income inequality between farmers and urban workers aggravate this inequality in the longer run by increasing the farm population, a proportion of which would have migrated out of the countryside in the absence of such policies. As a result, high income countries in Asia (e.g. Japan, Taiwan, and Korea) have retained small farms and lost comparative advantage in agriculture, and thereby massively increasing their imports of grain.[1]

What will happen to Chinese agriculture, if wage rates continue to increase? Since the average farm size in Chinese agriculture is extremely small and individual land ownership rights are absent, farm size expansion may not take place sufficiently fast. If China becomes a major importer of grain in future, world grain prices will shoot up and poverty is expected to deepen in low-income countries which import grain. This study examines what should be done to prevent this tragic outcome.

---

[1] Grain self-sufficiency ratio declined to about 25% in these countries starting with near self-sufficiency in the 1960s (Otsuka, 2013).

49.2 Dynamics of change in the optimum farm size

When labour is abundant relative to land, labour-intensive methods of cultivation are socially efficient. In such cultivation systems, no major indivisible inputs are used and, hence, there is no major source of scale economies. Roughly speaking, a farm of 1–2 hectares can be managed efficiently by family labour consisting of a few workers. Beyond that scale, hired labour must be employed. However, the monitoring cost of hired labour is high and it increases more than proportionally with an increase in the cultivation size (Feder, 1985; Hayami and Otsuka, 1993). This explains why family farms dominate agriculture in most countries (Eastwood et al., 2009).[2] Thus, the optimum farm size in low-wage economies is bound to be small because of the limited availability of family labour and the costly substitution of capital for labour. Indeed, an inverse correlation between farm size and yield per hectare has been widely observed in south Asia and sub-Saharan Africa (Lipton, 2009; Larson et al., 2014).

As the real wage rate increases, the opportunity cost of family labour increases. In order to reduce labour costs, labour must be substituted by machinery. In order to operate machinery more efficiently, the farm size must be increased. Since large machines are indivisible, scale advantages arise.[3] Thus, larger farms become more efficient than smaller farms. Renting is a practical way to transfer land into a smaller number of large farms. In fact, typically, landlords are small farmers and tenants are large farmers not only in high-income economies but also in South America, Eastern Europe, and Central Asia (Deininger and Byerlee, 2012).

When farm size is adjusted optimally by land renting as well as by land sales, we will not observe 'scale-economies', as all the existing farms are more or less equally large and efficient. Scale economies tend to be observed empirically when inefficient small farms and efficient large farms co-exist (Hayami and Kawagoe, 1989). This will be observed in the dynamic process of farm size adjustments and also when institutional constraints and government regulations impede such adjustments (Hayami, 2005).[4]

49.3 Farm size and food self-sufficiency in China

The most important lesson that can be drawn from the experience of Japan, Taiwan, and Korea is that significant inefficiency in agricultural production arises if farm sizes remain

---

[2] Large farms employing hired workers, however, are common in the land-abundant formerly socialist countries (Rozelle and Swinnen, 2004).

[3] The development of machinery rental markets will lessen the scale disadvantages, but the use of large machinery on a number of small farms will be more costly than on a small number of large farms.

[4] According to a recent study of Foster and Rozensweig (2010), large farms have become more productive than small farms in India due to rising wage rates and large-scale mechanization.

small in a high-wage economy (Otsuka, 2013). If the option of land tenancy is unrestricted, however, tenancy transactions will play an important role in transferring land from inefficient to efficient farm households, thereby contributing to the achievement of higher production efficiency. This view stands in sharp contrast to the conventional view that tenancy is inefficient (Otsuka et al., 1992).

Following the introduction of the household responsibility system since 1978, household farming now prevails in China (e.g. Lin, 1988). Since land is collectively owned in China, however, the land market does not operate freely and, in view of the increasing number of migrants from rural to urban areas, differences in factor endowments among farm households have emerged. Although the Chinese government has strengthened individual land rights (Kung, 1995; Yao, 2000), it appears that the provision of land rights is insufficient to achieve efficient land allocation (Kimura et al., 2011).

The Chinese economy has been rapidly growing over the last three and half decades, and the wage rate has been rising sharply since 2003 (Zhang et al., 2011). Thus, the agricultural wage rate or opportunity cost of family labour in farming must have been rising and will continue to rise, which will induce large-scale mechanization, thereby creating scale advantages. Indeed, the use of riding tractors and combine harvesters is becoming common (Yang et al., 2013). In these circumstances, the production inefficiency of small farms will increase, making it necessary to adjust farm size appropriately through tenancy transactions. Yet the average farm size remained at 0.6 hectare in 2010, increasing only by 0.05 hectare per year since 2000, even though land rental markets have become increasingly active (Huang et al., 2012).

As reported in Figure 49.1, the importing of soybeans has been rapidly increasing in China, particularly since the late 1990s. The high level of soybean imports is explained by increasing demands for feed for livestock production associated with the shift of people's diets from grains to livestock products. However, what is potentially also important is the preservation of small farm size, which is creating decreasing efficiency. The production cost of such small farms will certainly increase in the production of all major grains including maize, rice, and wheat, which may lead to an increase in imports of these grains in the future.[5]

In the case of Japan, imports of both soybean and maize have continuously increased since 1961, in contrast to their declining domestic production. This increased dependence on imports of soybean and maize occurred despite a heavy subsidy programme by the government. There is, therefore, no question that Japan has almost completely lost its comparative advantage in these crops over the last several decades, even though farm size has increased from 1.0 hectare to 1.8 hectares (Otsuka, 2013).

The extremely small farm size presents a major challenge for Chinese agriculture. For example, in order to establish a 10 hectare farm, a typical farmer must rent land from as

---

[5] So far, China has been largely self-sufficient in rice and wheat.

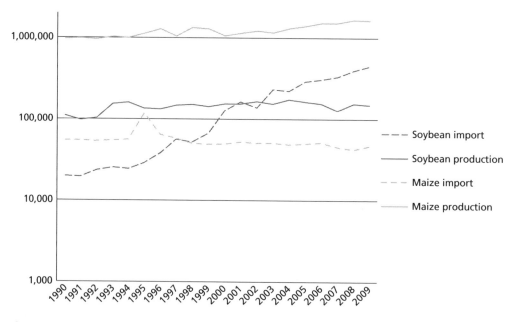

Figure 49.1. Changes in domestic production and imports of maize and soybean in China (semi-log scale)

many as sixteen other farmers. Such tenancy transactions are likely to be very costly. Also, if rented fields are scattered, the potential scale advantages of large-scale mechanization will not be fully realized. Thus, renting is unlikely to be the major means to create large farms in China. Since 2008, the Chinese government has allowed the consolidation of village farmlands, which are managed by a small number of selected full-time farmers. In this arrangement, ex-farmers who now work in the non-farm sector own shares, from which they receive a certain level of dividends. Whether and to what extent such new arrangements will work to create new efficient larger farms remains to be seen.[6]

49.4 **Concluding remarks**

As is shown by the cross-country regression analysis of Otsuka et al. (2013), the grain self-sufficiency ratio tends to decline with GDP growth in Asia, particularly those with meagre land endowment. This finding indicates that grain imports increase with economic growth, because of the increasing inefficiency of small farms. What is clear is that unless drastic measures are adopted to enlarge the average farm size, China, which is a

---

[6] Actually such a system seems to work efficiently in land-rich transition economies (Rozelle and Swinnen, 2004; Swinnen, 2009).

large country, is likely to become a major importer of grain on the world market, leading to increases in world grain prices.

■ **REFERENCES**

Deininger, Klaus and Derek Byerlee. 2012. The rise of large farms in land abundant countries: do they have a future? *World Development* 40(4), 701–14.

Eastwood, Robert, Michael Lipton, and Andrew Newell. 2009. Farm size. In *Handbook of Agricultural Economics*, Volume 4, edited by P. Pingli and R. E. Evenson, 3323–97. Amsterdam: Elsevier.

Feder, Gershon. 1985. The relation between farm size and productivity. *Journal of Development Economics* 18(2–3), 297–313.

Foster, Andrew D. and Mark R. Rosenzweig. 2010. Barriers to Farm Profitability in India: Mechanization, Scale and Credit Markets. mimeo.

Hayami, Yujiro. 2005. An Emerging Agricultural Problem in High-Performing Asian Economies. Presidential Address to the Fifth Conference of the Asian Society of Agricultural Economists, Zahedan, Iran, 29–31 August, and also reproduced in Keijiro Otsuka and C. Ford Runge (eds), *Can Economic Growth Be Sustained? The Collected Papers of Vernon W. Ruttan and Yujiro Hayami*. Oxford: Oxford University Press, 2011.

Hayami, Yujiro and Toshihiko Kawagoe. 1989. Farm mechanization, scale economies, and polarization. *Journal of Development Economics* 31(2), 221–39.

Hayami, Yujiro and Keijiro Otsuka. 1993. *The Economics of Contract Choice: An Agrarian Perspective*, Oxford: Clarendon Press.

Huang, Jikun, Xiaobing Wang, and Huanguang Qui. 2012. *Small-Scale Farmers in China in the Face of Modernization and Globalization*. London: International Institute for Environment and Development.

Johnson, D. Gale. 1991. *World Agriculture in Disarray*, 2nd edn. Basingstoke, UK: Macmillan Press.

Kimura, Shingo, Keijiro Otsuka, Tetsushi Sonobe, and Scott Rozelle. 2011. Efficiency of land allocation through tenancy markets: evidence from China. *Economic Development and Cultural Change* 59(3), 485–510.

Kung, James K.-S. 1995. Equal entitlement versus tenure security under a regime of collective property rights: peasants' preference for institutions in post-reform Chinese agriculture.' *Journal of Comparative Economics* 21(1), 82–111.

Larson, Donald, Tomoya Matsumoto, Talip Kilic, and Keijiro Otsuka. 2014. Should African rural development strategies depend on smallholder farms? an exploration of the inverse productivity hypothesis. *Agricultural Economics* forthcoming.

Lin, Justin Y. 1988. The household responsibility system in China's agricultural reform: a theoretical and empirical study. *Economic Development and Cultural Change* 36(2), 199–224.

Lipton, Michael. 2009. *Land Reform in Developing Countries: Property Rights and Property Wrongs*. Abingdon, UK: Routledge.

Otsuka, Keijiro. 2007. Efficiency and equity effects of land markets. In *Handbook of Agricultural Economics*, Volume 3. edited by R. E. Evenson and Prabhu Pingali), Amsterdam: Elsevier.

Otsuka, Keijiro. 2013. Food security, income inequality, and the changing comparative advantage in world agriculture. *Agricultural Economics* 44(s1), 7–18.

Otsuka, Keijiro, Hiroyuki Chuma, and Yujiro Hayami. 1992. Land and labor contracts in agrarian economies: theories and facts. *Journal of Economic Literature* 30(4), 1965–2018.

Otsuka, Keijiro, Yanyan Liu, and Yamauchi. 2013. Factor endowments, wage growth, and changing food self-sufficiency: evidence from country-level panel data. *American Journal of Agricultural Economics* 95(5), 1252–8.

Rozelle, Scott, and Johan F. M. Swinnen 2004. Success and failure of reforms: insights from transition agriculture. *Journal of Economic Literature* 47(2), 404–56.

Swinnen, Johan F. M. 2009. Reforms, globalization, and endogenous agricultural structures. *Agricultural Economics* 40(S1), 719–732.

Yang, Jin, Zuhui Huang, Xiaobo Zhang, and Thomas Reardon. 2013. The rapid rise of cross-regional agricultural mechanization services in China. *American Journal of Agricultural Economics* 95(5), 1245–51.

Yao, Yang. 2000. The development of land lease market in rural China. *Land Economics* 76(2), 252–66.

Zhang, Xiaobo, Jin Yang, and Shenglin Wang. 2011. China has reached the Lewis Turning Point. *China Economic Review* 22(4), 542–54.

50 Agricultural R&D and extension

Jikun Huang and Scott Rozelle

50.1 Introduction

China's ability to feed a population growing in both size and income has been impressive. China's agricultural gross domestic product has grown at an average of 4.6 per cent annually over the past three decades (NBSC, 2011). This rate of growth was about four times the average annual growth rate of China's population.

While China's agricultural success in the past three decades has come from several major driving forces, agricultural productivity growth has been one of the primary sources of long-term agricultural growth (Jin et al., 2002). Although rises in productivity were in part from decollectivization and market liberalization, they cannot explain the steady growth of 2–3 per cent of all crop yields during the entire period of reform between 1978 and 2010 (NBSC, 2011).

Sustained rises in agricultural investments and sharp changes in technology and irrigation are responsible for a large part of this rise in productivity. After 1985, the empirical literature is clear that technological change has been the main engine of productivity growth (Huang and Rozelle, 1996; Fan and Pardey, 1997; Jin et al., 2002).

50.2 Agricultural R&D and extension

50.2.1 AGRICULTURAL R&D

China's agricultural R&D has many unique characteristics; it is a public system, large in size, decentralized, and based on aggressive investment in both conventional and biotechnology. Agricultural R&D is almost completely organized by the government and based on public investment. Because of the role of the public, the goal of the system is to push the nation's agriculture towards the goal of national food security.

China has the largest agricultural R&D system in terms of staff in the world. Research staff increased from about 22,000 in 1979 to a peak of 102,000 in 1985 when China was preparing to enter an era of the 'Spring of Science' in the early reform period. However, overburdened with many poorly trained staff who lacked sufficient funding, the number of research staff has fallen since 1985. By 2010 we estimate that China still had at least 68,000 research staff working in the public agricultural R&D system. More than 65 per cent of the scientists are working in the crops sector, in particular, on rice, wheat, and maize.

While at one time China's agricultural R&D was underfunded, in recent years investment has increased. After a short period of stagnated growth in the mid-1990s, growth accelerated steadily thereafter. The annual growth rate of public spending on agricultural R&D in real terms increased from an average of 5.5 per cent in 1995–2000 to more than 16 per cent in 2000–11. In 2010 China's public agricultural R&D system is estimated to have spent about 30 billion RMB.

In contrast, the private sector is much smaller, although growth rates have been high in the past decade. A survey conducted by the Center for Chinese Agricultural Policy of the Chinese Academy of Sciences showed that domestic private agricultural research investment reached 3.5 billion in 2006 (about 25 per cent of public agricultural R&D), with average annual growth of 27 per cent in real terms between 2000 and 2006.

Recently, investing in biotechnology has become one of China's major priorities. In the mid-1980s, China initiated its programme on genetically modified (GM) crops and animals. Since the mid-1990s, the growth of China's agricultural biotechnology research investment has accelerated. Investment increased from US$33 million in 1995 to nearly US$200 million in 2003 (Huang et al., 2005). In 2008, the State Council approved a new, major twelve-year 'Special Program' to support GM rice, wheat, maize, soybean, cotton, hogs, cows, and sheep with a total budget of 26 billion yuan (or US$3.8 billion).

There has been a distinct mix in the sources of technologies between domestic and foreign. Because China's agricultural R&D has been mainly dominated by the government and has had a goal of national food security, public investment in domestic technologies has mainly focused on staple foods, cotton, and edible oil crops. In contrast, technologies for horticulture and livestock have relied more on foreign technology.

Regardless of the source (domestic or foreign) or type of technology (cropping or livestock), returns to agricultural R&D investment have been high. China's crop yields are generally higher than the world average. China supported more than 20 per cent of the world's population and achieved nearly 98 per cent overall food self-sufficiency in 2010 (despite a per capita water availability that is only one-quarter of the world average and an arable land area that is only 8 per cent of the world total).

While it has been successful, China's R&D is also facing great challenges. Huang and Hu (2008) show that, in comparison to other sectors in China, the public agricultural R&D is relatively short of top scientists. There is also evidence that the system does not appropriately respond to the new and changing demands of farmers for technologies. Moreover, public R&D focuses not only on basic and strategic research, it is also doing a lot of applied research and development of technologies that can be undertaken by the private sector.

In response to the challenges, China has released the 2012 Number 1 Document specifically focused on innovation in agricultural science and technology and boosting agricultural productivity. China is planning not only to increase its spending on agricultural R&D at an even higher growth rate than in the past, but also to further reform its R&D system by trying to create a clear division between public and private roles.

50.2.2 AGRICULTURAL EXTENSION

China has the largest agricultural extension system in the world. Inherited from the period prior to the reforms when China had a top-down, decentralized public agricultural extension system in the 1980s, the number of extension staff rose to more than 450,000 in the late 1980s. After several rounds of reforms, the system still had about 700,000 staff members in 2010.

In contrast to the experience of China's agricultural R&D, the extension system has experienced a twisting path of reform. In the 1980s, the expansion in extension staff—especially those who were drawing a wage whose numbers were rising during the early reform period (in the 1980s and 1990s)—was not accompanied with a corresponding rise in the budget. The size of the extension staff fell to less than 300,000 by 1992.

However, this fall in agricultural extension was accompanied by a short period of stagnation in grain production in the early 1990s. This stagnation drew the attention of the leaders. A movement to re-establish a strong public extension started in 1993. As a result, the extension staff reached a peak of more than 1 million in 1999.

The build-up of agricultural extension faltered in the late 1990s. The lack of sufficient budgetary support induced extension agents in many provinces to seek to support themselves by carrying out commercial activities, particularly running businesses in agricultural inputs. Such activities distracted the attention of agents when they were doing their jobs and distorted the incentives to provide unbiased, objective extension advice. Huang et al. (2009) showed that on average the extension staff at township extension stations spent only 24 per cent of their time on public extension during this time.

After 2000, another set of reforms sought to curtail the problems faced by the extension system. To do so, extension staff were divided into two segments: those in full-time extension work and those engaged in commercial activities. The results, again, were mixed.

In response to the variable results of early rounds of the extension reforms, in recent years China has started a number of new reforms. The new reforms have been aimed at providing better services to farmers and to stimulate the adoption of technology among farmers by separating commercial activities from public extension services, increasing the incentives and responsibilities of the extension staff, shifting personnel management from the township level to the county level, and increasing budgetary support. Recent research shows evidence of a more engaged and more effective extension.

50.3 Impact of technological change on agricultural productivity

In part, at least, due to the investments into agricultural R&D and extension, technological change has occurred in nearly every sub-sector of agriculture. China was one of the first developing countries to develop and extend Green Revolution technology—in rice, wheat, and maize—in the 1960s to 1980s. Hybrid rice was developed by China's scientists in the late 1970s.

Technological innovations in wheat, maize, and cash crops have also been impressive. For example, the average annual growth rate in the production of wheat (3.0 per cent) and maize (2.1 per cent) was even higher than that of rice (1.6 per cent) between 1978 and 2010 (NBSC, 2011). The growth rate was even higher for many cash crops (e.g. 3.2 per cent for cotton) during the same period. Productivity in the animal sector has also increased. Moreover, for the entire reform period, trends in agricultural labour productivity, measured as output per farm worker, parallel those of yield but are higher since labour input per unit of land has fallen over time (NBSC, 2011).

Since the mid-1990s, China has also relied on innovation from plant biotechnology. The most prominent innovation was China's production and extension of domestically produced GM cotton varieties (Huang et al., 2002). Bt cotton has become one of most successful stories in the use of GM technologies in the developing world, a technological change that has benefited millions of farmers. China also approved the commercialization of GM tomatoes, sweet peppers, poplar trees, and papaya. In 2009, the national biosafety committee issued biosafety certificates for Bt rice and phytase maize.

Evidence from the literature shows that total factor productivity (TFP) trends have moved largely in the same direction as yields (Jin et al., 2009). Research on TFP demonstrates that TFP has steadily risen at rates of around 2 per cent per year for grain and is even higher for most horticulture and livestock commodities (Fan, 1997; Jin et al., 2002, 2009). These levels of growth in TFP are high by international standards.

While there are several sources of growth in TFP, research has shown that technological change accounts for most of the rise in TFP after the mid-1980s. For example, Jin et al. (2009) show that technical change accounts for nearly all the rise for fifteen major crops in 1995–2004. The new varieties that China's breeders were producing in the nation's breeding programme during the 1980s were making their way into the fields of farmers. The rise of technical change-based TFP growth in cotton and horticultural crops after 1995 not only shows the effectiveness of China's domestic breeding programmes, it also suggests that opening China up to the import of new varieties from outside of China is an effective way to improve technology and TFP.

50.4 **Concluding remarks**

China is one of a few major countries in the world during the past several decades that has been able to maintain a steady growth in public spending on agricultural technology. According to plans of the government as revealed in key policy documents, China can be expected to continue to invest in agricultural technology as one of the main ways it will seek to maintain food security.

But, the story of China's investment into agricultural R&D and extension shows that success relies on more than the allocation of public funds. Government officials have continuously experimented with different ways to reform its public-based R&D and extension systems in their search for a more innovative-based system. China's R&D, however, is continuing to face many challenges. In forthcoming years, the reforms not only need to be continued within the public R&D and extension system, but also need to focus on creating a better environment for the engagement of the private sector.

■ **REFERENCES**

Fan, S. 1997. Production and productivity growth in Chinese agriculture: new measurement and evidence. *Food Policy* 22(3), 213–28.

Fan, S. and P. Pardey. 1997. Research productivity and output growth in Chinese agriculture. *Journal of Development Economics* 53(June), 115–37.

Huang, J. and R. Hu. 2008. Development and Reform of National Agricultural Research System: Policy Evaluation and Recommendation. Policy Brief: PB-07–3, CCAP, Beijing: Chinese Academy of Sciences.

Huang, J. and S. Rozelle. 1996. Technological change: the re-discovery of the engine of productivity growth in China's rural economy. *Journal of Development Economics* 49, 337–69.

Huang, J., S. Rozelle, C. Pray, and Q. Wang. 2002. Plant biotechnology in China. *Science* 295, 674–7.

Huang, J., R. Hu, S. Rozelle, and C. Pray. 2005. Insect-resistant GM rice in farmer fields: assessing productivity and health effects in China. *Science* 308, 688–90.

Huang, J., R. Hu, and H. Zhi. 2009. Development and reform of local agricultural extension system in the past 30 years: policy evaluation and recommendation. *Journal of Agrotechnology Economics* 1, 4–10.

Jin, S., J. Huang, R. Hu, and S. Rozelle. 2002. The creation and spread of technology and total factor productivity in China's agriculture. *American Journal of Agricultural Economics* 84, 916–30.

Jin, S, H. Ma, J. Huang, R. Hu, and Scott Rozelle. 2009. Productivity, efficiency and technical change: measuring the performance of China's transforming agriculture. *Journal of Productivity Analysis* 8, 1–17.

NBSC (National Bureau of Statistics of China). 2011. *China Statistical Yearbook*. Beijing: China Statistics Press.

51 Rural credit in China

Calum G. Turvey

51.1 Credit conditions of farm households

The perspective on rural credit in China presented in this chapter comes from a series of surveys conducted in China between 2007 and 2010 in the western and central provinces of Gansu, Shaanxi, and Henan on which we have a chronology of survey results. In Turvey and Kong (2009) a 2007 farm household survey ($N = 400$) in Shaanxi indicated household income of CNY13,147 with 70 per cent of income from farming, RCC debt of CNY6,973 and an average farm size of 5 mu (1 mu = 1/6th acre). In surveys of 1,565 farm households conducted across Gansu, Shaanxi, and Henan in 2007 and 2008 (Turvey and Kong, 2010) we found average household income of CNY11,477 across an average of 5.52 mu with 58.71 per cent of income from farming. On average, informal loans between friends and relatives were CNY10,395 and formal loans were CNY22,003. In Turvey et al. (2011) and Turvey (2010) we report on a survey conducted in 2009 ($N = 897$) that found 16 per cent of Shaanxi and Gansu farmers borrowed on average CNY8,452 from friends; 39 per cent borrowed CNY11.642 from relatives, and 34 per cent borrowed CNY21,611 from RCCs. Average household incomes were CNY21,422 on 6.50 mu.

In unpublished work (Verteramo Chiu, Khantachavana and Turvey, 2014)—a survey of 730 farm households in Shaanxi conducted in 2010—we find that a typical farm household had CNY23,796 in household income, CNY29,329 in debt, and a farm size of 4.9 mu. In that study we explicitly set out to measure the degrees of risk rationing, quantity rationing, and price rationing (see Boucher et al., 2008) and found that of farm households that indicated a demand for credit, risk rationed households comprised 6.5 per cent of farm households, 14 per cent were quantity rationed, and the remaining 80 per cent were price rationed.

These results indicate that in general farm incomes are low. A household income of CNY23,796 translates into about $US3,761 and household debt of CNY29,329 translates into about $US4,635. While low by Western standards, the role of credit is critically important for not only production but also consumption. In Turvey et al. (2011) we find that an additional RMB of debt increases household income by 0.073 RMB, or 7.3 per cent from debt use. In terms of credit demand, I report in Turvey (2010) a range of credit demand elasticities with mean point estimates of about –0.6. We find that nearly

20 per cent of farm households have nearly perfectly inelastic demands for credit but we also find that nearly 20 per cent have elasticities above –0.75, including some 15 per cent that have elasticities greater than –1.0. We also find that credit for consumption is more elastic than credit for production.

There is much heterogeneity in credit demand and we would argue that a full spectrum of targeted credit policies can be used to address differences across farms. Credit demand is highly variable in terms of the amount required and the sensitivity of borrowing that amounts to changes in interest rates. The amount depends on the size of the farm, what is actually grown, what investments are required to sustain or grow production, and what technological improvements are necessary for sustained production or growth. Not all farmers are interest rate insensitive. Non-borrowers may mobilize savings or curtail consumption in order to avoid debt use. They may not need credit at all, or may have a demand for credit but fail to borrow it because of a risk of collateral loss (risk rationed). Others might have a demand for credit but do not borrow because of guarantee requirements (policy rationed). Others may appear to be non-responsive to interest rates but cannot obtain all of the credit desired at the prevailing rates because of restraints placed upon the farm by the lender (credit rationing), and others reveal a range of demands that are highly unresponsive to changes in interest rates (inelastic demand for credit) while others are very responsive to changes in interest rates (elastic demand for credit). There is no such thing as an average or typical borrower!

51.2 **The role of credit policy**

For too long development economists have decried any form of credit policies especially credit policies that impose ceilings or subsidize interest rates (Ladman and Tinnermeier, 1981; Gonzales-Vega, 1982; Adams et al., 1984; Besley, 1994). The reality from our own observations across China is that it is unrealistic to dispense to China forms of banking and financial institutions that have evolved over centuries in Europe and the Americas subsequent to post-independence reforms in 1978, 1984, 1992, and particularly post-2003 reforms that have increased micro-credit loans to farm households.

With the focus on industrial growth rather than agricultural growth over the past thirty years, agricultural finance was much neglected. Up until 2003 when serious reforms were put in place, many local agricultural economies were suppressed through lack of credit. The purchase of production inputs were sub-optimally constrained to savings or informal (or familial) borrowing amongst friends and relatives. In Turvey and Kong (2010) we argue that familial lending within villages is economically significant. As a pro-poor policy (Dorward et al., 2004), it is in the public good to substitute informal credit for formal credit which can increase not only agricultural productivity (an income leverage effect), but also the consumption of non-agricultural goods and services by reducing the need for precautionary savings and releasing capital tied up in familial loans.

Even under current economic conditions the credit demands from non-farm sources are so large that providing small, costly, and risky loans to agriculture is not economically efficient. Instead, as in the USA, Canada, and elsewhere, the hand of government will need to be visible to encourage the reallocation of resources to their socially optimum levels. Thus a policy of interest rate subsidization targeted towards lower income communities may be justifiable on the basis of repairing institutional flaws that have suppressed one group of individuals to the benefit of another. This view is clearly in line with Lin (2011) and Stiglitz (2008, 2011). That financial liberalization in China would miraculously find credit widely available to rural clients and farm households without government intervention is somewhat naïve. China must implement (and in fact has) policy, governance, oversight, and a regulatory structure to address rural credit issues according to the institutions and conditions that are the reality.

51.3 **Rural credit reforms**

The current landscape of rural credit includes not only an expanded role for policy banks such as the Agricultural Development Bank of China, but also changes in regulations and oversight of existing banks such as the Agricultural Bank of China (ABC) and rural credit cooperatives (RCC). Since 2003 China has not only seen an initial public offering of shares in ABC, opportunities for RCCs to convert to rural commercial banks (RCB) with joint stock capital from other individual investors and financial institutions, but also a myriad of different financial institutions, with some accepting deposits and others being joint-stock companies that provide lending-only services. The range of new types of financial institutions include a vast number of micro-finance operators (MFI) that loan primarily to small and medium-sized enterprises, Urban Commercial Banks and Guarantee Companies (UCB & GC), Rural Financial Institutions (RFI),[1] China Development Bank (CDB) and Harbin Commercial Bank (HCB), Microcredit Companies (MCC), Village Banks (VB), Rural Mutual Credit Cooperatives (RMCC), Lending Companies (LC), Postal Savings Banks, and other types most surely to follow in the coming years.

The new era of institutional reform in China's credit markets is designed to increase capital flows into rural areas and improve financial deepening (Shaw, 1973; McKinnon, 1973; He and Turvey, 2009). Of particular interest is the provision of credit to agriculture.

[1] The Chongqing Rural Commercial Bank Co. (3618.HK) raised US$1.48 billion in its Hong Kong initial public offering TtSSPp on 16 December. It is the first to get an IPO among the current 84 rural commercial banks in China.

But an 'agricultural loan' in rural China does not necessarily mean that loans are being made to farm households, but rather to businesses and individuals in an agricultural region. Nonetheless, the expansionary policy has several modes of operation including centrally regulated interest rates and interest rate ceilings designed to induce demand at potentially lower rates than would otherwise be offered. This is a sensible policy. In the credit demand study referred to earlier, we found that as interest rates fall demand for credit becomes more elastic. Increased supply is encouraged by interest rate subsidies paid directly to lenders in direct proportion to increases in agricultural loans over the previous year. But it is also hoped that by expanding the number and types of financial institutions in rural areas there will be a degree of downscaling in which increased supply will find its way to farm households. Additionally, provincial ministries of agriculture, in partnership with counties and the Peoples Bank of China, will establish specific funding arrangements with RCCs for targeted development. These include capital for the development of self-help cooperatives or direct interest rate subsidies for farmers' expansion into new areas of agriculture including fruit orchards (e.g. converting grain land to kiwi orchards) and greenhouses for vegetable production.

As indicated, with the breadth of new and old financial institutions there are also substantial policy differentials between them. The Agricultural Bank of China and rural credit cooperatives have a legislated rate of between 0.9 and 2.3 times the PBC basic rate. At the time of writing (January 2012) the base interest rate is 6.56 per cent so that the range of interest that can be charged to farmers is between 5.904 per cent and 15.088 per cent. RCCs dominate agricultural finance in rural China, but for commercial banks, there is no effective ceiling. Village banks and other financial institutions face the same floor on interest rates but the upper ceiling of four times the base rate is (at the time of writing) 26.24 per cent.

51.4 Concluding remarks

The artificial ceiling is often viewed as an implicit subsidy for farmers, but care must be taken with this interpretation. In our surveys in Shaanxi and our investigation of credit demand we conclude, with quite decisive evidence, that the ceiling of 15.088 per cent is not binding in the sense that at that rate of interest the demand for credit is virtually zero (Turvey et al., 2012).

On the other hand, there are several justifiable reasons for supporting ceilings on agricultural loans. First is the principle of food security and a second is the principle of income equality. On the first measure the policy objective is to encourage farm households to borrow in order to purchase inputs to increase outputs. Assuming that this can be done profitably, the principal benefit would be an increased supply of domestically produced foods, which would reduce food prices, lead to a reduction in food imports, and perhaps increase food or processed food exports. The secondary benefits would be to increase the livelihoods of farm households, lift them out of poverty, and reduce the urban–rural income inequality and rural unrest.

■ REFERENCES

Adams, D. W., D. H. Graham, and J. D. Von Pischke. (eds) 1984. *Undermining Rural Development with Cheap Credit.*, Boulder and London: Westview Press.

Besley, T. 1994. How do market failures justify interventions in credit markets. *The World Bank Research Observer* 9(1), 27–47.

Boucher, S., M. Carter, and C. Guirkinger. 2008. Risk rationing and wealth effects in credit markets: theory and implications for agricultural development. *American Journal of Agricultural Economics* 90, 409–23.

Dorward, A., J. Kydd, and J. Morrison. 2004. A policy agenda for pro-poor agricultural growth. *World Development* 32(1), 73–89.

Gonzales-Vega, C. 1982. Cheap Agricultural Credit: Redistribution in Reverse. Discussion Paper 10, Colloquium on Rural Finance, 1–3 September 1981. Washington DC: Economic Development Institute, World Bank. (Revised 11 January 1982)

He, L. and C. G. Turvey. 2009. Financial repression in China's agricultural economy. *China Agricultural Economics Review* 1(3), 260–74.

Ladman, J. R. and R. L. Tinnermeir. 1981. The political economy of agricultural credit: the case of Bolivia. *American Journal of Agricultural Economics* 63(1), 66–72.

Lin, J. Y. 2011. New structural economics: a framework for rethinking development. *The World Bank Research Observer* 26, 193–221.

Mckinnon, R. I. 1973. *Money and Capital in Economic Development*, Washington, DC: Brookings Institution.

Shaw, E. S. 1973. *Financial Deepening in Economic Development*. New York: Oxford University Press.

Stiglitz, J. E. 2008. China: Towards a new model of development. *China Economic Journal* 1(1), 33–52.

Stiglitz, J. E. 2011. Rethinking development economics. *The World Bank Research Observer* 26, 230–6.

Turvey, C. G. 2010. Risk, Savings and Farm Household Credit Demand Elasticities in Rural China (5 May 2010). Available at SSRN: <http://ssrn.com/abstract=1601111> or <http://dx.doi.org/10.2139/ssrn.1601111>.

Turvey, C. G. and Rong Kong. 2009. Business and financial risks of small farm households in China. *China Agricultural Economic Review* 1(2), 155–72.

Turvey, C. G. and R. Kong. 2010. Informal lending amongst friends and relatives: Can microcredit compete in rural China? *China Economic Review* 21(4), 544–56.

Turvey, C. G., Guangwen He, Rong Kong, Jiujie Ma, and Patrick Meagher. 2011. The 7 Cs of rural credit in China. *Journal of Agribusiness in Developing and Emerging Economies* 1(2), 100–33.

Turvey, C. G., Rong Kong, Jiujie Ma, Guangwen He, and P. Meagher. 2012. Farm credit and credit demand elasticities in Shaanxi and Gansu, People's Republic of China. *China Economic Review* 23(4), 1020–35.

Verteramo Chiu, L. V., S. V. Khantachavana, and C. G. Turvey. 2014. Risk rationing and the demand for agricultural credit: a comparative investigation of Mexico and China, *Agricultural Finance Review* 74(2), 248–270.

52 Farmer cooperatives in China

Development and diversification

Huang Zuhui

Since 2006, farmer cooperatives in China have been developing rather quickly.[1] There were 484,300 farmer cooperatives in China by September 2011, but only about 100,000 in the year 2006. The number of farmers who have joined cooperatives is 38.7 million, accounting for 15.5 per cent of all farmers in China. Farmer cooperatives are involved in various industries including crop farming, livestock-raising, farming machines, forestry, plant protection, information technology, handicrafts, biogas services, agro-tourism, and so on. Among them, 43.3 per cent of cooperatives are engaged in crop farming, and 29.7 per cent in livestock-raising (Zhao, 2011).[2]

In practice, farmer cooperatives are an important way to organize scattered farmers, improve agricultural production, and help farmers get access to markets. According to data from 'Report on the Development of China Farmer Cooperatives (2006–2010)', the average income of members of farmer cooperatives was 20 per cent higher than it was for non-members (Sun Zhonghua et al., 2011).

52.1 Function of farmer cooperatives in China

China has a huge population but fragmented land. It is not possible in a short period of time for China to achieve the large-scale land operations seen in European and American countries, despite the shift of the agricultural labour force. Therefore, China has to adopt the methods of small-scale farming and large-scale production, which is also how developed countries without abundant land resources develop their agriculture. Farmer cooperatives

[1] The paper is supported by a project funded by the Natural Science Foundation of China (Grant No. 71333011). Thanks to Shenggen Fan and Xiaobo Zhang for the polishing up the article.
[2] Zhao Tieqiao, Current situation and tasks of the development of China farmer cooperatives, 23. 06. 2011.

can realize this goal. The specialized division and social services of cooperatives result in small-scale production from individual farms and large-scale services from the cooperative as a whole. That is to say, the large-scale operation of agriculture is not necessarily achieved through the large-scale operation of land. Large-scale operations can be realized in services, brands, and marketing—a more sustainable direction that should be advocated.

With increasing market competition, it has become harder for small farmers in China to adapt to competitive markets. The development of farmer cooperatives has played an important role in easing this difficulty. Farmer cooperatives not only connect small agricultural producers to big markets, but they also help farmers develop agriculture under small-scale production.

Farmer cooperatives are agricultural operation systems that maintain the advantages of the household operation of agriculture while mitigating its disadvantages. As an economic organization for mutual help among farmers, farmer cooperatives effectively organize scattered capital, the labour force, land and markets through united production and large-scale operations, without changing the independent operational agency of farmers. On the one hand, cooperatives enable small farmers to gain access to and adapt to big markets, increasing the added values of their produce. On the other hand, the development of cooperatives resolves the conflicts between independent household operation and agricultural-scale operation, between individual farmers and organizational enterprises, therefore promoting the vertical operation of agriculture. By organizing scattered farmers, farmer cooperatives organize production according to market information, which promotes the large-scale and standardized operation of agriculture. Through equal provision of production materials and internal supervision and management of members, farmer cooperatives can provide an important guarantee on the quality and safety of their produce. This reputation, once established, improves sales for each member of the cooperative.

Meanwhile, farmer cooperatives also improve the negotiating power of individual farmers in the market and extend industrial chains. In production, cooperatives can organize production according to market orders to avoid blind investments and unnecessary loss. In logistics, cooperatives can allow farmers direct access to supermarkets, wholesalers, and communities, lowering logistical costs and increasing their incomes.

52.2 Challenges for farmer cooperatives

At present, farmer cooperatives in China are a large market entity in the countryside, but due to misunderstandings and distortions of the cooperative system in the planned economy in the 1950s, farmer cooperatives were once cooperatives only in name, in fact resembling collectives, with indefinite property rights and low efficiency. During China's reform since 1978, the household responsibility system has replaced the low-efficiency collective system, improving agricultural productivity greatly. But the organization of farmer cooperatives did not develop at the same time. Only in the early twenty-first century after legislation on the farmer cooperatives, in July 2007, did farmer cooperatives undergo significant development. Therefore, farmer cooperatives in China are still in their preliminary stage and are facing many challenges on their way towards becoming powerful agricultural organizations that can connect farmers to domestic and international markets.

First, a lack of capable management and capital hinders the development of farmer cooperatives in China. Since China's market-oriented reform, many migrant rural labourers—about 230 million—have been engaged in non-agricultural sectors (National Bureau of Statistics of China, 2009). The majority of them are younger, either with a certain degree of education or with non-agricultural work experience. Those who stay in agriculture usually lack an awareness of the market economy, and their average education level is quite low. To resolve the lack of capable management, the Ministry of Agriculture has decided to train 15,000 people in the next ten years—1,500 people annually. They will also encourage rural youth and college graduates to become involved with cooperatives. In terms of financial support, the Ministry of Agriculture along with other related government departments initiated supportive policies, such as treating cooperatives under the same generous policies as individual farmers, offering exemption from certain taxes on the supply of materials provided by cooperatives, and favourable loan policies.

Second, it is still a difficult task for farmer cooperatives to help members sell their produce at reasonable prices. Besides facilitating the channels between farmers and consumers, cooperatives should also actively participate in various marketing activities such as produce trade fairs and group purchase fairs, and so on. If single small cooperatives are unable to access the market effectively, they should unite with other cooperatives in various ways, such as by establishing unions. Meanwhile, cooperatives should try to set up direct sales stores, chain stores, and outlet stores in urban communities and produce markets to create a seamless link from the farm to the dining table.

Furthermore, farmer cooperatives need guidance from professional agencies. With reference to successful practices in other countries, China should set up national and local agencies to guide and serve farmer cooperatives, integrate resources, and consequently promote the healthy development of cooperatives. To strengthen the cohesiveness of cooperatives, it is necessary for farmer cooperatives in China to be run with similar organizational structures. For example, this structure would include a member assembly, a board of directors, a board of supervisors, as well as a system for distributing earnings.

52.3 Further development of farmer cooperatives in China: key issues

First, it is crucial to understand the current status of diversified farmer cooperatives in China. Due to its short history and rapid development, cooperatives in China vary in quality, some are even regarded as fake. These 'fake' cooperatives are labelled as such because they differ from typical cooperatives. Some experts and officials think it is an urgent issue to identify and regulate them, but another possibility is that these cooperatives have simply been mis-labelled and misunderstood. Potentially fake cooperatives fall under three classifications.

The first type is usually formed by a few farmers who register a cooperative together without changing their activities. Their motivation is to take advantage of government subsidies and other lenient government policies. The second type of fake cooperative is organized by a strong enterprise or company. In such cooperatives, farmers do not have a strong position and the company or enterprise leads. It is nearly identical to contract farming which is dominated by a company or enterprise. The third type is a cooperative where the land contracted by farmers is leased out, and farmers then become employees or producers instead of independent operators. Rather than grouping these three types of non-standard cooperatives together as 'fake', we should treat each one individually. The first two types should be protected and improved. It is especially crucial to promote the transformation of the second type as it may bring about major innovation for coordination between cooperative operations and vertical integration in agriculture. The third type should never be supported, because they are truly fake cooperatives, similar to the low-efficiency agricultural collectives that were once experienced by China. The most important aspect of farmer cooperatives is that their members must retain their status as an independent operator, namely, they should still be independent household operators of agriculture. The household operation and the cooperative operation in agriculture should go hand in hand.

Second, the relation between the cooperative's operation and the corporation's operation in the vertical integration of agriculture should be handled properly. It is important to exert the cooperative in vertical agricultural integration. Generally speaking, there are two major models in the world. One is the European-American model which is characterized by cooperatives extending downstream and internalizing the entire industrial chains, such as the flower cooperatives in the Netherlands which cover all activities from flower planting to flower circulation and auction. The other is known as the Asian model and is characterized by cooperatives that mainly play a role in horizontal extension, and establish stable relations up- and downstream with processing or marketing enterprises. Both models have their advantages and disadvantages. The former has a strong ability to control the downstream market, but its internal governance is costlier, and also requires more capital. The latter has a comparatively weaker ability to control the downstream market, and higher vertical transaction costs, but it might be less costly in terms of internal governance, and require less capital overall. The European-American model is not suitable for the majority of current farmer cooperatives in China, and the Asian model seems more appropriate at the current time. However, it is worth pointing out that some agricultural companies and enterprises in China may play a role in the vertical integration of agricultural industrial chains by establishing cooperatives that extend upstream.

Agricultural corporations mainly operate downstream, especially in the processing stages. Agricultural processing and marketing enterprises are usually based in the corporation's operations. Even though the corporate operation of those enterprises has a role in the industrialization and vertical integration of agriculture, it is not enough. Several key issues need to be handled properly. Corporate operation is essential for agricultural industrialization, especially downstream. The application of the corporate operation system on agricultural industrialization has become an international trend, which can not only be seen downstream in areas such as processing enterprises, but is also demonstrated in farmer cooperatives in Western countries, which have become share-holding 'new-generation cooperatives'.

There have been instances of 'new-generation cooperatives' in China as well, but they have followed a different path. They have grown in the reverse direction, compared with European and American countries. In China, 'new-generation cooperatives' are usually driven by downstream enterprises or companies, instead of the farmer. Farmer cooperatives establish share-holding in order to extend upstream in agriculture. For such cooperatives in developed countries, the corporate operation must establish its role within a cooperative-dominated system. However, in China, the reverse is the case, and it is crucial for the cooperative operation to work out its role within the corporation in order to prevent members of the cooperative from losing their benefits. Meanwhile, they can form competitive 'new-generation cooperatives' with Chinese features.

Such institutional innovations within agricultural industrial organizations can improve the logistical efficiency of China's agriculture industry, increase the amount of vertical integration and international competitiveness, and justify farm cooperatives from a theoretical perspective. Therefore, the government should encourage and attach great importance to the development and perfection of farmer cooperatives dominated by corporations instead of urgently negating them. Research is needed to observe whether farmers are willing to work under such a corporate cooperative system. If most farmers are not against it, its existence becomes feasible to a certain degree. As long as a majority of the farmers are willing to join this type of cooperative while remaining independent producers and operators within the cooperatives, such an organization should be accepted. The key issue, at the initial stage of farmer cooperatives in China, is to persuade companies and enterprises downstream to help the farmer cooperatives upstream by providing support and services in terms of technology, skills, and capital. In recent years, there have been successful examples of such farmer cooperatives, and they promise to be valuable and deserving of proper development.

■ REFERENCES

National Bureau of Statistics of China. 2010. Migrant workers detection survey report 2009, 19 March.

Zhao Tieqiao. 2011. Current situation and tasks of the development of China farmer cooperatives, 23 June.

Zhonghua Sun, Tao Huaying, and Wei Baigang. 2011. Chinese farmers' professional cooperatives Development Report (2006–2010), *China Agriculture Press*, June.

53 Village governance in China

Nancy Qian

Throughout history, local governance has been one of the key challenges for the central authority of China, a large and heterogeneous country in terms of both its geographical size and its population. In this chapter, I briefly discuss a few of the most pressing issues of local governance for the current Chinese government, how they have addressed those issues, and the consequences of their policies. I focus on rural areas, which contain over two-thirds of the Chinese population; one dramatic policy reform—the introduction of elections for village government; and its consequences for three important issues for the rural population—the provision of local public goods, redistribution, and unpopular upper government policy enforcement. The material I discuss partly comes from my research, but is also based on the recent work of several political scientists and other economists.

The Chinese government, led by the Chinese Communist Party, is broadly ordered in a vertical hierarchy, from the central government in Beijing down to the rural levels that comprise counties and townships. Village governments are the lowest level of administration in rural China and directly oversee the welfare of the rural population. The communist government established village governments in the 1950s with two groups of leaders in each village. First, there is the village committee. It typically comprises three to five members and is led by the chairman. Second, there is the Chinese Communist Party branch in the village. It is similar in size to the village committee and is led by the village secretary. Before elections were introduced, all of these positions were filled by appointment by the county government and village party branch.

The village government is extremely important for the well-being of its citizens because it is responsible for village policies such as public goods provision and land allocation. The first local elections were introduced in the early 1980s soon after the dismantling of the commune system. The introduction was mainly motivated by two arguments. First, village elections would reduce the need for the central government to closely monitor local officials to prevent them from corruption or shirking. The worry that such behaviour could discredit the regime has been endemic in the centrally planned regime and was exacerbated by the widening regional differences caused by post-Mao market reforms. The hierarchical monitoring structure not only observed the actions of local leaders imperfectly, but also faced the difficulty of knowing the preferences and needs of each locality. The introduction of local elections was seen as a potential solution to this problem because it shifted the monitoring responsibilities onto villagers. Proponents argued that making local leaders accountable to villagers would impose checks on the chairman's behaviour and would also allow villagers to select the most competent candidates.

The second argument for introducing local elections was to improve the enforcement of centrally mandated policies at the village level. Proponents of reform claimed that elected village leaders would have more legitimacy and would better distribute the burden of these policies, which would increase overall compliance. It was also hoped that democratically accountable leaders would better determine which public goods investments were necessary and would better facilitate the local coordination necessary for providing them.

The initial introduction of elections changed the chairman's position from being appointed by the Party to being elected by villagers. The main legal requirements were that: (i) the number of candidates needed to exceed the number of positions; (ii) term lengths were to be three years; and (iii) the chairman must obtain 50 per cent of votes in the last round of voting. The last requirement ensured that the elected chairman had sufficient mandate. For example, elections with multiple candidates could have many rounds of votes. Each round removes the candidates with the least number of votes. This is done until one candidate has 50 per cent or more of the votes. Villagers may abstain from voting. There was no change in the selection method of the members of the village party branch and secretary positions, who continued to be appointed. The Party also maintained control over the villages by allowing the local Party branch to appoint candidates. Thus, the reform gave villagers the power to vote an unsatisfactory chairman out of office. In a second reform, villagers were allowed to nominate the candidates. Open nominations became national law in 1998.

The elections were implemented top-down. Each level of government would pilot the reform in a few select villages, and once the procedures and logistics were tested, the reform would be rolled out. Anecdotal evidence from interviews with county and province-level officials and the speed with which elections were implemented within provinces suggest that the roll-out was orthogonal to village characteristics in most cases. Statistics on the timing of election implementation imply that the average province was able to introduce reforms in 13,859 villages within three years and the average county was able to introduce elections in 143 villages within one year.

Researchers who study the effect of elections in rural China have employed a variety of econometric methods and used various different datasets. Despite this, there has been little controversy over the findings.

On average 57 per cent of villagers participate in elections and the rules of the reforms are well observed by villagers. Electoral procedures and the extent of corruption vary widely. It is not uncommon for elections to not have anonymous ballots or to have a roving ballot box. Despite this, elections have been found to be effective in shifting the accountability of the chairman from being wholly to the Party to being to both the Party and the constituent villagers. Moreover, village chairmen's de facto powers over village policies and the elections increased with the introduction of elections. This means that existing elites did not entirely circumvent the reform by removing the power of the newly elected leaders. The elected leaders tend to be younger and more educated than the former appointed leaders. They are mostly male and all from within the village.

In terms of policy outcomes, elections significantly increased local government expenditure and provision of public goods, such as irrigation and schooling. Also, public goods expenditure becomes more appropriate—that is, elections reduce investment in public goods in villages where the demand for such goods is presumably low, while they increase investment in villages where demand is presumably high. The increase in expenditures is funded by villagers and they are accompanied by an increase in the amount of local taxes paid by villagers. These effects contradict the traditional belief that democracy reduces the government's ability to provide public good investments because of short-term consumption demands from voters. Together with finding that public goods provision becomes more appropriate, these effects suggest that one of the reasons that elected leaders can increase taxes may be that they choose investments that correspond better to citizens' needs.

Next, we consider redistribution. Studies have found that elections significantly reduce inequality by redistributing income. To understand how the redistribution is achieved, it is important to note that village governments are legally prohibited from imposing recurring taxes, but control land allocation and the management and profit sharing of village enterprises. All land is publicly owned in China and granted to households for farming in long-term land contracts. The allocation of such contracts is one of the main responsibilities of village leaders. Since average households enjoy very small land allocations, a small increase in land can be extremely valuable. By law, the amount of land per household is supposed to depend on need and the ability to farm the land, and all rural households are entitled to enough farmland to guarantee subsistence. Households cannot rent out or sell their land rights. A small fraction of village land is retained under the direct control of the village government so that small adjustments in household land allocations can be made for demographic changes such as marriages or deaths without village-wide disruptions. This land can be leased to villagers for farming or non-farm activities, or leased to entities from outside of the village. The profits generated from these activities are typically reinvested or paid out to the villagers. Villagers who work in the enterprises also benefit from earning wages. It is generally believed that not all villagers benefit from these enterprises because they are either unprofitable or because the rents are not distributed equitably. For example, corrupt village leaders have been known to extract personal rents from land controlled by the village governments.

In terms of income, almost two-thirds of rural household income is earned through agriculture. The next most important source of income is wage income, which for most rural residents is earned by working for village enterprises. It is not surprising then, that elections caused significant redistribution of agricultural income, farmland, and wage income. The magnitude of change is quite large. Elections, on average, increased the ratio of income or household of the poorest 10 per cent to those who were the richest 10 per cent prior to the first election by almost 30 percentage-points. Also, elections drastically reduced the amount of land that is leased out to enterprises, which mostly benefited richer households in terms of providing them with higher wage income and income from profit sharing.

Elections are also found to benefit the well-being of villagers by reducing the enforcement of two very unpopular central government policies: the One Child Policy and upper government expropriation of village land. The village government is the ultimate enforcer of each policy. While the chairman is unlikely to openly resist the upper government, he can reduce or delay the enforcement of a policy by not exerting any effort to enforce them. In the case of the OCP, this means that he can simply not monitor pregnancies, cajole parents to abort, or impose fines. In addition, he can exert more effort to apply for legal exemptions from the upper government. For example, *State Council Document No. 7*, which was introduced in 1984, lists causes for obtaining legal exemptions. These include cases in which the first child is a girl or if the parents are handicapped. In the case of land expropriation, it means that the chairman does not block villagers' attempts to protest. Upper government land expropriation is always a highly contentious issue, which frequently results in the permanent loss of farmland to villagers. Village leaders are needed for reallocating remaining village land so that dispossessed households have farmland and occupation, as well as other activities to minimize the dissatisfaction of villagers with the central government. Therefore, while village leaders will rarely directly oppose land allocation, they can resist expropriation through non-cooperation. Elections significantly reduce the enforcement of each of these policies.

Whether elections improved local governance depends on the objectives of the government. From the perspectives of the villagers, all of the evidence suggests that elections improved governance—they improved public goods provision and redistribution while they reduced unpopular central government policies. For the autocratic central government, the evidence implies that there is a tradeoff in introducing local elections. On the one hand, elections can improve villagers' satisfaction with the regime. On the other hand, they reduce the enforcement of central objectives when they conflict with villager preferences.

54 Local governance and rural public good provision

Loren Brandt

54.1 Background

Throughout much of Chinese history, a highly autocratic state has ruled the countryside only indirectly. During the Ming (1468–1644) and Qing (1644–1911), for example, the formal bureaucracy extended no further than the county (*xian*), and county-level magistrates governed largely through ties and relationships to the local gentry and elite. Formal state taxation, primarily in the form of a land and head tax, was also relatively modest. Light taxation was generally seen as an essential part of good rule, a principle dating back to Mencius (372–289 BCE) and often reiterated, as in a memorial to the new Qianlong Emperor (1735–96) on the death of his father: 'There is a fixed amount of wealth on heaven and on earth. If it does not belong to the officials then it belongs to the people' (Zelin, 1984: 276).

Beginning with the Republican period (1911–49), and then with the establishment of the People's Republic of China (PRC) in 1949, the state penetrated much further. In the post-1949 era, this process began with land reform, and accelerated with the collectivization of agriculture in the mid-1950s. Formal state power was extended to the township—the administrative unit below the county—through the People's Communes, and through the Chinese Communist Party (CCP) down to the village (production brigade). State control of rural areas was critical to taxation, grain procurement for the cities, and the enforcement of tight restrictions on mobility between the countryside and the cities. In the Mao era, the countryside was highly marginalized, and left to fend for itself after resources were extracted by the state for the cities and development of industry. In the process, a huge gap emerged between the cities and the countryside in terms of the standard of living (Rawski, 1982), and in the countryside between regions (Vermeer, 1982).

54.2 Early governance reform

In the wake of the break-up of the communes and the de-collectivization of agriculture, a serious political vacuum formed in the countryside, the home in the late 1970s of nearly

80 per cent of China's population. From the perspective of upper levels of government, the village was now critical to the collection of tax revenue, for the delivery of food, and for enforcement of the household registration system and family planning. How the village functioned was equally important to the welfare of rural citizens. Land in rural China, for example, is 'collectively' owned at this level, and under the Household Responsibility System (HRS), villages allocated households usufruct rights for terms that, in principle, are governed by national land laws. Villages have also owned and managed local enterprises—a key source of dynamism in the rural economy through the 1990s—and often played an important role in organizing supply and marketing services for agriculture. Finally, under China's highly decentralized fiscal system, villages were the most important funder and provider of local public goods, most notably, primary education and health services, and often basic infrastructure. They were not part of the 'formal' government apparatus, however, and thus had no formal fiscal budget. It is only more recently that resources from above have come to play a dominant role in the financing of local fiscal expenditures.

In 1987, after several years of intense debate, the Draft Village Organic Law was passed. These reforms confirmed the role of the Communist Party as the 'core' leadership within the village (through the Party secretary and Party branch), but called for village 'self-government', and laid out a set of rules regarding the composition, election, and responsibilities of village governments (VCs, or village committees). By 1997, a majority of provinces had adopted local versions of the law, and in 1998 a formal version of the Organic Law was passed by the National People's Congress or NPC.

Support for these reforms among higher level government officials was mixed. Early proponents saw the elections and governance reforms as offering new channels through which villagers' own interests could better be expressed, and the most egregious of local cadre behaviour held in check. Others argued that an elected village government might actually make it easier for higher levels of government to carry out their mandates. But from the very outset there was regional and local opposition to the 'reintroduction' of self-government into China's villages (O'Brien and Li, 2000). Some of it came from local Party organizations, which now feared that their authority and power would be contested by elected village governments. With cadre remuneration and career prospects linked to fulfilling targets at this level (Whiting, 2001), government officials were often less than enthusiastic about reforms that gave power to individuals whose interest might not be aligned with their own. Other officials likely saw improved governance as a constraint on their own rent-seeking behaviour.

Village elections and the 'introduction of democracy' have become synonymous with local governance, much to the neglect of other factors, including those at the township and county level. Elections were originally experimented with in Guangxi province as early as 1980, and soon became the heart of the push for self-government by the Ministry of Civil Affairs (MOCA), the key executing government agency for the new law. Estimates differ, but by 1997 in upwards of 80 per cent of all villages in China had likely begun elections. And by 2012 all but a small percentage of villages in China had several elections as part of three-year election cycles.

By most measures, the quality of elections in rural China has been far from uniform. Incentives of local officials to interfere in village elections and the selection process of candidates are ever present. Data collected on key election protocols for a sample of a hundred villages for elections in the early 2000s are illustrative: the role of villagers in the candidate nomination process is often limited; eligible voters, especially women, often do not fill out their own ballot; rather they are filled out by other family members; rules regarding absentee balloting—increasingly important with migration—are not enforced, nor is the use of secret ballots. In general, 'good' protocols are bundled together, reflecting the important role (and influence) of upper level governments in the implementation of local elections.

Even when elections are 'clean', a good case can be made that 'ultimate' authority in a village does not reside in elected officials. In a majority of villages this power resides with a Party secretary, complicating the agency relationship between villagers and elected officials. Moreover, the selection process for the Party secretary and oversight exercised by the local Party branch can also differ across villages (Li, 1999). Some parts of the country, for example Guangdong, are now encouraging consolidation of the two positions by requiring the village Party secretary to run in the election for village chief. Promotion of elected village leaders to village Party secretary has also been a common occurrence.

54.3 In whose interests?

Across China's villages, we observe significant heterogeneity in the property rights in land that households enjoy, the level and incidence of taxation, and the organization and financing of local public goods. With respect to land, this is captured in differences in the frequency of village-wide land reallocations and the security of land tenure, the freedom of households to rent out land without risk of losing it and more recently, land seizures (Brandt et al., 2004). Village and township fiscal surveys covering the period up to the recent Tax for Fee Reform also point to sizeable differences in fiscal expenditures between localities, largely reflecting the ability to mobilize local resources. Utilizing survey data for 2000 covering a hundred villages in five provinces, Brandt et al., (2005) find that the gap in per capita fiscal revenue between villages in the richest and poorest quintiles was five to one. Over their full sample, average per capita village fiscal revenue was a meagre 68 RMB, or 2.1 per cent of the National Bureau of Statistics (NBS) estimates of rural per capita incomes in 2000. Significant local differences also exist in the level of educational attainment that is tied to local funding, and the costs and quality of local schooling (Connelly and Zhang, 2003). Between 1990 and 2000, inequality in rural educational attainment widened (Qian and Smyth, 2005).

These differences in village outcomes reflect some combination of endowments, preferences, and the local political economy. Unbundling their effects empirically has been very difficult so far, and a very mixed picture emerges on their respective roles. Research by Wang and Yao (2007), and Luo et al. (2007), for example, argues for a significant role for the introduction of elections in village decision making with respect to public goods. Tsai (2008) offers an important dissenting perspective. Utilizing village data that run through 2001, she contends that elections have not influenced how local officials behave. Rather, mirroring early work of North (1990) and Putnam (1993), Tsai argues that it is differences in the level of social capital, notably, the strength of kinship and religious ties in which cadre relations with the local community are embedded, that are the key here. Both of these institutions have deep historical roots.

Tsai's work can be criticized for the limited role of these ties in good parts of rural China. But clearly, history and informal institutions matter for how villages behave. For the pre-1949 era, Huang (1989) argues that differences in patterns of land ownership gave rise to significant differences at the village level between the Yangzi delta and the North China plain in the interrelationship among the state, elite, and households that mattered for the quality of local governance. Cataclysmic events of the last half century, including civil war, land reform, collectivization, the Great Leap Famine, as well as the Cultural Revolution have likely had lasting impacts on village cohesion, and solidarity as well.

54.4 Tax for fee reform and China's new socialist countryside

In the mid-1990s, China carried out a major recentralization of the fiscal system that once again put significant resources in the hands of the centre (Wong and Bird, 2008). Prompted by concerns over the growing rural–urban divide, arbitrary imposts and rural households' 'fiscal burdens', and their link to reports of growing rural discontent (Bernstein and Lü, 2003), attention has now turned to the countryside.

Beginning in 2000, China implemented the rural tax-for-fee (*fei gai shui*) reform. The original aim of these initiatives was to replace the informal, ad hoc collection of fines and fees paid by villagers with a single tax that, combined with the agricultural tax on land, would be capped at 5 per cent of local household incomes. Within a few years, all local levies paid by villagers, including those at the township and village level (*tongchou* and *tiliu*) and the educational levies were abolished, as was the agricultural tax. The responsibility for running and financing primary schools, which in the past was financed out of a combination of tuition fees and village funds, was also shifted upwards to the county. These reforms were complemented by a massive increase in central government investment in China's villages as part of a policy of developing the New Socialist Countryside. New rural medical and pension programmes, as well as old-age security, have also been introduced. Remaining village expenditures were to be financed by transfers from above and the mobilization of village funds for public investment on a case-by-case basis.

There is much to commend in these initiatives, but larger issues can be raised. Estimates of the farmers' burden (*nongmin fudan*) on which these reforms were predicated leave much to be desired. A significant portion of the taxes that were collected, including the national agricultural tax, was used to finance expenditure that was controlled by the centre and did not benefit villagers. The state (and urban residents) was also the major beneficiary of the implicit taxation associated with the grain quotas. On average, local taxes and fees were probably not much in excess of 5 per cent of household income. Moreover, half of this was remitted to townships, and some covered the services provided. The role of the village in the excessive taxation of villagers is much less than meets the eye.

Survey data covering the period up to the end of 2007 show poorer villages benefited most from these new programmes and funding from above. However, overall inequality in fiscal expenditure at the village level has actually widened, not decreased. This reflects more generous transfers from above in richer localities, but also the differences between villages in their ability to mobilize resources from non-tax revenue, for example village enterprises, and land. The percentage of villages experiencing deficits has also increased, as earmarked transfers from above did not fully compensate for the loss of *tiliu*. Land and village asset sales have also increased, and become a more important source of village revenue as they try to balance their books. This has also become a growing source of contention. In the long run, this is not sustainable.

In the context of a recentralization of state powers, these reforms represent a serious curtailment of the experiment with village governance reform. Village governments are now much less important, with limited tax collecting authority and discretion. The choice that has been made is interesting. Rather than more aggressively implement expanded governance reforms that would have acted as further constraints on local power, including that of elected officials, the Party and the township, and in the process better align the interests of the governed and governing, China decided to centralize with a single cut of the knife (*yidao qie*). Today, an increasing array of decisions is made by higher level bureaucrats even further removed from villagers. In this process, the township appears to be losing power and authority relative to the county, and the county to the province. It may only be coincidental, but the experiment in local governance appears to have ended at the same time that resource flows between the state and China's villages have been reversed.

■ REFERENCES

Bernstein, Thomas and Xiaobo Lü. 2003. *Taxation without Representation in Contemporary Rural China.* Cambridge: Cambridge University Press.

Brandt, Loren, Scott Rozelle, and Matthew Turner 2004. Local government behavior and property rights formation in rural China. *Journal of Institutional and Theoretical Economics* 160(4), 627–62.

Brandt, Loren, Scott Rozelle, and Linxiu Zhang. 2005. Tax Reform and Village Fiscal Health and Investment. Prepared for the World Bank.

Connelly, Rachel and Zhenshen Zheng. 2003. Determinants of school enrollment and completion of 10 to 18 year olds in China. *Economics of Education Review* 22(4), 379–88.

Huang, Philip. C. 1989. *The Peasant Economy and Social Change in North China.* Stanford: Stanford University Press.

Li, Lianjiang. 1999. The two ballot system in Shanxi Province: subjecting party secretaries to popular votes. *The China Journal* 42(July), 375–93.

Luo, Renfu, Linxiu Zhang, Jikun Huang, and Scott Rozelle. 2007. Elections, Fiscal Reform and Public Goods Provision in Rural China. Working Paper, Freeman Spogli Institute for International Studies, Stanford University.

North, Douglas. 1990. *Institutions, Institutional Change and Economic Performance.* New York: Cambridge University Press.

O'Brien, Kevin J. and Lianjiang Li. 2000. Accommodating 'democracy' in a one-party state: introducing village elections in China. *The China Quarterly* 162(June), 465–89.

Putnam, Robert. 1993. *Making Democracy Work: Civic Traditions in Modern Italy.* Princeton: Princeton University Press.

Qian, X. and Smyth, R. 2005. *Measuring Regional Inequality of Education in China: Widening Coast-Inland Gap or Widening Rural-Urban Gap.* Available at: <http://www.buseco.monash.edu.au/units/dru/papers/working-papers-05/1205-xl-china.pdf> accessed 25 January 2013.

Rawski, Thomas G. 1982. The simple arithmetic of Chinese income distribution. *Keizai Kenkyu* 33(1), 12–26.

Tsai, Lilly. 2008. *Accountability without Democracy: Solidary Groups and Public Goods Provision in Rural China.* New York: Cambridge University Press.

Vermeer, Eduard B. 1982. Income differentials in rural China. *The China Quarterly* 89, 1–33.

Wang Shuna, and Yang Yao. 2007. Grassroots democracy and local governance: evidence from rural China. *World Development* 35(10), 1635–49.

Whiting, Susan. H. 2001. *Power and Wealth in China: The Political Economy of Institutional Change.* Cambridge and New York: Cambridge University Press.

Wong, Christine and Richard M. Bird. 2008. China's fiscal system: a work in progress. In *China's Great Economic Transformation,* edited by Loren Brandt and Thomas G. Rawski, 429–66. Cambridge and New York: Cambridge University Press.

Zelin, Madeleine. 1984. *The Magistrate's Tael: Rationalizing Fiscal Reform in Eighteenth Century China.* Berkeley: University of California Press.

Part IX
Land, Infrastructure, and Environment

55 Land and development in China

Chengri Ding

Over the past couple of decades, perhaps, there are no other countries like China in which land is so controversial and commands so much attention in the policy arena. Land plays an important role in national policy in ways that there are unprecedented in human history. Land is not only used as a policy instrument to achieve social, economic, and environmental development goals, but more importantly is attached to many socioeconomic expectations that are root causes of or associated with many prominent issues and challenges. So the following questions arise: (1) what makes land distinctive? (2) what roles are played by land in national policy; and (3) what are the issues and challenges caused by or associated with land? This chapters will answer these questions in a concise way.

55.1 Land institutions

What makes land so distinctive is fundamentally related to unique institutions governing land ownership, land use, development, allocation, and land markets. China's institutional structure and settings with regard to land are distinguished in the following aspects (Ding, 2003). First, land ownership is geographically divided. Land in cities (including towns) is owned by the state whilst land in rural areas is owned by the collective villages residing on it.

Second, land markets are also geographically divided. In cities and towns for private users and investors are allowed to access the land use rights of state-owned land through the Land Use Rights (LURs) system, which effectively is a public land leasing system in which land use rights are separated from land ownership. The separation is restricted to the state-owned land and is not applicable to collectively owned land in rural areas. This implies that land development must take place at cities or towns, not rural areas (with limited exceptions).

Third, private users or investors must pay land conveyance fees, which are the leasing prices of the state land, in a lump sum and upfront. Acting as the representatives of the state government, cities and counties monopolize land leasing in their jurisdictions. The value of land revenues from land conveyance fees should not be underestimated because they are virtually the sum of leasing prices of 40–70 leased years, depending the type of land use.

Fourth, the combination of land development prohibition in rural areas and land markets only in cities and towns makes city and county governments an indispensable player in land development. This is because prior to land development, land ownership conversion must be undertaken by city and county governments. They exercise a policing power by paying farmers for their land at prices that are substantially lower than the land conveyance fees charged to developers. The price difference can be in the order of 10–20 times. In doing so, cities and counties are able to rely on land revenues to finance urban expansion and development.

Fifth and finally, land uses in the rural areas are also strictly regulated and managed. It is mandated that basic cultivated land should not be less than 80 per cent of total farmland within a province and cultivated land protection should be geographically designated and protected. Approval for land development in basic cultivated land must be obtained from the state council and its loss should be compensated from land reclamation from other types of land use.

55.2 **Land development**

Since the first introduction of LURs in the late 1980s in Special Economic Zones, public land leasing activities have grown exponentially. The total amount of leased land grew from slightly less than 950 ha in 1990 to 5,588 ha, and peaked in 2003 with more than 414 thousand hectares in 2003. It dropped by more than half in 2004 compared to the previous year due to national land policy and continued to decline in 2005. The total amount of land increased in 2006. The growth of land revenues from public land leasing followed a similar pattern. Land conveyance fees were only 2.69 billion RMB in 1993, but that figure rapidly rose to 29.05 billion RMB in 1996, to 52.17 billion RMB in 1999, and further to 111.27 billion RMB in 2003. The level dropped in 2004; decreased in 2005, and significantly increased again in 2006 and 2007 (China Land and Resources Almanac, 1999–2006; Ding, 2003). It should be pointed out that land conveyance fees are largely generated from a small proportion of total leased public land. This is because (1) land leasing to industrial development is heavily subsidized and (2) fully charged land leasing is applied only to commercial projects such as commercial housing and real estate development, which accounted for less than a quarter of total leased land in 2001–02.

The role of land in local development is three-fold. First, land is heavily used to support public finances at the sub-national government level. For instance, land revenues were equivalent to 44–55 per cent of local revenues (excluding intergovernmental transfers) during 2003–07 for all sub-national governments, which is equivalent to 60 per cent at a city level.[1] The second role of land is land-based financing of urban spatial expansion. Financing infrastructure through land leasing and bank loans securitized on land and property valuation accounts for 80–90 per cent of infrastructure financing by sub-national governments in China. Three cities surveyed in Zhejiang province show that cities heavily rely on land to finance urban expansion. For those cities, land financing directly (public land leasing) and indirectly (land used as collateral) accounts for 95–100 per cent of the construction of urban spatial expansion in 2005. It should be noted that the three Chinese cities with a population of about one-third of a million in 1998 grew fast around the turn of the twenty-first century. For instance, Shaoxing city doubled its population in eight years (1998–2006) while Jinhua city tripled.[2] The third role of land in local development is associated with land-based development and reform. Given skyrocketing land prices, land is used to (1) attract investment by providing free or subsidized land access; (2) support the reform of state-owned enterprises (privatization and bankruptcy); and (3) revitalize inner cities.

55.3 Land and national policy

Perhaps there are few countries in which land commands so much attention at the national level other than China. Land was used as a macro-economic control instrument in 2007 to cool off an overheated economy and to deal with potential bubbles in housing and manufacturing development. Those types of policy targets are usually achieved through monetary, fiscal, and exchange rate policies. It was not surprising to see that the usage of land as a macro-economic control tool was short-lived partly because of a lack of a theoretical foundation and partly because of a lack of effective implementation tools to deliver.

Land plays an extraordinary role in the national policy of food self-sufficiency. To achieve self-sufficiency of grain output, China adopts rigid farmland protection policies that include (1) a dynamic farmland balance, which is in fact a zero-net loss policy in farmland; (2) a mandate of 80 per cent of farmland as cultivated land that should be strictly protected, whose development requires approval from the State Council, and whose geographical boundaries should be explicitly delineated and marked on both the ground and maps; (3) a top-down allocation of land use and development quotas through administrative levels; and (4) a rigid requirement of approval for land use quotas and land supply to accommodate the land needed for urbanization and industrialization. The State Council approves the land use master plan for cities with populations of more than one million, whilst provincial governments approve land use master plans for cities with populations of less than one million. The core element of the land use master plan is eight land use quotas, such as permitted levels of construction on agricultural land, permitted

[1] <http://www.mof.gov.cn/zhengwuxinxi/diaochayanjiu/200806/t20080620_47504.html>.
[2] *China City Statistical Yearbooks*, 1999–2007.

2

2

levels of development on cultivated land, maximum per capita land consumption in cities and towns, and minimum levels of protected farmland and cultivated land.

55.4 **Land-related issues**

There are both enormous successes of economic development and outstanding issues and problems associated with land. Land-related issues and problems can be summarized as follows. First, there is rising social unrest in both land requisition in rural areas and land acquisition for urban redevelopment in existing built-up areas. In the former case, social unrest emerges partly because of market prices for land acquisition being far below the compensation level and partly because of an absence of social security, which is a role usually played by land in rural areas. In the latter case, social unrest usually emerges because of the high expectations of existing tenants in areas destined for urban redevelopment as they demand outrageous compensation or prices for resettlement in some cases. When their demands were not met for good reasons, some existing tenants committed suicide in the course of court-backed demolitions. A lack of due processes in land acquisition is a part of the problem.

Second, land-related economic bubbles threaten sustainable growth in China. There are two types of economic bubble. One is the over-capacity of manufacturing industries as cities race to the bottom in industrial land leasing to attract investment and business (Ding and Lichtenberg, 2011). Severe over-capacity is found in sectors such as steel, automobiles, aluminium, ferroalloys, coke, calcium carbide, automobile, copper, cement, electrical power, coal, textiles, petrochemicals, paper cartons, chemical fertilizers, domestic electric appliances, micro-computers, and shipbuilding. The other is housing bubbles. Housing prices in many big cities have increased by 200–500 per cent from 2004 to 2010. As a result, the central government ordered many cities to take extreme measures at the beginning of 2011 to control skyrocketing housing prices by imposing commercial housing purchase quotas.

Third, land-driven or -motivated development causes inefficient land use and allocation. In 2004, many land lots in various designated industrial and economic development parks/districts were cancelled and returned to agricultural use due to a lack of investment. And finally, land is often associated with problems such as corruption, fraud, and abuses of public finance (land revenues), and chaotic and uncoordinated development.

55.5 **Land policy challenges**

China has undertaken dramatic land policy reforms, such as LURs. These reforms have helped to improve efficiency in land resource allocation and management and to resolve disputes and conflicts over land. Because of its gradual nature, China's piece-meal approach to land reform has caused a number of side-effects and new issues and challenges have emerged. Among the primary challenges are:

1. How best to (re)-define public interests to justify land acquisition. Currently land requisition is the only effective way to supply land to accommodate urbanization and industrialization. This land supply scheme does not distinguish real public interests such as infrastructure from private economy-driven land demand.

2. How best to balance the property rights protection and public interests in land. Public awareness about the rights and interests behind land increases, as do government efforts to protect them. But China does not have explicit institutional arrangements to balance the protection of property (land) rights and public interest in land. Unless such institutions are put in place, any policy initiatives moving in the direction of property rights protection may imply huge socioeconomic costs and lead to social disorder and unrest.

3. How best to deal with the multiple and often conflicting development objectives attached to land. Land is used as a policy instrument to achieve self-sufficiency in food, to control an overheating economy, and to finance urban spatial development and urbanization. This issue should be addressed partly because land is influencing areas which it is not supposed to and partly because there are other policy instruments that can produce better outcomes. One example is that food security can, and should be, better achieved through agricultural policy, such as income or price subsidies and not through farmland protection (Lichtenberg and Ding, 2008).

4. How best to address the risk arising from land-based public financing. One alternative is to introduce a property tax. The Chinese tax system should be modernized to match its social wealth structure, which has been remarkably reshaped.

All of these challenges are fundamental and profound. Political barriers to any reforms are extremely strong and how the Chinese government responds remains to be seen. It is uncertain when and what policy measures will be introduced. But it is certain that whatever policy reform is chosen may have a profound impact on the trajectory of China modernization and growth.

■ **REFERENCES**

China Land and Resources Almanac, 1999–2006. China Geological Press, Beijing, 1999–2006.

Ding, C. 2003. Land use policy reform in China: assessment and prospects. *Land Use Policy* 20(2), 109–20.

Ding, C. and E. Lichtenberg. 2011. Land and urban economic growth in China. *Journal of Regional Science* 51(2), 299–317.

Lichtenberg. E., and C. Ding. 2008. Assessing farmland protection policy in China. *Land Use Policy* 25(1), 59–68.

56 Infrastructure in China

Sylvie Démurger

要想富，先修路
Yào xiǎng fù, xiān xiū lù
Wanna be rich? Build roads first!

56.1 Concept and terms

Though the concept of 'infrastructure' is extensively used in economic literature, it has no precise and generally accepted definition. As comprehensively reviewed by Fourie (2006), infrastructure can be defined in a variety of ways that may overlap. A prevailing distinction made by economists is between economic infrastructure and social infrastructure. The former is defined as infrastructure capital that promotes economic activity and its role is understood through the services provided to households and firms. The main components of economic infrastructure are transportation (by land, water, and air), telecommunications (including ICT), utilities (water and sanitation), and power supply. Social infrastructure, which will not be the focus here, includes institutions and services that 'promote the health, education and cultural standards of the population' (Fourie, 2006: 531) such as the healthcare system, the educational and research system, or recreational and cultural infrastructure.

The role of economic infrastructure is commonly characterized by both the quantity and the quality of supplied services. These two additional dimensions are important since they delineate the access to and the reliability of the corresponding services.

56.2 Infrastructure in numbers: where does China stand?

As in many other domains, superlatives characterize China's infrastructure provision. In the transportation sector, massive spending on road and railway construction projects over the past years has given China an extensive, and to some extent high quality and modern, network. China's expressway network is the second largest in the world, with a total length of about 85,000 km in 2011.[1] China's railway network covered about 93,000 km in 2011 and records by traffic volume the world's second busiest freight railway and busiest passenger railway (Amos and Bullock, 2011). As for its shipping industry, five of the world's ten busiest ports of 2010 were located in China, with Shanghai port ranking first. With regards to telecommunication or power supply, similar observations can be made. China ranks first in the world in terms of the number of telephone users, with a total of 1.27 billion users recorded at the end of 2011, an increase of 118 million compared with the end of 2010. Of these, 285 million are fixed-line subscribers and 986 million mobile customers. The number of Internet users has surged since 2002, from 4.6 users per 100 persons to 38.3 users per 100 persons in 2011, a level slightly above the world average. By 2010, China's power generation capacity reached 900 million kilowatts, ranking second in the world. The country has the world's largest hydropower capacity of about 200 million kilowatts.

Given the size of the country, inequality also characterizes infrastructure provision in China. Although significant progress has been made in reducing regional imbalances in infrastructure stock in transportation and telecommunication in the past decade, both the coastal–inland divide and the rural–urban divide in terms of access to quality infrastructure remain significant. Although road construction and telecommunication services grew faster in the western region than in the nation as a whole since the early 2000s (Yao, 2009: 232), the regional dispersion in terms of quality infrastructure is high. For example, while the ten coastal provinces accounted for 25 per cent of the highway network in 2010, their national share of higher quality road was much higher, accounting for 36 per cent of the expressways and 61 per cent of class one highways. In contrast, 58 per cent of the network of highways below class four were in the twelve western provinces.

56.3 Infrastructure spending policy in China

Infrastructure spending is regarded as a major policy priority by the Chinese Central government since the mid-1990s and its importance has been consistently recognized throughout the successive Five-Year Plans. The rationale is twofold. First, infrastructure development is necessary to support the rapid economic growth of the country that fuels an ever-increasing demand for infrastructure services. Second, infrastructure development is needed to fight worsening regional inequality by promoting the catch-up of lagging inland provinces with coastal provinces. As a consequence, after a long period of

---

[1] Data cited in this part are official figures provided by the National Bureau of Statistics of China. The interested reader can refer to <http://www.stats.gov.cn/english/>.

low investment in infrastructure (Démurger, 2001), ambitious programmes have been successively launched to accelerate infrastructure development throughout the whole country and to reduce regional imbalances.

In an attempt to minimize the impact of the Asian financial crisis in 1997–98, the central government announced a massive public investment plan in February 1998 to improve the country's infrastructure and stimulate economic growth. This was followed by the implementation of two region-specific large-scale programmes: the 'Go west' policy (*xibu da kaifa*) and the programme for 'Reviving the Northeast' (*zhenxing dongbei*), launched in 2000 and in 2003 respectively. The former particularly emphasized transportation infrastructure investment as a mechanism for improving the accessibility of the vast, land-locked west. Between 2000 and 2005, the cumulative investment in the twelve western provinces reached one trillion yuan (Yao, 2009). More recently, in response to the 2008 global financial crisis, the Central government announced a stimulus package of four trillion yuan to be invested in infrastructure and social welfare by the end of 2010 with a specific target of the rural and interior regions.

56.4 **The economic impact of infrastructure spending**

Economic infrastructure has long been recognized as playing a key role in economic development and poverty alleviation. In its latest competitiveness report, the World Economic Forum (2010) explicitly identified infrastructure as one of the major pillars of productivity and competitiveness. 'Extensive and efficient infrastructure is critical for ensuring the effective functioning of the economy, as it is an important factor determining the location of economic activity and the kinds of activities or sectors that can develop in a particular economy' (World Economic Forum, 2010: 4).

A well-developed network of transportation and telecommunication infrastructure is believed to stimulate economic activities by reducing distance and transaction costs, facilitating trade, accelerating industrial agglomeration, and improving the flow of information. Better infrastructure is also argued to have an impact on poverty reduction through multiple channels including lower prices of intermediate and final goods, higher agricultural productivity, higher wages, as well as improved opportunities for off-farm employment (Mu and Van de Walle, 2007).

Since the seminal work of Aschauer (1989), the core rationale for infrastructure investment is that in a standard production function framework, public investment in infrastructure raises the productivity of other capital used in production. As recently reviewed by Straub (2008), a large number of empirical studies on the relationship between infrastructure investment and economic growth followed Aschauer's work and generally found evidence of a substantial impact of infrastructure on economic growth.

Despite its obvious importance as part of China's national development strategy, the impact of infrastructure development on economic growth and poverty alleviation in China remains a rather under-studied area in academic research. Nevertheless, the available literature generally finds evidence of positive returns to investment in infrastructure, possibly higher in remote areas. With regard to economic growth, there is evidence of a beneficial impact of transportation infrastructure on regional economic growth (Démurger, 2001; Hong et al. 2011); of telecommunication infrastructure on regional economic growth (Démurger, 2001; Fleisher et al., 2010); of rural transportation and telecommunication infrastructure on rural non-farm productivity (Fan and Zhang, 2004); and of higher returns to telecommunication investment in the developed eastern regions (Fleisher et al., 2010). With regards to poverty reduction and improved living standards, empirical research by economists has mostly focused on the impact of roads. Jalan and Ravallion (2002) found evidence of higher consumption growth rates at the farm-household level in areas with higher road density. Fan et al. (2002) showed that improved rural roads, together with electrification and telecommunications, have all contributed to growth in rural nonfarm employment. Echoing these findings on the impact of road density on poverty, Fan and Chan-Kang (2008) analysed the impact of roads of different quality. They estimated that low-grade roads elevate far more rural and urban poor above the poverty line per yuan invested than do high-grade roads. They also highlight a tradeoff between growth and poverty reduction when investing in different regions: road investment is found to yield the highest economic returns in eastern and central China while its contribution to poverty reduction is greatest in western China.

56.5 **Future challenges**

Although huge progress has been made over the last fifteen years in the domain of infrastructure development, China nevertheless faces a number of major challenges for the future, among them availability, congestion risks, and reliability. First, very remote regions in western and northern China remain under-equipped, one reason being that it is extremely costly to build infrastructure there, with potentially low and decreasing marginal returns. Eradicating poverty will necessitate ensuring a wider access to core economic activities and markets. Hence, extensiveness of infrastructure networks remains on the agenda. Second, the rapidly growing urban population is adding huge pressure to the urban infrastructure, with potentially critical levels of urban congestion. For example, China's upsurge of private vehicle ownership has greatly outpaced the growth of the country's highway system, leading to spectacular traffic jams such as the one recorded on China National Highway 110 in August 2010. Last, as the Wenzhou accident on a high-speed train in July 2011 showed, the safety and reliability of transportation networks are far from being secured. More generally, the country faces the need to enforce a sound operation and maintenance of its rapidly growing stock of infrastructure. How China accommodates its infrastructure development is critical to both sustaining its economic growth and ensuring the well-being of its population.

■ REFERENCES

Amos, Paul and Richard Bullock. 2011. Governance and structure of the railway industry: three pillars. *China Transport Note Series* 02, Beijing: World Bank Office.

Aschauer, David A. 1989. Is public expenditure productive? *Journal of Monetary Economics* 23(2), 177–200.

Démurger, Sylvie. 2001. Infrastructure development and economic growth: an explanation for regional disparities in China? *Journal of Comparative Economics* 19, 95–117.

Fan, Shenggen and Connie Chan-Kang. 2008. Regional road development, rural and urban poverty: evidence from China. *Transport Policy* 15(5), 305–14.

Fan, Shenggen and Xiaobo Zhang. 2004. Infrastructure and regional economic development in rural China. *China Economic Review* 15(2), 203–14.

Fan, Shenggen, Linxiu Zhang, and Xiaobo Zhang. 2002. Growth, Inequality, and Poverty in Rural China: The Role of Public Investments. *Research Report* 125, Washington DC: IFPRI.

Fleisher, Belton, Haizheng Li, and Min Qiang Zhao. 2010. Human capital, economic growth, and regional inequality in China. *Journal of Development Economics* 92(2), 215–31.

Fourie, Johan. 2006. Economic infrastructure: a review of definitions, theory and empirics. *South African Journal of Economics* 74(3), 530–56.

Hong, Junjie, Zhaofang Chu, and Qiang Wang. 2011. Transport infrastructure and regional economic growth: evidence from China. *Transportation* 38(5), 737–52.

Jalan, Jyotsna and Martin Ravallion. 2002. Geographic poverty traps? A micro model of consumption growth in rural China. *Journal of Applied Econometrics* 17, 329–46.

Mu, Ren and Dominique van de Walle. 2007. Rural roads and poor area development in Vietnam. *Policy Research Working Paper Series* 4340, Washington DC: The World Bank.

Straub, Stéphane. 2008. Infrastructure and Growth in Developing Countries: Recent Advances and Research Challenges. *Policy Research Working Paper Series* 4460, Washington DC: The World Bank.

World Economic Forum. 2010. *Global Competitiveness Report 2010–2011*. Geneva.

Yao, Yang. 2009. The political economy of government policies toward regional inequality in China. In *Reshaping Economic Geography in East Asia*, edited by Yukon Huang and Alessandro M. Bocchi. Washington DC: The World Bank.

57 Doing good while doing well

China's search for environmentally sustainable economic growth

Trevor Houser

Chinese President Xi Jinping and Premier Li Keqiang, leaders of the fifth generation of Communist Party leadership, begin their tenure facing two seemingly irreconcilable challenges. Economic growth in 2012 slowed to 7.8 per cent, its lowest level in more than two decades with the exception of one year in the late 1990s.[1] Government stimulus helped China sail through the financial crisis relatively unscathed, but has created longer-term economic challenges. And the global economy is still struggling to recover from its post-crisis recession, limiting growth in international demand for Chinese goods. As leadership's legitimacy with the Chinese people has been predicated largely on its ability to deliver greater economic prosperity, the Xi–Li administration comes to power in search of ways to shore up Chinese economic growth.

At the same time, the environmental costs of China's past economic success are mounting and creating new sources of tension between China's government and its people. Much of Central and Eastern China started 2013 blanketed in some of the worst air pollution in recorded history (Wong, 2013). In Beijing, school children were ordered to stay indoors and hospitals coped with a spike in respiratory illnesses. The public outcry over air pollution has reached new levels, both on the Internet and in the streets. Chinese leaders must find a way to deliver both the economic growth Chinese citizens expect and the environmental protection the country's growing middle class now demands. Fortunately these two goals are not as much at odds going forwards as they were in the past. In fact, the right prescription for keeping China's economy afloat will help address many of the country's environmental ills along the way.

---

[1] National Bureau of Statistics of China, available online at <http://www.stats.gov.cn>.

57.1 **The cost of unbalanced growth**

For the first two decades of China's reform period, environmental protection was not a serious consideration in economic policy making. The first generation of Chinese leadership, led by Mao Zedong, was defined by economic chaos rather than economic growth. So when the second generation, led by Deng Xiaoping, took the reins the overwhelming policy priority was improving the standard of living of the average Chinese citizen (see Naughton, 2007).

The reforms launched in the late 1970s and early 1980s did just that, and more successfully than anyone expected. The economy grew at an average annual rate of 10 per cent during the 1980s and 1990s and millions of Chinese were lifted out of poverty. And this growth occurred without straining the country's energy resources. Economic reforms such as price liberalization and state-owned enterprise restructuring dramatically improved the efficiency with which Chinese industry used energy. And it was labour-intensive light manufacturing that drove China's growth during this period, as opposed to the energy-intensive development strategy pursued by Mao Zedong when he tried to achieve Soviet-style industrialization.

As a result, the energy-intensity of the Chinese economy (the amount of coal, oil, gas, nuclear, and renewable energy consumed for each unit of economic output) fell by 65 per cent between 1979 and 2000. That meant China accounted for only 10 per cent of global energy demand at the turn of the century, rather than the 25 per cent it would have been had the country stayed at pre-reform levels of energy intensity. China was not much of a factor in international energy markets and air pollution was not on the leadership's political radar. And since the Chinese economy was still four to five times more energy intensive in the year 2000 than the average developed country, most analysts (both inside and outside the country) thought China could continue these impressive energy-intensity reductions for another decade and continue to grow without butting up against natural resource constraints (Rosen and Houser, 2007).

Then the structure of the Chinese economy began to change. One of the reforms undertaken during the 1980s and 1990s was a loosening of the *Hukou* system that restricted where Chinese citizens could live, work, and receive social benefits. And during the late 1990s, China's integration into the global economy created demand for labour in light manufacturing along the country's coast. This touched off the largest migration in human history, as over 100 million Chinese citizens moved from the country to the city in search of work. And dozens of new cities were built on what used to be countryside.

The urbanization boom created tremendous demand for energy-intensive building materials. In 2000 China accounted for 16 per cent of global steel demand. By 2010 it accounted for 45 per cent (World Steel Association, 2011). China's share of global demand in other energy-intensive products such as cement, aluminium, and glass experienced similar growth. And investment in steel mills and cement kilns outpaced the already breakneck pace of investment in property and infrastructure, turning China into the world's largest producer and exporter of energy-intensive goods. Driven by property, infrastructure, and the heavy industries that supply them, investment's share of the Chinese economy rose from 35 per cent in 2000 to 48 per cent in 2010, while private consumption's share fell from 46 per cent to 35 per cent.[2] And China started to run a significant trade surplus thanks in large part to import substitution and the export of steel and other energy-intensive products.

While the investment and export-led economic growth over the past decade nearly tripled the size of the Chinese economy, it is unsustainable. Investment in property, infrastructure, and manufacturing has come at the expense of government spending on essential social services and expansion of the private service sector. And that investment has been made possible by a financial system that provides very low real returns for savers, making it difficult for households to prepare for future healthcare or retirement costs (Lardy, 2012).

One of the most significant consequences of unbalanced Chinese growth has been on the country's resource needs and environmental quality. Chinese growth was twice as energy intensive over the past decade as during the 1980s and 1990s. Since 2001, the country has accounted for 75 per cent of energy demand growth globally and become a major force in international energy markets (IEA, 2013). Heavy industry has led the increase in energy demand, with metals, cement, glass, and chemicals manufacturing consuming close to half the country's energy supply. Chinese energy consumption doubled between 2000 and 2008 and the country overtook the USA as the world's largest energy consumer in 2009. In 2010, the International Energy Agency in Paris revised its projections for Chinese energy demand in 2030 upwards by 79 per cent relative to their outlook only a few years earlier (IEA, 2010).

Since most of China's energy supply comes from coal, air pollution has increased dramatically. Chinese coal demand has grown from 1.5 billion tons in 2001 to 3.5 billion tons in 2011, half the global total.[3] China has added nearly 50 gigawatts a year of coal-fired power generation to the grid on average, more than the rest of the world combined. Rapid growth in oil demand, driven primarily by commercial trucking, has also contributed to China's air quality woes. The World Bank estimates that air pollution in China is responsible for more than 700,000 premature deaths each year (World Bank, 2007). It lowers agricultural yields by blocking out sunlight, and imposes billions of dollars in health costs. And to China's middle class, growing in number, wealth and worldliness, it is no longer an acceptable price to pay for rapid economic growth.

---

[2] National Bureau of Statistics of China, available online at <http://www.stats.gov.cn>.
[3] National Bureau of Statistics of China and BP Statistical Review of World Energy.

57.2 **The environmental promise of a rebalanced China**

Fortunately, Chinese leaders do not need to choose between economic growth and environmental protection. There is an emerging consensus that for China to sustain current growth rates (7–8 per cent) policy makers must rebalance the economy, away from past over-reliance on investment, exports and heavy industry, towards domestic consumption, government spending, service sector activities, and high value added manufacturing. This is no small task. It requires improving education, building a modern social safety net, and a renewed focus on rural development. Most importantly, it requires fundamental reform of the financial system, so that households earn a decent return on their savings (which will allow them to consume more) and the private sector companies that dominate the services sector have the same access to capital as industrial state-owned enterprises. That means taking on vested interests in the state sector that have grown accustomed to low-cost capital. And those interests have grown stronger and more politically powerful in recent years.

But the economic benefits of more rational investment and more balanced economic growth are profound. A 2007 IMF Working Paper authored by David Dollar and Shang-Jin Wei found that investments made by wholly and majority private-owned Chinese companies were far more productive and profitable than those made by their state-owned peers (Dollar and Wei, 2007). Redirecting capital to more productive sectors and firms should allow China to reduce investment's role in the economy while not sacrificing overall economic growth. A recent World Bank study conducted with the Development Research Center under the State Council of the Chinese Government found that economic rebalancing could grow annual Chinese domestic consumption by $10 trillion by 2020—roughly the size of total US private consumption today (World Bank and Development Research Center, 2012).

And rather than exacerbate China's environmental challenges, a consumption-led Chinese economic future would actually put the country on a much more sustainable path. Rebalancing the economy away from investment means less infrastructure and property construction, and thus lower metal, glass, and cement demand. And redirecting investment from state-owned enterprises to private Chinese companies means less metal, glass, and cement production. Even though higher levels of domestic consumption mean more automobiles and appliances, the energy needs of these consumer products in China pales in comparison to heavy industry.

Combined with existing government efforts to improve energy efficiency and increase the supply of natural gas, nuclear, and renewable energy, successfully rebalancing China's economy could, within a few years, bring coal demand growth to a halt. This would give recently adopted environmental regulations in the power generation and industrial sectors time to catch up and make a significant dent in Chinese air pollution. It would by no means solve China's environmental problems. New regulations are needed, as well as better enforcement. But it would make a much larger dent than any other single intervention, and deliver meaningful economic and public health benefits and put the country on a more environmentally sustainable path.

■ REFERENCES

Dollar, David and Shang-Jin Wei. 2007. *Das (Wasted) Kapital: Firm Ownership and Investment Efficiency in China*. Washington, DC: International Monetary Fund.

IEA. 2010. *World Energy Outlook*. Paris: Organization for Economic Cooperation and Development.

IEA. 2013. *World Energy Balances*. Paris: Organization for Economic Cooperation and Development.

Lardy, Nicholas R. 2012. *Sustaining China's Economic Growth After the Global Financial Crisis*. Washington, DC: Peterson Institute for International Economics.

Naughton, Barry J. 2007. *The Chinese Economy: Transitions and Growth*, Cambridge, MA: Massachusetts Institute of Technology Press.

Rosen, Daniel H. and Trevor Houser. 2007. *China Energy: A Guide for the Perplexed*. Washington, DC: Peterson Institute for International Economics.

Wong, Edward. 2013. Beijing Takes Steps to Fight Air Pollution as Problem Worsens. *New York Times*, 30 January.

World Bank and Development Research Center of the State Council. 2012. *China 2030: Building a Modern, Harmonious, and Creative High-Income Society*, Washington, DC: The World Bank.

World Bank. 2007. *Cost of Pollution in China: Economic Estimates of Physical Damages*. Washington, DC: The World Bank.

World Steel Association. 2011. *Steel Statistical Yearbook 2011*. Brussels: Worldsteel Committee on Economic Studies.

58 Sustainable water resources management in China

Critical issues and opportunities for policy reforms

Ximing Cai and Michelle Miro

58.1 Introduction

The concept of water resources sustainability sits at the confluence of environmental, economic, and social systems. In China, the strong coupling of these anthropogenic and natural drivers has caused simultaneous increases in water demand and limitations in water availability, leading to heightened water stress and leaving water resources in a critical state in many regions. Yet the nation's livelihood, ecological integrity, and economic growth are highly dependent on water. This is particularly evident in northern China where the Huai, Hai, and Huang River Basins (3-H basins) contribute half of the nation's gross domestic production and support about half of China's population, yet contain only 18 per cent of the nation's available water. Situations such as this illustrate the need for sustainable management and planning of water resources at the regional and national level for multiple objectives, including: improving drinking water and health, ensuring sustainable urbanization and economic growth, reaching food self-sufficiency, and protecting the environment. These objectives, often representing inconsistent needs of the society, the economy, and the environment, compete for water at the regional and even national level, complicating water resources planning and management in China. This chapter suggests an overall shift in the philosophy and approach of water resources planning and management, emphasizing policy reform to promote social equity and environmental recovery.

58.2 Challenges to water resources sustainability

58.2.1 AGRICULTURAL DEVELOPMENT

Strong economic growth compounded by the high temporal and spatial variability of China's water resources has amplified the need for measures to decrease agricultural water demand, particularly as it constitutes about 65 per cent of the nation's demand for water (FAO, 2010). Until the late 1990s, flood irrigation made up 85 per cent of irrigation methods in practice (MWR, 2004). Advancing irrigation technology is key to improving water-use efficiency, including drip and sprinkler systems, irrigation scheduling based on a crop's physiological processes and weather forecasts, and the use of less water-intensive crops (Deng et al., 2006). However, the water saving potential of these methods should be assessed with caution given the reuse of return flow from upstream water withdrawals in a river basin context (Cai and Rosegrant, 2004). Actually, water productivity, or food production per unit of water consumption, remains about average compared to the rest of the world (Rosegrant et al., 2002).

Given the need to reduce the proportion of water used for agriculture, sustaining or even expanding rain-fed agriculture in China has emerged as a realistic tool for curbing the expansion of irrigated agriculture. Rain-fed agriculture in northern China has been practised for hundreds of years, supported by a synchronized pattern of precipitation and solar energy, that is, peak rainfall and evapotranspiration coincide during the crop growth season so rainfall is more effectively used by crops (Cai and Rosegrant, 2005). 'Green water', or water held in the soil, is a highly valuable resource for rain-fed agriculture (Falkenmark and Rockstrom, 2006). However, difficulties are beginning to arise as rainfall patterns are changing and the impacts from human land use—soil erosion and salinization—are felt more strongly. Crop yield increases in rain-fed areas, improvements in water harvesting, and investment in research on rain-fed areas will be crucial to the future growth of rain-fed agriculture.

58.2.2 ENGINEERING INFRASTRUCTURES

The management of water resources in China has been dominated by large engineering works and heavy investment in engineering infrastructures during the past 60 years. In the 3-H basins in northern China, the total reservoir storage far exceeds total annual runoff. However, many of the irrigation districts operate below their potential, and are unable to produce a consistent crop yield; moreover the majority of small-scale districts are very limited by funding and technology. Today, questions also arise as to how much can be gained from additional engineering facilities as their marginal cost increases over time. The heavy burdens placed on the environment by these infrastructures may even outweigh their economic gains.

Smaller-scale, distributed management engineering investments, including the implementation of best management practices (BMPs), can better safeguard the environment and ensure the needs of people at the local level, especially poor groups. One BMP already in practice in northern China is rainfall harvesting, the accumulation and storage of rainwater, which has been used traditionally to supply households with water and supplement irrigation. Research is still needed, though, to assess their cost-effectiveness, operational feasibility, and environmental impacts with widespread implementation. Another important BMP is water and sediment catchments in the Loess Plateau of China. These catchments have been successfully used as cropland for local agriculture and to reduce the sediment load to the Yellow River (Li et al., 2002). However, the risk of landslide disasters that might be caused by extreme floods must be assessed carefully.

In summary, a shift from centralized, large-scale engineering development to more decentralized, smaller-scale management is expected to improve water sustainability by ensuring environmental protection and social equality while still retaining economic merit.

58.2.3 WATER ALLOCATION

At the core of water allocation strategies are the competing needs within and among the economy, society, and the environment. This can also be seen in the high degree of interrelation between the agricultural value of water, national policies aimed at food security, and the capacity for water saving. Thus, policies targeted at effective water transfer, social equity, and environmental protection could impact multiple sectors. Recommendations made by China's Ministry of Water Resources have been advancing demand management, seeking an appropriate balance between demand and supply management (Wang, 2003).

58.2.3.1 Sectoral water transfer

With growing demands from municipal and industrial sectors, the perspective is gradually shifting from considering agricultural dominated water demand alone to a competitive agricultural, municipal, industrial, and environmental water demand. Today, China's water management is still dominated by inefficient agricultural water use with a growing unmet water demand from industry and society. Requiring farmers to maintain levels of food production while decreasing water use is not an easy task given the complex nature of food and water pricing and the cost of agricultural inputs and technology adoption. Past water transfer failures led to economic and environmental losses that hurt farmers and slowed the flow of water needed by industry and cities. A 'smooth' water transfer may take a long time before a clear delineation of water rights arises, but certain actions are needed immediately to protect the basic water needs of both rural and urban residents and to prevent environmental disasters. Ultimately, from an economic perspective, the real value of the very limited water resources in northern China must be acknowledged in a broad national economic context for successful water transfers to occur. This will require that the entire society pay more for water and the goods that it produces so that farmers are able and willing to save water by adopting new technologies. The political philosophy that supports social harmony as a fundamental goal can serve as a basis on which Chinese policy can shift to encourage more equitable water rights and allocation (Cai, 2008).

58.2.3.2 Environmental protection

In many areas of China, particularly in the north, the environment has felt the most dramatic impact of extensive water use and development. With land use changes and intensive water use, soil erosion and dramatic decreases in water availability have become evident in many regions. The increasing use of pesticides and fertilizers, along with increasing industrial and municipal wastes, has caused significant amounts of pollutants to enter the nation's waterways, posing risks to human health. More so, China's capacity for water treatment is low, at a rate of 5–13 per cent in the late 1990s (Qian and Zhang, 2001), with some development during the past decade.

Facing the risk of large-scale, irreversible environmental damage, China has shifted its ideology away from 'human power over nature' towards a spirit of 'human harmony with nature,' On-going ad hoc, case-by-case administrative efforts are successful in restoring environmental water flow (e.g. the Hei River, Liu et al., 2005), but with large transaction costs. The key challenge will be converting these short-term emergency measures into long-term sustainable policies. Assessing environmental costs in both short-term and long-term contexts and taking into account the cost to gross domestic production will be a crucial step for reversing the environmental degradation and sustaining ecosystem services in the country.

58.3 Discussions

58.3.1 CLIMATE CHANGE IMPACTS

Climate change seems to bring both challenges and opportunities to China. Already, China has experienced some dramatic changes in climate in the form of multi-year droughts and more frequent floods. Projections of how climate changes will impact China regionally show significant decreases in water availability and more intensive periods of drought in southern China (Cai and Lall, 2012) while increases in temperature and precipitation may lead to a significant amount of land becoming suitable for agriculture in northwestern China (Zhang and Cai, 2011). Uncertainties regarding these changes and their impact on future water requirements make planning and policy making challenging.

58.3.2 THE COMPLEXITIES OF ACHIEVING FOOD SECURITY

Achieving food security implies a tradeoff with the environment. For example, eliminating intensive groundwater pumping in northern China (30 km^3) would reduce food production by 17 metric tons, or about 4 per cent of the total food demand (Rosegrant et al., 2002). The current national policy of food self-sufficiency requires more food production from less available land and water, which may challenge the ability of technology to improve water efficiency (Rosegrant et al., 2002). If there is no way to meet all the needs of food production, environment restoration, and non-agricultural water demand, a critical issue is whether and what compromises should be considered. Hoekstra and Hung (2002) identified China as one of the top ten countries that import 'virtual water', which is the transfer of water at the global scale via food export and import (Allan, 1998). A better understanding of the role of water in economic growth in northern China, the tradeoffs between food security and environmental integrity, and the range of possibilities for institutionalizing water allocation decisions would serve to better inform upcoming policy reforms.

58.3.3 A SHIFTING PHILOSOPHY

Importantly, sustainable management implies new ethics and a philosophy that promotes an equitable society, the needs of poor and underrepresented groups, and harmony between society and nature. Meeting the basic needs of China's poorest groups needs to be at the forefront of policy change. To make steps towards this goal, the whole society needs to be involved in water savings. Promotion of more small-scale distributed projects can make significant headway in improving environmental systems and distribute some responsibility and power to the local level. In this way China may ensure sufficient water resources for both society and the environment into the future.

■ **REFERENCES**

Allan, T. 1998. Moving water to satisfy uneven global needs: trading water as an alternative to engineering it. *International Commission for Irrigation and Drainage Journal* 47(2), 1–8.

Cai, X. 2008. Water stress, water transfer and social equity in northern China: implications for policy reforms. *Journal of Environment Management* 87, 14–25.

Cai, X. and L. Lall. 2012. Water resources sustainability in China. In *A New Economic Growth Engine for China : Escaping the middle-income trap by not doing more of the same*, edited by W. T. Woo et al., 239–88. Singapore: World Scientific.

Cai, X. and M. Rosegrant. 2004. Optional water development strategies for the Yellow River basin: balancing agricultural and ecological water demands. *Water Resources Research* 40, W08S04, doi:10.1029/2003WR002488.

Cai, X. and M. Rosegrant. 2005. Water management and food production in *China* and *India*: a comparative assessment. *Water Policy* 7(6).

Deng, X. L. Shan, H. Zhang, and N. C. Turner. 2006. Improving agricultural water use efficiency in arid and semiarid areas of China. *Agricultural Water Management* 80(1–3), 23–40.

Falkenmark, M. and J. Rockstrom 2006. The new blue and green water paradigm: breaking new ground for water resources planning and management. *Journal of Water Resources Planning and Management* Editorial, 132, 129–32.

FAO (Food and Agricultural Organization of the United Nations). 2010. China. *AQUASTAT*. FAO: Rome.

Hoekstra, A. Y. and P. Q. Hung 2002. Virtual water trade: A quantification of virtual water flows between nations in relation to international crop trade, Research report. IHE delft.

Li, X., J. Gong, and X. Wei 2002. In-situ rainwater harvesting and gravel mulch combination for corn production in the dry semi-arid region of China. *Journal of Arid Environments* 46: 371–82.

Liu, H., X. Cai, L. Geng, and H. Zhong 2005. Restoration of pastureland ecosystems: a case study of western Inner Mongolia. *Journal of Water Resources Planning and Management* 131(6), 420–30.

Li, X., Gong, J., and Wei, X. 2002. In-situ rainwater harvesting and gravel mulch combination for corn production in the dry semi-arid region of China, *Journal of Arid Environments* 46, 371–382.

MWR (Ministry of Water Resources of China) 2004. *The Annual Book of Water Resources in China*. Beijing: China Water Press.

Qian, Z. and G. Zhang (eds) 2001. Strategy study on sustainable water resources development in China, general report, Beijing: China Water Resources and Hydropower Press.

Rosegrant, W. M., X. Cai, and S. Cline 2002. *World Water and Food to 2025: Dealing with Scarcity*. Washington, DC: International Food Policy Research Institute.

Wang, S. C. 2003. *Resource-based Water Management—Human Harmony with Nature*. Beijing: China Water Press.

Zhang, X. and X. Cai 2011. Climate change impacts on global agricultural land availability. *Environmental Research Letters* 6, 014014.

59 Benefit–cost analysis of ambient water quality improvement in China

Hua Wang

59.1 Introduction

Over the past decades, China had been deliberately allowing environmental deterioration in exchange for economic development, but now this strategy has to be revised.[1] Environmental quality in China has been reduced to extremely serious levels, while people's incomes have been increased significantly. Currently in most areas of China, any further deterioration of environmental quality will not be tolerated by society, and people are demanding significant improvements almost everywhere.

The Chinese government is responding to people's call for environmental improvement. However, a number of economic questions have not been sufficiently answered with regard to environmental improvements in China. For example, how strong, economically, is the demand for environmental improvement, by different groups of people and in different areas? What are the associated costs? Which areas of environmental improvements should public investments go to first, in order to be more economically efficient? A better understanding of the benefits and the costs associated with environmental quality improvements in China is critically important, because in the long term, economic development will still be a priority in China, as there are still hundreds of millions of people to be further lifted out of poverty. Investments in environmental quality improvements in China must be made wisely.

59.1 Water quality and economic valuation

Water resources in China are abundant, but scarce in per capita terms and in some regions. China's renewable water resources on a per capita basis is estimated at 2,156 m³/

---

[1] This chapter draws on the findings in Ojeda et. al. (2008); Wang et. al. (2013); Xu et al. (2003); Yang et al. (2008).

year in 2007, only one-quarter of the world average of 85,49 m³/year. In the northern part of China, water availability is even poorer, only 757 m³/year per person. At the same time, water demand is increasing due to continuing economic growth, population increases, industrialization, and urbanization.

Accompanying the water scarcity problem is the problem of water quality deterioration in China's extensive water systems. Caused by pollution from the vast discharges of industrial and domestic wastewater, indiscriminate solid waste disposal and the runoff from the agricultural sector and its excessive use of fertilizers and pesticides and large-scale livestock breeding, about 25,000 square kilometres of Chinese lakes fail to meet the water quality standards for aquatic life and about 90 per cent of examined sections of lakes around urban areas have become seriously polluted. Among the 412 sections of the seven major lakes monitored in 2004, 42 per cent meet Grade I–III (acceptable water quality) standards, 30 per cent met Grade IV–V (significantly polluted) standards, and the rest 28 per cent failed to meet Grade V (worst level of pollution) standards. In 2011, the percentage was about the same as in 2004 for the Grade I–III surface water, but the proportion water with the worst pollution levels decreased from 28 per cent to 8 per cent. The remaining 50 per cent was at Grade IV–V, which was significantly polluted. For the major rivers, 61 per cent of the 469 sections monitored by the state in 2011 met the Grade I–III standard and 25 per cent were significantly polluted at the levels of Grade IV and V. The remaining 14 per cent were the most polluted with a quality failing to meet the Grade V standard.

Empirical estimations of the economic values associated with water quality improvements in the lakes and the rivers in China are very limited and of varying quality. Most of the studies used the contingent valuation method, with which willingness to pay (WTP) surveys are designed and executed, to measure people's demand for water quality improvements. Many of the existing studies reported high percentages (from 70 per cent to 95 per cent) of respondents who are willing to contribute a positive amount to water quality improvements. This actually demonstrates the fact that most of the Chinese people are aware of the seriousness of the water pollution problems in China. The reported willingness to pay varies between 0.21 per cent and 8 per cent of annual household income. However, no serious benefit–cost analyses of water quality improvement projects are found in China.

59.3 **The case of Yunnan**

In Yunnan, a southwest province of China, the accelerating urbanization process and rapid development of tourism during the last several years have exceeded the carrying capacity of the current municipal environmental infrastructure, putting great pressure on the ability to continuously increase urban general welfare. The lakes in Yunnan are largely contaminated by organic pollutants; some suffer particularly from eutrophication. Among the twenty-two main lakes and water basins, the clean and the comparatively clean lakes (Grade I–III) make up only 54.6 per cent; the polluted lakes (Grade IV) and the seriously polluted lakes account for over 45.4 per cent. There were only thirty-eight wastewater treatment facilities in Yunnan in 2007, ten of which are located in the municipality of Kunming, the capital of the province. Ninety counties and municipalities in the province had no wastewater treatment facilities in 2007.

In 2007, the Yunnan Provincial Government formally launched the 'Initiative to Protect Colorful Yunnan' to rehabilitate Yunnan, and one of the main projects is the Yunnan Urban Environment Project (YUEP). The proposed project components are expected to generate a number of positive externalities by providing much needed urban infrastructure and enhancing watershed management; in particular it should promote local economic development (including tourism), increase property values, increase the output of livestock and fishing, and increase the biodiversity of the watersheds. In addition, the project will also improve public health by reducing water-borne diseases and enhance the quality of life of project beneficiaries. For example, the project component for Lake Puzhehei in Qiubei County is to protect the lake from further and perhaps irreversible degradation and to enhance access to basic environmental infrastructure. The sub-project will first purify the wastewaters at the four intake rivers by building artificial wetlands, collect and treat wastewaters and solid wastes from nearby villages, and return some of the farming lands to wetlands. This sub-project should have a significant impact on the water quality in the lake and rivers and on the overall ecological conditions and natural environment. Even though it is difficult to precisely predict the impact on water quality, estimates show that the water quality of the surrounding rivers will be improved by one grade level, that is, from the current Grade IV to III. The water quality in the lake will not deteriorate further, and part of the water will be improved from the current Grade III to II.

Benefit–cost analyses have been conducted for three sub-projects, including the ones in Huaping County, Qiubei County, and Dali City, where the water quality has been deteriorating rapidly in the past ten years. The economic value of the benefits associated with water quality improvement projects are estimated using the contingent valuation method. The potential costs are estimated from the project data. On the cost side, investment, operation, and maintenance costs are included in the analysis. Interest payments, repayments of principals, taxes, and subsidies are excluded from the project costs, as they are merely transfers of resources within a society. Investment costs include the costs of works and the indirect costs of investment such as the costs of administration, supervision, and physical contingencies (6 per cent of the total project cost). The estimated yearly investment costs are determined in line with the project implementation plans of six years and disbursement schedules. Operational and maintenance (O&M) costs include the costs of labour, power, and maintenance. The standard conversion factor for China is assumed to be 1.0, as major equipment and material inputs are acquired through international competitive bidding and no major domestic input has an economic price above its financial price. In addition to standard project-related costs, other costs associated with the implementation of the project are examined, such as potential income loss for farmers from the closure of fishery ponds in the lake areas, and these are found to be marginal. Finally, the project cycle is assumed to be a twenty-year period in order to capture the long-term benefits of the projects.

In Huaping County, people are found to be willing to pay 67 yuan per household per month (or 5.2 per cent of income) continuously for five years for an improvement in water quality in the two major local rivers from the current medium-level pollution of Grade IV to an acceptable water quality of Grade III, which is the water quality of ten years previously and is suitable for swimming and fishing. A higher WTP is found if the water quality can be improved to meet the standards of Grade II (suitable as a source of drinking water), but the increase in WTP is marginal and only about 2 yuan per month. The economic internal rate of return of this project component is estimated to be 21 per cent.

In Qiubei County, WTP is estimated for the improvement of the water quality of Lake Puzhehei by one grade level, that is, from the current Grade III to Grade II in the lake and from the current Grade IV to Grade III in the surrounding rivers. The lake is located far from big cities in a rural area of Qiubei county. The results show that on average a household is willing to pay about 30 yuan per month continuously for five years to implement the project, with a median value of 11 yuan per month. This WTP is equivalent to roughly 2.9 per cent of household income. The economic internal rate of return is estimated to be 18 per cent.

In Dali, the WTP study aimed to estimate the total value of the project to improve the water quality of Erhai Lake by one grade level, that is, from the current Grade III to Grade II in the lake and from the current Grade IV to Grade III in the surrounding rivers. The lake is a famous tourist site and surrounded by cities and towns. The results show that on average a household located in Dali is willing to pay about 27 yuan per month continuously for five years to implement the project, with a median value of 14 yuan per month. This WTP is roughly equivalent to 1.6 per cent of household income. The economic internal rate of return of the project is estimated to be 13 per cent.

59.4 **Conclusion**

China is facing serious environmental issues even though the economy still needs to be developed much further. The challenges involved in making smart decisions when balancing the environmental improvement and economic development are huge. Careful economic analyses need to be systematically conducted on all the major investment projects, so that economic efficiency criteria can be met and investment priorities can be established, so that the well-being of the Chinese people of both the current and future generations can be maximized.

For the case in Yunnan Province, when the magnitude of water quality improvement in the lakes is about one grade level, that is, from the current Grade III to Grade II in the lakes and from the current Grade IV to Grade III in the surrounding rivers, people's willingness to pay for the improvement is between 1.6 per cent and 5.2 per cent of income. The elasticity of WTP with respect to income is between 0.2 and 0.3, and the economic internal rate of return is between 13 per cent and 21 per cent. These figures demonstrate that the demand for water quality improvement is very strong in China and people's valuation of ambient water quality improvement is far greater than the necessary cost.

■ REFERENCES

Ojeda, M., A. Mayer, and B. Solomon. 2008. Economic valuation of environmental services sustained by water flows in the Yaqui River Delta. *Ecological Economics* 65(1), 155–66.

Wang, Hua, Y. Shi, Y. Kim, and T. Kamata. 2011. Valuing water quality improvement in China: A case study of Lake Puzhehei in Yunnan Province. *Ecological Economics* 94, 56–65.

Xu. Z., X., G. Cheng, Z. Zhang, Z. Su, and J. Loomis. 2003. Applying contingent valuation in China to measure the total economic value of restoring ecosystem services in Ejina region. *Ecological Economics* 44, 345–58.

Yang, W., J. Chang, B. Xu, C. Peng, and Y. Ge. 2008. Ecosystem service value assessment for constructed wetlands: a case study in HangZhou, China. *Ecological Economics* 68(1–2), 116–25.

60 Climate change

Ye Qi

60.1 Definition

Climate change generally refers to significant and lasting variations or fluctuations in the averaged properties of a climate system in a region or of the entire Earth over a period of decades or more. It is shown in fluctuations in air temperature, precipitation, disastrous weather events, and causes numerous consequences in nature and society. A climate system usually maintains relative stability over decadal and centennial scales, but climate change has been commonplace over a longer period in the Earth's history. Climate change as a popular term in contemporary science and daily life usually refers to the variations caused by the worldwide warming effect of greenhouse gases, and covers a wide range of changes way beyond temperature increase. Changes in precipitation, wind velocity and frequency, vapour and cloud, monsoon, flood and drought, and weather patterns are some of the major properties observed and analysed in climate change science.

Climate change impacts are widespread and profound, including the melting of glaciers and permafrost, sea level rise, variation of air and ocean circulations, acidity and salinity of sea water. Numerous evidences and observations have pointed to the fact the climate change may have major impacts on agriculture, fishery, ecosystem structure and function, biodiversity, buildings and infrastructure, as well as disaster prevention and relief. All nations have taken action, individually and collectively, since 1992 when the United Nations Framework Convention on Climate Change (UNFCCC) was formulated. While national governments have been working diligently to reach global agreements on actions and responsibilities, many initiatives and action have been taken in communities, cities, and regions by citizens and organizations. Knowledge, technology, and financial resources, as well as desires for materials, wealth, and comfort, are some of the major obstacles that have been holding society back from greater achievement on climate change mitigation.

60.2 **Climate change in China**

The overall pattern of climate change in China is similar to that of the Northern Hemisphere and the globe. Instrumental measurements have shown a distinct trend of warming in the past century. The mean annual average of land surface temperature increased 0.5–0.8 °C, slightly higher than the global increase (0.6 +/–0.2 °C). Similar to the seasonal patterns of the temperature change of the globe, winter and spring showed a greater increase and summer very little change or even a slight decrease in temperature. There has been an accelerated warming trend in China in recent decades, and the warming has been much stronger than the global average, indicating greater climate changes in China.

Like the rest of the world, no significant temporal trend of precipitation has been observed as part of the climate change. However, there seemed to be a growing number of extreme weather events shown in more frequent occurrences of flood and drought in certain regions. In recent decades, northern China experienced a distinct period of drought, while western China has enjoyed a significant increase of precipitation. More rain storms have been falling in the middle and lower reaches of the Yangtze River. The change of precipitation pattern in China may be related to a declining trend of East Asian Monsoons. Summer monsoons in China showed a consistent increase from the 1920s through to 1960, and a trend of decline since 1960. This change is considered to be responsible for the drying trend in northern China.

Sea levels have been on rise worldwide. On average, a 2 mm annual increase has been observed in the last half a century with an accelerated trend in recent decades when the annual rise has gone up to 3 mm. There have been regional variations in sea level rises. The Western Pacific and the Eastern Indian Oceans have had a much greater increase, while the Eastern Pacific and Western Indian Oceans appeared to have a lowered sea level. China, at the Western coast of the Pacific, suffers more from a sea level rise.

60.3 **Climate change impacts in China**

China's susceptibility to climate change can be inferred from its geography. The majority of the country's population, economy, and urban built structure are located within 200 miles of the eastern coastlines. The damage by and economic loss from climate change would be devastating for China. Therefore, China is classified as a 'high risk' country according to the Climate Change Vulnerability Index. Historically, the agrarian economy was both blessed and cursed by the East Asian Monsoon, which brings rain for growing crops during the summer and blows wind across the continent in winter. With climate change, however, the East Asian Monsoon may have significantly dampened and thus aggravated the drought in northern China and flooding in the south. The glacial mountains in the west will eventually be so affected that it will reduce their capacity to supply water for the rivers that have been watering the thirsty land and people for thousands of years.

Climate change has already affected farming in China by shifting the locations of crop planting. Due to the warming trend of climate, the world's largest rice cropping nation has found the northern boundary of rice planting has been consistently moving northward by up to 60 kilometres in recent decades. The northern boundary of the wheat crop has moved several hundreds of kilometres to the north. Despite such examples which help to expand the areas of crop planting, it is estimated that the overall impact of climate change on farming is negative.

60.4 **China's climate policies and action**

Despite significant early involvement in the scientific research, the issue did not become a policy priority in China until 1990 when the National Coordination Group on Climate Change (NCGCC) was established under the State Council's Environmental Protection Committee (SCEPC). This government institution was formed to coordinate national policy and action on climate change and to prepare for China's national position on the issue in the formation of the UNFCCC during the World Conference on Environment and Development in Rio de Janeiro in 1992. The Group has evolved to reflect the growing significance of climate change in the national policy agenda. Shortly after the release of the Fourth Assessment of the Inter-governmental Panel on Climate Change (IPCC) in 2007, China formed a National Leading Group on Climate Change, led by the Premier and consisting of almost all ministries of the central government. This major shift of government attention is also reflected at local levels of government. All provinces and most municipalities now have their own leading groups on climate change led by the heads of the appropriate governments.

During the last two decades, China's climate policy and action has focused on mitigation of rather than adaptation to climate change. Due to the fact that the vast majority of greenhouse gas emission is from fossil fuel burning, particularly coal use, China's climate policy has emphasized improving energy efficiency and using renewable energy for power generation. In fact, energy efficiency improvement and renewable energy development are consistent with other policy goals such as energy security and economic growth. As a result, China's energy efficiency, as measured by economic productivity of energy use, has been steadily increasing for more than three decades, with only a short-term bump from 2002 to 2005. The government made a voluntary commitment at the Copenhagen Conference on Climate Change to reduce carbon intensity by 40–45 per cent from 2005 to 2020. If achieved, China would have avoided several billion tons of carbon dioxide emission as compared to a 'no policy' scenario.

The National People's Congress passed the first Renewable Energy Law in 2005. The legislation encouraged the use of renewable sources for power generation, buildings, and transportation by providing mandates and financial incentives. China has become a world leader in renewable energy development in the last decade. China has invested more than any other country in the development of renewable energy for three consecutive years. China's share in the photovoltaic (PV) market grew from 1 per cent to 35 per cent between 2002 and 2010, and currently China produces roughly half of the solar PV panels installed in the world. Wind power installation capacity increased by more than forty-fold in the five years from 2005 to 2010. Wind has become the third major source of power following coal and hydropower.

Carbon capture and sequestration (CCS) was advanced as a component of low-carbon development in recent decades. Afforestation and reforestation have been key approaches to sequestering atmospheric carbon dioxide. In the decade from 2000, forest cover in China increased nearly 4 per cent, from 16.6 per cent to 20.4 per cent. In the five-year period covered by the 11th FYP (2006–10), the growth in forest cover sequestered an average of 4.5 million tons of CO_2 per year. Looking to 2015, the government has planned to increase national forests by another 12.5 million hectares. Investment in CCS technology has also been a salient development in low-carbon strategy. CCS technology was incorporated into China's National Medium- and Long-term Science and Technology Plan—a key government policy blueprint covering the years 2006–20—in 2005.

To encourage innovations for climate policy and action, China established a pilot programme in selected provinces and cities for low carbon development. In addition, China has selected two provinces and five cities as pilots for a carbon market in designs similar to the EU-ETS. It is expected that a nationwide cap and trade programme will be in place by 2016.

60.5 **China in the global climate governance**

China has been a key engaging partner in the development of global governance on climate change, and its role has been increasing due to the size of the Chinese economy and the scale of China's emissions. Since China surpassed the USA and became the largest emitter of carbon dioxide, it has been expected, and on many occasions demanded, to show greater leadership in making new climate regimes. China seems to have been working hard to meet these international expectations and demands. During the Copenhagen Conference in 2009, The Chinese Premier worked with other world leaders, especially heads of states of the BASIC countries (including Brazil, South Africa, India, and China) as well as the USA to devise the basic terms of the Copenhagen Accord. However unsatisfying then, the Copenhagen Accord has served as a foundation that has helped to maintain goodwill and momentum in international climate negotiations. China joined other key parties to agree on the Durban Platform that started a new process for making a global agreement that involves all parties in commitment and action on cutting greenhouse gas emissions beyond 2020.

China is often seen by the developed countries as a less proactive or even resistant player in international climate negotiations. This reflects the differences in economic and social challenges faced by the developed countries on one side and developing countries on the other. Despite impressive economic growth in recent decades, China as a whole is still a developing country that has a huge obligation to lift its people out of poverty. According to the newly defined (2011) poverty standard (per capita annual income under 2300 yuan RMB in rural areas), 122 million people are under the poverty line. Although China has surpassed Japan in terms of national GDP and become the second largest economy in the world, the proportion of the population living in poverty is just about the same size as the total population in Japan. Most of the poverty-hit regions suffer from an adverse natural environment and thus economic development is particularly difficult. China faces daunting challenges for employment, including the employment of 10 million rural workers who are eager to enter the cities and six million college graduates flooding onto the job market annually. Adding to the difficulty, the rapid growth of the ageing population places a huge demand on economic and social resources. So far, China is the only country in the world with more than 100 million senior citizens. Most of the regions in China are still in the early stages of the industrialization and urbanization, technology is less advanced. These factors are often cited by Chinese negotiators as the reasons why economic growth, and thus energy consumption and carbon emissions, are expected to grow up significantly before they decline. The hard fact is that neither China nor the world can afford such a growth in carbon emission. China's 12th Five-Year Plan on energy development has made it clear that it wishes to set an overall cap of energy use of 4.1 million tons coal equivalent. The national government has recently declared its intention to make green and low carbon development a new mode of development of the nation's economy.

Part X
Population and Labour

61 What challenges are demographic transition bringing to China's growth?

Fang Cai

61.1 Introduction

The unprecedented rapid growth of the Chinese economy since the late 1970s can be seen as a typical dual economic development, as proposed by Arthur Lewis (1954). During this process huge numbers of labourers have migrated from agricultural to non-agricultural sectors, from rural to urban areas, and from central and western to coastal regions. The Chinese economy has thus been able to achieve increases in productivity through reallocating labour among sectors and rural and urban households have increased their incomes by the expansion of labour participation. Overall, such demographic change has spurred China's industrialization and urbanization and allowed China to benefit from economic globalization throughout the reform period.

The Lewisian type dual economic growth is merely a phase of economic development—namely, a transition from a Malthusian poverty trap to Solowian neo-classical growth (Hansen and Prescott, 2002; Aoki, 2012). There are two empirical turning points that help us to observe the change in development stages when considering dual economic development. First, when the growth rate of labour demand exceeds the growth rate of labour supply, the Lewis turning point characterized by constant labour shortages and wage increases is reached. Second, when the working age population shifts from expanding to reducing and the dependence ratio from declining to increasing, the turning point at which demographic dividend ends is reached. At the arrival of such two turning points, the previous sources driving economic growth become exhausted. As China enters its new stage of demographic transition and economic development, particularly after the arrival of these two turning points, such a pattern of growth will eventually end.

This chapter reveals that the Chinese economy reached its Lewis turning point in 2004 and the point when the demographic dividend will disappear is 2013, at the latest. This is a warning that China must prepare for a fundamental transformation from dual economic growth to neo-classical growth, which requires the substitution of growth sources and reforms of social and economic systems.

61.2 **Demographic transition and turning points**

As early as the 1970s, China's total fertility rate began to decline, from around 6 births per woman in 1970 to less than 3 in 1980. As a result of the implementation of the one-child policy and, more importantly, of rapid social and economic developments spurred by the reform and opening-up policy, the fertility rate has since declined to 2.1—the replacement level—in the early 1990s and to as low as 1.4 in 2006, which put China among the countries with the lowest fertility rates in the world.

As a consequence of a long decline in fertility, the population age structure has dramatically changed—that is, the working-aged population (between 15 and 64) has so far continued to grow, though at a diminishing rate, is predicted to stop growing in 2013, and fall thereafter. Similarly, the population dependence ratio will bottom out in 2013 and rise rapidly thereafter. Those changes will have a significant impact on the speed and pattern of Chinese economic growth.

Prior to 2004, when labour shortages first appeared in China, labour-intensive industries in the coastal areas could benefit from a ready supply of cheap labour—the migrant workers who have made a substantial contribution to the rapid economic growth and international competitiveness of manufacturing goods. The numbers of migrant workers, defined as those who left their home townships for more than six months, increased from 84 million in 2001 to 159 million in 2011, nearly double in 10 years.

Since 2004, however, labour shortages have become widespread throughout the country, and the wages of ordinary workers have constantly increased. In the period 2004–11, the real wage rate of migrant workers increased at an annual rate of 12.7 per cent. While the high speed of economic growth continues and 2013 gets closer, the labour shortage becomes more serious. In 2011 and early 2012, for example, Chinese enterprises confronted both unprecedented difficulties recruiting workers and the fastest rate of growth in the wages of unskilled workers.

Taking 2004 as the representative year of the arrival of the Lewis turning point and 2013 as the representative year of the disappearance of demographic dividend is a useful way to understand the challenges facing the Chinese economy. It appears that the length of time between the two turning points is affected by the Chinese characteristics of the demographic transition, and it raises an alert for China to tackle the resulting challenges.

Compared to other East Asian countries, the unique feature of the premature population ageing—or to put it another way, 'growing old before becoming rich'—makes the length of time between the two turning points especially short in China. The Japanese economy passed through its Lewis turning point around 1960 (Minami, 1968), and its population dependence ratio began to rise after 1990. That is, it took more than thirty years for Japan to pass between the two points. South Korea passed its Lewis turning point in 1972 (Bai, 1982), and it will reach the demographic turning point in 2013, giving the country over forty years to bridge the two points. The time span between the two corresponding turning points allows China only nine years. The uniqueness of this situation can help us understand why labour shortages, once they appeared, spread so quickly, accompanied by dramatic wage inflation, and why this indicates the urgency for China to transform its growth pattern.

61.3 The growth engine in the post-demographic dividend era

When labour shortages become a regular constraint, the opportunity for reallocative efficiency to be gained through labour mobility from the agricultural to the non-agricultural sectors becomes limited, which tends to reduce the potential GDP growth rate. Cai and Lu (2012) estimate that due mainly to the declining contributions of employment, capital investment, and total factor productivity, China's potential GDP growth rate is predicted to drop from 105 per cent in the 11th Five-Year Plan period (2006–10) to 7.2 per cent in 12th Five-Year Plan period (2011–15) and further to 6.1 per cent in 13th Five-Year Plan period (2016–20).

In response to the fundamentally changed stage of development, entrepreneurs and investors instinctively seek to substitute machines for labourers—namely, to enhance the capital–labour ratio in production, while governments, especially those which are viewed as 'developmental states', tend to employ a variety of policy measures, including investment programmes, industrial policies, regional development strategies, and stimulus packages, to spur economic growth, resulting in a capital deepening of the economy. That is what happened in Japan in the 1980s and 1990s when it was losing demographic dividend, and China has witnessed a similar trajectory in recent years as it approaches the same turning point.

According to estimations by Kuijs (2009), the contribution of the capital–labour ratio to the growth of labour productivity increased from 45.3 per cent in 1978–94 to 64.7 per cent in 2005–09, and it is predicted to increase to 65.9 per cent in 2010–15. Correspondingly, the contribution of total factor productivity to the growth of labour productivity dropped from 46.9 per cent to 31.8 per cent and will further drop to 28.0 per cent, respectively, in the same three periods. This reveals that there is a risk that China will duplicate the Japanese trajectory. After losing demographic dividend as the engine of Japanese economic growth, the contributive share of capital deepening to labour productivity improvement jumped as high as 94 per cent, while the contributive share of total factor productivity became negative (–15 per cent) in the period of 1991 to 2000 (APO, 2008), which resulted in long-term stagnation—known as the lost decade.

In fact, as capital input plays an ever greater role in spurring growth and labour productivity, improvement depends more and more on capital deepening in the Chinese economy; under the condition of labour shortages, the marginal return on capital has been diminishing since 1993 (Cai and Zhao, 2012). That suggests that the sustainability of economic growth is confronted by acute challenges and that the transformation to a total factor productivity-driven pattern is more urgent.

First, as a large economy, China still has opportunities to gain resource reallocation efficiency through industrial transfer among regions, in particular the transfer of labour-intensive industries from coastal to inland regions. There is a great variety of development levels, resource endowments, and demographic characteristics among the thirty-one mainland provinces, which allow for the forming of a domestic flying geese pattern so that the relatively abundant, cheap labour in the central and western regions can be exploited and the comparative advantage of labour-intensive industries maintained.

Comparing the average share of agricultural labour in countries with per capita GDP between US$6,000 and US%12,000—that is, 14.8 per cent in 2007—38.1 per cent of Chinese agricultural labour by official statistics in 2009—or 24.7 per cent by scholarly estimation—is still too high. In the next decade up to 2020, China will fall into a similar stage of development with per capita GDP of US$6,000–12,000. That is, it will have to release surplus labour force from agriculture at a rate of 1 percentage point or so per annum. To encourage a continuing shift of labour, reform of the *Hukou* system, as a necessary institutional stimulus, should be accelerated.

Second, the government should bring to an end its current intervention in economic growth whereby it directly invests in competitive sectors and subsidizes inefficient state enterprises. Instead, the government should be responsible for establishing a 'creative destruction' environment in which the well functioning markets of production factors and competition encourage the factors of production to move across sectors to seek more productive employment so that the most efficient enterprises survive and expand while inefficient enterprises die. Only the enterprises with good total factor productivity dominate, but the economy as a whole remains healthy.

Last but not least, enhancing the skills of workers, or more generally, improving the human capital of the country is vital for the Chinese economy to sustain its growth. While the inadequacy of resources is still the main constraint of the development of education and training, the demand side constraint sets in as the Lewis turning point arrives. That is, as the wages of ordinary workers grow and the wage rates of skilled and unskilled workers converge, the incentive for the young to continue at school weakens. Based on three waves of survey in twelve Chinese cities, Cai and Du (2011) estimate the relative return on education, taking junior high school as a reference, and find that the additional return to senior high school relative to junior high declined from 25.9 per cent in 2001 to 17.3

per cent in 2005 and 16.9 per cent in 2010, which implies a labour market failure—that is, there is a diminishing incentive for households to invest in education. Therefore, as the demographic dividend disappears, the national education policy should expand its focus not only on the supply side but also on the demand side.

61.4 **Conclusions**

The demographic dividend has facilitated China's transition from dual economy development to neo-classical growth over a period of thirty years. As a result of demographic transition and economic development, such a conventional growth driver is disappearing. The challenge facing China is to sustain its growth and avoid the middle-income trap by implementing further reforms that will eliminate institutional barriers to labour mobility, productivity improvement, and human capital accumulation.

■ REFERENCES

APO (Asian Productivity Organization). 2008. *APO Productivity Databook 2008*, The Asian Productivity Organization, 1–2–10 Hirakawacho, Chiyoda-ku, Tokyo 102–0093, Japan.

Aoki, Masahiko. 2012. The five-phases of economic development and institutional evolution in China and Japan. In *The Chinese Economy: A New Transition*, edited by Masahiko Aoki and Jinglian Wu. Basingstoke: Palgrave Macmillan.

Bai, Moo-ki. 1982. The turning point in the Korean economy. *Developing Economies* 2, 117–40.

Cai, Fang and Yang Du. 2011. Wages increase, wages convergence, and Lewis turning point in China. *China Economic Review* 22(4), 601–10.

Cai, Fang and Yang Lu. 2012. What growth rate will China realize in the next decade? In *Bluebook of China's Economy, 2012*, Chen, Jiagui et al. Beijing: Social Sciences Academic Press.

Cai Fang and Zhao Wen. 2012. When demographic dividend disappears: growth sustainability of China. In *The Chinese Economy: A New Transition*, edited by Masahiko Aoki and Jinglian Wu. Basingstoke: Palgrave Macmillan.

Hansen, G. D. and E. Prescott. 2002. Malthus to Solow. *American Economic Review* 92, 1205–17.

Kuijs, Louis. 2009. China Through 2020—A Macroeconomic Scenario. World Bank China Research Working Paper No. 9.

Lewis, Arthur. 1954. Economic development with unlimited supplies of labor. *The Manchester School* 22(2), 139–91.

Minami, Ryoshin. 1968. The turning point in the Japanese economy. *The Quarterly Journal of Economics* 82(3), 380–402.

62 Rural–urban migration in China

Xin Meng

62.1 History and institution

One of the most important forces driving China's miraculous growth is rural–urban migration (Bosworth and Collins, 2008). Hundreds of millions of unskilled workers have moved from low-productivity agricultural sectors to high-productivity urban sectors, creating significant productivity gains in China.

Although the total number of rural–urban migrants reached 145 million in 2009 (National Bureau of Statistics, 2010), accounting for over a quarter of the urban labour force, the large scale rural–urban migration is a rather new phenomenon. In 1990 the number of rural–urban migrants was only 25 million,[1] and after 9 years by 1999 it had doubled to reach 52 million, and a decade later it had tripled (World Bank, 2009).

Rural–urban migration has been a controlled process since the early 1950s when the Communist Party rose to power. Since then, the Chinese economy has been divided into rural and urban economies. During the Mao era, rural people received lower incomes and no welfare from the state, while city-dwellers had higher incomes and a state-provided welfare system. This rural–urban segregation was sustained by the household registration system—*Hukou*. Individuals born in rural areas received 'agriculture or rural *Hukou*' while those born in cities received non-agriculture or urban *Hukou*. Only urban *Hokou* holders were allocated food coupons. Without food coupons, one could not purchase any food in cities. This way rural–urban migration was easily controlled, and the need to do so was partly related to the sustainability of the very unequal treatment of the rural and urban populations.

It was not until the 1990s when the influx of foreign direct investment generated significant demand for unskilled labour that the government loosened its control over rural–urban migration. However, even today the *Hukou* system still restricts labour mobility, although in a more subtle way. Migrants in cities are treated differentially from their urban *Hukou* counterparts. They often obtain lower-end jobs and are not entitled to social welfare and social services which are available to urban *Hukou* people. As such, migrants and their families have no access to unemployment, healthcare, or pension support in cities; and their children only have limited access to urban public schools.

---

[1] Author's own calculation based on a 1 per cent sample of the 1990 population census data.

62.2 **Who migrates and how they are doing in cities**

In response to institutionalized discrimination, most migrants come to cities alone, leaving their families behind in the rural villages. For example, data from the RUMiCI[2] 2009 migrant survey indicate that of the 5,214 migrant household heads, around 56 per cent are married, and of these only 63 per cent have their spouse with them. Among children of migrants who are aged below 16, 56 per cent are left behind in rural villages. Because of these left-behind families, migrants have a special demographic structure.

Migrants normally come to cities in their late teens and return to their home village at marriage and child-bearing age for women (around 25–30 years of age) and when children start schooling for men (in their mid to late 30s). RUMiCI rural household survey data indicate that at the age of 25, 58 per cent and 50 per cent of the male and female rural labourers, respectively, had migrated out of their own counties to work in 2009, whereas at 35 years of age, only 30 per cent males and 20 per cent of females had migrated. In total 22 per cent of the rural labour force worked in cities in 2009 (Meng, 2012).

On average, migrants in cities in 2009 are 32 years of age, and around 59 per cent are male. Their mean years of schooling is 9.2 years whereas for urban *Hukou* workers it is 11.5 years.

Migrants work extremely long hours, mainly as manual labourers, and earn much lower wages than their urban counterparts. This was true in the 1990s (Meng and Zhang, 2001) and is still the case now. In 2009, 31 per cent of urban workers held a professional or managerial job while the proportion for migrants is a mere 3 per cent; 91 per cent of migrants work as production or service workers, while the proportion for urban workers is 35 per cent (Frijters et al., 2011b). Migrants, on average, work 63 hours a week, while their urban *Hukou* counterparts work 43 hours, almost one-third less. Although this difference may seem to be due to the fact that more migrants are self-employed (28 per cent) than their urban counterparts (6 per cent), the difference remains large when comparing hours of work for wage-salary workers (57 vs 42 hours). The average hourly wage for migrant wage-salary earners is 7.4 yuan in 2009, while for their urban counterparts it is 16.6 yuan.

None of the above differences can be fully explained by the observed differences in human capital (such as age, city work experience, and education); physical capital (height and health); or regional variations (cities where they work). For example, after controlling for these observed differences migrant wage-salary earners still earn 6.4 yuan less per hour than their urban counterparts, almost 40 per cent (Frijters et al., 2011a). Furthermore, the RUMiCI survey shows that only 13.5 per cent of migrants have unemployment

[2] Rural–Urban Migration in China and Indonesia (RUMiCI) project is sponsored by the Australian Research Council, AusAID, and the Ford Foundation and was carried out by the Research School of Economics, Australian National University. See <http://rse.anu.edu.au/rumici/> for detailed information on the project.

insurance, only 17 per cent have work injury insurance, and only 12 per cent have city health insurance. These ratios for urban local workers are 66 per cent, 87 per cent, and 64 per cent, respectively.

Institutional discrimination increases the rural workers' opportunity cost of migration. As a result, the number of rural–urban migrants may be significantly smaller than it could have been. Had there been no institutional restrictions deterring marriage and child-bearing aged rural women, parents of school-aged children, and children of elderly parents from migration, the proportion of rural workers who would choose to migrate might well be double its current level.

62.3 **Turning point?**

As the demand for unskilled labour increases in cities, and institutional restrictions to migration keep many rural workers from migrating, the Chinese are beginning to experience unskilled labour shortages and the wages of unskilled workers have begun to rise. Since 2004, many scholars have argued that China has reached the Lewisian turning point, whereby the rural surplus labour was absorbed and urban and rural unskilled wages began to rise.

The argument that China has reached the turning point is based on increases in the wages of unskilled migrant workers in the past decade and the belief that an oncoming period of rapid ageing will lead to a labour shortage. There is some evidence that rural wages are also increasing. Furthermore, it has also been argued that improvements in rural education will reduce the supply of unskilled workers (Zhao and Wu, 2007; Cai, 2010; Du and Wang, 2010; Zhang et al., 2011).

Not all scholars believe that the Lewisian turning point has arrived (Minami and Ma, 2010; Yao and Zhang, 2010; Knight et al. 2011; Golley and Meng, 2011; Ge and Yang, 2011). In particular, using household level data these studies provide evidence that the relative wages of unskilled to skilled workers in cities have been decreasing rather than increasing over the period 2000–09; only around 20–23 per cent of the rural *Hukou* labour force permanently moved out of their own county into urban cities. Those who migrated stayed in cities, on average, for only around seven years. Golley and Meng (2011) suggest that if institutional change can reduce the churning of migrants so that the average duration of migration is doubled, the supply of migrant workers in cities would be doubled. In fact, the RUMiCI survey asks migrants to state the length of time they would like to spend in cities if the policy allows them to choose. A figure of 63 per cent reply that they would choose to stay in the cities forever. In other words, government policy can do a great deal to ease the migrant supply 'shortage'.

62.4 **Future challenges**

As a result of the institutionally induced 'labour shortage', city firms are moving towards more capital- and technology-intensive technologies. Labour intensive investment has begun moving to other developing countries and new investments have much higher human capital requirements. Will China's future labour supply be well equipped for this important change?

To answer this question, one needs to know the primary source of the future labour force. The One-Child Policy (OCP) was strictly enforced for the urban *Hukou* population but not for the rural *Hukou* population. Consequently urban *Hukou* births shrank significantly after the OCP. The 2000 Population Census data indicate that for the population aged 20–29 (those who were born just before the OCP) the ratio of urban to rural *Hukou* population is 38 per cent, whereas for those who were aged 10–19 and 0–9 in 2000 the ratios reduced to 25 per cent and 23 per cent, respectively. The population pyramids in Figure 62.1 show that the future labour force will mainly come from the current rural *Hukou* population.

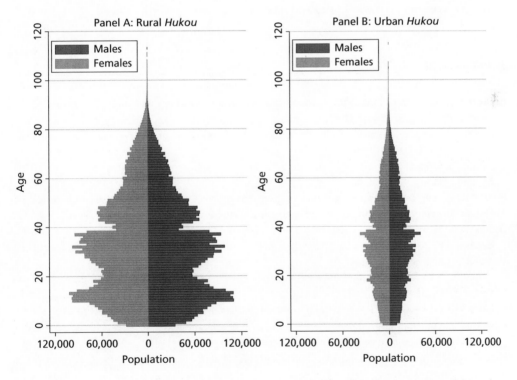

Figure 62.1. Population pyramids for rural and urban *Hukou* populations, 1 per cent of the 2000 Census data

Source: Extracted from Meng (2012).

How well is the rural *Hukou* population equipped for the future changes? The answer to this question is not very encouraging. In 2000, the rural *Hukou* population between 20 and 65 years of age had on average seven years of schooling while their urban *Hukou* counterparts had eleven years. Nineteen per cent of the urban *Hukou* population has education to a three years of college or above, while this ratio is 0.24 per cent in the rural population. Among the younger generation, for those born between 1970 and 1980, the ratio of urban *Hukou* population with a three-year college degree or above is 28 per cent while for rural population it is 0.54 per cent.

The significant rural–urban divide in education, together with the transition of Chinese industry towards a capital- and technology-intensive structure induced by institutional restrictions on migration, pose enormous challenges for China's future rural–urban migration and economic growth. If the institutional restrictions on migration cannot be dismantled quickly and rural education continues to lag behind, many rural workers will be confined to rural areas, the urbanization process will slow down, and rural underemployment and urban labour shortages will co-exist for a long time (Meng, 2012). Thus, an important challenge facing the Chinese government in the next few decades is to make policy changes so that the rural and urban populations are treated equally in all dimensions and to speed up the quantity and quality of education in rural areas.

■ REFERENCES

Bosworth, B. and S. M. Collins. 2008. Accounting for growth: comparing China and India. *Journal of Economic Perspectives* 22(1), 45–66.

Cai, F. 2010. Demographic transition, demographic dividend, and Lewis turning point in China. *China Economic Journal* 3(2), 107–19.

Du, Y. and M.Y. Wang. 2010. A discussion on potential bias and implications of Lewisian turning point. *China Economic Journal* 3(2), 121–36.

Frijters, P., T. Kong Tao, and X. Meng. 2011a. Migrant Entrepreneurs and Credit Constraints under Labour Market Discrimination. IZA Discussion Papers 5967, Institute for the Study of Labor (IZA).

Frijters, P., X. Meng, and B. Resosudarmo. 2011b. The effects of institutions on migrant wages in China and Indonesia. In *Rising China: Global Challenges and Opportunities*, edited by Golley Jane and Ligang Song, 245–84. Canberra: ANU ePress.

Ge, S. and D. T. Yang. 2011. Labour market developments in China: A neoclassical view, *China Economic Review* 22(4), 611–25.

Golley, J. and X. Meng. 2011. Has China run out of surplus labour? *China Economic Review* 22(4), 555–72.

Knight, John, Quheng Deng, and S. Li. 2011. The puzzle of migrant labour shortage and the rural labour surplus in China. *China Economic Review* 22(4), 585–600.

Meng, X. 2012. Impact of economic reform on labour market outcomes in China. *Journal of Economic Perspectives* 26(4), 75–102.

Meng, X. and J. Zhang. 2001. Two-tier labour markets in urban China: Occupational segregation and wage differentials between urban residents and rural migrants in Shanghai. *Journal of Comparative Economics* 29, 485–504.

Minami, Ryoshin and Xinxin Ma. 2010. The turning point of Chinese economy: compared with Japanese experience. *China Economic Journal* 3(2), 163–80.

National Bureau of Statistics. 2010. *China Statistics Yearbook*. Beijing: China Statistical Press.

World Bank. 2009. *From Poor Areas to Poor People: China's Evolving Poverty Reduction Agenda*. Washington, DC: World Bank

Yao, Y. and K. Zhang. 2010. Has China passed the Lewis turning point? a structural estimation based on provincial data. *China Economic Journal* 3(2), 155–62.

Zhang, X., J. Yang, and S. Wang. 2011. China has reached the Lewis Turning Point. *China Economic Review* 22(4), 542–54.

Zhao C. B. and Z. G. Wu. 2007. Special report: analysis of wages of rural–urban migrants. In *Green Book of Population and Labor (2007) Lewisian Turning Point and Its Policy Challenges*, edited by Cai Fang and Du Yang (in Chinese). Beijing: Social Science Academic Press (China).

63 The Lewis turning point

Is there a labour shortage in China?

Yang Yao

One of the driving forces behind China's phenomenal growth has been rural–urban migration. When China started economic reform in 1978, 71 per cent of the population was in the countryside. The rural reform allowed agriculture to absorb much of the rural labour force in the initial several years, but soon labour surplus became evident when marginal returns to labour diminished. Large-scale migration began to occur from the early 1990s; as a result, industrial development has enjoyed an almost unlimited supply of labour, that is, the labour supply curve has been kept almost flat at a constant wage rate.

However, the wage rate of migrant workers began to rise in the early 2000s, and from 2008 it has been increasing by double-digit rates. This has propelled some authors to question whether China has passed the Lewis turning point, that is, the point beyond which surplus labour is depleted and the industrial labour supply is no longer indefinite (Cai, 2010; Zhang et al., 2011). However, other scholars disagree. From example, Knight et al. (2011) fit the characteristics of a large sample of rural residents in a Probit model of migration and estimate that there were still 80 million potential migrants in the countryside in 2007. Yao and Zhang (2010) estimate a system of structural equations for the demand and supply of migrant workers based on provincial data. Their approach is to impose a flat portion to the supply curve to make it account for the Lewis turning point. It transpires that the demand curve has crossed the supply curve on the latter's flat portion up until 2007, the last year they have estimated, implying that the Lewis turning point had not arrived by that year.

The most cited reasons for China having passed the Lewis turning point are the following. The first is the rising wage rate paid to migrant workers. By Lewis' original formulation, the wage rate should stay constant if there is surplus labour in agriculture. Therefore, rising wage rates are a sign that an economy has depleted the surplus labour. The second reason is the depletion of young workers in the countryside. Both newspaper reports and more serious academic surveys have shown that the number of young people in the countryside has declined rapidly. Those left behind tend be women older than 40 years old and men who are even older. Their skills are regarded as inadequate for industrial employment. The third reason is the widespread cries of labour shortages in the coastal provinces. To attract workers, factories have to provide better dormitories and other living amenities in addition to offering higher salaries. In addition, labour shortages seem to have spread to some inland provinces. Local factories have begun to increase salaries to attract migrant workers who come home for the Spring Festival to stay and work there instead.

China passed the highest point of labour growth in 2010, and the size of its labour force will begin to decline by 2020. Therefore, there are reasons to believe that migrants' wages will continue to grow in the future. Nevertheless, more careful analysis is needed to find out whether the Lewis turning point has been passed. As the first step, it is worthwhile to revisit Lewis' concept of surplus labour and unlimited supply of labour.

In his original formulation, Lewis defines surplus labour as the labour whose marginal product is zero (Lewis, 1954). In the meantime, he assumes that there exists a subsistence wage that is paid based on surplus labour. However, he does not define how this subsistence wage is formulated in agriculture. One possibility is that the family pays it; another possibility is that the community as a whole pays it. The evidence for this kind of institutional arrangement, though, is scant, at least in today's China. In addition, this formulation has to face a conceptual problem. A labour surplus can only be found at the aggregate level; one cannot name who is surplus and who is not in any particular village. Therefore, Lewis' notion of surplus labour can only be made consistent if the subsistence wage is applied to everyone in the community, that is, if it is the average income in the community. However, this creates a further inconsistency between the notion of surplus labour and the unlimited supply of labour to industry. The latter is created because surplus labour is willing to work at the subsistence wage, which is assumed constant. However, the average income, and thus the subsistence wage, will increase as labour is being drawn out of agriculture, so that the labour supply curve is no longer flat.

Sen (1969) proposes a way out of this inconsistency. In the framework of family production, he assumes that farmers' real wage rate—that is, the marginal utility of their leisure time—is constant in a reasonable range of labour supply to agriculture. Under this assumption, a family will maintain the optimal total amount of working hours when a member moves out. The output of this family does not decline, and the person moving out is surplus labour. In the meantime, industrial labour supply is infinitely elastic at farmers' real wage rate.

As in Lewis' original formulation, the industrial wage rate must be constant under Sen's notion of an unlimited supply of labour. However, migrants' real wages have increased in the last twenty years in China—although the growth was modest before 2004 (Lu, 2011). This means that China's industrial labour supply has never been unlimited if one uses either Lewis' or Sen's formulation. This is apparently contradictory to conventional wisdom and inconsistent with the fact that there has been a large amount of labour in the countryside despite how quickly the share of agricultural output in GDP has declined.

One way to arrive at a notion of an unlimited supply of labour that is consistent with rising real industrial wages is to modify Sen's model by giving up the assumption that farmers' real wages are constant. Instead, we can assume that there is a convention on per-unit labour input—for example, fifty days in a year—that each farm household follows. The marginal utility of leisure is variable in a range so family members are willing to increase labour days when one of them is moved out. To be exact, let us assume that farm household i has a constant-return-to-scale production function $PAF(T_i, L_i)$, where P is the price of agricultural output, A is an index of technological efficiency, T_i is the amount of land, and L_i is working days. Using the property of constant returns to scale, the marginal product of labour hours can be written as $PAf'(l^*)$, where l^* is labour days per unit of land and $f(.)$ is the per-unit land production function. It is immediately clear that this wage rate will increase when agriculture receives positive shocks, such as technological progress and increase of agricultural prices, and so on, but it is independent of the amount of labour moving out as long as surplus labour exists. That is, wage growth alone cannot be taken as evidence for an economy to have passed the Lewis turning point. Realizing this, one may find two alternative explanations to the growth of migrant wages, both related to the growth of rural income.

One explanation is the central government's direct subsidies to farming and abolition of agricultural taxes. On average, each mu of land devoted to grain production receives 100 yuan of subsidy from the central government. This means that an average farm household can get an extra 700 yuan in cash income. In addition, it recaptures 300 to 400 yuan because of the abolition of agricultural taxes. Those two sources of income are not trivial for an average farm household because the average per-capita net income in the countryside was less than 6000 yuan as late as 2010.

The other explanation is related to the different rates of inflation in agricultural products and other products. In every period of inflation, agricultural prices grew first. In the most recent round of inflation since 2010, the growth of food prices accounted for two-thirds of the growth of the Consumer Price Index (CPI). Apparently, this unbalanced pattern of inflation benefited farmers and largely explained why rural income grew faster than urban income in 2010 and 2011. As a matter of fact, the growth of rural net income has been closely linked with the CPI. In particular, rural households' agricultural income did not grow during the period 1997–2003 when China experienced deflation; its meagre growth was entirely brought about by off-farm employment. In contrast, rural income began to grow by more than 8 per cent per annum since 2004 when the decline of CPI was reverted.

In addition to the above two alternative explanations for wage growth, the other two reasons cited for China's loss of surplus labour also need to be scrutinized carefully. It is true that most of the young people originating in the countryside have moved to the city, but the claim that older workers are not employable in the city seems to be unwarranted. They may not be suitable to work on the assembly line, but there is no reason why they cannot work in the service sector. For example, gated communities in the city hire many young people as security guards. There is almost no skill involved to become a security guard and a man in his late 40s or 50s can easily qualify. In the end, the hindrance to their mobility is the *Hukou* system. Older workers have families, but the *Hukou* system does not allow them to settle permanently in the city, so they opt to stay in their home villages.

The shortage of workers in coastal regions also needs to be qualified. A shortage is always relative. If wage rates are adjusted upwards swiftly, a shortage will be eased or even eliminated. In addition, one needs to pay attention to the structure of the labour shortage. There is a clear shortage of skilled workers, but the supply of unskilled workers is still relatively abundant. Lastly, demographic changes among the workers can be an important force to drive up the wage rate and thus the relative shortage of labour supply. Young workers born after 1990 are quickly becoming the bulk of the workforce. Their attitudes towards work and life are quite different from their parents. Compared with their parents, they are less likely to tolerate inferior working conditions, care less about current income, and tend to pay more attention to quality of life. These changes translate into demand for higher wages, better working and living conditions, and more humane treatment, all of which drive up the costs faced by employers.

The central government announced a new *Hukou* policy on 23 February 2012. According to this new policy, small cities at the county level or below are open to anyone who has a stable job and residency (including rental homes); medium-size cities are open to people who have worked and lived in the city for three consecutive years; and large cities maintain the current *Hukou* restriction. When it is implemented, this policy will provide a perfect experiment to test whether there is still a labour surplus in the countryside. If we see a large outflow of people into the cities, then we have to conclude that there is still a labour surplus in the countryside, and vice versa.

In any case, more serious studies are needed to determine whether there is still a labour surplus in rural China. As a first step, we need to come up with a new concept of surplus labour that is consistent with rising real wages as well as an unlimited supply of labour. Then we need to extend the study from the aggregate level to the household level.

■ **REFERENCES**

Cai, Fang. 2010. Demographic transition, demographic dividend, and Lewis turning point in China. *China Economic Journal* 3(2), 107–20.

Knight, John; Quheng Deng, and Shi Li. 2011. The puzzle of migrant labour shortage and the rural labour surplus in China. *China Economic Review* 22(4), 585–600.

Lewis, Arthur. 1954. Economic development with unlimited supplies of labour. *The Manchester School of Economic and Social Studies* 22(2), 139–91.

Lu, Feng. 2011. *A Report on China's Labor Shortage.* National School of Development, Peking University.

Sen, Amartya. 1969. Peasants and dualism with or without surplus labor. *Journal of Political Economy* 74(5), 425–50.

Yao, Yang and Ke Zhang. 2010. Has China passed the Lewis turning point? A structural estimation based on provincial data. *China Economic Journal* 3(2), 155–62.

Zhang, Xiaobo, Jin Yang, and Shenglin Wang. 2011. China has reached the Lewis turning point. *China Economic Review* 22(4), 542–54.

64 Labour and employment in China

Yaohui Zhao

64.1 Introduction

The dualistic nature of the Chinese economy has been widely noted. The urban sector, characterized by much higher incomes, formal employment with social security, and much better social services, is clearly superior to the rural sector. This division is sustained by the household registration system which has restricted mobility by depriving certain social services to non-native residents. The urban–rural divide is most evident in the area of labour and employment. Urban residents start working at an older age and retire earlier, while rural residents start working at younger ages and retire later. For the young cohorts, higher school enrolment rates among urban residents explain most of the delay in labour market entry. For the older cohorts, the differential treatments by retirement policies are likely to be the main explanation. Overall, in terms of labour supply, urban China behaves like a welfare society in Western Europe while rural China behaves like a low income developing country. Unemployment is also mainly an urban phenomenon.

64.2 Labour force participation

The labour force participation (LFP) rate is higher among rural residents at all ages, but the difference is higher at two ends. Urban youths start working at a much later age than their rural counterparts. According to the 2010 population census, the LFP rate of rural youths aged 16–19 was 43.2 per cent, while that of urban (defined as cities plus towns) youths was only 24.9 per cent (Table 64.1). At ages 20–24, the LFP rate among rural residents rose to 82.6 per cent, while that among urban residents rose to 64.4 per cent.

The large difference in LFP between urban and rural youths mainly reflects different school attendance rates between urban and rural residents. Schooling enrolment rate among rural youths aged 16–19 was 52.6 per cent, and that among urban youths was 72.3 per cent. At ages 20–24, the gap becomes larger: 10.0 per cent for rural and 27.8 per cent

Table 64.1 Labour force participation rates, China 2010

				Men		Women	
	All	Rural	Urban	Rural	Urban	Rural	Urban
All ages	71.0	77.8	64.3	83.4	73.1	72.2	55.5
16–19	33.5	43.2	24.9	44.9	25.7	41.4	24.0
20–24	72.8	82.6	64.6	86.6	67.7	78.6	61.5
25–29	88.9	91.6	86.8	97.2	94.7	85.9	79.2
30–34	90.2	93.3	87.8	97.9	96.4	88.6	79.2
35–39	90.7	94.2	87.8	97.9	96.1	90.5	79.3
40–44	90.7	94.3	87.1	97.8	95.2	90.8	78.8
45–49	87.7	93.0	82.2	97.3	93.0	88.7	71.0
50–54	76.3	89.2	62.6	95.5	83.7	82.7	41.0
55–59	67.1	84.1	46.3	91.9	65.8	76.0	27.2
60–64	49.5	68.7	24.3	77.8	31.8	59.2	16.9
65–69	36.3	51.5	15.5	61.5	20.9	40.9	10.3
70–74	19.7	29.2	7.3	37.1	10.2	21.2	4.7
75 +	8.2	11.9	3.0	16.7	4.2	8.2	2.1

Source: Calculated from 2010 census tabulations.

for urban people (Table 64.2). It is also interesting to see that the large gender difference in education observed in older Chinese has virtually disappeared among young cohorts—men aged 20–24 only have a slightly higher enrolment rate than women while the reverse is true of the age cohort of 16–19 year olds.

Schooling is not the only explanation for non-participation in the labour force among young adults. Housework becomes an important source of non-participation, especially for women. Take the 20–24 year olds for example, among urban residents, housework accounts for 14.8 per cent of non-participation among women, only 0.5 per cent among men, and among rural residents it accounts for 37.2 per cent of non-participation among women, only 2.6 per cent among men. Notice that housework is twice as important in explaining female non-participation in rural as in urban areas. The difference is likely to be due to earlier marriage among rural women. In 2010, 41.2 per cent rural female aged 20–24 are married, in comparison to 24.7 per cent in urban areas (Table 64.2).

At ages 25–29 the urban–rural gap in LFP narrows to the lowest point—91.6 per cent for rural residents and 86.8 per cent for rural residents (Table 64.1). The peak of LFP is reached at 40–44 for rural residents and 35–39 for urban residents for both men and women. After this point, the urban–rural patterns start to diverge. Withdrawal from the labour force occurs most rapidly among urban women, who show a sharp decline in participation by 7.8 percentage points to 71 per cent between ages 40–44 and 45–49, then

Table 64.2 Selected statistics of 16–19 and 20–24 year olds

	Labour force participation rate	School enrolment rate	Share of housework of non-participation	Marriage rate
Ages 20–24				
Urban	64.6	27.8	8.6	18.8
Male	67.7	28.4	0.5	12.9
Female	61.5	27.2	14.8	24.7
Rural	82.6	10.0	24.1	32.1
Male	86.6	10.5	2.6	22.8
Female	78.6	9.6	37.2	41.2
Ages 16–19				
Urban	24.9	72.3	0.5	3.4
Male	25.7	71.5	0.2	1.6
Female	24.0	73.2	0.9	4.3
Rural	43.2	52.6	2.1	9.6
Male	44.9	51.6	0.7	5.3
Female	41.4	53.8	3.6	15.3

Source: Calculated from 2010 census tabulations.

by another large (30 percentage points) decline to 41 per cent at 50–54. The trajectory of retirement by urban men traces that of urban women by five years, showing a decline of 9.3 percentage points in LFP between ages 45–49 and 50–54 to 83.7 per cent, and 17.8 percentage points to 65.8 per cent at ages 55–59, then a dramatic 34 percentage point reduction to 31.8 per cent at ages 60–64. At the same time, the LFP among rural workers has declined very gradually. At ages 65–69, 61.5 per cent of rural men and 40.9 per cent of rural women are still working, compared to merely 20.9 per cent of urban men and 10.3 per cent of urban women. It is thus evident that the urban–rural difference in employment is most extreme for the elderly population.

Summing up LFP rates for all years up to age 74 (ignoring work for those aged 75 and older), we derive the length of working life for an average person—45.6 years for a rural resident and 33.6 years for an urban resident. This means that a rural resident works 11.7 years more years than an urban resident. The gap is larger among women—a rural woman works for 13.5 more years than her urban counterpart, and a rural man works 10.2 more years than his urban counterpart.

It is worth noting that the shorter working lives of urban people is not due to inferior health status—in general, urban residents are healthier than their rural counterparts in almost all aspects of health, be it physical or mental (Lei et al., forthcoming). The large difference between urban and rural LFP is also not compensated by shorter working hours among rural people (Giles et al., 2012).

64.3 **Retirement policy in urban and rural areas**

Perhaps the largest institutional divide between urban and rural employment is that until very recently government-sponsored social security was available to urban workers only. The urban social insurance system was established in the 1950s to provide social security to urban workers, while agricultural workers were left to fend themselves. In the collectivization era, rural social security (healthcare and elderly support) was provided by the collectives (usually administrative villages comprised by several natural villages) but this layer of protection fell through with agricultural de-collectivization in the early 1980s. In the decade of the 1990s the government tried to implement a mainly contributory rural pension scheme but it was very insignificant and soon abandoned. Rural health insurance made some headway after 2003 by the New Rural Cooperative Health Insurance Scheme. It has now reached nearly universal coverage but the level of protection is much lower than that in urban areas.

In urban areas, mandatory retirement ages are low: men retire at age 60, female workers retire at age 50, and female cadres 55. These extremely young retirement ages were set in the 1950s and have not changed despite the fact the life expectancy has increased by more than twenty years. Given the rapid ageing of the Chinese population, this will be unsustainable.[1] Moreover, even these extremely young retirement ages are not rigorously enforced. As has been revealed by the China Health and Retirement Longitudinal Study, a substantial number of workers were allowed to retire and draw a pension well ahead of the official retirement ages (Giles et al., 2012).

The huge gap in social protection between urban and rural residents is probably the most significant factor contributing to the large difference in urban–rural labour force participation rates among the elderly. Future policy reform should encourage urban workers to stay in the labour force longer and give the rural elderly the freedom to retire.

Starting in late 2009, the government started to institute a New Rural Pension Programme. Because the government subsidizes participation by immediately paying a pension to those aged 60 and older and subsidizes premiums for those under 60, the coverage has expanded rapidly. The programme is expected to cover all counties by the end of 2012.

Nevertheless, like the New Rural Health Insurance Scheme, the level of protection afforded to the NRPS is minimal in comparison to those schemes in urban workers.[2] The true effect of these schemes on retirement is yet to be assessed.

---

[1] The share of the Chinese population aged 65 + is projected to rise to 25.6 per cent in 2050, up from 7.0 per cent in 2000 (United Nations, 2010).

[2] According to the China Health and Longitudinal Study, a representative sample of Chinese residents aged 45 and older, conditional on positive pension income, the median amount of pension among rural people was 720 yuan per year while that of urban workers was 18,000 yuan per year (CHARLS Research Team, 2013).

64.4 **Unemployment**

The 2010 population census allows for the calculation of unemployment rates according to internationally acceptable standards. The long-form survey first asks about work status during one week prior to the census ('Did you work for pay for at least one hour during October 25 and 31, 2010', with answers being (1) yes, (2) no but was in vacation, training, or temporary or seasonal work stoppage, and (3) no.) Those who answered (3) were further prompted by the question whether he/she looked for work during the past three months and whether he/she could start working within two weeks if offered a job.

Tabulations from the 2010 census show that the overall unemployment rate was 2.9 per cent, with urban areas being higher at 4.8 per cent and rural areas 1.2 per cent (Table 64.3). As is the case in other countries, young people report the highest rates of unemployment, which reflects greater difficulties in job matching in the earlier stage of careers, as well as higher reservation wages due to the availability of parental support. Note also that even among young people, the unemployment rate is significantly higher among urban than rural residents—64.4 per cent higher among 16–19 year olds and 157 per cent higher among 20–24 year olds. Interestingly, as rural workers grow older, the unemployment rate falls drastically to below 1 per cent after the age of 30, but the unemployment rate falls

Table 64.3 Unemployment rates, China 2010

	All			Men		Women	
		Rural	Urban	Rural	Urban	Rural	Urban
All ages	2.9	1.2	4.8	1.1	4.3	1.3	5.5
16–19	7.6	6.0	9.9	6.0	10.7	6.0	9.0
20–24	6.1	3.4	8.8	3.1	8.6	3.8	9.1
25–29	3.6	1.7	5.1	1.4	4.5	2.0	5.9
30–34	2.6	1.0	3.8	0.8	3.1	1.2	4.8
35–39	2.4	0.7	3.9	0.6	3.1	0.9	4.9
40–44	2.2	0.6	3.9	0.5	3.2	0.7	4.8
45–49	2.3	0.6	4.3	0.5	3.8	0.6	5.1
50–54	1.9	0.5	4.1	0.5	4.4	0.5	3.6
55–59	1.4	0.4	3.6	0.4	3.9	0.4	2.9
60–64	0.8	0.3	2.3	0.3	2.3	0.4	2.3
65–69	0.7	0.4	2.0	0.3	1.9	0.4	2.3
70–74	0.7	0.4	2.2	0.3	1.8	0.6	3.0
75 +	1.2	0.7	3.6	0.6	2.9	1.0	4.9

Source: Calculated from 2010 census tabulations.

very slowly among urban workers and hovers around 4 per cent even for people in their forties. This causes the ratio of the unemployment rate of urban to rural workers to continue to rise with age, reaching 8.8 for the group aged 55–59.

What causes the large gap in the unemployment rate between urban and rural workers? One possible explanation is that unemployment insurance is more widely available in urban areas; farmers do not qualify for employment-based social insurance with unemployment insurance being one of its components. But this is unlikely to be the main reason because unemployment insurance only applies to involuntary unemployment and involves substantial administrative red tape in the application process. It has been reported that unemployment funds have accumulated extremely large surpluses due to insufficient payouts. The most plausible explanation is the higher reservation wage afforded by higher family income and assets in urban households.

■ **REFERENCES**

CHARLS Research Team. 2013. *Challenge of Population Aging in China: Evidence from the National Baseline Survey of the China Health and Retirement Longitudinal Study (CHARLS)* <http://charls.ccer.edu.cn/uploads/document/public_documents/application/Challenges-of-Population-Aging-in-China-final.pdf>.

Giles, John, Xiaoyan Lei, Yafeng Wang, and Yaohui Zhao. 2012. Retirement Patterns in China. Working Paper, Peking University

Lei, Xiaoyan, Xiaoting Sun, John Strauss, Yaohui Zhao, Gonghuan Yang, Perry Hu, Yisong Hu, and Xiangjun Yin. forthcoming. Health outcomes and socio-economic status among the mid-aged and elderly in China: Evidence from the CHARLS National Baseline Data. *The Journal of the Economics of Ageing.*

United Nations. 2010. *World Population Prospects: The 2010 Revision*, Population Division of the Department of Economic and Social Affairs of the United Nations Secretariat. <http://esa.un.org/unpd/wpp/index.htm>.

Part XI
Dimensions of Well-being and Inequality

65 China's well-being since 1990

Richard A. Easterlin

What has happened to the well-being of the Chinese people in the transition from socialism to capitalism? If economic growth is taken as the criterion of well-being, then the answer must be unprecedented improvement. In the two decades since 1990 gross domestic product (GDP) per capita—the standard measure of economic growth—has doubled and then redoubled in real terms (that is, adjusted for changes in the level of prices)—the most rapid recorded economic growth in history.

Given this remarkable multiplication of real incomes in only two decades from an initially very low level, one might have expected many in China's population to be virtually dancing in the streets. Yet a recent scholarly assessment concludes that the 'Chinese people are deeply insecure about themselves and their future . . .' (Lemos, 2012: 3).

This seeming contradiction between the conclusion of a contemporary observer and the evidence on economic growth is largely explained by the fact that GDP per capita captures only one facet of people's lives—their material living level. Although living conditions are important for well-being, so too are numerous other concerns such as job security, family circumstances, and healthcare, all of which have been significantly and adversely affected by the transition. These other dimensions of well-being, along with material living conditions, are captured in the newly developed and more comprehensive measures of *subjective* well-being (SWB). The SWB measures ask respondents about their feelings of happiness or overall satisfaction with life, typically on a numerical response scale, for example 0 to 10. They have been subjected to intensive methodological scrutiny and have been validated as meaningful and comparable over time and among countries. Hence, data on SWB are used here to present a more comprehensive picture of the Chinese peoples' well-being in the course of the transition.

An attempt has been made to assemble and analyse all of the time series surveys of China's SWB during this period. Most of these surveys are disproportionally urban. But economic growth since 1990 has also been disproportionally urban, with urban incomes rising markedly relative to rural. Thus, while the life satisfaction data have an urban bias, so too does economic growth. In all of the surveys but one, data for the total population, rather than urban, are analysed, chiefly to maximize sample size in a country as vast as China. (For details on surveys, methods, and supporting material, see Easterlin et al., 2012.)

65.1 **Longer-term movement**

Taken together the surveys indicate that life satisfaction in China declined from 1990 to around 2000–05 and then turned upward, forming, for the period as a whole, a U-shaped pattern (Figure 65.1). Although a precise comparison over the full period is not possible, there appears to be no increase and perhaps some overall reduction in life satisfaction. A downward tilt along with the U-shape is evident in the two series with the longest time span, the World Values (WVS) and Horizon Surveys.

It is noteworthy that there is no evidence of a substantial uptrend in life satisfaction of the magnitude one might have expected due to the four-fold increase in GDP per capita. In the happiness literature the point-of-time (cross-section) relationship of happiness to GDP per capita is often used to infer the likely life satisfaction trend as GDP per capita increases over time. Based on the international cross-section relationship between life satisfaction and GDP per capita in the 1990 WVS data, one would have expected that from 1990 to 2012 life satisfaction in China would have increased by at least six-tenths of a point (on a 1 to 10 scale) due to the four-fold increase in GDP per capita. There is no indication of such a sizeable full-period increase in Figure 65.1.

One may reasonably ask how it is possible for life satisfaction not to improve in the face of the marked increase in material living conditions from a very low initial level. The

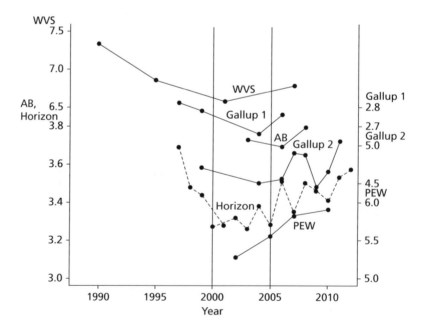

Figure 65.1. Mean life satisfaction, six series, 1990–2012

Source: Easterlin et al. (2012). The data are for the total population, except for the Horizon series (urban).

answer is, in part, that other factors have adversely affected life satisfaction. In addition, there is growing evidence of the importance of relative income comparisons and rising material aspirations in China that tend to negate the effect of rising incomes. This evidence is consistent with the view common in the happiness literature that the growth in aspirations induced by rising income undercuts the increase in life satisfaction due to rising income itself.

Recognition of the U-shape of China's changing life satisfaction explains the mixed results of previous studies of China's trend in SWB. Those who have claimed that the trend is downward analysed series that fell in the early, declining segment of the U (Kahneman and Krueger, 2006; Brockmann et al., 2009). Those finding a pattern of constancy examined series that straddled the 2000–05 trough (Burkholder, 2005; Crabtree and Wu, 2011; Knight and Gunatilaka, 2011). An uptrend finding resulted from a starting survey date falling in the 2000–05 trough (PEW Research Center, 2011).

China's long-term movement of life satisfaction is like that of the European transition countries, in that life satisfaction declines early in the transition and then recovers. China's initial decline in life satisfaction, 0.76 points (on a 1 to 10 scale) from 1990 to the 2001 trough WVS observation, is of the same order of magnitude but a little less than the average (0.91) of the six European transition countries for which similar peak to trough calculations can be made (the former GDR, Estonia, Latvia, Lithuania, Belarus, and Russia). Such sizeable declines in life satisfaction are quite rare.

65.2 **Socioeconomic differentials**

China has moved from one of the most egalitarian countries in life satisfaction to one of the least. The beneficiaries of the transition have been the higher income and better-educated segments of the population whose life satisfaction has increased. The lower segments of the distribution have experienced a substantial decline in life satisfaction. China's trend in the socioeconomic differential in life satisfaction is typical of transition countries generally and in terms of magnitude closely parallels the trend in Russia since the onset of its transition.

65.3 **Causes**

The factors chiefly responsible for China's life satisfaction trends are the developments in unemployment and the social safety net. The U-shaped pattern of life satisfaction largely mirrors an inverted U in the urban unemployment rate. The unemployment rate rose markedly in the 1990s, peaked in the 2000–05 period, and then declined somewhat, though remaining above its initially very low level.

The causality suggested by the inverse swings in life satisfaction and the unemployment rate is consistent with the common finding in the happiness literature that unemployment reduces life satisfaction. Moreover, life satisfaction is reduced not only for those who become unemployed but for employed persons as well, presumably due to the anxiety created by a worsening labour market.

The movement of China's unemployment rate is partly due to the state of the world economy. There was a significant slowdown in world economic growth at the start of the millennium, and countries substantially dependent on exports, such as China, felt the impact of declining foreign demand.

More importantly, however, the movement in China's unemployment rate is a result of government policy, and symptomatic of the deterioration in the social safety net that had prevailed under socialism. China's urban labour market prior to reform has been characterized as an 'iron rice bowl' and 'mini welfare state'. Workers in state-owned enterprises (SOEs), the firms that accounted for the bulk of urban employment, had permanent jobs and an extensive employer-provided social safety net. From an economic point of view, this system was highly inefficient and lacked incentives, but it ensured that urban workers had income security, and it was highly egalitarian.

In 1994, in the face of the continuing inefficiency and unprofitability of SOEs, the government initiated a restructuring programme that shortly evolved into what has been called 'a draconian policy of labor shedding' (Knight and Song, 2005: 22). The resulting rise in unemployment, although cushioned somewhat by an urban layoff programme that provided some temporary safety net benefits, was aggravated by a rising rural to urban labour movement as policies restricting internal migration were gradually relaxed. Along with a sharp rise in unemployment, SOE restructuring also meant the end of the 'iron rice bowl' of guaranteed life-time employment and benefits for urban workers.

Beginning around 2004, the rate at which SOEs were downsized diminished sharply. Between 1995 and 2003, reduced employment in SOEs far exceeded increased employment elsewhere in the urban sector; thereafter the situation was reversed and the unemployment rate declined modestly.

China's labour market developments are similar to those of the European transition countries—the emergence of substantial unemployment and the dissolution of the social safety net, developments that most severely affected the lower socioeconomic stratum of the population. Unlike Europe, however, average real wages in China rose markedly in the course of the transition, along with the very high rate of GDP growth. As in Europe, however, life satisfaction in China was dominated by employment and safety net circumstances.

65.4 **Summary**

Despite an unprecedented rate of economic growth, China's life satisfaction in the last two decades has largely followed the trajectory of the Central and Eastern European transition countries—a decline followed by a recovery, with a nil or declining trend over the period as a whole. There is no evidence of a marked increase in life satisfaction in China of the magnitude that might have been expected due to the enormous four-fold improvement in the level of GDP per capita. In its transition, China has shifted from one of the most egalitarian countries in the distribution of life satisfaction to one of the least. Life satisfaction has declined markedly among the lowest income and least educated segments of the population, while rising somewhat among the upper socioeconomic stratum.

The factors shaping China's life satisfaction are essentially the same as in the European transition countries—the emergence and rise of substantial unemployment and the dissolution of the social safety net. The fact that China's life satisfaction failed to increase despite its differing output experience—a rapid increase versus the collapse and recovery of output in the European countries—demonstrates that employment and the social safety net are of critical importance in determining people's feelings of well-being.

■ REFERENCES

Brockmann, H., J. Delhey, C. Welzel, and H. Yuan 2009. The China puzzle: falling happiness in a rising economy. *Journal of Happiness Studies* 10, 387–405.

Burkholder, R. 2005. *Chinese Far Wealthier Than a Decade Ago—but Are They Happier*. The Gallup Organization. Available at: < http://www.gallup.com/poll/14548/Chinese-Far-Wealthier-Than-Decade-Ago-They-Happier.aspx>, accessed 6 May 2014.

Crabtree, S. and T. Wu, 2011. China's Puzzling Flat Line. *Gallup Management Journal*. Available at: <http://gmj.gallup.com/content/148853/china-puzzling-flat-line.aspx#1>, accessed 1 February 2012.

Easterlin, R. A., R. Morgan, M. Switek, and F. Wang 2012. China's life satisfaction 1990–2010. *Proceedings of the National Academy of Science* 109(25), 9775–80.

Kahneman, D. and A. B. Krueger 2006. Developments in the measurement of subjective well-being. *Journal of Economic Perspectives* 20, 3–24.

Knight, J. and R. Gunatilaka 2011. Does Economic growth raise happiness in China? *Oxford Development Studies* 39(1), 1–24.

Knight, J. and L. Song. 2005. *Towards a Labour Market in China*. New York: Oxford University Press.

Lemos, G. 2012. *The End of the Chinese Dream, Why the Chinese People Fear the Future*. New Haven, CT: Yale University Press.

PEW Research Center 2011. Available from the 2011 Global Attitudes Project by the PEW Research Center <http://www.pewglobal.org/category/datasets/>.

66 Relative deprivation in China

Xi Chen

Relative deprivation (RD), also known as relative poverty,[1] an idea implicitly put forward by Adam Smith in *The Wealth of Nations* and formally conceptualized by Runciman (1966), refers to the discontent people feel when they compare their positions to others and realize that others in the group possess something that they do not have. RD is important to Chinese people as reflected in the traditional saying '*it is better to be the head of a chicken than the tail of a phoenix*', indicating that taking a relatively good position benefits people in Chinese society. RD is also a pressing issue for China after its three decades of unprecedented economic growth accompanied by inequalities at historically high levels. This chapter reviews key measures of RD and empirical findings for China. I also discuss some of the most pressing policy issues with regard to RD.

Reference group is crucial to RD measures. Reference groups can be defined quite differently in specific contexts. In a developed society, information flow is fast and efficient, such that reference groups are not straightforward. However, in an impoverished traditional community, poor public infrastructure drags resource flow, and the evolution of local norms strengthens reciprocity. These differences facilitate a much improved definition of reference group. Substantial ethnographic evidence documents social interactions more appropriate at the village level in less-developed rural communities. Mangyo and Park (2011) suggest that village reference groups are salient for residents living in close proximity in rural China, while relatives and classmates are salient reference groups for urban residents. Knight et al. (2009) find that two-thirds of rural respondents reported their own village as the main comparison group, whereas very few stated that their main comparison group is outside the village.

RD has been measured along various socioeconomic distributions, including general consumption, status goods consumption, income, other perceived economic welfare and financial status relative to peer group members.

Studies first attempt to measure RD at the community level. Some studies identify the effect of relative income by community average income. Carlsson and Qin (2010) conduct

---

[1] In contrast to absolute deprivation (or absolute poverty) that applies to all underprivileged people, relative deprivation comes from a comparison to the reference group. While economic growth may be accompanied by massive absolute poverty reduction, relative deprivation may not change as long as inequality persists.

a survey-based experiment to elicit people's preferences regarding relative standing. They find that poor Chinese farmers care about relative status to a high degree comparable to previous studies in developed countries. Mangyo and Park (2011) verify the negative impact of RD status on self-reported health and psychosocial health.

Meanwhile, the community Gini coefficient is often used since it can be derived from aggregation of RD. Li and Zhu (2006) find a significant inverted-U association between the Gini coefficient and self-reported health. Meanwhile, the Gini coefficient increases health-compromising behaviour such as smoking and alcohol consumption. The Gini coefficient does not explain any of the health outcomes and health behaviour investigated except high waist circumference among older adults (Ling, 2009). However, community inequality measures mask individual RD and mix the impact of inequality with that of RD by implicitly assuming even the richest people suffer from RD. Jin et al. (2011) investigate differential RD impacts between the rich and the poor.

Higher order community RD measures, such as skewness and kurtosis statistics, are also used. Both are good measures of local density in tails of income distribution. Brown et al. (2011) document that the relatively deprived rural households increase spending on funerals and gifts as competition for status intensifies. Moreover, lower ranked families of grooms (but not brides) increase spending on wedding ceremonies as local income competition intensifies.

Individual level measures gauge RD via the differences between own income and the incomes of the richer members of the group. One would feel more deprived as the number of individuals in society with higher incomes increases. To begin with, the RD of Absolute Income (RDA) sums the income differences and weighs with the number of people in a reference group. One concern is that it does not normalize for income scale across groups. Doubling everyone's income automatically doubles RD. Therefore, RDA overstates the RD of individuals in high-income reference groups. To improve on this, RD over Individual Income (RDI) divides RDA by the individual's own income. Using both RDA and RDI measures, Li and Zhu (2006) find an insignificant impact of RD on self-reported health status. Moreover, Wildman (2003) proposes a measure of individual-specific RD based on the Lorenz curve that incorporates the cumulative proportion of total income and population up to the individual. Ling (2009) finds that among older adults this measure imposes different effects on health behaviour and outcomes, and those less relatively deprived are not necessarily healthier than those more relatively deprived.

Deaton (2001) proposes a measure of RD to integrate the model of mortality and income with the animal and human evidence on inequality and health. The Deaton RD measure takes normalized differences between the average income of those with higher income and this individual's income weighted by the proportion of those with income higher than the individual. Stark and Yitzhaki (1988) develop an RD measure to explain distinctive migration patterns for the rich and poor. While the two measures are similar in form, the Deaton RD measure is further divided by average community income to normalize the RD index.

Four immediate advantages of the Deaton measure follow. First, a large amount of scientific evidence, in public health, psychology, animal science, economics, and so on, lays its foundation. Second, it normalizes for scale to avoid overestimating RD in high-income groups. Third, relative to some other RD indexes, it is more sensitive to income distribution. Fourth, it is bounded between 0 and 1, which facilitates interpreting the magnitude of empirical findings.

Ling (2009) concludes that higher Deaton RD lowers the odds of high waist circumference, increases nutritional intake, reduces the probability of being overweight, and raises the probability of ever smoking. However, the probability of being underweight, hypertension, and current smoking behaviour are not much affected. Chen et al. (2012) utilize gift books kept by rural households to document that the relatively deprived households spend much higher budgets on gifts and festivals, and status seeking accounts for much of the recent escalating household social spending. On average, these scarce resources are barely enough to cover wasteful status games, such as costly weddings and funerals. In consequence, children born to mothers in more relatively deprived households are more likely to suffer from malnutrition indicated by low height-for-age z-score and high stunting rate (Chen and Zhang, 2012).

Most *individual* level RD measures presume that the distance between two agents matters, either in proportional or absolute terms. However, studies on animals suggest rank over distance in terms of importance. Unlike most of the other measures, rank is unaffected by changes in the shape of the income distribution and ignores the magnitude of income differences among individuals. A higher rank corresponds to a lower RD. Li and Zhu (2006) and Sun and Wang (2012) utilize an individual's rank within the reference group. Li and Zhu (2006) find no rank-specific harmful effect of income inequality on health, though lower rank corresponds to worsened health outcomes. Sun and Wang (2013) find a negative relationship between income rank in the community and its consumption rate, and the impact on total consumption is mainly reflected in expenditure on housing, education, clothing, and eating out.

RD studies in China concentrate on three aspects—saving and consumption, health, and happiness. I relate the empirical findings to policy discourse and then discuss RD's implication for poverty alleviation and more general development policies.

Regarding saving and consumption, non-positional and positional consumption are distinguished. People signal wealth and educational attainment to improving social status that ties to large benefits in China. Worsening inequality raises the benefits and entry costs for high status and strengthens saving incentives to increase positional consumption, typically on housing, and reduces non-positional consumption, and cuts non-positional consumption, especially for poorer groups (Jin et al., 2011). Future research is expected to investigate the potential macro-economic impacts of RD status, such as high saving rates, low consumption, and escalating housing prices in China.

High RD raises the importance of social inclusion, which incurs high expenditure among the poor. There is a large literature documenting high spending on gifts and festivals among the poor that serve as essential social roles, and the consequences of refusing to participate are grave. Evidence from China has shown that the poor could spend more on basic food instead of festivals but failed to do so. The studies on RD and social inclusion shed light on why the nutritional status of the poor is stagnant amid rapid growth in developing countries (Chen and Zhang, 2012).

Most studies on RD and health point to its negative consequences. These findings indicate the unintended impacts of economic policies in stimulating growth disparities to affect individual health and health inequality. The issue is further complicated by findings from older adults (Ling, 2009) that being less deprived may not guarantee better health and neither do those who are more deprived have worse health. More research is needed to examine absolute and relative income effects on health inequalities along major health behaviour and outcomes.

Studies on RD and happiness attempt to account for the Easterlin Paradox: average happiness has remained constant over time despite sharp rises in income but, at the same time, positive correlations are found between individual income and subjective well-being. The two trends puzzle policy makers, and China studies confirm the important role played by RD (Knight et al., 2009; Mangyo and Park, 2011). To reconcile the two seemingly contradictory trends, we should know how RD works. RD may arise due to positional goods that give utility when most other people do not have them or aspirations formed by relative comparisons that affect utility. The former is evaluated relative to others (social comparison), while the latter is evaluated relative to oneself in the past (habituation) as well as to others (social comparison).

The strong evidence of RD in developing countries would point to an important trade-off for current development policies and therefore cast serious doubt on welfare justifications. Considering the case where relative income imposes a counteracting impact (equal to the positive effect of own income) on well-being, an equal proportionate increase in all incomes would have no impact on average well-being. In this case, promoting poverty reduction without considering their income gains on social comparators would entail welfare efficiency costs, as poor people face inefficiently high incentives to escape poverty without taking account of their negative spillover effect.

Finally, the idea of RD can be generalized to analyse social competition in other aspects. For example, owning a house was not a prerequisite to getting married twenty years ago. However, a skewed sex ratio favouring girls due to the combination of son preference and implementation of the One Child Policy has totally changed the landscape in the last decade. At present, families with a son, especially those without a house, are relatively deprived in the marriage market, which bears long-term impacts that are worth further investigation.

■ REFERENCES

Brown, P., E. Bulte, and X. Zhang. 2011. Positional spending and status seeking in rural China. *Journal of Development Economics* 96(1), 139–49.

Carlsson, F. and P. Qin. 2010. It is better to be the head of a chicken than the tail of a phoenix: Concern for relative standing in rural China. *The Journal of Socio-Economics* 39(2), 180–6.

Chen, X. and X. Zhang. 2012. Costly posturing: relative status, ceremonies and early child development in China. World Institute for Development Economic Research (UNU-WIDER) Research Working Paper No. 2012/70.

Chen, X., R. Kanbur, and X. Zhang. 2012. Peer effects, risk pooling, and status seeking: what explains gift spending escalation in rural China? CEPR Discussion Papers 8777.

Deaton, A. 2001. Relative deprivation, inequality, and mortality. NBER Working Paper 8099.

Jin, Y., H. Li, and B.Wu. 2011. Income inequality, consumption, and social-status seeking. *Journal of Comparative Economics* 39(2), 191–204.

Knight, J., L. Song, and R. Gunatilaka. 2009. Subjective well-being and its determinants in rural China. *China Economic Review* 20(4), 635–49.

Li, H. and Y. Zhu. 2006. Income, income inequality, and health: Evidence from China. *Journal of Comparative Economics* 34(4), 668–93.

Ling, D. 2009. Do the Chinese 'keep up with the Joneses'? implications of growing economic disparities and relative deprivation on health outcomes among older adults in China. *China Economic Review* 20(1), 65–81.

Mangyo, E. and A. Park. 2011. Relative deprivation and health: Which reference groups matter? *Journal of Human Resources* 46(3), 459–81.

Runciman, W. G. 1966. *Relative Deprivation and Social Justice*. London: Routledge and Kegan Paul.

Stark, O. and S. Yitzhaki. 1988. Labor migration as a response to relative deprivation. *Journal of Population Economics* 1(1), 57–70.

Sun, W. and X. Wang. 2013. Do relative income and income inequality affect consumption? Evidence from the villages of rural China. *Journal of Development Studies* 49(4) 533–46.

Wildman, J. 2003. Income related inequalities in mental health in Great Britain: analyzing the causes of health inequality over time. *Journal of Health Economics* 22, 295–312.

67 Poverty

Albert Park and Sangui Wang

67.1 China's record on poverty

Since the start of its economic reforms, China has successfully lifted hundreds of millions of its citizens out of poverty, an achievement of historical and global importance. Using the World Bank's preferred $1.25/day consumption poverty line, as seen in Figure 67.1 China reduced the number of people living in poverty from 835.1 million (84.0 per cent) to 173.0 million (13.1 per cent) during the period 1981–2008 (World Bank, 2012). During this same period of time, poverty in the rest of the world actually increased by 13.2 million even as the poverty rate fell from 40.5 per cent to 25.2 per cent. Without China, the world fell well short of the pace required to meet the Millennium Development goal to halve the 1990 poverty rate by 2015. With China, the world is on track to meet this objective (Chen and Ravallion, 2010).

The dramatic reduction of poverty in China is robust to using different poverty lines and poverty measures (World Bank, 2009; Chen and Ravallion, 2010). The Chinese government uses poverty criteria that incorporate both consumption and income data. For many years, China adopted a poverty line well below the World Bank's $1.25/day line (World Bank, 2001, 2009). Using this austere poverty line, China's official poverty count still fell dramatically from 250 million in 1978 to 14.8 million in 2007 (Figure 67.2). In 2000, the government established a higher 'low income' line very near to $1/day in order to identify additional near-poor populations to be targeted by policy; in that year 94.2 million people fell below the low income line compared to 32.1 million people who were below the official poverty line. In 2008 the low income line was adopted as the official poverty line. In 2011, the Chinese government nearly doubled the poverty line again to reach $1.8/day, which raised China's official poverty headcount to 122.4 million in 2011 from 26.9 million in 2010 (Figure 67.2). Thus, China has raised it poverty threshold twice to reflect rising incomes and aspirations.

67.2 Sources of poverty reduction

What factors contributed to China's remarkable record of poverty reduction? Although the Chinese government has invested significant resources in combating poverty through

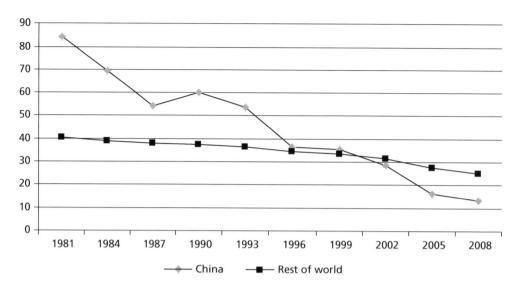

Figure 67.1. Poverty headcount rate (%) in China and the rest of the world, 1981–2008

Note: Based on consumption being below $1.25 a day based on 2005 PPP.

Source: World Bank (2012).

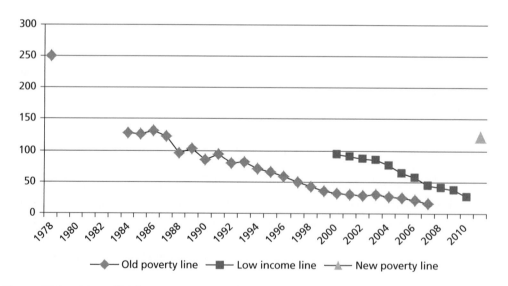

Figure 67.2. China official poverty count (millions), 1978–2011

Source: Leading Group Office for Poverty Alleviation and Development (LGOPAD).

a variety of targeted programmes, rapid economic growth and reforms that produced broad-based increases in rural incomes can explain most of China's reduction in poverty. Growth would have had an even greater anti-poverty impact if inequality had not increased so substantially (Ravallion, 2010).

China's flagship anti-poverty programme is a regionally targeted public investment programme initiated in 1986 under the direction of national, provincial, and county Leading Group Offices for Poverty Alleviation and Development (LGOPAD). The goal of the programme has been to increase the income-generating potential of households living in poor regions. Initially, the government targeted 328 nationally designated poor counties, which increased to 592 poor counties by 1993, accounting for 23.5 per cent of China's rural population (Park et al., 2002; LGOPAD, 2003). The 592 poor county designations were revised in 2001 and 2011. Starting in 2001, partly in response to criticism that nearly half of the poor did not live in official poor counties (World Bank, 2001; Park et al. 2002), China shifted from county-level to village-level targeting, focusing targeted public investments on 148,131 officially designated poor villages covering about 15 per cent of China's rural population (Park and Wang, 2010). Unfortunately, the shift to lower-level targeting actually worsened targeting accuracy due to political, institutional, and informational factors (Park and Wang, 2012). According to China's poverty reduction plan for 2011–20, China will concentrate public investment in fourteen key poor areas located in remote, mountainous regions (State Council News Office, 2011).

The main targeted investment programmes have been budgetary grants administered by the Ministry of Finance, a public works programme administered by the State Planning Commission and Development and Reform Commission, and a subsidized loan programme administered by the Agricultural Bank and Agricultural Development Bank. Funding amounts have increased over time, reaching 5 per cent of the national budget (including loan principal) during 2001–07 (World Bank, 2009). Rigorous evaluations find that the programmes have had a positive impact on consumption and incomes. Analysis of household panel data from four southern provinces in the late 1980s finds that living in a poor county increased the growth of consumption per capita by 1.1 per cent per year with a rate of return of 12 per cent (Jalan and Ravallion, 1998a). A study using panel data for all counties in China estimates that poor county designation increased rural income per capita by 2.3 per cent per year during 1985–92 and 0.9 per cent during 1992–95 with rates of return of 15.5 per cent and 11.6 per cent, respectively (Park et al., 2002). An evaluation of poor village targeting using nationally representative rural household panel data finds no statistically significant average impacts on income or consumption from 2001 to 2004; however, the programme did increase the consumption and income of richer households (above the median) by 6.1 per cent (Park and Wang, 2010). Overall, the programmes appear to have made a difference in the targeted areas, but there remains doubt about the extent to which the programmes have actually helped the poor living in those areas (Wang, 2005) and many poor live outside officially targeted areas and so do not realize any benefits (Park and Wang, 2012).

Broad-based rural income growth associated with market reforms and rapid economic development can explain most of the reductions in poverty. The introduction of the Household Responsibility System in the early 1980s returned authority for farm decisions to households, significantly increasing incentives and productivity. In combination with large agricultural price increases, this led to dramatic increases in rural incomes and a halving of the official poverty count from 250 million in 1978 to 125 million in 1985, the year *before* government poverty programmes were set up. Poverty reduction actually slowed in the late 1980s after the poverty programmes were in place. In general, poverty reduction in China has been strongly associated with agricultural growth, both across time and across regions (Ravallion and Chen, 2007; Montalvo and Ravallion, 2010). The importance of agricultural growth contrasts with Brazil and India where growth in the service sector is much more strongly associated with poverty reduction (Ravallion, 2010). This difference probably reflects China's relatively equitable land distribution. All rural households in China have access to land, unlike in India where there is a large landless class or Brazil where land is very unequally distributed. Agriculture is also important because many of the poor live in remote areas with few local off-farm wage opportunities and find it difficult to migrate out due to limited labour, poor human capital, or the need to care for children or the elderly (Du et al., 2005; World Bank, 2009). Nonetheless, over time the share of agricultural income in total rural household income has fallen steadily while the share of wage income has increased to over 40 per cent by 2011 thanks to robust growth in the demand for (and wages of) migrant workers. In many poor villages, young adults have nearly all out-migrated. For this reason, non-agricultural growth is likely to play an increasingly prominent role in poverty reduction in the future.

67.3 **Identifying and helping China's remaining poor**

China's official poverty headcount rate is calculated as a share of the population with rural residential registration (*Hukou*) and so excludes entirely the urban poor. This omission reflects China's large urban–rural divide dating from the socialist period. Urban residents were provided with wages, housing, education, and healthcare services that were far superior to those available to rural residents. However, with massive layoffs of state enterprise workers in the late 1990s and a massive surge in rural–urban migration, it has become more likely that those living in urban areas are poor. Still, efforts to quantify the extent of rural and urban poverty have generally found that rural poverty accounts for over 97 per cent of total poverty (Ravallion and Chen, 2007; World Bank, 2009). Poverty in China has always been and continues to be predominantly a rural phenomenon.

Poverty rates are much higher in western China, where the topography is mountainous, fertile land is scarce, and the distance to the ports and China's major cities is great. In 2003, the consumption poverty headcount rates using the $1/day line were 21 per cent and 29 per cent in the southwest and northwest compared to 6 per cent, 7 per cent, and 13 per cent in the coast, the northeast, and central China (World Bank, 2009). Minority villages and mountainous villages are concentrated in the west and have higher poverty rates than non-minority and non-mountainous villages (World Bank, 2009). Because of the geographic concentration of poverty in western China, the Chinese government has used regional targeting to guide its public investments for poverty alleviation.

However, given that most of China's population lives in the east, despite having a lower poverty rate the non-western regions account for nearly half of China's poor; these poor are much more dispersed spatially than in the west. A cluster analysis aimed at revealing different types of poor populations using 2003 rural household survey data identified six categories of the poor, the key features of which are living in a minority area (20.6 per cent), low land productivity (19.6 per cent), high dependency ratio (18.6 per cent), low work capacity (17.3 per cent), land scarcity (13.9 per cent), and remote location (8.6 per cent) (World Bank, 2009). The prevalence of these different poverty groups varies considerably across regions. Nearly all of China's poor can be characterized as working poor, with less than 0.5 per cent of the poor living in households with no able-bodied workers (World Bank, 2009). This diversity in the nature of poverty provides justification for developing a multipronged approach to poverty alleviation efforts that shifts the focus 'from poor areas to poor people' (World Bank, 2009).

Another important feature of poverty in China is that much of the poverty is transient in nature. An analysis of three years of household survey data from the early 2000s found that on average 17.8 per cent of the rural population was consumption poor, but 30.9 per cent were poor in at least one of the three years and only 6.9 per cent were poor in all three years (World Bank, 2009). A study using six years of rural panel data from southern China in the late 1980s found that 7 per cent to 13 per cent of the population were poor in a given year even though their mean consumption was above the poverty line (Jalan and Ravallion, 1998b). Both studies found that nearly half of poverty as measured by the poverty squared index is attributable to consumption variability. These findings suggest that social insurance and social protection programmes as well as improved access to insurance and credit services may be important for addressing the transient nature of poverty.

The Hu–Wen government (President Hu Jintao and Premier Wen Jiaobo) has recognized this challenge and has made significant efforts to expand social protection and social insurance programmes. Since the mid-2000s, China has aggressively expanded the rural minimum living standard (*dibao*) programme, administered by the Ministry of Civil Affairs, to cover the entire country. The programme in principle provides subsidies to bring household incomes up to the poverty line. However, the programme is decentralized and benefits are often low and unevenly provided across regions and households. The government also runs other social assistance programmes, including assistance to help pay medical fees, subsidies to support households lacking work capacity (*wubaohu* and *tekunhu*), and disaster relief. According to official statistics, rural health insurance now covers over 97 per cent of the rural population, and a new rural pension programme also is being scaled up nationally, with 326 million participants by year-end 2011.

■ REFERENCES

Chen, Shaohua and Martin Ravallion. 2010. The developing world is poorer than we thought, but no less successful in the fight against poverty. *Quarterly Journal of Economics* 125(4), 1577–625.

Du, Yang, Albert Park, and Sangui Wang. 2005. Migration and rural poverty in China. *Journal of Comparative Economics* 33(4), 688–709.

Jalan, Jyotsna and Martin Ravallion. 1998a. Are there dynamic gains from a poor-area development program?, *Journal of Public Economics* 67(1), 65–85.

Jalan, Jyotsna and Martin Ravallion. 1998b. Transient poverty in post-reform rural China. *Journal of Comparative Economics* 26, 338–57.

Leading Group Office of Poverty Alleviation and Development (LGOPAD). 2003. *An Overview of the Development-oriented Poverty Reduction Program for Rural China.* Beijing: China Financial & Economic Publishing House.

Montalvo, Jose G. and Martin Ravallion. 2010. The pattern of growth and poverty reduction in China. *Journal of Comparative Economics* 38: 2–16.

Park, Albert and Sangui Wang. 2010. Community development and poverty alleviation: an evaluation of China's poor village investment program. *Journal of Public Economics* 94(9–10), 790–99.

Park, Albert and Sangui Wang. 2012. Choosing the optimal level of geographic targeting: lessons from China. Mimeo.

Park, Albert, Sangui Wang, and Guobao Wu. 2002. Regional poverty targeting in China. *Journal of Public Economics* 86(1), 123–53.

Ravallion, Martin. 2010. A comparative perspective on poverty reduction in Brazil, China, and India. *World Bank Research Observer* 26, 71–104.

Ravallion, Martin and Shaohua Chen. 2007. China's (uneven) progress against poverty. *Journal of Development Economics* 82, 1–42.

State Council News Office. 2011. *China's New Strategy for Rural Poverty Alleviation*, 16 November.

Wang, Sangui. 2005. Problems in reaching the absolute poor in the implementation of village plans (in Chinese), Report to the Ministry of Finance.

World Bank. 2001. *China: Overcoming Rural Poverty.* Washington, DC: The World Bank.

World Bank. 2009. *From Poor Areas to Poor People: China's Evolving Poverty Reduction Agenda.* Washington, DC: World Bank.

World Bank. 2012. An update to the World Bank's estimates of consumption poverty in the developing world, <http://siteresources.worldbank.org/INTPOVCALNET/Resources/Global_Poverty_Update_2012_02-29-12.pdf>.

68 Inequality and the reform era in China

Carl Riskin

68.1 Income inequality at the end of the collective era

In 1979, on the threshold of the reform era, China had one of the most equally distrib-uted national incomes in the world. Economic equality was a hallmark of Maoist eco-nomic policy, in the form of narrowing the 'three great differences' between workers and peasants, city and countryside, and manual and mental labour. While *political* inequality was striking, especially between Communist Party or government cadres and ordinary people, income as conventionally measured was quite evenly distributed. In 1981, as the transition to a market economy was just beginning, the Gini ratio[1] for rural China was estimated at 0.25, and that of urban China at 0.18, signifying remarkably low levels of inequality. In the countryside there were sizeable income differences among localities, reflecting variations in physical conditions and proximity to markets. Moreover, the urban–rural gap was pronounced despite Mao's goal of reducing it, causing the overall national Gini ratio, at 0.28 in 1981, to exceed that of either urban or rural China, taken separately.

Urban bias has characterized China's economic policies for most years, both before and after the reform era. Its prime driver has been the *Hukou* (household registration) system, which kept people without specific permission to move in their place of birth. During the collective period, food rationing effectively ruled out illicit rural–urban migration; any-one moving without permission would be unable to obtain food in the host community. The urban labour force, thus shielded from competition, was virtually fully employed and subject to highly compressed national wage schedules. Urban residents were the beneficiaries of a cradle-to-grave social welfare system, receiving subsidized housing, education, healthcare, transport, and even food. Rural residents received none of these subsidies, although at the end of the collective period a rural cooperative medical system

---

[1] The Gini coefficient is a common measure of inequality that ranges from 0 for perfect equality to 1 (or 100, in index form) for complete inequality. See <http://data.worldbank.org/indicator/SI.POV.GINI>.

provided rudimentary healthcare to over 80 per cent of villages. Even without the inclusion of all subsidies, urban incomes still averaged 2.7 times rural incomes in 1978 (Khan et al., 1992; Carter, 1997; Khan and Riskin, 2008).

68.2 **Measurement issues**

In China, measurement of economic inequality is beset by several sampling issues: the concealment of high incomes; under-counting of very poor people living in remote and inaccessible regions; and under-reporting of migrants' incomes. There are also conceptual issues: whether and how to include imputed rent on owner-occupied housing in income, as is the international standard; whether to take into account price differences among provinces and between urban and rural areas in calculating incomes. Different solutions to these problems generate different estimates of income inequality, although the main trends are similar whatever the approach used. Such problems are not unique to China. The accuracy of national measures of inequality always depends upon national institutions and practices. Therefore, gaps between any two countries' Gini ratios must be quite large to signify real differences in inequality, rather than merely differences in institutions or practices that affect the Gini measure.

68.3 **The reform era**

The period of reform and transition began with a focus on the rural economy, a brief exception to the urban bias of Chinese economic and social policy. During the first half of the 1980s, new reform policies favoured the countryside, sharply raising farm prices and encouraging farmers to abandon the collective people's communes, return to family farming, and pursue income-maximizing opportunities, aided by expanding supplies of farm inputs. Rural income per capita more than doubled between 1978 and 1984, rising twice as fast as that of urban workers (Riskin, 1987: 293). Even though rural inequality widened as some people fared better than others in the new market economy, this was the only sustained period in China's contemporary history when the urban–rural disparity narrowed. The spurt, however, ended by 1985. Farm prices became less favourable and a new 'coastal development strategy' benefited eastern urban industries rather than farmers. The urban–rural income gap and the national Gini coefficient began to rise again.

While the Chinese government withheld estimates of income inequality for twelve years after 2000—on the grounds that income surveys under-counted very high incomes (Fang and Yu, 2012)—in January 2013 it released statistics showing the Gini coefficient rising to a high of 0.491 in 2008 and then declining to 0.474 in 2012. An independent estimate of the Gini for 2007, moreover, finds that, unadjusted for regional price differences, it had increased to about 0.5, one of the highest levels in Asia (Li et al., 2011),[2] and 79 per cent above the level of 1981. However, if concealed high incomes were included, the national 2007 Gini ratio would be higher by as much as four percentage points (Li and Luo, 2011). Depending upon which income definition is used, whether regional price differences are taken into account, and whether the migrant population is included, the result would be a Gini ranging from just below 0.5 to well above it.

A large and growing share of China's total inequality is still due to the urban–rural income gap. In 2007, the raw differential stood at 4-to-1, twice as high as among most developing countries, and it contributed about half of national income inequality. However, if urban–rural price differences are taken into account, the urban–rural income gap narrows to about 2.9-to-1 and its contribution to overall inequality declines to a still substantial 41 per cent (Li et al., 2011). Moreover, disparities among China's thirty-one provinces and province-level municipalities (excluding Hong Kong and Macao) are substantial: the richest province, Shanghai, has a per capita income ten times that of the poorest, Guizhou (Fan et al., 2011). Inequality in per capita incomes is accompanied by substantial disparities in wealth, infant mortality, and access to education and healthcare as well as to social protection and insurance programmes (Fan et al., 2011).

68.4 Market forces and government policies both affect inequality

The primary market force that has helped produce large income disparities is the downward pressure on wages exerted by the enormous pool of surplus labour with which China began the transition to a market economy around 1980. In addition, there is the 'Kuznets effect', which recognizes that initial modernization efforts open gaps between the modernizing and traditional sectors of the economy. However, government policies have also exacerbated growing inequality. Examples of such policies include the *Hukou* system, still surviving although in weakened form, which has impeded population mobility; and export subsidies and the 'coastal development strategy' of the mid-1980s. This policy succeeded brilliantly in attracting foreign direct investment, expanding exports and accelerating growth, but it also aggravated economic inequality, especially between

---

[2] The United Nations Development Programme's *Human Development Report 2011* (UNDP, 2011) lists the following Asian countries as having recent Gini ratios roughly the same as or greater than China's: Thailand (0.54), Nepal (0.47), Bhutan (0.47), Malaysia (0.46), Cambodia (0.44), Philippines (0.44), Hong Kong (0.43). However, China's own Gini is given as 0.415, undoubtedly a serious underestimate for 2011. If the independent estimate of 0.5 for China in 2007 is accurate, then only Thailand's Gini is greater in Asia. But see the text's discussion of problems with international comparisons of inequality.

the developed coastal regions and the under-developed interior and between urban and rural areas (Fan et al., 2011). Other aggravating policies include a regressive tax structure and the decentralization of the public finance system, which encouraged a local preference for capital investment and growth over all other objectives while ruling out any significant redistribution of resources from wealthier to poorer regions (Wong, 2010). To an unmeasurable extent, corruption in the form of families of high officials enriching themselves has played a role as well.

In the early 2000s, a new set of policies arose that affected income distribution. These fostered exceedingly high rates of capital investment and of net exports in GDP, and correspondingly low rates of consumption; and a burgeoning manufacturing sector but under-developed services. The repression of deposit interest rates to levels often below the rate of inflation effectively redistributed income from households to banks and large enterprises. Household income fell to a remarkably low 50 per cent of GDP. Profits, subsidized by the artificially cheap cost of capital, claimed a growing share of national income. The minority of incomes tied to profits grew faster than did labour incomes both because of the income transfer and because low rates encouraged the use of capital-intensive technologies, slowing job creation and the increase in wages. It is hard to see how income inequality could be reduced in China without reversing these imbalances.

68.5 Inequality and public opinion

Evidence suggests that the Chinese public may not much resent income inequality, per se (Whyte, 2009). Most Chinese have enjoyed large gains in living standards over the past few decades, and appreciation of absolute progress may dominate animus towards growing disparities. However, tens of thousands of 'mass incidents,' that is, protests or demonstrations, occur annually and with increasing frequency in China (Bloomberg News, 2011; Freeman, 2010). Many of these are responses to particular acts or events, such as local government seizures of peasant land for urban development, environmental despoliation from under-regulated local industries, or disputes over pay. Such causes do reflect increasing economic inequality, as well as the weak rule of law in China. The national government has been alarmed at the threat of social instability presented by large and growing disparities, and it has tried to stem their rise, but with little success.

68.6 Policies to reduce economic inequality

There are many policies aimed at reducing economic inequality, some already being undertaken by the government. Prominent among them are: reform of the public finance system to give local governments the incentive and means to pursue goals other than GDP growth (Wong, 2010); greater investment in education, healthcare, and infrastructure in poor regions; elimination of the *Hukou* system leading to full integration of migrants into their new urban environment, with access to the same public services as ordinary urban residents; reform of the fiscal system to reduce its regressiveness; and redress of the distorted relative costs of capital and labour by allowing interest rates on deposits to rise, which would transfer income flows from banks and enterprises to households. Effective policies to rebalance the economy, however, would engender resistance from powerful vested interests, including banks, coastal provinces, export industries, and heavy manufacturing companies that have benefited from economic imbalances and the inequality they have produced.

■ REFERENCES

Bloomberg News. 2011. China's Spending on Internal Police Force in 2010 Outstrips Defense Budget.

Carter, C. A. 1997. The urban–rural income gap in China: implications for global food markets. *American Journal of Agricultural Economics* **79**(5 (Proceedings Issue)), 1410–18.

Fan, S., R. Kanbur, and X. Zhang. 2011. China's regional disparities: experience and policy. *Review of Development Finance* (1), 47–56.

Fang, Xuyan and Lea Yu. 2012. Government Refuses to Release Gini Coefficient. Caixin (China Economy and Finance) <http://english.caixin.com/2012-2001-18/100349814.html>.

Freeman, W. 2010. The accuracy of China's 'mass incidents'. *Financial Times.*

Khan, A. and C. Riskin. 2008. Growth and distribution of household income in China between 1995 and 2002. In *Inequality and Public Policy in China*, edited by B.Gustafsson, S. Li, and T. Sicular, 61–87. New York: Cambridge University Press.

Khan, A. R., K. Griffin, C. Riskin, and R. Zhao. 1992. Household income and its distribution in China. *China Quarterly* 132, 1029–61.

Li, S. and C. Luo. 2011. Zongguo shouru chaju jiujing you duo da? (How unequal is China?). *Jingji Yanjiu* (4).

Li, S., C. Luo, and T. Sicular. 2011. Overview: Income Inequality and Poverty in China, 2002–2007. University of Western Ontario, CIBC Centre for Human Capital and Productivity Working Papers (201110).

Riskin, C. 1987. *China's Political Economy: The Quest for Development since 1949*. Oxford and New York: Oxford University Press.

UNDP. 2011. *Human Development Report 2011: Sustainability and Equity, A Better Future for All*. New York: UNDP.

Whyte, M. K. 2009. *Myth of the Social Volcano: Perceptions of Inequality and Distributive Injustice in Contemporary China*. Stanford, CA: Stanford University Press.

Wong, C. 2010. Fiscal reform: paying for the harmonious society. *China Economic Quarterly* 14(2), 22–7.

69 Inequality in China

John Knight

Starting from a very low level, inequality in China rose rapidly over the reform period: the Gini coefficient of household income per capita was 0.49 in 2007 (Li et al., 2013a), and China was found to have the joint highest inequality in Asia (Asian Development Bank, 2007).[1] Inequality has now become a matter of concern to the Chinese leadership.

There are two main sources of information on inequality over time: the annual national household income and expenditure surveys of the National Bureau of Statistics (NBS) and the periodic national household surveys of the China Household Income Project (CHIP). The NBS surveys contain many observations but have a limited number of questions, they cannot be used as a panel, and they are generally not available to researchers at disaggregated household and individual level. The CHIP surveys relate to the years 1988, 1995, 2002, and 2007; they use a sub-sample of the NBS surveys, and they ask many more questions. The two sources use different definitions of income, with the CHIP definition being more comprehensive. The NBS urban and rural surveys are based on local residence registration (*Hukou*), so excluding most rural–urban migrants (normally retaining rural *Hukou*) from the urban sample. By 2002 the number of rural–urban migrants exceeded 100 million: the 2002 and 2007 CHIP surveys added a separate sample of rural *Hukou* households in urban China.

China's poverty and its inequality fell dramatically in the years of rural reform 1978–85, when farming was decollectivized and household production was restored. According to the CHIP surveys, in 1988 the urban Gini (0.24) was very low by international standards, the rural Gini (0.33) reflected regional income disparities, and the national Gini (nearly 0.40) was higher than either owing to the contribution made by the high ratio of urban to rural income per capita. There appeared to be a lull in the rise, as the national Gini was 0.45 in both 1995 and 2002. However, in 2007 the urban Gini was 0.34, the rural Gini 0.36, and the national Gini no less than 0.50.[2] Adjusted for regional price differences, the Gini was 0.43 in 2007, having risen from 0.40 in 2002 (Li et al., 2013a).

---

[1] I am grateful to Ravi Kanbur, Martin Ravallion, Terry Sicular, and Li Shi for helpful comments.

[2] Excluding migrants, for comparison with earlier years. Including migrants, the urban and national Ginis were 0.33 and 0.49 in 2007 (Li et al., 2012).

Ravallion and Chen (2007), having partial access to the NBS microdata, also found growing income inequality: all three Gini coefficients increased by three percentage points over the six years 1995–2001; their estimate of the national Gini in 2001 was 0.45. Moreover, a national Gini coefficient based on grouped NBS data was estimated to rise by five percentage points between 2000 and 2008 (Lin et al., 2010).

The various estimates of income so far discussed are for disposable income. In fact, taxes and subsidies have done nothing to remedy factor income inequality, although the degree of fiscal regressivity has fallen as the reforms have progressed (for instance, Khan and Riskin, 2007). In 2007 the urban Gini for income after the deduction of direct taxes was only one percentage point lower than its pre-tax counterpart (Xu and Yue, 2013). Incomes at the top of the income distribution are likely to be understated. An ingenious attempt to measure this claimed to find much 'grey income' in the highest income group (Wang and Woo, 2010).

Although there was almost no personal wealth under central planning, the Gini coefficient of wealth in 2002 had reached 0.55 (rural 0.40, urban 0.48), considerably higher than that of income per capita (Zhao and Ding, 2007). The main contribution in both rural and urban areas came from housing, which in the latter case represented two-thirds of the inequality of net wealth. The acquisition or appropriation of state assets at below-market prices was a powerful disequalizing force. The divergence of wealth was also assisted by the fact that the household saving rate rises sharply with income.

The various dimensions and components of income inequality will now be considered, starting with the urban sector. As an urban labour market gradually emerged along with economic reform, the wage structure widened and wage inequality rose. For instance, the Gini coefficient was 0.21 in 1988, 0.33 in 1995, but still 0.33 in 2007 (Deng and Gustafsson, 2013). The rise was partly due to increasing rewards for productive characteristics and incentives for efficiency; for instance, the wage premium of a college degree over primary schooling was 9 per cent, 39 per cent, and 88 per cent, respectively. However, it was also partly due to new or growing forms of discrimination and segmentation—by sex, ownership, enterprise profitability, and region (Knight and Song, 2007). Estimates of urban inequality are complicated by the presence of rural–urban migrants. The CHIP survey of 2002 showed that inclusion of migrant households raised the Gini by two percentage points (Khan and Riskin, 2007) but this may be an understatement if migrants living in households have higher incomes than sojourners on their own.

Non-farm employment is important for rural income and its distribution. The share of wages in rural income rose sharply as, first, rural industry burgeoned and, second, migration accelerated. Wage income contributed 21 per cent of rural income inequality in 1988, 40 per cent in 1995, and 41 per cent in 2007 (Knight and Ding, 2012: ch. 10). The slowdown is due to the reduction in rural spatial income inequality as wage employment opportunities spread more widely across provinces and counties. An analysis, using the 2007 CHIP survey, of the effect on the income of rural households of having migrant members showed that migration reduced rural poverty and by implication inequality (Luo and Yue, 2010).

The rural–urban divide was not reduced by reform and marketization of the economy: the ratio of urban to rural household income per capita was greater than ever in 2007, being 4.10 according to the CHIP survey but reducing to 2.91 after adjustment for spatial differences in prices The corresponding CHIP ratios in 2002 were 3.35 and 2.28 (Li et al., 2013a: table 2.8). However, including various disguised subsidies (for healthcare, education, and pension contributions), the 2002 ratios become 4.35 and 3.10 respectively (Li and Luo, 2010: 119). Rural–urban differences in the cost of living are offset by hidden subsidies to urban people. The explanation for the high ratio is to be found in the underlying political economy that favours urban-dwellers and the control of migration (Knight and Song, 1999). The contribution to overall inequality made by the mean difference in rural and urban incomes rose from 37 per cent in 1988 to 54 per cent in 2007. Even when adjustment is made for spatial price differences, reducing the 2007 figure to 41 per cent (Li et al., 2013a), this is far higher than in most other developing countries.

It is an interesting question: is there regional divergence or convergence over time—are the processes of cumulative causation that produce 'polarization' outweighed by 'spread effects'? The evidence tends to favour absolute divergence but, in line with economic theory, conditional convergence. For instance, this pattern was found by Lau (2010) in examining income per capita among provinces over the period 1978–2005. Gustafsson et al. (2007b) found that the proportion of inequality in urban China that is due to between-province inequality fell from 29 per cent in 1988 to 19 per cent in 2002. The main gain came from within eastern China, where this more developed economy was becoming more spatially integrated. The contribution of between-province inequality to rural income inequality rose from 22 per cent in 1988 to 39 per cent in 1995 and remained at 39 per cent in 2002 (Gustafsson et al., 2007b). It appears that the initial polarization effects were being offset by the spread effects that were created by a growing scarcity of local resources.

How much concern is there for inequality in China? Consider first the people and then the government. Research on subjective well-being in China shows why people are indeed concerned about income inequality: 'relative deprivation' is a common phenomenon (for instance, Knight and Gunatilaka, 2011, using the 2002 CHIP survey). Regression analyses of happiness, or life satisfaction, in China produce well-fitting equations with understandable and significant coefficients. A consistent finding is the importance of relative income and also of the chosen reference group. Income inequality matters, but it is inequality at the local and not the national or regional level that matters to people (Knight and Gunatilaka, 2011). The underlying reasons for inequality also matter. Whyte (2010) concluded from a national sample survey of attitudes to inequality that Chinese people were less opposed to income inequality based on merit or effort (perhaps seeing it as providing opportunities) than to income inequality based on unfairness in opportunities (for instance arising from corruption or connections).

Government strategy for much of the reform period can be summed up in the words of a high official, Du Runsheng (1989: 192): 'prosperity to few, then to many, then to all'. In creating a 'developmental state', government gave overwhelming priority to economic growth. This strategy was adopted as the best way of maintaining political legitimacy and support. However, the rise in inequality created a new potential source of discontent. Owing to the narrowness of people's reference groups, it may be important for a government concerned about social instability to remedy the causes of income inequality at the local level. However, orbits of comparison are widening on account of the increasing use of the Internet and the explosion of migration. The leadership became more sensitive to rising inequality in the mid-2000s, when policies to promote a more 'harmonious society' were introduced. The economic measures included the abolition of the agricultural tax and of fees for basic (nine-year) rural education, rural infrastructure development, grain production subsidies, the extension of poverty relief (*dibao*), the introduction of a minimum wage policy, and the extension and improvement of social security provision. The rural tax rate was reduced from 2.9 per cent in 2002 to 0.3 per cent in 2007, and was made less regressive (Luo and Sicular, 2013).

Although the rise in national inequality is more related to the economic reforms than to the growth of income, it is consistent with the upward-sloping part of the hypothesized Kuznets curve relating inequality to income level (Kuznets, 1955). Can China be predicted to follow the downward-sloping part as well, that is, will inequality fall as future income rises? This will depend on the balance of countervailing forces. On the one hand, the various processes that have raised China's income inequality during the reform period will continue to operate. On the other hand, there are three main equalizing forces. It is predictable that the labour market will tighten as China enters the second stage of the Lewis model and the fruits of economic development are more widely spread (Knight and Ding, 2012: ch. 9).[3] The growing scarcity of labour and other resources can be predicted to transfer production from the coastal provinces to the, poorer, interior provinces. It appears that Chinese society is becoming more sophisticated and better informed, and that peoples' aspirations are rising. In that case government may well introduce stronger policies to diminish various dimensions of inequality as a protection against social instability.

■ **REFERENCES**

Asian Development Bank. 2007. *Inequality in Asia*, Manila: ADB.

[3] Moreover, the NBS national household surveys show rural growing faster than urban income per capita since 2009.

Deng, Quheng and Bjorn Gustafsson. 20132. A new episode of increased urban inequality in China. In *Rising Inequality in China: Challenge to the Harmonious Society*, edited by Li Shi, Hiroshi Sato, and Terry Sicular, ch. 7. Cambridge and New York: Cambridge University Press.

Du Runsheng. 1989. *China's Rural Economic Reform*. Beijing: Foreign Languages Press.

Gustafsson, Bjorn, Li Shi, and Terry Sicular. 2007a. Inequality and public policy in China: issues and trends. In *Inequality and Public Policy in China*, edited by B. Gustafsson, Li Shi, and Terry Sicular, 1–34. Cambridge and New York: Cambridge University Press.

Gustafsson, Bjorn, Li Shi, Terry Sicular, and Yue Ximing. 2007b. Income inequality and spatial differences in China, 1988, 1995, and 2002. In *Inequality and Public Policy in China*, edited by B. Gustafsson, Li Shi, and Terry Sicular, 35–60. Cambridge and New York: Cambridge University Press.

Khan, Aziz and Carl Riskin. 2007. Growth and distribution of household income in China between 1995 and 2002. In *Inequality and Public Policy in China*, edited by B. Gustafsson, Li Shi, and Terry Sicular, 61–87. Cambridge and New York: Cambridge University Press.

Knight, John and Sai Ding. 2012. *China's Remarkable Economic Growth*. Oxford: Oxford University Press.

Knight, John and Ramani Gunatilaka. 2010. The rural–urban divide: income but not happiness? *Journal of Development Studies* 42(7), 1199–224.

Knight, John and Ramani Gunatilaka. 2011. Does economic growth raise happiness in China? *Oxford Development Studies* 39(1), 1–24.

Knight, John and Lina Song. 1999. *The Rural–Urban Divide: Economic Disparities and Interactions in China*. Oxford: Oxford University Press.

Knight, John and Lina Song. 2007. China's emerging wage structure, 1995-2002. In *Inequality and Public Policy in China*, edited by B. Gustafsson, Li Shi, and Terry Sicular, 221–42. Cambridge and New York: Cambridge University Press.

Kuznets, Simon. 1955. Economic growth and income inequality. *American Economic Review* 45, 1–28.

Lau, C. K. M. 2010. New evidence about regional income divergence in China. *China Economic Review* 21, 295–309.

Lin, T., J. Zhuang, D. Garcia, and F. Lin. 2010. Income inequality in the PRC, 1995–2008. In *Poverty, Inequality and Inclusive Growth in Asia*, edited by J. Zhuang. London: Anthem Press.

Luo, Chuliang and Terry Sicular. 2013. Inequality and poverty in rural China. In *Rising Inequality in China: Challenge to the Harmonious Society*, Li Shi, Hiroshi Sato, and Terry Sicular, ch. 5. Cambridge and New York: Cambridge University Press.

Luo, Chuliang and Ximing Yue. 2010. Rural–urban migration and poverty in China. In *The Great Migration. Rural-urban Migration in China and Indonesia*, edited by X. Meng and C. Manning. Cheltenham: Edward Elgar.

Ravallion, Martin and Shaohua Chen. 2007. China's (uneven) progress against poverty. *Journal of Development Economics* 82(1), 1–42.

Shi, Li, and Chuliang Luo. 2010. Re-estimating the income gap between urban and rural households in China. In *One Country, Two Societies. Rural-urban Inequality in Contemporary China*, edited by M. Whyte. Cambridge, MA: Harvard University Press.

Shi, Li, Luo Chuliang, and Terry Sicular. 2013a. Overview: income inequality and poverty in China, 2002–2007. In *Rising Inequality in China: Challenge to the Harmonious Society*, Shi, Li, Hiroshi Sato, and Terry Sicular, ch. 2. Cambridge and New York: Cambridge University Press.

Shi Li, Hiroshi Sato, and Terry Sicular (eds) (2013b). *Rising Inequality in China: Challenge to the Harmonious Society*, Cambridge and New York: Cambridge University Press (forthcoming).

Wang, Xiaolu and Wing Thye Woo. 2010. The size and distribution of hidden household income in China. *Asian Economic Papers* 10(1), 1–26.

Whyte, Martin K. 2010. *Myth of the Social Volcano. Perceptions of Inequality and Distributive Justice in Contemporary China*. Stanford, CA: Stanford University Press.

Xu, Jing and Yue Ximing. 2013.'Redistributive impacts of personal income tax in urban China. In *Rising Inequality in China: Challenge to the Harmonious Society*, edited by Li Shi, Hiroshi Sato, and Terry Sicular. Cambridge and New York: Cambridge University Press.

Zhao, Renwei and Ding Sai. 2007. The distribution of wealth in China. In *Inequality and Public Policy in China*, edited by B. Gustafsson, Li Shi, and Terry Sicular, 118–44. Cambridge and New York: Cambridge University Press.

70 Overcoming the middle-income trap in China

From the perspective of social mobility

Hongbin Cai

70.1 How to overcome the middle-income trap

China's remarkable economic growth of the last three decades since the economic reform and opening-up policy was launched in 1978 has lifted China out of the 'poverty trap'.[1] As the second largest economy in the world, China is now a middle-income country with a per capita GDP of over US$5,000. However, how the Chinese economy is going to perform in the next 20–30 years is quite uncertain, and is a crucial question the answer to which affects not only more than 1.3 billion Chinese people, but also the whole world.

The future of the Chinese economy crucially depends on whether China can successfully overcome the so-called middle-income trap. What makes a country more likely to overcome the middle-income trap? One school of thought focuses on structural problems in the economy. It is a popular view in policy discussions in China that many structural problems, such as insufficient domestic consumption, income inequality, and over-reliance on export, pose serious obstacles for China to sustain growth in the future. However, a multivariate probit regression shows that whether a country successfully overcomes the middle-income trap is not correlated with any of its structural factors at the time it enters the rank of middle-income economies (Cai, 2011). This result should not be surprising. These structural variables reflect the current state of an economy, and will vary as economic policies and the economic situation of the economy change over time. As static and endogenous variables, structural factors do not predict, let alone determine, long-run economic growth.

Another school of thought about overcoming the middle-income trap focuses on economic policy. A typical argument is that countries fall into the middle-income trap

[1] I thank Yuyu Chen, Se Yan, and Li-An Zhou for helpful comments and Qing Gong, Guang Shi, and Rongzhang Wang for diligent research assistance. Much of the article is based on Cai (2011) on the Chinese journal *Bijiao* 2011(2).

because they adopt the wrong economic policies. However, this view lacks systematic evidence that countries who successfully climb out of the middle-income trap adopt the right set of policies, and vice versa. Import substitution and industrialization policies adopted by Japan and Korea during their taking-off periods are not considered a good recipe for other developing economies. On the other hand, many countries which are trapped have undertaken serious economic reforms. For example, Kehoe and Ruhl (2010) argue that Mexico has adopted the right set of economic reforms and opened up its economy, and yet failed to grow out of the middle-income trap.

Structural economic problems and economic policies are important issues for a country to maintain economic stability and promote growth, but there is no single recipe of a 'correct' economic structure or a 'right' set of economic policies that guarantees a country can climb out of the middle income trap.

70.2 Why is social mobility critical for overcoming the middle-income trap?

To ascertain what is critical for overcoming the middle-income trap, we need to go back to the basics of long-run economic growth. The institutional theory of economic growth argues that the most important factor of long-run economic growth is institutions that protect property rights (North, 1990). Only when property rights (including intellectual property rights) are protected do people have incentives to make investment and engage in technological innovations, thus ensuring capital accumulation and technological progress. However, this cannot account for the growth divergence of middle income countries. It is hard to argue that countries that fall into the middle-income trap (e.g. Latin American countries) have weaker protection of property rights than those who climb out of it (e.g. Japan and Korea in their taking-off periods).

Compared with the emphasis on incentives to make investment in capital accumulation and technological progress, less attention is paid to the *incentives to invest in human capital*. I argue that the key factor for a country to overcome the middle-income trap is for people in the country, especially young people, to maintain incentives to invest in human capital, which crucially depends on the social mobility of the country.

Social mobility, more specifically intergenerational mobility, is the extent to which parents' characteristics, such as earnings, occupations, and education, affect those of the next generation.[2] One common measure of social mobility is intergenerational correlation

---

[2] More general social mobility includes movements in income, occupation, and social status within generation. Here we focus on intergenerational mobility.

or elasticity, often obtained by regressing children's income and other characteristics on those of their parents. A high correlation suggests a strong persistence of socioeconomic status or low social mobility.[3]

Why is social mobility critical to escaping from the middle-income trap and sustained economic growth? Less social mobility means more persistent social and economic status across generations, which reduces incentives to make human capital investment. In a society with low social mobility, the disadvantaged see no hope of succeeding and have no incentive to exert any effort, and the advantaged do not have to make an effort to enjoy an easy life. In such a society, neither the disadvantaged nor the advantaged have the incentive to invest in human capital, resulting in a stagnant society.

A healthy level of social mobility is crucial for a society to maintain a strong incentive to invest in human capital, thus sustaining economic growth. This is especially important for middle-income countries. Why do so many countries fall into the middle-income trap? I argue that there is a general trend of declining social mobility in countries that have just climbed out of the poverty trap and entered the middle-income ranks, which leads to the middle-income trap. For a country just climbing out the poverty trap, the market mechanisms ensuring fair competition and the institutions ensuring equal opportunities have yet to be established, while conflicts of interests among different social and economic classes become more and more intense. Without strong measures and effort by the society to counterbalance the trend, inevitably the old and new elite class will seek to expand their advantages, often at the cost of opportunities for the disadvantaged. This leads to declining social mobility, where the elite class becomes more entrenched and the disadvantaged become more hopeless. Consequently, incentives to invest in human capital are stifled and the economy stagnates.

One piece of evidence supporting the above claim can be found from the comparison of an intergenerational correlation of education attainment across countries. Intergenerational education correlation coefficients in Latin American countries such as Peru, Chile, and Brazil are close to or exceeding 0.60. In these countries, the children of parents with poor education do not have a good chance of receiving a good education. As a sharp contrast, this coefficient in all the developed countries is significantly lower, below 0.4 in most European countries (the Netherlands, Norway, Finland, Ireland, and the UK). Although no data on Japan and Korea are available, it is reasonable to assume that the intergenerational education correlation in these countries is very low, given their known emphasis on education and education equality.

---

[3] For detailed information about measuring social mobility, see Solon (1999) and Black and Devereux (2010).

70.3 **The declining trend of social mobility in China in the recent decade**

China's social mobility should be quite high in the first two decades since 1978. As the centrally planned economy gradually gave way to a market-based economy, many people from relatively low social classes were able to take advantage of new opportunities offered by the market reforms and moved up the social ladder. For example, most entrepreneurs in the early stage of China's economic reforms were not from the elite class, but came from rural areas or the informal sector of urban areas.

However, evidence and casual observations suggest that social mobility in China has been declining at an alarming speed in recent years. For example, in a series of studies about the intragenerational income mobility of China, Khor and Pencavel (2006, 2008, 2010) find that income mobility declined significantly in the past decade. What is more, intergenerational education mobility in China has been declining in recent years. Using population census data, Liu (2008) finds that China's social mobility as measured by education correlation started decreasing substantially in the past decade. Li (2010) finds that while the percentage of college graduates in the total population increased substantially after college expansion since 1999, the gap in educational mobility between urban and rural areas widened. Such a gap is much wider in the very elite universities, as it is reported recently that only 10 per cent of students in those universities are from rural areas (the urbanization ratio is currently only about 50 per cent; Yang, 2006).

The decline of China' social mobility in recent years is consistent with the general trend in middle-income countries, as market mechanisms ensuring fair competition and institutions ensuring equal opportunities are yet to be established. Moreover, the legacies of central planning mean that the resources of Chinese society are highly centralized, allowing the elite class more easily to expand their interests at the cost of the disadvantaged. As a result, social mobility in China can decline at a much higher speed.

70.4 **Policy implications and further research**

After more than thirty years of fast economic growth, China is now facing many serious challenges to sustain growth to overcome the middle-income trap. I argue that the future of the Chinese economy crucially depends on whether China can reverse the declining trend of social mobility. This is not an easy task. It requires a comprehensive economic and social transformation, and systematic economic, social, and political reforms are needed. First and foremost, in order to develop a market mechanism ensuring fair competition and institutions ensuring equal opportunities, China needs to shift its attention from building physical infrastructure to building a market and legal infrastructure for

Chinese society. For example, the household registration system (*Hukou*) and regulatory entry constraints in the labour market and capital market should be eliminated in a timely and orderly fashion.

Second, the Chinese government should invest more in human capital, such as education and health, instead of physical capital. Moreover, much more attention should be paid to reducing education and health inequality. The most important factor for improving social mobility is that the young people in society, regardless of their family or ethnic backgrounds, enjoy equal educational and health opportunities. Closing the rural and urban gap in education and health should be top of the policy priorities in China.

Further research is needed in at least three areas: (i) the relationship between long-run economic growth and social mobility; (ii) a cross-country comparison of social mobility and economic performance; and (iii) intergenerational mobility in education, income, and occupation in China.

■ REFERENCES

Black, Sandra E. and Paul J. Devereux. 2010. Recent developments in intergenerational mobility. *Discussion Paper Series, Forschungsinstitut zur Zukunft der Arbeit* No. 4866.

Cai, Hongbin. 2011. China's economic transition and social mobility. *Bijiao* (in Chinese) April.

Kehoe, Timothy J. and Kim J. Ruhl. 2010. Why have economic reforms in Mexico not generated growth? *Journal of Economic Literature* 48(4), 1005–27.

Khor, Niny and John Pencavel. 2006. Income mobility of individuals in China and the United States. *Economics of Transition* 14(3), 417–58.

Khor, Niny and John Pencavel. 2008. Measuring income mobility, income inequality, and social welfare for households of the People's Republic of China. *Asian Development Bank Economics Working Paper* No. 145.

Khor, Niny and John Pencavel. 2010. Evolution of income mobility in the People's Republic of China: 1991–2002. Asian Development Bank Economics Working Paper No. 204.

Li, Chunling. 2010. Expansion of higher education and inequality in opportunity of education: a study on effect of Kuozhao Policy on Equalization of Educational Attainment. *Sociology Studies* (Shehuixue Yanjiu) 2010(3), 82–113.

Liu, Jingming. 2008. Changing patterns of inequality of educational opportunity in basic education in China. *China Social Sciences* (Zhongguo Shehui Kexue) 2008(5), 101–16.

North, Douglas. 1990. *Institutions, Institutional Change and Economic Performance*. Cambridge: Cambridge University Press.

Solon, Gary. 1999. Intergenerational mobility in the labor market. In *Handbook of Labor Economics*, edited by Orley C. Ashenfelter and David Card, Vol. 3A, 1761–800. Amsterdam: North-Holland.

Yang, Dongping. 2006. *The Target and the Reality of Education Equality in China* (Zhongguo Jiaoyu Gongping de Lixiang yu Xianshi). Beijing: Peking University Press.

71 Trends in food consumption and nutrition in China

Baorui Wan

The next decade will see accelerated industrialization, urbanization, and agricultural modernization in China. During this time, a 1 per cent increase in the annual urbanization rate will result in the relocation of tens of millions of rural–urban migrants, which will further reshape the rural–urban structure and expand domestic consumption demands. The booming urban population will, in particular, stimulate the demand for food, so the food industry must increase commercial production and streamline the supply chain, in order to accommodate the increasing demand for safe and high-quality processed and convenient foods.

It is estimated that by 2020, when the population of China reaches about 1.45 billion, grain production will top 540 million tons[1] and the output of meat, eggs, dairy products, aquatic products, vegetables, and fruit will also grow. Furthermore, per capita daily protein intake is expected to be 80 g, which translates to 2200–2300 kCal of energy, at least 50 per cent of which will come from cereals.[2] Finally, shrinking arable land, further demographic shifts, aggravating climate change impacts, and deteriorating international food supply and demand problems are expected to heighten pressure on future food security and the supply–demand balance of major agricultural products.

Although China's urban–rural gap in food and nutrition is narrowing, dietary imbalance is an increasing problem throughout the country. A considerable number of people suffer from sub-optimal health. While chronic diseases associated with over-consumption—such as obesity, high blood pressure, and diabetes—are afflicting more, and younger, people, there is still a high incidence of diseases associated with under-consumption—such as anaemia and malnutrition—among the 36 million rural poor. It is therefore imperative that public health measures be designed according to the common and specific needs of different groups and regions if they are to be effective and successful.

---

[1] According to National Food Security Long-term and Mid-Term Plan (2008-2020), China's cereal production would maintain at the level of 500 million tons and above in 2010 and reach 540 million tons by 2020.

[2] This number is imputed based on 'China food and nutrition development outline' issued by China State Council.

There are a number of particularly pressing food consumption and nutrition challenges in China.

71.1 Challenges related to awareness and mindset

First, overeating is a major health awareness issue. Many people are unaware of the importance of a balanced diet and nutritional requirements and believe that eating more is the only way to improve their nutrition. Second, refined foods are mistakenly assumed to be healthy. Many people choose to eat refined, processed foods, not realizing that these may not have the minerals, vitamins, or other nutrients of their unrefined counterparts. Moreover, the refining process also leads to waste. Third, there is a common misconception that the more expensive food is, the healthier it must be.

71.2 Challenges related to food safety

Some food items are low-quality and do not meet safety standards. People need food that is safe, fulfils quality standards, and is clearly labelled. There are also some problems with agricultural inputs, such as pesticides and veterinary drug residues, as well as issues with unapproved additives in processed foods. There are also tainting problems in some food processing plants caused by quality control loopholes in rural areas.

71.3 Challenges related to unbalanced diets

Some rural areas are underdeveloped, thus food consumption there is low. Emerging towns, with their rapidly changing life styles and sudden ability to consume food at will, serve as the ground zero for nutritional diseases such as obesity, high blood pressure, and diabetes. Pregnant women, infants and babies, children and teenagers, and the elderly remain high-risk groups that require special supplements delivered through food and nutrition policies.

71.4 Challenges related to lack of knowledge

A sound knowledge and understanding of nutrition is instrumental in preventing diseases associated with malnutrition and overconsumption. In recent years, gaps in information dissemination resulted in poor public health awareness. This lack of awareness has led to unhealthy dietary patterns, demonstrated by people of all ages especially at banquets and dinner parties. China also exhibits a severe shortage of nutritionists. Additionally, some public media outlets are biased in their presentation of nutrition and health-related topics. Finally, commercials for food and functional food are often misleading.

In the early 1990s, China promulgated the *Outline on the Reform and Development of China's Dietary Patterns of 1990's* and the *Development Outline on China's Food and Nutrition (2001–2010)* to enhance food safety and to improve the nation's nutritional profile. These two documents have played an important role in promoting China's food production, food safety, and public nutritional status. While ensuring supply, consumption will be guided by increasing awareness of nutrition and letting consumption determine production, so as to reduce unwanted production and irrational consumption. The production, processing, distribution, and consumption of food should all be science-based, with control measures throughout the whole industrial chain.

To this end, China should:

First, attach an equal emphasis to food quantity and quality. Policy support should be strengthened to prioritize food quality and safety, while increasing food supply in a steady way. Given that consumption has changed and life has improved, a new outline for food and nutrition should be developed and implemented to balance food consumption and production. Legislative action on food safety and nutrition improvement should be accelerated to provide more guidance and support for better food and nutrition intake.

Second, establish programmes to improve dietary nutrition. Dietary nutrition improvement programmes should be designed to include regular dietary nutrition surveillance, nutritional intervention, targeted guidance, and consumption steering. It is also crucial to emphasize the professional management of a voluntary and participatory approach that is science-based. Dietary nutrition improvement should be better incorporated into public health initiatives. The production of safe agri-food, green food, organic food, and Geographical Indication (GI) food as well as the development of processed instant food and fortified food should be accelerated to support schemes promoting food nutrition, health surveillance, dietary nutritional intervention, and a nutritious diet. The development of key and quality food products should be highlighted, in order to guarantee the safe supply of food to key areas and dietary nutrition improvement for targeted groups.

And third, disseminate knowledge of food and nutrition. Based on government endorsement and promotion, public outreach activities should be carried out to encourage a balanced diet, healthy nutritional intake, and proper physical exercise, and to raise awareness of the importance of a healthy diet and life style practices. The state should issue group-targeted dietary guidance and nutrition manuals to disseminate appropriate nutritional concepts and dietary patterns and to cultivate a culture of dietary health. Experts, industrial and academic associations, and NGOs should be organized to provide knowledge of food and nutrition in communities. The media should be better supervised. Publications and publicity materials on nutrition and health should receive expert review to ensure that the knowledge and information contained are science-based and accurate.

72 The Great Chinese Famine

Douglas Almond

The Great Famine of 1959–61 was the 'greatest peacetime disaster' of the twentieth century (Eberstadt, 1997). In terms of both mortality and failed policy, the Famine was an outlier.[1] Around 30 million died, which ranks as the worst famine in modern history. Although weather was initially blamed, the draconian policies of Mao's Great Leap Forward are now accepted as the primary culprit. The Famine was an avoidable 'social catastrophe' (Smil, 1999) whose damage persists to this day.

72.1 Causes and manifestations

72.1.1 CAUSES

The Famine was caused by a breakneck attempt at industrial development. Seeking to overtake Britain and eventually the USA, Mao launched the Great Leap Forward in 1958, an ambitious set of centrally orchestrated reforms intended to promote heavy industry. Labour was diverted from agriculture, including to the famously inefficient 'backyard' furnaces. Grain procurement from rural areas was increased. Simultaneously, the further collectivization of agriculture production, intended to 'free up' rural labour for capital investments and industry, merged 740,000 cooperatives into 26,000 communes (Spence, 1990). Just as the abandonment of collective farming in the early 1980s would finally increase agricultural productivity, its intensification during the Great Leap Forward reduced productivity.[2] The political environment led provincial leaders to exaggerate reported grain production levels despite growing starvation. Exaggerations led to higher diversion of grain from rural areas to cities. China was a net grain exporter throughout 1960. Wastage of food in mandatory communal dining rooms has also been widely noted.

The Great Leap Forward featured a bizarre dalliance with *faux* science, including 'close planting' and using broken glass to fertilize crops (Becker, 1998). More important for the disastrous human calamity that would ensue, the baseline nutritional status

[1] Financial support from National Science Foundation CAREER Award (award # SES-0847329) Health Determinants and Research Design is gratefully acknowledged.

[2] Lin (1990) focuses on lost right of exit from communes, which here are considered part of the policy failure of the Great Leap Forward.

of poor Chinese was precarious, with tens of millions living at subsistence. Even small changes in labour allocation, labour productivity, and procurement would have outsized impacts on health.

72.1.2 IMMEDIATE EFFECTS

Famine began in the fall of 1959 and touched all regions of China. Grain output fell 15 per cent in 1959 and an additional 15 per cent in 1960 (Li and Yang, 2005). Relative to an average food energy requirement of around 2,100 calories per person per day, average calorie availability fell from 2,200 in 1958 to 1,800 in 1959 before bottoming out at 1,500 in 1960 (Ashton et al., 1984). According to official numbers, rural death rates rose to 2.5 times pre-Famine levels. Urban residents were not spared, death rates in urban areas in 1960 were 80 per cent above pre-Famine levels (China Statistical Press, 2000). Central provinces in Anhui, Henan, and Sichuan suffered the most, while northeastern provinces like Heilong-jiang and Jilin were less affected. The death rates had returned to normal in over half the provinces in 1961, but remained high in southern provinces like Guangxi and Guizhou. All told, around 30 million died due to the 'systematic failure' of Mao's Great Leap Forward (Li and Yang, 2005). Thus, the Famine's death toll easily exceeds that of Word War I.

The Famine ended once the Great Leap Forward reforms were belatedly (and quietly) reversed. Most surreal perhaps, the outside world did not realize the enormity of the disaster for a generation. Until the 1982 Census and other demographic data were released during the early 1980s (Ashton et al., 1984), the scale of the Famine went 'unnoticed' outside of China (Chen and Zhou, 2007). Even as late as 1997, the *New Encylopedia Britanica* did not list the China Famine among its list of famines over the last 200 years (Smil, 1999).

72.2 **Long-term effects**

An obstacle to understanding the health effects of famine is that large-scale microdata on births and deaths is unavailable for the famine period. The 'statistical blackout' (Lin, 1990) in China has encouraged researchers to look for traces of the Famine in data collected twenty or more years after the Famine's end, much in the sleuthing spirit of 'forensic economics' (Zitzewitz, 2012). While born of necessity, this approach is sensible in that most of those who went hungry due to the Famine managed to survive. Below, the effect of famine on childbearing and the health of surviving cohorts is summarized. Other important long-term effects of the famine, for example retribution during the Cultural Revolution against those who opposed Mao's Great Leap Forward policies, are omitted.

72.2.1 FERTILITY

Dyson's (1991) study of South Asian famines reveals that conceptions decrease prompt-ly and dramatically in response to famines. Indeed, the decrease in the number of births occurring nine months later is arguably a better metric of famine severity than informa-tion on grain prices.

The massive reduction in Chinese births is readily seen in Figure 72.1, which reveals a roughly one-third drop in surviving births during 1959–61 (as captured by the 1990 census data). The result was roughly 30 million delayed or prevented births, relative to previous cohort trends.

72.2.1.1 Developmental effects

The 'fetal origins' literature posits persistent health effects among famine survivors, now in their early 50s or older. Such effects are expected to be especially pronounced for cohorts exposed to famine in early childhood (see, e.g., Almond and Currie, 2011, and references). The basic reason for such persistent effects is that growth is most rapid dur-ing early childhood. If this rapid growth is disrupted, it is not always possible to 'catch up' with compensatory growth later on.

As such, the Famine also provides an opportunity/crucible to understand the impor-tance of developmental effects that occur outside of famines.[3] Absent a famine, poor

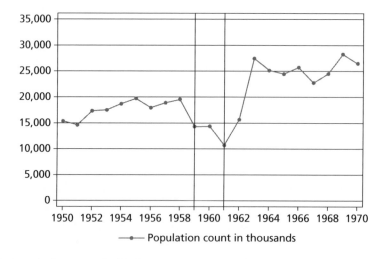

Figure 72.1. Population count by birth year

---

[3] Nutrition's effect on survivors is of interest because in the 20 years following the famine, nutrition in China was little improved above and beyond that achieved during the 1930s (White, 1991). While land reform of the early 1980s improved agricultural output and productivity, poor nutrition persisted for many. For example, Hesketh et al. (2002) found that in rural areas, 21 per cent of boys had moderate anemia (hemo-globin concentrations below 120 gl-1) and fully 55 per cent of girls.

nutritional status is correlated with a host of other negative factors that might impact a child's subsequent health (e.g. parental education). Randomized control trials could conceivably break this correlation and deliver causal estimates of nutrition, assigning starvation during pregnancy is not ethical. Using observational data, famines can furnish a natural experiment that helps with causal inference. Currie (2009) states that 'the most compelling examinations of the fetal origins hypothesis look for sharp exogenous shocks in fetal health that are caused by conditions outside the control of the mother'. While survivors are clearly a selected sample, it is generally thought that those missing were the weakest. Therefore, excluding those who died (or were not born) tends to make damage estimates on survivors conservative.[4]

Focusing on hard-hit Annhui, St Clair et al. (2005) found that the risk of schizophrenia more than doubled for the cohort exposed prenatally to the Famine. Looking nationally, Chen and Zhou (2007) found that the 1959 birth cohort would have been 3 cm taller absent the famine. Furthermore, they find that the famine reduced the labour supply and earnings of cohorts exposed in early childhood. Almond et al. (2010) found that men exposed to the famine in utero were 9 per cent more likely to be illiterate, 6 per cent less likely to work, and 6.5 per cent less likely to be married. Almond et al. (2010) also found an 'echo' effect on the next generation: mothers exposed to famine in utero were more likely to give birth to daughters some 20–35 years after the Famine. Mu and Zhang (2011) argued that female survivors showed more famine damage since they were less likely to suffer 'survivor bias' than males. Gorgens et al. (2012) likewise found that children who survived the famine were shorter.

Overall, findings from the China famine indicate that in addition to the tremendous death toll, children who survived the Famine were (and are) permanently scarred. This replicates findings from the better-measured Dutch famine of 1944–45, which also was more sudden, shorter, and therefore a 'cleaner' natural experiment. Beyond the 100-fold larger population, long-term effects from China's famine are noteworthy because: (i) 'economic' outcomes (e.g. labour force participation) show long-term damage, alongside the better-established long-term health consequences,[5] and (ii) the severity of the China Great famine remained hidden from the outside world for so long.

■ **REFERENCES**

Almond, Douglas and Janet Currie. 2011. Killing me softly: The fetal origins hypothesis. *The Journal of Economic Perspectives* 25, 153–72.

Almond, Douglas, Lena Edlund, Hongbin Li, and Junsen Zhang. 2010. Long-term effects of the 1959–61 China Famine: mainland China and Hong Kong. In *The Economic Consequences of Demographic Change*

---

[4] Despite the high mortality rate, selection into childbirth is more important empirically to subsequent cohort size than postnatal mortality.

[5] Notwithstanding Scholte et al.(2012).

in East Asia, NBER-EASE, edited by Takatoshi Ito and Andrew Rose, 321–350. University of Chicago Press, Chicago.

Ashton, Basil, Kenneth Hill, Alan Piazza, and Robin Zeitz. 1984. Famine in China, 1958–61. *Population and Development Review* 10(4), 613–645.

Becker, Jasper 1998. *Hungry Ghosts: Mao's Secret Famine*. New York: Owl Books. Henry Holt.

Chen, Yuyu and Li-An Zhou. 2007. The long term health and economic consequences of 1959–1961 famine in China. *Journal of Health Economics* 26(4), 659–681.

China Statistical Press. 2000. Comprehensive statistical data and materials on 50 years of new China. Technical report. Beijing: China Statistical Press.

Currie, Janet. 2009. Healthy, wealthy, and wise: is there a causal relationship between child health and human capital development? *Journal of Economic Literature* XLVII(1), 87–122.

Dyson, Tim. 1991. On the demography of South Asian famines: Part i. *Population Studies*, 45(1), 5–25.

Eberstadt, Nicholas. 1997. Book review: Hungry ghosts: Mao's secret famine (Jasper Becker). *The New York Times*, February.

Gorgens, Tue, Xin Meng, and Rhema Vaithianathan. 2012. Stunting and selection effects of famine: A case study of the Great Chinese Famine. *Journal of Development Economics* 97(1), 99–111.

Hesketh, Therese, Qu Jian Ding, and Andrew M. Tomkins. 2002. Disparities in economic development in eastern china: Impact on nutritional status of adolescents. *Public Health Nutrition* 5(2), 313–318.

Li, Wei and Dennis Tao Yang. 2005. The Great Leap Forward: anatomy of a central planning disaster. *Journal of Political Economy* 113(4), 840–877.

Lin, Justin Yifu. 1990. Collectivization and China's agricultural crisis in 1959–1961. *Journal of Political Economy* 98(6), 1228–1252.

Mu, Ren and Xiaobo Zhang. 2011. Why does the Great Chinese Famine affect the male and female survivors differently? Mortality selection versus son preference. *Economics & Human Biology* 9(1), 92–105.

Scholte, Robert S., Gerard J. van den Berg, and Maarten Lindeboom. 2012. Long-run effects of gestation during the Dutch hunger winter famine on labor market and hospitalization outcomes. IZA Discussion Papers 6307, Institute for the Study of Labor (IZA).

Smil, Vaclav. 1999. China's famine: 40 years later. *British Medical Journal* 319, 1619–1621.

Spence, Jonathan D. 1990. *The Search for Modern China*. London: Hutchinson.

St Clair, David, Mingqing Xu, Peng Wang, Yaqin Yu, Yoorong Fang, Feng Zhang, Xiaoying Zheng, Niufan Gu, Guoyin Feng, Pak Sham, and Lin He. 2005. Rates of adult schizophrenia following prenatal exposure to the Chinese famines of 1959–1961. *Journal of the American Medical Association* 294(5), 557–562.

White, Tyrene. 1991. Birth planning between plan and market: the impact of reform on China's One Child Policy. In *China's Economic Dilemmas in the 1990s: The Problems of Reforms, Modernization, and Interdependence*, edited by Joint Economic Committee. Washington, DC: US Government Printing Office.

Zitzewitz, Eric. 2012. Forensic economics. *Journal of Economic Literature* 50(3), 731–769.

73 An emerging new form of social protection in twenty-first-century China

Martin Ravallion

China's economic transformation has come with a dramatic change in the nature of social protection, which has switched from employer-based security arrangements (the so-called 'iron rice bowl') to an increasing role of governments at all levels.[1] This has been a policy response to fundamental changes in the urban labour markets, themselves stemming from policy changes.

A new form of open unemployment—found in many other economies but new to China—emerged in urban China in the late twentieth century, in the wake of retrenchments of workers in unprofitable state-owned enterprises since the mid-1990s. Not surprisingly, those least able to work, including the disabled or unhealthy, tended to be the first to go. Having previously been protected by their work units, they were now exposed to market forces. Using a 2000 survey, Appleton et al. (2002) found persistently high unemployment amongst retrenched workers, who tended to have fewer skills, less education, poorer health, and to be women and middle-aged. Less secure, less regular forms of part-time work have also become more common in urban China (Solinger, 2002; Park and Cai, 2011).

A new form of social policy based on targeted income transfers has also emerged. In an effort to address concerns about unemployed and vulnerable workers, and the social instability that they might create, the central government introduced the Minimum Livelihood Guarantee programme, popularly known as the *dibao* (DB) programme, in 1999. The programme aims to provide locally-registered urban households with an income per person below predetermined local DB 'poverty lines' (*dibao xian*) with a transfer payment sufficient to bring their incomes up to that line.[2] The programme started in Shanghai in 1993, spread to other cities, and became a national policy in 1997, with formal regulations

---

[1] The author is grateful to Philip O'Keefe, John Knight, and Dorothy Solinger for comments on this chapter.
[2] Obtaining registration in a new location is generally a difficult and lengthy process in China (not least for the poor), so in practice DB eligibility is confined to well-established local residents.

issued by the State Council in 1999.[3] The programme then expanded rapidly to include about 20 million participants in 2002, then expanded more slowly to 23 million in 2009. The programme is administered by the Ministry of Civil Affairs (MOCA).[4]

Like many social spending programmes in China, *dibao* relies on decentralized implementation. While the national and provincial governments provide guidelines and co-financing (to all except the well-off coastal provinces), the selection of beneficiaries is under municipal control. Each municipality determines its own DB line and finances the transfers in part at least from local resources. Claimants must apply to the local (county-level) Civil Affairs office for DB assistance, and they typically do this through their local community committee, which administers the programme on a day-to-day basis. There is also a community-level vetting process whereby the names of proposed participants are displayed on local notice boards and community members are encouraged to identify any undeserving applicants.

73.1 Incentives, targeting, and coverage of the *dibao* programme

In aiming to provide a guaranteed minimum income, there is a concern about behavioural responses to the DB programme. Some of those eligible may well be deterred by the application process (including the use of community notice boards). The World Bank (2007) reports the results of a survey of DB participants in Liaoning province, which found that only 10 per cent said they were ashamed or uncomfortable with disclosure of their household information in the application process. However, this calculation may well understate the extent of the problem since the survey could not include those deterred by public disclosure. Stigma effects may well be a problem but we do not really know.

Work disincentives are another concern. A strict interpretation of the design of the programme suggests that it could well create a *poverty trap*, in that participants would face a 100 per cent marginal tax rate, and so face no pecuniary incentive to escape poverty by their own means. However, the evidence to date is not consistent with this view. The quantitative results of Ravallion and Chen (2013) confirm my qualitative observations from field work suggesting that the way the programme operates in practice greatly attenuates the incentive effects implied by its design. Local DB officials actively smooth DB payments relative to income changes, such as by continuing payments for a few months

---

[3] On the history of the programme see Hammond (2009).

[4] In 2007 a new rural version of the *dibao* programme emerged, although much less is currently known about this programme. World Bank (2010) studies the rural DB programme in its early stages in four provinces. This suggests that the same issues discussed here regarding the urban programme have salience for the new rural programme.

after a participant finds a job. Using panel data on DB participants, Ravallion and Chen (2013) estimate that the benefit withdrawal rate is 12–14 per cent per annum, that is, a 100 yuan increase in income for DB participants results in only a 12–14 yuan drop in transfer receipts over one year, on average. Some cities have higher benefit withdrawal rates than others, with a range from 6 per cent to 27 per cent.

Based on these research findings, it appears that the incentives built into the programme *as it works in practice* are very unlikely to create a poverty trap. Indeed, when viewed in the light of the literature on the optimal design of targeted programmes (Kanbur et al., 1995), the programme's rate of benefit withdrawal in practice is clearly too low.

The programme is good at avoiding leakage to the non-poor. DB recipients are more likely to be poor—by multiple criteria, including disability and ill-health—and unemployed (Wang, 2007; Chen et al. 2008; Gustafsson and Deng, 2011).

Coverage of the poor is the bigger problem.[5] Despite the programme's aims, it is clearly not reaching the majority of those households with a reported income (net of DB) below the DB line (Chen et al. 2008). Gao et al. (2009) estimate that the programme only reaches half of its intended beneficiaries. Chen et al. (2008) estimate that the programme only covers about one-eighth of the aggregate income gap relative to the DB lines. The benefit levels for retrenched workers are clearly well below their prior wages.

Because of its weak coverage and low benefit levels the scheme's impact on poverty is modest. Using survey data for China's thirty-five largest cities in 2004, Ravallion (2009b) estimates that the proportion falling below the DB lines fell from 7.7 per cent to 7.3 per cent after DB transfers. While, in theory, this programme would eliminate poverty (based on the DB lines), the real impact is small.

73.2 Pros and cons of decentralized implementation

Decentralized implementation of a programme such as DB relieves the centre of the need to identify eligible recipients, which local authorities are presumably in a better position to do. The fact that local authorities retained power over the DB thresholds undoubtedly reflects in part the centre's lack of information. Government officials (in interviews with the author) said that the advantage of involving local community groups in this process is their greater knowledge of local conditions, including the cost of living. This type of central reliance on local governments is a long-standing feature of China's social policies.

Decentralization has its costs too. The choices made by local authorities in deciding who is eligible need not be consistent with the centre's objectives and will be constrained

---

[5] The authorities know this as the 'ought to protect, not protecting' (*yingbao weibao*) problem (Hammond, 2009).

by local resources. While the centre covers half or more of the cost nationally, the share financed locally varied across provinces. Evidence is incomplete, but there are indications that an effort is made to set higher central cost shares in poorer provinces.[6]

On combining evidence from an unusually large household survey (representative for each of the thirty-five largest cities) with administrative data on the DB lines chosen by local authorities, Ravallion (2009a) finds that better-off cities have higher poverty lines for programme eligibility and hence higher participation rates at given levels of absolute need. This could reflect either differences in the resources available or differences in perceptions of what 'poverty' means; the two explanations are hard to distinguish empirically. Either way, the inter-city income gradient in DB lines is large enough to roughly cancel out the effect of the inter-city differences in need for the programme. (The overall income gradient in programme spending is still negative, although small and statistically insignificant.) The variation in poverty lines associated with the decentralized eligibility criteria attenuated the programme's overall poverty impact, although the incomplete coverage of the 'DB poor' is clearly a bigger problem from this perspective (Ravallion, 2009a).

As a consequence of the income effect on the eligibility thresholds, equally poor families in different cities can have very different levels of access to the programme, with the poor in poor cities typically faring the worst. This happens even though the centre provides differential cost-sharing favouring poorer municipalities. The extent of this horizontal inequality suggests that it may create incentives for migration by China's poor. For now, the country's registration system and the low level of DB payments are constraining these incentives for migration.

73.3 **Social protection going forward**

The *dibao* programme is a good start, but there is still a long way to go. *Dibao* coverage needs to expand and benefit levels increase. Looking further ahead, likely reforms to the registration system (that would help free up the country's labour markets) and efforts to expand outlays and coverage will probably require a more unified, and horizontally equitable, system of social assistance.

■ REFERENCES

Appleton, Simon, John Knight, Lina Song, and Qingjie Xia. 2002. Labor retrenchment in China: determinants and consequences. *China Economic Review* 13(2–3), 252–75.

[6] World Bank (2007: 11) reports that the share of central financing relative to in-province financing for 2002 ranged from zero in coastal provinces to 100 per cent in Tibet, and 88 per cent in Ningxia.

Chen, Shaohua, Youjuan Wang, and Martin Ravallion. 2008. Does the *dibao* program guarantee a minimum income in China's cities? In *Public Finance in China: Reform and Growth for a Harmonious Society*, edited by Jiwei Lou and Shuilin Wang. Washington DC: World Bank.

Gao, Q., Garfinkel, I.. and Zhai, F. 2009. Anti-poverty effectiveness of the minimum living standard assistance policy in urban China. *Review of Income and Wealth* 55, 630–55.

Gustafsson, Bjorn A. and Quheng, Deng. 2011. Dibao receipt and its importance for combating poverty in urban China. *Poverty & Public Policy* 3(1), Article 10.

Hammond, Daniel Robert. 2009. Explaining Policy Making in the People's Republic of China: The Case of the Urban Resident Minimum Livelihood Guarantee System, 1992–2003. PhD thesis, University of Glasgow.

Kanbur, Ravi, Michael Keen, and Matti Tuomala. 1995. Labor supply and targeting in poverty-alleviation programs. In *Public Spending and the Poor*, edited by Dominique van de Walle and Kimberly Nead. Baltimore, MD: Johns Hopkins University Press for the World Bank.

Park, Albert and Fang Cai. 2011. The informalization of the Chinese labor market. In *From Iron Rice Bowl to Informalization*, edited by Sarosh Kuruvilla, Ching Kwan Lee, Mary E. Gallagher. Ithaca, NY: Cornell University Press.

Ravallion, Martin. 2009a. Decentralizing eligibility for a federal antipoverty program: a case study for China. *World Bank Economic Review* 23(1), 1–30.

Ravallion, Martin. 2009b. How relevant is targeting to the success of the antipoverty program? *World Bank Research Observer* 24(3), 205–31.

Ravallion, Martin and Shaohua Chen. 2013. Benefit incidence with incentive effects, measurement errors and latent heterogeneity. Policy Research Working Paper 6573, Washington DC: World Bank.

Solinger, Dorothy. 2002. Labour market reform and the plight of the laid-off proletariat. *The China Quarterly* 170, 304–26.

Wang, Meiyan. 2007. Emerging urban poverty and effects of the Dibao Program on alleviating poverty in China. *China & World Economy* 15, 74–88.

World Bank. 2007. *Urban Dibao in China: Building on Success*. Social Protection Group, East Asia Human Development Unit, Washington, DC: World Bank.

World Bank. 2010. *Social Assistance in Rural China: Tackling Poverty through Rural Dibao*. Social Protection Group, East Asia Human Development Unit, Washington, DC: World Bank.

Part XII
Health and Education

74 Economics of health transitions in China

Gordon G. Liu and Samuel Krumholz

74.1 Introduction

Over the past three decades, Chinese demand for medical services has increased much faster than the overall economy. This change is primarily due to China's epidemiological transition, the growth in available medical technology, and other changes related to Chinese income growth. In the face of growing demand, the Chinese health system struggled to increase healthcare supply and adjust healthcare financing, leading to serious cost and access problems for Chinese patients. In response, the government launched a nationwide health reform in 2009, aiming to make the system more responsive to the needs of Chinese citizens. To support this reform, the government allocated an additional 1.2 trillion CNY (Chinese yuan) to the health system between 2009 and 2011. Additionally, according to the State 12th Five-Year Health Reform Blueprint, the government will contribute no less than 1.2 trillion CNY to the health system between 2012 and 2015.

74.2 The epidemiological transition in population health

Since 1949, China has undergone a significant epidemiological transition in which degenerative, chronic, and man-made diseases have replaced infectious disease as the primary cause of morbidity and death. A recent review by Yang et al. (2008) indicates that the share of deaths caused by communicable diseases and maternal and perinatal conditions fell from 27.8 per cent in 1973 to 5.2 per cent in 2005. Over the same time period, the proportion of deaths caused by cerebro-cardiovascular disease, cancers, and chronic obstructive pulmonary disease (COPD) increased from 41.7 per cent to 74.1 per cent. Additional studies have shown the increasing growth of individual chronic diseases such as diabetes, coronary heart disease, and hypertension over the past thirty years (Wu et al., 2008; Yang et al., 2010).

China's disease transition has been influenced by three major societal shifts: life style, demographic, and environmental. First, recent research has shown that levels of physical activity among the Chinese population have decreased substantially over the past thirty years, especially among those living in urban areas (Munter et al., 2005; Ng et al., 2010; Cui et al., 2011). Similarly, carbohydrates have decreased as a percentage of total energy intake, while fats have increased (Popkin, 2008). These dietary and activity trends are reflected in the fast growth of China's overweight and obese population since 1990 (Wang et al., 2007). China has also undergone a major demographic shift. China's elderly population has been growing rapidly, with life expectancy increasing from 67 years in 1980 to 73 years in 2010, contributing to higher levels of chronic and degenerative disease (World Bank, 2010). The elderly are more susceptible to chronic and degenerative diseases; therefore as a country's elderly population grows, its non-communicable disease burden should also grow. Finally, air pollution in China increased drastically through the 1980s and 1990s. Chen et al. (2004) report that air pollution leads to higher rates of cerebrovascular disease, respiratory ailments, and COPD. Several other sources demonstrate the negative effects of increased water pollution in China on citizens' health, especially in rural areas (Wang et al., 2006; Wu et al., 1999; Ebenstein, 2012).

74.3 The inelastic response of China's old health system

74.3.1 HEALTHCARE FINANCING

Prior to 1978, China tightly controlled both the pricing and financing of healthcare through three major health financing programmes: the Government Insurance Scheme (GIS) and Labor Insurance Scheme (LIS) for the urban population and the Cooperative Medical Scheme (CMS) for the rural population. Limited availability of medical services and public provision of care kept overall costs low for patients. In 1980, only 21 per cent of total medical expenditures were financed by individuals, 43 per cent by social insurance programmes, and 36 per cent by the government (China Ministry of Health, 2010).

However, the period of Opening and Reform ushered in by the 1978 economic reforms saw dramatic changes in the Chinese Health System. By the late 1990s, only 9.5 per cent of rural residents still had insurance and the uninsured made up nearly half the urban population. The confluence of decreasing insurance coverage and increasing demand for medicine, led to a dramatic rise in out-of-pocket expenditures for Chinese patients (Liu, 2004; Yip and Hsiao, 2008). For example, in the year 2000, out-of-pocket payments made up 59 per cent of total health expenditures, compared with just 26 per cent for social insurance, and 16 per cent for the government (China Ministry of Health, 2010).

74.3.2 HEALTHCARE DELIVERY

China's healthcare delivery system also failed to adapt to increasing demand. For example, there were 3.5 times more inpatients in 2009 relative to1985, but, the number of hospital beds slightly more than doubled during the same time period (China Ministry of Health, 2010). Similarly, the number of medical personnel in China has barely kept pace with the growth in population even though demand has increased exponentially; the rate of doctors and health workers in urban areas per 1,000 population is lower today than it was in 1990, and in rural areas the growth rate has been only marginal.

One major reason for China's limited supply of healthcare is the regulatory and managerial environment within the health sector. The Chinese hospital industry has been largely dominated by public providers; private entry has been tightly controlled, limiting potential sources for healthcare expansion. At the same time, multiple government agencies exert control on different aspects of public hospital management, leaving public hospitals with little room and incentives to be responsive in other ways to market demand. These government agencies often work at cross-purposes, and no one agency is accountable for overall hospital performance. Compounding matters further, many of these agencies also have responsibility for regulating different aspects of the local healthcare market, creating many potential conflicts of interest.

China's inelastic healthcare supply is exacerbated by poor allocation of existing healthcare resources. Two main policies contribute to this misallocation: physician single-site practice, and restrictions on private entry into the market. In China, physicians are only allowed to practise at a single site; since urban tertiary hospitals offer physicians the most social and professional benefits, they attract the large majority of high-quality doctors. Thus, it can be difficult for primary care providers to find good physicians, leading many patients to seek care at tertiary facilities, even for minor illnesses. The over-reliance on tertiary care is compounded by medical provider ownership patterns. In China, public hospitals dominate the tertiary market, while private facilities are often limited to supplemental and specialty services in areas under-served by public hospitals thereby inverting the conventional comparative advantages.

74.4 The state health reform roadmap and future trends

These supply constraints led to significant discontent with the Chinese healthcare system among a large subset of citizens. In response, the Chinese government has made health reform a national priority. After extensive discussions and debates, the state health reform roadmap was launched in 2009, with five core components: (1) establishing a universal health insurance policy; (2) implementing a state essential drug policy; (3) strengthening the primary care delivery system; (4) improving the availability and equity of public health services; and (5) reforming the public hospital system (Liu 2009; Yip et al., 2012). After completion of the phase-one reform from 2009 to 2011, the government published the State 12th Five-Year Health Reform Blueprint, calling for a policy focus from 2012 to 2015 on three main agendas: universal insurance policy, the state essential drug policy, and public hospital reform.

74.4.1 THE UNIVERSAL INSURANCE POLICY

To improve demand-side healthcare financing, the government has established three national insurance programmes: Urban Employee Basic Medical Insurance (UEBMI), Urban Resident Basic Medical Insurance (URBMI), and the New Rural Cooperative Medical Scheme (NCMS). UEBMI mandates that urban employers provide employees in urban areas with insurance. On average, the total insurance premium is about 10 per cent of a worker's salary, with 8 per cent contributed by the employer, and 2 per cent by the employee. Both inpatient and outpatient care are covered. Although UEMBI's enrolment had reached 216 million employees by 2011, many urban residents including the retired, children, the unemployed, self-employed, and those working for small companies outside the formal sector remain ineligible (Lin et al., 2009; Eggleston, 2012).

To reach rural residents and urban residents ineligible for UEBMI, the government established NCMS and URBMI. Participation in both URBMI and NCMS are voluntary, and enrolment is heavily subsidized by government. In 2011, the government contributed 300CNY towards an individual's NCMS yearly premium, with the remaining individual contribution ranging from 20CNY to 50CNY (Yip et al., 2012). By 2011, NRCMS enrolment had reached over 832 million people. With similar levels of government contributions, URBMI has also grown rapidly; enrolment increased from 43 million in 2007 to over 247 million in 2011 (Yip et al., 2012). However, both NRCMS and UEBMI have relatively low funding levels per enrolllee. As a result, coverage is often quite shallow and is primarily focused on inpatient services, with higher deductibles and co-payment rates (Wagstaff et al., 2009). Additionally, for all three programmes, there is considerable autonomy at the local level in terms of premium rates, deductible/copayment levels, and benefit schemes.

By 2011, total enrolment in the three insurance programmes had reached nearly 1.3 billion or over 98 per cent of the Chinese population. Looking forward, the next stage of reforms will focus on three main tasks. First, the three insurance programmes should become better integrated, allowing different insurance plans to be portable and reimbursable at providers nationwide. This integration would benefit migrants and increase labour mobility. Second, commercial insurance companies should play a greater role by not only offering supplemental insurance, but also by helping to manage the primary insurance programmes. Third, in order to limit long-term cost inflation that may threaten the long-term fiscal health of government insurance programmes, it is critical to start physician payment reforms, aimed at moving from retrospective payments towards prospective payments such as Diagnostic-Related-Groups (DRGs) or capitation.

74.4.2 THE STATE ESSENTIAL DRUG POLICY

Overprescribing is endemic in China. Prescription drug spending makes up more than 40 per cent of total health expenditures, far higher than rates in most other countries. High prescription rates arise partially from China's drug policy: medical providers are required to charge low government set prices for medical services, but may charge a 15 per cent mark-up on drugs, incentivizing overprescribing. In 2009 the government launched an Essential Drug List (EDL) covering 307 medications in an effort to control drug spending. Drugs listed on the EDL are available for purchase at community and village health centres with no mark-up, and are reimbursed at a higher rate by the primary insurance programmes (Eggleston, 2012). However, the EDL eliminates health centres' prescription drug mark-ups without creating stable new sources of revenues, potentially threatening community health centres' financial sustainability. Rigorous empirical evaluations are necessary to determine the effects of this policy and provide guidance on further changes.

74.4.3 PUBLIC HOSPITAL REFORMS

The transformation of the public hospital system is essential to the success of the state health reform. Public hospital reforms focus on three main policies. First, separation reform in public hospitals describes the separation of regulatory and management responsibilities into different governmental entities. In general, regulatory responsibilities remain under the umbrella of the Ministry of Health, while management responsibilities shift to an independent government or non-government entities. A recent analysis by Liu et al. (2012) finds some evidence indicating a significant supply increase in response to the separation reform, although the success of separation reform also depends strongly on other reforms by local government. Second, the government has begun to carry out reforms allowing licensed physicians to practise medicine at multiple sites. With this reform, the government expects to see top quality physicians legally practise at primary and secondary care facilities, while still retaining their positions at tertiary hospitals. In an empirical study by Liu et al. (2012), data show that hospitals with an influx of secondary-sites had a concurrent increase in patient volume. Finally, private investment in the hospital market will be encouraged, from both domestic and international sources.

74.5 **Conclusion**

Over the past three decades, the Chinese population has undergone a significant health transition, creating a surge in healthcare demand. Although this demand initially put extreme strains on the Chinese healthcare system, in recent years the Chinese government has instituted a series of healthcare reforms meant to increase the system's responsiveness to Chinese patients' needs. Most significantly, the reforms include a commitment to universal insurance coverage and a transformation of public hospital management. Although these reforms address significant gaps in the current system, early empirical results examining their effects on healthcare access, cost and outcomes have been mixed. A continued emphasis on reform will be necessary to further promote accessible, affordable, and quality healthcare among the Chinese population.

■ **REFERENCES**

Chen, Bingheng, Chuanjie Hong, and Haidong Kan. 2004. Exposures and health outcomes from outdoor air pollutants in China. *Toxicology* 198(1–3), 291–300.

China Ministry of Health Statistical Digest. 2010. Available at: <http://www.moh.gov.cn/publicfiles/business/htmlfiles/zwgkzt/ptjty/digest2010/index.html> Accessed 5 August 2012.

Cui, Zhaohui, Louis L Hardy, Michael J. Dibley, and Adrian Bauman. 2011. Temporal trends and recent correlates in sedentary behaviours in Chinese children. *International Journal of Behavioral Nutrition and Physical Activity* 8, 93–100.

Ebenstein, Avraham. 2012. The consequences of industrialization: evidence from water pollution and digestive cancers in China. *Review of Economics and Statistics* 94(1), 186–201.

Eggleston, Karen. 2012. Health Care for 1.3 Billion: An Overview of China's Health System. Stanford Asia Health Policy Program Working Paper No. 28.

Lin W., G. G. Liu., and G. Chen. 2009. The urban resident basic medical insurance: a landmark reform towards universal coverage in China. *Health Economics* 18, S83–S96.

Liu, G. G. 2009. *Beijing's Perspective: The Internal Debate on Health Care Reform*. Washington, DC: Center for Strategy and International Studies (CSIS).

Liu, G. G., J. Pan, and C. Gao. 2012. Does separating government regulatory and management roles in public hospitals lead to greater supply capacity? Peking University China Center for Health Economic Research Working Paper.

Liu, Yuanli. 2004. Development of the rural health insurance system. *Health Policy and Planning* 19(3),159–65.

Munter, Paul, Dongfeng Gu, Rachel P. Wildman, Jichun Chen, Wenqi Qan, Paul K. Whelton and Jiang He. 2005. Prevalence of physical activity among Chinese adults: results from the International Collaborative Study of Cardiovascular Disease in Asia. *American Journal of Public Health* 95(9), 1631–6.

Ng, Shu Wen, Edward C. Morton, and Barry M. Popkin. 2010. Why have physical activity levels declined among Chinese adults? Findings from the 1991–2006 China Health and Nutrition Surveys. *Social Science & Medicine* 68(7), 1305–14.

Popkin, Barry M. 2008. Will China's nutrition transition overwhelm its health care system and slow economic growth? *Health Affairs* 27(4), 1064–76.

Wagstaff, Adam, Magnus Lindelow, Gao Jun, Xu Ling, and Qian Juncheng. 2009. Extending health insurance to the rural population: An impact evaluation of China's new cooperative medical scheme. *Journal of Health Economics* 28(1), 1–19.

Wang, Mark, Michael Webber, Brian Finlayson, and Jon Barnett. 2006. Rural industries and water pollution in China. *Journal of Environmental Management* 86, 648–59.

Wang Y., J. Mi, X. Y. Shan, Q. J. Wang, and K. Y. Ge. 2007. Is China facing an obesity epidemic and the consequences? The trends in obesity and chronic disease in China. *International Journal of Obesity* 31, 177–88.

The World Bank. 2010. Life expectancy at birth, total (years). Available at: <http://data.worldbank.org/indicator/SP.DYN.LE00.IN>. Accessed 3 August 2012.

Wu, Changhua, Crescencia Maurer, Yi Wang, Shouzheng Xue, and Devra Lee Davis. 1999. Water pollution and human health in China. *Environmental Health Perspectives* 107(4), 1999.

Wu, Yangfeng and the China NNHS Steering Committee and the China NNHS Working Group. 2008. Prevalence, awareness, treatment and control of hypertension in China. *Circulation* 118, 2679–86.

Yang, Gonghuan, Lingzhi Kong, Wenhua Zhao, Xia Wan, Yi Zhai, Lincoln C Chen, and Jeffery P. Koplan. 2008. Emergence of chronic non-communicable diseases in China. *The Lancet* 372(9650), 1697–705.

Yang, Wenying, and the China National Diabetes and Metabolic Disorders Study Group. 2010. The prevalence of diabetes among men and women in China. *The New England Journal of Medicine* 362(12), 1090–101.

Yip, Winnie and William Hsiao. 2008. MarketWatch: the Chinese health system at a crossroads. *Health Affairs* 27, 460–8.

Yip, W. C., W. C. Hsiao, W. Chen, S. Hu, J. Ma, and A. Maynard. 2012. Early appraisal of China's huge and complex health-care reforms. *The Lancet* 379(9818), 833–42.

75 The changing landscape of rural health services in China

Ling Zhu

75.1 Introduction to the structure of the Chinese healthcare system

The modern incarnation of the Chinese healthcare system began in the 1960s, with the creation of a three-tiered healthcare system. County-level hospitals were funded by the government, while township and village-level hospitals were a cooperative healthcare system, funded by the public welfare fund of communes and production teams. When communes were abolished in the economic reforms of the 1980s, the cooperative healthcare system nearly collapsed. Although the county government was responsible for covering the operational cost of hospitals at the county level and clinics at the township level, the government capped individual wages as well as funding in general. Village health workers (also known as 'barefoot doctors') transformed themselves into self-financed doctors, by the guidance and supervision of village health centres (Wei and Zhu, 2008).

At the county level, the Public Health Bureau both monitors the health industry and directs public health institutions (for example, by selecting hospital directors and approving investment plans). Since early 2003, it has also been responsible for the promotion of a new rural cooperative medical system (similar to health insurance, with a coverage rate of 97 per cent). In addition, all medical insurance companies and health institutions must be approved by the Health Bureau. To date, even though private doctors, clinics, and hospitals can enter the medical service market, they are excluded from the medical insurance system, so they are unable to compete with public institutions. Public hospitals alone dominate the market. Within the medical services market, they account for 77 per cent of total hospital beds, 79 per cent of health personnel, and 86 per cent of total operating income.

75.2 **Distortion of incentives in the supply delivery industry**

In the medical services ecosystem, village clinics bear the responsibility of providing rural residents with public health and basic healthcare services. However, public health project funding and other government subsidies are 'trickle down', and as money is filtered through multi-layered regulatory agencies much of the money is claimed by intermediaries. Village doctors, at the bottom of the chain, often fail to receive their full compensation. Moreover, they are required to pay township hospitals and county health bureau management fees (Zhu, 2011). Not only does this discourage existing doctors and affect their performance, but it hinders the ability of the health sector to attract trained doctors. Not only do private healthcare providers suffer from institutional and policy disadvantages, but villagers themselves often find it difficult to obtain high-quality healthcare.

Under this system where healthcare providers only receive a portion of their allotted subsidy, public medical institutions have evolved into a for-profit enterprise. Government price control bureaus, operating under a command economy mindset, underestimate the costs of providing medical services, the human capital investments of doctors, and the high-risk and high-intensity nature of the job. To compensate, medical fees and drug prices have skyrocketed.

The distortion is most visible in the pharmaceutical industry. With the industry's liberalization, public hospitals have wielded their state-protected monopoly to induce drug manufacturers to set higher prices while driving common low-cost drugs out of the market—reducing patients' options even further. The healthcare reform of 2009 abolished hospitals' ability to collude with pharmaceutical companies to set retail prices much higher than wholesale prices, but this has directly impacted on the income of these medical institutions. The general quality of service has decreased in hospitals.

With the establishment of the new rural medical cooperative system, 'third-party payers' have been introduced into the process of running medical institutions. Although the government institutions that allocate medical funding have attempted to establish some sort of control through reviewing prescriptions and checking reimbursements, they have not been effective. First of all, regulatory agencies lack the necessary technology and manpower to conduct serious audits—they can only outsource to corporate health insurance companies. Second, under fiscal decentralization, medical insurance is administered at the county level, resulting in a high degree of fragmentation. For example, a migrant worker's healthcare coverage is provided by his home county. If he gets sick in a city and visits a hospital there, it would be difficult for him to receive reimbursement, if any. Thirdly, the amount of funding is low (230 yuan per capita in 2011), and the number of medical institutions that received funding is low. This virtually prohibits patients and fund managers from 'voting with their feet' to influence hospitals and doctors.

75.3 **Conclusion**

The ideal medical services ecosystem would consist of healthy competition between multiple service providers, along with basic universal health insurance. To create this system, the government first needs to open up the healthcare market to private investors and destroy the public monopoly. Then the government should cease using price controls and intervening in operation of hospitals. Lastly, the current taxation system requires reform, and different forms of health insurance should be combined. To do so involves disturbing many groups with vested interests, and will therefore inevitably be difficult. However, without these institutional changes, pouring more money into the system will not cause it to unknot itself. For example, the Chinese government invested 1.1 trillion yuan in medical services reform, but it did not notably improve the availability of quality healthcare, and therefore it is unsurprising that it failed to alleviate public dissatisfaction with the entire healthcare system.

■ REFERENCES

Grossman, M. 2000. The human capital model. In *Handbook of Health Economics*, Volume 1A, edited by Anthony J. Culyer and Joseph P. Newhouse, 347–408. Amsterdam: North-Holland, Elsevier Science.
Wei, Z. and L. Zhu. 2008. *Reducing Health Vulnerability in the Economic Globalization: A Case Study from Rural China*, Beijing: Publishing House for Economic Management. In Chinese.
Zhu, H. 2011. The logic of medical reforms at grassroots. *Weekly Magazine of the New Century (Xinshiji Zhoukan)* 50, 78–9. (In Chinese.)

76 Human capital, economic growth, and inequality in China

James J. Heckman and Junjian Yi

China's rapid growth was fuelled by substantial physical capital investments applied to a large stock of medium-skilled labour acquired before economic reforms began.[1] As development proceeded, the demand for highly skilled labour has grown, and, in the past decade, China has made substantial investments in producing it. Egalitarian access to medium-skilled education, characteristic of the pre-reform era, has given rise to substantial inequality in access to higher levels of education. China's growth will be fostered by expanding access to all levels of education, reducing impediments to labour mobility, and expanding the private sector.

The complementarity between the abundant medium-skilled labour and the large inflow of physical capital induced by the Open Door policy has fostered China's economic growth since 1979. The high saving rate, fast accumulation of physical capital, and integration of China into the world economy during the 1980s and 1990s increased the demand for highly skilled workers. The return to education increased dramatically. The government implemented a radical expansion of higher education in 1999 in response to the substantial increase in the demand for highly skilled labour. As a result, the skills of the labour force have been substantially increased in the first decade of the twenty-first century. However, the restrictive household registration (*Hukou*) system and segmented labour market distort the incentive to invest in human capital and have created a large pool of 'left behind' children in rural areas. Moreover, reliance on family resources to finance children's education beyond primary level, the lack of capital markets, and substantial increases in tuition and accommodation fees have restricted opportunities for children from poor families to attain higher education. These factors reduce social mobility and perpetuate inter-generational poverty.

---

[1] Medium-skilled labour refers to those with primary or secondary education. The illiterate or semi-illiterate are referred to as low-skilled labour. Tertiary education graduates are defined as highly skilled labour. For an insightful discussion of China's economic reforms and its policies, see Lin (2011).

76.1 Complementarity between abundant medium-skilled labour and the large inflow of physical capital initiated China's economic growth since 1979

The extraordinarily high primary and middle school enrolment rates before the 1979 economic reform have not been fully appreciated in the literature studying China's economic growth. For example, in 1975 the primary school enrolment rate was 96 per cent, and the middle-school enrolment rate was 60 per cent (NBS, 2010). Adjusting for stages of economic development, the primary and secondary completion rates were much higher in China than in other Asian countries, such as South Korea and Taiwan, in the early stage of their economic take-off (Becker et al. 2012). Further, the Chinese pupil–teacher ratio of primary school in 1976 was 29, ranking 51st in the world and second in South and East Asia, next to Japan (World Bank, 2011).

However, in 1976, per capita GDP in China was about 2 per cent of that in the USA, ranking at the bottom across the world. In contrast with the abundance of labour, physical capital was extremely scarce in the 1970s. For example, the net foreign exchange reserve was at the negligible level of 0.58 billion US dollars in China in 1976 (NBS, 2010). The Open Door policy induced a huge inflow of physical capital since 1979. The total amount of FDI was US$1,096.6 billion from 1979 to 2008 (NBS, 2010). Adjusting for the stage of economic development, the per capita FDI was higher in China than in South Korea and Taiwan at a comparable stage of economic development.

76.2 Fast accumulation of physical capital endogenously increased the demand for higher education

However, the stock of highly skilled labour was low. Tertiary education was suspended during the Cultural Revolution from 1966 to 1976. Tertiary school enrolment rates hovered around 1.5 per cent to 2.5 per cent from 1979 to 1995 (NBS, 2011a). With economic growth and rapid accumulation of physical capital, the return to education increased (Wang, 2013). China, as with other East Asian countries, maintained a national gross saving rate as high as 35–55 per cent throughout the entire economic reform period, dramatically increasing the marginal productivity of labour, especially highly skilled labour. The newer technology was strongly complementary of higher skilled labour (Liang, 2011).

The increase in the demand for higher education led the government to implement a radical policy of expansion of higher education in 1999. The total number of fresh college graduates increased more than six-fold from 960,000 in 2001 to 6,350,000 in 2010, at an annual increment of 1 million per year (NBS, 2011a). Tertiary school enrolment rates jumped from less than 3 per cent to almost 19 per cent during the same period. Moreover, the increase in the stock of domestic college graduates is only one part of the entire picture. Constant et al. (2013) show that the number of Chinese students studying abroad had also increased dramatically. In 2000, less than 40,000 Chinese students went overseas. This number increased more than four-fold to almost 180,000 in 2008. China's impressive stride in human capital investment and its notable achievements in education have been less appreciated by the literature.

76.3 The widening inequality in education in China

Along with rapid economic growth and the expansion of higher education, inequality in education in China has increased drastically. Public schooling is funded mainly at the local level. Rich provinces tend to produce more human capital per capita than poor provinces. Resource constraints affect access to the schooling of individuals in different parts of China differentially, bringing disadvantages to rural areas and those in the west. Moreover, the place of a person's birth is one of the most important determinants of that person's adult skill level (Fleisher et al., 2011). This creates serious regional disparities and is a powerful source of cross-sectional and intergenerational inequality in Chinese society (Heckman, 2003, 2005).

This inequality is reinforced by the *Hukou* system. Based on the 1 per cent sample of the 2005 Census, there are about 140 million rural–urban migrants working in urban areas. Most of these migrants are not able to acquire urban residency due to the *Hukou* system. Thus, most of the children of these migrants are deprived of the right to attend free public schools in urban areas. Those able to attend public schools in the city have to pay a substantial tuition fee above what is required of locals. As a consequence, many migrant workers leave their school-age children behind to attend schools in their home villages. These 'left-behind' children are usually taken care of by grandparents or other relatives. According to research commissioned by the All-China Federation of Women, the estimated number of 'left-behind' children is 58 million (Ye et al., 2005). The rapid increase and large number of 'left-behind' children have caused serious concerns for Chinese society and the government. The schooling quality of these 'left-behind' children is not the only source of concern. The substantially negative effect on the children's psychological development and human capital caused by parental absence is another serious issue. The *Hukou* system has led to a segmented labour market (Fleisher and Wang, 2004; Meng and Zhang, 2001). In this system, *Hukou* status is a major determinant of an individual's salary, which distorts the incentive to investment in human capital (Heckman, 2005).

The ratio of government investment in schooling over GDP has historically been very low, and was 3 per cent in 2007, despite the fact that tertiary school enrolment rates increased from less than 2 per cent in 1990 to almost 19 per cent in 2010. A child's tertiary education in China is mainly financed by the family. In addition, tuition fees have also increased substantially with the rapid expansion of higher education. In the early 1990s, higher education was almost entirely subsidized by the government. However, the tuition fee plus accommodation fee for an ordinary college student exceeded RMB10,000 per year in 2010. Since the annual income of rural residents is only RMB5,919, and the annual disposable income of urban residents is RMB19,109 in the same year (NBS, 2011b), the cost of attending college has become a heavy burden for ordinary families, particularly for rural families. The lack of any capital market to finance the college education of children has further widened inequality in education. Li aet al. (2014) find that relative to other groups, the minority females and children from the central-western region and rural areas are much less likely to enter college. Wang et al. (2010) report evidence of the growing influence of private financial constraints on decisions to attend college as tuition costs have risen. Moreover, educational reform without the concomitant capital market reform and government support for the financially disadvantaged exacerbates the increase in inequality.

In addition, educational choice is a sequential process. Increase in the cost of attending tertiary schools discouraged children from poor and rural families from attending secondary school, because the option value of attending secondary school decreased. In recent years, secondary school enrolment in rural areas has deteriorated (NBS, 2011a).

76.4 Policies to foster human capital, promote economic growth, and decrease inequality

Although notable achievements in education have been made in the past decades, China still faces serious challenges in decreasing the inequality in education, fostering a highly skilled workforce, and promoting economic growth.

Faced by these challenges, government expenditure on education needs to increase. The current ratio of government expenditure on education to GDP is too low. A child's tertiary education is financed mainly by their families. This is neither efficient nor fair. On the one hand, investment in human capital has strong positive external effects on society. Private investment in human capital will never reach an efficient level. On the other hand, relying on family resources to finance a child's education leads to persistent intergenerational poverty.

The Chinese government should balance human capital investment across regions and across rural and urban areas. Schooling should be expanded in middle and western regions, as well as in rural areas. More primary and secondary schools should be built in urban areas to accommodate children of rural–urban migrants. Education for the large number of 'left behind' children should also be a priority in the government budget. More investments should be used to support the publicly supported college loan system to allow students to borrow against their future earnings, thereby allowing children from poor families to have the opportunity to attend college (Heckman, 2005). The tertiary school completion rate in China is still very low compared that in many developed countries, such as the USA, South Korea, and Japan. Moreover, the rapid expansion of tertiary education has also led to a deterioration of its quality (NBS, 2011a).

Increasing government expenditure is not the only way to enhance the quality of education. A lesson learned from studies in the USA, Europe, and other countries around the world is the value of competition among schools and incentives to improve the performance of educational institutions (Heckman, 2000). Thus, it is better to allow more private and foreign educational organizations to operate as it will undoubtedly promote competition between public and private schools and enhance the resources available to support the expansion of education. Even if the government is cautious in permitting private and foreign educational institutes to enter the market, more competition among the existing public schools should be encouraged because competition will increase the quality of education. Such competition will foster the development of curricula that feature job-relevant skills. So will development of closer links between formal educational institutions and the workplace. The current emphasis on academic education to the exclusion of job-relevant vocational education leads to shortages of medium-level skills.

Another important way to foster human capital that would entail less direct cost to the government would be to free up the labour market. The segmented labour market induced by the *Hukou* system reduces the incentive to invest in human capital in China. Current practices restrict labour mobility across regions. The government should remove these artificial barriers to achieve an integrated and efficient labour market. A free labour market allows individuals to reap the fruits of their skills, and thus allows the forces of market incentives to operate.

76.5 Summary

China's rapid economic growth was initiated by the complementarity between a solid base of a medium-skilled labour force and a huge inflow of FDI. It has been sustained by rapid physical capital accumulation and rapid human capital formation. However, China is now facing serious challenges. The Chinese government should take firm action to enhance public expenditure on education and to equalize educational opportunities between coastal and inland areas and between urban and rural areas. It should enhance the quality of education and foster a highly skilled labour force, remove inefficient institutional barriers, and develop an integrated and efficient labour market.

■ REFERENCES

Becker, G., K. Ye, and J. Yi. 2012. Rapidly growing human capital investment in China. Presentation at at the 2012 AEA Meeting.

Constant, A., J. Meng, B. Tien, and K. Zimmermann. 2013. China's latent human capital investment: Achieving milestones and competing for the top. *Journal of Contemporary China* 22(79), 109–130.

Fleisher, B., H. Li, and M. Q. Zhao. 2011. Human capital, economic growth, and regional inequality in China. *Journal of Development Economics* 92(2), 215–31.

Fleisher, B. M. and X. Wang. 2004. Skill differentials, return to schooling, and market segmentation in a transition economy: The case of mainland China. *Journal of Development Economics* 73(1), 315–28.

Heckman, J. J. 2000. Policies to foster human capital. *Research in Economics* 54(1), 3–56.

Heckman, J. J. 2003. China's investment in human capital. *Economic Development and Cultural Change* 51(4), 795–804.

Heckman, J. J. 2005. China's human capital investment. *China Economic Review* 16(1), 50–70.

Li, S., J. Whalley, and C. Xing, C. 2014. China's higher education expansion and unemployment of college graduates. Forthcoming, *China Economic Review*, <http://dx.doi.org/10.1016/j.chieco.2013.08.002.>

Liang, J. 2011. Evolution of the labor market in a rapidly developing economy. Unpublished manuscript, Graduate School of Business, Stanford University.

Lin, J. Y. 2011. *Demystifying the Chinese Economy*. Cambridge: Cambridge University Press.

Meng, X. and J. Zhang. 2001. The two-tier labor market in urban China: Occupational segregation and wage differentials between urban residents and rural migrants in Shanghai. *Journal of Comparative Economics* 29(3), 485–504.

National Bureau of Statistics. 2010. *China Compendium of Statistics 1949–2008*. Beijing: China Statistics Press.

National Bureau of Statistics. 2011a. *China Education Yearbook*. Beijing: China Statistics Press.

National Bureau of Statistics. 2011b. *China Statistics Yearbook*. Beijing: China Statistics Press.

Wang, L. 2013. How does education affect the earnings distribution in urban China, *Oxford Bulletin of Economics and Statistics* 75(3), 435–54.

Wang, X., B. M. Fleisher, H. Li, and S. Li. 2010. Access to higher education and inequality: The Chinese experiment. University of Hawaii, unpublished manuscript.

World Bank. 2011. World Bank Data Catalog. Available at: <http://data.worldbank.org/indicator>.

Ye, J., J. Murray, and Y. Wang. 2005. *Left-behind Children in Rural China: Impact Study of Rural Labor Migration on Left-behind Children in Mid-West China*. Beijing: Social Sciences Academic Press.

77 Human capital

Schooling

Haizheng Li and Qinyi Liu

While human capital can be accumulated via different channels, formal schooling still constitutes a major form of investment in the formation of human capital. As the Chinese economy has grown, China's educational system has also expanded rapidly, and the Chinese people currently enjoy unprecedented access to education.

77.1 Formal school system

The basic educational system in China is governed by the Compulsory Education Law (1986), which provides a free, mandatory nine-year education (six years primary school and three years middle school). The compulsory education system has increased enrolment significantly and helped largely eliminated illiteracy. The enrolment of school-aged students in primary school reached 98.6–99.7 per cent during 1999–2010.[1] The admission rate to middle school was 74.6 per cent in 1990,[2] and had risen to 98.7 per cent by 2010.[3]

After middle school, students can apply for high schools or middle-level technical schools. The admission rate of middle school graduates into high school has risen from 42.6 per cent in 1991 to 87.5 per cent in 2010.[4] It takes three years to complete high school, and students can choose to concentrate on humanities or sciences, and need to pass standardized tests for graduation.

Higher education consists of colleges and four-year universities that provide bachelor's, Master's, and doctoral degrees. In order to earn acceptance into higher education, graduating high school students need to take a national college entrance examination.

With a bachelor's degree, students are qualified to apply for a Master's programme. For admission, students must either pass the national entrance examinations for graduate study or seek approval for exemption from the school. In 2010, the total number of

[1] Ministry of Education of PRC: <http://www.moe.edu.cn/publicfiles/business/htmlfiles/moe/s6200/201201/129608.html>.

[2] Chinese Government's official website: <http://www.gov.cn/test/2005-06/27/content_10052.htm>.

[3] Ministry of Education of PRC website: <http://www.moe.edu.cn/publicfiles/business/htmlfiles/moe/s6200/201201/129607.html>.

[4] Ministry of Education of PRC website: <http://www.moe.edu.cn/publicfiles/business/htmlfiles/moe/s6200/201201/129607.html>.

students enrolling on a Master's programme reached approximately 1.3 million, 11–12 times of that in 1994.[5]

Basically, students with only a bachelor's degree cannot apply directly to a doctoral programme. A Master's level education is usually required. Students gain admission to a doctoral programme by passing an entrance examination or by receiving a waiver. There is no national entrance examination for doctoral study and each university sets its own standards for admitting doctoral students. In 2010 the total number of students enrolling on a doctoral programme was 258,950, an increase of 10–11 times compared to that in 1994.

Since China's opening up, studying abroad has become a more prominent path of formal education for Chinese students. In 2010, the total number of Chinese individuals studying abroad reached 284,700.[6] From 2000 to 2011, the average annual growth rate of students studying abroad was 25.1 per cent.[7] Before 1992, most students studying abroad were funded either by the government or by financial aid from the host school. As family income rapidly increased, the reliance of Chinese students on financial aid has been significantly reduced. Now many Chinese students study abroad with funding from their own families.[8]

In the 1980s and 1990s, a majority of Chinese students studying abroad were for doctoral degrees. In recent years, however, there has been an increasing flow of Chinese students going abroad to study for their Master's or bachelor's degree, or even to study in high school and middle schools. In 2000, 80.1 per cent of all Chinese students studying in US universities were pursuing a graduate degree, while in 2010, graduate students accounted for only 48.8 per cent.[9]

77.2 From education for the elite to education for the masses

Traditionally, higher education in China was designed to train the elite. Entry was highly selective and all tuition was paid for by the government. However, universities began to charge in 1989. The tuition fee level is relatively high compared to family incomes,

[5] In this chapter, unless otherwise specified, the data are from the *China Statistic Yearbook* and the *China Educational Statistic Yearbook*, various years.
[6] *China Statistic Summary* (2011), published by China Statistics Press.
[7] New China 60 Year Compiled Statistics (1949–2008), and official website of Ministry of Education of the People's Republic of China.
[8] Ministry of Education: <http://www.moe.edu.cn/publicfiles/business/htmlfiles/moe/moe_863/201202/130328.html>.
[9] Open Doors Fact Sheet: China, Institute Of International Education, Educational Exchange Data from Open Doors 2011.

especially for those living in rural areas. In 1997, the average tuition cost per student was about 28 per cent of per capita GDP, and this ratio reached 46 per cent in 2002 (Li, 2010). In 2009, the average fee per student was 22 per cent of per capita GDP, accounting for 32.3 per cent of the average annual disposable income of urban households and 107.3 per cent of the average income of rural households.[10]

In the meantime, the higher education system has undergone significant expansion. From 1978 to 2010, the number of regular higher education institutions has grown from 598 to 2,358. The number of students enrolled increased from 0.86 million to 22.32 million. In 2010, there were 6.6 million new students admitted into colleges and universities, which exceeded the total enrolment of 2000.[11]

The accelerated growth of higher education began in 1999 due to a central government initiative. In that year alone, the enrolment of new undergraduate students increased by 47 per cent. For the five-year period from 1999 to 2003, the average annual growth in new enrolments was 29 per cent.[12] The growth in enrolments has declined since then and the average annual growth for 2004–10 was 6.8 per cent. In 2010, the number of undergraduate students who completed their degree was nearly 5.8 million, almost equalling the total number of students who graduated in the fifteen years from 1978 to 1992.

For graduate programmes, the new enrolment in 2010 was 6.6 times higher than in 1999, reaching 0.47 million. This sector also experienced rapid expansion during the period 1999–2004, with an average annual growth of 27.8 per cent in new enrolments; and for the next six-year period, 2005–10, the average annual growth rate remained at 8.9 per cent. At the Doctoral level, new enrolments in 2010 were 63,762, around three times that of 1999.

The rapid expansion of higher education significantly increased the chance of getting into a university. At the undergraduate level, among those who participated in the National College Entrance Examinations, the rate of admission was below 10 per cent before 1981. From 1981 to 1998, the admission rate was in the range 10–40 per cent.[13] During 1999–2010, the admission rate was in the range 55–70 per cent, and reached 72.3 per cent in 2011.[14]

College education has become widely available and the proportion of young people studying in higher education has increased. The urban population with a college

[10] *China Educational Finance Statistic Yearbook* 2010; *China Statistic Summary* (2011), published by China Statistics Press.

[11] Comprehensive Statistics of 55 Years of New China; Official website of Ministry of Education of the People's Republic of China.

[12] In the chapter, the average annual growth rate is calculated based on the simple average of annual growth rate for each year in the time period.

[13] Admission rates are from <http://www.neea.edu.cn/>.

[14] <http://gaokao.eol.cn/html/g/report/report1>.

education or above accounted for 3.9 per cent of the total urban labour force population in 1982,[15] and this ratio had increased to 21.1 per cent by 2010.[16]

77.3 **Restructuring higher education**

The expansion and transition of higher education has raised a number of challenges. First, how should universities restructure their curriculums in order to meet the demands of the market and prepare their ever-increasing numbers of graduates for a variety of different jobs? Second, how should the higher education system maintain its role in advanced training that supports the development of world-class researchers and innovators as well as a highly skilled labour force?

77.3.1 THE DILEMMA OF THE MASTER'S PROGRAMME

During the years when higher education was a luxury in China, a Master's degree was considered to be elite. In the 1980s, an individual with a Master's degree could be a professor and researcher in a university. Master's programmes at the time were designed to train researchers. However, the situation has changed significantly with the mass enrolment of Master's students and the establishment of large-scale doctoral programmes. The role of the Master's programmes in training researchers has dramatically diminished. The majority of graduate students with Master's degrees now enter non-research jobs, while universities and research institutes require a doctoral degree for faculty.

However, Master's programmes have not caught up with those changes yet. They are still intended to train researchers, with a strong research component in the curriculum. More specifically, most Master's students are paired with faculty advisers, and are required to write a thesis with a formal proposal defence and final defence in front of a committee. Many programmes even require publication for graduation. Therefore, there now exists an inconsistency between the professionally focused outcome of Master's students and the outdated design of their curriculum.

Such an inconsistency creates a huge waste of valuable resources. Faculty spend time participating in thesis defences and evaluating student papers that mostly have little research value; and students take a great deal of time doing something that may not directly benefit their future job placement. This incentive structure produces low-quality

---

[15] The labour force represents the population aged 16–54 for females and 16–59 for males.

[16] Population data by age, education level, and urban–rural area are from *China Population Statistic Yearbook*, Bureau of Statistics, various years.

theses and low quality advising, and even more serious problems of academic dishonesty. In order to meet the publication requirement for graduation, some students pay publishers in exchange for publication. This has created a market for a large number of low quality journals, which take papers for money.

Therefore, the Master's programme needs to be overhauled, specifically the mandated research requirements should be removed. The programme should be flexible and leave the choice to students and faculty, as is the case for most Master's programmes in the USA. More specifically, a Master's programme should serve as a bridge to both the job market and doctoral programmes. The new Master's structure would have a thesis and a course-only option, and the duration can be from one and a half years to three years. Some aspects of the curriculum, such as defences and faculty advising, should be dropped.

77.3.2 CHALLENGES FOR DOCTORAL PROGRAMMES

Doctoral programmes are mostly designed to train those who have the potential to become highly skilled for research, and a doctoral degree represents the highest level of training in a field. A major problem for doctoral programmes in China is that the training they give graduates for research is insufficient. In particular, most doctoral programmes only require three years to complete, which is much shorter than the 4–7 years in US universities. Moreover, doctoral students are not required to take many courses before starting their dissertation; while in the USA, students spend the first 2–3 years taking courses. As a result, in China, doctoral students do not receive the necessary new training in theory or quantitative techniques, and are poorly equipped for advanced research.

This problem is aggravated by the prevalence of 'on-the-job part-time' doctoral students. It is common for universities in China to admit part-time doctoral students, especially in the field of the humanities and social sciences. These students are mostly government officials and company executives. Many of them do not formally take any classes, and even worse, some may hire others to do their dissertation work. This phenomenon has serious consequences. First, it produces low quality research and doctoral programmes. Second, it creates a negative impact on academic integrity among professionals. The disrepair of the nation's doctoral programmes is a reason for the widespread culture of cheating and plagiarism in academia in China. An even more severe consequence is that high-quality students with research potential are discouraged from pursuing a doctoral degree in China, and some of them go overseas to further their studies. Therefore, it creates a vicious cycle: low quality doctoral programmes admit low quality students, which further lowers the quality of doctoral programmes.

Problems with the quality of doctoral programmes have resulted in very low market value for domestic doctorates, in comparison to foreign trained doctorates. A doctorate from a US research university would be in great demand in China. Many universities set up special policies to attract them, while domestically trained doctorates have difficulties in securing employment. The salary gap is even more dramatic. In 2012, the starting salary for new, US-trained doctorate in economics was around RMB 350,000 yuan for an assistant professor position in China; in comparison, domestically trained doctoral graduates only earn about 1/6–1/3 of that amount.

In the long term, the inferior doctoral programmes will impede the development of higher education, and thus restrain China's capacity for research and innovation, eventually its competitiveness in the world.

77.4 **The effect of education**

Although higher education has expanded substantially, it remains extremely difficult to get into a top undergraduate programme. And the training from undergraduate programmes in the top schools has been both stable and of consistently good quality. As a result, the labour market increasingly focuses on an individual's bachelor-granting school, even after they have received a Master's or doctoral degree. Those graduating from elite universities for their undergraduate degrees were received much more favourably than their peers from non-elite schools in the job market. Some employers even automatically filter out job applicants whose undergraduate schools are not in the top 100.

This phenomenon shows that employers do not have confidence in the training an individual has received in a post-graduate programme, and that education only seems to be an effective signal at the undergraduate level. Graduate students often take various professional tests outside of the university, such as certificates in accounting, finance, information technology, and English, in order to create signals that improve their competitiveness in the job market.

Yet, despite the various problems in the Chinese educational system, the rates of return to education have been rising since the start of economic reform, with a rate of 1–3 per cent in the 1980s to 8–12 per cent after 2000. It is unclear, though, how much of this rise is due to higher demand from the labour market, the rising private costs of attending education, or a vintage effect, that is, the higher quality of the education received in school, if any.

Additionally, education plays an important role in the growth of China's human capital. For the period of 1985–2008, the average annual contribution of education to the growth of human capital is 0.86 percentage points, and this contribution primarily came from expanding education beyond middle school level (Li et al., 2013). Moreover, studies also find strong positive externalities of education in China (Liu, 2007) due to the effect of overall education in a city in increasing an individual's earnings, as well as strong positive effects of investing in education in reducing regional inequality (Fleisher et al., 2010). Therefore, it is important for the Chinese government to continue to increase their investment in education.

The rising private returns to education will continue to provide strong incentives for individuals to invest in schooling and to pursue higher levels of education. The social and political benefits of education should also encourage the Chinese government to increase spending on education. However, in order to utilize those resources effectively, there are a number of opportunities to reform and restructure the higher education systematically, so that it can provide productivity-enhancing education to a large number of people as well as highly advanced training that can support a dynamic and technologically innovative economy.

■ REFERENCES

Fleisher, Belton, Haizheng Li, and Minqiang Zhao. 2010. Human capital, economic growth, and regional inequality in China. *Journal of Development Economics* 92(2), 215–31.

Li, Haizheng. 2010. High education in China—complement or competition to US universities. In *American Universities in Global Competition*, edited by Charles T. Clotfelter (NBER) invited book chapter), 269–304. Chicago: University of Chicago Press.

Li, Haizheng, Yunling Liang, Barbara Fraumeni, Zhiqiang Liu, and Xiaojun Wang. 2013. Human capital in China, 1985–2008. *Review of Income and Wealth* 59(2), 212–34.

Liu, Zhiqiang. 2007. The external returns to education: evidence from Chinese cities. *Journal of Urban Economics* 61(3), 542–64.

78 The commanding heights
The state and higher education in China

Rong Wang

78.1 Introduction

'The commanding heights' was first used by Lenin as a defence of his New Economic Policy, which included permitting profit-making enterprises in some areas of the economy. In persuading his suspicious colleagues, Lenin proclaimed at a convention in 1922 that the reforms were rather modest, and the new Soviet state would always retain its control over what he called the 'commanding heights' of the economy. By 'the commanding heights', Lenin meant the critical sectors that dominated economic activity—primarily electricity generation, heavy manufacturing, mining, and transportation. In other words, the state would control the most important elements of the economy by commanding the heights.

The commanding heights as a military metaphor once again gained audience when Daniel Yergin and Joseph Stanislaw used the term as their book title and their unifying thread to analyse the battle between government and the marketplace in twentieth-century economic history (Yergin and Stanislaw, 1998). One is easily reminded of the book and the metaphor when China's development stories become the target of scrutiny.

The dramatic expansion of higher education in China has already attracted enormous attention worldwide. Among developing countries, China has perhaps made the most impressive progress, at least in quantitative terms, in the shortest period of time. Total enrolment in China's higher education system increased from 1.02 million in 1980 to 31 million in 2010 (UNESCO, online sources).[1]

The expansion of higher education in China is in need of a good narrative. A good narrative explains what has happened and helps to organize thinking for the future. There are already several story lines in the available literature.

---

[1] <http://data.uis.unesco.org/#>.

1. *The developmental state story*. The legitimacy of the Chinese state is rooted in its ability to maintain growth of its economy, with human capital being an increasingly important determinant. The expansion of higher education in China is a state-led process, which by design primarily serves the political objective of sustaining state legitimacy.

2. *The retreating state story*. The Chinese state has embraced the ideology that market mechanisms are more effective and efficient than totalitarian controls by the state in the planned economy. Under the guidance of this ideology, education reforms have been undertaken, with the powers of the state curtailed in this sector.

3. *The responsive state story*. This could also be called the market transition story. Higher education expansion is largely seen as a response from the state to the increase in private demand for education from citizens. The state, from this perspective, behaves in a very responsive manner and follows the collective will of citizens. The expansion is essentially a market phenomenon, and individual demand is the driving force behind it. Scholars so inclined make strenuous efforts to provide evidence that private rates of returns to higher education in China keep rising, sustaining the expansion.

In this chapter we propose a different story line utilizing the military metaphor of 'the commanding heights' as used by Yergin and Stanislaw (1998). We argue that what has happened in higher education in China is essentially a change of strategy by the state, and for the state. By commanding the heights, the state retains its reign.

78.2 **The commanding heights of higher education in China**

China's higher education under the planned economy is a system where the state controls every aspect wherever feasible. Higher Education Institutes (HEIs) functioned as a state apparatus that specialized in training. Students were provided with free education at HEIs which were all publicly owned and operated, as private institutions were rapidly eradicated in the 1950s soon after the Peoples' Republic of China was founded. What is of paramount importance to the system is that graduates of colleges, universities, and three-year polytechnics were commonly under the control of direct state assignment, through which they were guaranteed jobs in the state sector.

The decades after economic reform witnessed a transition of this strategy by the state, from the control-all strategy to the commanding heights strategy. There are several important dimensions to the commanding heights strategy as identified by the state in action, including: the commanding heights of the HEI hierarchy, and the commanding heights of the mechanisms of intervention.

78.2.1 THE COMMANDING HEIGHTS OF THE HIERARCHY OF HEIs

How has the expansion in China's higher education been achieved? There are two reforms adopted by China's central government. One is to loosen their grip on the mass of HEIs and decentralize them towards local governments, the other is to prioritize support to elite institutions.

For the first reform, the major policies include: (1) localization of HEIs which used to belong to central-level industry ministries; (2) structural streamlining and centralization of the regulatory and management responsibilities to a two-tier system of management, consisting of two central organizations including the Ministry of Education and the provincial education bureaus; (3) localization of the accreditation authority for three-year vocational and professional institutions (polytechnics) to provincial governments.

The above policies were quick to take effect. The number of HEIs belonging to the central government declined from more than 400 in the early 1990s to only 111 in 2001. After local governments were given autonomy for accreditation, 584 polytechnics were established in the next four years.

For the second strategy of 'the commanding heights', there are several important features:

1. Enrolment of HEIs that belong to the central government, that is the Ivy League of the Chinese higher education, was under rigorous control despite the dramatic expansion of the whole system. The non-elite institutions, that is those belonging to local governments, have been relied upon to absorb the mass of students. Due to different rates of expansion of the two tiers, between 1998 and 2006, the share of central HEIs in total enrolment (four- and three-year regular programmes) drastically declined from 33.76 per cent to 9.52 per cent during the period.

2. Another symbol of the added commitment of the Chinese government to the commanding heights was when, on 4 May 1998, President Jiang Zemin declared that 'China must have a number of world class universities' in his speech at the conference celebrating Peking University's centennial. Thus, in addition to the on-going 'Project 211',[2] Project 985 came into being in 1999. The project involves both national and local governments allocating large amounts of funding to a certain number of designated and best universities. Specific project grants such as Project 985 and Project 211 have comprised a substantial proportion of total annual public financing for elite institutions since the projects started.

---

[2] Project 211 is a project initiated in 1995 by the Ministry of Education of the People's Republic of China, with the intent of raising the research standards of high-level universities. The name for the project comes from an abbreviation of the twenty-first century and 100 (approximately the number of participating universities).

78.2.2 THE COMMANDING HEIGHTS OF INTERVENTION MEASURES

There is a consensus that the adoption of cost-sharing policies and charging individuals tuition fees are the most important reform policies over the past three decades in China's higher education sector.

Yet it should be noted that cost-recovery policies were implemented before instead of for the expansion of higher education. In the 1980s, the Chinese government started to promote 'a multi-channel approach' to financing the education sector. Schools at every level were allowed to charge tuition fees,[3] which have since become an increasingly important source of revenue particularly for HEIs. The share of government appropriations in total educational revenues for higher education declined from 59.38 per cent in 1998 to 53.88 per cent in 2000, which is made up by the increasing share of student tuition fees, from 14.29 per cent to 22.04 per cent, and the proportion climbed further to more than 33 per cent in 2009.

Yet, in hindsight, it is clear that the state has adopted differential treatment towards different aspects of university governance. In brief, the state allows HEIs more leeway in fund raising, but takes measured steps to allow private institutions to proliferate, meanwhile it develops more comprehensive rules of quality assurance, and keeps its hands-on approach to HEIs' personnel management firmly unchanged. Despite the fact that the financial aspect of the reform has attracted much attention, comparatively speaking, it is less important, and less relevant to the commanding heights strategy, for the state to retain the basics of its control over HEIs.

78.2.2.1 Ownership reform of HEIs

Although reform to promote the development of private education was started in 1980s, enrolment at private HEIs only reached 13.4 per cent by 2005. During this period, China's education development model can be described as 'small private sector, large private finance'.

The prominence of independent colleges with hybrid ownership structures in the private education sub-sector has largely escaped the attention of scholars outside China. Such institutions are usually created and operated by public colleges or universities. In fact, many of the independent colleges are creations of central HEIs and top local HEIs. For instance, of the 320 independent colleges established by 2006, 83 of them were founded by Project 211 HEIs. By relying on institutions with hybrid ownership, China presents a very different development model of private education compared to those in other East Asian countries. It indicates a conservative if not distrustful attitude towards ownership reform of HEIs by the state.

[3] China stated to implement free compulsory education in 2006.

78.2.2.2 **Quality assurance**

The state has developed a more sophisticated and comprehensive quality assurance system of mechanisms to hold HEIs accountable. The evolution of higher education assessment in China during the expansion period can be separated into two phases. The first phase is the Discipline Assessment Phase lasting from 1985 to 1994, with a focus on specific disciplines. The Comprehensive Assessment Phase lasted from 1995 to 2001, the objective of assessment turned to the educational capacities of HEIs. Furthermore, a new procedure for evaluating all the four-year HEIs—including both elite and non-elite institutes—was started in 2002 amid opposition and suspicion. Under the procedure, every university is to be evaluated once every five to six years (OECD, 2003).

78.2.2.3 **Personnel management and allocation of talents**

The state exerts strong control through the appointment of its agents at HEIs. According to Article 39 of China's Higher Education Law, 'In every publicly funded higher education institution there shall be a committee of the Communist Party of China that leads the institution while the president is responsible for the administration.' For internal administration of HEIs, the committee representative of the Party is responsible for the selection and training of senior cadres and for managing a large legion of Party members consisting of students and professors. For instance, Party member students accounted for 24 per cent and 29 per cent respectively at Peking University and Tsinghua University. The proportions of the Party member faculty are even higher. Also by stressing Party importance at elite institutions, the state retains the commanding heights over the allocation of talents, and 'the lure of officialdom', continues to attract the best and the brightest of the young into the mandarin ranks.

78.3 **Conclusion and discussion**

This chapter is not intended to provide a thorough and in-depth analysis of what has happened in China's higher education system, but focuses upon a selected few aspects of the change that, in opinion of the author, have largely escaped attention. It is argued that institutional differentiation in the Chinese system is a result of the state strategy of 'the commanding heights'; specific grants such as Project 985 and Project 211 are efforts to consolidate the grip of the state over elite institutions. In the available literature the shifting of the responsibility to finance HEIs from the state towards individuals has been identified as the most important feature of China's reform, it is argued in this chapter that in fact it is less important, and less of the nature of the commanding heights strategy, for the state to retain the basics of its control over HEIs. Control over the rules which assess the quality of HEIs and their branch disciplines and control of the hiring and promotion of faculty and senior cadres inside HEIs are representative of the commanding heights approach.

What are the policy implications? First, horizontal competition among local governments, which is viewed by some economists as the most important engine of economic growth in China, is hampered in the arena of education. Local higher education systems are restrained by the fact that the top HEIs in their territory invariably belong to the central government. Second, vertical differentiation of the higher education system is consolidated. The dynamics behind institutional development is essentially vertical and oriented to bureaucratic rules. HEIs wishing to climb up to join the commanding heights league have to compete according to the terms of various kinds of projects and credentials set out by the state, another tool which strengthens the prowess of the state. However, for elite HEIs already at the top, there is path-dependence inertia. The state and public interests could very well become 'captured' by these HEIs. Third, as operational definition of 'the commanding heights' is subject to the discretionary authority of bureaucrats, political manoeuvre and rent seeking behaviour are very much encouraged by both bureaucrats and institutions. Four, social equity is negatively affected. Those enrolled in elite universities who are much more likely to be from privileged families enjoy a higher quality service which is financed with more tax revenue.

■ REFERENCES

OECD. 2003. *OECD Review of Financing and Quality Assurance Reforms in Higher Education in The People's Republic of China*. Paris: OECD.

Yergin, D. and Stanislaw, J. 1998. *The Commanding Heights: The Battle Between Government and the Marketplace that is Remaking the Modern World*. London: Simon & Schuster.

79 Economics and business education in China

Yingyi Qian

79.1 Economics and business majors in Chinese colleges

Every year in early June, nearly 10 million high school graduates take China's College Entrance Exam. In 2013, more than 6 million got a place in college, a drastic increase from just 1 million only 15 years ago (Figure 79.1). In 1998, the raw college enrolment rate calculated for the population of 18–21 year-olds was only 5 per cent. That rate increased to 26 per cent in 2011. The turning point of 1998 was accidental to some extent: China's economy was adversely affected by the Asian financial crisis in that year, and the government wanted to delay the employment of high school graduates by expanding college enrolment.

Economics and business are two very popular subject categories for majors in college. Moreover, they attract high-scoring high school graduates. In other parts of the world, medicine and law (or pre-medicine or pre-law if colleges do not offer bachelor's degrees in medicine and law) are two frequently selected majors, but this is not the case in China. In China, doctors are not paid well, and the legal profession has yet to develop. As a consequence, many talented high school graduates choose economics or business as their major instead of law or medicine.

Even if studying other subjects as their major, many Chinese college students choose economics or business as their second degree (or minor) in addition. As well as the usual reason that students want to gain a knowledge of economics and business in addition to their major, say engineering, there is another reason that is specific to China: it is very difficult for students to change their majors in college. Many Chinese students accept the assigned major because this is the only way they can enrol in the university of their choice. So they enrol in a second-degree programme as a substitute for changing a major. Among the second-degree programmes in colleges, economics and business are the most popular.

All research universities in China are public, and a great majority of them are nationally supervised by the Ministry of Education. Two universities, Tsinghua and Peking, each enrolling around 3,000 undergraduates annually, are extremely selective. Take the

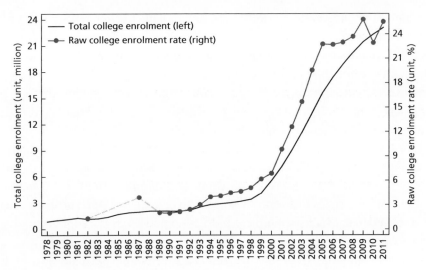

Figure 79.1. College enrolment and raw college enrolment rate in China

Notes: The raw college enrolment rate is calculated for the population of 18–21 year-olds.

Source: China Statistical Yearbook 2010, China Population Statistical Yearbook (various years).

example of Tsinghua University School of Economics and Management (Tsinghua SEM). It combines the Economics Department with the Business School under one roof and enrols around 200 freshmen each year. In China, each college applicant takes one of two tracks, science or humanities, in the College Entrance Exam. Then each province has 10 in the top 10 in each track and thus has 20 in the top 10 in the two tracks combined, and each province has also two number 1 applicants in the two tracks combined. As mainland China has thirty-one provinces, the entire country has about 620 in the provincial top 10 and 62 provincial number 1 applicants. In the last seven years, each year about 100 students of the 200 freshmen enrolled at TsinghuaSEM were ranked in the provincial top 10, and around 20 were ranked provincial number 1 in the College Entrance Exam.

79.2 **Undergraduate curriculum reform: from specialized education to general and specialized education**

College courses in China run four years, not three as in Europe. But college students in China are specialized, as in Europe. First, the assignment of a major subject is made at the entrance to college, and it is very hard for students to change to a different major later. Second, a major is more narrowly defined than it is in US colleges. In the category of economics, majors include economics, public finance, international economics and world economy, regional economics, finance, etc. In the category of management, majors include business management, marketing, accounting, management information system, public management, library management, etc. Third, the total number of credits required for a major is far higher than in US colleges.

Over the last decade, economics and business education incorporated many of the standard courses as in the US colleges, and in many cases professors used US textbooks translated into Chinese. For example, students in economics and finance majors were required to take Principles of Economics in the freshman year, Intermediate Microeconomics, Intermediate Macroeconomics, and Econometrics in the sophomore year, and field courses throughout the four years.

Those students who want to go abroad to undertake PhD studies usually do the following to demonstrate their qualification: first, they take mathematics as a second degree and, second, they spend at least one semester at an overseas university, preferably in a US university.

American universities are envied around the world mainly or exclusively for their research and graduate schools. But its college education, especially in liberal arts or general education in the first two years of college, are not appreciated enough.

In recent years, some leading universities in China have started to put a greater emphasis on general education in college. For example, at Tsinghua SEM, the following general education courses, mostly in the humanities and social science, were incorporated into its undergraduate curriculum: Chinese Writing, Communications, Chinese Civilization, Western Civilization, Critical Thinking and Moral Reasoning, Arts and Aesthetics, and China and the World.

Incorporating general education into the curriculum is not easy in Chinese universities. Among many challenges, the lack of teaching faculty is one problem. Ironically, it is relatively easy to find people to teach English or Western Civilization in China, but rather difficult to find someone to teach freshmen Chinese Writing and Chinese Civilization. Tsinghua SEM has to hire a lecturer from outside to teach Chinese Writing, and the same is true for the Chinese Civilization course. The reason is that the faculty in Chinese literature, history, and philosophy departments are only interested in teaching students who are majoring in these fields, and are not interested in teaching general education courses. And these departments do not have a large faculty either.

79.3 MBA and executive MBA: a case of leapfrogging

China started MBA education in 1991, with a total enrolment of 94 nationwide in that year (Figure 79.2). By 2013, annual MBA enrolment had increased to more than 35,000.

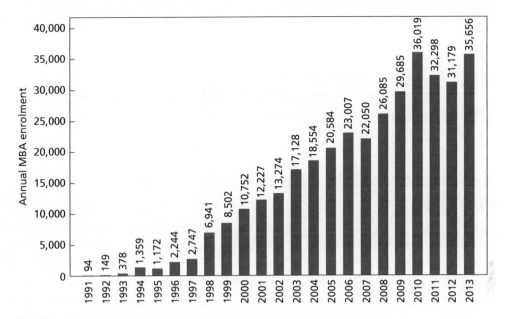

Figure 79.2. Annual MBA enrolment in China

Source: China National MBA Education Supervisory Committee.

While the regular MBA education is catching up quickly, the more impressive development is in the Executive MBA, or EMBA, programme, which is a part-time MBA programme for executives. EMBA has become an exceptionally successful programme in China, even by international standards.

In the respected *Financial Times* global ranking of EMBA programmes, three out of the top ten programmes were from mainland China universities in 2012 and 2013. In fact, among several *FT* business programme rankings, EMBA is the only category that has more than one mainland Chinese business school ranked in the top ten.

This is in part for the following reason. Some top ranked business schools in the USA (such as Harvard and Stanford) do not offer EMBA programmes for fear of diluting their precious MBA brands. Some other top-ranked business schools either have small EMBA programmes (for example Wharton) or have just started their EMBA programmes recently (for example MIT Sloan). Therefore, rankings for EMBA programmes are not as crowded as the rankings for MBA programmes.

But there are other reasons as well. In China, EMBA students are in their forties, and they could not have had an MBA education when there were young. On the other hand, thanks to the rapid growth of the Chinese economy in the past two decades, entrepreneurs and business executives have been very successful in growing their businesses, and they demand a business education as well as new networking opportunities. So there is a demand. On the supply side, business schools in China are innovative in creating EMBA programmes to suit the needs of senior executives. And the government regulations have so far allowed the universities to have the autonomy to run EMBA programmes. Tsinghua SEM enrols 400 EMBA students each year. One programme, the all English Tsinghua-INSEAD dual degree EMBA programme, is exceptionally successful. In 2012, this programme, only five years old, appeared in the *FT* ranking for the first time and was ranked No.4 globally. And in 2013 it was ranked No.2 globally.

79.4 **The strengths and weaknesses of Chinese higher education**

In China, from elementary school to high school, the emphasis of education is on basic skills and imparting knowledge. In these aspects discipline and learning through rote memory help. In a recent OECD programme for international student assessment (PISA) test which assessed the competencies of 15-year-olds in the three key subjects of reading, mathematics, and science, Chinese students from Shanghai scored among the top performing students.

In college, the traditional emphasis is also on knowledge transfer and skill development, especially in English and mathematics. Students at Tsinghua SEM used to joke that SEM stands for School of English and Mathematics. Not surprisingly, the strength of Chinese higher education is the high average level of basic skills such as mathematics.

This advantage served China well over the last thirty years as its economic development was catching up with other countries. When an emerging market economy is at a lower stage of development, a high level of basic skills in the work force is conducive to the 'copy and improve' strategy to work. It is not bad at all.

Now China's economy is entering a middle-income level. Looking ahead, to sustain China's economic growth and to become a leading economy in the world, China has to depend more on innovation than on imitation. But innovation cannot come from the people who lack creativity, curiosity, critical thinking, independent thinking, and different thinking. This is the area that shows major weaknesses in the Chinese higher education system. On these measures, China's higher education has a long way to go.

Part XIII
Gender Equity

80 Gender and China's development

Xiao-yuan Dong

80.1 Introduction

Gender refers to the 'socially constructed roles and socially learned behaviours and expectations associated with females and males' (World Bank, 2001). In almost all countries, socially prescribed gender roles and expectations systemically favour men over women and give rise to gender inequalities in rights, resources, and power. Gender inequality is one of the most pervasive forms of socioeconomic inequality because gender intersects with all other forms of disadvantage, including class, race, ethnicity, location, parenthood, and so on, frequently exacerbating the injustices associated with them.

Gender equality is a prerequisite for broad-based development (World Bank, 2001, 2012). Gender equality matters in its own right because the goal of development is to improve capabilities, agency, and well-being for all people and create just and equitable societies. Gender equality and women's empowerment are also instrumental for achieving broader development goals such as sustainable economic growth, poverty alleviation, health, education, and human well-being.

Economic development expands opportunities and releases constraints for women and improves women's position in society (World Bank, 2012). However, gender gaps in rights, resources, and power do not automatically decrease with rising income. Economic development may even be accompanied with transformations that can aggravate gender inequalities and reverse the hard-achieved progress. This is because inequitable gender norms and expectations are deeply rooted in social and individual consciousness and are therefore resistant to change. Traditional gender norms influence policy making and the choice of development strategies; public policies that appear gender neutral often unintentionally reproduce, strengthen, and legitimize unequal gender relations. Hence, a fundamental transformation of the social structures that place women in a subordinate position requires more than rapid economic growth. The experience of urban Chinese women during the economic transition offers an important lesson in this regard.

80.2 **Women's status under socialism**

Prior to the founding of the People's Republic of China, Chinese women had been oppressed by a Confucian patriarchy system for many centuries. During Mao's era (1949–76), women's status in society improved considerably. Women's full participation in the labour force played a central role in the leadership's agenda to eliminate gender discrimination in China. To support working women, the leadership implemented a wide range of policy measures from subsidized childcare, paid maternity leaves, healthcare, to retirement pensions. The lifetime employment guarantee and centralized wage structure—two salient features of the labour regime under central planning—also acted to minimize the market 'penalties' on women for their family responsibilities. As a result, China's female labour force participation rate was among the highest in the world, and the gender wage gap was remarkably small by international standards.

However, the progress in gender equality during Mao's era has proved to be unsustainable because it was achieved within a state system of labour allocation which created huge inefficiencies and redundancy. Moreover, the progress of gender equality in the workplace did not spill into the home and women's responsibility for care and housework remained unchallenged. Even in the workplace, gender segregation remained prevalent; women were concentrated in the sectors that offered lower wages and fewer benefits and over-represented in the positions that had less decision-making power and fewer opportunities for career advancements.

80.3 **Women's status during the economic transition**

China embarked on the transition to a market-oriented economy starting in the late 1970s. The market reforms and economic opening to the world market have brought about rapid economic growth and lifted more than 500 million people out of poverty. The sharp increase in income and decline in poverty have contributed to a narrowing of gender gaps in education and an improvement in women's health. For instance, from 1990 to 2005, the mean years of schooling increased from 7.4 to 8.4 years for males, up by one year, and from 5.5 to 7.3 years for females, up by 1.8 years (NBS, 2007: 64). The maternal mortality rate fell sharply from 88.9 deaths per 100,000 live births in 1990 to 41.1 in 2005 (NBS, 2007: 105).

While men and women have both gained much from rapid growth, the reforms appear to have worked to women's disadvantage in the urban labour market. The decentralization and privatization of the state-owned enterprise (SOE) sector have brought an end to the era of lifetime employment and egalitarian labour compensation for urban workers. While the restructuring of the SOE sector is imperative for a well functioning labour market, the reform unintentionally destroyed the institutional mechanism that protected women's reproductive role under central planning and did not put forth adequate measures to replace it. Under pressure for profits, enterprises are increasingly reluctant to accommodate employees' care-giving needs; as a consequence, having young children places mothers at risk of losing earnings or being dismissed from the job altogether. Moreover, the dismantling of the employer-based socialist welfare system has led to a substantial decline in state and employer support for childcare, shifting care responsibilities predominantly to the family (Liu et al., 2008; Cook and Dong, 2011).

The declining influence of socialist ideology has also led to a re-emergence of traditional patriarchal values, increasing pressures on women to return to the home. According to the Surveys of Chinese Women's Status conducted by the All China Women's Federation, the proportion of the respondents who agreed with the statement 'men should play a major role in society while women should play a major role at home' rose from 53.9 per cent in 2000 to 61.6 per cent in 2010 among men and from 50.4 per cent to 54.8 per cent among women. As a reflection of the growing influence of traditional gender values, many Chinese economists held the view that Chinese women's labour force participation is too high to be justified by market forces, and hence the withdrawal of some working-age women from the labour force, permanently or periodically, would be a solution to rising unemployment in the cities (Yee, 2001). During the SOE-sector restructuring, gender-differentiated mandatory early retirements were widely applied, forcing a larger number of women in their late forties than their male counterparts to leave the labour force.

Labour reform policies appear to be gender insensitive. For instance, during the SOE sector restructuring, a reemployment programme was introduced to assist laid-off workers coping with employment turbulence. Primarily targeting displaced state workers, the programme overlooked the collective sector in which women were concentrated and were the hardest hit by labour restructuring (Du and Dong, 2009). Unequal access to social assistance by non-state workers in conjunction with the historical pattern of gender segregation created gender inequality in access to reemployment assistances and consequently led to a greater gap in reemployment between displaced male and female workers. Moreover, in policy circles, rising urban unemployment following the SOE sector restructuring has led to a stronger justification of less secure, 'flexible' forms of employment as reemployment measures especially in sectors where women predominate (Cook, 2010).

In consequence, the market reform has inadvertently worsened the terms under which women participated in the labour market. Women faced increasing discrimination in accessing employment, including those at high levels of education. Women were more likely than men to be laid off in the process of SOE-sector restructuring and less likely to be reemployed (Appleton et al., 2002; Giles et al., 2006; Du and Dong, 2009). Women have withdrawn from the labour force at much higher rates since the 1990s (Maurer-Fazio et al., 2007). The decline in women's labour force participation was concentrated among wives with low-earning husbands, mothers with preschool children, and daughters with disabled elderly parents (Ding et al., 2009; Liu et al., 2010; Maurer-Fazio et al., 2011). The increase in labour market mobility does not benefit women and men equally either. Women were more likely than men to undergo downward occupational changes but less likely to experience upward mobility (Song and Dong, 2013). A growing number of urban workers, predominately women, have been pushed into the informal sector where jobs are typically temporary, insecure, and low paid (Yuan and Cook, 2010).

Moreover, the gender wage gap has been on a steady increase leading to greater income differentials, especially among less-educated, blue-collar workers (Gustafsson and Li, 2000; Chi and Li, 2008; J. Zhang et al., 2008). Mothers are found earning substantially less than childless women in the emerging private sector (Jia and Dong, 2013). Analysts show that women's family responsibilities have played a more important role than their disadvantage in human capital in terms of increasing gender inequalities in employment and wages in the post-reform urban labour market (Y. Zhang et al., 2008).

Clearly, women have not benefited equally from the market reform, and women who are less well educated, from low-income families, and with family responsibilities are the hardest hit in the reform process.

80.4 **Conclusion**

The experience of urban Chinese women has demonstrated that economic growth does not automatically lead to greater gender equality and may increase women's vulnerability under certain circumstances. The setbacks in Chinese women's hard-won battle for gender equality teach us two important lessons. First, a sustainable progress in gender equality requires a fundamental transformation of the deep-rooted societal mindsets that view taking care of family members as 'the natural duty of women' and women's own private matters. Gender equitable public policy must fully recognize women's reproductive role and its contribution to national well-being and properly distribute caregiving responsibilities among the state, employers, and the family, and within the family, between women and men, in the new market economy. Second, a top-down approach to gender equality is vulnerable to policy reversals; women must play an active role in challenging ideologies and institutions that place them in a subordinate position and empower themselves both economically and politically.

■ **REFERENCES**

Appleton, Simon, John Knight, Lina Song, and Qingjie Xia. 2002. Labor retrenchment in China: determinants and consequences. *China Economic Review* 13(2/3), 252–75.

Chi, Wei and Bo Li. 2008. Glass ceiling or sticky floor? examining the gender earnings differential across the earnings distribution in urban China. *Journal of Comparative Economics* 36, 243–63.

Cook, Sarah. 2010. Informality and gender inequality: the challenge of China's labor market restructuring. In *Gender Equality and China's Economic Transformation: Informal Employment and Care Provision*, edited by Xiao-yuan Dong and Sarah Cook, 27–47. Beijing: Economic Science Press.

Cook, Sarah and Xiao-Yuan Dong. 2011. Harsh choices: Chinese women's paid work and unpaid care responsibilities under economic reform. *Development and Change* 42(4), 947–66.

Ding Sai, Xiao-Yuan Dong, and Shi Li. 2009. Employment and earnings of married women and family income inequality during China's economic transition. *Feminist Economics* 15(3), 163–90.

Du, Fenglian and Xiao-Yuan Dong. 2009. Why women have longer unemployment durations than men in post-restructuring urban China? *Cambridge Journal of Economics* 33(2), 233–52.

Giles, John, Albert Park, and Fang Cai. 2006. Re-employment of dislocated workers in urban China: the roles of information and incentives. *Journal of Comparative Economics* 34(3), 582–607.

Gustafsson, Björn and Shi Li. 2000. Economic transformation and the gender earnings gap in urban China. *Journal of Population Economics* 13(2), 305–29.

Jia, Nan and Dong Xiao-Yuan. 2013. Economic transition and the motherhood wage penalty in urban China: investigation using panel data. *Cambridge Journal of Economics* 37(4), 819–44.

Liu, Bohong, Yongying Zhang, and Yani Li. 2008. *Reconciling Work and Family: Issues and Policies in China.* ILO, Asia.

Liu, Lan, Xiao-Yuan Dong, and Xiaoying Zheng. 2010. Parental care and married women's labor supply: evidence from urban China. *Feminist Economics* 13(3), 169–92.

Maurer-Fazio, Margaret, James Hughes, and Dandan Zhang. 2007. Gender, ethnicity, and labor force participation in post-reform urban China. *Feminist Economics* 13(3–4), 189–212.

Maurer-Fazio, Margaret, Rachel Connelly, Lan Chen, and Lixin Tang. 2011. Childcare, eldercare, and labor force participation of married women in urban China, 1982–2000. *Journal of Human Resources* 46(2), 261–94.

National Bureau of Statistics of China (NBS). 2007. *Women and Men in China: Facts and Figures 2007.* Beijing: China Statistical Press.

Song, Yueping and Xiao-yuan Dong. 2013. Gender and Occupational Mobility in Urban China during the Economic Transition. *Research in Labour Economics* 37, 93–122.

World Bank. 2001. *Engendering Development: Through Gender Equality in Rights, Resources, and Voice.* Washington, DC: World Bank.

World Bank. 2012. *World Development Report 2012: Gender Equality and Development.* Washington, DC: World Bank.

Yee, Janice. 2001. Women's changing roles in the Chinese Economy. *Journal of Economics* 27(2), 55–67.

Yuan, Ni and Sarah Cook. 2010. Gender patterns of informal employment in urban China. In *Gender Equality and China's Economic Transformation: Informal and Care Provision*, Xiao-Yuan Dong and Sarah Cook, 48–68. Beijing: Economic Science Press.

Zhang, Junsen, Jun Han, Pak-wai Liu, and Yaohui Zhao. 2008. Trends in the gender earnings differential in urban China, 1988–2004. *Industrial and Labor Relations Review* 61(2), 224–43.

Zhang, Yuping, Emily Hannum, and Meiyan Wang. 2008. Gender-based employment and income differences in urban China: considering the contributions of marriage and parenthood. Social Force 86(4), 1529–60.

81 High sex ratio in China

Causes and consequences

Hongbin Li and Lingsheng Meng

The population of China is characterized by a significant sex imbalance that favours males. As reported in population censuses, the sex ratio (defined as the number of males per 100 females) at birth has drastically increased from 108.5 in 1982, to 113.8 in 1990, and to 119.9 in 2000 and 118.9 in 2010, which is much higher than the biological norm of 105.

Recent studies have found that the increase in sex ratio at birth in China has been a result of a combination of son preference, a decrease in fertility induced by the One Child Policy, and the diffusion of sex selection technology. Chinese people's preference for sons has deeply rooted cultural reasons. Historically, parents refrained from having more children when the desired number of sons was reached. However, China's national family planning programme, enacted in 1979 and commonly known as the One Child Policy, dramatically altered the situation. In essence, the stringent birth control policy placed a legal limit on family size, preventing individuals from having multiple children to ensure the birth of a son (or sons). The opportunity cost of raising more children of an unwanted sex increases substantially. Consequently, son preference manifests itself through sex-selection practices.

Li et al.'s (2010) study aims to identify the causal effect of the One Child Policy on sex ratio. They employ a difference-in-differences (DD) approach based on a plausibly exogenous differential treatment between the Han and minorities under the One Child Policy. In the quasi-experimental design of the DD estimator, both the ethnic-specific heterogeneity and the effects of socioeconomic development have been swept out. Therefore, the DD estimate allows one to identify the causal effect of the One Child Policy on sex ratio imbalance in China.

The One Child Policy stipulates that each couple is allowed only one child. Couples are given birth quotas, and they are penalized for 'above-quota' births. However, a unique feature of the One Child Policy was that minority women were generally allowed to have at least two children whereas the Han could only have one child. The differential treatment of the One Child Policy across different ethnic groups has been embodied in various regulations. In addition, the motivation of the differential treatment of the One Child Policy across ethnic groups has evidently been exogenously imposed. Therefore, the consistently differential treatment of the One Child Policy between the Han and other minorities provides us a unique opportunity to identify its causal effect on the sex ratio imbalance in China.

Using the Chinese population census in 1990, the estimated treatment effect on the probability of being a boy is as large as 1.01 percentage points for the 1980s birth cohort. This means that the strict enforcement of the One Child Policy has causally increased the sex ratio by 4.4 which accounts for about 94 per cent of the increase in sex ratios during this period. The authors further conduct the DD estimation using both the 2000 census and 2005 mini-census. Their DD estimates suggest the One Child Policy has increased the sex ratio by about 7.0 for the birth cohort of 1991–2005. The policy effect accounts for about 57 per cent and 54 per cent of the increase in sex ratios for the birth cohorts in the 1990s and 2001–05, respectively.

Chen et al.'s 2013 study seeks to understand the instrument for achieving the observed sex imbalance in China. Previous literature suggests that the biased sex ratio may have been caused by sex-selective abortion—a procedure that has become possible thanks to modern science. However, no previous study has shown large-sample evidence of the link between sex-selective abortion and sex imbalance.

Chen et al. (2013) construct a unique dataset that tracks the differential diffusion of diagnostic ultrasound in China, which has created variation in access to prenatal sex determination technology that may be orthogonal to demand factors. The data are obtained from numerous issues of the *Local Chronicle*, which provides a record of Chinese local history, to identify the year in which ultrasound machines were introduced in approximately 1,500 Chinese counties. Subsequently, this dataset was matched with a large micro dataset (from the Chinese Children Survey) that contains the records of more than 500,000 live births in China from 1975 to 1992, a period of rapid expansion in ultrasound technology access.

To estimate the effect of access to selective abortion on the sex ratio at birth, the study employs a DD approach that exploits the variation in the timing of ultrasound technology adoption across counties. During the study period, induced abortion was legal and abortion services were offered in public health facilities throughout China, in the same manner as other medical procedures. Therefore, access to sex-selective abortion depended crucially on the availability of ultrasound equipment capable of prenatal sex determination. Women who became pregnant after the introduction of ultrasound technology were more likely to have knowledge of foetal sex than those who became pregnant prior to its introduction. Therefore, it is possible to estimate the effects of better access to sex-selective abortion by comparing changes in the sex ratio at birth in counties that had adopted ultrasound technology relative to those that had not.

The chapter finds that the adoption of ultrasound technology had a significant effect on the sex ratio at birth in China. The estimates from their preferred specification imply that on average, the introduction of ultrasound technology in a county increased the probability of a male birth by 1.3 and 2.4 percentage points for second-order and third- or higher-order births, respectively. If no sons had been born previously, having local access to ultrasound technology raised the probability of having a male child by 4.8 percentage points for second births, and 6.8 percentage points for third births. These findings indicate that roughly 40–50 per cent of the increase in sex imbalance at birth during the 1980s can be explained by local access to ultrasound technology. These findings are interpreted as clear evidence of prenatal sex selection in China during the period under consideration. Furthermore, the study also finds that ultrasound technology affected only those who were subject to the One Child Policy, suggesting an interacting effect of the two variables.

The adoption of ultrasound removed the technological constraints on sex selection in China. Female infanticide is regarded more aversively than prenatal sex selection, and the availability of prenatal sex determination allows those who otherwise would not have sex-selected to sex-select. Importantly, the new technology makes low-cost prenatal sex determination possible at an earlier stage of gestation, and the process of technology diffusion is generally irreversible. As a result, one may expect persistently high sex ratios in China and elsewhere.

As a follow-up analysis, Almond et al. (2012) examine whether the knowledge of foetal gender during pregnancy alters parental investment. Observationally, deliberate sex selection by parents may obscure the effect of knowing foetal gender on early childhood investments. The diffusion of ultrasound technology across China during the 1980s allowed parents to observe and exercise son preference through sex-selective abortion. If some Chinese parents had a stronger son preference than others, those choosing to abort females might have a stronger son preference than those who delivered daughters despite newfound access to ultrasound. Thus, Chen et al.'s result suggests that with increased sex ratios, parents were increasingly sorted according to son preference. In this respect, parents of girls may have benefited from increased investments.

Applying a DD approach to the same datasets as Chen et al. (2013), Almond et al. (2012) compare outcomes of females versus males before and after the introduction of ultrasound. Furthermore, the data allow them to restrict comparisons to those within the family by including maternal fixed effects, which can address biases arising from differences across families. In their richest specification, the effects of ultrasound availability are identified using variation in ultrasound between children in the same families, after controlling flexibly for year fixed effects, county fixed effects, county time trends, and observed characteristics of the mother. They find that postnatal investments do not seem to change as a result of preference-sorting induced by the availability of ultrasound. Nevertheless, they find a sizeable increase in female neonatal mortality relative to male neonatal mortality following ultrasound availability. No significant effects are found for post-neonatal mortality measures, which imply that the effects of the availability of ultrasound on child health are concentrated soon after birth. Overall, these mortality results suggest that parents withheld investment in female foetuses relative to males after pre-natal sex determination became available.

The biased sex ratio not only has profound ethical implications for women's welfare, but can also cause adverse social consequences that are long lasting. Apparently, a high sex ratio will disturb the marriage market. For cohorts born between 1980 and 2000, there are around 22 million more males than females. A majority of the excess men are expected to fail to ever marry. However, the social impact of the sex imbalance will not be confined to the marriage market.

Edlund et al. (2013) focus on the effect of surplus men on crime. As sex ratios rose markedly in China in the last two decades, crime rates nearly doubled. The authors present empirical evidence linking the rise in crime to rising sex ratios. Employing province-level annual data covering the period 1988–2004 they uncover a strong rela-tionship between the sex ratios of 16–25 year-olds and criminality. This relationship holds up in the face of province and year fixed effects, province specific time trends, and a battery of time-varying controls, including the sex ratios of other age groups, meas-ures of the economic climate such as income, employment rate, education, inequality, and urbanization rate. In their preferred specification, they find that the rise in sex ratios can account for one-seventh of the overall rise in criminality during the study period. Edlund et al. (2013) also find that with rising sex ratio, men are less likely to get married, and if they marry, they tend to marry women who are younger and have fewer years of schooling. They also find that men invest more in human capital in response to higher sex ratios. Employing the Chinese Urban Household Surveys for the period of 1988–2006, Edlund et al. find that, for men, higher sex ratios are associated with higher education, and a higher probability of being employed or being professional (relative to women).

High sex ratio is also found to be one of the causes of high saving rates in China. Wei and Zhang (2011a) hypothesize that as the sex ratio rises, the pressure in the marriage market increases and it becomes harder for a Chinese man to find a wife. In response, families with sons compete with one another by saving a higher fraction of their income, hoping to improve their sons' likelihood of getting married. This competitive saving motive may have a spillover effect to other households when housing prices are bid up.

Wei and Zhang (2011a) find that across regions, there is a positive correlation between local savings rate and sex ratio. An instrumental variable approach that accounts for the endogeneity of the sex ratio also confirms a positive effect of the sex ratio on savings. Using household level data, the authors also show that in a region with a biased local sex ratio, the presence of a son is associated with a higher savings rate. Finally, they provide evidence that in a certain region, a higher sex ratio is associated with larger house sizes and higher house prices, which supports the proposed spillover effect of saving. Accord-ing to their estimates, the rise in the sex imbalance could account for about half of the increase in household savings during the same period.

In a separate paper, Wei and Zhang (2011b) identified a potentially positive effect of a higher sex ratio in China. As competition intensifies in the Chinese marriage market, men (or households with sons) may work harder and engage in more entrepreneurial activities, hoping to enhance their prospect in the marriage market by accumulating more wealth. In the long run, the entire economy may grow faster thanks to the rise in entrepreneurship. First, using the two most recent censuses of manufacturing firms in China (in 1995 and 2004), the authors find that a local sex imbalance is a strong predictor of local entrepreneurial activities. According to their estimates, a one-standard-deviation increase in the sex ratio can explain about half of the emergence of new private firms across regions. Second, using the 2005 Inter-Census Population Survey, the authors show that parents with a son are more likely to be business owners in areas with a more severe sex imbalance. Third, using a survey of rural households in 2002, the authors find that parents with a son are more likely to take dangerous jobs for higher pay in areas with a higher sex ratio. Finally, using provincial level data, they demonstrate that around 20 per cent of GDP growth in recent years can be attributed to an increase in the sex ratio.

■ REFERENCES

Almond, Douglas, Hongbin Li, and Lingsheng Meng. 2012. Son Preference and Early Childhood Investments in China. Working Paper.

Chen, Yuyu, Hongbin Li, and Lingsheng Meng. 2013. Prenatal sex selection and missing girls in China: evidence from the diffusion of diagnostic ultrasound. *Journal of Human Resources* 48(1), 36–70.

Edlund, Lena, Hongbin Li, Junjian Yi and Junsen Zhang. 2013. Sex ratios and crime: evidence from China's One Child Policy. *Review of Economics and Statistics* 95(5), 1520–34.

Li, Hongbin, Junjian Yi, and Junsen Zhang. 2010. Estimating the effect of the one-child policy on the sex ratio imbalance in China: identification based on the difference-in-differences. *Demography* 48(4), 1535–57.

Wei, Shang-Jin and Xiaobo Zhang. 2011a. The competitive saving motive: evidence from rising sex ratios and savings in China. *Journal of Political Economy* 119(3), 511–64.

Wei, Shang-Jin and Xiaobo Zhang. 2011b. Sex Ratios, Entrepreneurship, and Economic Growth in the People's Republic of China. NBER Working Paper No. 16800.

82 Gender and family

Yu Xie

82.1 Traditional Chinese family and gender roles

The family, a group of individuals connected by either marriage or blood, is the most elementary social, economic, and residential collective unit in a human society. While family as a social institution is universal, its manifestation and significance vary both across societies and over time. Ample evidence indicates that the traditional Chinese family, in its ideal form, is distinctive from what is commonly known as the modern family that evolved in Western Europe.

One distinctive feature of the traditional Chinese family is the paramount importance of family lineage (Chu and Yu, 2010). In this tradition, individuals are no more than temporary carriers that perpetuate familial male lines, with ancestors assuming spiritual roles. Ancestors are believed to be active in their afterlives and need to be worshiped, offerings made to them, and they should be respected through family rituals. In return, they provide protection and assistance to their living offspring. Thus, ancestors assume a god-like status in Chinese culture, with each large family clan essentially having its own folk religion (Thompson, 1989). The god-like status of ancestors also carries practical implications for everyday life in the form of filial piety. The core value in a Chinese family, filial piety, dictates that children or grandchildren should respect and care for their parents or grandparents (Thornton and Lin, 1994; Whyte 2004).

The traditional Chinese family has long been characterized as patriarchal, patrimonial, patrilineal, and patrilocal, putting women at a severe social disadvantage relative to men (Thornton and Lin, 1994). Indeed, in a classic paper on the influence of Chinese family structure on gender inequality, Greenhalgh (1985: 265) stated that 'Traditional Confucian China and its cultural offshoots, Japan and Korea, evolved some of the most patriarchal family systems that ever existed.' There are rational bases for this gender inequality. In this family system, sons are permanent members of their natal family and retain lifetime financial relationships with their parents. They are expected to contribute to their parents' economic well-being even after they are married themselves. Thus, it is in their self-interest for parents to invest in sons because they may reap returns from the investment in the long term. In contrast, daughters are only temporary members of their natal family before marriage, upon which a woman serves her husband's extended family

(Whyte and Xu, 2003). Thus, due to the limited time during which daughters serve their natal families, parents often extract resources from unmarried daughters, for example in terms of remittances from daughters' market labour or household work, to improve the family budget and invest in sons. In Greenhalgh's (1985: 276) words, 'Put baldly, parents' *key strategy* was to take more from daughters to give more to sons and thus get more for themselves'.

82.2 **Empirical evidence and social changes**

Researchers have found empirical evidence, mostly based on data from Taiwan, to illustrate the traditional Chinese family system. For example, two studies report that Taiwanese families tend to sacrifice older daughters' educations to benefit the educational outcomes of younger sons (Parish and Willis, 1993; Chu et al., 2007). Furthermore, several studies have found that married sons provide larger amounts of financial support than married daughters to elderly parents in Taiwan (Lee et al., 1994; Hermalin et al., 2003; Lin et al., 2003) and in rural China (Yang, 1996). More evidence is given in books by Chu and Yu (2010) and Thornton and Lin (1994).

China has undergone major social changes in the last six decades, due to several revolutionary movements, most notably the Communist Revolution that resulted in the founding of the People's Republic of China (PRC) in 1949, the 1966–76 Cultural Revolution, and the economic reform that began in 1978. In 1950, China instituted the Marriage Law, which formally legalized free-choice marriage and explicitly equalized wives' rights and interests with those of husbands. As I will show below, changes in education, the pension system, and the economic structure have also greatly altered family life in contemporary China. There are also good indications that a substantial fraction of Chinese parents today, especially educated ones, no longer subscribe to the traditional Chinese value of maintaining family lineage (Wu and Xie, 2013).

82.3 **Gender inequality in contemporary China**

Since the founding of the PRC in 1949, women's socioeconomic status has significantly improved. This is most significantly shown in education. While women's education fell far below that of men in the early years of the PRC, women's educational attainment has gradually caught up with that of men (Hannum and Xie, 1994; Wu and Zhang 2010; Li and Xie 2013). For instance, in 1982, the percentages receiving postsecondary education were respectively 1.24 per cent for men and 0.64 per cent for women; these percentages increased to 6.72 per cent and 5.63 per cent in 2005 (Mu and Xie, 2014). Women's employment has been nearly universal throughout the history of the PRC, although severe segregation in occupations has persisted for non-agricultural jobs over time (Wu and Wu, 2008). Although the gender gap in earnings was low among urban workers, especially educated urban workers, in the early years of the reform era (Xie and Hannum, 1996), the gender gap has increased over time (Hauser and Xie, 2005). A recent study based on data from 2010 and 2012 estimates women's earnings to be 70 per cent of those of men, without any controls (Li and Xie, 2013). The same study also reports gender differences, in favour of men, in middle- and higher-level administrative/managerial positions and political participation.

An explanation of the paradox of women's large improvement in educational attainment being accompanied by lower economic standing for women than for men, especially for high-level positions, lies not only in the labour market but also in the family. Yu and Xie (2012) report large gender gaps in household work in contemporary China, with the lion's share falling on the shoulders of the wife rather than the husband. It is quite possible that this traditional division of labour in the household, with women being mainly responsible for caring for children and the household, may impede the realization of their full potential in the labour market.

82.4 **Marriage behaviours**

The rapid improvement in women's social status has important implications for marriage behaviour in China. The median age of first marriage rose steadily for women, from twenty in the 1940s birth cohort to 23 in the 1980s birth cohort; by comparison, the increase for men was smaller, from 24 in the 1940s birth cohort to 25 in the 1980s birth cohort (Mu and Xie, 2014). Despite the delay in marriage, marriage has remained nearly universal, except for less educated men in the most recent birth cohort, to be discussed in the next paragraph (Yu and Xie, 2013).

Status hypergamy—the tendency of women to marry men of higher social status— has been a traditional practice in China (Thornton and Lin, 1994; Xu et al., 2000). This cultural norm has remained in place in contemporary China, although mate selection has largely been transformed from being arranged by parents to being based on love (Xu and Whyte, 1990). In the past, hypergamy was achieved by women marrying men of higher educational attainment. With women now closing their overall educational gap with men, however, hypergamy cannot be achieved easily through educational hypergamy. Instead, the trend observed now suggests an increase in the age gap between husband and wife to allow prospective husbands to accumulate more economic resources than prospective wives of a similar level of education (Mu and Xie, 2014).

Mu and Xie (2014) propose that high consumption aspirations resulting from the recent economic boom in China have exerted economic pressures on young persons entering marriage. Consistent with this conjecture, Yu and Xie (2013) find that, defying the universal marriage norm, more than a quarter of men with primary school education who were born after 1974 remained single after age 32, while similarly educated men in earlier birth cohorts did achieve universal marriage. Through multivariate analysis of the hazard of marriage entry, Yu and Xie conclude that economic factors have increased in importance as determinants of entry into marriage during the economic reform era. Most directly, they report evidence that housing prices affect marriage entry: higher housing prices at the city level are associated with later age at marriage and a more positive effect of education on marriage entry. Wei and Zhang (2011) argue that the economic pressure for marriage comes from China's rising sex ratios. But this pressure may actually be generated by a combination of broader factors, such as hypergamy, an improvement in women's socioeconomic status, and rising consumption aspirations. Thus, economic pressure, combined with a hypergamy culture, will make marriage difficult to attain for two groups: men with little education and highly educated women.

82.5 Cohabitation, divorce, and the second demographic transition

By the 1990s, China had completed its first demographic transition from a regime with high fertility and high mortality to a regime with low fertility and low mortality (Xie, 2011). The second demographic transition refers to the social trends of increases in non-traditional family practices such as cohabitation, divorce, and childbirth out of wedlock (Lesthaeghe, 2010). Has China experienced such a second demographic transition?

Out-of-wedlock childbirths remain almost absent in China. However, the rates of both premarital cohabitation and divorce have risen. For example, the crude divorce rate increased from 0.3 per thousand in 1979, to 0.7 per thousand in 1990, to 1.0 in 2000, and 2.1 in 2010 (*Fa Zhi Wan Bao*, 2010). The latest data from the China Family Panel Study (CFPS) indicate that premarital cohabitation, virtually absent for marriage cohorts before 1980s, has reached almost a third for the most recent marriage cohort in 2010–12 (Xu et al., 2013). Cohabitation rates are much higher in more developed coastal regions, such as Shanghai and Guangdong, than in less developed inland regions, such as Gansu (Xu et al., 2013). Furthermore, the same study also finds that cohabitation is positively associated with education. These results reveal that premarital cohabitation has become a more socially accepted form of living arrangement before formal marriage in China.

82.6 **Coresidence and elderly support**

CFPS data from 2012 show that about one-third of the Chinese population still lives in multi-generational families (Xu et al., 2013). Data from the China Health and Retirement Longitudinal Study (CHARLS) 2011–12 baseline survey reveal that about 43 per cent of elderly persons aged 60 and above still lived with a child, the proportion being higher in rural than in urban China (Lei et al., 2013). However, this number may substantially underestimate the social support that elderly people receive from their children, as another 31 per cent have a child living in the same neighbourhood, and 13 per cent more in the same county but not in the same neighbourhood (Lei et al., 2013). When the elderly co-reside with children, they are far more likely to co-reside with sons than with daughters (Chu et al., 2011).

There are two main explanations for a higher percentage of Chinese elderly persons living with children. First, the traditional Chinese family is patrilinear and patrilocal. Indeed, surveys show that a large portion of the elderly prefer or expect to live with their children (Chu and Yu, 2010). Second, largely due to a lack of public support, a significant portion of Chinese elderly still count on their children for old age support (Logan and Bian, 1999; Chu and Yu, 2010; Chu et al., 2011; Lei et al., 2013). Both CFPS and CHARLS data show a high frequency of financial transfers between elderly parents and their children. With China's further economic development and better provision of public support for the elderly, the rate of the elderly's co-residence with children may decline in the future.

82.7 **Conclusion**

Both gender relations and family forms have undergone tremendous changes over the past decades in China. Women's socioeconomic status has greatly improved and indeed reached parity with that of men by some indicators, although women remain disadvantaged relative to men in terms of labour income, positions of authority, and household labour. Marriage behaviours in China have trended increasingly towards patterns observed in the West, such as later marriages, more cohabitation, and more divorce. However, a high proportion of extended families with elderly parents living with their sons remains a distinct characteristic of the Chinese family today, as are parents' expectations that their adult children will provide them with old age support. Another pattern peculiar to Chinese marriages is social hypergamy, which remains in effect despite a significant improvement in women's socioeconomic status. The cultural expectation of hypergamy, coupled with rising consumption aspirations and rapid increases in housing prices in many parts of China, exerts intense economic pressure on young men contemplating marriage. This pressure leads to a marriage squeeze for two demographic groups: low-status men and high-status women, who may find it increasingly difficult to fulfil their desires for marriage.

■ REFERENCES

Chu, C. Y. Cyrus and Ruoh-rong Yu. 2010. *Understanding Chinese Families: A Comparative Study of Taiwan and Southeast China*. Oxford: Oxford University Press

Chu, C. Y. Cyrus, Yu Xie, and Ruoh-rong Yu. 2007. Effects of sibship structure revisited: evidence from intra-family resource transfer in Taiwan. *Sociology of Education* 80, 91–113.

Chu, C. Y. Cyrus, Yu Xie, and Ruoh-rong Yu. 2011. Coresidence with elderly parents: a comparative study of southeast China and Taiwan. *Journal of Marriage and Family* 73, 120–35.

Fa Zhi Wan Bao. 2010. Ministry of Civil Affairs: Divorce Rate in China Has Continuously Increased for 30 Years. Available at <http://news.163.com/10/1003/13/6I2T8NPB0001124J.html> accessed 6 October 2013.

Greenhalgh, Susan. 1985. Sexual stratification: the other side of 'growth with equity' in East Asia. *Population and Development Review* 11, 265–314.

Hannum, Emily and Yu Xie. 1994. Trends in educational gender inequality in China: 1949–1985. *Research in Social Stratification and Mobility* 13, 73–98.

Hauser, Seth and Yu Xie. 2005. Temporal and Regional variation in earnings inequality: urban China in transition between 1988 and 1995. *Social Science Research* 34, 44–79.

Hermalin, Albert I., Mary-Beth Ofstedal, and S. P. Shih. 2003. Support received by the elderly in Baoding: the view from two generations. In *China's Revolutions and Intergenerational Relations*, edited by M. Whyte, 121–42. Ann Arbor, MI: Center for Chinese Studies, University of Michigan.

Lee, Yean-Ju, William L. Parish, and Robert J. Willis. 1994. Sons, daughters, and intergenerational support in Taiwan. *American Journal of Sociology* 99, 1010–41.

Lei, Xiaoyan, John Strauss, Meng Tian, and Yaohui Zhao. 2013. Living Arrangements of the Elderly in China: Evidence from the CHARLS National Baseline. Department of Economics, Texas A&M University. Unpublished manuscript. Available at: <http://econweb.tamu.edu/common/files/workshops/PERC%20Applied%20Microeconomics/2013_2_27_John_Strauss.pdf> accessed 6 October 2013.

Lesthaeghe, Ron J. 2010. The unfolding story of the second demographic transition. *Population and Development Review* 36(2), 211–51.

Li, Wangyang and Xie, Yu. 2013. Gender differences (性别差异). In *Wellbeing Development Report of China 2013* 《中国民生发展报告2013》(in Chinese), edited by Y. Xie, X. Zhang, J. Li, X. Yu, and Q. Ren谢宇、张晓波、李建新、于学军、任强, 215–49. Beijing: Peking University Press. 北京大学出版社。

Lin, I-Fen, Noreen Goldman, Maxine Weinstein, Yu Hsuan Lin, Tristan Gorrindo, and Teresa Seeman. 2003. Gender differences in adult children's support of their parents in Taiwan. *Journal of Marriage and Family* 65, 184–200.

Logan, John R. and Fuqin Bian. 1999. Family values and co-residence with married children in urban China. *Social Forces* 77, 1253–82.

Mu, Zheng and Yu Xie. 2014. Marital Age Homogamy in China: A Reversal of Trend in the Reform Era? *Social Science Research* 44, 141–57.

Parish, William L. and Robert J. Willis. 1993. Daughters, education, and family budgets Taiwan experiences. *The Journal of Human Resources* 28, 863–98.

Thompson, Lawrence G. 1989. *Chinese Religion: An Introduction* 4th edn. Belmont, CA: Wadsworth.

Thornton, Arland and Hui-sheng Lin. 1994. *Social Change and the Family in Taiwan.* Chicago, IL: University of Chicago Press.

Wei, Shang-Jin and Xiaobo Zhang. 2011. The competitive saving motive: evidence from rising sex ratios and savings rates in China. *Journal of Political Economy* 119, 511–64.

Whyte, Martin. 2004. Filial obligations in Chinese families: paradoxes of modernization. In *Filial Piety: Practice and Discourse in Contemporary East Asia*, edited by C. Ikels, 106–27. Stanford, CA: Stanford University Press.

Whyte, Martin and Qin Xu. 2003. Support for aging parents from daughters versus sons. In *China's Revolutions and Intergenerational Relations*, edited by M. Whyte, 167–96. Ann Arbor, MI: Center for Chinese Studies, University of Michigan.

Wu, Qiong and Xie, Yu. 2013. Attitudes and values (态度和观念). In *Wellbeing Development Report of China 2013* 《中国民生发展报告2013》(in Chinese), edited by Y. Xie, X. Zhang, J. Li, X. Yu, and Q, Ren谢宇、张晓波、李建新、于学军、任强, 27–53. Beijing: Peking University Press. 北京大学出版社。

Wu, Xiaogang and Zhuoni Zhang. 2010. Changes in educational inequality in China, 1990–2005: evidence from the population census data. *Research in Sociology of Education* 17, 123–52.

Wu, Yxiao and Xiaogang Wu. 2008. A study on the sex segregation in non-agricultural occupations in China in 1982–2000. (1982–2000: 我国非农职业的性别隔离研究) *Society*《社会》 28, 5.

Xie, Yu. 2011. Evidence-based research on China: a historical imperative. *Chinese Sociological Review* 44(1), 14–25.

Xie, Yu and Emily Hannum. 1996. Regional variation in earnings inequality in reform-era urban China. *American Journal of Sociology* 101, 950–92.

Xu, Qi, Jianxin Li, and Xuejun Yu. 2013. Marriage and family (婚姻与家庭). In *Wellbeing Development Report of China 2013* 《中国民生发展报告2013》(in Chinese), edited by Y. Xie, X. Zhang, J. Li, X. Yu, and Q. Ren谢宇、张晓波、李建新、于学军、任强, 305–43. Beijing: Peking University Press. 北京大学出版社。

Xu, Xiaohe and Martin Whyte. 1990. Love matches and arranged marriages: a Chinese replication. *Journal of Marriage and the Family* 52, 709–22.

Xu, Xiaohe, JianJun Ji, and Yuk-Ying Tung. 2000. Social and political assortative mating in urban China. *Journal of Family Issues* 21, 47–77.

Yang, Hongqiu. 1996. The Distributive norm of monetary support to older parents: a look at a township in China. *Journal of Marriage and the Family* 58, 404–15.

Yu, Jia and Yu Xie. 2012. The varying display of 'Gender Display'. *Chinese Sociological Review* 44(2), 5–30.

Yu, Jia and Yu Xie. 2013. Changes in the Determinants of Marriage Entry in Post-Reform Urban China. PSC Research Report 13–802 (September). University of Michigan, Ann Arbor, MI.

83 Women and agricultural labour in China

Alan de Brauw

83.1 Women and agricultural labour in China

Throughout the developing world, observers suggest that more and more agricultural labour is being supplied by women.[1] From the perspective of women's welfare, there are several concerns. Returns to agricultural labour typically lag returns in all other sectors (McMillan and Rodrik, 2011), so women's economic status might suffer as a consequence. Furthermore, women may provide the agricultural labour within a household, but men may still make managerial decisions or even control the proceeds from crop sales. When women do control decisions about agricultural production, they face several potential limitations in agricultural market participation. Women often have less access to all types of inputs—physical inputs such as fertilizers or improved seeds; high quality or irrigated land; human capital; or even social and political capital, including social networks (Peterman et al., 2010). Consequently, if the proportion of land controlled by women is increasing, overall agricultural production could stagnate or decline, potentially affecting food security within a country.

The feminization of agriculture has been an important issue in discussions about China's rapid economic growth. Rural–urban migrant flows have not been gender balanced; rather, migrants are more likely to be male (e.g. Cai et al., 2009). Consequently, as rural–urban migration flows have grown over time, one consequence appears to be that female participation in agricultural labour and in managing agricultural activities increased during the 2000s (e.g. Mu and van der Walle, 2011; de Brauw et al., 2013). In this chapter, I describe the trend towards increasing agricultural labour by women in China, its likely implications, and policy implications as China continues to modernize.

[1] The author would like to thank Markus Goldstein, Jikun Huang, Ren Mu, Agnes Quisumbing, Scott Rozelle, and Linxiu Zhang, who have all indirectly made substantial contributions to this chapter. All views are held by the author and are not necessarily the views of the International Food Policy Research Institute.

83.2 **The feminization of the agricultural labour force in China**

To initially consider how agricultural labour force participation has changed, we use the China Health and Nutrition Study (CHNS) data, which have been gathered intermittently between 1991 and 2009. Although the questions asked about agricultural labour in the CHNS are sparse, the important thing is that they have been asked the same way in the same villages (and households) over a long period of time, so the biases in the data should at least be consistent over time.

The data indicate several interesting trends (Table 83.1). First, conditional on reporting positive hours worked, households have decreased their allocation of labour to farming substantially, from over 3,500 hours in 1991 on average to less than 1,400 hours in 2009. Simultaneously, an increasing proportion of sample households do not farm; whereas 11 per cent of households did not farm in 1991, the figure in the 2009 survey is 35 per cent of households. Consequently, it appears that by 2010 households in rural China spent substantially less time on average completing tasks on the farm.

Whereas the total amount of farmwork being completed is declining, among households doing farmwork two further trends are apparent from the data. First, prior to 1997, it is not clear that the feminization of farmwork was occurring; the proportion of farmwork done by women appears to have been constant. However, after 1997, we observe an increase in the proportion of work done by women. While the average number of hours spent by women on the farm declined from 1,192 hours per year in 1997 to 748 hours per year in 2009, the total hours worked by the household declined faster. Consequently, the average share of farmwork performed by women increased from 53 per cent in 1997 to 59 per cent in 2009. Second, there was substantial gender specialization in farmwork. Whereas women do all of the farmwork in a rapidly increasing proportion of households, reaching 29.1 per cent of households in 2009, the proportion of households in which men do all the farmwork increased between 1997 and 2009 as well, from 11.1 to 14.2 per cent of households. Since households tend to be small in rural China relative to other developing countries, these figures suggest that in a rising proportion of households one working member does all the farmwork while other members specialize in off-farm work.

Whilst the above statistics demonstrate a substantial decrease in reported hours of farmwork completed, a decreasing proportion of households farming, and the specialization in farmwork by women or men (but usually women) within households, they do not shed light on decision making about farming. For example, a husband can manage the farm *in absentia* by making decisions about what crops to grow, what inputs to purchase, and how much to sell.

If farm management is also being taken over by women, one might be concerned that agricultural yields might suffer or stagnate, for one of several reasons. It could be that

Table 83.1 Participation in farm work by men and women, China Health and Nutrition Survey, 1991–2009

	Year						
	1991	1993	1997	2000	2004	2006	2009
Average total reported hours of farm work, household, conditional on positive farmwork	3527.8 (174.3)	2743.3 (133.1)	2355.7 (127.4)	1975.8 (145.6)	1755.6 (145.2)	1557.1 (120.3)	1399.2 (126.3)
Percentage of rural households reporting no farm work	11	12.7	18.8	24.7	29.6	35.2	35
Average hours of farmwork done by women, conditional on farmwork done by household	1862.6 (96.7)	1430.7 (69.2)	1191.6 (63.7)	1057.8 (76.4)	926.8 (75.7)	867.1 (63.5)	748 (63.7)
Percentage of farmwork done by women	53.1%	55.2%	52.9%	55.3%	57.2%	60.2%	59.1%
Percent of households, women do all farmwork	14.3	14.3	16.3	17.9	24.4	30.4	29.1
Percent of households, men do all farmwork	10.7	9.9	11.1	11.5	12.3	12.5	14.2
Number of observations	2290	2236	2393	2389	2338	2355	2385

Notes: Cluster corrected standard errors in parentheses for average hours.
Source: China Health and Nutrition Survey.

women have too many other tasks to do within the household, and so the time spent making decisions about farming is limited. Their knowledge base about farming might be lower, either because of less intergenerational transfer to women or because women have not received as much training as men in farming. To at least indirectly test whether women's management of farms reduces yields, de Brauw et al. (2013) use data collected in the same households in both 2000 and 2009 to regress plot-level yields for major grains on an indicator for female-headed households, household and plot-level characteristics, and village or household fixed effects. The female-headed household indicator proxies in their regressions for female management. Once they control for village-level fixed effects, they find no difference in yields between male- and female-headed households; this lack of a difference is suggestive that in China, women appear to be as good at managing farms as men.

Although de Brauw et al.'s findings are quite suggestive that female-headed households are equally as productive as male-headed households, there are two concerns. First, female headship is not a perfect proxy for female management; women might receive advice from their absent husbands about what to plant, what inputs to use, and men might even control the proceeds from any cash sales. To more appropriately study female management of farms in China, a more detailed questionnaire than was used in their study would be necessary. Further, they report that female-headed households tend to be less wealthy than male-headed households, measured through asset holdings. Part of this difference is due to locational differences; female headship is more common in poorer areas. Nonetheless, this difference suggests that although female-headed households are just as productive as male-headed households from an agricultural perspective, they may still lag behind male-headed households from an overall welfare perspective.

These findings could be explained as follows. China's rural market environment is so competitive and efficient that women are provided with the services, inputs, markets for selling their produce, and information that they need to efficiently operate and succeed in agriculture (Huang et al., 2004). Moreover, unlike in other countries, women who head households tend to have human capital levels nearly equal to levels among male heads of households, which allows them to take equal advantage of agricultural opportunities.

83.3 The future of women in agriculture in China

Undoubtedly China will continue to further urbanize over the next ten years, both through current processes as well as new government programmes to induce additional urbanization. Consequently, it is likely that the feminization of the agricultural labour force will continue at least in the relatively near future, particularly as *Hukou* restrictions remain in place tying rural labourers to their land. Since a feature of changes in the agricultural labour force is specialization within the household, it is important to consider how specialization (largely by women) could affect agricultural productivity growth.

The findings in de Brauw et al. (2013) might suggest that China should largely continue the policies and actions that have allowed China's markets to flourish. Government interference in China's farming sector has been minimal over the past two decades, but it has invested heavily into the infrastructure required by agricultural markets to function well: roads, communications, and accessible wholesale marketing facilities. This environment has led to strong market competition among traders, which would suggest a lack of gender discrimination; margins among traders are too low to discriminate against women.

Assuming that female headship is a reasonable proxy for female management, women are equally as productive as men when managing the farm. To ensure that women continue to be as productive as men, China's government should consider policies to promote women as farmers. For example, it would be worthwhile to foster initiatives promoting female agricultural extension agents. Overall, less than 30 per cent of extension agents are women, though the proportion is higher among younger women. Ensuring that extension agents are well-versed in adult education techniques and are gender sensitive would help to continue to foster productivity gains among all farmers in China as more people leave farming overall.

Further research could also help to clarify the types of policies that would enhance women's welfare and continue agricultural productivity growth. Research on the tasks being managed within agriculture by men and women would help to tailor gendered components of extension programmes. Furthermore, regional heterogeneity is not explored here. The feminization of agricultural labour or farm management may differ by region, or by rich and poor areas. Additional research on areas with more female headship or agricultural specialization could also help to inform better policy.

■ REFERENCES

Cai, F., Du, Y., and Wang, M. 2009. Migration and Labor Mobility in China. UNDP Human Development Report Research Paper 2009/09.

de Brauw, A., J. Huang, S. Rozelle, and L. Zhang. 2013. Feminization of agriculture with Chinese characteristics. *Journal of Development Studies* 49(5), 689–704.

Huang, J., S. Rozelle, and M. Chang. 2004. The nature of distortions to agricultural incentives in China and implications of WTO accession. *World Bank Economic Review* 18(1), 59–84.

Jin, S., H. Ma, J. Huang, R. Hu, and S. D. Rozelle. 2009. Productivity, efficiency and technical change: measuring the performance of China's transforming agriculture. *Journal of Productivity Analysis* 8, 1–17.

McMillan, M., and D. Rodrik. 2011. Globalization, Structural Change, and Productivity Growth. Working Paper, International Food Policy Research Institute.

Mu, R. and D. van de Walle. 2011. Left behind to farm? women's labor re-allocation in rural China. *Labour Economics* 18(supp. 1), S83–S97.

Peterman, A., J. Behrman, and A. Quisumbing. 2010. A Review of Empirical Evidence on Gender Differences in Nonland Agricultural Inputs, Technology, and Services. International Food Policy Research Institute Discussion Paper 975.

Part XIV
Regional Divergence in China

84 Regional divergence

Kai-yuen Tsui

84.1 Introduction

Travelling along Highway 318 offers a kaleidoscope of contrasts and extremes. At the eastern end stands the gleaming modern skyline of cosmopolitan Shanghai, brazenly reminding the world of her imminent membership to the club of riches. Languishing at the western end of the journey is Lhasa, which seems barely to be emerging from her mystical past. Why is there persistence in regional disparities? What are the forces shaping regional divergence or convergence? To what extent do history and institutions matter?

84.2 Big picture of regional divergence

Tests of *unconditional* convergence, which postulate poorer regions growing faster, are at most mixed (e.g. Jian et al., 1996), depending on the period under study. Likewise, using different measures of inequality, previous studies—for example. Tsui (2007)—have converged to a nuanced picture. Using the mean logarithm deviation index, Figure 84.1 depicts an *oscillatory* trend with respect to gross regional product per capita for the period 1952–2010. Further decomposing the trend reveals a widening coastal–inland gap in the same figure. The coastal–inland dichotomy masks the rural–urban divide as another important facet of spatial inequalities. As shown in Figure 84.2, the ratio of urban to rural consumption per capita fluctuates, echoing a similar message from previous studies such as Kanbur and Zhang (2005).

What are the obstacles standing in the way of long-term convergence? The early Lardy–Donnithorne (Donninthorne, 1976; Lardy, 1976) debate largely dwelled on the spatial allocation of investments and fiscal resources. The coastal–inland divide suggests that geography, transport infrastructure, and openness are obstacles; the rural–urban gap points to obstacles due to industry having higher productivity than agriculture. Another factor immediately coming to mind is education. According to the 1964 census, 41% per cent of those aged between age 13 and 40 were illiterate, the rate for Beijing was 14% per cent as opposed to Gansu's 60% per cent. Many western provinces were not far behind Gansu 国家统计局人口统计司 (1986).

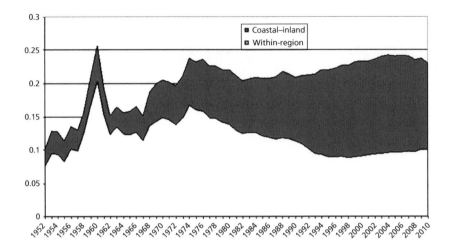

Figure 84.1. Overall interprovincial inequality with respect to gross regional product per capita and decomposition

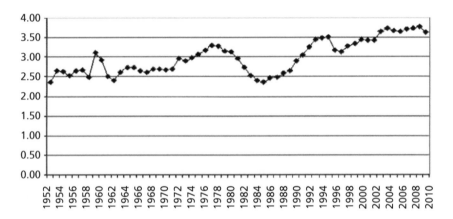

Figure 84.2. Ratio of urban to rural consumption per capita

The recent burgeoning literature using growth regressions, by and large, confirms that the above factors are significantly correlated with regional growth (e.g. Démurger, 2001; Fleisher and Chen, 1997; Fleisher et al., 2010; Jian et al. 1996). But these correlates of growth, while illuminating, are just a first step towards a deeper understanding of why regional inequality is persistent. The growth accounting approach often has a large and unexplained residual which has been shown to exert an important impact on regional growth and thus regional inequality (Tsui, 2007). While this black box is often interpreted as an index of technological progress, institutional arrangements are also influential.

84.3 **History, institutions and oscillating regional inequality**

The ebb and flow of regional economic fortunes driving the oscillatory trend in inter-provincial inequality (Figure 84.1) could not be divorced from China's Maoist past and the subsequent reform since 1978. Teetering on the brink of disintegration after more than a century of foreign aggression and civil war, there emerged in 1949 a strong communist state putting the far-flung corners of the empire firmly under one administrative rubric. At the core was a Soviet-style planning machine capable of swift and large-scale resource mobilization to achieve quick results. Besides the oft-cited flaws of central planning, certain aspects of such a top-down system had important ramifications on regional disparities. For a large country as China, rigid planning from above could easily squeeze regions with widely varying endowments and comparative advantages into a straight-jacket. Furthermore, incentives embedded in a top-down system were inimical to horizontal coordination when local cadres carried out mandates from above. Their careers were (and still are) tied to regional development, breeding local protectionism impeding horizontal flows in factors and goods.

Last but not least, the top-down industrialization 'big push' also drove a large wedge into the rural–urban divide. A compulsory grain procurement system rigged the rural–urban terms of trade to guarantee cheap materials to support industrialization. The household registration system tying peasants to their hometowns was introduced in the 1950s partly to prevent them flooding into cities where residents enjoyed better public services and secure employment. It has since become a hindrance to labour mobility.

The above institutional backdrop offers clues as to why pre-reform regional income disparity was not on a diminishing trend as in Figure 84.1 and Figure 84.2. It is not that regional issues were off the radar screen of the Chinese leadership. Mao declared gaping coastal–inland imbalances to be one of the ten cardinal relationships calling for action. The First Five-Year Plan (1953–57) located two-thirds of the major projects in the interior (Yang, 1990), with the inland share of fixed asset capital formation by and large rising during that period. Then came the defence-related Third Front Campaign, lasting from 1964 to 1971 and massively transferring industrial facilities inland, with a surge of investment skewed towards the inland provinces. These spatial tilts in investment did not, however, translate into sustained declines in regional income disparities, showing that there is more to development than investment. Even worse, the Third Front Campaign, overwhelmed by immense logistical problems, ended in tremendous economic losses (Naughton, 1988), while scarcely making a dent in regional inequality.

If the rhetoric to close regional gaps did not turn into reality, bouts of top-down initiatives and political campaigns more often than not aggravated regional disparities. As if to show how planning and big-push industrialization could go terribly awry, Mao herald-ed the Great Leap Forward to leapfrog the West only to find the economy being thrown into disarray. With the administrative machine to squeeze the rural sector in support of industrialization up and running, the movement increased rural exploitation by herding peasants into communes, pushing production targets up to unrealistic levels, and hand-ing down excessive grain procurement quotas. Slumps in grain production and fam-ine ensued. Hardest hit were the grain bowls particularly in central and western China, leaving behind an indelible mark registered as a sharp jump in regional inequality as in Figure 84.1.

Then, just as the disequalizing impact of the Great Leap Forward was subsiding, the eruption of the Cultural Revolution in 1966 set off a decade of further regional divergence. The upward trend is as much driven by increases in coastal–inland inequality as it is by within-region and rural–urban inequality. Particularly worth mentioning is a policy turn towards administrative decentralization and regional self-reliance undermining what was already weak horizontal coordination under the top-down administrative system. The march of the nation in lockstep towards self-sufficiency paid scant attention to spe-cialization or regional comparative advantage. As pointed out by Lardy (1983) on grain self-sufficiency, the cost of such a distortion was not equally shared among the regions. What is known now lends credence to Donnithorne's hypothesis that the fragmentation of China into what she called a 'cellular economy' was a recipe for regional divergence (Donnithorne, 1972).

Navigating the pre-reform institutional landscape, overall regional inequality ironic-ally peaked at the end of the alleged egalitarian Maoist era. Coastal–inland as well as rural–urban income inequalities reached historic highs. The unfolding of reform since 1978 has unleashed new forces which have altered the dynamics of regional inequality. Pulling back from Maoist excesses at the dawn of reform brought a respite to the rise of regional inequality. The retreat from self-reliance rewound its negative impact on region-al inequality. On the reform front, the curtain raiser was the liberalization of the rural sector with peasants extricating themselves from abject poverty thanks to their newfound freedoms. The household responsibility system let peasants sell their crops at market pric-es after fulfilling the state compulsory grain delivery quotas. Next came a blossoming of township and village enterprises as another stimulus to rural off-farm employment and income. Not surprisingly, a rapid growth in rural income and consumption quickly translated into a conspicuous narrowing of the rural–urban gap up to the mid-1980s (see Figure 84.2 and Kanbur and Zhang, 2005).

The decline was, however, short-lived. Amid spectacular success and euphoria, rural reform lost steam before mustering enough political support to remove the remaining vestiges of the urban-biased pre-reform institutions. Although less stringent, the house-hold registration system continued to erect hurdles blocking rural-to-urban labour mobility. The dualistic land administration system truncated peasants' rights over their land, with their precarious hold over their land tenure threatened by land acquisition for rapid urbanization. In the meantime, unfunded mandates from above and local fiscal systems suffering from revenue–expenditure mismatches led to local predatory charges falling on peasants in the 1990s.

With rural reform stalling in the 1990s, overall inequality resumed its inexorable ascent, this time mainly driven by a rapidly widening coastal–inland gap. With China increasingly opening up to the rest of the world, local governments rolled out the red carpet to foreign investors, showering them with preferential policies. With its better infrastructure and cheap land and labour, the coastal region was best positioned to tap opportunities offered by the global supply chain, fuelling an export bonanza. Manufacturing clusters such as the Pearl and Yangze Delta became magnets for overseas investment and export-oriented firms. Thanks to such agglomerative forces as economies of scale, low transport costs, and a large market, the concentration of manufacturing activities along the coast has fed on itself shaping a core–peripheral structure reminiscent of the lessons from the New Economic Geography.

Towards the end of the 1990s, overall regional inequality as well as its coastal–inland and rural–urban components reached unprecedented levels (Figure 84.1 and Figure 84.2). Indeed, the contribution of a coastal–inland gap to overall inequality shot up from 34 per cent in 1978 to 61 per cent in 2000 (Figure 84.1). Compared with a low of about twofold (in real terms), urban consumption per capita exceeded that of rural residents by three times at the turn of the millennium.

As regional disparities again climbed to historic heights, the Chinese leadership was prompted into action. Starting with the Western Development Programme, initiatives targeting central and north-eastern provinces followed. On the rural front, the plight of peasants moved up the policy makers' agenda. Starting with the fee-to-tax reform to combat local arbitrary charges under the premiership of Zhu Rongji, the succeeding Hu–Wen administration elevated the problems of the 'three rurals' (i.e. agriculture, peasant, and village) to the core of their policy platform. Again reviewing Figure 84.1 and Figure 84.2, it appears that the upward trends in coastal–inland/rural–urban disparities have been arrested.

84.4 Conclusion

The empirical evidence on long-term regional convergence reveals that the long quest for a redress in regional imbalances is still elusive. While correlates of regional growth in terms of investment, schooling, transport infrastructure, and so on, have been shown to affect regional growth and convergence, one should not lose sight of institutions which could have an equally if not more important impact. The analysis in this chapter links the fluctuations in regional inequality to China's evolving institutional landscape. It is also interesting to note that, despite their raison d'être evaporating, the persistence of some pre-reform institutions, such as the household registration system, has continued to be in the spotlight not least because of its alleged impact on interjurisdictional factors and resource mobility and thus on regional convergence.

■ REFERENCES

Démurger, Sylvie. 2001. Infrastructure development and economic growth: an explanation for regional disparities in China? *Journal of Comparative Economics* 29, 95–117.

Donnithorne, Audrey. 1972. China's cellular economy: some economic trends since the Cultural Revolution. *The China Quarterly* 52, October–December, 605–19.

Donnithorne, Audrey. 1976. Comment. *The China Quarterly* 66, 328–40.

Fleisher, Belton and Jian Chen. 1997. The coast–noncoast income gap, productivity, and regional economic policy in China. *Journal of Comparative Economics* 25, 220–36.

Fleisher, Belton, Haizheng Li, and Min Qing Zhao. 2010. Human capital, economic growth, and regional inequality in China. *Journal of Development Economics* 92, 215–31.

Jian, Tianlun, Jeffrey D. Sachs, and Andrew M. Warner. 1996. Trends in Regional Inequality in China. NBER Working Paper 5412.

Kanbur, Ravi and Xiaobo Zhang. 2005. Fifty years of regional inequality in China: a journey through central planning, reform, and openness. *Review of Development Economics* 9(1), 87–106.

Lardy, Nicholas R. 1976. Replies. *The China Quarterly* 66, 340–54.

Lardy, Nicholas R. 1983. *Agriculture in China's Modern Economic Development*. Cambridge: Cambridge University Press.

Naughton, Barry. 1988. The third front: defence industrialization in the Chinese interior. *The China Quarterly* 115, September, 351–86.

Tsui, Kai-yuen. 2007. Forces shaping China's interprovincial inequality. *Review of Income and Wealth* 53(1), 60–92.

Yang, Dali. 1990. Patterns of China's regional development strategy. *The China Quarterly* 122, June, 230–57.

85 China's political-economic institution

Regionally decentralized authoritarianism (RDA)

Chenggang Xu

Regionally decentralized authoritarianism (RDA) is a concise description of China's most fundamental institution, which deeply affects incentives and behaviours at all levels of government in China.[1] The RDA regime is characterized as a combination of political centralization and economic regional decentralization. The basic governance structure of the RDA regime originated from the Chinese empire and has evolved over 2,000 years, allowing the empire to last much longer than any other empire in world history, and leaving a long lasting impact on the governance of China today.

On one hand, the Chinese political and personnel governance structure has been highly centralized in the RDA regime. The central government is constitutionally empowered to delegate power to regions, and also to rescind this power. The backbone of the centralized political control is the Chinese Communist Party (CCP), which rules the appointment and removal of officials at sub-national government level and commands high economic sectors (e.g. banking, energy, telecommunications, railways, etc.), as well as managing ideology and the mass media.

On the other hand, the governance of the national economy is delegated to sub-national governments. Regional economies (provinces, municipalities, and counties) are relatively self-contained, and sub-national governments have overall responsibility for initiating and coordinating reforms, providing public services, and making and enforcing laws within their jurisdictions. Under the political and personnel control of the central government, sub-national governments run the bulk of the Chinese economy. They initiate, negotiate, implement, divert, and resist reforms, policies, rules, and laws. China's reform trajectories have been shaped by the RDA regime. Spectacular performance on the one hand and grave problems on the other hand are all determined by this governance structure.

[1] This chapter is a summary of Xu (2011).

Within the RDA regime, Chinese regional leaders are appointed by upper-level governments through the CCP system, despite devolution of much power over economic matters to the sub-national governments. The central government dictates regional officials' career paths, maintaining a powerful incentive structure. In practice, the central government makes decisions on the appointment and removal of provincial leaders, for example governors. Similarly, most municipal leaders, for example mayors, are directly controlled by corresponding provincial governments. This nested network extends the central government's personnel control to officials at all levels of the regions, from provincial to municipal to county to township governments. A set of performance criteria for officials at each sub-national government level is stipulated by the level of government above it. The success of regional officials is measured by their fulfilment of the tasks and targets laid down by their superior level of government. Level by level, each level of sub-national government negotiates performance targets with their subordinate sub-national government.

This personnel control approach is the major instrument used to make regional officials comply with the central government's policy, and also to provide incentives for regional experimentation. Moreover, through this mechanism, the central government has maintained considerable influence in consensus-building with sub-national governments in order to push through policies that are favourable to the central government. It is important to point out that although the formal structure is hierarchical between central and regional governments, the authority of the central government is endogenized insofar as the power of the national leadership depends on the collective support of the regional leaders as well. Furthermore, the personnel control and power delegation is highly incomplete, designed to encourage more local initiatives from local governments, while still remaining open to central control as the central government retains the power to intervene. Depending on their gains and losses, sub-national governments have a certain degree of freedom to choose to manoeuvre against, or to comply, with policies of the central government.

On the aspect of policy implementation, sub-national governments are granted sizeable de jure control rights and endowed with even greater de facto control rights over most administrative matters, economic issues, and resources within their jurisdictions. It has been well observed that it is the sub-national levels of government that implement China's national development agenda. Nearly 70 per cent of total public expenditure in China takes place at the sub-national level, of which more than 55 per cent takes place at sub-provincial levels. For most administrative and economic matters, as long as the central government does not declare an explicit policy, the regional governments are given the default position to make decisions within their jurisdiction.

Sub-national governments were encouraged to try out reforms and promote economic growth. Consequently, regional competition has been a major component of China's three decades of reform. When one region has a higher growth rate than others, the head of the region will enjoy greater power and is more likely to be promoted. One of the most important initiatives taken by many sub-national governments was the development of non-state firms, including foreign direct investment (FDI) and indigenous firms.

In contrast to the prevalence of regional competition and initiatives taken by sub-national governments in Chinese reforms, officials in other reforming countries and transitional economies were not given similar competitive incentives and were generally less active in taking the initiative than their Chinese counterparts. Moreover, decentralization does not inherently create strong incentives to regional officials for regional economic growth. It is the structure of the RDA regime that makes China special in providing strong incentives for regional officials to encourage economic development.

First, Chinese sub-national officials are subject to incentive schemes managed by the central government. With centralized personnel management for sub-national officials, regional competition under this institutional structure is qualitatively different from regional competition in a federalist system where local officials are elected.

Second, the Chinese national government not only possesses superior powers of appointment, promotion, and dismissal of subordinate government officials, but it is also strong enough to eliminate collusion between lower level sub-national governments. This preserves tournament-like regional competition, since collusion among sub-national officials can make competition impossible.

Third, Chinese regions, particularly county or higher level regions, have historically been and remain relatively self-sufficient in that each region contains multiple economic sectors. Therefore, most Chinese regions are alike in their economic structures, a critical condition for tournament-like competition (Maskin et al., 2000). Moreover, this greatly weakens interdependence among Chinese regions, and enables sub-national governments to coordinate most of the economic activities within their jurisdictions.

Finally, Chinese sub-national governments are both enabled and empowered to take responsibility for economies within their jurisdictions. They are granted a fairly high degree of autonomy on economic activities. Enablement and empowerment themselves are vital sources of incentive. Incentives for officials only work when officials are enabled and empowered to take reform initiatives or growth-enhancing measures, and so on.

Chinese sub-national governments not only compete against quantifiable targets, such as GDP growth rate, they also often compete in initiating or testing new reform policies, that is, regional reform experiments. They have been given considerable responsibility for regional coordination, and such decentralized coordination has facilitated regional reform experiments. Since sub-national governments are closer to experimentation sites, they are much better-informed about local information than the central government, and are therefore more capable of effective coordination. Region-based coordination also makes economy-wide coordination failures less likely when there are external shocks. This makes it easier to experiment with institutional changes locally without causing disruption to the rest of the economy. Most importantly, by incorporating regional experiments as an essential part of the central decision making process, the political risks of advancing reforms are substantially reduced, and political opposition to reforms is significantly weakened. Indeed, almost all successful reforms in the past three decades were introduced through local experiments. Furthermore, regional experimentation is an essential part of the central decision making process in China. Almost every major step on the path of reform was piloted in a few regions before being launched nationwide.

One of the major uncertainties of reform is the challenge of political resistance. Under certain conditions, regional reform experiments are used as a strategy to weaken political resistance. A successful experimental outcome not only provides feedback on which reform programme works, but can also be used to support the reform and to persuade the unconvinced. Moreover, compared with full-blown nationwide reform, the consequences of failure can be contained within the experimental region. In addition, compromise and compensation schemes may be attempted as a way to ease the opposition of a given policy. That is, the option value carried with regional experimentation may bear the necessary weight to tip the political balance in favour of reforms which might otherwise have been discarded.

The key potential benefit of experimenting is to reduce the uncertainties of reform. This requires experiments to avoid disturbing the rest of the economy, particularly in case an experiment fails. It turns out that how an experiment is coordinated determines whether the experiment will be fruitful, and in turn, the way experiments are coordinated is determined by the way the economy and the government are organized. In the RDA regime, a typical Chinese region is relatively self-contained and a sub-national government is responsible for most of the economic activities within its jurisdiction. Thus, sub-national governments are assigned the power and the resources to initiate and to coordinate regional reform experiments. Moreover, given that interregional dependence is relatively weak in China, when a regional experiment fails, its impact on the rest of the national economy is minimal. Qian et al. (2006) explain how the Chinese RDA regime creates conditions that alleviate coordination problems in reforms and allows for flexible experimentation.

However, most of the current major problems in China, from the economic structure to social problems, are also created by the RDA regime. As previously stated, regional competition and regional experimentation have been the driving forces of reform and rapid economic growth in the past three decades. Under the RDA regime, the central government sets the ultimate objective of the government, which guides the direction of the competition. When China is poor, economic growth or the GDP growth rate are important objectives, which can easily be agreed upon by elites and citizens alike. However, when China enters a low–medium income level and when China becomes increasingly more unequal, social and economic issues beyond the GDP become more vital. That is, the government must simultaneously face multiple tasks.

Regional competition is an enormously powerful mechanism that can be vitally constructive as well as destructive. Due to information and incentive problems, it is impossible for the central government to fully control its consequences. Faced with multiple tasks, regional competition in the RDA regime creates 'multiple equilibria', which generate polarizing outcomes. Facing multiple tasks, sub-national governments strategically choose to ignore some tasks in the competition. Regional competition may lead to a 'race-to-the-top' equilibrium, in which regional governments compete intensively for GDP growth rate. It may also lead to a 'race-to-the-bottom' equilibrium, in which regional governments compete ferociously in seeking more rents, grabbing more land by suppressing citizens' rights, and so on (Xu, 2012). Any reform to mitigate these problems will meet the intrinsic conflict of interests of the government itself at all levels in the regime. China's future depends on a fundamental transformation of the institution itself.

■ REFERENCES

Maskin, Eric, Yingyi Qian, and Chenggang Xu. 2000. Incentives, information, and organizational form. *Review of Economic Studies* 67(2), 359–78.

Qian, Yingyi, Gerard Roland, and Chenggang Xu. 2006. Coordination and experimentation in M-form and U-form organizations. *Journal of Political Economy* 114(2), 366–402.

Xu, Chenggang. 2011. The fundamental institutions of China's reforms and development. *The Journal of Economic Literature* 49(4), 1076–151.

Xu, Chenggang. 2012. Institutional foundations of China's structural problems. In *Proceedings of 2011 International Economic Association World Congress*, edited by Masa Aoki. Forthcoming.

86 China's regional development strategy

Ying Du

As a vast country, China naturally exhibits large variations in natural conditions and levels of development. Uneven development is a basic national condition. Promoting balanced regional development has always been an important aspect of China's economic policy.

Since the founding of modern China, the Chinese government has attached great importance to the issue of regional disparity, trying out many different strategies to remediate it throughout history. From the early days of reform and opening up, the dominant strategy was balanced development. In order to speed up interior development, the government pushed the industrial layout inland from the coast—the first steps in counteracting an extremely uneven starting distribution of industrial layout. From the beginning of reform until the mid-to-late 1990s, non-balanced development became the dominant strategy, allowing the coast to lead development to raise the entire country's economic competitiveness. Since the late 1990s the dominant strategy has been coordinated development—attempting to resolve the growing problem of regional inequality. China's plan for coordinated development consisted of plans to promote the western region, to revitalize old industrial bases in the northeast, to promote development in the central region, as well as allowing the eastern region to continue to lead development. Through this plan, China has effectively curbed the expansion of regional inequality, as well as strengthened the coordinated nature of its development.

In recent years, under the guidance of the coordinated development strategy, the country has introduced a series of major plans, policy documents, and pilot programmes dedicated to solving the problem of regional inequality. The government's grasp over regional economies has become finer in detail, giving regional policy a more area-specific, realistic, and nuanced direction. Thanks to differentiated treatment and guidance, different areas have been able to express their competitive advantage to the fullest, increasing guidance and support for development in the two types of regions: on one hand, for regions that naturally fulfil the potential for industry and development, the importance lies in rapidly developing and opening up. The focus should be on changing the means of development, enhancing overall strength and competitiveness, and fostering the creation of economic poles, whose benefits will spill over to nearby areas, leading to their development. On the other hand, in minority, border, poverty-stricken, and other undeveloped regions, the focus lies on increasing support initiatives, strengthening weak links, breaking through developmental bottlenecks, improving the environment's potential for development, increasing developmental self-efficacy, and narrowing their gaps with other regions.

While promoting the development of key areas, we should also promote domestic coordination, international and interregional cooperation, international and domestic opening up, and the optimization of large-scale resource allocation. To further improve regional policy institutions, we should strategically flesh out the basic developmental trajectory of key areas, clarifying leadership on which areas we wish to innovate, focus, restrict, or prohibit development. Since the 12th Five-Year Plan, China's central and western areas have drastically increased development vigour and speed. In the four years after 2008, the western, central, and north-east regions all showed faster development than the east, reversing the trend of China's development being led by the east. At the same time, the east has shown remarkable development in terms of openness and overall economic quality, with the Yangtze River Delta, the Pearl River Delta, and the Bohai Rim zones accounting for half of all economic development in the country, remaining leaders in China's economic growth.

Promoting coordinated regional development is still one of China's most urgent socio-economic tasks in the 12th Five-Year Plan. Although in recent years regional development coordination has improved significantly, there are still many pressing issues that require attention, such as the still-large regional developmental gap, the special difficulties of lagging regions, imperfect institutional mechanisms for promoting balanced regional development, and so on. More region-oriented policy efforts are required. According to China's 12th Five-Year Plan, coordinated regional development is an objective that involves implementing both a strategy for overall coordination and a strategy focused on developing the main functional areas, as well as initiatives to prevent GDP gaps from increasing beyond moderate ranges. In order to provide basic public services of equal quality, to allow regions to exercise their comparative advantages, and to provide harmonious and cooperative development between man, region, and nature, regional economic strengths need to be capitalized, main functions need to be positioned strategically, and a new ecological and harmonious pattern of development needs to be encouraged.

There are six major tasks involved in promoting regional development:

1. Following national and regional strategic guidelines by promoting another round of development in western regions, revitalizing old industrial bases in the northeast, aiding the rise and development of central China, and continuing to support the leadership role of the eastern region.

2. Implement a comprehensive strategy related to developing key functional areas. Following the requirements outlined in the 'National Plan for the Development of Main Functional Areas',

we should further standardize the developmental sequence, control the intensity of development, and support the development of efficient coordination and sustainable land development systems.

3. Continue promoting the opening up and development of economic hotspots, cultivating new economic growth poles to assume leadership and exemplary roles, radiating out support and stimulation for the development of other areas. At the same time, vigorously support impoverished areas, ethnic minority areas, and border areas to improve development, production, living conditions, and self-efficacy.

4. Deepen interregional economic cooperation, encourage cooperation in general, promote orderly industrial change across regions, unify interregional development, vigorously promote the marine economy, continuously opening up towards the outside world, coordinate the advancement and opening up of coastal, border, and inland areas, and create a new model of comprehensive opening up.

5. Close the interregional gaps in the quality of public services by increasing funding in under-developed regions, accelerating construction of basic public service infrastructure. This will improve overall quality of life and reduce the amount by which under-developed areas lag behind in terms of public services.

6. Improve the public policy making apparatus by strengthening the top-down structure of regional development and integrating regional policy with tax, investment, industry, land, environmental protection, and population control policies. Moreover, we should clean up regional policy making by implementing a classification and management system, accelerating the formation of laws and regulations that promote coordinated regional development.

Part XV
China's Provinces: Selected Perspectives

87 Anhui

Economic and social development

Peikun Dai

87.1 Basic profile

Anhui province, 'Wan' for short, is located in the southeast of China. As a hinterland province close to the Yellow China Sea and across the Yangtze River, Anhui lies to the west of Jiangsu and Zhejiang, to the east of Hubei, bordering Jiangxi in the south, and neighbouring Shangdong and Henan to the north. Straddling the Yangtze and Huaihe Rivers, Anhui is naturally separated into three geographical regions, Huaibei, Huainan, and Jiangnan. Two of the five largest freshwater lakes in China, the Hongze Lake and the Chaohu Lake, are in Anhui, along with beautiful scenery, a rich culture, fertilized lands, and numerous rivers. The lower Yangtze area and Huaihe River areas are regarded as 'lands flowing with milk and honey'. The province covers an area of 139,600 square kilometres. By the end of 2011, it had a resident population of 68.76 million and a permanent population of 59.68 million people, with an urbanization rate of 44.8 per cent. In 2011, the disposable income of urban residents and rural residents in Anhui province were 18,606 yuan and 6,232 yuan, respectively. There are various landforms in Anhui that divide the province into five natural areas: the Huaibei Plain, Jianghuai Hill, Dabieshan Mountain area, the Lower Yangtze Plain area, and the mountain area of south Anhui.

Anhui province maintained fast economic growth in recent years. Measured with constant prices, Anhui had a GDP of 1,511.03 billion yuan in 2011—a growth rate of 13.5 per cent over the previous year. Its GDP per capita reached 25,340 yuan ($3923 USD), with an increase of 4,452 yuan over 2010. By the end of 2011, the total deposits of financial institutions (in RMB) in Anhui was 1,940.43 billion yuan, 303.82 billion yuan more than the previous year.

In 2011, the total fixed asset investment of Anhui was 1,212.63 billion yuan, increasing by 27.6 per cent from the previous year. Of this, 1,135.09 billion yuan was urban investment and 77.54 billion yuan was rural investment, with growth rates of 27.6 per cent and 27.3 per cent, respectively. A total of 29.47 billion yuan was invested in upgrading IT and industry and 79.37 billion yuan were privately invested—an increase of 41.8 per cent and 37.1 per cent, respectively.

The fiscal income of Anhui province was 26.33 billion yuan in 2011, showing 27.6 per cent growth on the previous year, in which local fiscal income was 14.63 billion yuan, with a growth rate of 27.3 per cent. The total retail sales of consumer goods were 49.01 billion yuan, an increase of 18 per cent, along with an increase in consumer price of 5.6 per cent. Moreover, the gross import and export value of Anhui was $31.34 billion, an increase of 29.1 per cent, of which total exports numbered $17.08 billion and total imports $14.25 billion, with growth rates of 37.6 per cent and 20.2 per cent respectively.

87.2 Anhui's advantages for economic development

87.2.1 A GOOD ENVIRONMENT AND NATURAL RESOURCES

Anhui has 4.08 million hectares of arable lands and 1.05 million acres of water (0.48 million acres of which are aquacultureable). There are 10,917 species in Anhui, including 30 national key-protected woody plants, 54 rare wild animals, 368 second-grade state protected animals, and 18 first-grade state protected animals, such as the precious Chinese alligator and white fin globefish. The total water quantity of Anhui is around 68 billion cubic metres, ranking Anhui twentieth nationwide.

By 2011, 158 kinds of minerals had been discovered in Anhui province (non-metallic minerals included), and 126 have proved reserves (including common stone construction materials), comprising 5 energy minerals, 19 metal minerals, 96 non-metal minerals as well as two hydrosphere minerals. In 2011, 95 geological research programmes (provincial level) were conducted by geological exploration departments, and 30 reserves with large and medium-sized minerals were newly discovered (excluding mid- and large-sized symbiotic minerals).

The exploration of mineral resources in Anhui province plays an important role in the national economy. Coal, iron, copper, limestone cement, and pyrite are massively explored, forming the five basic industries of energy, construction materials, metallurgy, nonferrous metals, and chemicals. Anhui is a national base for the materials industry and the energy supply base of eastern China. Moreover, Lianghuai (an aggregation of Huainan and Huaibei) coalfield is the largest coal production centre in southern China.

87.2.2 A GOOD LOCATION AND CONVENIENT TRANSPORTATION

Traversed by large rivers such as the Huaihe and Yangtze, and bordering Jiangsu to the east and Hubei to the west, Anhui is an important pivotal hinterland of the Yangtze Delta Plain. Anhui has a road density more than double the national average, as well as a total freeway length of more than 3,000 kilometres. The north and the south are connected by the Tongling Yangtze, Wuhu Yangtze, and Anqing Yangtze River Bridges. Anhui ranks second in its road transportation ability and third in its inland water transportation ability among the provinces of central China. Traversed by the Beijing–Shanghai railway, Beijing–Kowloon railway, and the Eurasian Continental Bridge, Anhui has a total railway length of over 2,800 kilometres, ranking first in eastern China. For air-transportation, Anhui possesses six airports in Heifei, Huangshan, Wuhu, Anqing, Bengbu, and Fuyang. Anhui also leads in the areas of postal services and telecommunications, being the third province in China that managed to digitize communication in all its counties.

87.2.3 A DIVERSE COLLECTION OF PROJECTS

With the pace of '861' planning and the effect of some leading projects, Anhui is experiencing a burgeoning development impetus, with significant achievements in the construction of industrial bases and other key projects.[1] In 2011, Anhui arranged 3,871 '861' projects, with a total investment of 533.38 billion yuan. Several key projects, such as the eighth generation TFT-LCD production line of Xinsheng Co., Ltd in Hefei, the industrialization project of San'an Optoelectronic Co., Ltd in Huainan, the PV system project of Haode Co., Ltd in Chuzhou, the PV system project of LDK Solar Power Group Co., Ltd, the project of industrializing modern Traditional Chinese Medicine by Jiren Pharmaceutical Co., Ltd in Bozhou, the crane chassis project of Liugong Group Co., Ltd in Bengbu, the 100,000 per year 6AT gearbox project of Chery Automobile Co., Ltd, the 1.2 million ton per year cold-rolled plate project of Maanshan Iron & Steel Company Ltd, the Hui culture and art promenade of Huang Mountain, the Nanxiang International Logistic Park in Wuhu, the Nanjing Bay Advanced Business Park in Lai'an, Yuexi–Wuhan Expressway in Anhui province, and the project of the Hefei Comprehensive Center of SPD Bank were under construction. Some other important projects, such as the sixth generation liquid crystal assembly line of BOE Technology Group Co., Ltd in Hefei, the TFT-LCD glass substrate project of IRICO Group Electronics Co., Ltd, the Longyuan 200,000 KWH wind power field project in Lai'an, the CAMC productivity expansion project of 30,000 heavy trucks per year in Maanshan, the expansion project of Hitachi excavator and related parts in Hefei, the first phase project of the salt chemical factory in Dingyuan, the first phase project of the Huayi coal-based co-production fine chemical factory in Wuwei, and the Continental tyre project were successfully accomplished. In year 2011, the total coal capacity increased by 6.3 million tons, and the total installed capacity of electricity was 3.39 million KWH.

---

[1] The 861 programme refers to a government plan that aims to develop eight key industrial clusters, construct six infrastructure projects, and achieve the goal of 10 trillion yuan of GDP in Anhui Province by 2010.

87.2.4 BEAUTIFUL SCENERY AND EXCELLENT TOURISM

Anhui has a colourful culture and history, which is known for its legacy of many eminent people, such as Lao Tzu, Chuang Tzu, Cao Cao, Zhu Xi, Chen Duxiu, Tao Xingzhi, and other prominent thinkers, politicians, militarists, and educationalists. Meanwhile, Anhui is also among the provinces with the richest tourist resources, including ten national scenic spots and historical sites, such as the Huang, Jiuhua, Tianzhu, Langya, and Xiyun Mountains; Caishi Rock; Chaohu Lake, and the Huashan Mysterious Grottoes—Jianjiang River, Taiji Cave, and Huating Lake. The province also contains four national historical and cultural cities—Xixian, Shouxian, Bozhou, and Anqing—six national natural reserves, twenty-eight national forest parks, and thirty-six national historical relics. Moreover, Huang Mountain is a world cultural heritage site, a world natural heritage site, and a world geological park; Xidi and Hongcun ancient dwellings are world cultural heritage sites, and the Huang, Jiuhua, and Tianzhu Mountains are all national 5-A tourist attractions. By the end of 2011, there were 380 A-level tourist sites in the province.

In 2011, international tourism and domestic tourism attracted 2.65 million and 225.35 million people, with growth rates of 33.6 per cent and 46.8 per cent, respectively. Anhui province achieved a total tourist income of 190.1 billion, increased by 65.5 per cent over the previous year, $1.32 billion of which was foreign exchange tourist income and 181.5 billion yuan of domestic tourist income—showing growth rates of 60.5 per cent and 65.8 per cent, respectively.

87.2.5 TRANSFERRING INDUSTRY

On 12 January 2012, the planning of the Industrial Transfer Demonstration Zone in Anhui Yangtze River City Belt was approved by the State Council. By constructing solid platforms and optimizing the economic structure, Anhui has received industries transferred from elsewhere. By holding conferences of Hui Merchants and trading communications with Hong Kong, the province continues to construct multi-dimensional and diversified trading platforms, as well as propagating the Anhui Yangtze River City Belt. As a result of focusing on crucial industries and leading enterprises, along with optimizing the structure of foreign investment, 263 foreign-funded firms were newly accepted in 2011, a decrease of 6.4 per cent compared to the previous year; contracted foreign direct investment reached $3.44 billion, and realized foreign direct investment achieved $6.63 billion, with growth rates of 59.1 per cent and 32.2 per cent, respectively. By the end of 2011, Anhui had attracted fifty-seven foreign Fortune 500 companies to invest in its region. Moreover, a national service outsourcing demonstration city and three national and two provincial service outsourcing demonstration districts have been constructed in the province.

88 Guangdong

Maintaining leadership in China's next round of reforms

Wanda Guo

As one of the pioneers of China's reform, Guangdong has a significant strategic role in the next round of opening-up and reform. Guangdong's head start has made it one of the most developed provinces in China. In 2011, its GDP amounted to RMB 5.3 trillion,[1] the highest of all provinces in the country. Per capita GDP was US$7,819. According to the income standard of the World Bank, Guangdong already ranks among medium- and high-income economies globally.

In the 1980s, Guangdong was identified as a candidate for market-oriented economic reform, a pilot programme undertaken by the nation. Because of its success, Guangdong's experience was promoted across the country in the 1990s, making market-oriented economic reform the primary direction of the nation. Therefore, market-oriented reform is also known as 'the Guangdong model'.

As the origin of China's market economic reform, Guangdong has encountered almost all of the conflicts, problems, and challenges that have occurred during the socioeconomic development of the nation. Particularly, as the 'world's factory', which has lately become a nickname for China itself, Guangdong has experienced rapid industrialization and urbanization in the past three decades, overtaking Henan to be the province with the largest population.[2] With a large number of immigrants, Guangdong is notorious for increasingly difficult problems and conflicts related to these 'migrant workers'. For example, in 2011, local citizens in Wukan Village, Shanwei City staged protests against corrupt village cadres who sought personal benefit from public land transactions. It was covered extensively by the domestic and international media as the 'Wukan Incident'. The

---

[1] Statistics Bureau of Guangdong Province, 'Guangdong Statistical Yearbook 2011': <http:www.gdstats.gov.cn>.

[2] According to the results of the 6th National Population Census announced by the National Bureau of Statistics of China, Guangdong, with 104.30 million citizens in total, is the only province with a population over 100 million. In addition, Guangdong has an above-average urbanization rate—amounting to 66 per cent.

situation was settled with democratic elections of village cadres in mid-March, 2012, but the serious social impact was irreversible.

The incident raised a question for the top officials of the provincial government: how should the next round of reforms be initiated to mitigate conflict and improve the economic competitiveness of the province? In my view, the environment and foundation for Guangdong's economy at the present time is significantly different from that in the early 1980s when the reform began. On one hand, China has been converging with the global economy with unparalleled depth and breadth. On the other hand, Guangdong is currently at a critical juncture for the transformation of its economic structure and growth model, and acceleration of its social reform. Therefore, the next round of reforms should be staged not only in the economic domain, but also within the government system.

Guangdong's governmental reform is an exploration of a new political system, targeted at building a more open and transparent government, and a more flexible culture and value system. An open, transparent government should provide regulated, internationalized, impartial government services, while developing regulations in accordance with the law. Its power for social development and management should be strictly limited, and it should adopt a more flexible and diversified culture and value system.

This reform will take place in four ways. First of all, Guangdong should transform into a service-oriented government by building a regulated, internationalized, fair business environment. In addition to its economic benefits, this will provide Guangdong with international recognition for achieving a 'complete market economy'. It should develop and improve economic management and an operation system in line with international practice and WTO rules, referencing the business regulations, management, and trading practices of developed countries. It should identify factors, standards, and indices of trade remedies, while developing regulations and implementation rules in accordance with practices generally accepted in the international market.

Second, Guangdong should ensure a 'rule of law' government. Efforts will be made to enhance governmental functions in accordance with the law. It is necessary to advocate the spirit of rule of law, contractual obligation, and business credibility. Economic issues should be solved with laws. A 'government of the law' should be built to improve the ability of social management by the law. Local legislation that is not consistent with WTO rules should be revoked or revised to enhance the transparency of legislation and law enforcement. Efforts should be made to explore and improve legislation and enhance the working mechanisms for anti-monopoly practices. An IPR protection system should be developed from the legislative, judicial, and executive aspects to resolve conflicts between employers and employees, and protect the rights and interest of workers in accordance with the law.

Third, Guangdong needs to further ease restrictions for the registration of non-governmental organizations (NGOs) while reducing the size of government. More governmental powers should be transferred to NGOs. Efforts should be made to drive in-depth reform of the NGO registration system by gradually expanding the scope of direct registration to create a well-established structure, multiple layers, and more complete functions. It is necessary to support the development of philanthropic and public welfare organizations, and encourage the involvement of independent, professional third-party organizations in the development of public policies. Industrial rules and standards should be developed referencing generally accepted international practices to lead NGOs on a regulated, healthy path of development through pro-active guidance and regulation.

Fourth, Guangdong needs to build a more open and flexible cultural and value system, while increasing tolerance in government. It is necessary to learn and draw from advanced civilizations from around the world. The traditional culture of China should be integrated with the modernization process of the nation. In this way, it would be possible to build a diversified, open, flexible culture and value system. There should be means for the people to perform watchdog duties on the government. While keeping existing rules, it is necessary to break out-of-date mindsets about government documents and meetings, in an effort to shape a new trend of proactive, innovative governmental practice.

89 Guangxi

Rapid development

Zhongren Cui

Guangxi Zhuang Autonomous Region, in southern China, is the only autonomous region that connects China and the Association of Southeast Asian Nations (ASEAN) through both land and sea. It is China's hub towards the south-west, positioned advantageously along the coast, river, and border of the ethnic minority autonomous regions. Inhabited by such nationalities as Zhuang, Han, Yao, Miao, Dong, Mulam, Maonan, Hui, Jing, Yi, Shui, Gelao, and more, Guangxi possesses one of the largest ethnic minority populations of the provinces in China. The population was 46 million at the end of 2011—32.8 per cent of the population of the province—with minorities accounting for 38.3 per cent.

For more than thirty years, Guangxi has been reforming and opening up and has achieved remarkable economic and social development, especially since the time of the 11th Five-Year Plan. Guangxi has seized the initiative in China's western development strategy and built the China–ASEAN free trade zone. It has been the destination for historically important relocations of international and domestic industries, exercising its unique advantages in terms of location, resources, and policy while strengthening its construction infrastructure, vigorously developing industrial advantages, and accelerating the pace of reform and opening up.

Since the 11th Five-Year Plan, Guangxi has accelerated its industrialization, urbanization, and agricultural modernization, achieving rapid and sound economic development. Guangxi has achieved average annual GDP growth of 13.9 per cent, 3.1 per cent faster than the average growth rate in the 10th Five-Year Plan. Annual fiscal revenue increased by 20.9 per cent, 4.4 per cent faster than the 'Fifteen'. Average annual fixed asset investment rose 34.7 per cent, 12.9 per cent faster than the 'Fifteen' and 9 per cent faster than the national average. In addition, twelve major economic indicators have more than doubled. In 2011, the region's seven economic indicators of GDP, total fixed asset investments, total industrial output value, total large-scale industrial output value, total large-scale industrial business income, total savings balance, and total loan balance have exceeded one trillion yuan, ushering in a golden socioeconomic period.

In recent years, Guangxi has upgraded its basic infrastructure and capacity, constructing a number of high-speed railways, highways, and ports, transforming Guangxi from a peripheral player into the key connection between China and the ASEAN countries, as well as being a hub for south and southwest China. Nanning is the current centre of

Guangxi with primarily ports and airports, but also railways, highways, and waterways, providing the overall transportation framework to both surrounding provinces and the ASEAN countries.

Guangxi has seized the initiative provided by China's international strategy by taking full advantage of its proximity to the ASEAN countries. It has actively participated in and supported the China–ASEAN free trade zone, establishing itself as an international channel of transportation, communication, and cooperation between the ASEAN countries and the other provinces of China. Since 2004, acting as the main driver of the China–ASEAN free trade zone, Guangxi has been the location of eight China–ASEAN expos, sponsored by China and eleven other nations. After eight successful sessions, the China–ASEAN expo has become a key element of friendly China–ASEAN exchange, trade promotion, and interdisciplinary cooperation. It is a platform for dialogue between domestic provinces and the ASEAN countries—a crucial channel for expanding trade. Guangxi is also a leader in relations with Taiwan, successfully holding large-scale commercial and cultural exchange activities, achieving overall communication and connections. Relations with Hong Kong and Australia continue to deepen, and the effectiveness of inter-provincial cooperation is continuously demonstrated by the effectiveness of Guangxi's participation in the Pan-Pearl River Delta, Big Southwest, Yangtze River Delta, and Bohai Rim regions.

As the China–ASEAN free trade zone was fully completed in 2010, and development of the Pan-Beibi Gulf Economic Cooperation and the Guangxi Beibi Gulf Economic Zone became national strategy, Guangxi's comparative advantages and strategic role have become more prominent.

Guangxi enjoys special treatment under regional national autonomy, the China western development policy, the coastal area opening-up policy, and the border trade policy. Since 2008, the state has promulgated the 'Guangxi Beibu Gulf Economic Zone Development Plan', 'A number of views on further promotion of economic and social development in Guangxi', and other major policies. At the same time, eastern Guangxi industries have continued to be approved for relocation to demonstration zones; the national service sector in Guilin has been approved for comprehensive reform; the national mineral resources park in Wuzhou has become a demonstration site for recycling technology; and ecological initiatives have been undertaken within the aluminium industry and other industrial parks in Baise—all unprecedented strategic opportunities for Guangxi's developmental leap.

Moreover, Guangxi possesses rich resources for tourism. Guangxi has blue skies and water, beautiful mountains, and fresh air. The region's forest coverage is 54.2 per cent, ranking fourth in the country. There are 12.56 million mu of coastal mangroves, accounting for 38 per cent of total mangrove coverage, ranking second in the country. Thirty-one municipalities (districts and counties) within Guangxi participate as pilot areas for national ecological demonstrations, and within them, Guangxi has seventy-six nature reserves, thirty-four scenic spots, twenty-six national forest parks, and six national geological parks. Over 80 per cent of Guangxi meets or exceeds tier two urban air quality standards, and over 90 per cent of rivers and lakes exceed the three water quality compliance standards. A good ecological environment is a major advantage for Guangxi—and a point of pride.

Within the magic and beauty of Guangxi, the Zhuang, Han, Yao, Miao, Dong, and seven other native ethnicities worked together to create a rich tapestry of history and culture. Guangxi culture is an important part of Chinese culture—a flower in a garden, so to speak. We should expand on the 'clear mountains, pure waters, and ecological beauty' aspects of the Guangxi 'brand' by coordinating development to accelerate the construction of its economy, resources, and eco-industries. Moreover, we should protect the beautiful natural environment and preserve the harmonious balance between man and nature with ecological civilization demonstration zones, striving to create an ecologically strong area and a path of green development. To strengthen Guangxi's ecology, we should accelerate the development of the recycling economy, strengthen ecological improvement and environmental protection, and strengthen society's ecological consciousness and environmental institutions.

Presently, Guangxi is at the beginning of a new historical era. Its overall strength has improved considerably, its developmental potential is growing, and it is faced with major opportunities, such as, but not restricted to, the Western development strategy and the China–ASEAN free trade zone development strategy. These opportunities mean that Guangxi finds itself in a critical catch-up period. In order to fulfil the ideal of a 'well-off society', Guangxi should complete its assigned mission of building a new highland of international and regional economic cooperation, creating a new economic pole along the coast, leading Western implementation of scientific concepts of development, and being the first to achieve the goal of building a moderately prosperous society. In the next five to ten years, Guangxi should strive to create a wealthy and strong populace, quadruple the regional GDP and per capita GDP, increase urban and rural residents' incomes and reduce the gap between them, and make significant improvement in three aspects: basic public services, sustainable development, and social civilization. Guangxi should also accelerate construction of strong Western economic zones, strong areas of national culture, demonstration zones for social harmony and stability, demonstration zones for ecological civilization, and demonstration zones for national unity and progress.

90 Inner Mongolia Autonomous Region

Strategies and considerations of development

Chenhua Yang

Inner Mongolia, established in 1947, is China's oldest ethnic minority autonomous region and has sixty years of varied history. The region has total land mass of 1.183 million square kilometres, stretching 2,400 kilometres from east to west, and 1,700 kilometres from north to south. On the eastern, southern, and western borders, Inner Mongolia borders the eight provinces of Heilongjiang, Jilin, Liaoning, Hebei, Shanxi, Shaanxi, Ningxia, and Gansu. It is close to the northeast, north, and northwest parts of China, and close to Tianjin and Beijing as well. Inner Mongolia shares its northern border with Mongolia and the Russian Federation. Its border is 4,221 km in length. The population of Inner Mongolia is 24.722 million, with a minority population of 5.317 million, of which 4.411 million are Mongolian—17.9 per cent of its total population.

Since China's opening up and reform, and especially since the implementation of the western development strategy, Inner Mongolia's economy has seen rapid growth, structural optimization, increased efficiency, and a continuous increase in overall strength. The frontier region, as a whole, has improved drastically. As Inner Mongolia undergoes rapid economic development and widespread social progress, the standard of living is constantly improving, all of which serves to maintain national unity, social harmony, and tranquility on the northern border.

From 2002 to 2011, the Inner Mongolia Autonomous Region economy increased from 172.5 billion yuan to 1.4246 trillion yuan—the largest improvement among China's five autonomous regions, as well as the second of China's twelve western provinces and cities to achieve an economy of one trillion yuan. GDP per capita increased from 7,233 yuan to 57,515 yuan, increasing its national rank from sixteenth to sixth. Local fiscal revenue increased by 11.3 billion yuan to 135.7 billion yuan. The per capita income of farmers and herdsmen increased from 2,086 yuan to 6,642 yuan.

From a structural point of view, between 2000 and 2011 the proportions of the economy based in agricultural, industrial, and service sectors changed from 22.8 per cent,

37.9 per cent, and 39.3 per cent to 9.2 per cent, 56.8 per cent, and 34 per cent, respectively. The contribution of industry to the economy rose from 31.5 per cent to 50.3 per cent, and the urbanization rate increased from 42.7 per cent to 56.6 per cent. Of the twelve cities in Inner Mongolia, seven have more than 60 per cent of its population living in urban areas. The Inner Mongolian economy has also undergone important structural transformation. The foundations of agriculture and animal husbandry have been solidifying; industry has strengthened and consolidated its leadership; the service industry has continuously improved; new villages and pastoral areas have been steadily constructed; and urban and rural development has achieved positive results.

The increase in infrastructure construction has laid the foundation for economic development. Total operational railway mileage reached 10,789 km in 2010, with eight of the twelve major cities now connected to highways, 90 per cent of counties connected to cities by secondary roads, 94 per cent of towns connected by asphalt roads, and 84 per cent of administrative villages connected by any type of road. Additionally, there are now twelve public airports in Inner Mongolia.

After tireless long-term ecological construction efforts, the overall deterioration of the ecological health of Inner Mongolia has slowed, with significant improvements in key targeted areas. According to the seventh annual national forest inventory, forest coverage reached 20 per cent, outpacing planning benchmarks, and improving by 5.18 per cent since 1998. Overall groundcover continues to improve. In addition, energy conservation and emissions reductions initiatives have made solid progress, with energy consumption per capita decreasing on target with state control objectives, and total pollutant emissions decreasing at a rate faster than state control objectives.

There have been social welfare initiatives, too. General welfare projects are still in motion, receiving more than 180 billion yuan in funding between 2005 and 2010. The projects that have been implemented have increased the standards of living for people of all ethnic groups in the area. Moreover, job creation and income-generation initiatives have created 1.114 million urban jobs, with 2.24 million farmers and herdsmen switching over to urban jobs annually. The region's average urban and rural incomes rank tenth and sixteenth in the country, respectively. The third initiative has been to strengthen the social security system and gradually expand coverage, raising the standards of the urban and rural poor to meet or exceed the national average. The fourth initiative has been expanding investment in public services and improving the basic standards of education, science, and technology, public health, and other services concurrently.

At the same time, we must clearly recognize that despite the clear improvement in economic strength, the situation of regional economic underdevelopment has not changed and remains a primary challenge. Compared with more developed regions, there is a large gap. For instance, there is insufficient industrial development in Inner Mongolia. Its industry has a single focus, not enough development occurs in emerging industries, the service industry lags behind, and industrial competitiveness and resilience are lacking.

A large gap exists both between regions and between rural and urban areas in terms of development and speed of development, and closing this gap is a difficult task. Basic developmental needs are not yet met by the infrastructure—the irrigation facility is weak and unreliable, public services are rather weak, urban–rural incomes lag behind economic development, per capita income is below the national average, and a proportion of low income people struggle to live. The quality of basic public services is too low—social development and government administration need to be strengthened.

During the 12th and 13th Five-Year Plans, as Inner Mongolia continues to expand its economy and increase the quality of its products, decisive steps must also be taken to protect people's living standards, one of the most pressing issues facing contemporary society. According to the outline of the 12th Five-Year Plan, Inner Mongolia should follow through on its strategic objectives for all-around increases in prosperity and affluence. The comprehensive improvement of quality of life should be a primary objective, as well as strongly supporting scientific development, adjusting and restructuring the economic system, increasing coordination between urban and rural areas, and accelerating the multitude of developments that characterize a modern industrial system. Moreover, urban systems should be upheld with multi-polar structures, the basic public service system should be solidified and improved, social security and institutions of technological and scientific innovation should be decisively strengthened, and Inner Mongolia should commit to an overall, comprehensive development and opening up.

There are several major components to improving Inner Mongolia's economic development. First, the fields of modern agriculture and animal husbandry should be developed. Healthy changes in these fields are to be encouraged, for example the development of high-yield, high-quality, efficient, ecological, and safe modern products. Consolidation of the six leading industries—milk, meat, wool, vegetable oil, potato, and livestock feed—should also be encouraged. The quality, efficiency, risk tolerance, and competitiveness of agricultural and livestock product markets need to be significantly enhanced. All of these steps should consolidate and strengthen the relative status of the agricultural and animal husbandry industries.

Second, Inner Mongolia should build a multi-faceted modern industrial system with coordinated development of resource-based and non-resource based industries, and a deep integration of industry with information technology. On one hand, Inner Mongolia must strengthen its resource-based industries, transforming them into major production bases to fulfil the nation's demand for energy, chemicals, non-ferrous metals, and environmentally friendly agricultural products. On the other hand, the non-resource based industries should also be vigorously developed, focusing on new materials, advanced equipment manufacturing, biomedical innovation, alternative energy, clean coal, information technology, and environmental initiatives such as conservation and recycling. Promoting the non-coal energy industry and other strategic emerging clusters could create new sources of economic growth in Inner Mongolia.

A third route to enhancing economic development would be to build a modern service industry, centred on improving the core of the traditional service industry: tourism and commerce, for example producer services such as logistics, financial services, business services, and high-tech services. Inner Mongolia should research and formulate guidelines for promoting service industry clusters in autonomous regions and promote the concentration, clustering, and intensive development of the service industry. The quality and level of service industry development need to be improved. Promoting the specialization and socialization of the service industry will increase its development speed, relative importance, competitiveness, and structural efficiency.

A fourth component of development will be to continue emphasizing the priority of wealthy and strong districts, using the protection and improvement of livelihood as both a fundamental starting point and goal. The main tasks are to expand employment, raise incomes, and improve the social security system and at the same time foster the basic elements of safety, growth, and diversity, so that minority groups can also fully benefit from the fruits of reform and development.

Fifth, by coordinating regional development, districts can complement each other's regional advantages and create synergistic patterns of cooperation, allowing them to express their comparative advantages, strengthen weak links, and concentrate their energies around the most necessary areas. On one hand, for regions with more abundant production factors and greater growth potential, the focus is on accelerating development and opening up, evolving modes of development, and enhancing strength and competitiveness. These regions will be the main drivers for economic growth in Inner Mongolia, pulling other areas forwards as they develop. A key plan is the integrated development of Hohhot, Baotou, and Ordos, making this area a central focus in the economic zone alongside the Yellow River. This will create a group of viable industrial clusters that will lead the rest of western Inner Mongolia in industrial upgrading and economic restructuring, increasing overall competitiveness.

On the other hand, the development of eastern Inner Mongolia should be actively promoted, with a focus on increasing institutional innovation, improving intra-regional cooperation, and promoting inter-city cooperation. Large, trans-regional industrial parks should be created with several distinct industries, improved administrative mechanisms, and clear competitive advantages. To promote intra-regional competition, the cooperation agreements signed by the regions and provinces and cities should be sought out and spurred into action. Both international and domestic enterprises should be encouraged to build industrial parks. Inner Mongolia might develop a number of large-scale industrial clusters with dotted development (limited to a narrow location), surface protection (a large area can be protected), and centralized layout, while increasing ecological protection efforts, improving environmental resilience, and decisively tackling the issue of sustainability.

A sixth means to enhance economic development would be to construct a bridge to the north, comprehensively opening up to the world. This would serve to consolidate and improve relations with Russia and Mongolia. In addition, Inner Mongolia should speed up the construction of the free market pilot areas of in Manzhouli and Erenhot, strengthen key ports, cooperative zones, and international channels, strongly develop border and port economies, and promote the construction of inland ports.

91 Jiangsu

Pattern change and structural adjustment

Futian Qu

Located on the north side of the Yangtze Delta, Jiangsu is among the most developed provinces in China. It is regarded as the origin of China's national industry. It has also been known as 'a land flowing with milk and honey' since ancient times. With an area of 102,600 km², a total population of 78 million people, and an urbanization rate of 61.9 per cent, Jiangsu reached a total GDP of US$762 billion in 2011, ranking second in China. Meanwhile, income exceeded $9,500 GDP per capita, reaching the economic development standards of higher middle-income countries.

91.1 Basic economic development profiles of Jiangsu Province

Jiangsu Province has the highest population and economic density of any province in China. With only 1.1 per cent of the nation's territory, Jiangsu holds 5.9 per cent of China's population, produces 5.6 per cent of its food, and generates 10.3 per cent of its GDP. As a paragon of the more developed coastal regions, Jiangsu's economic development process has had the following unique characteristics.

First, it has experienced solid and rapid regional economic growth for over thirty years. Regarded as one of the fastest growing provinces, in China Jiangsu sustained an average economic growth rate of 12.6 per cent from China's reform and opening up in 1978 to 2011, a rate higher than the national average by 3 per cent. The economic development of Jiangsu Province has had significant characteristics. During the 1980s, the booming township industry led Jiangsu to transition into an industrialized economy, with an annual growth rate of 8.5 per cent. In the 1990s, with the introduction of foreign direct investment (FDI) and the development of an export oriented economy, Jiangsu reached an annual growth rate of 11.2 per cent and opened up its economy. In the new millennium, Jiangsu has focused more on its high-tech and modern service industries, striving towards an innovation-based economy, reaching 15.1 per cent economic growth per year.

Second, its industrial structure modernized around the service industry. The shares of the agricultural, industrial, and service sectors in Jiangsu were 6.3 per cent, 51.5 per cent, and 42.2 per cent, respectively. As the third most important agricultural province in China, Jiangsu covers 6.4 per cent of the nation's agricultural added value. Jiangsu's industrial structure also possesses a competitive manufacturing industry. With an industrial added value of $397 billion, Jiangsu owns 13.2 per cent of the nation's total industrial value and 1.5 per cent of the world's. It is responsible for 23.5 per cent of information technology (IT) output value, as well as 33 per cent of IT exports. Moreover, the value added of new emerging industries, such as new energy, new materials, and new medical products, constituted over 10 per cent of Jiangsu's total GDP. Meanwhile, the service sector is booming. With a higher than average growth rate, its effect as a driver of economic growth and employment has increased significantly over the past five years.

Third, international trade and FDI have had significant impacts on economic growth. Benefiting from a favourable location and rapid reform, Jiangsu established an open economy with a two-way exchange of factors and resources earlier than other regions. In 2011, Jiangsu reached a gross trade value of $539.76 billion—14.8 per cent of the total amount in China, with a foreign trade dependency of 71.4 per cent. Meanwhile, it had a total FDI of $32.13 billion—27 per cent of China's total. The rapid expansion of trade and FDI not only contributed to economic growth, but also had a far-reaching influence on the transformation of Jiangsu's industrial structure.

Fourth, human capital and technological development made a significant contribution towards Jiangsu's economic growth. Four to five hundred thousand students graduate from college in Jiangsu per year—the largest higher education system in China. The number of scientists and technological workers per 10,000 people in Jiangsu is 172, nearly twice the national average. In addition, R&D investment in Jiangsu comprised 2.2 per cent of its total GDP, and scientific and technological development contributed 55.2 per cent towards Jiangsu's economic growth—higher than the national average by 8 per cent.

Fifth, multidimensional reform of the market economy created institutional advantages in regional economic development. The township and village-owned enterprises (TVE) started the process of rural industrialization through market reform in southern Jiangsu. The 'Southern Jiangsu Pattern' once served as a role model for the entire Chinese economy. In 2011, with a rapid property rights reform, the private sector reached 41 per cent of the total economic value of Jiangsu, accompanied by higher growth incentives, while state-owned and foreign enterprises only covered 33.9 per cent and 25.1 per cent, respectively. As a result of persistent reform, Jiangsu has generally developed the factor markets of labour, land, capital, and technology that are consistent with the requirements of a modern market economy.

91.2 **Change of growth patterns and adjustment of the economic structure: the major thesis of economic growth in Jiangsu**

Jiangsu will develop into the post-industrialization stage in the following 5–10 years, the first Chinese province to advance into a modern, creative, and high-income society. With the reduction of comparative advantages in labour-intensive industries and changes in international economic circumstances, Jiangsu is also facing the problems of a decelerating growth rate, a reduction of growth impetus, a slowing down of structural transformation, and the splitting of the economy into a rural–urban dichotomy, to the extent that the traditional path of economic growth is being challenged. Analysing the problems and finding solutions are crucial for Jiangsu sustainable development.

91.2.1 THE CHANGE OF ECONOMIC GROWTH DYNAMICS AND THE CHOICE OF GROWTH PATTERN

Jiangsu had a higher economic growth rate than average over the past thirty years. However, with its change of developmental stage and the lingering effects of the financial crisis, Jiangsu is experiencing a decreasing impetus of economic growth.

In terms of the drivers behind Jiangsu's economic growth, from 1980 to 2006, the contribution rate of investments and net exports increased from 27.6 per cent and 8.8 per cent to 40.8 per cent and 15.3 per cent, respectively, serving as the major determinant of Jiangsu's economic growth, while the contribution of consumption decreased from 63.7 per cent to 43.9 per cent (Sun and Wang, 2008). After the financial crisis, the export growth rate in Jiangsu decreased from 27 per cent in 2007 to –16.6 per cent in 2009. Meanwhile, the contribution rate of net exports in 2009 was –10.5 per cent, and back to merely 1 per cent in 2011. Despite the increase of the contribution rate of consumption to 51 per cent in 2011, the impetus of consumption was still not high enough in comparison with the contribution rates of 60–80 per cent in Europe, the USA, and India. At the same time, the investment effect coefficient also decreased from 2.2 in 2004 to 1.83 in 2009 (Men et al., 2011). If a new growth impetus cannot be found, growth in Jiangsu will experience a faster decline, considering its high dependency on exports and investment.

As for factor input, the contribution rate of capital was 54.2 per cent in 1978–98, the main source of growth. After entering the 2000s, the contribution rate of labour and capital decreased gradually, while the contribution rate of total factor productivity (TFP) increased, reaching 55.2 per cent in 2011. However, unlike developed countries where technical progress covers 70–80 per cent of the total economic contribution rate, technical innovation in Jiangsu has not been able to effectively replace the role of capital and labour and generate a powerful influence on the economic growth of Jiangsu (Hong, 2009). Meanwhile, along with the disappearing demographic dividend (Cai, 2004), the cost of labour and land will continue to rise, and their marginal contribution rates will experience further declines. The present growth model that relies on low labour costs is unlikely to be sustained.

Therefore, changing the growth pattern will become inevitable for Jiangsu's further economic development. On the one hand, we need to improve the contribution of consumption toward economic growth, increase the quality of foreign trade, and optimize the dynamic structure of Jiangsu's economy. On the other hand, we should raise the contribution rate of TFP, transform knowledge and technology into the primary sources of economic growth, and develop an innovative economy that can achieve endogenous economic growth (Romer, 1990).

91.2.2 A SKETCH FROM THE BOTTOM-UP: INDUSTRIAL UPGRADE AND STRUCTURAL TRANSITION

The transformation of an economy from low-productivity sectors to high-productivity sectors facilitated the rapid growth of Jiangsu's economy. As a result of its rapid industrialization, the industrial sector contributed 73 per cent of total economic growth from 1978 to 2006. In 2006–11, Jiangsu quickly adjusted its industrial structure: the service sector experienced fast growth, with its relative weight rising from 36.4 per cent to 42.2 per cent, increasing by 1.16 percentage points per year. The high-tech industries covered 35.3 per cent of total industrial output, increasing by 10.4 per cent. In this period, the industrial and service sectors contributed 59.6 per cent and 38.6 per cent of GDP growth, respectively, serving as important drivers of economic development. Currently, Jiangsu is experiencing a transition from traditional to modern manufacturing industries, as well as from a manufacture-based economy to a service economy.

Despite boasting a GDP per capita above $9,500, Jiangsu has not yet formed an industrial structure centred on the service sector. The share of the service industry in total GDP is low—42.2 per cent, which is even less than the worldwide average of 67.3 per cent. In particular, Jiangsu is facing a drawback in its producer services, such as financing, modern logistics, and IT services. In Jiangsu, the development of a service industry is largely dependent on consumption, as intermediate demand, FDI, and net exports do not show sufficient impetus to drive the growth of the service industry on their own. It is notable that 61.4 per cent of total FDI is centred in the second industry. Mainly used for equipment imports, such FDI inhibits direct demand on the service industry. Moreover, as an important component of the 'Made in China' brand, Jiangsu attracted international subcontractors via its cheap land and labour force. Jiangsu positioned itself on the lower rungs of the global value chain at first, and remained locked there for a long time, lacking the ability to upgrade, creating a problem for the intention to transform and improve its manufacturing industry. At the same time, low-level manufacturing industry has limited demand for a high-level service industry, making it difficult to achieve mutual and reciprocal development between the two (Liu, 2010).

The fact that Jiangsu's economic growth relied excessively on the strength of its second industry inhibited the potential growth effect of a more efficient service industry. The industrial value added rate of Jiangsu is around 20 per cent, which is lower than the average rate of 35 per cent among developed countries. Moreover, it also led to excessive exploration of land and other environmental resources (Qu and Tan, 2010). Jiangsu's land exploration strength has been over 18 per cent, surpassing 7.9 per cent in Japan and 11 per cent in Germany. The energy intensity per GDP of Jiangsu is also 2.1 times the average worldwide, suggesting that the environmental Kuznets turning point has not been reached. Meanwhile, the land and labour dividends are disappearing, and the present industrial structure is losing its comparative advantage and competitiveness. Now, policies that would establish a modern industrial system centred around a service economy include adjusting the industrial development strategies by striving towards the upper part of the global value chain as well as constructing a parallel national value chain enhancing technical innovation and the standards of opening-up, advocating the combined development of advanced manufacturing industry and service industry, motivating the development of industrial clusters, and establishing favourable factor prices and taxing policies for the development of the service industry.

91.2.3 THE CHALLENGES AND POTENTIAL STRATEGIC ADJUSTMENTS OF AN EXPORT-ORIENTED ECONOMY

The high correlation between foreign trade and FDI in Jiangsu not only significantly influences the dynamics of economic growth, but also deeply affects the direction of industrial structural transformation. From 2000 to 2008, the contribution rate of net exports towards Jiangsu's economic growth increased every year, with an average annual increase of 10.4 per cent. Consisting of 20 per cent of the total amount of investments in fixed assets, FDI had a higher contribution rate than domestic capital towards the growth of southern Jiangsu and the second industry. In Jiangsu, foreign enterprises generated 30 per cent of the total GDP and covered 60 per cent of the total export value. Moreover, more than 60 per cent of the FDI went into manufacturing industries, promoting their development. On one hand, by introducing advanced technology and crucial devices, foreign investments have supported the development of new industries. About 20 per cent of the FDI went into electronic and communication device manufacturing, growing it into one of the three leading industries in Jiangsu. On the other hand, the boom of foreign investment has led to a spatial integration of leading industries, forming many industrial clusters such as the IT industry along the Shanghai–Nanjing line, equipment manufacturing along the Yangtze River, and the processing industry along the coast. Twenty-two national and 103 provincial economic development zones were established, accounting for 75.7 per cent and 75.8 per cent of the total gross trade and FDI in Jiangsu, respectively. The clustering effects of FDI are becoming increasingly obvious. Meanwhile, the development of foreign enterprises also improved the structure of export products. In 2011, advanced technological and electromechanical products accounted for 41.4 per cent and 66.5 per cent of the provincial export, respectively, increasing by 20.6 per cent and 20.3 per cent compared to 2000. Admittedly, the FDI of Jiangsu mainly focuses on the lower end of manufacturing industry, which inhibits the development of the service industry directly and indirectly.

Jiangsu's export-oriented economy is facing a severe challenge after the financial crisis. First, exports experienced a rapid reduction, and the contribution rate of net exports towards economic growth contracted, even becoming negative. Second, the FDI attracted by Jiangsu was mostly focused on the lower parts of global industrial divisions, and further export trade faces significant risks. Specifically, processing trade covers 60 per cent of total exports in Jiangsu. Only a few industries and enterprises have independent brands and independent intellectual property—market competitiveness and profitability are not enough. Meanwhile, FDI centred around the manufacturing industries, creating a crowding-out effect on domestic investment in these more competitive export-oriented industries. In the short term, the 'two ends abroad' situation in the processing trade cannot be easily changed (Wang, 2009). Third, as a result of increasing domestic factor costs and emerging competitive advantages in the surrounding areas, Jiangsu will likely face a problem of FDI outflow.

Several factors cause such problems. First, a dependency on cheap factors in the international division inhibits firms' self-innovation and the introduction of advanced parts into the system. Second, the fundamental path of capital introduction inhibits the introduction of technological and human resources. In Jiangsu, the positive technological spillover of FDI is not high. The investment ratio of technology introduction and re-innovation is merely 1:0.42, much lower than the 1:8 ratio of Japan and Korea. Third, policy preference does not encourage foreign enterprises to upgrade their production structure. Facing a declining world economy and a weak external market, Jiangsu's export-oriented economy cannot be easily sustained with its previous comparative advantage of cheap labour costs and land.

Facing such challenges, the following aspects deserve special consideration in the development of foreign trade and FDI in Jiangsu: ensure that the promoting economic growth does not rely solely on trade and investment, but also includes consumption in its forward planning; increase the weight of common trade, in order to promote the transition and upgrade of processing trade; encourage FDI to invest in fields with high technological intensity and product value added; stress the introduction of advanced technology and top-level employees and establish domestic brands and independent intellectual properties in order to accelerate Jiangsu's transition from the lower end to the upper end of the global value chain; cultivate Jiangsu's own multinational enterprises to transform the one-way, inward flow of foreign capital into a two-way flow of domestic and foreign capital.

91.2.4 THE REFORM AND FRAMEWORK INNOVATION OF AN RURAL–URBAN DUALISTIC ECONOMY

Reducing the rural–urban gap is an important topic for the adjustment of the economic structure of all developing regions and countries, and is crucial to their economic development. By establishing township and village-owned enterprises (TVEs) and letting peasants share the benefits of industrialization, Jiangsu led China's rural–urban reform, with the income ratio between urban and rural citizens decreasing to 1.52:1 in 1988. However, since the economy was centred around the dualistic framework of domicile control, the peasants in TVEs could be emancipated from the land, but not from their hometown. Such situations hindered the transition from the dualistic economy and, in the 1990s, the income gap between rural and urban citizens increased, with an income ratio of 2.43:1 in 2011.

Compared to the nationwide rural–urban income ratio of 3.3:1, Jiangsu is among the provinces with the lowest income gap. With the rapid industrialization of the past several decades, Jiangsu achieved an urbanization rate of 66.7 per cent; 90 per cent of the agricultural labour force in Southern Jiangsu has been employed in non-agricultural departments, and the rural–urban income ratio decreased in recent years. With rigid constraints on the dualistic framework, the transition speed of the agricultural labour force decreases and the dualistic economic attributes become obvious. First, the employment structure lags behind the industrial structure. In 2011, the added value of agriculture was 6.3 per cent of total GDP, while the agricultural labour force accounted for 21.5 per cent, and the comparative labour productivity was merely 0.293. Second, urbanization falls behind industrialization. In 2011, the ratio between the urbanization and industrialization rates was 1.2, lower than the international reasonable interval of 1.4–2.5 and the average global standard of 1.95 in 2010 (Zhou, 2012). Third, the phenomenon of peri-urbanization is severe, whereby a large number of the estimated urban citizens are not real urban citizens; instead, they travel between the urban and rural areas in their daily life. In 2011, the weight of urban citizens was 61.9 per cent, while only 40 per cent had a real urban household registration. That is to say, for one-third of urban citizens, approximately 17 million people (12.7 million of which came from Jiangsu), rural household registration prevented them from accessing the common welfare services of urban citizens, such as education, medical care, housing, and social security. The industrialization lag and peri-industrialization prevents the transition from peasant to urban citizen, which not only makes it difficult to acquire a high-quality labour force for the transition and upgrading of industry, but also deters the reform of traditional agriculture, for peasants cannot leave their land and rural areas completely. Nowadays, Jiangsu has an agricultural labour force of 8.7 million, operating on 4.467 million acres of land, with a mere 0.51 acre of land per labourer, which is much lower than the 0.93 average of Korea and Japan. As a result, most of the agricultural labourers are peasants older than 50, with fewer income opportunities. The small scale of agricultural operations as well as the low quality of the labour force makes it difficult to accomplish traditional agricultural reform by attracting advance production factors.

In addition, the present framework of rural land and social security are also restrictions on any labour transition in rural areas. With obscure land property rights and a shortage of an effective land market, peasants can hardly receive adequate price compensation for their land (Tan et al., 2011). When peasants have little or no standard endowment and medical security, land becomes the most important source of insurance in their life. This creates two situations: either the peasants are not willing to enter urban areas, or they go to the urban areas without abandoning their land. Admittedly, their old age, low educational status, and weak technical abilities also prevent them from transitioning into non-agricultural employment.

The restriction of rural labour transition by a dualistic economy not only delays the industrialization process and the upgrading and transition of industry, but it also hinders reform of traditional agriculture and improvement of peasants' income. In order to break down the dualistic economy, Jiangsu needs to accelerate its reform on land, social security, and the household registration system, so as to achieve a free flow of labour, land, and other production factors between rural and urban areas, and an equilibrium of the public services allocated between the two areas.

91.3 **Policy prospects of Jiangsu's economic growth**

In order to step into the club of developed countries and regions by 2020, as well as sustain a leading position in the modernization of China, it is necessary for Jiangsu to promote an economic transition towards endogenous growth via reform and policy adjustment. Meanwhile, Jiangsu needs to make many adjustments in the realms of industrial upgrading, structural transformation, and the rural–urban relationship.

Jiangsu should reform technology policies to promote independent innovation, and to help realize the goal of transforming human resources and technical factors into the main impetuses of economic growth. Fiscal support of technological innovation should be increased, so as to promote R&D and the investment of human resources. In particular, support is needed for innovative technological enterprises to integrate their innovative resources. Enhancing basic educational standards and emphasizing vocational skill training is required to raise the quality of the labour force. To raise the standards of environment protection, it will be necessary to improve the portfolio of production factors and increase the costs of material resources. An improvement in the protection for intellectual property, clarification of systematic contract arrangements, and relative financial products are needed to guarantee the long-term profits of technical innovation.

Further measures include reform of industrial and tax policies with the aim of improving and transforming industry into a '321' structure. The industry menu needs to be changed and the development of a modern service industry, advanced manufacturing industry, and modern agriculture promoted. The development of industries with a high dependency on the investment of human capital, technological capital, and knowledge capital should be advocated, with restrictions on industries which require high consumption of resources and energy and record high levels of emissions. Reform of business tax to a value added tax in the service industry so that it receives the same tax rate as other industries should be promoted. For those restricted industries, stricter permission standards, along with a diversified land, tax, and pricing policy, should be applied to enhance their operation costs.

Trade and FDI policies need to be adjusted with the aim of closely integrating with the global value chain and achieving a worldwide allocation of production factors. The development path of foreign trade could be changed to promote the transition from processing trade to common trade, from general industrial product exports to advanced product exports, and from goods trade to service trade. Imports of advanced products and equipment should be increased to promote mutual development between imports and exports. The introduction of people with high-tech skills and top-class potential needs to be emphasized, as well as the cultivation of domestic brands and independent intellectual property rights. Approval of overseas investments should be relaxed in order to encourage enterprises to establish institutions for raw material purchase, production, R&D, and marketing. It would also be beneficial to remove the double tax for transnational operations.

Reform of the dual rural–urban system, promoting the rural labour transition and the integration of rural and urban development, is needed. An integrated household registration system based on living areas should be established so as to disconnect it from the urban welfare system. The land property rights of rural areas need to be clarified via land property registration. Promoting the emerging land market of rural areas, protecting the land profit rights of peasants, and enlarging the scale of the agricultural land market is also necessary, as is reform of the traditional land requisition system and the formation of an integrated construction land market between rural and urban areas. The construction of an integrated rural–urban social security system and equality among basic public services should be promoted. Peasants' cultural and technical qualities should be enhanced via vocational training.

There are a number of spatial policies that should be emphasized to promote industrial clustering and achieve sustainable development. A focus on construction within the four industrial bends—along the Shanghai–Nanjing line, the Yangtze River, the coastal areas, and the east Longhai railway—should be prioritized to increase their economic and urban density. The main functional strategy for the region must be applied in order to control extensive spatial development. Moreover, for those important developing areas, specific industrial bases and service clusters need to be constructed and modern industrial clusters cultivated, mainly via the creation of development zones. In restricted and forbidden regions, exploitive activities should be strictly controlled, and a greater focus needs to be placed on modern agriculture and environmentally friendly industries in order to protect green and open spaces.

Continuing improvement in the market economy system is needed, with the aim of achieving market allocation of factor resources. State-owned enterprises should be encouraged to leave competitive areas and reform of monopolized industries introduced, which will enable a private economy to develop allowing more firms to enter the realms of infrastructure, public affairs, financial services, and social affairs on an equal footing. The investment management framework as well as and the procedures regulating administrative approval need to be reformed. In addition, the micro-direct intervention of the government concerning factors such as land, capital, and finance should be reduced in order to allow the market to influence resource allocation.

■ REFERENCES

Cai, Fang. 2004. Demographic transition, population dividend, and sustainability of economic growth: minimum employment as a source of economic growth. *Population Research* 28(12), 2–9.

Hong, Yinxing. 2009. Transition towards an innovative economy: thoughts from a post-crisis period. *Social Sciences in Nanjing* 11, 1–5.

Liu, Zhibiao. 2010. *Economic Integration of Yangtze River Delta*. Beijing: China Renmin University Press.

Men, Kepei, Zhao Kai, and Zhu Shudan. 2011. A forecast research on China's economic development in the twelfth five-year plan period. *Yuejiang Academic Journal* 2, 58–65.

Qu, Futian and Rong Tan. 2010. *Sustaining Governance of Land Use Conversion*. Beijing: Science Press.

Romer, P. 1990. Endogenous technological change. *Journal of Political Economy* 98, 71–102.

Sun, Guofeng and Jiaxin Wang.2008. Consumption, investment, net export and economic growth: an empirical analysis on Jiangsu. *Financial & Trade Economics* 12, 85–90.

Tan. R., F. Qu, N. Heerink., and E. Mettepenningen. 2011. Rural to urban land conversion in China—how large is the over-conversion and what are its welfare implications? *China Economic Review* 22(4), 474–84.

Wang, Ying. 2009. FDI and economic growth in Jiangsu: an empirical analysis on total FDI and industrial distribution. *Industrial Technology and Economy* 28(10), 151–5.

Zhou, Qiren. 2012. Leading industrialization and lagging urbanization. *The Economic Observer* 4/20.

92 Ningxia

Poverty alleviation and development

Dongyu Qu

Since the beginning of the twenty-first century, poverty alleviation in Ningxia has been guided by a scientific outlook on development, prioritized to improve farmers' income and aimed at the self-development of poor regions and poor populations. A series of methods have been used, such as combining local poverty alleviation and reallocation, developing and protecting natural resources, constructing infrastructure and social projects; and integrating these alleviation programmes with intelligent development. The impact has been remarkable. Farmer's net incomes in the eight key counties identified as being in need of poverty alleviation were increased from 987 yuan (US$119, $1 = 8.3 yuan in 2000) in 2000 to 3,415 yuan ($542, $1 = 6.3 yuan in 2010) in 2010, a net increase of 2,428 yuan ($385) and annual growth of 13.2 per cent, much higher than the average in China and in other counties in Ningxia. The average farmer income was over 3,800 yuan ($603) in 2011.

92.1 Main measures and their effects

92.1.1 THE REMARKABLE EFFECTS OF SPECIAL PROGRAMMES FOR POVERTY ALLEVIATION

92.1.1.1 Promote the whole village as the key measure for improving the basic working and living conditions of local farmers

According to the general requirements of reducing poverty, increasing income, decreasing the differences, promoting the development and constructing a harmonious society, up to 2010, three groups totalling 777 key villages were promoted and a total of 1.33 billion yuan ($211 million) was invested, 1.7 million yuan ($270,000) for each village. In 2011, the first group of 248 key villages was included in this effort during the 12th Five-Year Plan with a total investment of 520 million yuan ($82.5 million), that is, 2.09

million yuan ($332,000) for each village. As a result, the working and living conditions for local people were improved greatly, their spirits uplifted, and their capabilities for self-development remarkably increased.

92.1.1.2   Support poverty alleviation by industrializing to increase the farmer income

A number of meetings on how to plan the development of the central dry regions and Guyuan region were organized in the autonomous region. A number of industry projects were launched, such as the Animal Husbandry Project for 100,000 Poverty Households, the Planting Grass for 1 million Mu (one Mu is 666.7 sqm) Project, the Supporting Animal Husbandry by Micro-Credit with Government Guarantee, Four-million Mu Project, and the Upgrading Leading Enterprises Project. Animal husbandry, potato cultivation, labour service, and tourism were growing to become leading industries in the region and special industries for planting watermelons in sand fields, medicinal herbs, red onions, mushrooms, wolfberries, and dates have begun to take shape.

92.1.1.3   Focus on training for labour transfer to improve the capability of people living in poverty for self-development

Since the start of the twenty-first century, a number training projects have been implemented, such as Training for One Million Farmers, Training for 10,000 Labour Transfer, the Sunlight Project, and the Employment Training for the Poor Rural Labour Transfer in Mid- to Long-term Period. Up to now, 24,880 farmers have been trained by the mid- to long-term training project. The stable employment rate has been raised to over 90 per cent for people who have been trained.

92.1.1.4   Using migration of people living in poverty as a means of widening their living space

To solve the problem of the survival and development of the population living in poverty once and for all, the Ningxia party committee and government, based on past experience, launched projects for ecological relocation, labour service relocation, and educational relocation. During the 12th Five-Year Plan, 350,000 poor people who are living in regions where basic survival is extremely difficult and the conditions for development are missing will be re-settled to other suitable locations, which is known as ecological relocation. Other favourable policies have been designed to encourage students from poor regions to receive a better education. High quality schools such as Liupanshan Senior High School,

Yucai High School, and a number of professional training bases have been built with governmental investment to serve students from the poorer areas.

92. 1.1.5 Develop mutual help funds within villages as a major way to solve the problem of development fund shortages

Up to now, the village mutual help fund project has covered 970 villages in 128 towns in 22 counties. Over 80,000 farmers have joined the development mutual fund cooperatives and over 400,000 people have benefited from the project. The total mutual fund was over 400 million yuan ($63.5 million). Furthermore, a new mechanism combining the mutual fund with introduced financial capital was explored. A financial innovation poverty alleviation project to provide 'credit for a thousand villages and mutual help fund' was launched. This strategic cooperative agreement was signed between the Ningxia Poverty Alleviation Office and the Yellow River Commercial Bank.

92.1.2 STEADILY PROMOTE POVERTY ALLEVIATION BY INDUSTRY

To accelerate social and economic development in poor regions, taking 'the poverty alleviation and development project for a thousands of villages' and the whole village poverty alleviation and development work as a starting point, resource integration among different sectors was enhanced, mainly focusing on the regions with the most poverty. Significant success has been achieved. The obligation to provide nine years of education passed the national inspection. Access to water, electricity, and roads were made possible. Clinics, technological, and cultural centres have been built in each village. Drinking water projects for humans and livestock were established where the average per capita basic farmland exceeded 2.7 mu (0.18 ha). A number of advanced practical production technologies were extended, and the working and living conditions for local people in poor rural areas were improved significantly.

92.1.3 WIDELY CONDUCT POVERTY ALLEVIATION THROUGH SOCIAL ORGANIZATIONS

Nearly 100 million yuan ($15.9 million) were invested in the designated regions by the Ministry of Railways, China Soong Ching Ling Foundation, and other central government organizations (enterprises). More than 500 million yuan ($79.4 million) were invested by Fujian province along with her partner counties. More than 300 million yuan

($47.6 million) was invested by other organizations from Ningxia. All these efforts have bolstered the local economy and social development and created a good social atmosphere.

92.1.4 THE CENTRAL GOVERNMENT HAVE INCREASED POVERTY ALLEVIATION FUNDS

With the implementation of the strategy for the development of the western part of China and 'several suggestions on further promoting economic and social development in Ningxia' issued by the State Council, the poverty alleviation funds distributed by State Council Leading Group Office of Poverty Alleviation were increased from 300 million yuan ($47.6 million) per year at the beginning of this century to 799 million yuan ($126.8 million) in 2011. The poverty alleviation fund per capita was at the forefront of the whole country.

92.2 **Future plans**

In Ningxia, implementing the 'Rural Poverty Alleviation and Development Program of China (2011–2020)' and following instructions from the conference for poverty alleviation and development organized by central government, the poverty alleviation and development drive is guided by a scientific outlook on development, and has as its primary tasks solving the key issues for poor people: eating, clothing, and heating in the winter season and access to compulsory education, basic healthcare, housing, and safe drinking water. A campaign for the poverty alleviation of a million poor people will be launched in the Liupanshan region in Ningxia.

The Liupanshan (south of Ningxia) area is divided into three regions and special strategies for poverty alleviation will be designed for each of these regions. For the key development regions, including Yuanzhou District and nine counties, central towns, and ecological relocation zones, the strategies are to promote the concentration of industries and populations and to increase the integrated supporting capability through the development of the industrial and service sectors and urbanization. For the agricultural ecological regions, which include areas irrigated by pumping water from the Yellow River, areas irrigated by wells and reservoirs, and dry farming areas, the strategy is to eliminate poverty in-situ by supporting the special industries, modern agriculture, and the labour transfer service. For the ecological protection regions, such as Liupanshan Nature Reserve, the strategy is to eliminate poverty by developing the relevant industries (including eco-tourism) or settling populations ex-situ in order to protect the environment.

A large effort will be concentrated in two hard campaigns: ecological relocation and lifting one million people out of poverty. During the 12th Five-Year Plan, 350,000 poor people who are living in the regions where basic survival is extremely difficult and the conditions for development are poor will be settled ex-situ as ecological migrants, to help them get out of poverty and become rich in the next five years. For others who are living in the regions where survival is possible and the conditions for development are more favourable, strategies for whole village promotion and development in the contiguous areas will be introduced. Up to 2020, the objectives are to ensure that the basic needs of eating, clothing, and heating in the winter season, and for compulsory education, basic healthcare, housing, and safe drinking water are met. Six poverty alleviation projects including development of industry, labour force transfer and training, poverty alleviation by social organizations, mutual help funds, and poverty alleviation through family planning, will be organized and carefully implemented.

For the new round of poverty alleviation, we will highlight the key issues, promote development systematically, fully utilize the important role of the Yellow River Economic Area in leading development of other poor areas in the middle and south of Ningxia, improve the working, living, and ecological conditions in poor areas, and make Ningxia a well-off society in the same way as other regions of China.

93 Shandong

Scientific development and new prospects

Chuanting Zhang

Shandong is a place of junctions. It is a province with an important location on the eastern shore, located by the lower stretches of the Yellow River, the East Bohai Sea, the Yellow Sea, the Korean Peninsula, and the Japanese archipelago. It is at the intersection between north and east China, and between the Yellow River Economic Belt and the Bohai Rim Economic Zone—a pivotal position in the national economy. Shandong encompasses 157.1 thousand square kilometres of total land area, 3345 km of coastline, 95.79 million people, and it has jurisdiction over 17 cities in 140 counties. It is also a place with a rich heritage and history. Shandong's Provincial Party Committee Secretary Jiang Daming summarized Shandong's cultural legacy in a four line poem:

The place where the Tai Mountains surge forth, where the Yellow River returns to sea, where Confucius was born, and where the world sailed during the Beijing Olympics.

In recent years, under the leadership of the Communist Party of China's Central Committee and State Council, the Shandong Provincial Party Committee has embraced scientific development, uniting the people under a pragmatic and scientific approach. This was done in accordance with Deng Xiaoping's Theory of the 'Three Represents', and fulfilled the main requirements of China's 11th Five-Year Plan. In 2011, Shandong achieved a GDP of 4.5429 trillion yuan, and an annual average growth rate of 10.9 per cent. Other telling statistics include total fixed investments of 2.59284 trillion yuan (an annual growth rate of 17.3 per cent), total consumer good sales of 1.66759 trillion yuan (a 17.3 per cent annual growth rate), and a fiscal revenue of 345.57 billion yuan (25.7 per cent annual growth rate). Urban residents had an average disposable income of 22,792 yuan, a growth rate of 14.3 per cent, and rural residents had an average net income of 8,342 yuan, a growth rate of 12.1 per cent.

93.1 Accelerate economic growth and restructure industrial infrastructure

The first objective is to create new advantages and opportunities for rural areas. In order to increase farmers' income and productivity, we should optimize logistical institutions, improve quality standards, and strengthen supporting political institutions. It is also necessary to accelerate growth towards a high-yield, high-quality, high-efficiency, ecologically safe agricultural system. Lastly, we need to improve overall grain production capacity, improve production efficiency, increase the scale and quality of the production of agricultural equipment, raise quality standards, encourage industrialization, and protect water quality.

The second objective is to encourage industrial growth using a method of 'two-pronged encouragement'. On one hand, existing infrastructure should be transformed and upgraded, and industry should continue striving to improve. On the other hand, we should embrace new innovations in energy, material science, information technology, medicine, and marine technology. Strategic, emerging industries should be nurtured and developed to have the momentum to compete with existing industries.

The third objective is to promote development in service industries across the board, using innovations in service to catalyse change in other industries. The ten essential industries that must be managed towards growth are finance and insurance, logistics and management, wholesale and retail food products, information technology, business services, home services, real estate, tourism, community service, and rural services. Priority should be placed on the 50 major urban areas, 100 industrial parks, 100 key enterprises, and 100 large projects that constitute the 'Big Four' vectors of development.

93.2 Open up markets to increase domestic demand as a means to increase Shandong's developmental momentum

Shandong must firmly grasp the strategic importance of increasing domestic demand. While maintaining external demand, we must consider every possible method of increasing domestic demand, paying special attention to the roles of consumer demand on economic growth. This is to ensure a steady and rapid pace of economic development.

The first goal is to optimize the domestic investment structure. The government must express leadership when it comes to investment, focusing priority on the fields of modern agriculture, technological innovation, energy (conventional and alternative), transportation, environmental protection, the modern service industry, and other fields associated with improving the livelihood of the people. Moreover, the government should stead-fastly implement policies and measures that encourage private investment, while limiting investment in the Big Two industries, construction and production, to prevent redundant and low-quality construction projects and the over-production of goods caused by the over-expansion of industry.

The second goal is to increase consumer demand. This is achieved by increasing income, establishing mechanisms that encourage long-term and steady growth in con-sumption, and enhancing the consumption capacity of the people. At the same time, the government should formulate policies that encourage consumption, that strongly culti-vate the creation of consumption hotspots, and that upgrade and optimize the consump-tion infrastructure.

The third goal is to actively open up and expand the market. By speeding up the dis-tribution networks and innovating new methods of distribution, new markets can be encouraged to develop. Also, enterprises should be encouraged to invest in factories and turnkey engineering projects in western Shandong, to advantageously drive production capacity towards the west.

93.3 Strongly implement an area-centric strategy focused on bringing economic development to new areas

The 'Peninsula Blue Economic Zone' and 'Yellow River Delta High-Efficiency and Eco-logical Economic Zone' have been designated by the national government as strategic hotspots, and are also important components of Shenzhen's economic engine. Both Shan-dong's Provincial Party Committee and government attach great importance to initiatives that can support the two zones' development. In the Peninsula Blue Economic Zone, we are striving to establish the marine economic demonstration zones with advanced inter-national standards, and to establish them as a major economic growth pivot for the entire region. Likewise, the Yellow River Delta High-Efficiency and Ecological Economic Zone is striving to become the model for high-efficiency and ecological economic zones in all of China, a crucial industrial base, an important supply of reserve land resources, as well as an important growth area along the Bohai Gulf.

Moreover, Qingdao's leadership can be used to raise construction standards on the Jiao-dong Peninsula to match higher-end industrial areas. By accelerating economic develop-ment in the provincial capital area, the surrounding area will grow as a whole. National approval should be acquired to allow the old Yimeng revolutionary base area to enjoy the policies and opportunities of the central region, allowing the area to prosper and develop. At the same time, Shandong should promote modern urbanization, focus more on improving the layout and form of urbanization, develop intercity agglomerations, use scientific design principles for both cities and towns, and encourage symbiotic urban–rural relationships by coordinating the development of infrastructural systems.

93.4 Strengthen environmental and ecological practices and encourage sustainable development

The provincial government has always attached great importance to environmental conservation and ecologically minded construction practices, and innovation in ways of resource usage, developing a circular and ecologically efficient economy, and following the path of development, prosperity, and ecological development. To build an ecological province, we should implement the 'Beautiful Neighborhoods' programme, increase environmental remediation efforts across urban and rural areas, and strongly promote the six initiatives for constructing aquatic ecosystems. Moreover, we should strengthen institutional accountability, refine supporting policies, firmly eliminate the outdated production capacity of the 'Big Two' industries, and use regulation to control expansion. We should strengthen efforts in conservation and efficient resource use, while continuing to conserve land, water, and raw materials. We should quickly adopt environmentally conservative life styles and consumption patterns. With raising the efficiency of resource production in mind, we should promote circular economy demonstration projects, as well as encourage habits of re-using and recycling resources, scale resource usage, and using high value added resources.

93.5 Implementing science education and fostering talent to increase provincial innovation

There are three main components of this objective:

1. Encourage scientific and technological innovation. Continue encouraging independent innovation, focusing on fostering important breakthroughs, encouraging development, and being at the forefront of the future. At the same time, increase investments in technology while focusing on specific game changing and mission critical technologies. Create a platform for scientific and technological innovation, at both the national and provincial level, and vigorously encourage scientific and technological achievements in industry.

2. The high priority of education development must be maintained. In order to foster development, nourish human capital, reform and innovate, promote equality, and enhance overall quality, we must necessarily deepen educational reform, promote educational equality,

develop effective pre-school education, comprehensively improve the quality and standards of compulsory education, accelerating the speed at which students fulfil the core curriculum in high school. Simultaneously we must develop strong vocational education programmes while comprehensively improving the quality of higher education, and encouraging the application of scientific innovation to the field of education.

3. We must foster and harness our province's talent. Continue adhering to the guiding principles of developing the service industry, placing a high priority on human talent, putting the customer first, innovating with institutions, developing effective leadership, and encouraging overall development. This will allow an overall improvement in the quality of human capital and teamwork in the government, in business leadership, in professional and technical trades, in highly skilled personnel, in rural management, and in social work personnel, allowing Shandong to become a hotbed for talent and high-quality workers.

93.6 Improve social institutions and support structures to ensure streamlined socioeconomic development

Guaranteeing and improving the livelihood of the citizenry is an important result of scientific development, as well as being a crucial method of accelerating economic development and spurring change and the optimization of economic institutions. This requires work in five areas.

1. Expand the employment market. Implement more active employment policies, develop labour-intensive and service industries, foster small enterprises, develop employment opportunities through multiple channels, encourage entrepreneurs to make start-ups, and encourage full-time employment.

2. Improve the social security system for both rural and urban residents. Implement a new, full-coverage rural pension insurance system, and improve the existing pension insurance system for urban workers and residents.

3. Reform the medical and health services industry. Deepen the coverage of the healthcare system, improve medical insurance institutions, extend medical insurance coverage to all urban and rural citizens, and, using the national pharmaceutical supply infrastructure as a model, improve our own drug supply system.

4. Promote cultural development and prosperity. Making full of use Shandong's rich cultural resources, accelerate development of a 'High-Culture Shandong', improve the public cultural service system, strengthen the development of cultural industries, encourage cultural innovation, and promote the coordinated development of cultural undertakings and industries.

5. Strengthen and innovate social administration. Using the development of 'Peaceful Shandong' as the pivot, improve social administration institutions, promote fairness and justice, and protect social harmony and stability.

94 Shenzhen

From labour-intensive to innovation-driven economic growth

Jie Tang

That China's economic rise over the last three decades has lasted for so long and grown so quickly is nothing short of miraculous. Now most economists believe that China had been near a turning point, transitioning from the old labour-intensive pattern to a new innovation-driven pattern. China's transforming economy is an increasingly important topic both within the field of economics and in the global economy. Shenzhen, the first Special Economic Zone in China, is a telling example. Shenzhen was a very small town near the border between Hong Kong and mainland China with a population of only 30,000 people. Now it is a booming city with nearly 14 million people. Shenzhen has transitioned from a traditional agricultural economy to an industrial economy, from processing and assembling to creating, and from being labour-intensive to knowledge-intensive. The path of innovation started with imitation and gradually developed into autonomous innovation.

94.1 Characters of economic development in Shenzhen

A rather contradictory phenomenon is that despite China's obvious interests in economic globalization, there still exist arguments that China is exploited by foreign capital and thus can only make 'blood money'. Shenzhen is an example of a good outcome from the comparative advantage trap in globalization.

The first defining characteristic of Shenzhen is that it maintained both a sustainable yet high speed of economic growth and allowed a healthy private sector to become the core of its economy. Shenzhen has transformed from a small border town to a high-tech city in thirty years, ascending to the 30th place among cities worldwide in terms of GDP; Shenzhen's GDP was only 0.3 per cent of that in Hong Kong, now it is nearing 70 per cent, and it is projected to surpass Hong Kong in ten years. Shenzhen undoubtedly benefited from the reform and opening up policy in China in the early 1980s, but the proportion of foreign direct investment (FDI) in its economy is far lower than in other outward-looking cities of China. State-owned enterprises (SOE) also occupy a very limited share, equalling only one-third of Shanghai's and one-seventh of Beijing's economy.

The second characteristic is that Shenzhen continuously carried out extraordinary structural upgrades. OEM (original equipment manufacturer) was rapidly replaced by ODM (original design manufacturer). Traditional manufacturing, including machinery, watches, furniture, gold jewellery, textiles, printing, and toys, have transitioned from being low-end production to high-end designing and brand management. High-tech industries have replaced traditional manufacturing industries to become leading industries, from a start point of 0 per cent to accounting for over 33 per cent of the city's GDP. Companies in Shenzhen can produce almost any supporting components needed in the IT field. Its output of laptops, mobile phones, and PBX ranks number one, and Shenzhen is at the forefront of biological and super-material research.

The third characteristic is that Shenzhen allowed autonomous innovation. The total number of patent applications was near zero in 1990, exploding to 40,000 by 2010. The PCT (Patent Cooperation Treaty) applications of Shenzhen account for almost half of all of China's applications. In 2009, research and development accounted for 3.6 per cent of its GDP, with over 300,000 specialized technical staff engaging in high-tech R&D, including more and more Chinese returned from overseas. Huawei technology and ZTE communication, two of the famous private enterprises in the world and major contributors in the field of R&D, are located in Shenzhen.

The fourth characteristic is it allowed cost-effective and small private IT companies to begin with low-end imitations, giving them the opportunity to ease into autonomous innovation. Autonomous innovation happened not only in the high-tech industry, but also in more traditional fields, such as clothing. For example, since the clothing industry embraced clasp-nailing and sleeve-seaming technologies, nearly half of the world's production of clothing for women has been produced in China. But after digital jet printing and colorimetric technology were applied, 5,000 fashion designers have clustered in Shenzhen to engage in brand development and management. Now the average price of fashion clothing is ten times that of ten years ago.

94. 2 **An endogenous specialized labour growth model explaining the story of Shenzhen**

We can begin to explain the Shenzhen case with the theory of comparative advantage, which predicts that countries maximize their benefits by concentrating on their areas of comparative advantage under free trade; but the obvious weakness is that this relies on a static perspective. We can use the framework of Krugman and Fujita's new spatial economics, leaving more room for external economies and the effects of agglomeration, which allows for developing countries to gain benefits by participation in globalization. However, it still hints that developing countries will always follow the path of developed countries, like the 'flying-geese' model based on the experience of Japan's economy surging then diffusing into 'four little dragons' (South Korea, Singapore, Taiwan, and Hong Kong) and Mainland China.

Adam Smith (1776) put forward the idea that the division of labour is limited by the extent of the market. This means that the division of labour causes productivity improvement, accompanied with income growth and market extension, then an extended market accelerates a further division of labours, so that the division of labour is not only the cause but also the consequence of economic growth. Following this theorem, we explore a specialized labour model in which the specialized labour created by division, without any undifferentiated human capital, and the increase of types of specialized labour indicates the deepening of division of labour. The source of economic backwardness in poor regions lies in the lack of specialized labour. The greater the quantity and/or types of specialized labour that a region has, the faster knowledge is created and accumulated, and the more the pattern of development speeds up. Once opened up, developing regions are generally able to attract FDI owing to low labour costs. FDI brings advanced technologies and management skill. This new knowledge is absorbed to generate diversified specialized labours so that specialized labour teams can be formed. The new specialized labours thus are able to catalyse imitative and original innovation, expanding the division of labour even further.

We assume that any product only needs two factors, that is, general labour and specialized labour, and the costs are wages and licence fees, respectively, as charged by R&D firms. Three variables exist in the model: general labour, proprietary technology, and output. The production function is generalized by a Cobb–Douglas function. The model has an endogenous growth feature, meaning that specialized labour should correspond to proprietary technology, thus specialized labours are heterogeneous and the quantity of types of specialized labour is dynamic within a symmetrical condition. A newcomer with the advantage of requiring lower wages can take advantage of R&D competition. By combining Ramsey–Cass–Koopmans' function with the dynamic innovative function, economic growth can be seen as a function of the division of labour.[1] The growth rate will be a function of the rate of division of labour, and the equilibrium path is no longer related with higher savings ratios.

While specialized skills are learned through advanced education, most educational experience comes from learning by doing and R&D. Reducing the cost of social R&D and

---

[1] The Ramsey–Cass–Koopmans function is a neoclassical model of economic growth based primarily on Ramsey (1928) with significant extensions by Cass (1965) and Koopmans (1965).

innovation by adopting efficient polices to increase the quantity of specialized labour is an essential strategic choice for developing countries to promote innovation and accelerate growth. This way, developing countries will surpass the traps of development, and potentially catch up with developed countries.

This model emphasizes that developing countries are able to catch up and even surpass developed countries through 'learning by doing' and starting off by focusing on imitative innovation. Practically speaking, the deepening of the division of labour is very complicated. No country is able to undertake isolated R&D in the era of globalization in which modular division becomes mainstream. Outsourcing may cause an unfair vertical division of labour across countries; it also accelerates a horizontal deepening of the division and only gradually brings R&D opportunities for developing countries.[2] Modular division narrows enterprise boundaries and enlarges industrial boundaries, replacing an internal division of labour with a social division of labour. Accompanied by market segmentation and technological penetration, the final goods can be restructured in the form of modularization. Innovation can trigger a wave of related innovations both within an industry and across other industries. We can define these phenomena with a new concept of boundary-less industry for the expansion of technology that involves mutual penetration and unrestricted entry for new competitors. Even traditional industries with clear boundaries could be permeated by innovations in design.

94.3 **Specialized labour growth in Shenzhen**

In the next three paragraphs we would like to analyse the evolutionary process of the deepening divisions of labour and the improvement of specialized labours.

Phase one is specialization of process; it is exactly what Adam Smith (1776) described with his pin-making story and represents a kind of evolution of the division of labour. During this process manufacturing flow disintegrates into incremental steps. The major target is to ensure that production can be processed with high quality, high efficiency, and the lowest possible cost. Because of large-scale input OEM during a nascent stage of economic development, Shenzhen quickly mastered the skills and technologies to disintegrate the manufacturing process, the techniques to control this process, and the effective use of cheap specialized labour so that the capability of socialized production and competitiveness were built up in very short period of time. Despite its important role in fostering rapid economic growth in Shenzhen during the early period, this kind of division of labour could not be deepened further.

---

[2] Modular division is abstracted and concluded by Masahiko Aoki (2010), and this could not only be applied to product design and the management of the supply chain, but also to the study of the evolution of labour division.

Phase 2 is specialization of product innovation. Product innovation from specialized labour will occur once R&D becomes a reliable investment, because there must be open and common technological standards across industries so that differently modulated products can be compatible. There are a small number of rivals for a monopoly modulus product provider in the world, so innovation firms could keep their sole ownership of their internal innovation and avoid special knowledge disclosure. A new economic framework mainly made of civilian high-tech firms is then rapidly founded. Spatial competition then changes to take advantage of scale economy in each sector of the industry chain rather than comparative advantages. In Shenzhen, the explosive interaction between the deepening of the division of labour and scale economy created the 'Shenzhen miracle'. Although there were still obvious imitations when it came to product innovation, Shenzhen showed unparalleled creativity in process specialization. With rising labour productivity and state-of-the-art production technology, Shenzhen has quickly climbed up the industrial value chain. The specialized competencies of the enterprises allowed them to upgrade from OEM to ODM, while patent application and brand registration have boomed since 1990.

Phase 3 is innovation specialization. Shenzhen was initially able to break into the IT industry because of its competitive labour costs, and it then expanded its ground with massive production and a focus on research. Innovation in each IT industry is mutually encouraged. Innovative firms and areas often surpassed the leaders of old through original innovation. The openness of the system also allowed for a rapid diffusion of technology. Huawei Technologies Co., Ltd, ZTE Corporation, Tencent, and BYD all rose rapidly because they seized the opportunity of open innovation and modular division of labour to place themselves at the cutting edge of innovation. Today, Shenzhen does not only feature industrial giants like Huawei and ZTE, but also a promising mass of innovative small firms. With the expansion of the market, these creative small businesses will spawn a batch of large businesses with excellent core technique, brand management, and industrial organization. Meanwhile, even more of these creative small businesses will be competing and cooperating simultaneously, creating several interconnected clusters within high-growth industries.

Shenzhen's experience suggests that protecting property rights, fostering competitive innovation, and encouraging patent application, are fundamental aspects of a growth-fostering industrial policy.

As Shenzhen's story is retold in other mainland cities, the deepening divisions of labour will bring sustainable benefits for China to surpass the comparative advantage trap and create good case studies for economists.

■ REFERENCES

Aoki, Masahiko. 2010. *Corporations in Evolving Diversity: Cognition, Governance, and Institutions*. Oxford: Oxford University Press.

Cass, David. 1965. Optimum growth in an aggregative model of capital accumulation. *Review of Economic Studies* 32 (3), 233–40.

Koopmans, Tjalling C. 1965. On the concept of optimal economic growth. In *The Economic Approach to Development Planning*, 225–287. Chicago: Rand McNally.

Ramsey, Frank P. 1928. A mathematical theory of saving. *Economic Journal* 38(152), 543–59.

Smith, Adam. 1776. *An Inquiry into the Nature and Causes of the Wealth of Nations*. Chicago: University of Chicago Press. Reprinted in 1977.

95 Sichuan

A west-China province undergoing rapid development and change

Changwen Zhao

Sichuan Province is located in southwest China, by the upper reaches of the Yangtze River. It covers an area of 485,000 square kilometres, accounting for 5.1 per cent of the area of mainland China, placing it fifth in terms of total area after Xinjiang, Tibet, Inner Mongolia, and Qinghai. According to the population census in 2010, the total number of residents had reached 80.4 million, placing it fourth after Guangdong, Shandong, and Henan Provinces. The capital city—Chengdu—has been acclaimed by residents as the friendliest city in China. Sichuan remains the most important province in western China for its resources, developments in science and technology, economy, and culture.

Four aspects of Sichuan's social and economic development of the past decade deserve special attention.

1. Under the 'Grand Strategy of West China Development', Sichuan Province has achieved overall improvement in terms of its social and economic development.

2. Although the 2008 earthquake did drastic damage to Sichuan, the reconstruction also brought a rare opportunity for adjusting industrial structures and the public service system.

3. As a designated 'National Experiment Area for Balancing Urban and Rural Development and Integrated Support Reform', the capital city of Chengdu acquired experience and practice in balancing the interaction between the city and the country, providing an excellent model for urbanization in China.

4. 'The west isn't wild': An open and cooperative Sichuan is developing.

These four aspects will now be considered in turn.

95.1 Sichuan Province and the 'Grand Strategy of West China Development'

The 'Grand Strategy of West China Development' has improved Sichuan's social and economic development across the board. This can be seen from four major perspectives. First, the general economic power of Sichuan has strengthened as it enters the middle stage of industrialization. Its GDP has nearly quadrupled in the past decade, reaching RMB2102.7 billion in 2011 with per capita GDP over US$4,000. Second, the incomes and living standards of rural and urban residents have dramatically increased. In 2011, the average disposable personal income of urban residents was RMB17,899, and the net income of farmers was RMB6128.6 per capita. The third factor is increased urbanization. Although Sichuan's overall urbanization is below the national average, it increased by 6 per cent during the past decade. The proportion of the population living in urban areas was 41.83 per cent in 2011. Finally, Sichuan has been playing an increasingly important role in leading west China towards social and economic development. In 2011, Sichuan's GDP was the 8th highest in China, accounting for 21.16 per cent among the twelve provinces in west China—including Inner Mongolia and Guangxi. Among the world's top 500 firms, 164 foreign enterprises have investments in Sichuan, ranking it first in central and west China in terms of foreign investment.

95.2 The aftermath of the 2008 earthquake

On Monday, 12 May 2008, an earthquake that registered 8.0 on the Richter scale struck Sichuan, with its epicentre in Wenchuan County. This earthquake, the most devastating natural disaster in the area since 1949, resulted in 69,227 casualties with 374,643 people injured and 17,923 missing. Residential, transportation, and industrial infrastructure was thoroughly damaged. The direct loss was reported to have exceeded RMB1 trillion.

After the event, the Sichuan government adopted the following guiding principles towards reconstruction: develop industry, support job creation, assist the poor, protect the environment, and facilitate social development. In the following three years, 33,000 projects were completed. The total capital injected for recovery and reconstruction was RMB1.7 trillion for the 142 impacted counties. Due to the fact that most of the impacted areas were in rural mountain regions, the government-initiated reconstruction has greatly promoted local economic development.

In the three years of reconstruction, people in affected areas moved into new neighbourhoods; the infrastructure in the towns and countryside were generally rebuilt; public service facilities were fundamentally improved; industrial structures were optimized and upgraded; and resource-based industries and advantaged industries as well as strategic emerging industries became the foundation for sustainable development in the region. In general, the infrastructure, basic living conditions, and social development have all increased well beyond pre-earthquake levels. Average personal income has nearly doubled since 2007.

95.3 Chengdu—a designated 'National Experiment Area for Balancing Urban and Rural Development and Integrated Support Reform'

A prominent feature of the Chinese economy is the separation between city and country. Economic and social development in the countryside has lagged far behind the city. Thus issues related to agriculture and farming are the core obstacles in the general modernization of China.

Sichuan is a large agricultural province with a significant amount of land dedicated to agriculture and a big agrarian population. Chengdu, its capital city, was approved by the State Department as a 'National Experiment Area for Balancing Urban and Rural Development and Integrated Support Reform'. It has undertaken eight years of 'Trial and Error' pilot programmes, and has achieved a series of significant breakthroughs in terms of land use policy, urban and rural planning, industrial layout, infrastructure construction, and integration of public services. Therefore, public resources and facilities have been well allocated between the city and the country, and elements of production can also move freely between the two. Thus through progress in urban and rural balancing, and by embracing an innovative attitude towards development, Chengdu has achieved parallel development and mutual prosperity between the city and the country.

Chengdu's experience is valuable to the central government as a successful example of promoting integrated development of the city and the country. In 2011, the net per capita income growth rate of farmers in Sichuan was 4.7 per cent higher than the average disposable personal income of urban residents, and the ratio of urban and country income decreased to 2.92:1.

95.4 'The west isn't wild': an open and cooperative Sichuan

As an inland province, Sichuan was an early adopter of an open and cooperative strategy for economic development. In terms of opening up to the domestic market, Sichuan has focused on welcoming industry, becoming an important destination for coastal enterprises.

Sichuan has several natural advantages, namely a rich supply of natural resources, low costs, a sturdy industry for auxiliary parts, strong market potential, and a capacity for research. Based on these advantages, Sichuan has selected some key industries for development, such as electronic information, biotechnology, aerospace, modern Chinese medicine, advanced manufacturing such as industrial equipment and automobiles, the oil and gas chemical industries, agricultural product processing, modern service sector industries such as logistics, trade, and exchange, and labour-intensive industries such as textiles, garments, and leather.

In 2011, Sichuan attracted total investment of more than RMB700 billion from other provinces. Thus a large number of new energy, new material, and green industries have set up in Sichuan, optimizing the industrial structure for sustainability, laying a solid foundation for long-term development.

In terms of economic exchange with foreign countries, Sichuan attracted US$11 billion worth of foreign direct investment (FDI) in 2011, the highest of any western province. Currently, of companies in the world's top 500, including Chinese companies, 212 have established headquarters, agencies, or branch offices in Sichuan. Chengdu, the capital city, has been acclaimed by the World Bank, *Fortune*, and *Forbes* as a benchmark city for the investment environment in China, the best global emerging business city, and the leading city for future development in the next ten years.

The total volume of imports and exports was US$ 47.7 billion in 2011, with exports at US$29 billion, and imports at US$18.7 billion. During recent years, industrial products have been rising in international trade, accounting for more than 90 per cent of both exports and imports. Of total imports and exports in 2011, the European market accounted for 21.0 per cent, North America 14.6 per cent, and Asia 55.7 per cent.

96 Tianjin
The third growth pole of China

Chen Zongsheng

96.1 Tianjin, the third largest city in China

The name Tianjin means Emperor's Port. When Tianjin became a city in 1404, it was already serving as a key hub linking economic activities between the north and south of China. Upon the founding of the People's Republic of China in 1949, Tianjin became a municipality directly under the control of the central government.

In terms of population, in 2011 Tianjin had more than 13 million people, and was the third largest city in China, just smaller than Shanghai and Beijing. Tianjin is a modern industrial and commercial city and in recent years accelerated the development of its economy by 15 per cent annually. In 2011 per capita GDP reached US$14,000.

Tianjin is situated in the east of the North China Plain, geographically covering an area of 11,900 square kilometres. Tianjin is located so close to Beijing (the Chinese capital) that you can make the trip between the two cities in just 28 minutes by express-train or one hour by car.

96.2 Tianjin is a window on modern China

A 600-year-old city does not qualify as ancient in China. But for Tianjin, its six centuries of history have marked it as the gateway through which the modern Western world first entered the country. This port city was among the first Chinese locations where Western society became accepted, endowing it with a unique place in the country's history.

Because Tianjin is one of the earliest coastal cities in north China to open up to the outside world in modern times, many late-arriving technologies to China were first introduced to the country through Tianjin, such as trains, telegrams, postal services, telephones, trolley cars, and so on.

The same holds true for education. 'Peiyang Martial School', the first military academy that trained modern army recruits, was founded in Tianjin in 1885. The earliest university of China 'Peiyang University of Western Studies' opened in Tianjin in 1895. In 1919, the country's most successful private university, Nankai University, opened its doors.

As a metropolis, Tianjin has its own uniqueness derived from China's modern history. During the past 100 years, the city has witnessed the introduction of modern education, technology, architecture, and financial systems, even political, military, cultures, and so on, which are all worth looking at.

So it is not easy to summarize Tianjin's historical resources in one single sentence, since the city is truly multifaceted. But people always say if Xi'an is well known for its 5,000-year historical heritage and Beijing is famous for its glorious 1,000 years, then Tianjin may boast 100 years of China's cultural, social, and economic elements. Tianjin can show you many modern Chinese historical points and tell you many historical stories.

95.3 Tianjin grows as the economic hub of north China

Ever since the Binhai New Area was embodied into the national development strategy, the expected image of Tianjin as the future economic centre of north China has gradually taken shape.

The State Council endorsed the 'Overall Planning of Tianjin Municipality (2005–20)' on 27 July 2006, giving clear definition to Tianjin's future position as an international port city, north China's economic centre, and an eco-friendly city suitable for human habitation in the next ten years. Tianjin should be the centre of the Bohai Bay rim region, and the city should give priority to the development of its Binhai New Area.

After years of construction and development, Tianjin has grown into one of the most potentially robust economies nationwide. Tianjin's per capita GDP reached $14,000 in 2011.

More than 20,000 foreign enterprises have invested in Tianjin. Among the world's top 500 enterprises, 168 have set up branches in Tianjin.

With electronics, automotives, petrochemicals, metallurgy, biotechnology, pharmaceuticals, new energy, and environmental protection as its pillar industries, Tianjin has become the most important modern manufacturing hub of north China.

Tianjin enjoys the advantages of a good geographical location, developed industrial layout, strong research and development capabilities, and a modern logistics base and air cargo transport hub in north China.

Together with Beijing, Tianjin is to lead the high-profile campaign to develop an economic circle encompassing Beijing, Tianjin, and Hebei province and the entire Bohai Bay rim region, which are growing to become the third economic growth pole of China after Shenzhen and Pudong.

From the perspective of regional economic development, Shanghai and Shenzhen are the engine cities, driving up the development of the Yangtze River Delta and Pearl River Delta regions. North China also needs an economically robust city, which can play a role similar to the one played by Shanghai and Shenzhen within their economic circles.

The long-term development goal of China is to quadruple its gross domestic product (GDP) of 2000 by 2020. This target requires high-speed growth of the nation's economy during the next decade. To fully drive up China's economy, it is absolutely necessary to have a new growth engine, which is more powerful and influential. Positioning Tianjin as the future economic centre of north China is a key strategy to balance the economic gap between China's north and south and enhance regional economic coordination.

It is expected that the Bohai Bay rim region, led by Tianjin, will soon become one of the top three national economic engines, alongside the Yangtze River Delta and Pearl River Delta regions.

96.4 **The Binhai New Area is a shining star**

Since the development of the Binhai New Area was included in the national development strategy in recent years, Tianjin has undoubtedly become a shining star in China's regional economic development.

The Binhai New Area covers a planned area of 2,270 sq km and after several years of development and construction, the area's major economic indexes have been growing at annual rate of more than 20 per cent.

In 2011, the local gross domestic product (GDP) of the Binhai New Area totalled 6206.9 billion yuan, with accumulative overseas investment in place amounting to $223.1 billion.

Key projects have been proceeding well. The zone of the Sino-Singaporean Eco-city and Dongjiang Bonded Port Area, several one-million-ton ethylene cracker projects and the Airbus A320 assembly line are also in full swing. The Binhai New Area is expected to become an international shipping centre for north China and an international logistics hub.

The Binhai New Area is also expected to become a technological innovation hub. It will include the International Bio-Pharmaceutical Innovation Park and Civil Aviation Science & Technology Industrialization Base, thirty-three national engineering centres, and more than 120 R&D centres.

A high-tech industry cluster has initially taken shape, involving electronic information, bio-pharmaceuticals, and new materials. This cluster boasts a strong capacity to conduct R&D projects in the areas of biochips, membrane technology, electrical vehicles, stem cells, nanometer technology, and so on.

96.5 **Tianjin Harbour ranks as the world's fourth largest in annual throughput**

Located at the entrance to the Bohai Bay from the Haihe River, Tianjin Port is one of the world's best artificial deep-water harbours with the most advanced facilities and the most complete functions in China.

In 2011, the port had an annual throughput of more than 453 million tons, ranking it fourth among major ports of the world. Its annual container throughput reached 9.1 million twenty-foot equivalent units (TEUs) last year, making the port one of the world's top twenty container ports.

Tianjin Port is situated at the intersection of the Jingjin (Beijing and Tianjin) city zone and the Bohai Bay economic rim, and can handle 250,000-ton ships easily and 300,000-ton ships at tides.

Among all ports around the Bohai Bay, it is the nearest one to the inland areas including northern and northwestern China. This international port plays an instrumental role in facilitating foreign trade for northern China. It is also the link connecting northeast Asia and central-west Asia, and is the eastern starting point of the Euro-Asia Continental Bridge.

The port has extensive contacts with the world, establishing sister-port relationships with twelve ports including those in Japan, South Korea, the USA, and the Netherlands, and trading with more than 500 ports in more than 180 countries and regions.

Tianjin Port is one of the most functional coastal ports in China, in possession of container, iron ore, charcoal, petrochemicals, general cargo, roll-on roll-off, general grain, general chemical fertilizer, international passenger, and a variety of other specialized terminals.

It will become a modernized international deep-water port with advanced facilities, comprehensive functions, scientific management, high efficiency, and a harmonious, ecological and livable environment, and the biggest comprehensive port in the area around the Bohai Bay.

96.6 **Tianjin creates a modern financial service system**

In 2006, the State Council approved a proposal for Tianjin Binhai New Area to lead national comprehensive reform and experimental development and encouraged it to carry out financing reform and innovation. Therefore, Tianjin Binhai New Area, and the whole Tianjin will grow faster than before, and will become a financial services base.

The State Council clearly points out that financial reform and innovation in Tianjin Binhai New Area is encouraged. All major reforms such as financial enterprises, financial business, financial markets, and financial products can first be launched and tested in Tianjin.

According to the Plan, some financial markets will be based in Tianjin Binhai New Area, such as Tianjin Equity Exchange, Tianjin Ore Ownership Exchange, Bohai Commercial Goods Exchange, Tianjin Climate Exchange, and so on, which are significant capital markets.

In addition to all these efforts, Tianjin still has lots of projects to be completed to achieve the overall aim of financial reform and innovation, such as the pilot reform of foreign exchange management, establishing an International Financial Holding Group, developing a comprehensive financial service base in Tianjin. This series of measures shows that a modern financial service system is being built in Tianjin.

Thus the Binhai New Area can play a vital role in promoting the development of Tianjin, the Bohai Bay rim region, and northern China, and provide experience and a demonstration project for the development and reform of the whole nation.

96.7 **Tianjin becomes a private equity fund and financial leasing centre**

From establishing the first private equity fund, Bohai Industry Fund, to getting the approval for a shipping industrial fund—the 20 billion yuan shipping industrial fund—Tianjin has become the pilot city winning most fund approvals from the State.

In June 2011, the fifth China International Private Equity Forum was held in Tianjin when nearly 5,000 excellent enterprises from China and more than 1,500 private equity funds from all over the world took part. The first meeting was in June 2007 and this forum is now an annual event in Tianjin.

Tianjin has been pinpointed to develop a private equity fund centre in China. The city is taking action and perfecting policies and measures to attract fund enterprises. So far, there are more than 2,408 private equity and 250 venture capital funds in Tianjin. The city is advancing to become China's fund centre with financial innovation advantages entrusted by the Chinese government.

In addition, the development of a leasing industry in Tianjin is among the best and most rapid in China. In 2011 the balance of financial leasing contracts was approximately 230 billion yuan, accounting for a quarter of the total business in China; a plan was made to make the Dongjing Free Trade Port Zone of Tianjin the largest centre of financing leasing in China in about three years.

Tianjin is becoming the third growth pole of China. So, welcome to Tianjin, come to visit us, to join us, to share the dream with us.

97 Western regions
Ideas of cultural industry development

Qingsheng Xie

97.1 An overview of China's cultural industry development

With China's rapid economic growth and increasing economic integration, it has become increasingly important to maintain a balance of speed and quality, equity and efficiency.[1] In 2009, the State Council issued a 'Cultural Industry Promotion Plan', aiming to develop the cultural industry into an emerging strategic industry, featuring a wide variety of elements, a high scientific and technological content, innovation, and strong competitiveness. The past few years have witnessed phenomenal growth in the industry. From 2004 to 2008, the sector's value added output grew by 23.3 per cent annually on average. During the period 2008–10, the surveyed industrial entities reported an annual increase of 24.2 per cent in value added output, significantly higher than other sectors and industries. International experience suggests that China's annual consumption of culture can reach 40 trillion RMB, although current consumption stands at only 10 trillion RMB, suggesting that there is room for growth. It is expected that the cultural industry, being instrumental in transforming the mode of economic development, will account for about 5 per cent of the country's GDP. The Ministry of Culture expects to see an annual growth rate of over 20 per cent in the industry during the period 2011–15—a reasonable target.

In recent years, China has accelerated its reform and innovation in its cultural system and has transformed some cultural institutions into for-profit enterprises. This has energized the market and enabled the integration of culture and science and technology, culture and finance, as well as culture and tourism. An emerging cultural industry featuring

[1] I am grateful to Shang-jin Wei and Xiaobo Zhang for their helpful advice

digital and Internet infrastructures has gained momentum. As such the cultural industry is becoming a new growth pole in the Chinese economy. The central government has further clarified its goal of building a modern cultural industry and turning it into a pillar industry in order to better meet the diversified, multi-level spiritual and cultural needs of the people. According to the cultural development plan released by the Ministry of Culture, eleven main industries were highlighted: the performing arts, entertainment, animation, gaming, cultural tourism, art, arts and crafts, exhibition, creative design, cyber culture, and digital cultural service industries. The plan also encouraged enterprises to participate in the international cultural trade in accordance with international market demands by exporting an enriching variety of cultural products and services.

97.2 The differences in the development of the cultural industry in western Chinese regions

Western China covers an area of 5.46 million square kilometres, accounting for 57 per cent of the total area of the country, and is home to 23 per cent of the country's population. Most of the fifty-five ethnic minority groups live there. Remarkable gaps still exist in cultural industry development, parallel to gaps in regional economic development, when compared with the eastern regions. According to the data released by the National Bureau of Statistics of China in 2008, the eastern regions hold 59 per cent of the country's cultural industry legal entities, 67 per cent of the employees, 75 per cent of the total assets, 78 per cent of the operating income, and 69 per cent of added value. In terms of its contribution to the national economy, the added value of the cultural industry in the eastern regions takes up 2.73 per cent of local GDP, whereas in the central and western regions the added value accounts for only 1.63 per cent and 1.34 per cent, respectively.

In order to promote the cultural industry development of China's western regions, differentiated strategies need to be implemented. Within these vast territories are diversified eco-environments and rich ethnic cultures, boasting natural ecological resources and ethnic cultural resources, which are suitable for developing tourism, leisure industries, as well as distinctive cultural industries. Combined with comparatively low labour costs, cultural industries in the western regions demonstrate a great potential for local economic development. The regions should take full advantage of their unique natural, historical, and cultural resources, make specific cultural industry promotion plans, and turn their cultural industry into a new pillar of economic growth.

97.3 **The cultural industry development plan of China's western province—Guizhou**

As an economically underdeveloped province in China's western region, Guizhou's economic and social development rank among the lowest in the country. However, with its seventeen native ethnic minorities such as the Miao, Dong, and Buyei, it is a region with a well-preserved ethnic diversity. The provincial government has set an overall development goal for the cultural industries in Guizhou, which will bring its multi-cultural resources into full play to establish a vibrant cultural industry with distinctive products, including a complete supply chain and an integrated market. Both the private and public sector play a role in forming the cultural industry. In 2010, the province's annual growth in the added value of the culture industry reached 11.221 billion RMB and accounted for 2.44 per cent of its GDP. Despite this low level, its growth rate has exceeded that of the national average, promising strong growth prospects. Guizhou will accelerate its development of the cultural industry, striving to turn it into one of the pillar industries of the province's economy by 2020.

Guizhou's cultural industry development strategy is as follows. First, on the basis of preserving and celebrating the ethnic cultural heritage, the development of ethnic cultural resources and ethnic characteristics should be stressed. Second, competitive industries and areas should be properly selected, and an enabling environment should be created to facilitate the development of cultural industries. Different areas may adopt different strategies: major cities should make use of their own comparative advantages to develop new industries with high technology content and high added value; rural areas should take advantage of their unique natural and cultural resources to develop new industries with distinctive characteristics. Third, some areas may consider setting up special cultural industrial zones to nurture competitive cultural-related enterprises and promote major cultural industry projects. Fourth, the related service sector, such as scientific and technological support, supporting industries, consulting services, and civic culture, should also be promoted. Fifth, the market should play a fundamental role in resource allocation to facilitate the integration of culture and science and technology, culture and finance, and culture and traditional industries, while the role of government is to create an enabling market environment, such as building basic infrastructure and enforcing law and order. Cultural products that reflect diverse cultures and that meet the demands of the international market should be highly promoted. Sixth, it is important to train high-quality human capital in related fields such as culture, science and technology, and management, in order to improve the competiveness and quality of the cultural industry, turning it into a pillar industry for Guizhou.

98 Zhejiang

Economic development

Jinchuan Shi

Zhejiang Province, located in the southern part of the Yangtze Delta on the southeast coast of China, is one of the most densely populated provinces in China, with a population density of approximately 540 people per square kilometre, that is, 55 million residents living in a land area of only 101.8 thousand square kilometres. However, since the introduction of economic reform and the opening-up policy in China in 1978, the economy of Zhejiang has undergone a higher growth trend: from 1978 to 2011, the regional nominal gross domestic product (GDP) rose from RMB12.3 billion (US$1.9 billion) to RMB3,200 billion (US$495 billion) with an average annual growth rate in real terms of approximately 13 per cent, while the regional nominal GDP per capita rose from RMB331 (US$51) to RMB58,665 (US$9,083); the residential building areas per capita in 2011 for urban and rural residents were 60 square metres and 36 square metres, respectively. By 2011, the level of urbanization of Zhejiang Province had reached 60 per cent and the value added of the primary industry, secondary industry, and tertiary industry accounted for 4.9 per cent, 51.3 per cent, and 43.8 per cent of regional GDP, respectively. Through these data we can see that Zhejiang Province has entered into the middle or later stage of industrialization.

During the past thirty years, the most powerful driving force for the rapid growth of industrialization and urbanization in Zhejiang Province has been the growth of the private economy as a result of successful reforms in the economic system. Zhejiang Province had no private enterprises in 1978 (Shu, 2010; Shi et al., 2004a). However, 2,257 private enterprises appeared in 1988, and the number of private enterprises in 2009 had increased dramatically to over 5,666,000, 250 times more than the number in 1988. This rapid growth of the private sector in Zhejiang Province has accelerated the flow of production factors such as capital and labour, optimized the allocation of resources, and promoted regional industrialization and urbanization. Currently, the private sector accounts for 70 per cent of regional GDP, 60 per cent of government tax revenues, 45 per cent of the export trade volumes, and 90 per cent of newly created jobs.

Why has the private sector in Zhejiang Province been able to grow so quickly over the past thirty years? From the perspective of historical and comparative institutional analysis (HCIA), there are three fundamental and special characteristics associated with Zhejiang Province (Shi et al., 2004b), discussed in the next three sections.

98.1 Natural resource endowment

Zhejiang Province is one of the smallest provinces in China in terms of land area, with mountain and hilly areas accounting for 70 per cent of this area, leaving even less land for agriculture. Meanwhile, mineral resources, which are crucial inputs for various industry sectors, are extremely scarce in Zhejiang Province. China's rural economic reform was launched in 1978, and since then Chinese farmers have been released from the strict bond of the people's communes (modes of collective organization of production), having become independent decision makers on agricultural production who are free to move from agricultural jobs to non-agricultural jobs. Although rural economic reforms initially stipulated incentives for farmers to engage in agricultural activities and to improve agricultural productivity, the farmers in Zhejiang Province were forced to transform from agricultural sectors to non-agricultural sectors, such as family trading companies and family firms, due to the scarcity of good, arable land. Therefore, the private sector in rural areas (initially the township and village enterprises) in Zhejiang Province began to appear and grow, promoting industrialization in rural areas and the booming of small towns and finally driving the industrialization and urbanization across the whole province.

98.2 Historical and cultural 'genes' and human resource endowment

Historically, several intensive commodity trading centres were located in Zhejiang Province. The area's well-respected mercantile culture can be traced back to the Southern Song Dynasty (1127–1279). The region of Zhejiang was the first place to experience the seeds of capitalism in China during the period of the late Ming Dynasty (1368–1644) and early Qing Dynasty (1644–1911), with a large number of active business groups. From 1840, Zhejiang was the first region to release overseas trade restrictions, allowing a large number of industrial investments from private capital investors. This human resource endowment with traditional commercial awareness did not disappear in the planned economy, rather it lay dormant. Therefore, at the beginning of the economic reforms, these people with traditional commercial awareness showed extremely strong vitality and creativity, and thus acted as an important driving force to promote economic growth in the private sector, witnessed by typical examples such as the rise and development of Yiwu (a city in central Zhejiang Province), an International Commodity Market, and the regional development pattern of Wenzhou (a city in southeastern Zhejiang Province) known as the 'Wenzhou model' (Shi et al., 2004b).

98.3 The 'legacy' of the planned economy and policies of local governments

China maintained a centrally planned economy and implemented a development strategy of prioritizing heavy industries from 1949, until the introduction of the economic reform and opening-up policy in 1978. The highly centralized Chinese central government controlled and allocated all resources to promote industrialization through mandatory plans, while local governments played only an auxiliary role in implementing those plans. However, since Zhejiang Province was located on the southeast coast of China, directly in the area of military confrontation with Taiwan, the local governments in Zhejiang Province lacked opportunities to develop the regional economy by implementing the mandatory industrialization plans of the central government as they received almost no investment in the region from the central government. It can be said that the local governments in Zhejiang province did not receive much 'legacy' from the central government at the beginning of the economic reform and opening-up period. The primary attitude of the local governments in Zhejiang Province after 1978 towards the private sector was significantly influenced by that historical fact. Largely ignored by central government during the command economy, local governments and officials at all levels in Zhejiang province naturally sought driving forces of regional economic growth from the private sector instead of the state sector when the country's economic system transformed into a market-based economy. The local governments in Zhejiang Province were actually the first ones to tolerate, protect, and support the development of the private sector in China.

98.4 Summary

In summary, the biggest driving force for the rapid economic growth achieved during the process of industrialization and urbanization in Zhejiang Province was the rapid emergence of the private sector with market-oriented economic reforms (Shi and Luo, 2000). Based on observations of Zhejiang's experience, the combination of regional natural resource endowment, historical and cultural 'genes' and human resource endowment, and regional policies of local governments, along with the interaction between local governments and private enterprises, could explain quite well the growth of the private sector and regional economic development in Zhejiang province.

■ REFERENCES

Shi, Jinchuan and Weidong Luo. 2000. *Study on Modernization Road of Zhejiang Province (1978–1998)*. Hangzhou: Zhejiang People's Publishing House.

Shi, Jinchuan, Wei Wang, and Tao Qian. 2004a. *Private Economy and Institutional Innovation: A Study of the Taizhou Phenomenon*. Hangzhou: Zhejiang University Press.

Shi, Jinchuan, Xiangrong Jin, Wei Zhao, and Weidong Luo. 2004b. *Institutional Transformation and Economic Growth: A Study of the Wenzhou Model* (2nd edn). Hangzhou: Zhejiang University Press.

Shu, Guozeng. 2010. *Overview of Zhejiang: Economy*. Hangzhou: Zhejiang People's Publishing House.

■ INDEX

McKibbin, Warwick 97 n.
McMillan, Margaret 502
Means, Gardner C. 38 n.
mechanization 6, 309, 310 n., 311, 312
medical care
  access to 547
  cost of/prices for 180, 453, 457
mega-cities 227, 229
Mencius 334
Mendoza, Enrique G. 140 n.
Meng Xin 4, 230, 231, 383, 384, 386, 461
MEP (Ministry of Environmental Protection) 12
mergers and acquisitions 260, 288
Mexico 166, 213 n., 429
  maquiladoras 105
Mexico City 229
MFN (most-favoured nation) status 115, 116, 125,
  157, 158, 159
Miao (nationality) 532, 534
middle-income countries 91, 104, 178, 482
  fledgling economy 42
  higher 540
  young people in rural areas 226–7
middle-income transition 80–9
middle-income trap 23
  China's chances of falling into 11, 62, 64–5
  overcoming 428–32
  sustaining growth and avoiding 381
migrant workers 64, 245, 461
  demand for 388, 414
  difficult problems and conflicts related to 529
  effective urbanization of 77
  healthcare coverage 457
  higher domestic consumption by 77
  implicit per capita labour tax rate on 34
  living conditions made difficult 229
  numbers of 4, 237, 378
  remittances from 4
  salary increases to attract 389
  share in the urban labour force 225
  supply of 388
  underclass of 1
  wages of 214–15, 378, 384, 388, 414
migration 13, 37, 71–2, 76, 77, 336
  accelerated 423
  control of 424
  cost of 226, 227
  distinctive patterns for rich and poor 407
  explosion of 425
  fair rules for 34
  incentives for 444
  interregional 301
  large-scale 230, 387
  largest in human history 354
  legal 226
  mass, business people 289

  means of widening living space 552–3
  permanent 10
  Probit model of 388
  restrained 225, 226–7
  restricted 181, 404
  rural poverty reduced by 424
  temporary 226, 230
  see also migrant workers; rural–urban migration
Ming dynasty (1468–1644) 334
Ming Su 200, 201, 202
Minimum Livelihood Guarantee, *see* DB programme
Ministries:
  Agriculture 282, 327
  Communications 133
  Culture 576, 577
  Education 51 n., 134, 465–7 nn., 474, 478
  Foreign Affairs 133, 134
  Foreign Economic Relations 133
  Health 134, 450, 451, 453
  Human Resources and Social Security 244 n., 246 nn.
  Railways 133, 553
  Trade 133
  Water Resources 360
  see also MEP; MOCA; MOF; MOFCOM; MOFERT;
    MOFTEC
Ministry of Disinvestment (India) 291
Mishra, Prachi 130
Mitchell, Derek J. 18, 19
MNCs (multinational corporations) 16, 21, 159, 258,
  546
  Chinese firms successfully competing with 259
  gradual phase-out of tax advantages for 165
  impact/effects on Chinese clusters 264, 265
  initiatives that envisage restricted roles for 256
  outsourcing by 263, 265
  US 122, 275
MOCA (Ministry of Civil Affairs) 335, 415, 442
MOF (Ministry of Finance) 113, 134, 135, 146 n., 245,
  282, 413
MOFCOM (Ministry of Commerce) 122 n., 133, 134,
  135 n.
MOFERT (Ministry of Foreign Economic Relations
  and Trade) 133, 156
MOFTEC (Ministry of Foreign Trade and Economic
  Cooperation) 133
Moganshan 48
monetary policy 38, 194–9
  contractionary 221
  exchange rate the anchor for 77
  normalization in developed countries 177
  potential complications for 22
  pressures on 123
money supply:
  excessive 203
  huge 34
  pressure on 201

Printed and bound by CPI Group (UK) Ltd, Croydon, CR0 4YY